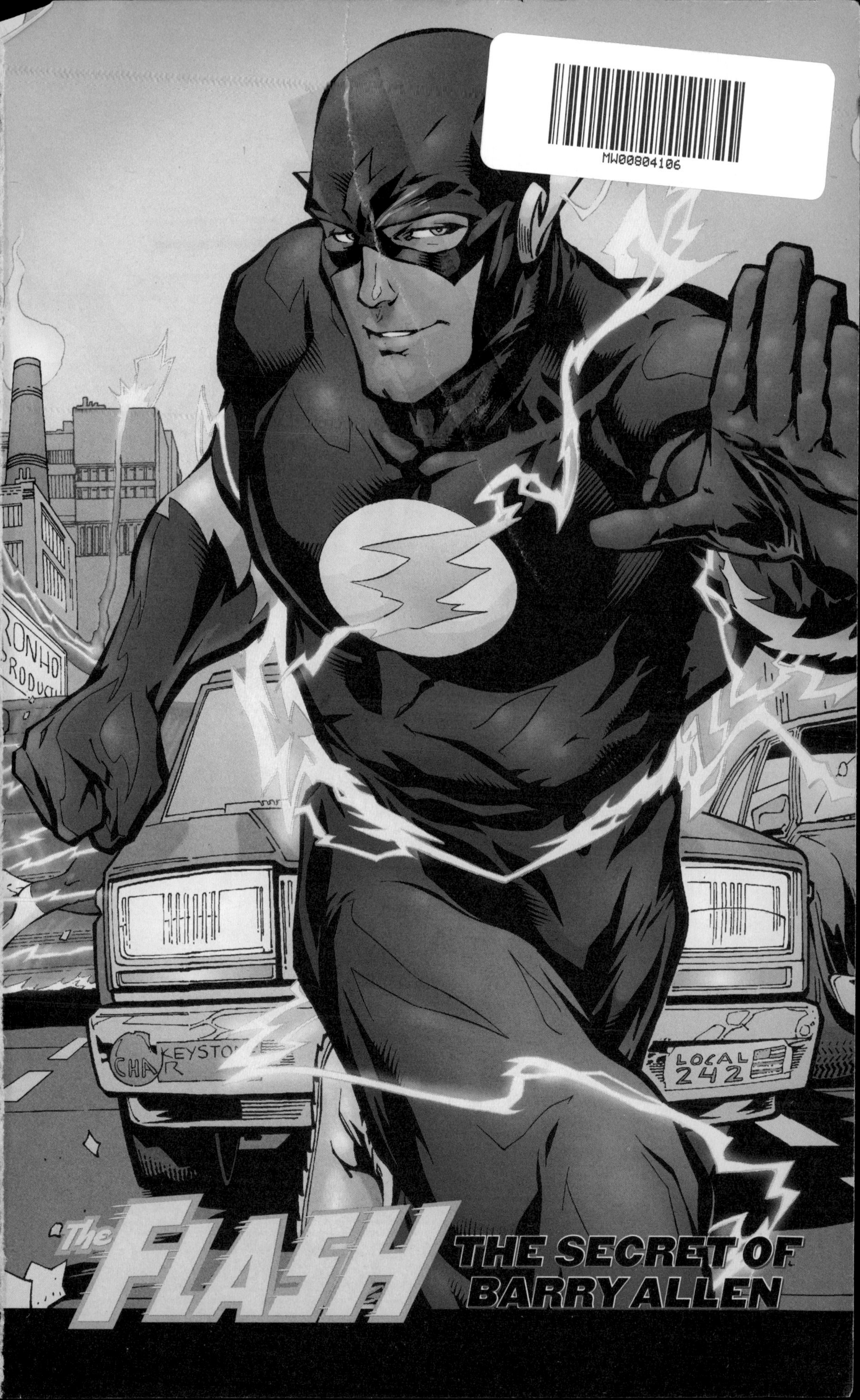
LOCAL
242
The FLASH
THE SECRET OF
BARRY ALLEN

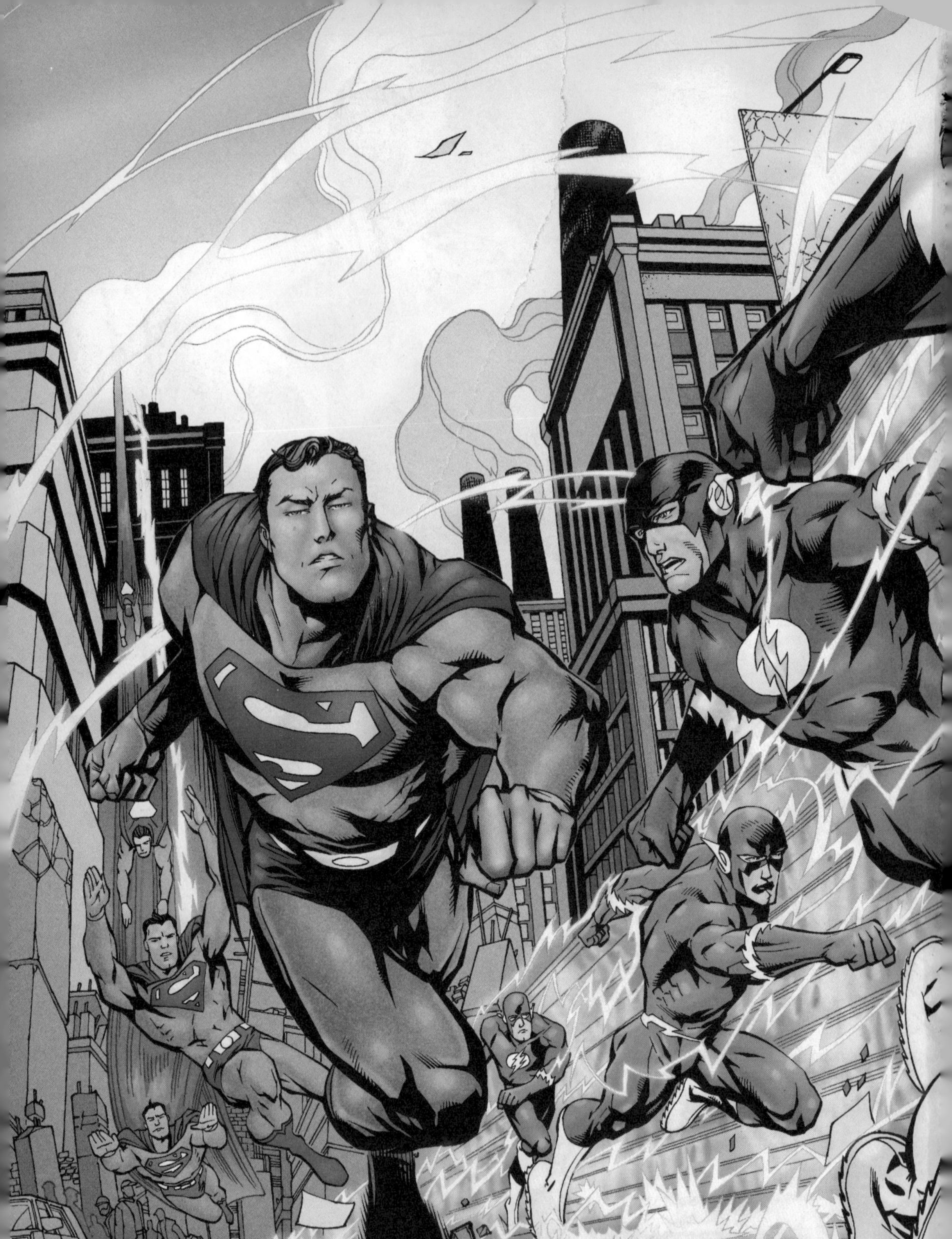

Dan DiDio VP-Executive Editor Joey Cavalieri Editor-original series Harvey Richards Rachel Gluckstern Assistant Editors-original series Robert Greenberger Senior Editor-collected edition Robbin Brosterman Senior Art Director Paul Levitz President & Publisher Georg Brewer VP-Design & Retail Product Development Richard Bruning Senior VP-Creative Director Patrick Caldon Senior VP-Finance & Operations Chris Caramalis VP-Finance Terri Cunningham VP-Managing Editor Stephanie Fierman Senior VP-Sales & Marketing Alison Gill VP-Manufacturing Rich Johnson, VP-Book Trade Sales Hank Kanalz VP-General Manager, WildStorm Lillian Laserson Senior VP & General Counsel Jim Lee Editorial Director-WildStorm Paula Lowitt Senior VP-Business & Legal Affairs David McKillips VP-Advertising & Custom Publishing John Nee VP-Business Development Gregory Noveck Senior VP-Creative Affairs Cheryl Rubin Senior VP-Brand Management Bob Wayne VP-Sales

THE FLASH: THE SECRET OF BARRY ALLEN

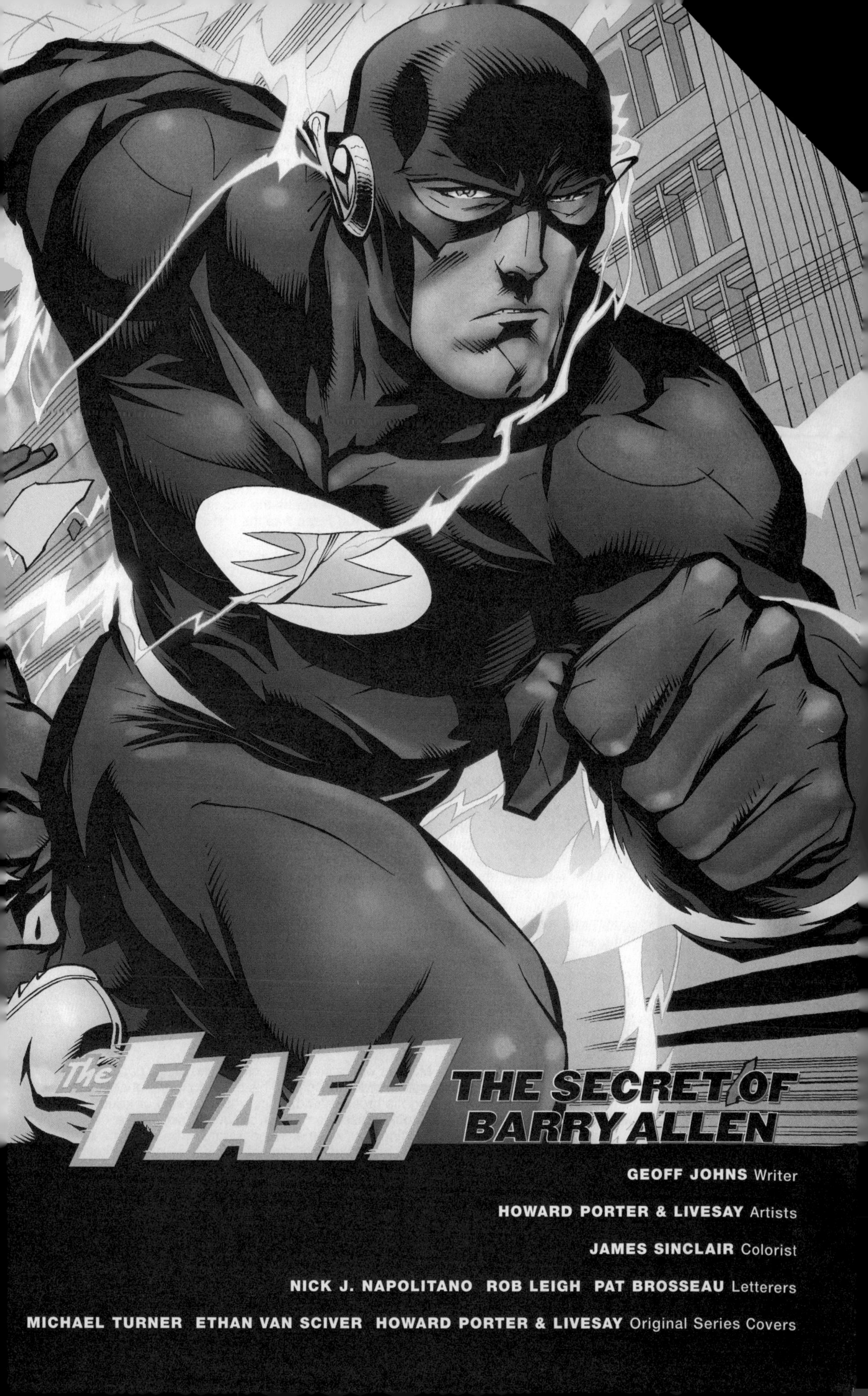

The Flash: The Secret of Barry Allen

GEOFF JOHNS Writer

HOWARD PORTER & LIVESAY Artists

JAMES SINCLAIR Colorist

NICK J. NAPOLITANO ROB LEIGH PAT BROSSEAU Letterers

MICHAEL TURNER ETHAN VAN SCIVER HOWARD PORTER & LIVESAY Original Series Covers

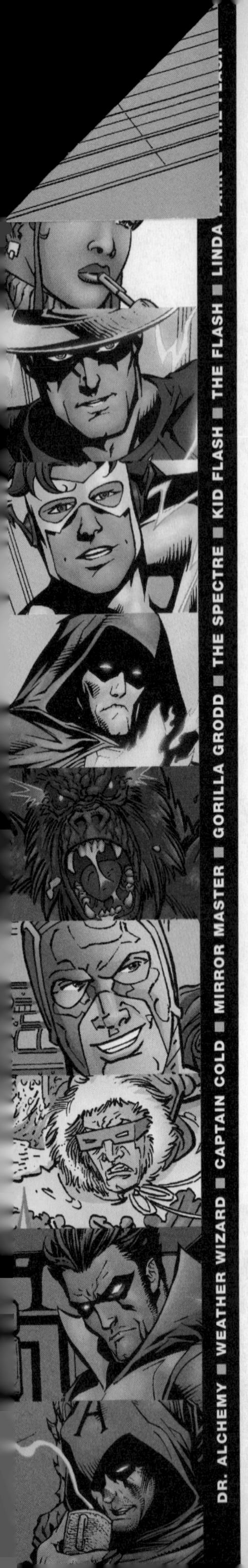
DR. ALCHEMY ■ WEATHER WIZARD ■ CAPTAIN COLD ■ MIRROR MASTER ■ GORILLA GRODD ■ THE SPECTRE ■ KID FLASH ■ THE FLASH ■ LINDA

C H A R A C T E R   B I O S

THE FLASH: In a bizarre accident, teenager Wally West was struck by a bolt of lightning and bestowed with the gift of incredible super-speed. After years of training as Kid Flash to Barry Allen's Flash, Wally inherited the mantle of the Scarlet Speedster following the death of his mentor. Now, protecting Keystone City, he carries on the legacy of the fastest man alive — Wally West is the Flash!

LINDA PARK: Linda Park originally thought Wally to be brash and arrogant — which he was. But Linda also saw something else in him, the spark of a better man. As their relationship developed, that spark turned into a flame of love that led them to marry. So strong is their bond that it has enabled Flash to find his way home, regardless of time, dimension, or location. Recently, Linda discovered she was pregnant, only to lose the twins when she was assaulted by Zoom. It's been a slow, painful recovery these last few months.

THE FLASH: The first in a long line of super-speedsters, Jay Garrick was the victim of a lab accident that imbued him with impossible speed. He is capable of running at velocities near the speed of light. Retired from his career in the lab, Garrick is one of the more sought-after mentors of his generation.

KID FLASH: Bart Allen has quite a legacy to live up to. His grandfather was Barry Allen, the second Flash. Born in the 30th century, Bart was brought to the 21st century by his grandmother to be properly schooled in the use of his natural super-speed. For a time, he operated as Impulse, under the tutelage of Max Mercury, Zen master of speed. After recent events, Bart decided it was time to grow up, and toward that goal he has speed-read and memorized the contents of the San Francisco Public Library. He has the knowledge but now needs the experience to be worthy of the Flash mantle. Changing his name to Kid Flash was the first step in the process.

THE SPECTRE: God's Spirit of Vengeance has had several human hosts over the millennia. Currently, the host is Hal Jordan, Earth's former Green Lantern. His tortured soul was corrupted but by quelling a threat to humanity, he voluntarily took possession of the Spirit. With sheer will power, he has turned Vengeance to Redemption. When Wally and Linda lost the twins to Zoom, the Spectre granted a boon and erased the world's knowledge that Wally was the Flash.

THE ROGUES

GORILLA GRODD: Somewhere deep in the jungles of Africa lies a city of highly intelligent and evolved gorillas. The citizens of this Gorilla City would like nothing more than to peacefully exist hidden from humankind — all, that is, save Grodd, a power-hungry megalomaniac who believes he should be ruling Gorilla City and the world. Despite his superior telepathic abilities and unbelievable strength, it is usually the Flash who puts an end to Grodd's plans.

MIRROR MASTER: Just as Wally is the third generation Flash, there have been several incarnations of the Mirror Master. Currently wearing the costume is Evan McCulloch. Hired and equipped by the government as an enforcer, he quickly outgrew the need for direction and banished his superiors to a mirror world. He has used the reflecting ability of mirrors in ways that Sam Scudder, the original Mirror Master, never dreamt of. McCulloch will do anything for a price.

CAPTAIN COLD: Leonard Snart was never more than a common thief until the day he was taken down by the Flash. Len promised himself he would face the Flash when he got out of prison. The opportunity came after Snart stole an experimental cryogenic engine. He then created a cold-gun, donned a costume, and renamed himself Captain Cold. During his years of battling with the Flash, Cold saw his sister Lisa slide into his shadow as the villainous Golden Glider. Today, he remains guilt-ridden over her death and has grown even colder towards his fellow man. Cold is the most underestimated of the Flash's Rogues.

WEATHER WIZARD: Mark Mardon was a small-time crook who either got lucky or was a murderer. A prison escapee, Mardon headed to his older brother's observatory for shelter, where he either found his brother dead (from a heart attack) or killed him. What is indisputable is that he took possession of his brother's invention, a device capable of controlling weather. Using ths "weather wand," Mardon became the thief known as Weather Wizard. He has battled various incarnations of the Flash, improving his control over the wand's properties with experience.

DR. ALCHEMY: After coming into possession of the transmuting talisman known as the Philosopher's Stone, criminal Albert Desmond, once known as Mr. Element, adopted a new alter ego, Dr. Alchemy. He met defeat at the hands of the Flash and served his time. His psychic twin, though, Alvin Desmond, took up the Stone and Dr. Alchemy persona and has continued committing heinous acts ever since.

C H A R A C T E R B I O S

CAPTAIN BOOMERANG: George "Digger" Harkness left his native Australia as a child, being raised in America. He learned his craft well and was hired to demonstrate boomerangs for a toy manufacturer. Along the way, he committed petty crimes until he decided to try stealing full-time, using an array of enhanced boomerangs to help him. Ever since, he has been one of the most amoral rogues to confront the Flash. Recently, after a string of failures and loss of stature in the super-villain community, Boomerang learned he had a grown son.

THE TOP: Thomas O'Neil was once a politician with a promising career. That all changed when the spirit of Roscoe Dillon – the original rogue known as The Top — possessed his body, imbuing it with Dillon's metahuman ability to spin at amazing speeds.

ABRA KADABRA: Kadabra is one of the original rogues, hailing from the 64th century. Craving adulation for his exploits, he uses his sophisticated technology to perform "magic acts." He has opposed and been routinely defeated by first Barry Allen and more recently, Wally West.

TAR PIT: Unexceptional as a kid, Joey Monteleone discovered, while serving a prison term at Iron Heights, that he was a metahuman. He could project his astral self and inhabit inanimate objects. At night he roamed free, "joyriding" with random acts of violence until his form became stuck in a pool of tar.

FALLOUT: Neil Borman is a walking nuclear man, his body radiating immeasurable radiation. Sentenced to Iron Heights, Borman had been trapped in the bowels of the prison, providing the energy the prison needed. The Flash intervened, seeing to it that in exchange for such energy, he was well supplied with books and comforts, as his cell channels his energy as the prison's primary power source.

PLUNDER: While trapped in a "mirror world" within his wife's diamond ring, the Flash was tracked by a bounty hunter calling himself Plunder. Realizing he was trapped in a reflection, which was destined to fade away, Plunder escaped "Wonderland" on the heels of the Flash. Plunder is a "reflection" of somebody in the real world, Flash's ally and friend Detective Jared Morillo.

TRICKSTER II: Rebellious teen Axel Walker was recruited by Blacksmith to use the Trickster's old gear in new ways. After earning his way into the criminal community, the new Trickster has plagued not only Flash in Keystone but also Robin in Blüdhaven.

THE FORMER ROGUES

HEAT WAVE: Mick Rory developed a fondness for heat and warmth after being locked in an industrial freezer as a child. Developing a warm suit and a stylized pistol-shaped flamethrower, Heat Wave took to the streets of Central City as one of the Flash's original rogues. After a time, he decided to reform his life, earning Barry Allen's trust. Rory served as Security Chief at Project Cadmus and after that operation closed, joined the Trickster at the FBI.

TRICKSTER I: Giovanni Giuseppe was a brilliant inventor and circus acrobat with a fear of heights. Eventually he turned to crime, only to meet repeated defeat at the hands of the Flash. After outwitting the demon Neron, Giovanni, now known as James Jesse, decided to walk a straighter path and now works in Chicago for a special department of the FBI.

PIED PIPER: Hartley Rathaway was born deaf, but after modern medical science restored his hearing he fell in love with music. That love of music fueled an interest in sonics that ultimately led the wealthy youth to assume the costumed guise of the Pied Piper. Rathaway seemed more interested in challenging the second Flash than in committing crimes, and he ultimately turned away from that path. Today, as a friend to Wally West, he is a champion of civil and social rights across Keystone and Central City. Recently, he's been recruited to work at the FBI.

THE POLICE

It takes a special breed of cop to patrol the streets of Keystone City. With all the metahuman and above-average criminal activity, Keystone's police force formed the Department of Metahuman Hostility, staffed by two officers. Often driven by his short temper, Officer Fred Chyre has been suspended for excessive force several times. Most of his anger stems from the death of his first partner, Joe Jackam. Jared Morillo, his current partner, was the chief homicide detective in Los Angeles. When his wife wanted to start a family, they moved to Keystone where Morillo was unimpressed by his peers. Quickly becoming disliked, he was placed in the new department of metahuman hostility. They work closely with The Flash as well as Iron Heights warden Gregory Wolfe. Aiding their work is the FBI's metahuman profiler Ashley Zolomon, recently transferred to the city after her ex-husband, Hunter Zolomon, became the criminal known as Zoom.

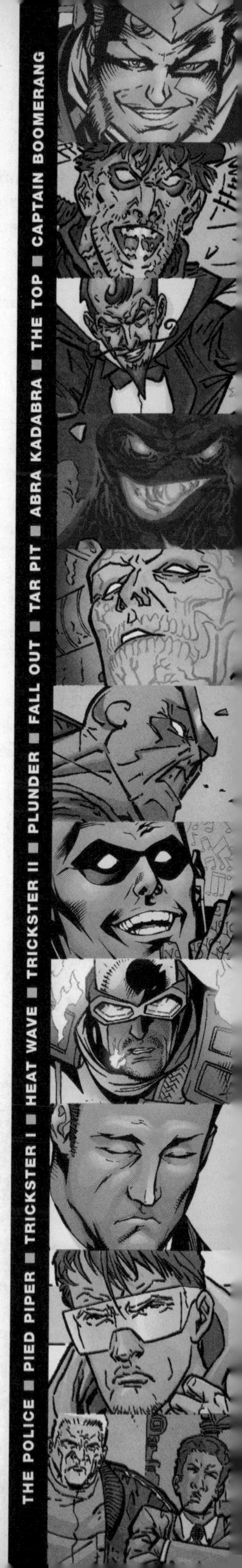
THE POLICE ■ PIED PIPER ■ TRICKSTER I ■ HEAT WAVE ■ TRICKSTER II ■ PLUNDER ■ FALL OUT ■ TAR PIT ■ ABRA KADABRA ■ THE TOP ■ CAPTAIN BOOMERANG

Wally West inherited the mantle of the Flash, fastest man alive, and has strived to be worthy of the power and name. He does this by protecting the citizens of Keystone City from an ever-growing number of powered criminals, by serving as a member of the JLA, and by employing the lessons he learned from his mentor, the second Flash, Barry Allen.

It hasn't been easy.

Even though he is supported by his loving wife, Linda Park, and the first Flash, Jay Garrick, the threats to his city have only increased. Keystone has done its part by building the fortress known as Iron Heights, where the common and not-so-common criminals are incarcerated. Ruled strictly by the warden, Gregory Wolfe, the criminals are kept locked up tight, with little effort made to rehabilitate the rogues, known for their recidivism.

Recently, Wally and Linda were attacked by former police profiler Hunter Zolomon, who had become the deranged speedster Zoom. Zolomon's body, frozen in a moment of time, was encapsulated at Iron Heights, leaving Wally to grieve at the damage done and question the public identity, given the high cost. The Spectre chose to give Wally a gift: he made the entire world forget that Barry Allen was the Flash and that Wally West was his successor. For two months now, the Flash has been absent from the city while Wally, also unaware of his heroic persona, has come to enjoy his nighttime job as a Keystone Police mechanic.

But circumstances led Wally to rediscover his skills and his heritage. After accidentally befriending Captain Cold, Wally cleared the rogue of murders that were committed by someone using Mr. Element's weapon. Now, Wally has to put his life back together.

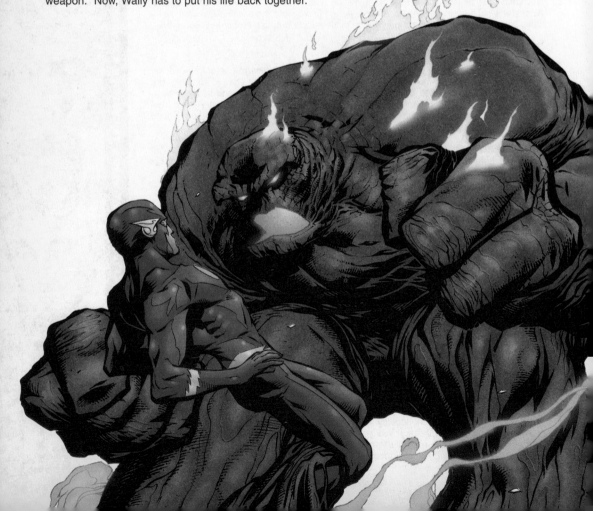

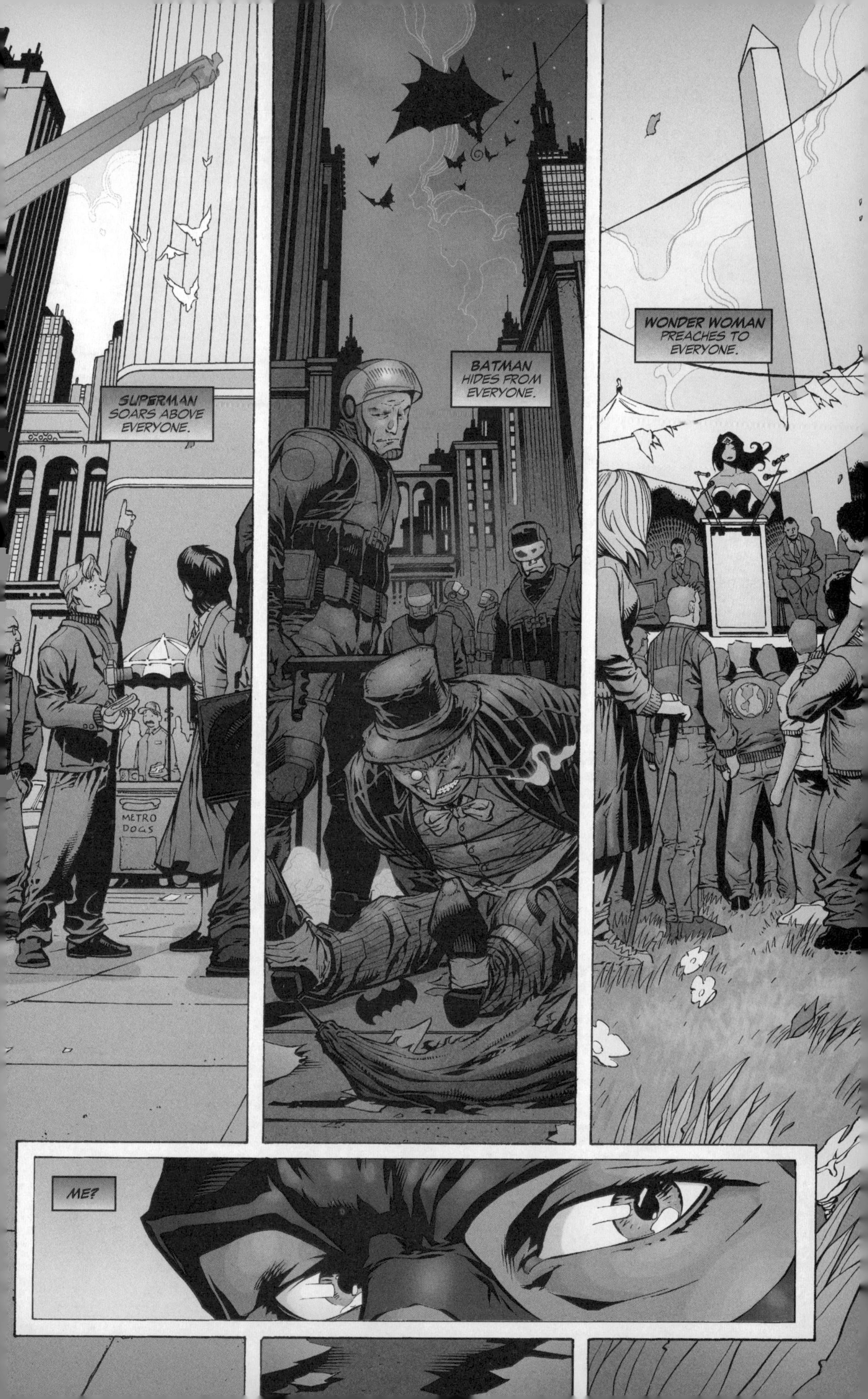
SUPERMAN SOARS ABOVE EVERYONE.
METRO DOGS
BATMAN HIDES FROM EVERYONE.
WONDER WOMAN PREACHES TO EVERYONE.
ME?

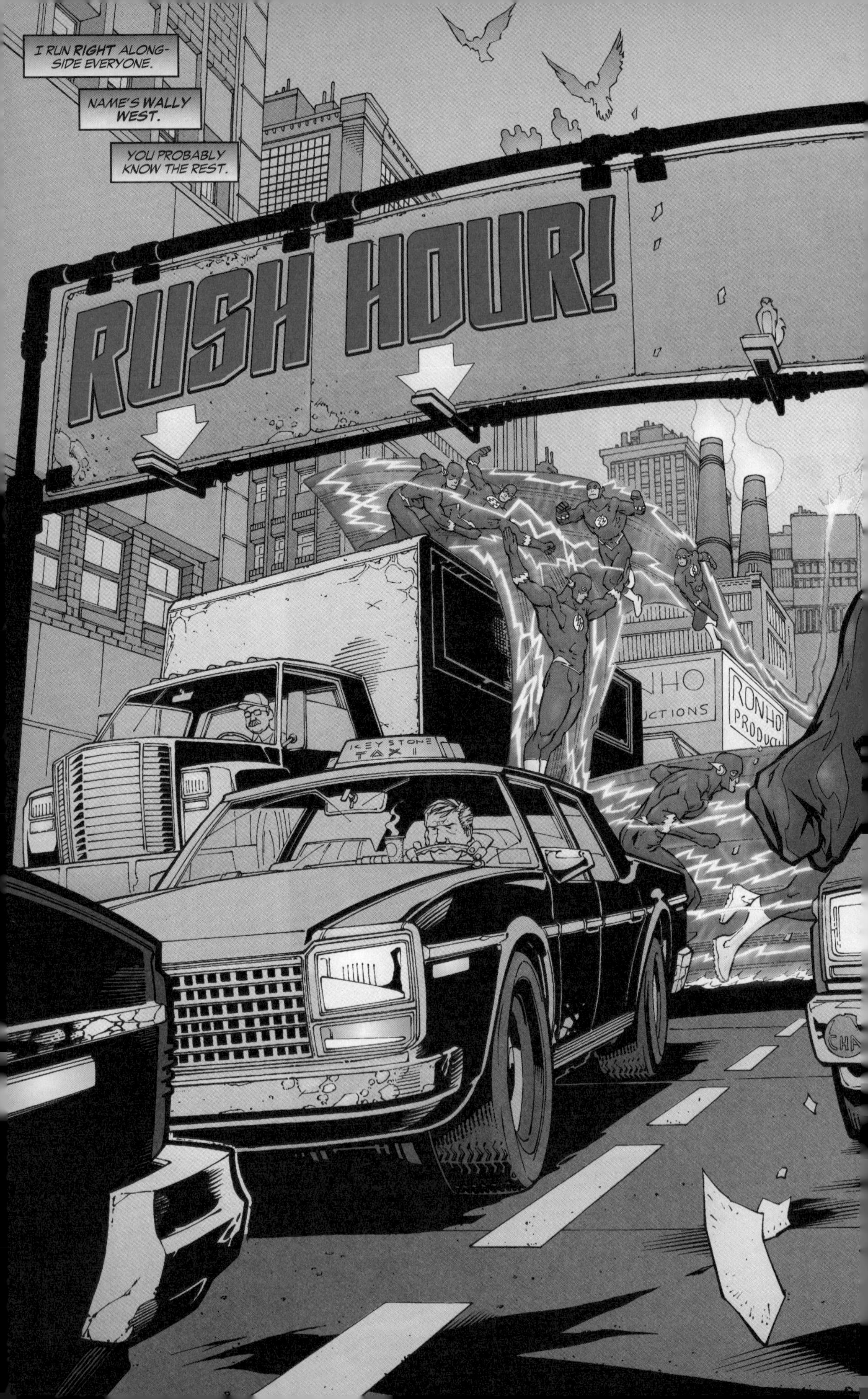
I RUN RIGHT ALONG-SIDE EVERYONE.
NAME'S WALLY WEST.
YOU PROBABLY KNOW THE REST.
RUSH HOUR!
KEYSTONE TAXI
RONHO PRODUCTIONS

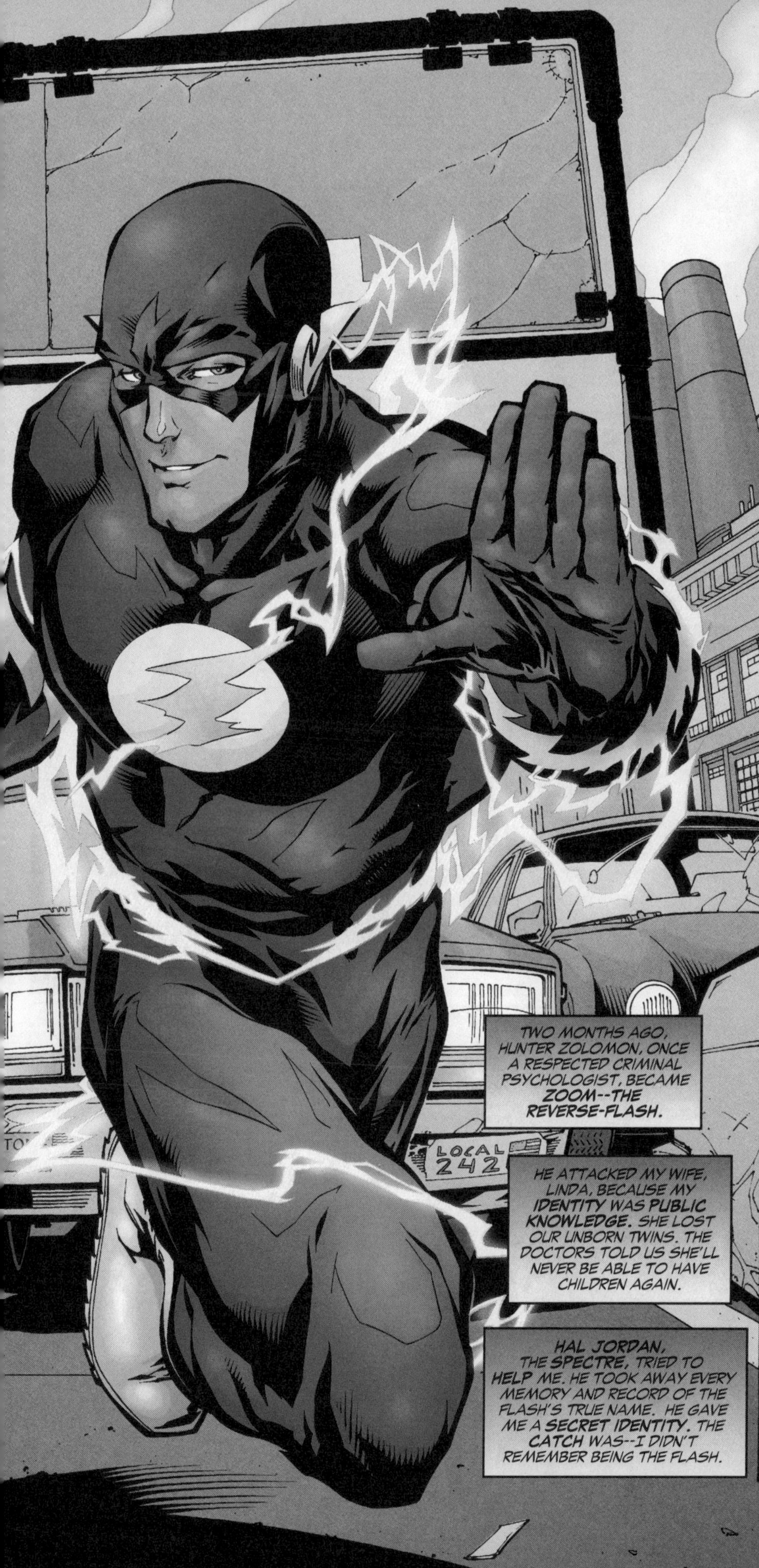

TWO MONTHS AGO, HUNTER ZOLOMON, ONCE A RESPECTED CRIMINAL PSYCHOLOGIST, BECAME ZOOM--THE REVERSE-FLASH.
LOCAL 242
HE ATTACKED MY WIFE, LINDA, BECAUSE MY IDENTITY WAS PUBLIC KNOWLEDGE. SHE LOST OUR UNBORN TWINS. THE DOCTORS TOLD US SHE'LL NEVER BE ABLE TO HAVE CHILDREN AGAIN.
HAL JORDAN, THE SPECTRE, TRIED TO HELP ME. HE TOOK AWAY EVERY MEMORY AND RECORD OF THE FLASH'S TRUE NAME. HE GAVE ME A SECRET IDENTITY. THE CATCH WAS--I DIDN'T REMEMBER BEING THE FLASH.

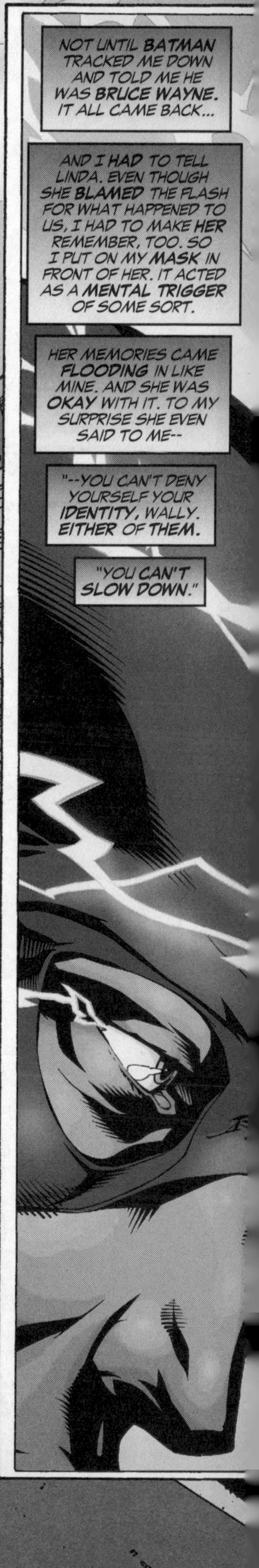

NOT UNTIL BATMAN TRACKED ME DOWN AND TOLD ME HE WAS BRUCE WAYNE. IT ALL CAME BACK...
AND I HAD TO TELL LINDA. EVEN THOUGH SHE BLAMED THE FLASH FOR WHAT HAPPENED TO US, I HAD TO MAKE HER REMEMBER, TOO. SO I PUT ON MY MASK IN FRONT OF HER. IT ACTED AS A MENTAL TRIGGER OF SOME SORT.
HER MEMORIES CAME FLOODING IN LIKE MINE. AND SHE WAS OKAY WITH IT. TO MY SURPRISE SHE EVEN SAID TO ME--
"--YOU CAN'T DENY YOURSELF YOUR IDENTITY, WALLY. EITHER OF THEM.
"YOU CAN'T SLOW DOWN."

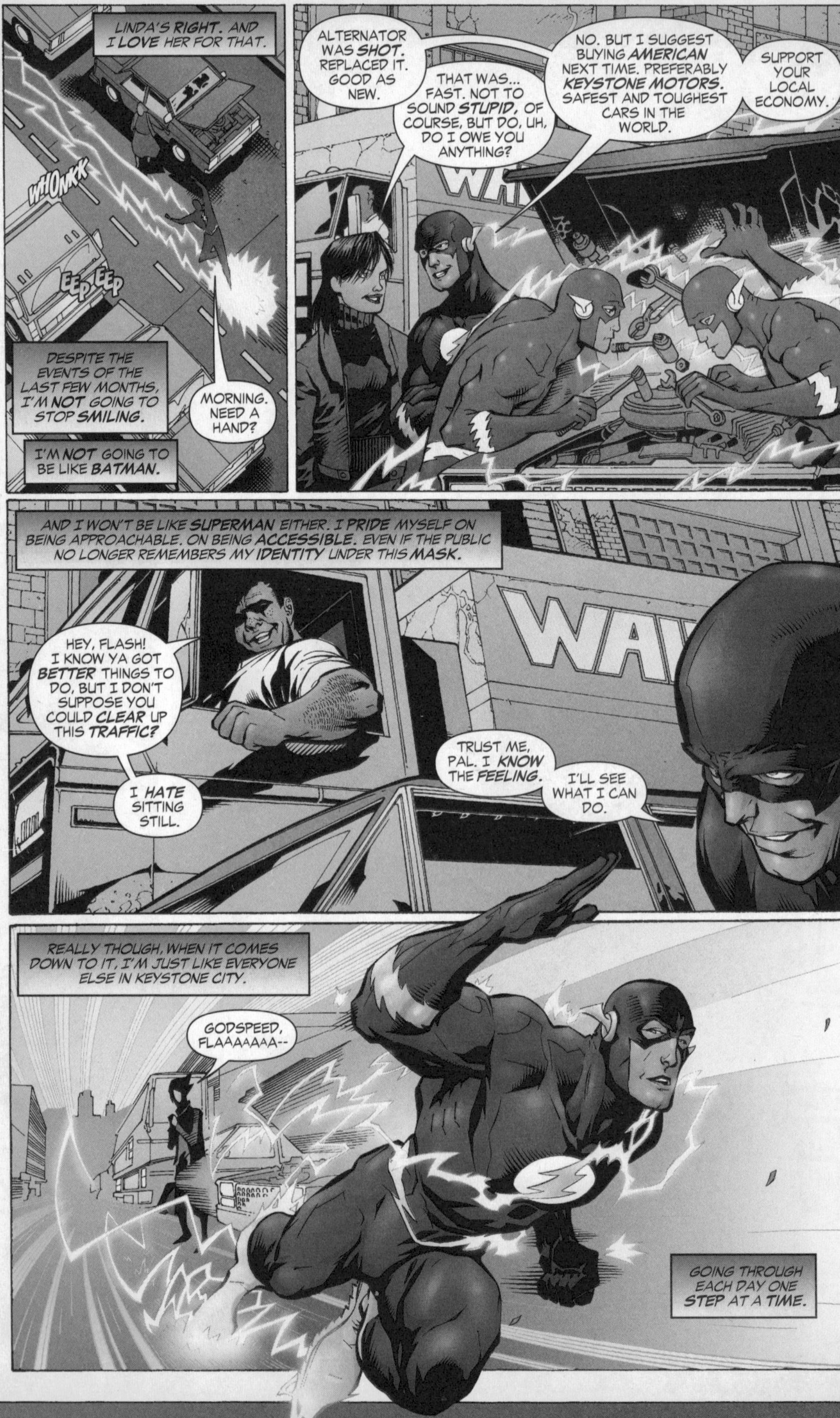

LINDA'S RIGHT. AND I LOVE HER FOR THAT.
WHONKK
EEP EEP
DESPITE THE EVENTS OF THE LAST FEW MONTHS, I'M NOT GOING TO STOP SMILING.
I'M NOT GOING TO BE LIKE BATMAN.
MORNING. NEED A HAND?
ALTERNATOR WAS SHOT. REPLACED IT. GOOD AS NEW.
THAT WAS... FAST. NOT TO SOUND STUPID, OF COURSE, BUT DO, UH, DO I OWE YOU ANYTHING?
NO. BUT I SUGGEST BUYING AMERICAN NEXT TIME. PREFERABLY KEYSTONE MOTORS. SAFEST AND TOUGHEST CARS IN THE WORLD.
SUPPORT YOUR LOCAL ECONOMY.
AND I WON'T BE LIKE SUPERMAN EITHER. I PRIDE MYSELF ON BEING APPROACHABLE. ON BEING ACCESSIBLE. EVEN IF THE PUBLIC NO LONGER REMEMBERS MY IDENTITY UNDER THIS MASK.
HEY, FLASH! I KNOW YA GOT BETTER THINGS TO DO, BUT I DON'T SUPPOSE YOU COULD CLEAR UP THIS TRAFFIC?
I HATE SITTING STILL.
TRUST ME, PAL. I KNOW THE FEELING.
I'LL SEE WHAT I CAN DO.
REALLY THOUGH, WHEN IT COMES DOWN TO IT, I'M JUST LIKE EVERYONE ELSE IN KEYSTONE CITY.
GODSPEED, FLAAAAAAA--
GOING THROUGH EACH DAY ONE STEP AT A TIME.

OFFICER... RICHARDS, IS IT?

WHAT'S GOING ON HERE? NEED ANY HELP?

FLASH! WOW. THIS IS... WOOOWWWW--

THROUGH THE YEARS, BEING ABLE TO **THINK** AT THE SPEED OF SOUND HAS TAUGHT ME A LOT OF **PATIENCE**. SITTING AND **WAITING** FOR PEOPLE TO ANSWER A QUESTION.

EVEN DURING **JUSTICE LEAGUE** MEETINGS. TOOK ALL MY CONCENTRATION NOT TO JUMP INTO SPEED-MODE AND **ZONE OUT**. ESPECIALLY WHEN **WONDER WOMAN** WOULD GET INTO IT.

I ALWAYS FELT GUILTY AFTER LISTENING TO HER. WHAT WITH THE RAIN FORESTS AND THE OIL SPILLS. ALL THE STEREOTYPICAL **WRONGS** IN THE WORLD THAT NEED TO BE RIGHTED. YET SHE BELIEVES A FOREST FIRE IS A GOOD THING?

AMAZONS.

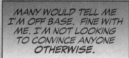

I'M ALL FOR PROTECTING OUR ENVIRONMENT. BUT AS FAR AS I'M CONCERNED, OUR **FIRST PRIORITY** SHOULD BE TO PROTECT **THE PEOPLE**.

MANY WOULD TELL ME I'M OFF BASE. FINE WITH ME. I'M NOT LOOKING TO CONVINCE ANYONE OTHERWISE.

IT'S JUST ONE MAN'S OPINION.

HIS MOUTH HANGS OPEN FOR A RELATIVE SEVEN MINUTES BEFORE HE FINALLY **SPEAKS** AGAIN.

--WW! THEY CLOSED DOWN THE ROAD. FOR **YOU**.

ME?

YEAH. DIDN'T YOU KNOW?

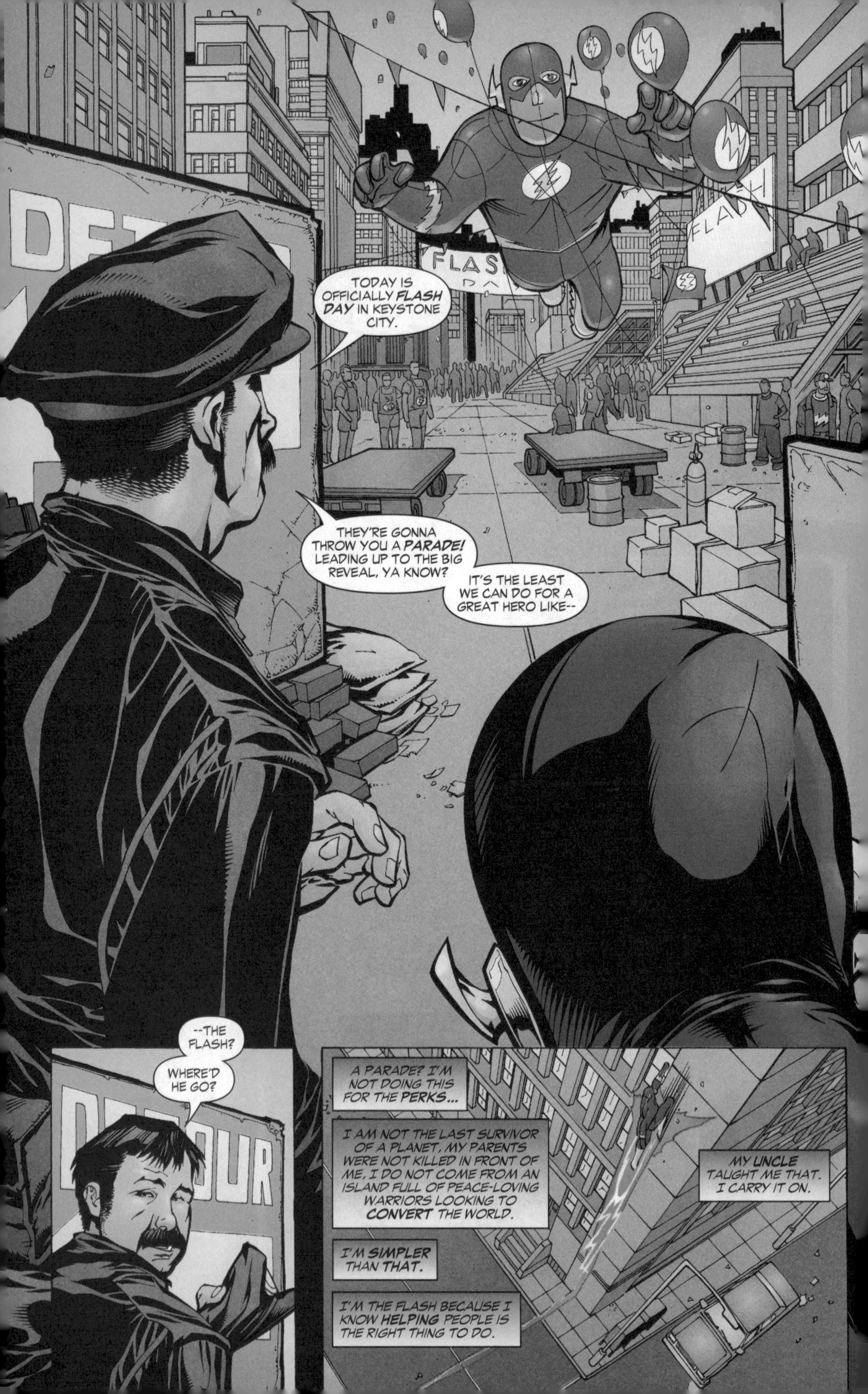

TODAY IS OFFICIALLY FLASH DAY IN KEYSTONE CITY.
THEY'RE GONNA THROW YOU A PARADE! LEADING UP TO THE BIG REVEAL, YA KNOW?
IT'S THE LEAST WE CAN DO FOR A GREAT HERO LIKE--
--THE FLASH?
WHERE'D HE GO?
A PARADE? I'M NOT DOING THIS FOR THE PERKS...
I AM NOT THE LAST SURVIVOR OF A PLANET, MY PARENTS WERE NOT KILLED IN FRONT OF ME, I DO NOT COME FROM AN ISLAND FULL OF PEACE-LOVING WARRIORS LOOKING TO CONVERT THE WORLD.
I'M SIMPLER THAN THAT.
I'M THE FLASH BECAUSE I KNOW HELPING PEOPLE IS THE RIGHT THING TO DO.
MY UNCLE TAUGHT ME THAT. I CARRY IT ON.

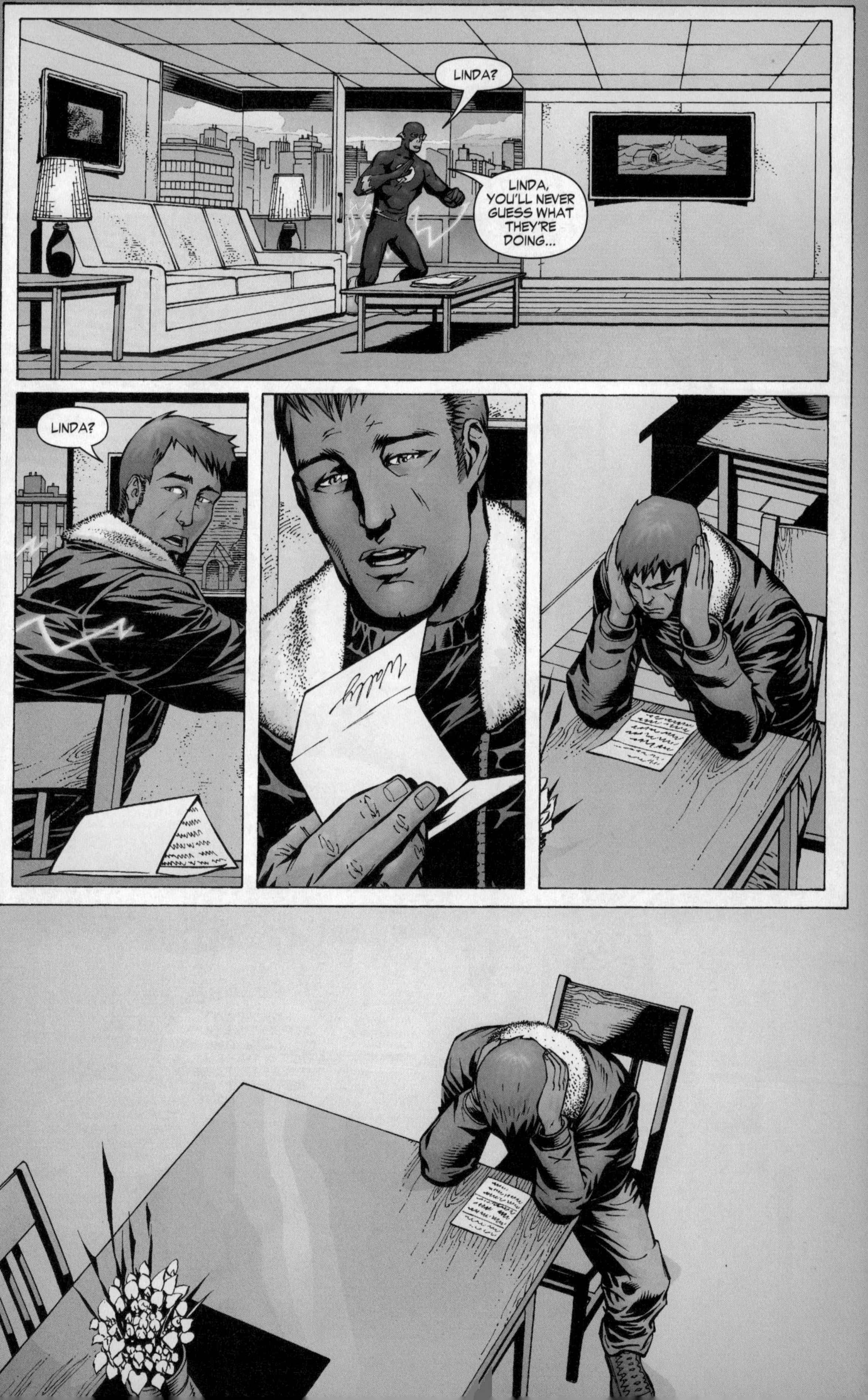

LINDA?
LINDA, YOU'LL NEVER GUESS WHAT THEY'RE DOING...
LINDA?
Wally

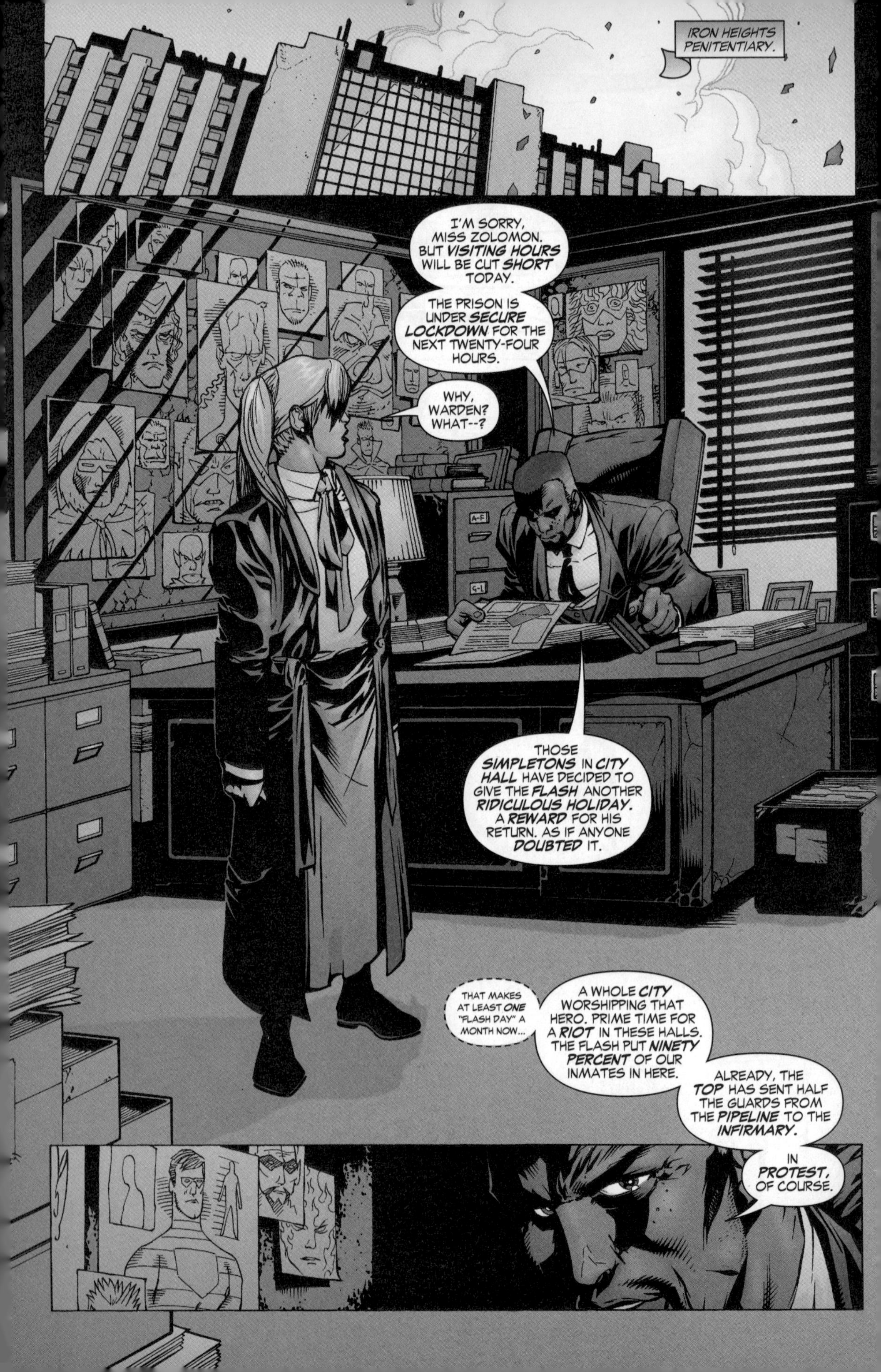
IRON HEIGHTS PENITENTIARY.
I'M SORRY, MISS ZOLOMON. BUT VISITING HOURS WILL BE CUT SHORT TODAY.
THE PRISON IS UNDER SECURE LOCKDOWN FOR THE NEXT TWENTY-FOUR HOURS.
WHY, WARDEN? WHAT--?
A-F
G-L
THOSE SIMPLETONS IN CITY HALL HAVE DECIDED TO GIVE THE FLASH ANOTHER RIDICULOUS HOLIDAY. A REWARD FOR HIS RETURN. AS IF ANYONE DOUBTED IT.
THAT MAKES AT LEAST ONE "FLASH DAY" A MONTH NOW...
A WHOLE CITY WORSHIPPING THAT HERO. PRIME TIME FOR A RIOT IN THESE HALLS. THE FLASH PUT NINETY PERCENT OF OUR INMATES IN HERE.
ALREADY, THE TOP HAS SENT HALF THE GUARDS FROM THE PIPELINE TO THE INFIRMARY.
IN PROTEST, OF COURSE.

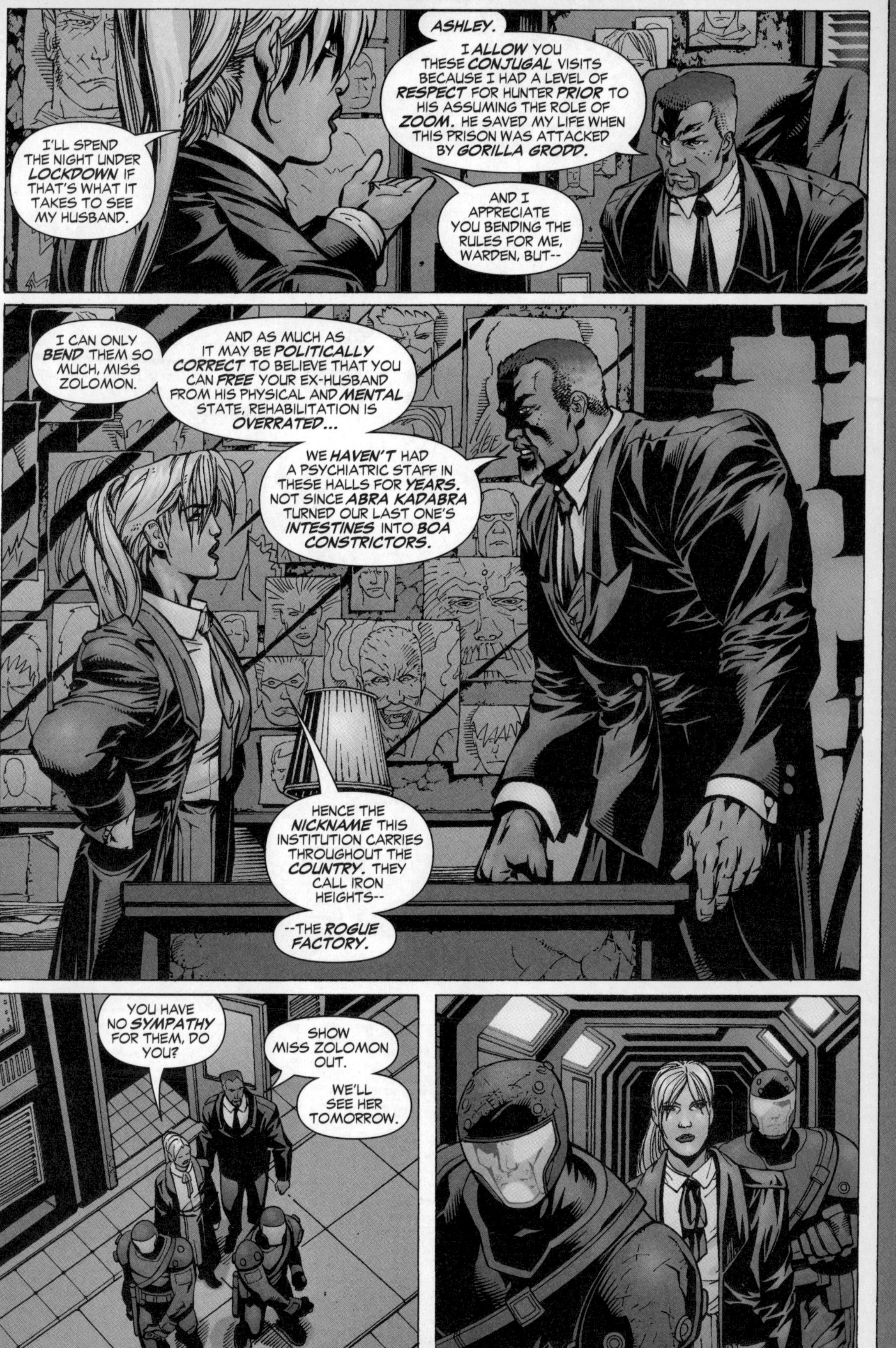

ASHLEY.
I ALLOW YOU THESE CONJUGAL VISITS BECAUSE I HAD A LEVEL OF RESPECT FOR HUNTER PRIOR TO HIS ASSUMING THE ROLE OF ZOOM. HE SAVED MY LIFE WHEN THIS PRISON WAS ATTACKED BY GORILLA GRODD.
I'LL SPEND THE NIGHT UNDER LOCKDOWN IF THAT'S WHAT IT TAKES TO SEE MY HUSBAND.
AND I APPRECIATE YOU BENDING THE RULES FOR ME, WARDEN, BUT--
I CAN ONLY BEND THEM SO MUCH, MISS ZOLOMON.
AND AS MUCH AS IT MAY BE POLITICALLY CORRECT TO BELIEVE THAT YOU CAN FREE YOUR EX-HUSBAND FROM HIS PHYSICAL AND MENTAL STATE, REHABILITATION IS OVERRATED...
WE HAVEN'T HAD A PSYCHIATRIC STAFF IN THESE HALLS FOR YEARS. NOT SINCE ABRA KADABRA TURNED OUR LAST ONE'S INTESTINES INTO BOA CONSTRICTORS.
HENCE THE NICKNAME THIS INSTITUTION CARRIES THROUGHOUT THE COUNTRY. THEY CALL IRON HEIGHTS--
--THE ROGUE FACTORY.
YOU HAVE NO SYMPATHY FOR THEM, DO YOU?
SHOW MISS ZOLOMON OUT.
WE'LL SEE HER TOMORROW.

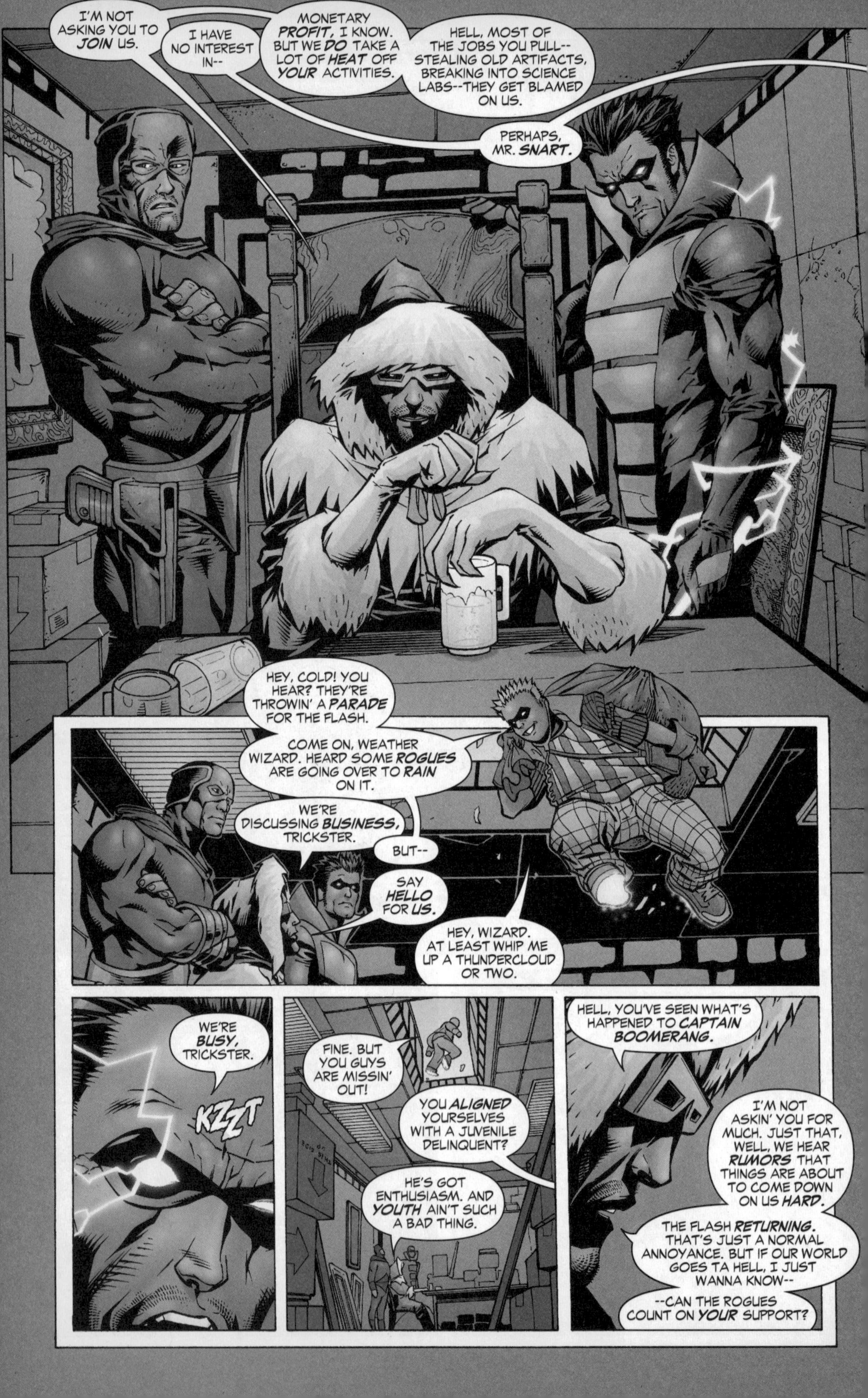
I'M NOT ASKING YOU TO JOIN US.
I HAVE NO INTEREST IN--
MONETARY PROFIT, I KNOW. BUT WE DO TAKE A LOT OF HEAT OFF YOUR ACTIVITIES.
HELL, MOST OF THE JOBS YOU PULL--STEALING OLD ARTIFACTS, BREAKING INTO SCIENCE LABS--THEY GET BLAMED ON US.
PERHAPS, MR. SNART.
HEY, COLD! YOU HEAR? THEY'RE THROWIN' A PARADE FOR THE FLASH.
COME ON, WEATHER WIZARD. HEARD SOME ROGUES ARE GOING OVER TO RAIN ON IT.
WE'RE DISCUSSING BUSINESS, TRICKSTER.
BUT--
SAY HELLO FOR US.
HEY, WIZARD. AT LEAST WHIP ME UP A THUNDERCLOUD OR TWO.
WE'RE BUSY, TRICKSTER.
KZZT
FINE. BUT YOU GUYS ARE MISSIN' OUT!
YOU ALIGNED YOURSELVES WITH A JUVENILE DELINQUENT?
HE'S GOT ENTHUSIASM. AND YOUTH AIN'T SUCH A BAD THING.
HELL, YOU'VE SEEN WHAT'S HAPPENED TO CAPTAIN BOOMERANG.
I'M NOT ASKIN' YOU FOR MUCH. JUST THAT, WELL, WE HEAR RUMORS THAT THINGS ARE ABOUT TO COME DOWN ON US HARD.
THE FLASH RETURNING. THAT'S JUST A NORMAL ANNOYANCE. BUT IF OUR WORLD GOES TA HELL, I JUST WANNA KNOW--
--CAN THE ROGUES COUNT ON YOUR SUPPORT?

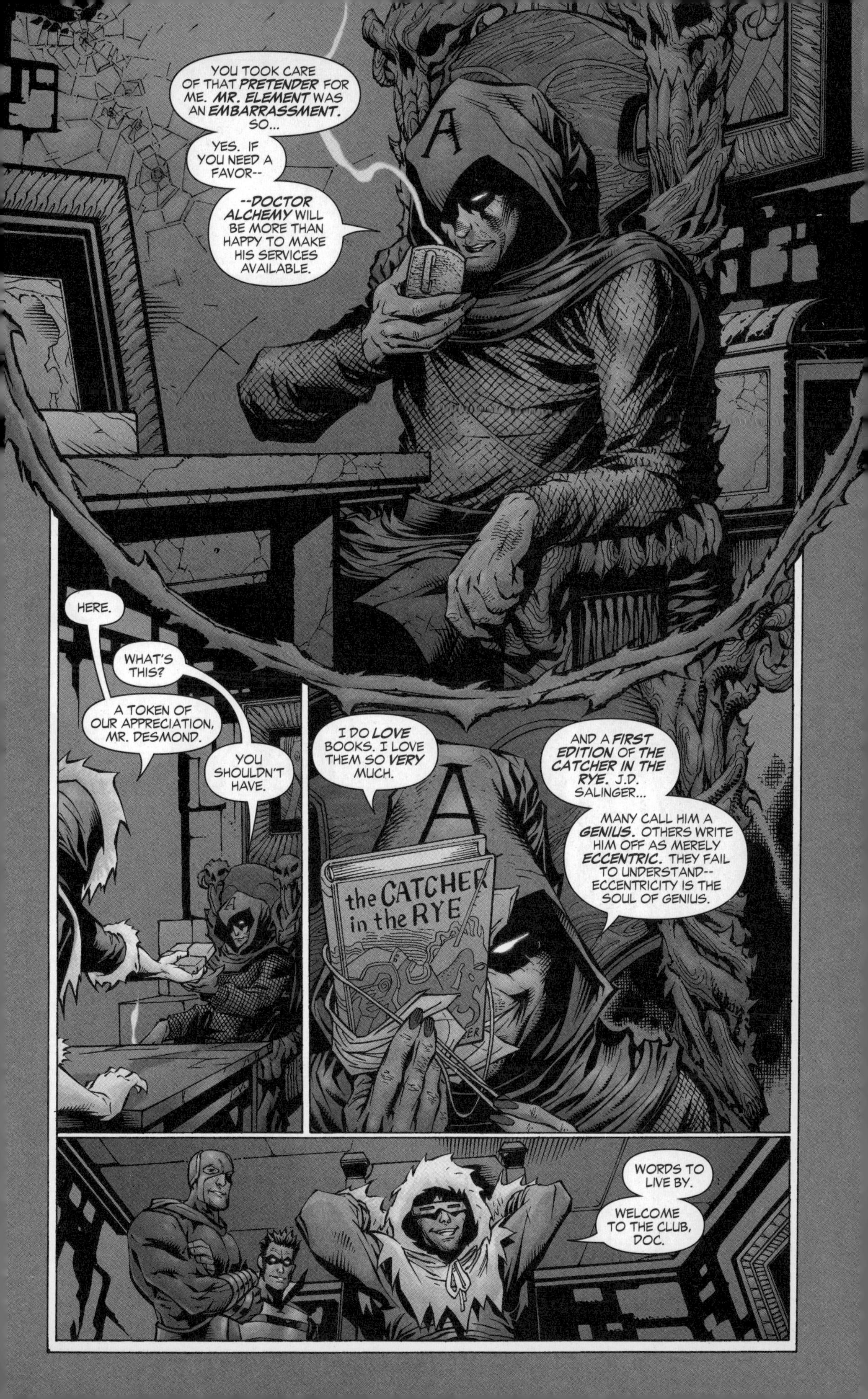
YOU TOOK CARE OF THAT PRETENDER FOR ME. MR. ELEMENT WAS AN EMBARRASSMENT. SO...
YES. IF YOU NEED A FAVOR--
--DOCTOR ALCHEMY WILL BE MORE THAN HAPPY TO MAKE HIS SERVICES AVAILABLE.
HERE.
WHAT'S THIS?
A TOKEN OF OUR APPRECIATION, MR. DESMOND.
YOU SHOULDN'T HAVE.
I DO LOVE BOOKS. I LOVE THEM SO VERY MUCH.
the CATCHER in the RYE
AND A FIRST EDITION OF THE CATCHER IN THE RYE. J.D. SALINGER...
MANY CALL HIM A GENIUS. OTHERS WRITE HIM OFF AS MERELY ECCENTRIC. THEY FAIL TO UNDERSTAND-- ECCENTRICITY IS THE SOUL OF GENIUS.
WORDS TO LIVE BY.
WELCOME TO THE CLUB, DOC.

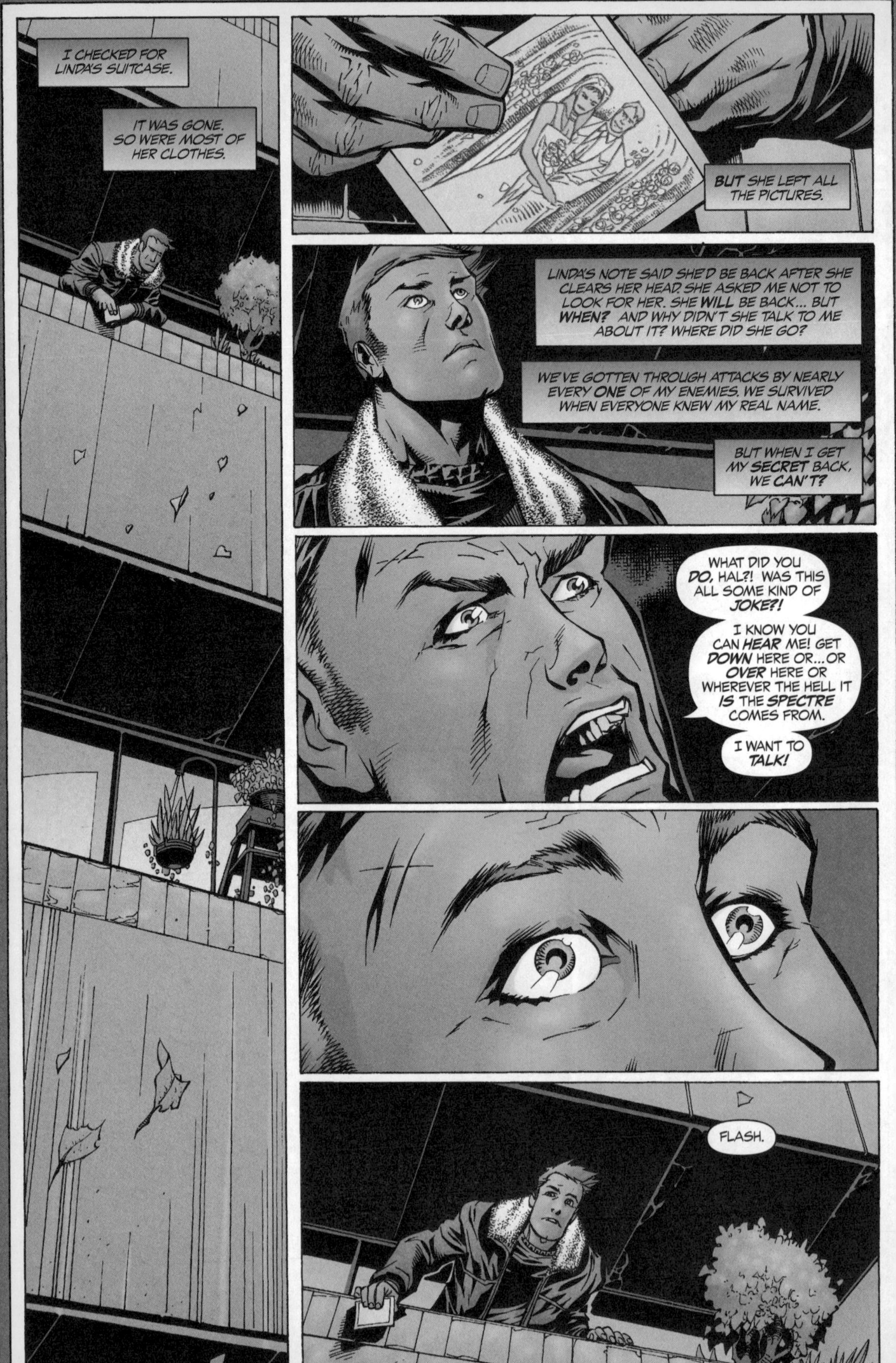
I CHECKED FOR LINDA'S SUITCASE.
IT WAS GONE. SO WERE MOST OF HER CLOTHES.
BUT SHE LEFT ALL THE PICTURES.
LINDA'S NOTE SAID SHE'D BE BACK AFTER SHE CLEARS HER HEAD. SHE ASKED ME NOT TO LOOK FOR HER. SHE WILL BE BACK... BUT WHEN? AND WHY DIDN'T SHE TALK TO ME ABOUT IT? WHERE DID SHE GO?
WE'VE GOTTEN THROUGH ATTACKS BY NEARLY EVERY ONE OF MY ENEMIES. WE SURVIVED WHEN EVERYONE KNEW MY REAL NAME.
BUT WHEN I GET MY SECRET BACK, WE CAN'T?
WHAT DID YOU DO, HAL?! WAS THIS ALL SOME KIND OF JOKE?!
I KNOW YOU CAN HEAR ME! GET DOWN HERE OR...OR OVER HERE OR WHEREVER THE HELL IT IS THE SPECTRE COMES FROM.
I WANT TO TALK!
FLASH.

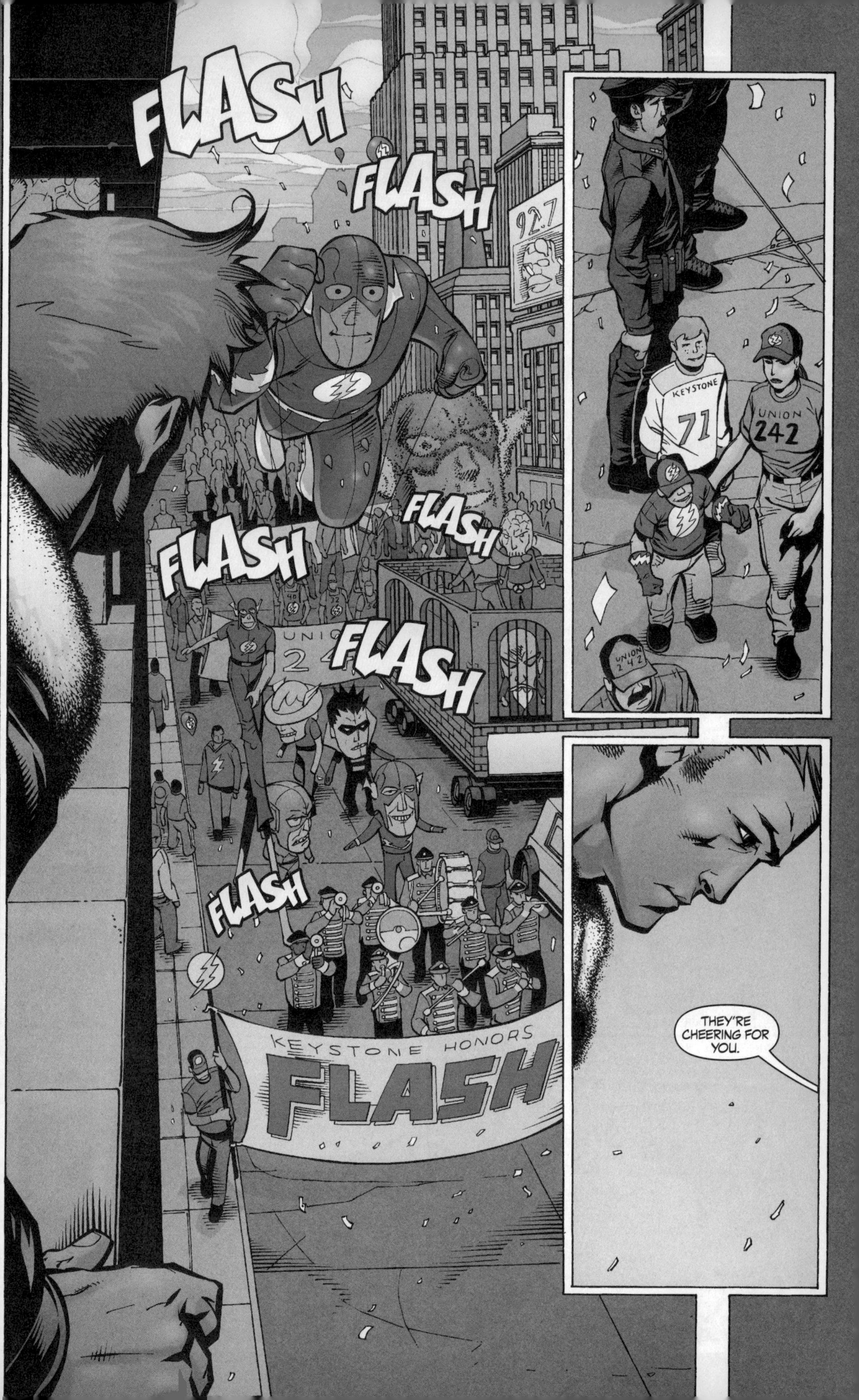

FLASH
FLASH
92.7
KEYSTONE
71
UNION
242
FLASH
FLASH
UNION
2
FLASH
UNION
242
FLASH
KEYSTONE HONORS
FLASH
THEY'RE CHEERING FOR YOU.

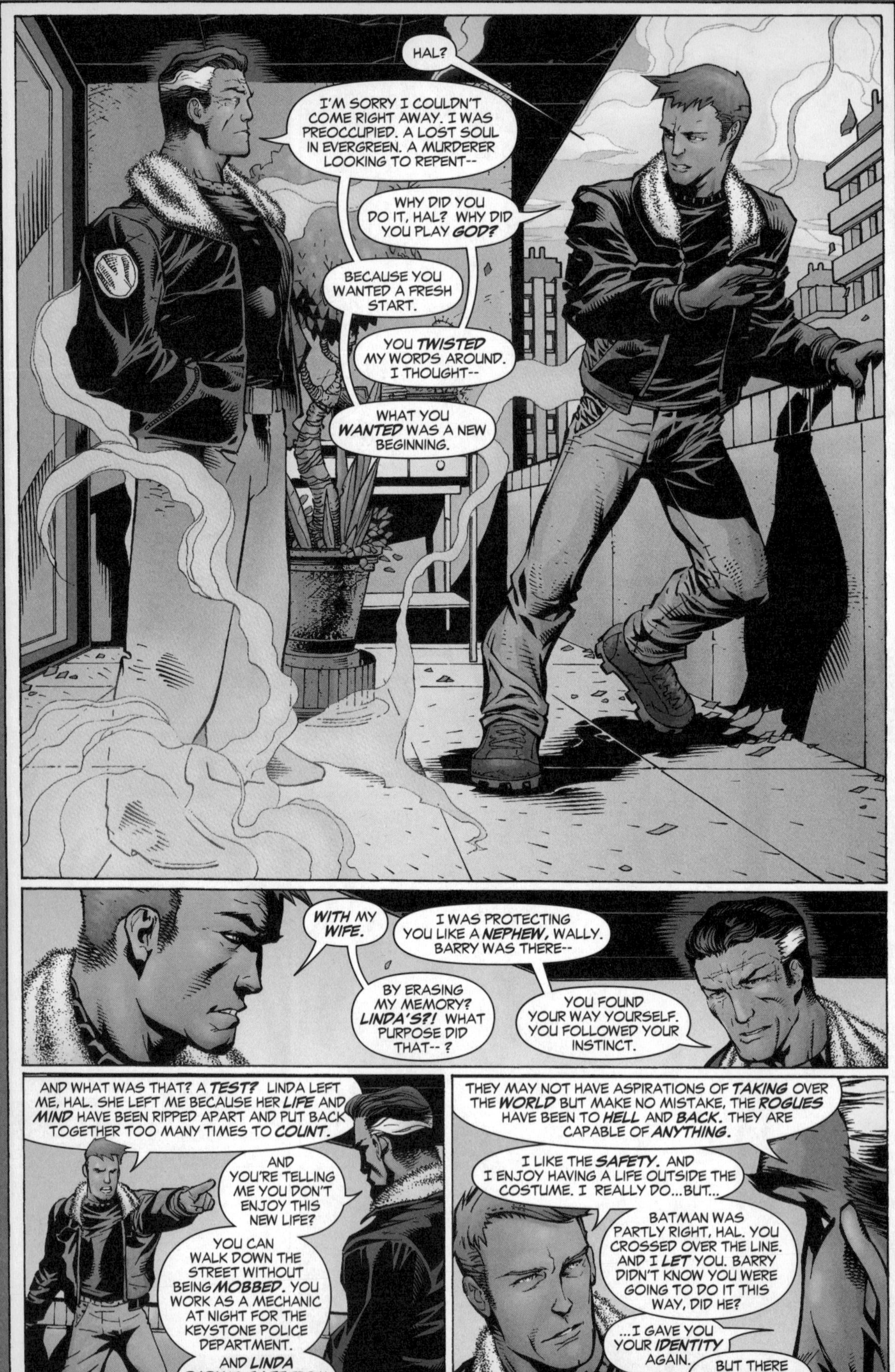
HAL?
I'M SORRY I COULDN'T COME RIGHT AWAY. I WAS PREOCCUPIED. A LOST SOUL IN EVERGREEN. A MURDERER LOOKING TO REPENT--
WHY DID YOU DO IT, HAL? WHY DID YOU PLAY GOD?
BECAUSE YOU WANTED A FRESH START.
YOU TWISTED MY WORDS AROUND. I THOUGHT--
WHAT YOU WANTED WAS A NEW BEGINNING.
WITH MY WIFE.
I WAS PROTECTING YOU LIKE A NEPHEW, WALLY. BARRY WAS THERE--
BY ERASING MY MEMORY? LINDA'S?! WHAT PURPOSE DID THAT-- ?
YOU FOUND YOUR WAY YOURSELF. YOU FOLLOWED YOUR INSTINCT.
AND WHAT WAS THAT? A TEST? LINDA LEFT ME, HAL. SHE LEFT ME BECAUSE HER LIFE AND MIND HAVE BEEN RIPPED APART AND PUT BACK TOGETHER TOO MANY TIMES TO COUNT.
AND YOU'RE TELLING ME YOU DON'T ENJOY THIS NEW LIFE?
YOU CAN WALK DOWN THE STREET WITHOUT BEING MOBBED. YOU WORK AS A MECHANIC AT NIGHT FOR THE KEYSTONE POLICE DEPARTMENT.
AND LINDA PARK IS SAFE FROM THOSE MANIACS.
THEY MAY NOT HAVE ASPIRATIONS OF TAKING OVER THE WORLD BUT MAKE NO MISTAKE, THE ROGUES HAVE BEEN TO HELL AND BACK. THEY ARE CAPABLE OF ANYTHING.
I LIKE THE SAFETY. AND I ENJOY HAVING A LIFE OUTSIDE THE COSTUME. I REALLY DO...BUT...
BATMAN WAS PARTLY RIGHT, HAL. YOU CROSSED OVER THE LINE. AND I LET YOU. BARRY DIDN'T KNOW YOU WERE GOING TO DO IT THIS WAY, DID HE?
...I GAVE YOU YOUR IDENTITY AGAIN.
BUT THERE WERE STRINGS ATTACHED.

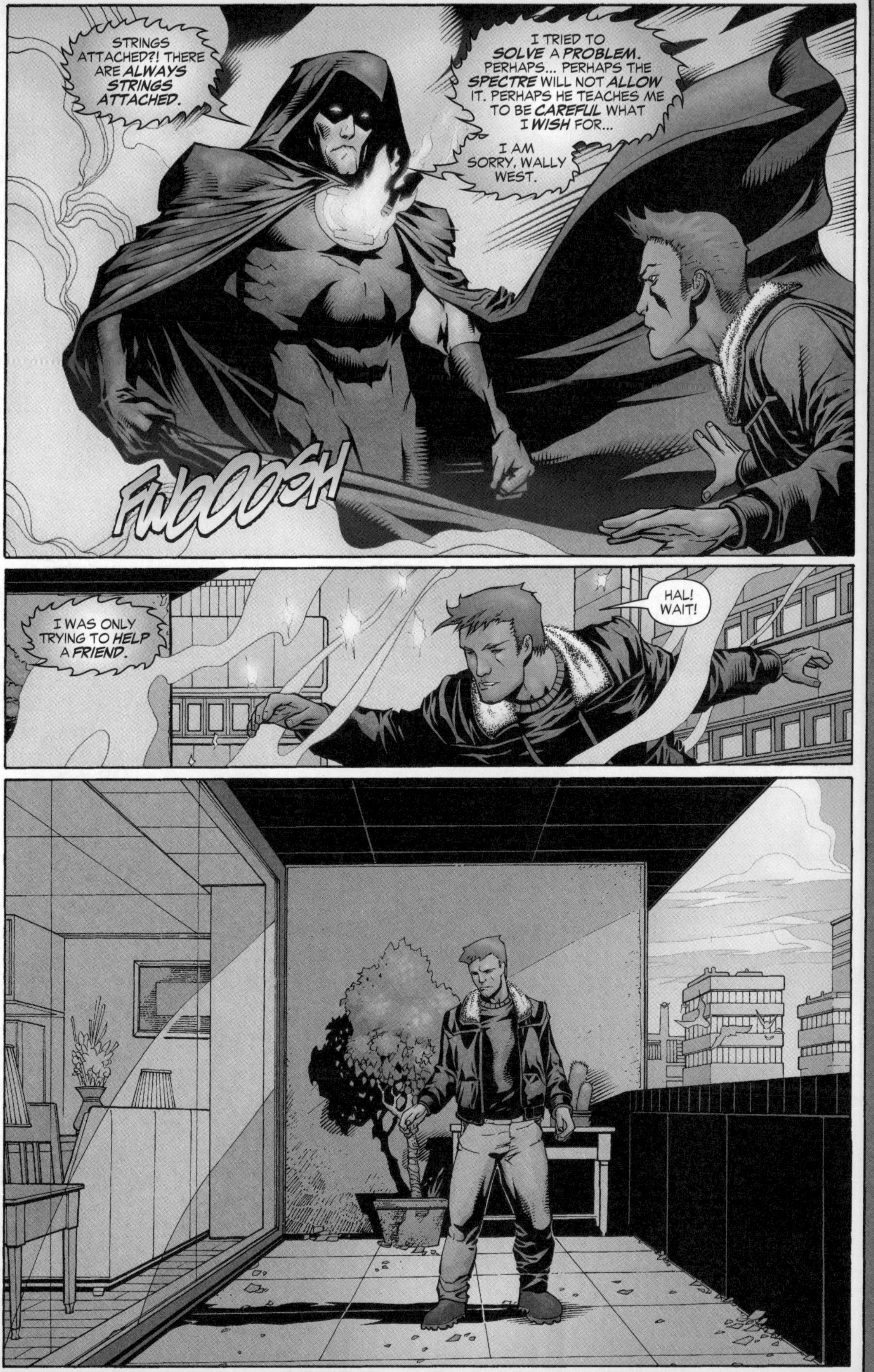

STRINGS ATTACHED?! THERE ARE ALWAYS STRINGS ATTACHED.
I TRIED TO SOLVE A PROBLEM. PERHAPS... PERHAPS THE SPECTRE WILL NOT ALLOW IT. PERHAPS HE TEACHES ME TO BE CAREFUL WHAT I WISH FOR...
I AM SORRY, WALLY WEST.
FWOOOSH
I WAS ONLY TRYING TO HELP A FRIEND.
HAL! WAIT!

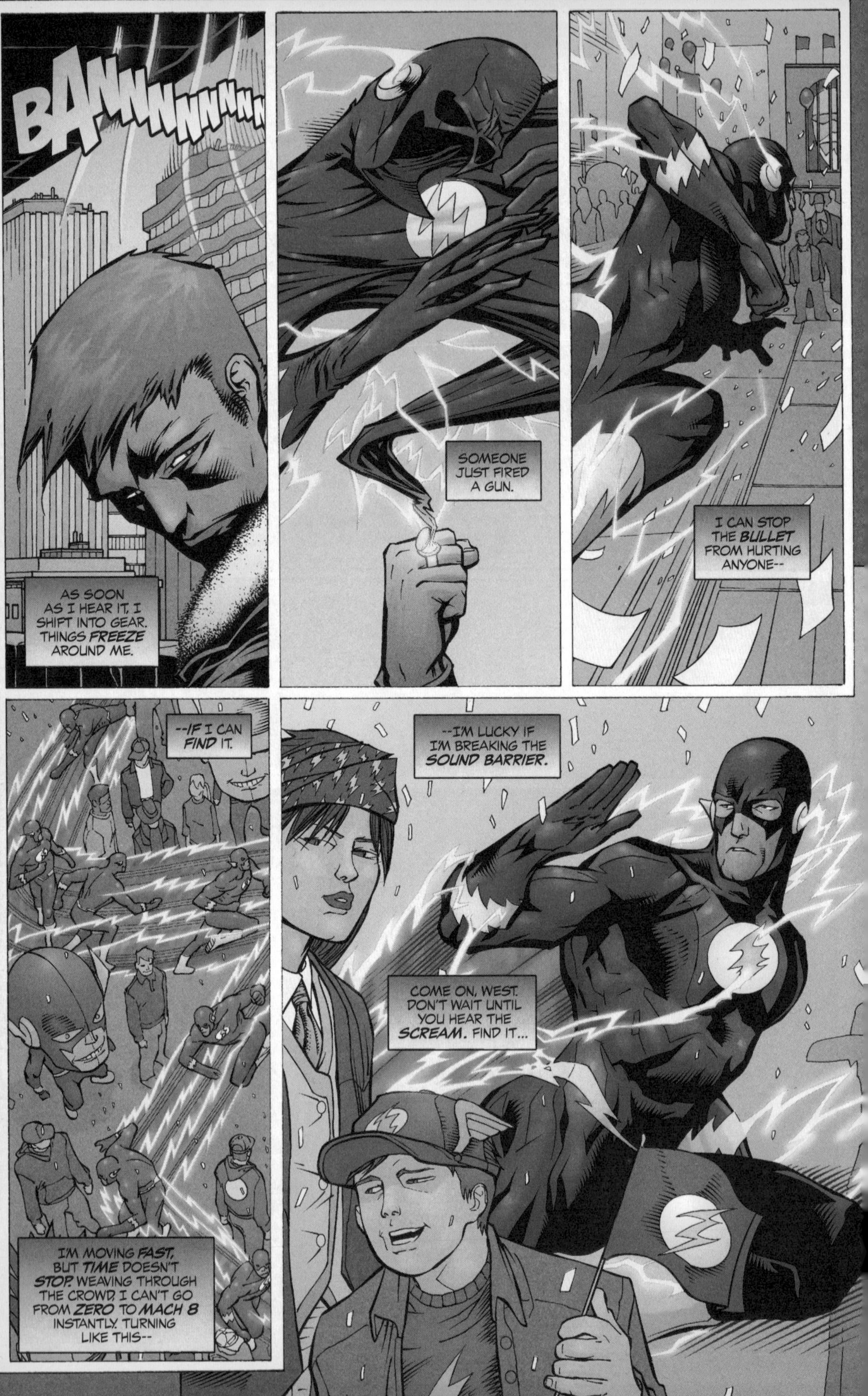
BANNNNNNNN
AS SOON AS I HEAR IT, I SHIFT INTO GEAR. THINGS FREEZE AROUND ME.
SOMEONE JUST FIRED A GUN.
I CAN STOP THE BULLET FROM HURTING ANYONE--
--IF I CAN FIND IT.
I'M MOVING FAST, BUT TIME DOESN'T STOP. WEAVING THROUGH THE CROWD, I CAN'T GO FROM ZERO TO MACH 8 INSTANTLY. TURNING LIKE THIS--
--I'M LUCKY IF I'M BREAKING THE SOUND BARRIER.
COME ON, WEST. DON'T WAIT UNTIL YOU HEAR THE SCREAM. FIND IT...

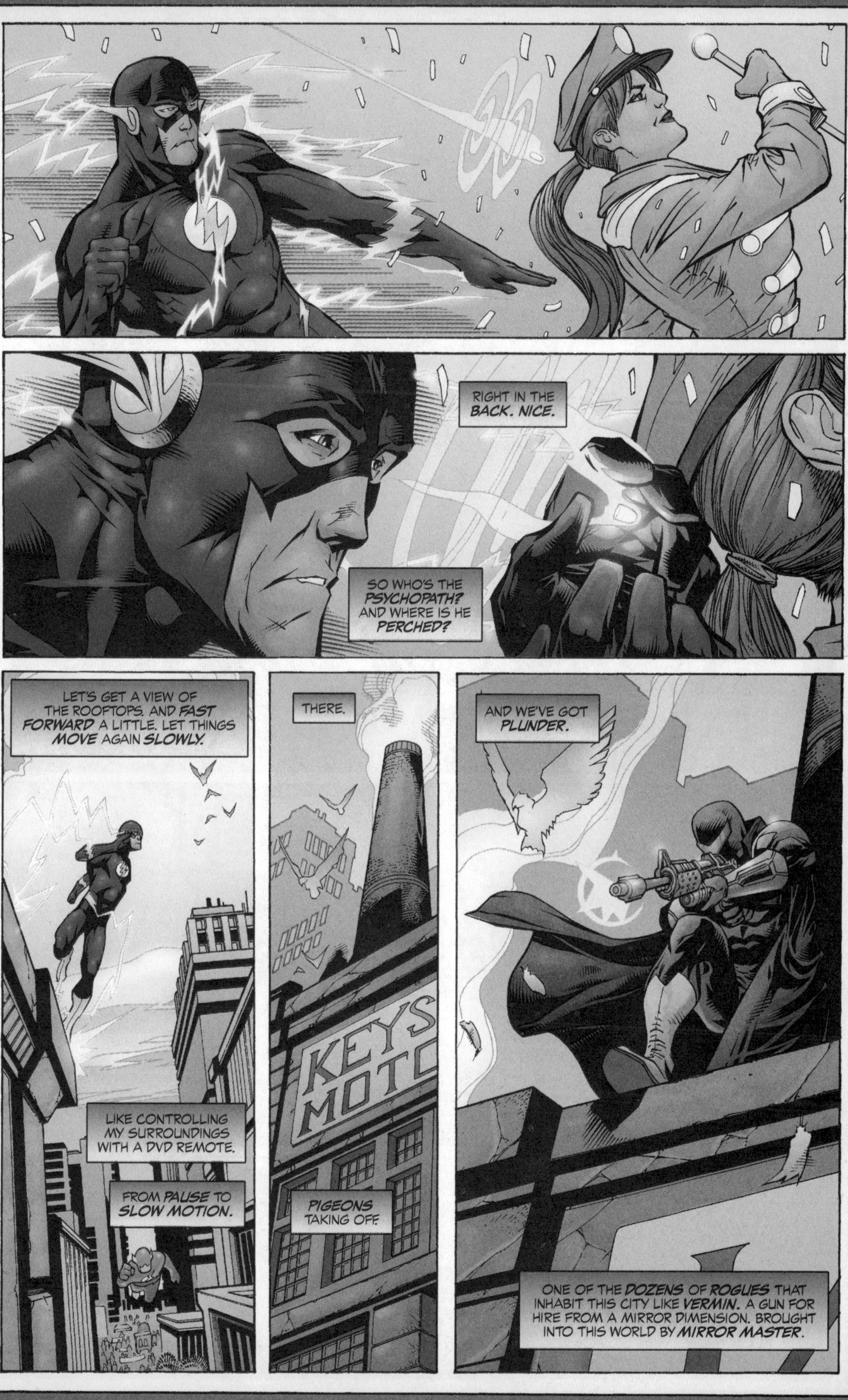
RIGHT IN THE BACK. NICE.
SO WHO'S THE PSYCHOPATH? AND WHERE IS HE PERCHED?
LET'S GET A VIEW OF THE ROOFTOPS. AND FAST FORWARD A LITTLE. LET THINGS MOVE AGAIN SLOWLY.
LIKE CONTROLLING MY SURROUNDINGS WITH A DVD REMOTE.
FROM PAUSE TO SLOW MOTION.
THERE.
KEYS
MOTO
PIGEONS TAKING OFF.
AND WE'VE GOT PLUNDER.
ONE OF THE DOZENS OF ROGUES THAT INHABIT THIS CITY LIKE VERMIN. A GUN FOR HIRE FROM A MIRROR DIMENSION. BROUGHT INTO THIS WORLD BY MIRROR MASTER.

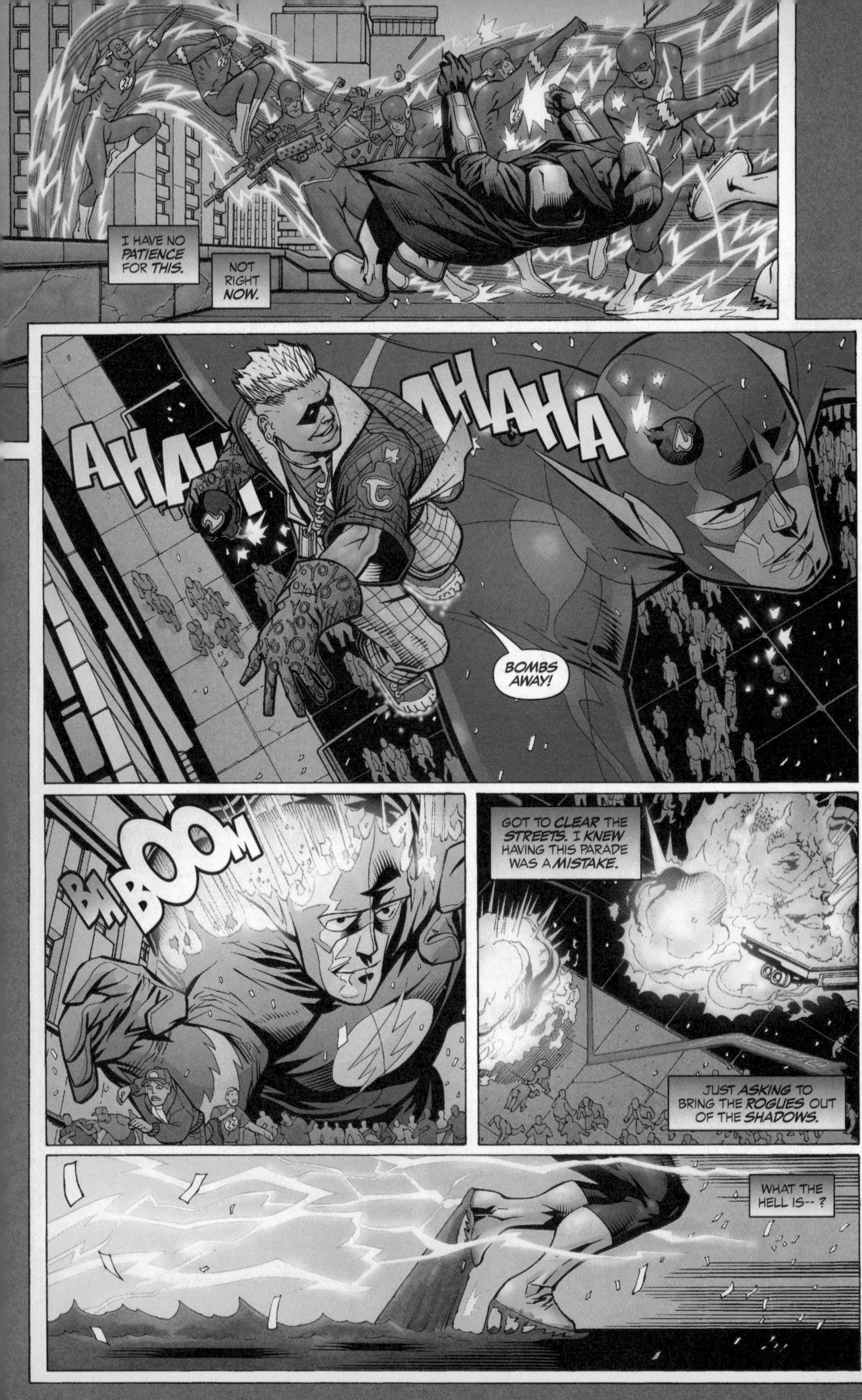
I HAVE NO PATIENCE FOR THIS.
NOT RIGHT NOW.
AHAHAHAHAHA
BOMBS AWAY!
BABOOM
GOT TO CLEAR THE STREETS. I KNEW HAVING THIS PARADE WAS A MISTAKE.
JUST ASKING TO BRING THE ROGUES OUT OF THE SHADOWS.
WHAT THE HELL IS-- ?

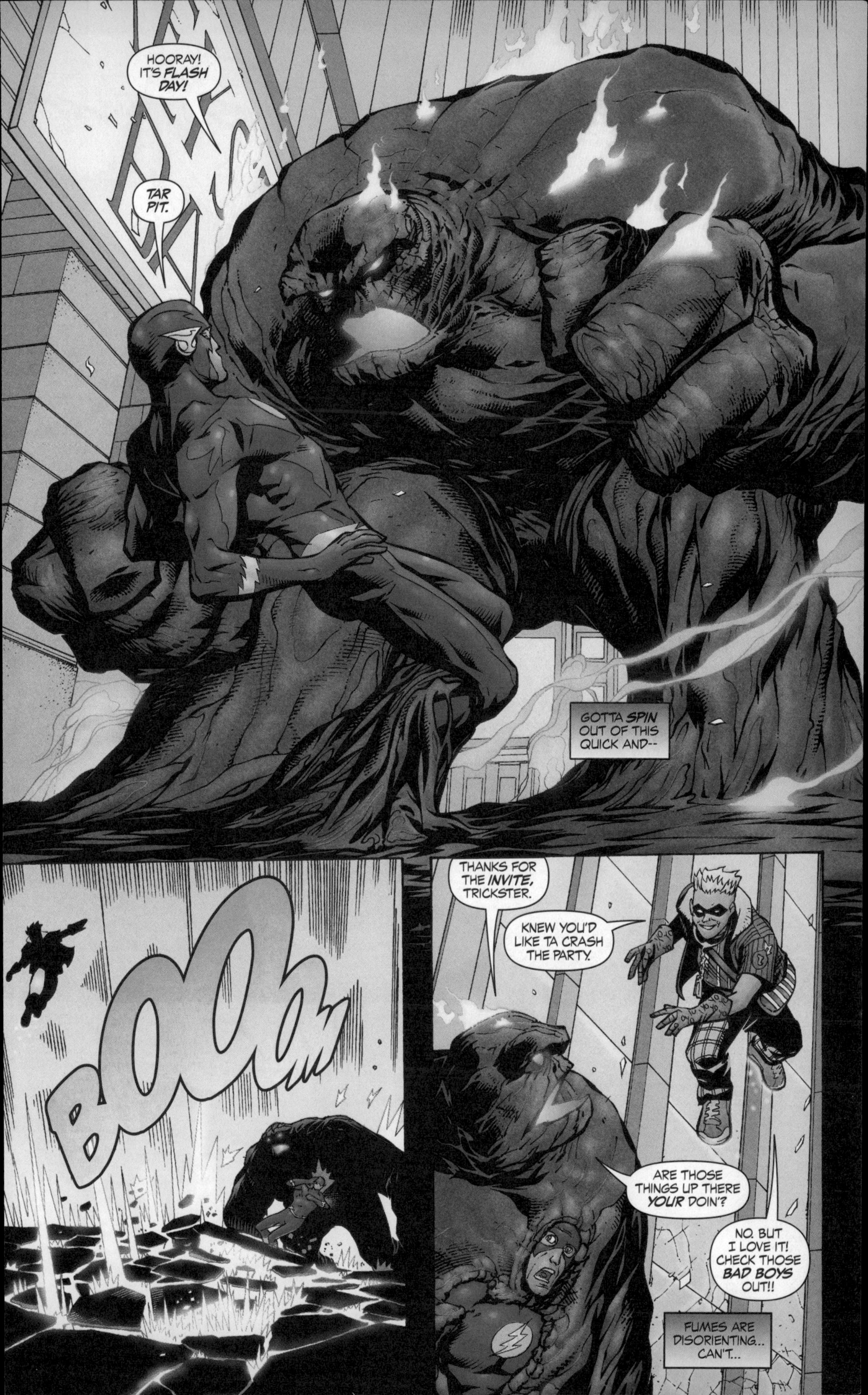
HOORAY! IT'S FLASH DAY!
TAR PIT.
GOTTA SPIN OUT OF THIS QUICK AND--
BOOM
THANKS FOR THE INVITE, TRICKSTER.
KNEW YOU'D LIKE TA CRASH THE PARTY.
ARE THOSE THINGS UP THERE YOUR DOIN'?
NO. BUT I LOVE IT! CHECK THOSE BAD BOYS OUT!!
FUMES ARE DISORIENTING... CAN'T...

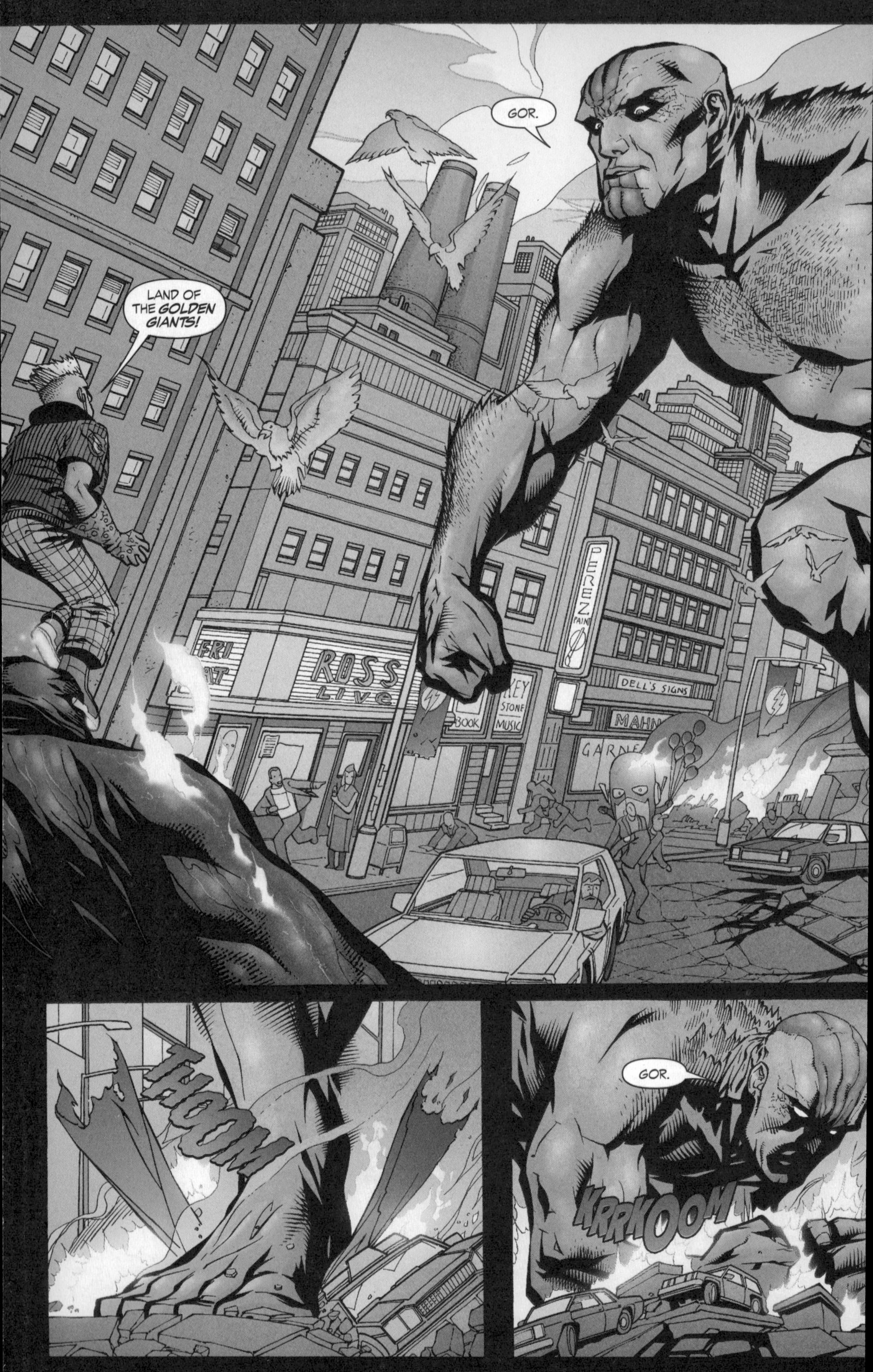
LAND OF THE GOLDEN GIANTS!
GOR.
ROSS LIVE
PEREZ
DELL'S SIGNS
STONE MUSIC
BOOK
THOOM
GOR.
KRRKOOM

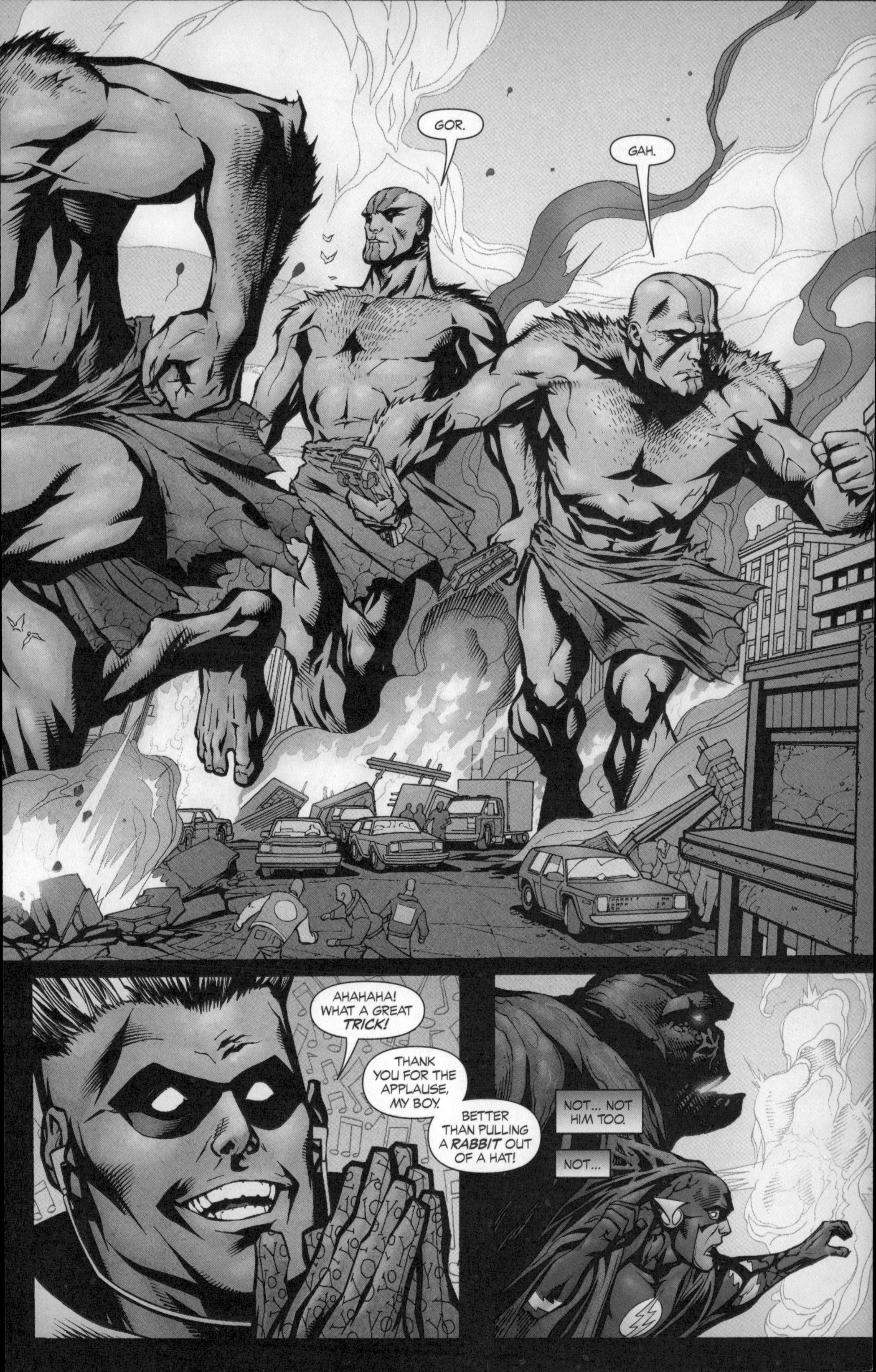

GOR.
GAH.
AHAHAHA! WHAT A GREAT TRICK!
THANK YOU FOR THE APPLAUSE, MY BOY.
BETTER THAN PULLING A RABBIT OUT OF A HAT!
NOT... NOT HIM TOO.
NOT...

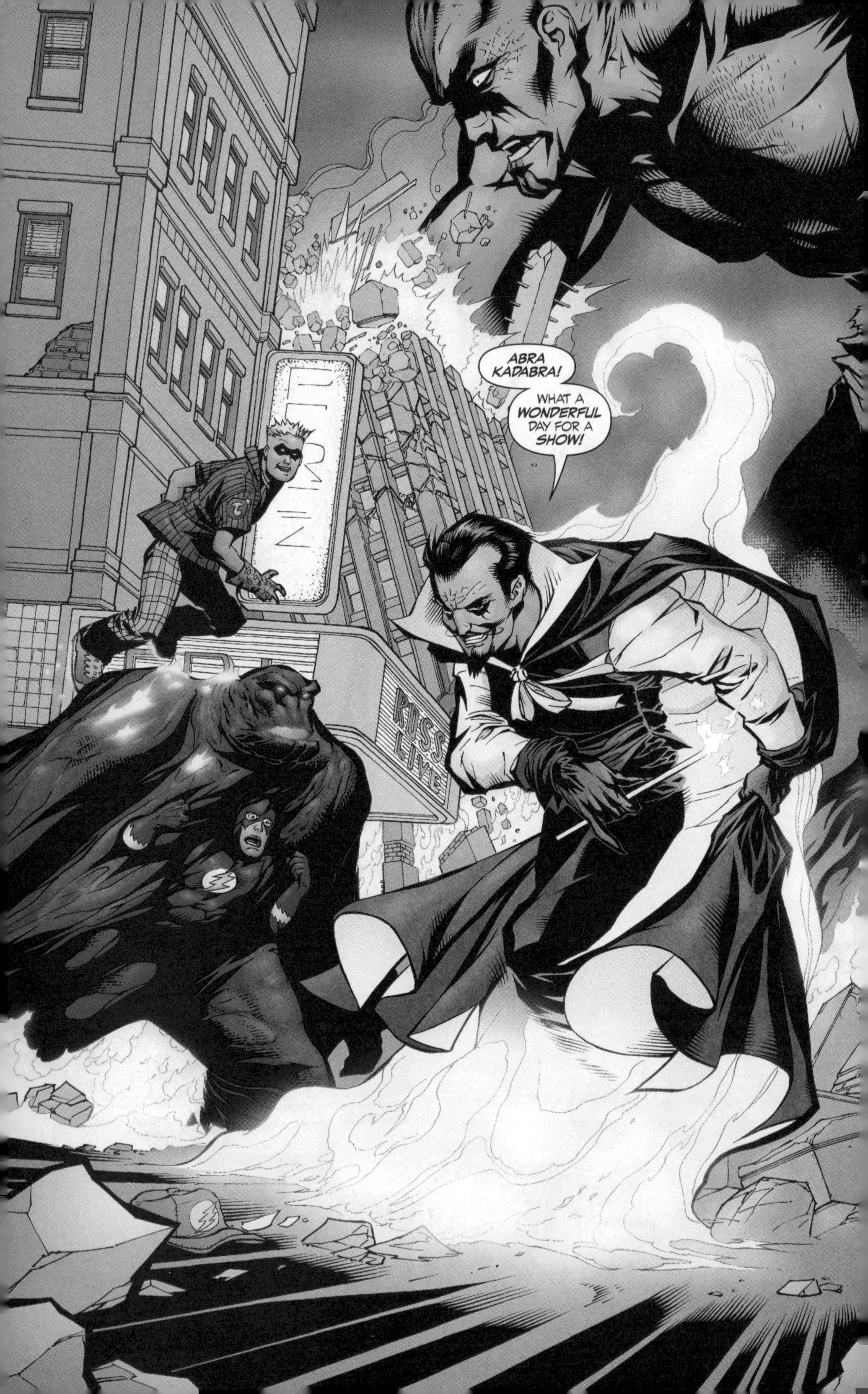
ABRA KADABRA!
WHAT A WONDERFUL DAY FOR A SHOW!

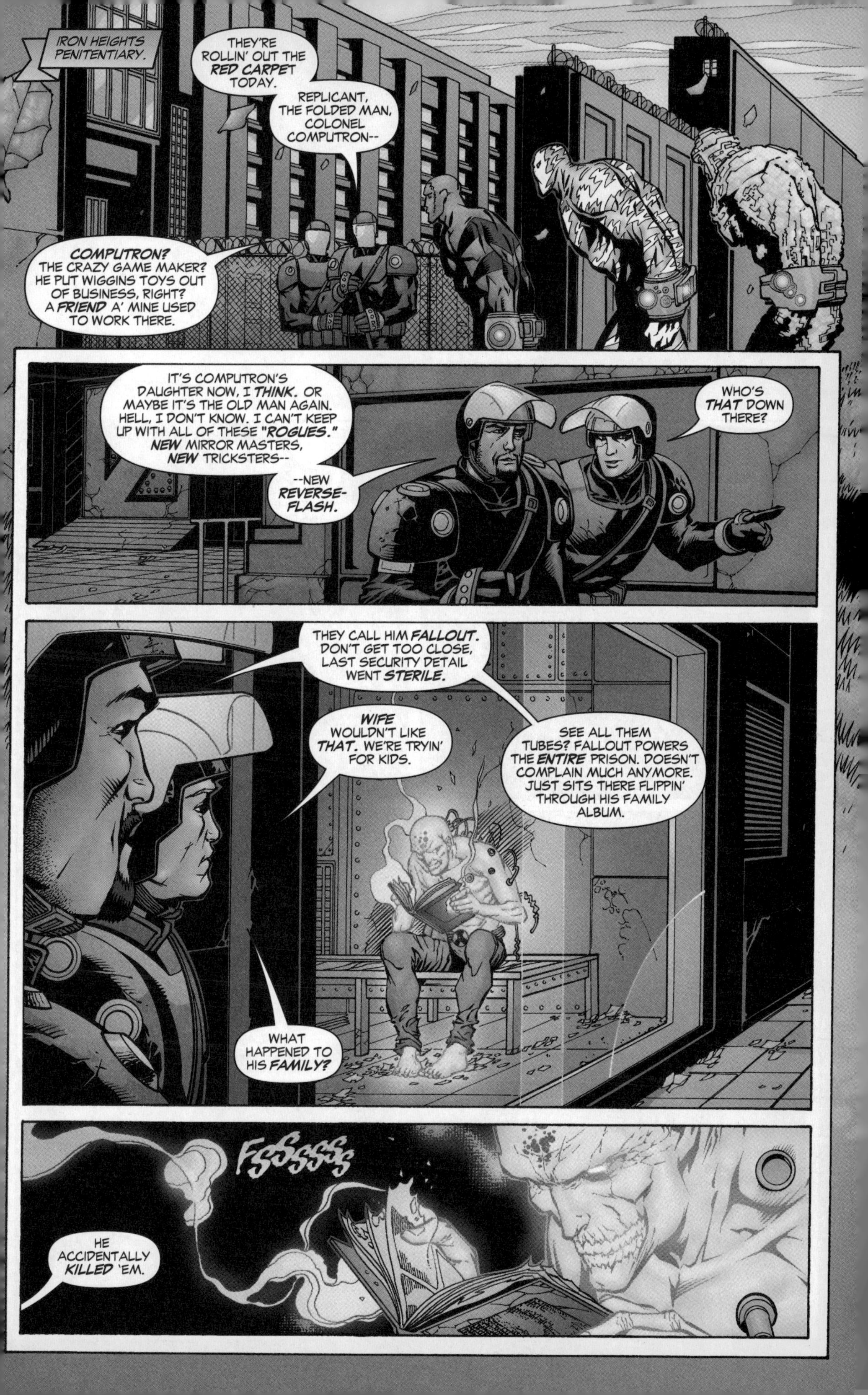
IRON HEIGHTS PENITENTIARY.
THEY'RE ROLLIN' OUT THE RED CARPET TODAY.
REPLICANT, THE FOLDED MAN, COLONEL COMPUTRON--
COMPUTRON? THE CRAZY GAME MAKER? HE PUT WIGGINS TOYS OUT OF BUSINESS, RIGHT? A FRIEND A' MINE USED TO WORK THERE.
IT'S COMPUTRON'S DAUGHTER NOW, I THINK. OR MAYBE IT'S THE OLD MAN AGAIN. HELL, I DON'T KNOW. I CAN'T KEEP UP WITH ALL OF THESE "ROGUES." NEW MIRROR MASTERS, NEW TRICKSTERS--
--NEW REVERSE-FLASH.
WHO'S THAT DOWN THERE?
THEY CALL HIM FALLOUT. DON'T GET TOO CLOSE, LAST SECURITY DETAIL WENT STERILE.
WIFE WOULDN'T LIKE THAT. WE'RE TRYIN' FOR KIDS.
SEE ALL THEM TUBES? FALLOUT POWERS THE ENTIRE PRISON. DOESN'T COMPLAIN MUCH ANYMORE. JUST SITS THERE FLIPPIN' THROUGH HIS FAMILY ALBUM.
WHAT HAPPENED TO HIS FAMILY?
FSSSSSS
HE ACCIDENTALLY KILLED 'EM.

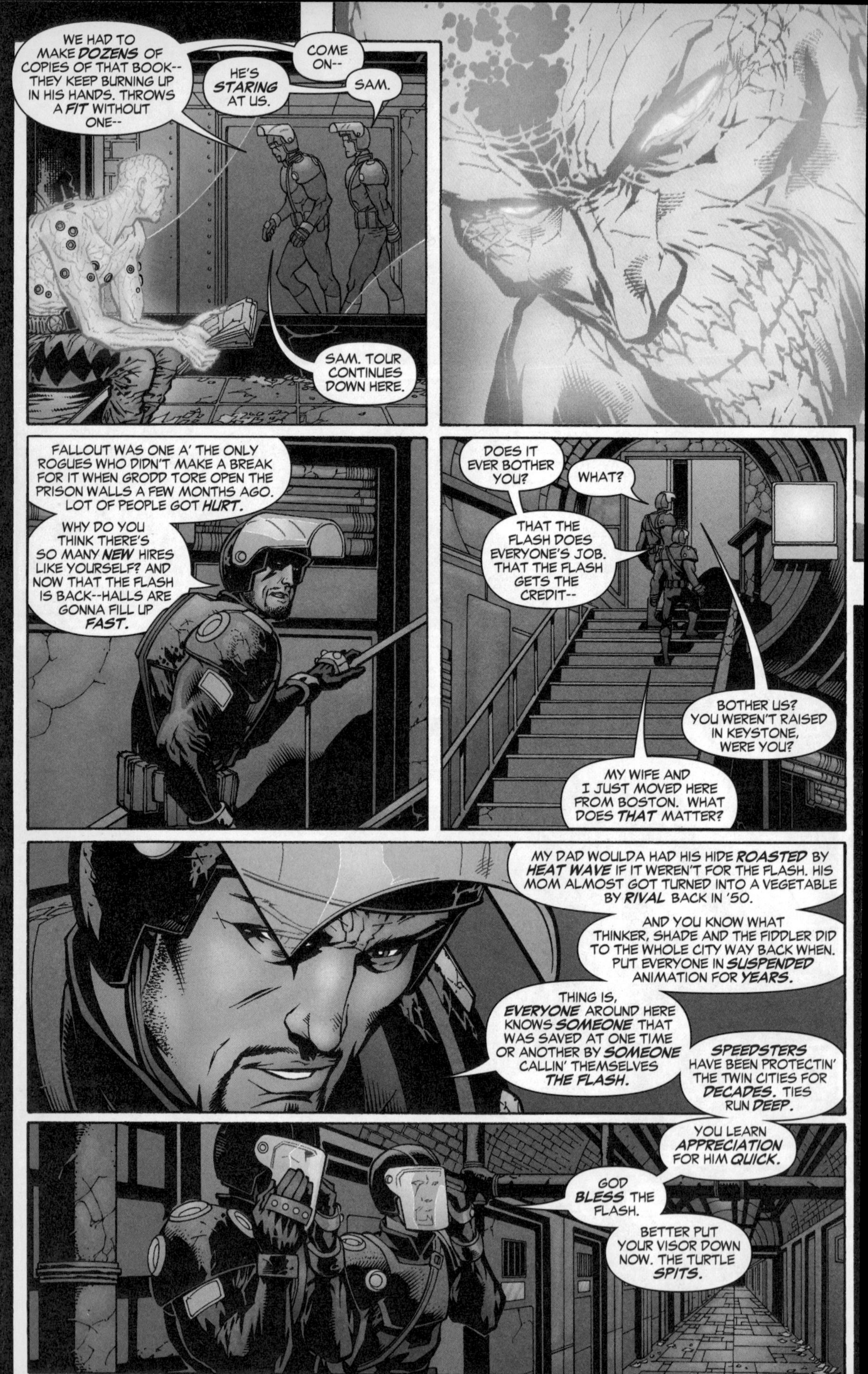
WE HAD TO MAKE DOZENS OF COPIES OF THAT BOOK-- THEY KEEP BURNING UP IN HIS HANDS. THROWS A FIT WITHOUT ONE--
COME ON--
HE'S STARING AT US.
SAM.
SAM. TOUR CONTINUES DOWN HERE.
FALLOUT WAS ONE A' THE ONLY ROGUES WHO DIDN'T MAKE A BREAK FOR IT WHEN GRODD TORE OPEN THE PRISON WALLS A FEW MONTHS AGO. LOT OF PEOPLE GOT HURT.
WHY DO YOU THINK THERE'S SO MANY NEW HIRES LIKE YOURSELF? AND NOW THAT THE FLASH IS BACK--HALLS ARE GONNA FILL UP FAST.
DOES IT EVER BOTHER YOU?
WHAT?
THAT THE FLASH DOES EVERYONE'S JOB. THAT THE FLASH GETS THE CREDIT--
BOTHER US? YOU WEREN'T RAISED IN KEYSTONE, WERE YOU?
MY WIFE AND I JUST MOVED HERE FROM BOSTON. WHAT DOES THAT MATTER?
MY DAD WOULDA HAD HIS HIDE ROASTED BY HEAT WAVE IF IT WEREN'T FOR THE FLASH. HIS MOM ALMOST GOT TURNED INTO A VEGETABLE BY RIVAL BACK IN '50.
AND YOU KNOW WHAT THINKER, SHADE AND THE FIDDLER DID TO THE WHOLE CITY WAY BACK WHEN. PUT EVERYONE IN SUSPENDED ANIMATION FOR YEARS.
THING IS, EVERYONE AROUND HERE KNOWS SOMEONE THAT WAS SAVED AT ONE TIME OR ANOTHER BY SOMEONE CALLIN' THEMSELVES THE FLASH.
SPEEDSTERS HAVE BEEN PROTECTIN' THE TWIN CITIES FOR DECADES. TIES RUN DEEP.
YOU LEARN APPRECIATION FOR HIM QUICK.
GOD BLESS THE FLASH.
BETTER PUT YOUR VISOR DOWN NOW. THE TURTLE SPITS.

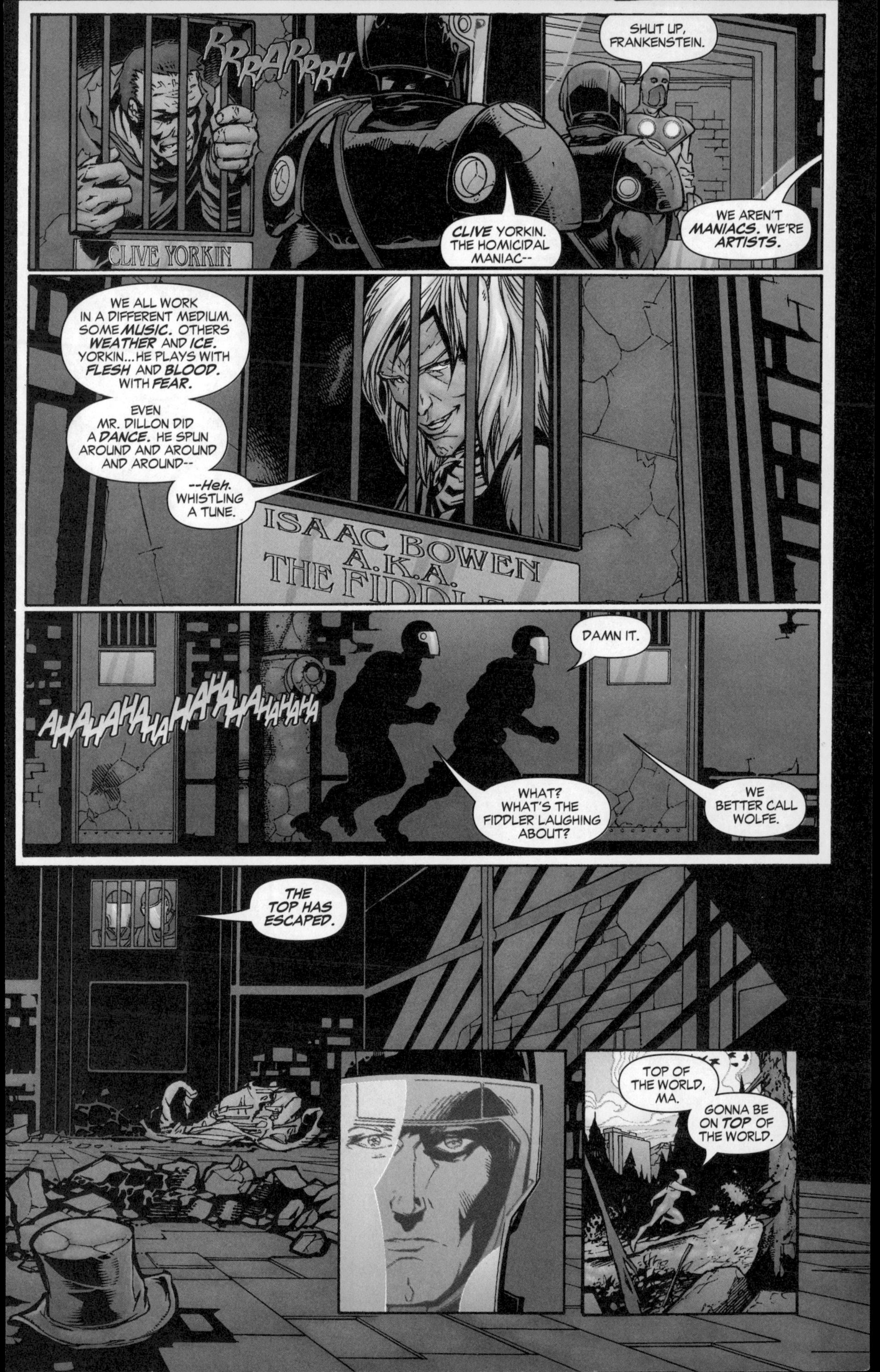
RRRAARRRH
SHUT UP, FRANKENSTEIN.
CLIVE YORKIN. THE HOMICIDAL MANIAC--
WE AREN'T MANIACS. WE'RE ARTISTS.
CLIVE YORKIN
WE ALL WORK IN A DIFFERENT MEDIUM. SOME MUSIC. OTHERS WEATHER AND ICE. YORKIN... HE PLAYS WITH FLESH AND BLOOD. WITH FEAR.
EVEN MR. DILLON DID A DANCE. HE SPUN AROUND AND AROUND AND AROUND--
--Heh. WHISTLING A TUNE.
ISAAC BOWEN A.K.A. THE FIDDLE
AHAHAHAHAHAHAHAHAHAHAHA
DAMN IT.
WHAT? WHAT'S THE FIDDLER LAUGHING ABOUT?
WE BETTER CALL WOLFE.
THE TOP HAS ESCAPED.
TOP OF THE WORLD, MA.
GONNA BE ON TOP OF THE WORLD.

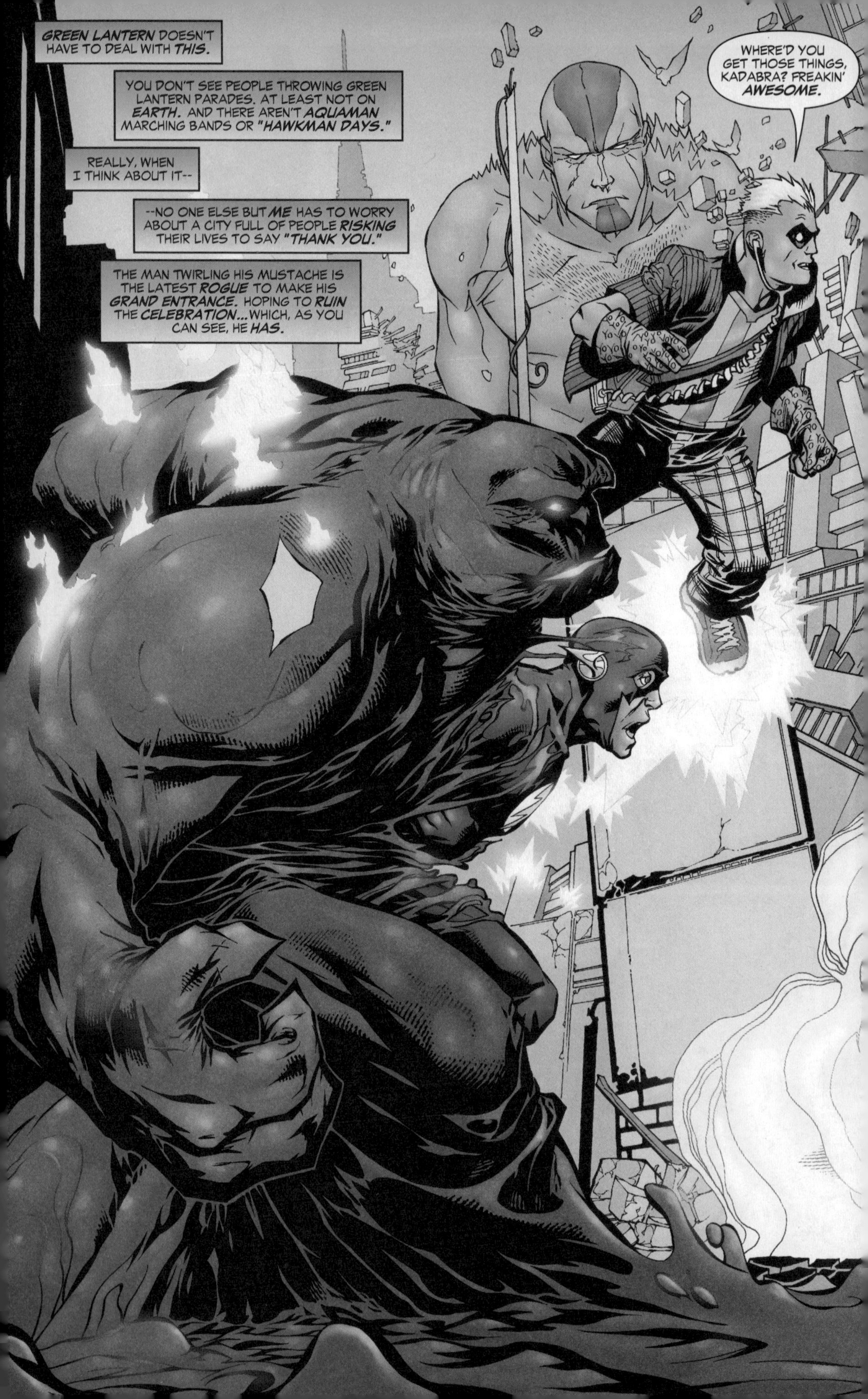
GREEN LANTERN DOESN'T HAVE TO DEAL WITH THIS.
YOU DON'T SEE PEOPLE THROWING GREEN LANTERN PARADES. AT LEAST NOT ON EARTH. AND THERE AREN'T AQUAMAN MARCHING BANDS OR "HAWKMAN DAYS."
REALLY, WHEN I THINK ABOUT IT--
--NO ONE ELSE BUT ME HAS TO WORRY ABOUT A CITY FULL OF PEOPLE RISKING THEIR LIVES TO SAY "THANK YOU."
THE MAN TWIRLING HIS MUSTACHE IS THE LATEST ROGUE TO MAKE HIS GRAND ENTRANCE. HOPING TO RUIN THE CELEBRATION...WHICH, AS YOU CAN SEE, HE HAS.
WHERE'D YOU GET THOSE THINGS, KADABRA? FREAKIN' AWESOME.

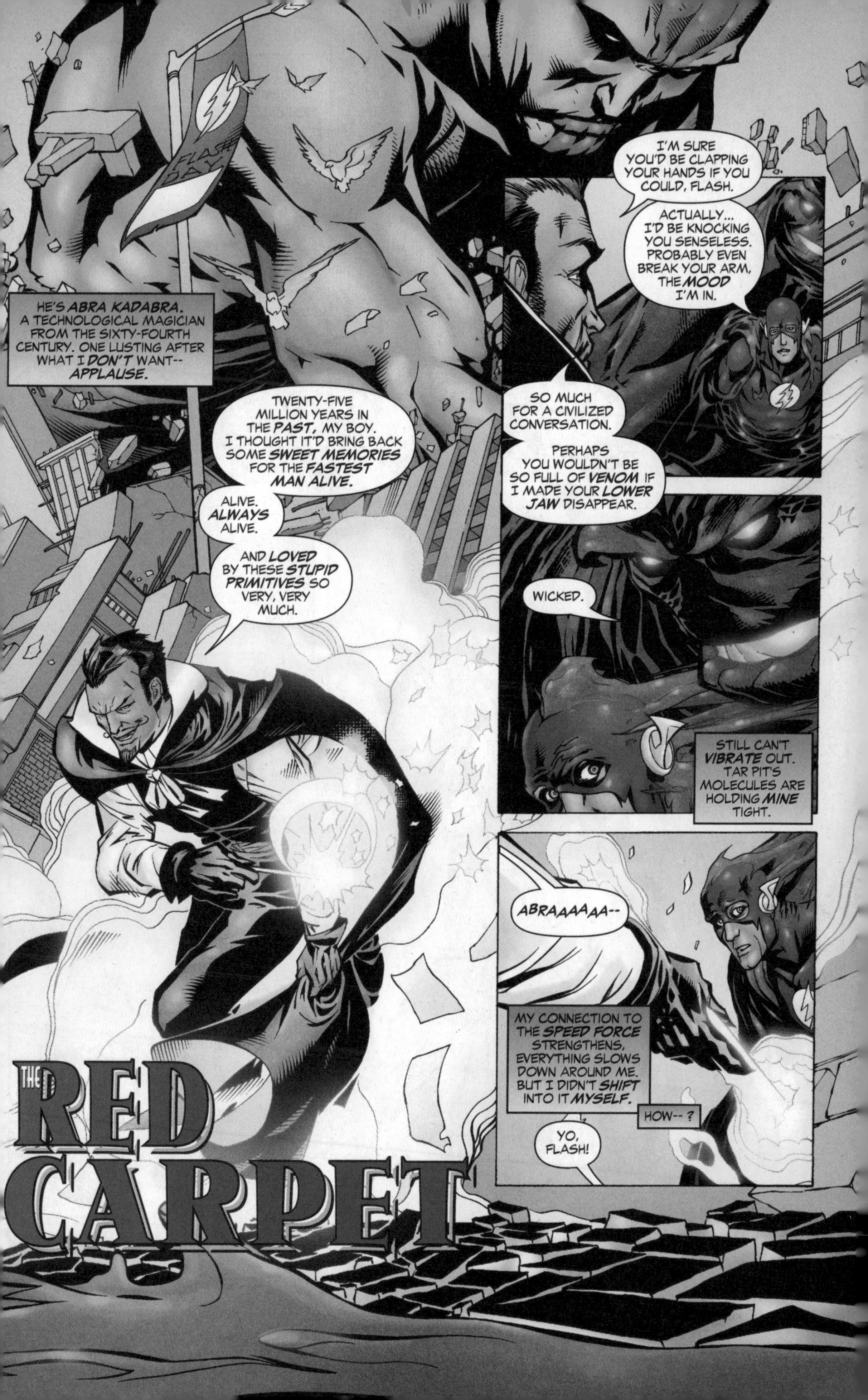

FLASH DAY
HE'S ABRA KADABRA. A TECHNOLOGICAL MAGICIAN FROM THE SIXTY-FOURTH CENTURY. ONE LUSTING AFTER WHAT I DON'T WANT-- APPLAUSE.
TWENTY-FIVE MILLION YEARS IN THE PAST, MY BOY. I THOUGHT IT'D BRING BACK SOME SWEET MEMORIES FOR THE FASTEST MAN ALIVE.
ALIVE. ALWAYS ALIVE.
AND LOVED BY THESE STUPID PRIMITIVES SO VERY, VERY MUCH.
I'M SURE YOU'D BE CLAPPING YOUR HANDS IF YOU COULD, FLASH.
ACTUALLY... I'D BE KNOCKING YOU SENSELESS. PROBABLY EVEN BREAK YOUR ARM, THE MOOD I'M IN.
SO MUCH FOR A CIVILIZED CONVERSATION.
PERHAPS YOU WOULDN'T BE SO FULL OF VENOM IF I MADE YOUR LOWER JAW DISAPPEAR.
WICKED.
STILL CAN'T VIBRATE OUT. TAR PIT'S MOLECULES ARE HOLDING MINE TIGHT.
ABRAAAAAA--
MY CONNECTION TO THE SPEED FORCE STRENGTHENS, EVERYTHING SLOWS DOWN AROUND ME. BUT I DIDN'T SHIFT INTO IT MYSELF.
HOW-- ?
YO, FLASH!
THE RED CARPET

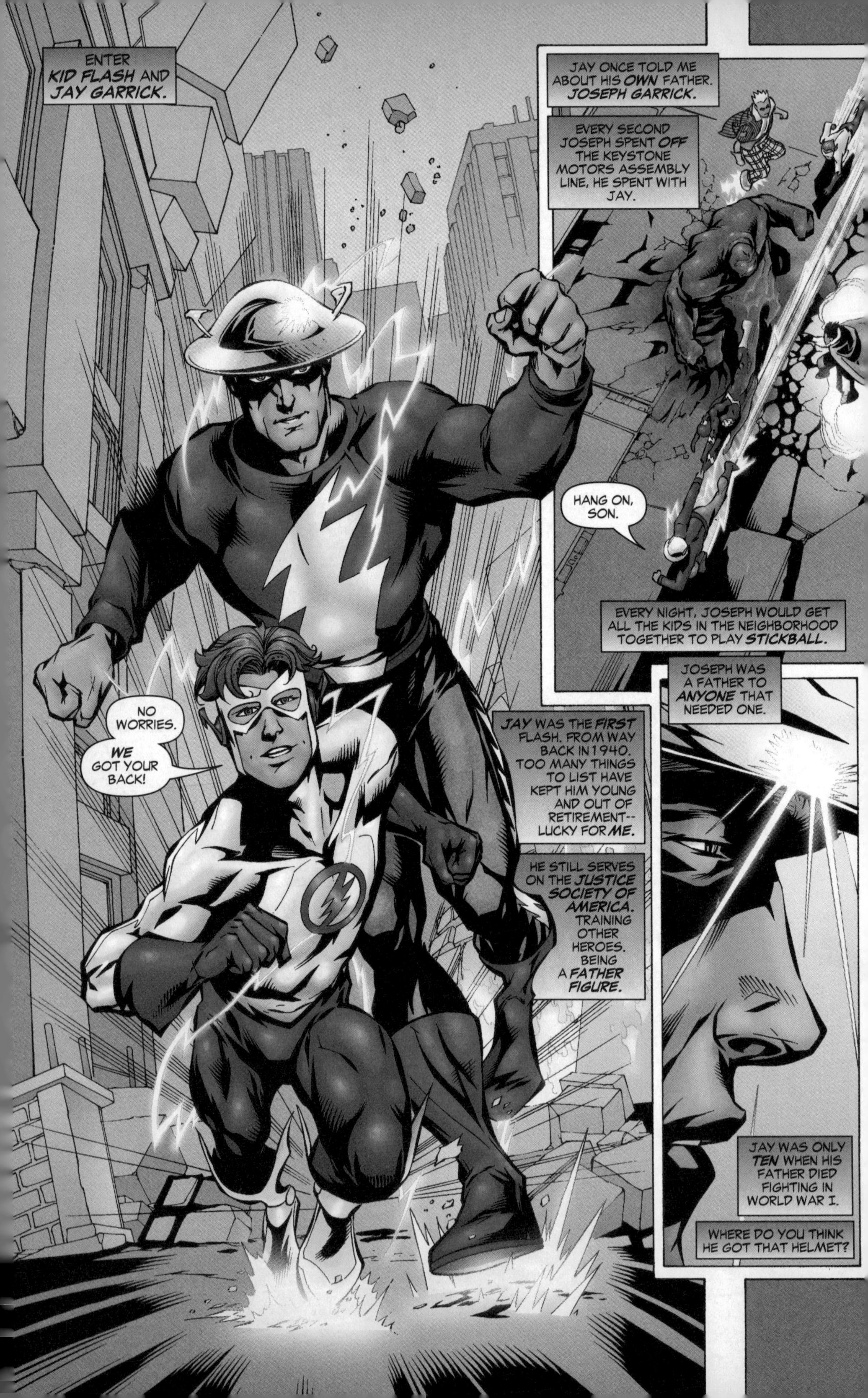
ENTER KID FLASH AND JAY GARRICK.
NO WORRIES.
WE GOT YOUR BACK!
JAY WAS THE FIRST FLASH. FROM WAY BACK IN 1940. TOO MANY THINGS TO LIST HAVE KEPT HIM YOUNG AND OUT OF RETIREMENT-- LUCKY FOR ME.
HE STILL SERVES ON THE JUSTICE SOCIETY OF AMERICA. TRAINING OTHER HEROES. BEING A FATHER FIGURE.
JAY ONCE TOLD ME ABOUT HIS OWN FATHER. JOSEPH GARRICK.
EVERY SECOND JOSEPH SPENT OFF THE KEYSTONE MOTORS ASSEMBLY LINE, HE SPENT WITH JAY.
HANG ON, SON.
EVERY NIGHT, JOSEPH WOULD GET ALL THE KIDS IN THE NEIGHBORHOOD TOGETHER TO PLAY STICKBALL.
JOSEPH WAS A FATHER TO ANYONE THAT NEEDED ONE.
JAY WAS ONLY TEN WHEN HIS FATHER DIED FIGHTING IN WORLD WAR I.
WHERE DO YOU THINK HE GOT THAT HELMET?

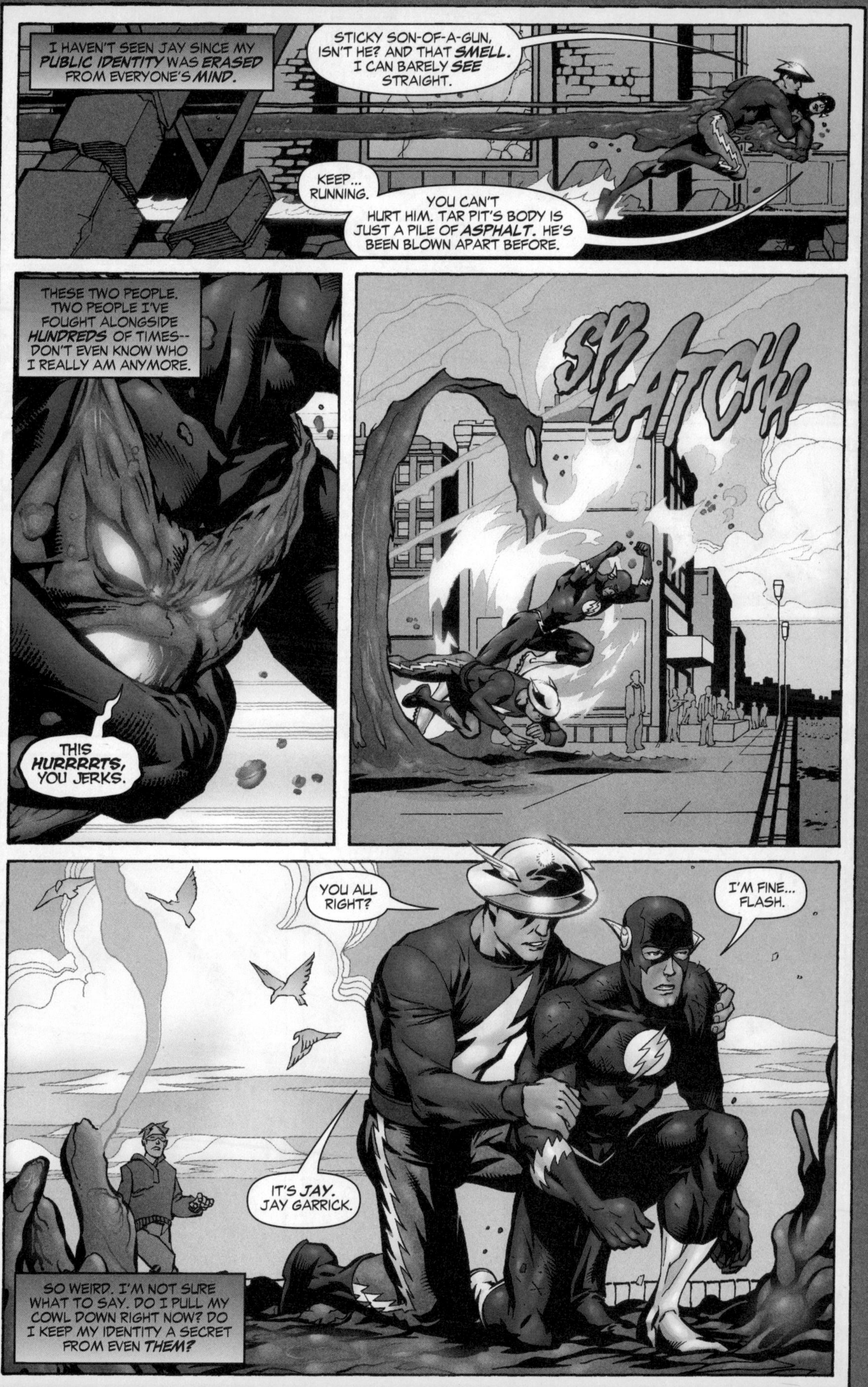
I HAVEN'T SEEN JAY SINCE MY PUBLIC IDENTITY WAS ERASED FROM EVERYONE'S MIND.
STICKY SON-OF-A-GUN, ISN'T HE? AND THAT SMELL. I CAN BARELY SEE STRAIGHT.
KEEP... RUNNING.
YOU CAN'T HURT HIM. TAR PIT'S BODY IS JUST A PILE OF ASPHALT. HE'S BEEN BLOWN APART BEFORE.
THESE TWO PEOPLE. TWO PEOPLE I'VE FOUGHT ALONGSIDE HUNDREDS OF TIMES-- DON'T EVEN KNOW WHO I REALLY AM ANYMORE.
THIS HURRRRTS, YOU JERKS.
SPLATCH
YOU ALL RIGHT?
I'M FINE... FLASH.
IT'S JAY. JAY GARRICK.
SO WEIRD. I'M NOT SURE WHAT TO SAY. DO I PULL MY COWL DOWN RIGHT NOW? DO I KEEP MY IDENTITY A SECRET FROM EVEN THEM?

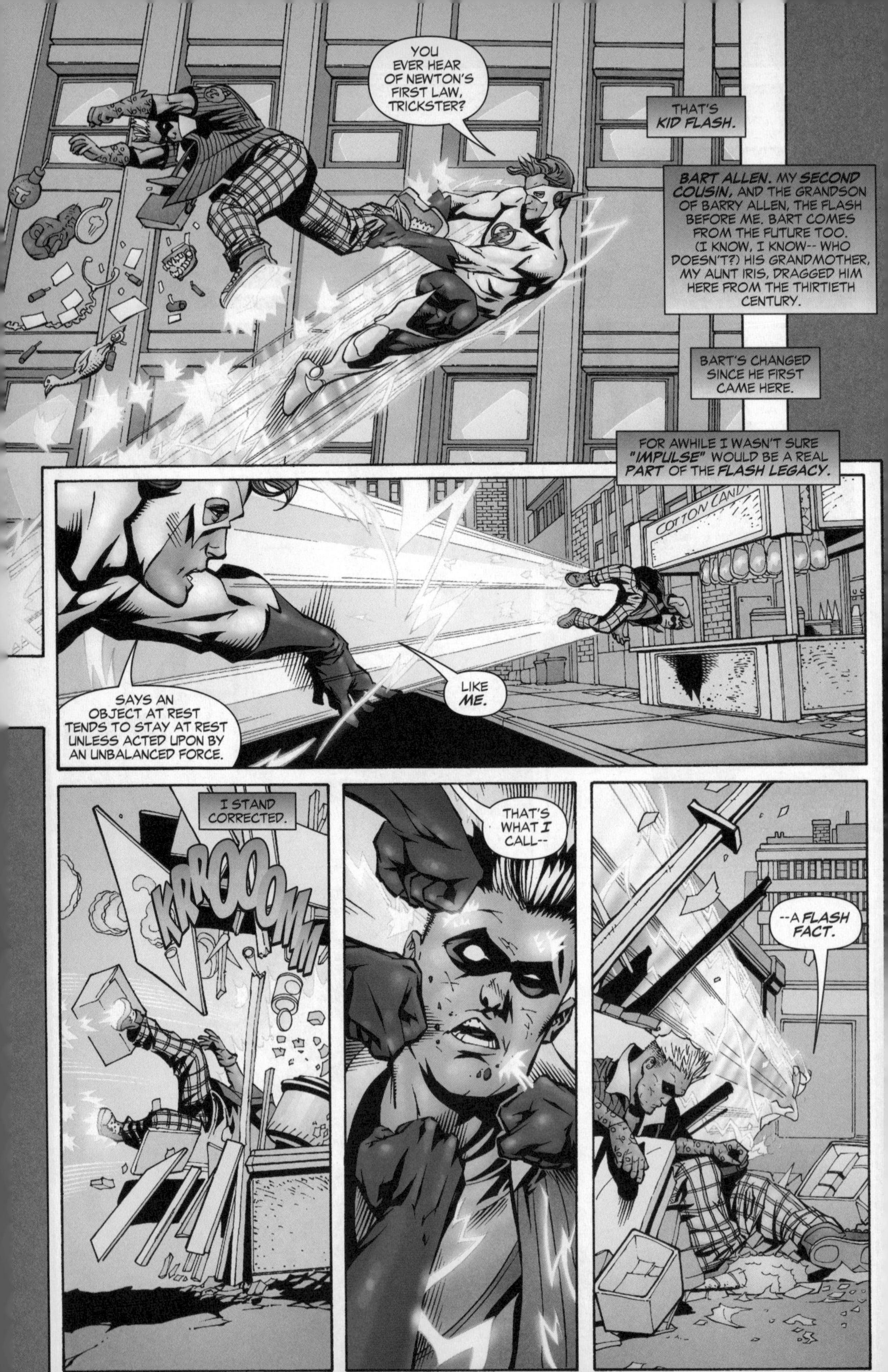
YOU EVER HEAR OF NEWTON'S FIRST LAW, TRICKSTER?
THAT'S KID FLASH.
BART ALLEN. MY SECOND COUSIN, AND THE GRANDSON OF BARRY ALLEN, THE FLASH BEFORE ME. BART COMES FROM THE FUTURE TOO. (I KNOW, I KNOW-- WHO DOESN'T?) HIS GRANDMOTHER, MY AUNT IRIS, DRAGGED HIM HERE FROM THE THIRTIETH CENTURY.
BART'S CHANGED SINCE HE FIRST CAME HERE.
FOR AWHILE I WASN'T SURE "IMPULSE" WOULD BE A REAL PART OF THE FLASH LEGACY.
COTTON CAND
SAYS AN OBJECT AT REST TENDS TO STAY AT REST UNLESS ACTED UPON BY AN UNBALANCED FORCE.
LIKE ME.
I STAND CORRECTED.
KRROOOOMM
THAT'S WHAT I CALL--
--A FLASH FACT.

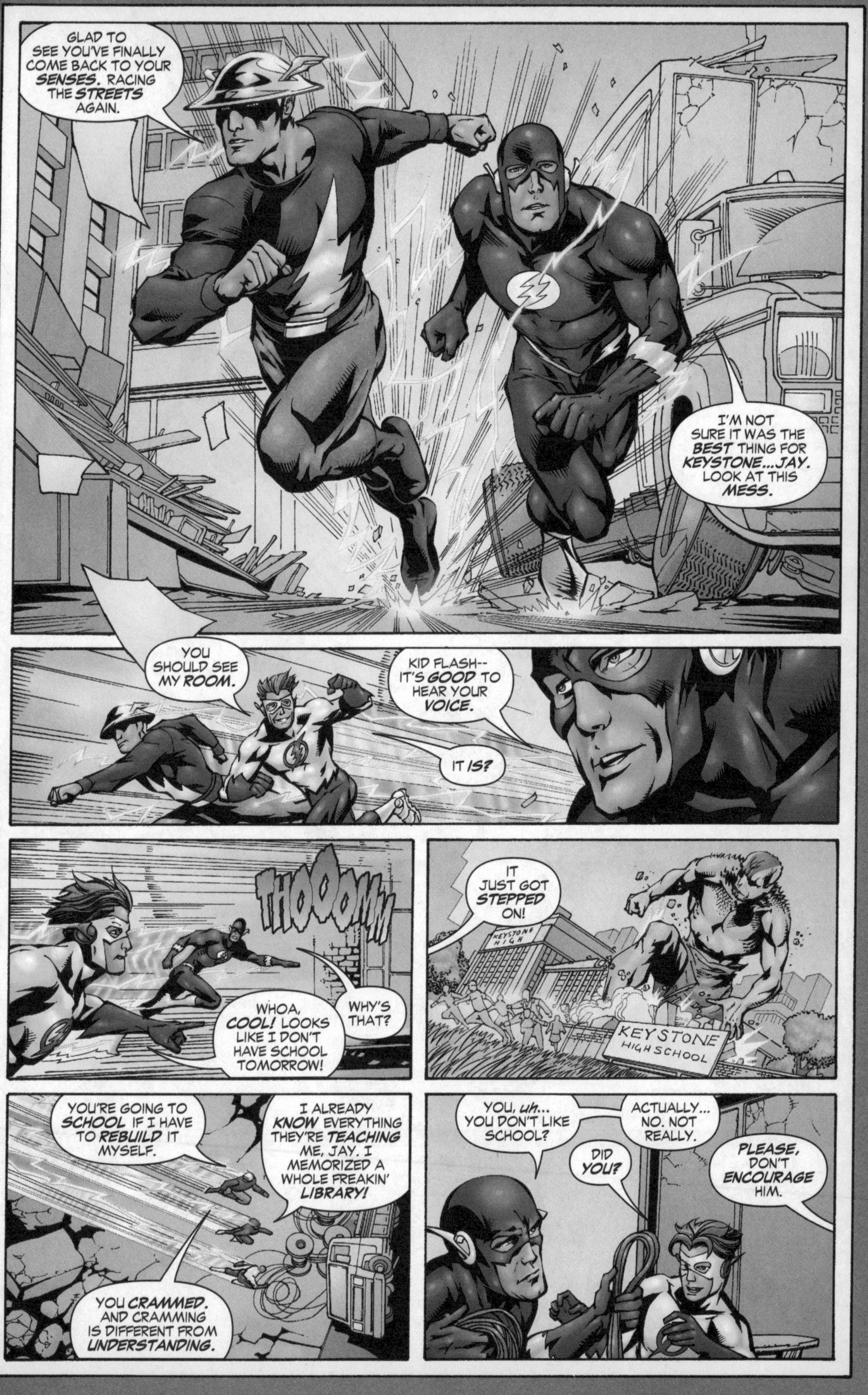
GLAD TO SEE YOU'VE FINALLY COME BACK TO YOUR SENSES. RACING THE STREETS AGAIN.
I'M NOT SURE IT WAS THE BEST THING FOR KEYSTONE...JAY. LOOK AT THIS MESS.
YOU SHOULD SEE MY ROOM.
KID FLASH-- IT'S GOOD TO HEAR YOUR VOICE.
IT IS?
THOOOMM
WHOA, COOL! LOOKS LIKE I DON'T HAVE SCHOOL TOMORROW!
WHY'S THAT?
IT JUST GOT STEPPED ON!
KEYSTONE HIGH
KEYSTONE HIGH SCHOOL
YOU'RE GOING TO SCHOOL IF I HAVE TO REBUILD IT MYSELF.
I ALREADY KNOW EVERYTHING THEY'RE TEACHING ME, JAY. I MEMORIZED A WHOLE FREAKIN' LIBRARY!
YOU CRAMMED. AND CRAMMING IS DIFFERENT FROM UNDERSTANDING.
YOU, uh... YOU DON'T LIKE SCHOOL?
ACTUALLY... NO. NOT REALLY.
DID YOU?
PLEASE, DON'T ENCOURAGE HIM.

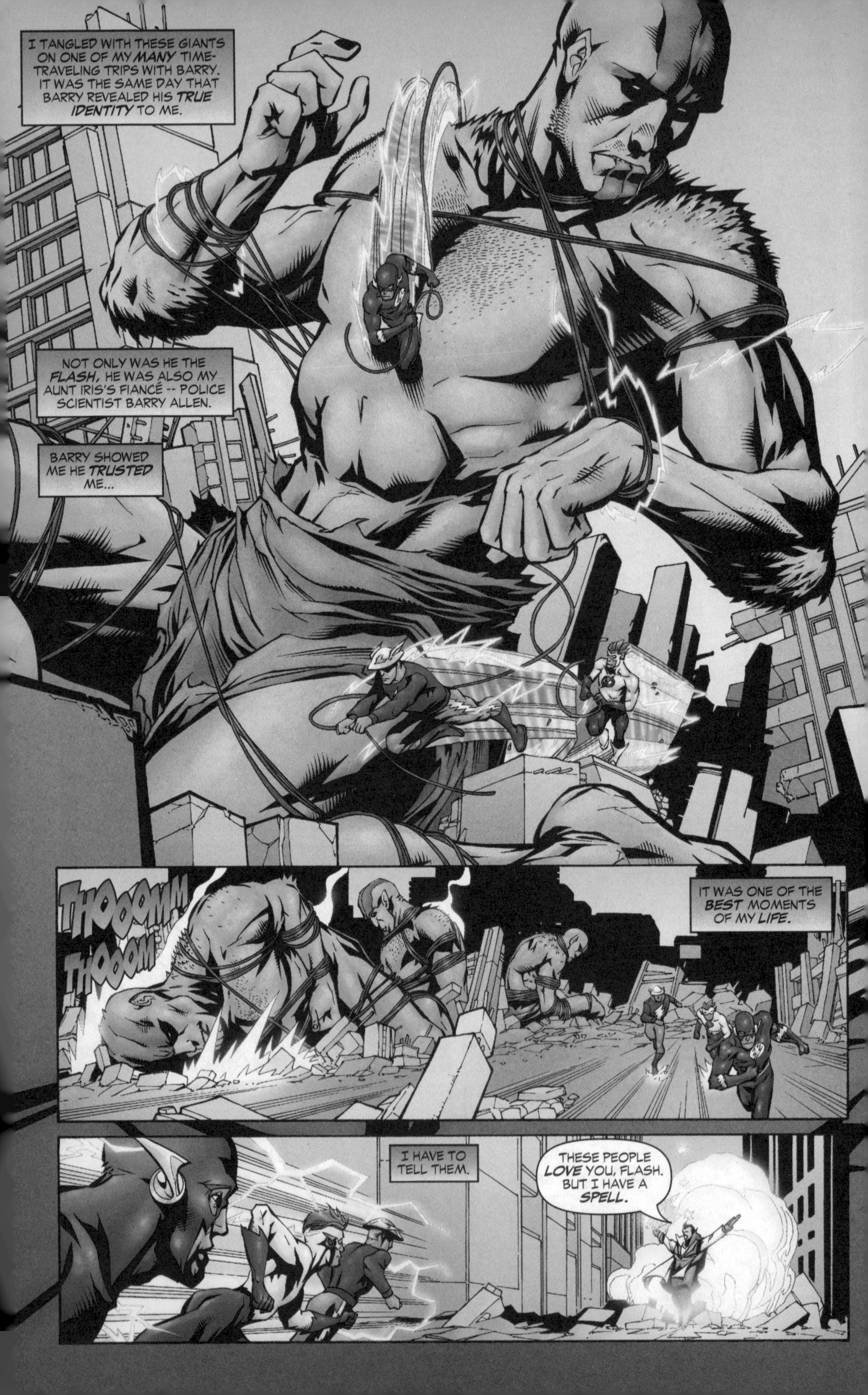
I TANGLED WITH THESE GIANTS ON ONE OF MY MANY TIME-TRAVELING TRIPS WITH BARRY. IT WAS THE SAME DAY THAT BARRY REVEALED HIS TRUE IDENTITY TO ME.
NOT ONLY WAS HE THE FLASH, HE WAS ALSO MY AUNT IRIS'S FIANCÉ -- POLICE SCIENTIST BARRY ALLEN.
BARRY SHOWED ME HE TRUSTED ME...
THOOOMM
THOOOM
IT WAS ONE OF THE BEST MOMENTS OF MY LIFE.
I HAVE TO TELL THEM.
THESE PEOPLE LOVE YOU, FLASH. BUT I HAVE A SPELL.

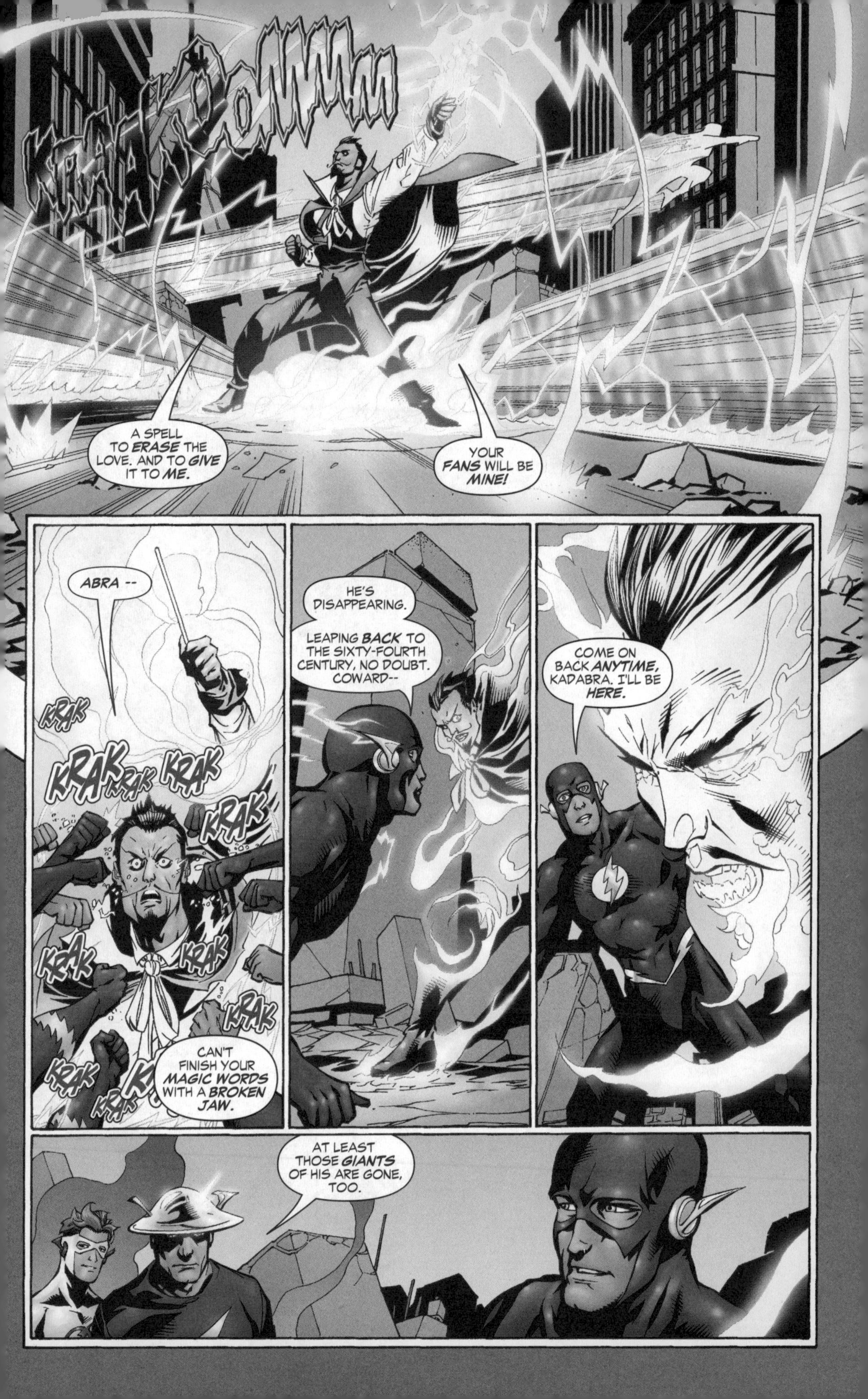
KRAKKOOMMM
A SPELL TO ERASE THE LOVE. AND TO GIVE IT TO ME.
YOUR FANS WILL BE MINE!
ABRA --
KRAK
KRAK KRAK KRAK
KRAK
KRAK
KRAK
KRAK
KRAK
KRAK
CAN'T FINISH YOUR MAGIC WORDS WITH A BROKEN JAW.
HE'S DISAPPEARING.
LEAPING BACK TO THE SIXTY-FOURTH CENTURY, NO DOUBT. COWARD--
COME ON BACK ANYTIME, KADABRA. I'LL BE HERE.
AT LEAST THOSE GIANTS OF HIS ARE GONE, TOO.

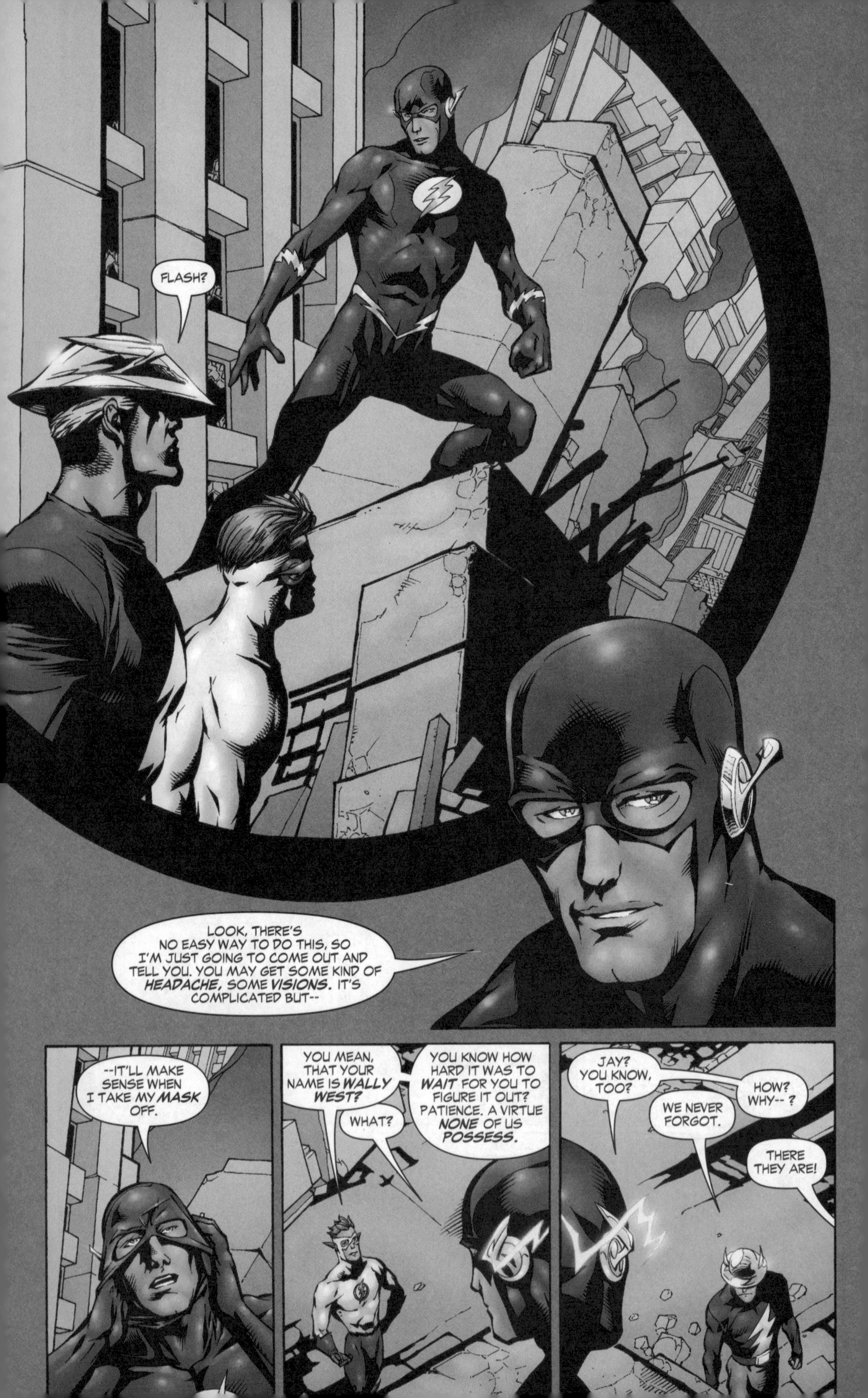
FLASH?
LOOK, THERE'S NO EASY WAY TO DO THIS, SO I'M JUST GOING TO COME OUT AND TELL YOU. YOU MAY GET SOME KIND OF *HEADACHE*, SOME *VISIONS*. IT'S COMPLICATED BUT--
--IT'LL MAKE SENSE WHEN I TAKE MY *MASK* OFF.
YOU MEAN, THAT YOUR NAME IS *WALLY WEST?*
WHAT?
YOU KNOW HOW HARD IT WAS TO *WAIT* FOR YOU TO FIGURE IT OUT? PATIENCE. A VIRTUE *NONE* OF US *POSSESS*.
JAY? YOU KNOW, TOO?
HOW? WHY-- ?
WE NEVER FORGOT.
THERE THEY ARE!

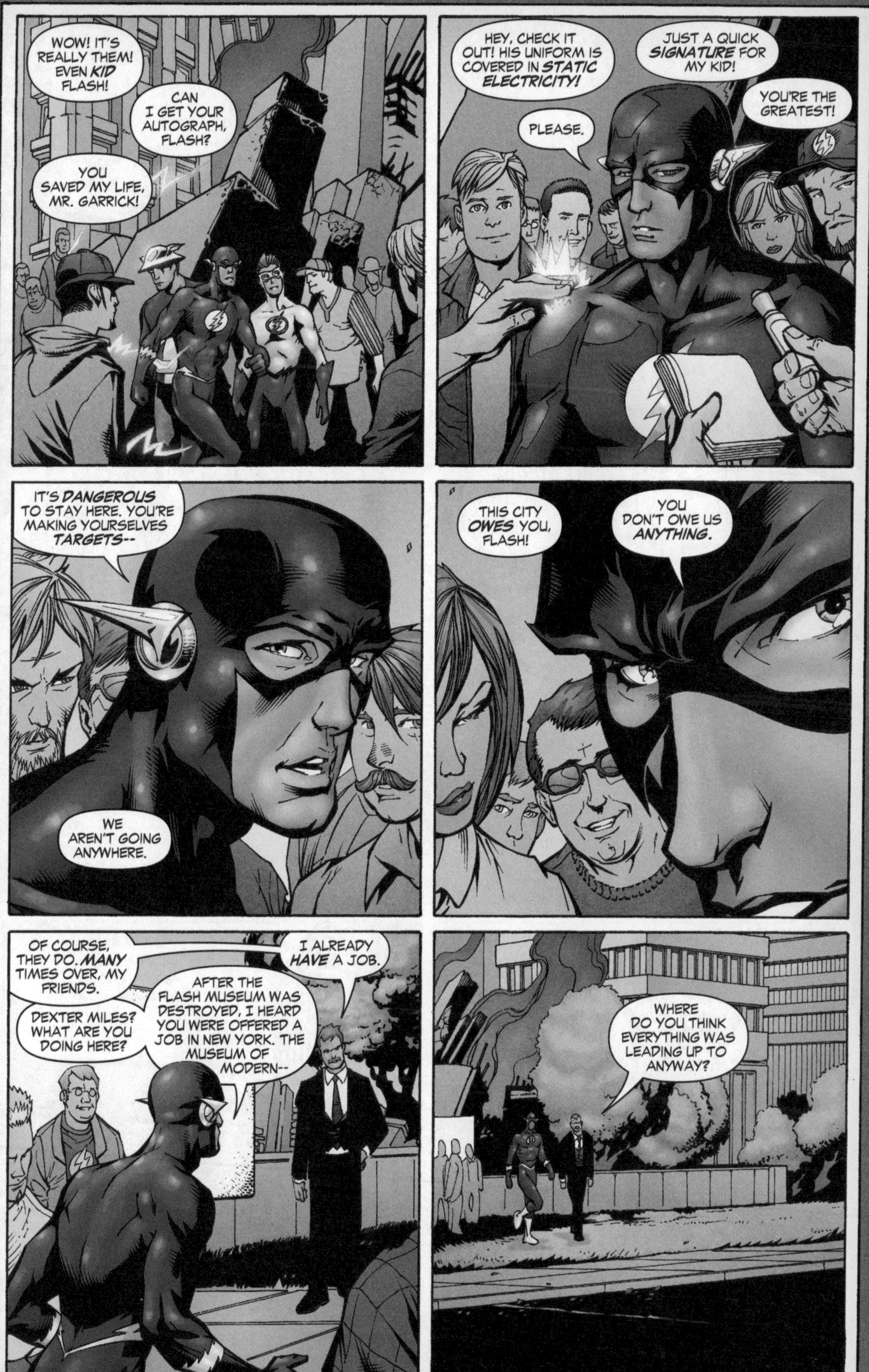
WOW! IT'S REALLY THEM! EVEN KID FLASH!
CAN I GET YOUR AUTOGRAPH, FLASH?
YOU SAVED MY LIFE, MR. GARRICK!
HEY, CHECK IT OUT! HIS UNIFORM IS COVERED IN STATIC ELECTRICITY!
JUST A QUICK SIGNATURE FOR MY KID!
YOU'RE THE GREATEST!
PLEASE.
IT'S DANGEROUS TO STAY HERE. YOU'RE MAKING YOURSELVES TARGETS--
WE AREN'T GOING ANYWHERE.
THIS CITY OWES YOU, FLASH!
YOU DON'T OWE US ANYTHING.
OF COURSE, THEY DO. MANY TIMES OVER, MY FRIENDS.
I ALREADY HAVE A JOB.
DEXTER MILES? WHAT ARE YOU DOING HERE?
AFTER THE FLASH MUSEUM WAS DESTROYED, I HEARD YOU WERE OFFERED A JOB IN NEW YORK. THE MUSEUM OF MODERN--
WHERE DO YOU THINK EVERYTHING WAS LEADING UP TO ANYWAY?

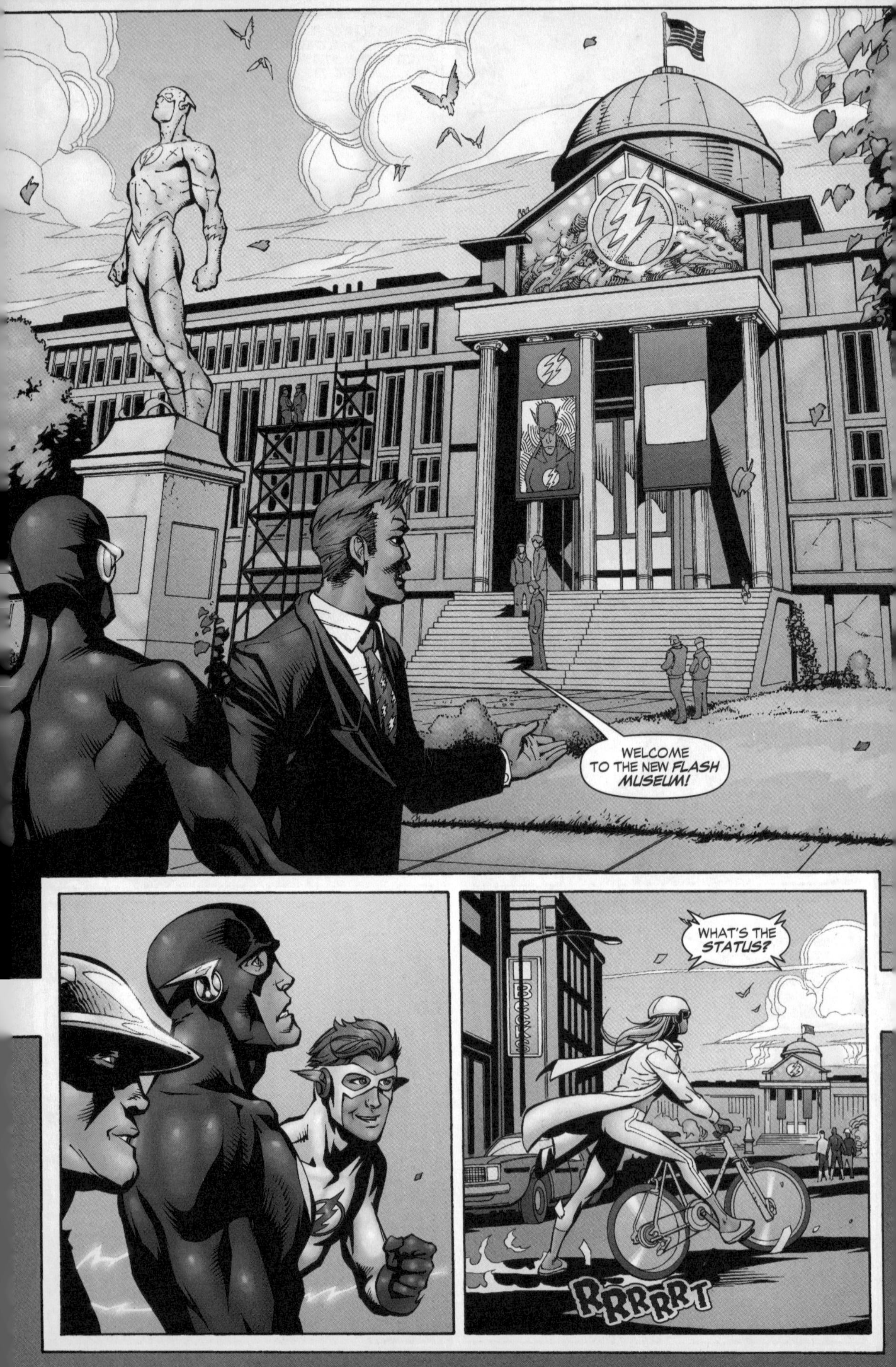
WELCOME TO THE NEW FLASH MUSEUM!
WHAT'S THE STATUS?
RRRRRT

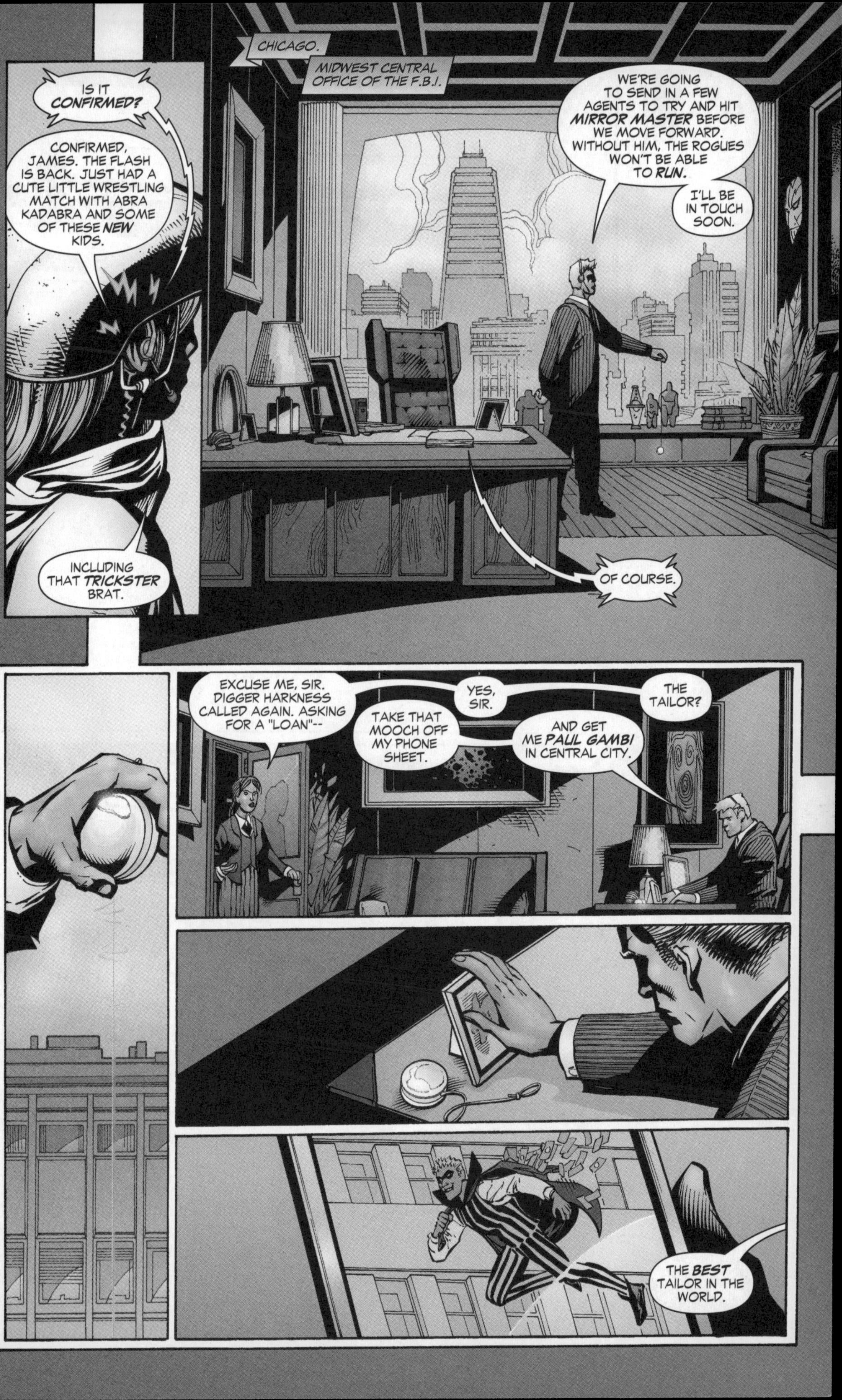
CHICAGO.
MIDWEST CENTRAL OFFICE OF THE F.B.I.
IS IT CONFIRMED?
CONFIRMED, JAMES. THE FLASH IS BACK. JUST HAD A CUTE LITTLE WRESTLING MATCH WITH ABRA KADABRA AND SOME OF THESE NEW KIDS.
INCLUDING THAT TRICKSTER BRAT.
OF COURSE.
WE'RE GOING TO SEND IN A FEW AGENTS TO TRY AND HIT MIRROR MASTER BEFORE WE MOVE FORWARD. WITHOUT HIM, THE ROGUES WON'T BE ABLE TO RUN.
I'LL BE IN TOUCH SOON.
EXCUSE ME, SIR. DIGGER HARKNESS CALLED AGAIN. ASKING FOR A "LOAN"--
TAKE THAT MOOCH OFF MY PHONE SHEET.
YES, SIR.
AND GET ME PAUL GAMBI IN CENTRAL CITY.
THE TAILOR?
THE BEST TAILOR IN THE WORLD.

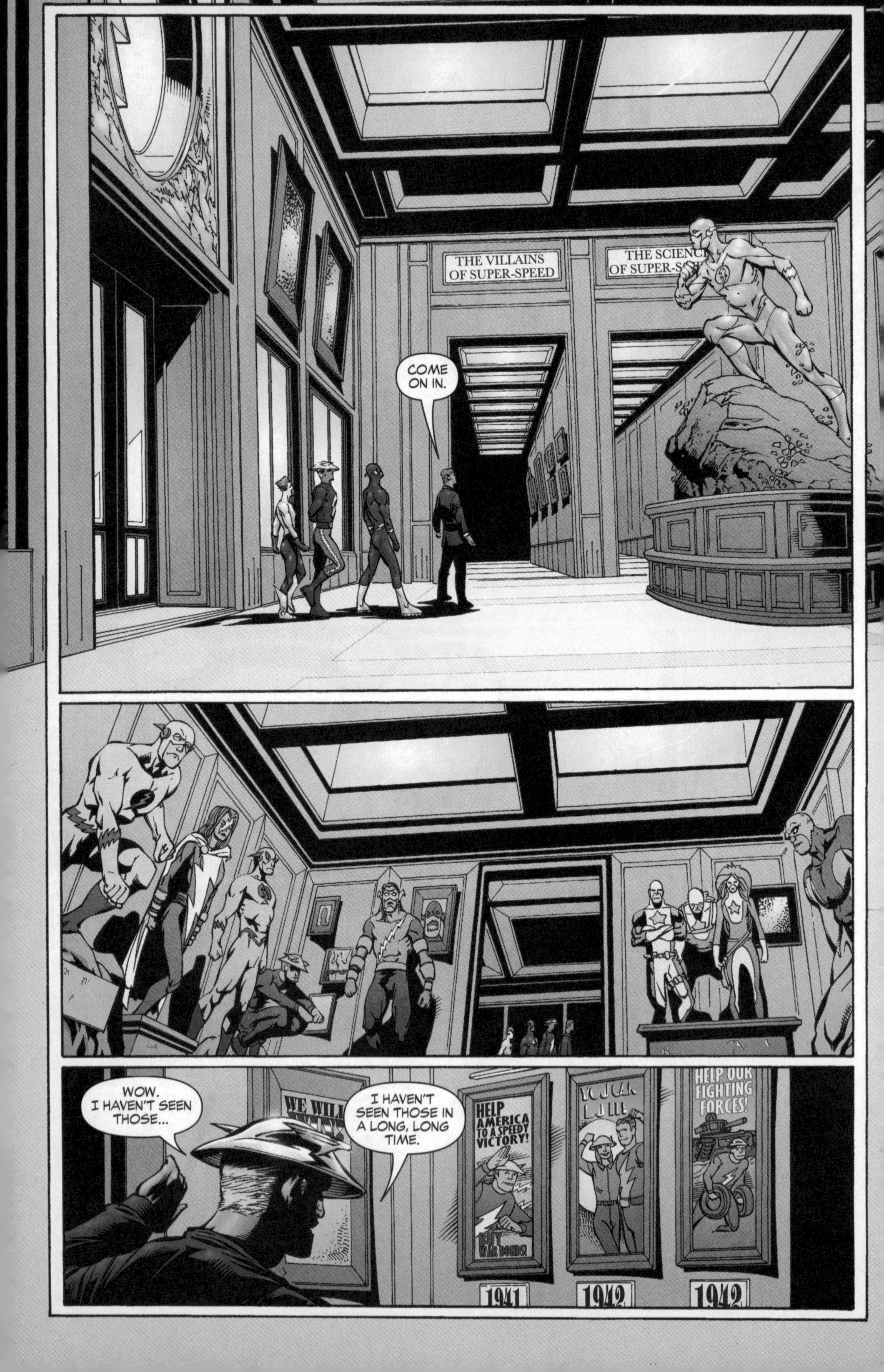
THE VILLAINS OF SUPER-SPEED
COME ON IN.
WOW. I HAVEN'T SEEN THOSE...
I HAVEN'T SEEN THOSE IN A LONG, LONG TIME.
HELP AMERICA TO A SPEEDY VICTORY!
BUY WAR BONDS!
HELP OUR FIGHTING FORCES!
1941
1942
1942

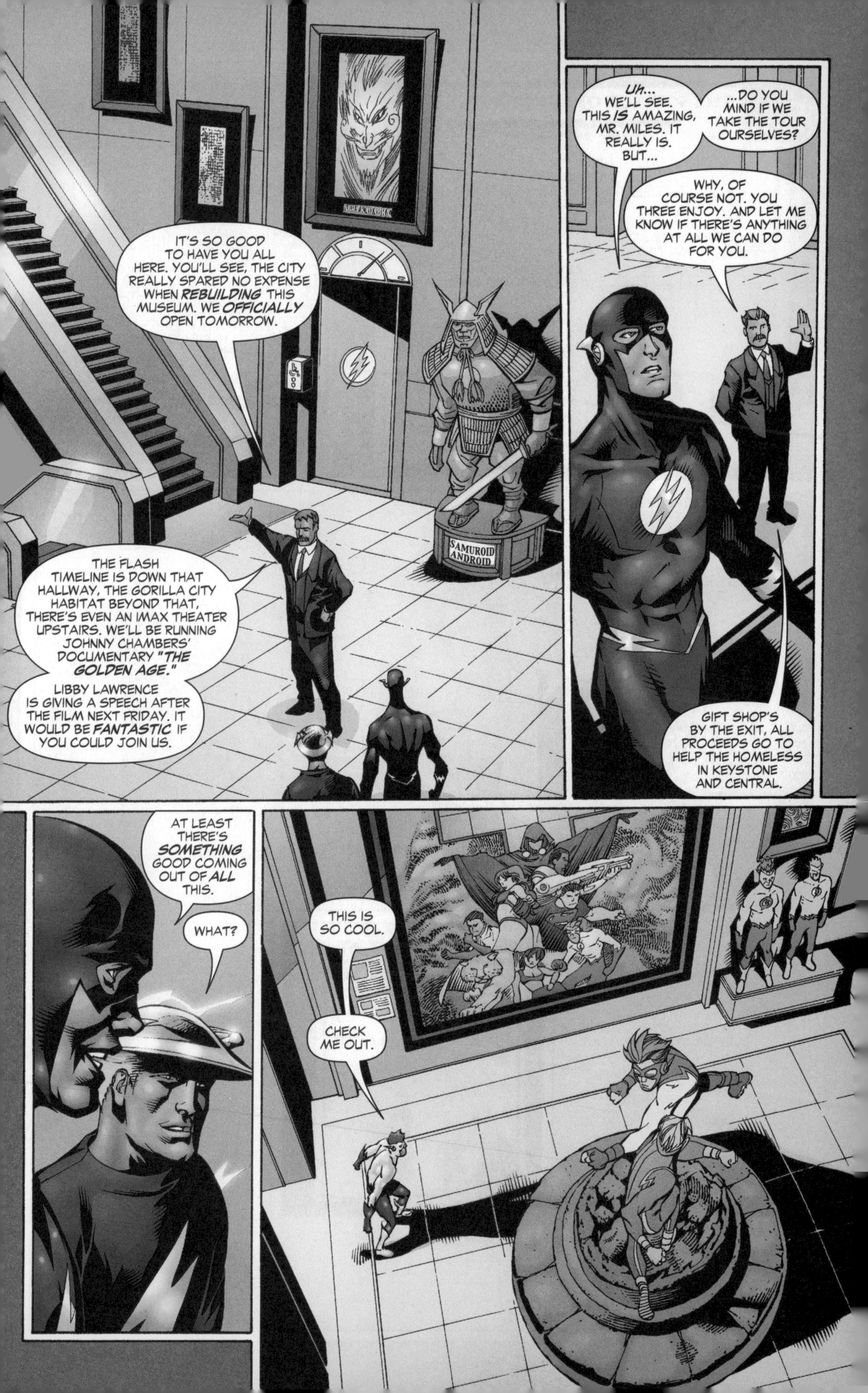
IT'S SO GOOD TO HAVE YOU ALL HERE. YOU'LL SEE, THE CITY REALLY SPARED NO EXPENSE WHEN REBUILDING THIS MUSEUM. WE OFFICIALLY OPEN TOMORROW.
SAMUROID ANDROID
THE FLASH TIMELINE IS DOWN THAT HALLWAY, THE GORILLA CITY HABITAT BEYOND THAT, THERE'S EVEN AN IMAX THEATER UPSTAIRS. WE'LL BE RUNNING JOHNNY CHAMBERS' DOCUMENTARY "THE GOLDEN AGE."
LIBBY LAWRENCE IS GIVING A SPEECH AFTER THE FILM NEXT FRIDAY. IT WOULD BE FANTASTIC IF YOU COULD JOIN US.
Uh... WE'LL SEE. THIS IS AMAZING, MR. MILES. IT REALLY IS. BUT...
...DO YOU MIND IF WE TAKE THE TOUR OURSELVES?
WHY, OF COURSE NOT. YOU THREE ENJOY. AND LET ME KNOW IF THERE'S ANYTHING AT ALL WE CAN DO FOR YOU.
GIFT SHOP'S BY THE EXIT, ALL PROCEEDS GO TO HELP THE HOMELESS IN KEYSTONE AND CENTRAL.
AT LEAST THERE'S SOMETHING GOOD COMING OUT OF ALL THIS.
WHAT?
THIS IS SO COOL.
CHECK ME OUT.

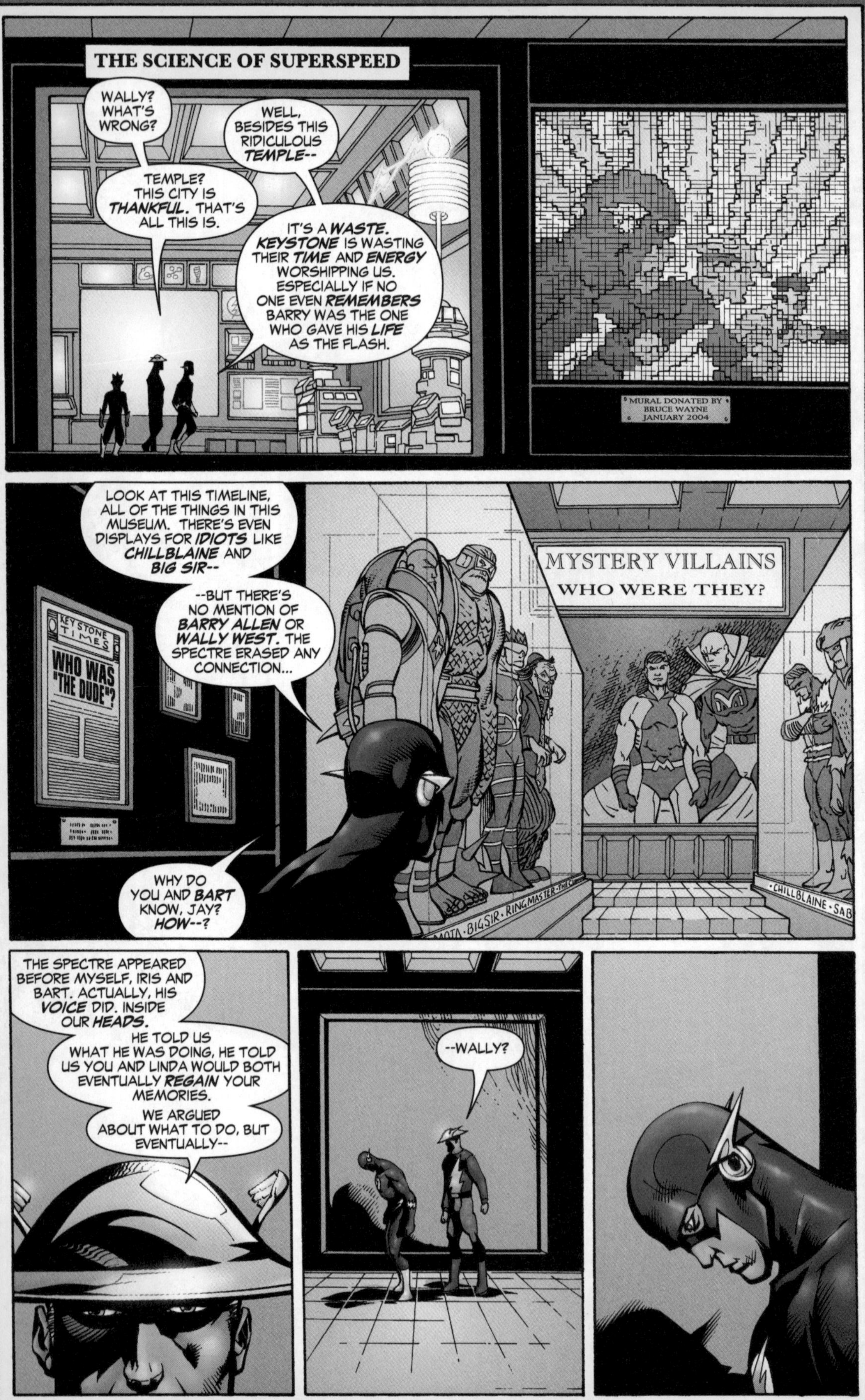
THE SCIENCE OF SUPERSPEED
WALLY? WHAT'S WRONG?
WELL, BESIDES THIS RIDICULOUS TEMPLE--
TEMPLE? THIS CITY IS THANKFUL. THAT'S ALL THIS IS.
IT'S A WASTE. KEYSTONE IS WASTING THEIR TIME AND ENERGY WORSHIPPING US. ESPECIALLY IF NO ONE EVEN REMEMBERS BARRY WAS THE ONE WHO GAVE HIS LIFE AS THE FLASH.
MURAL DONATED BY BRUCE WAYNE JANUARY 2004
LOOK AT THIS TIMELINE, ALL OF THE THINGS IN THIS MUSEUM. THERE'S EVEN DISPLAYS FOR IDIOTS LIKE CHILLBLAINE AND BIG SIR--
MYSTERY VILLAINS
WHO WERE THEY?
KEYSTONE TIMES
WHO WAS "THE DUDE"?
--BUT THERE'S NO MENTION OF BARRY ALLEN OR WALLY WEST. THE SPECTRE ERASED ANY CONNECTION...
WHY DO YOU AND BART KNOW, JAY? HOW--?
MOTA · BIG SIR · RINGMASTER · THE C
· CHILLBLAINE · SAB
THE SPECTRE APPEARED BEFORE MYSELF, IRIS AND BART. ACTUALLY, HIS VOICE DID. INSIDE OUR HEADS.
HE TOLD US WHAT HE WAS DOING, HE TOLD US YOU AND LINDA WOULD BOTH EVENTUALLY REGAIN YOUR MEMORIES.
WE ARGUED ABOUT WHAT TO DO, BUT EVENTUALLY--
--WALLY?

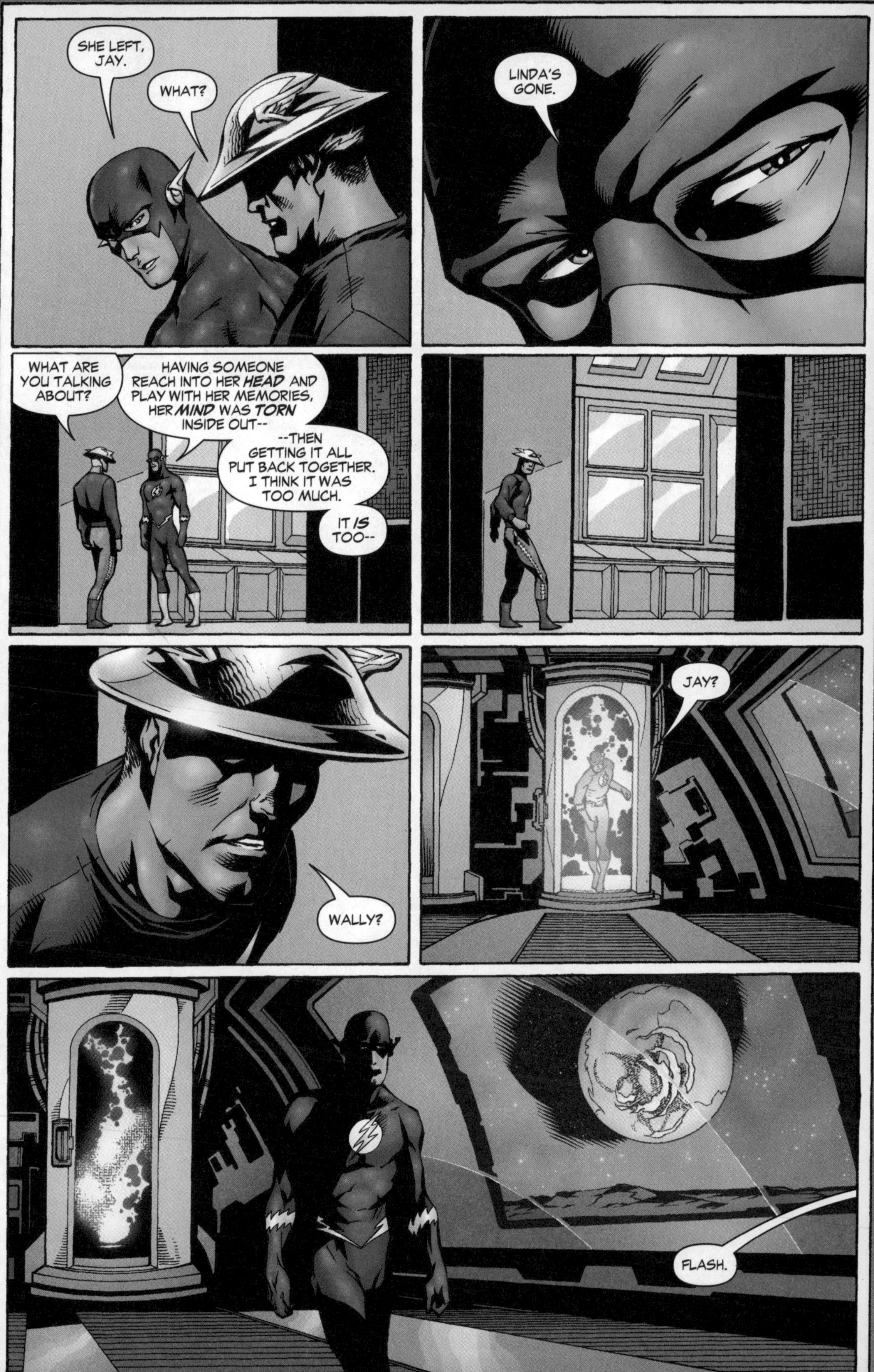
SHE LEFT, JAY.
WHAT?
LINDA'S GONE.
WHAT ARE YOU TALKING ABOUT?
HAVING SOMEONE REACH INTO HER HEAD AND PLAY WITH HER MEMORIES, HER MIND WAS TORN INSIDE OUT--
--THEN GETTING IT ALL PUT BACK TOGETHER. I THINK IT WAS TOO MUCH.
IT IS TOO--
WALLY?
JAY?
FLASH.

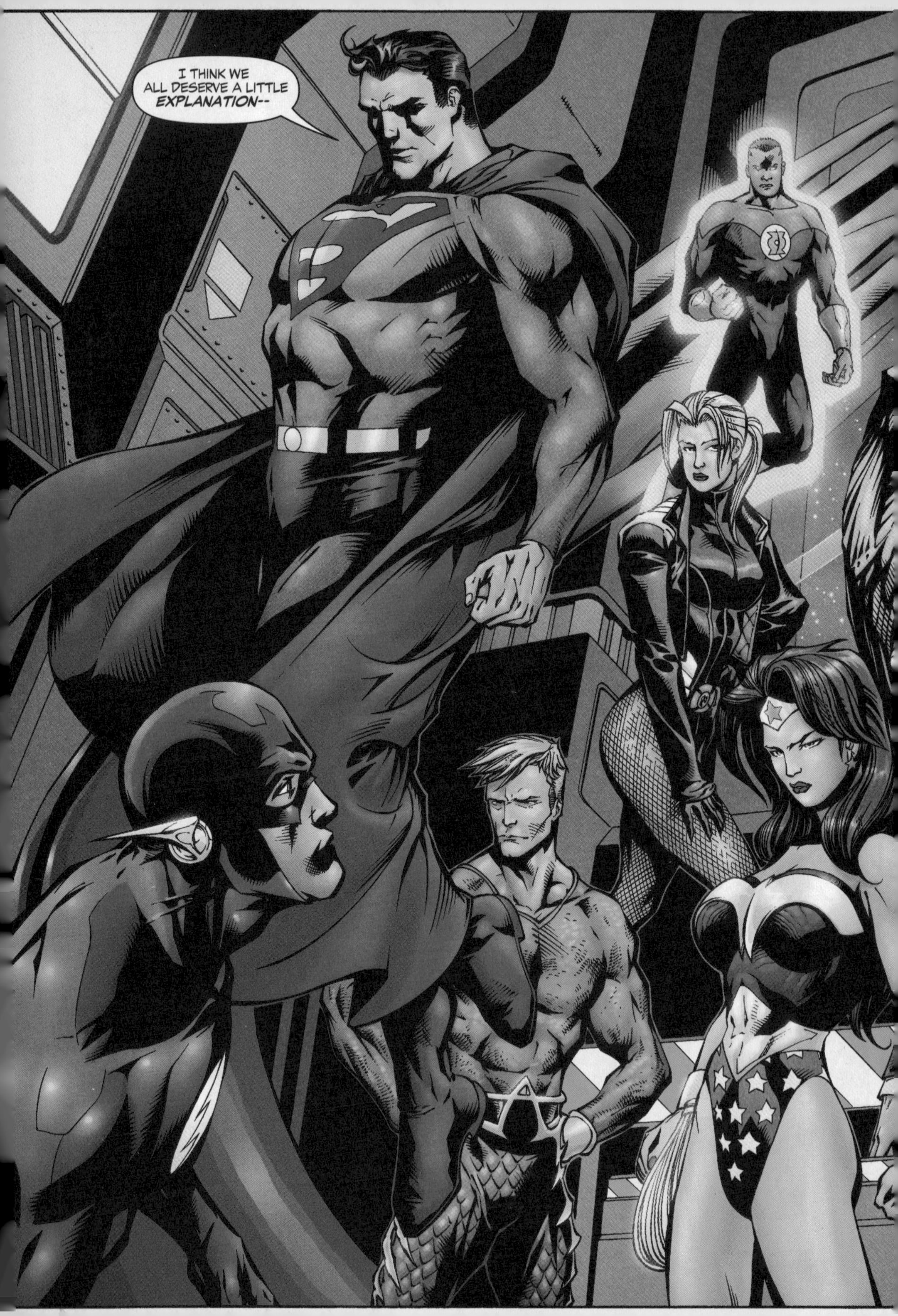
I THINK WE ALL DESERVE A LITTLE *EXPLANATION*--

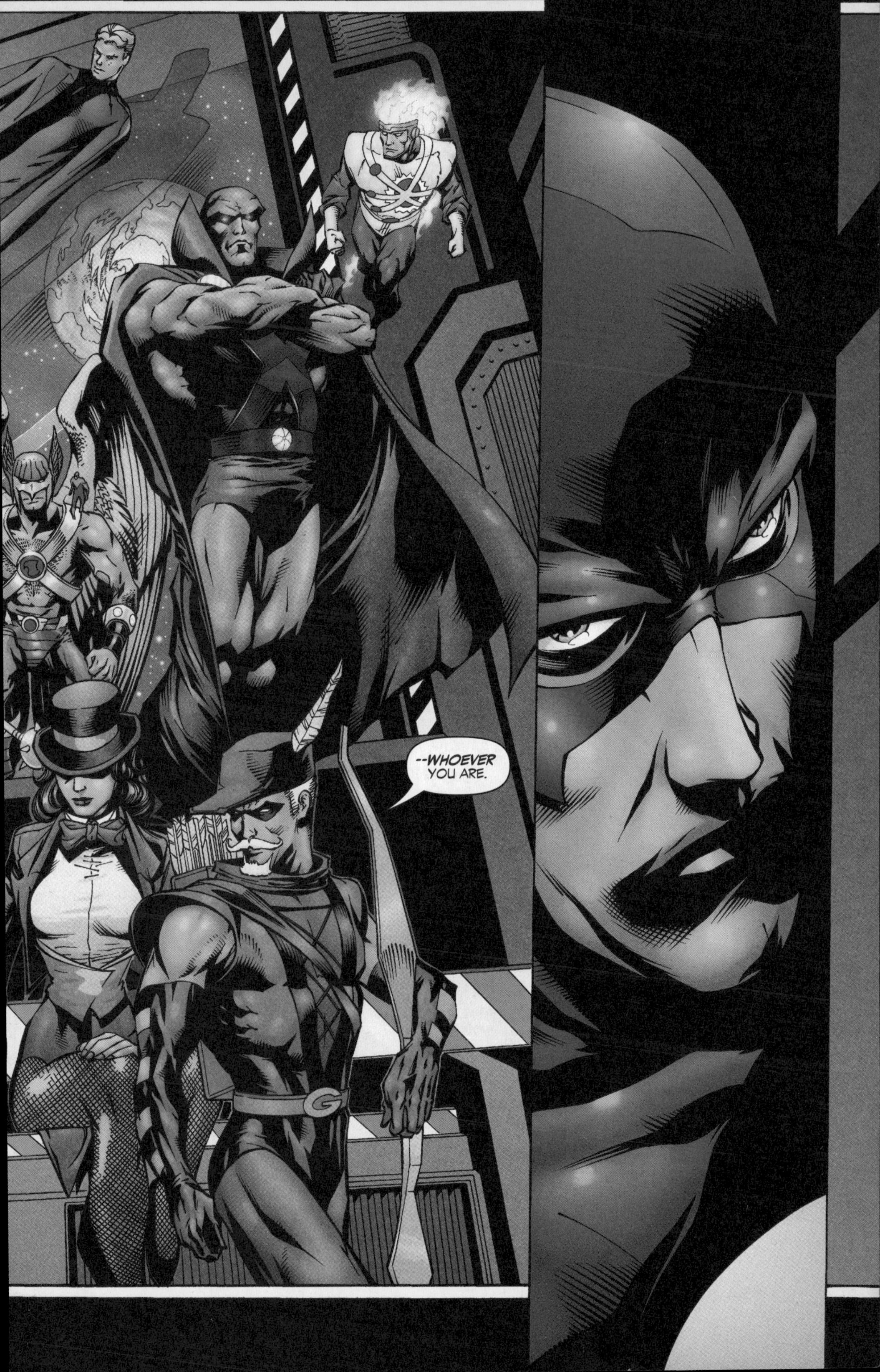
--WHOEVER YOU ARE.

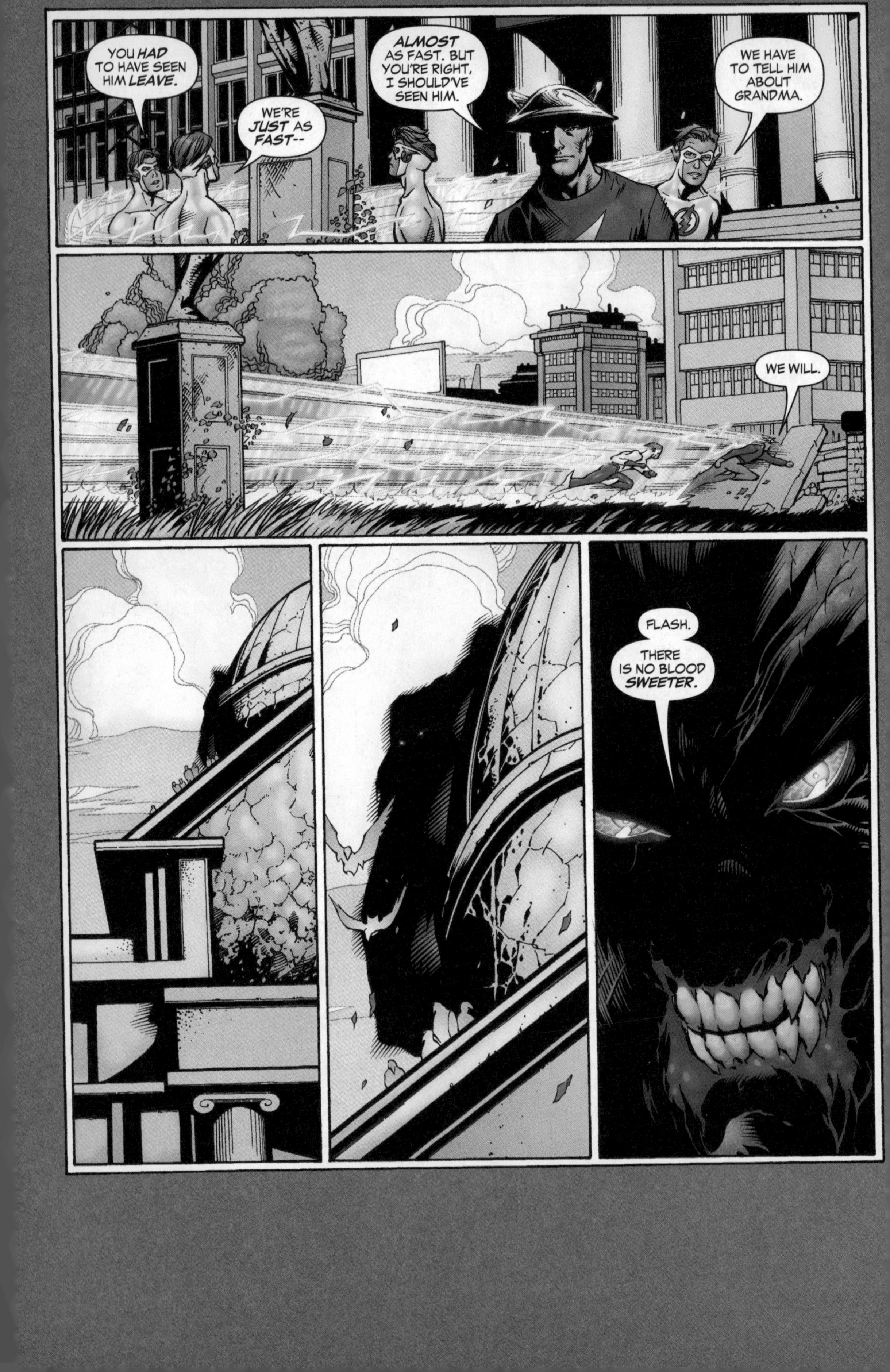

YOU HAD TO HAVE SEEN HIM LEAVE.
WE'RE JUST AS FAST--
ALMOST AS FAST. BUT YOU'RE RIGHT, I SHOULD'VE SEEN HIM.
WE HAVE TO TELL HIM ABOUT GRANDMA.
WE WILL.
FLASH.
THERE IS NO BLOOD SWEETER.

HE USUALLY DOES THIS WITH CRIMINALS.

HE'LL PUT HIS HANDS ON HIS HIPS, TILT HIS HEAD DOWN AND FILL HIS PUPILS WITH HEAT VISION.

MOST OF THEM GIVE UP RIGHT AWAY. I'VE EVEN SEEN A FEW GUYS WET THEMSELVES. LIKE THE TATTOOED MAN. BACK WHEN HE WAS A MEMBER OF THE INJUSTICE GANG. BACK WHEN BAD GUYS TEAMED UP AS OFTEN AS WE DO. NOT SO MUCH ANYMORE.

EXCLUDING THE ROGUES, OF COURSE.

MOST OF THE TIME, I DON'T BOTHER TRYING TO "TALK" CROOKS DOWN.

DON'T HAVE THE PATIENCE TO WAIT FOR THEM TO WEIGH THEIR OPTIONS. AND I'VE SEEN TOO MANY WEASELS PLAY POSSUM AND INNOCENTS GET HURT.

BLACK CANARY TRIES TO HOLD GREEN ARROW BACK, I CAN HEAR HIM MUTTERING UNDER HIS BREATH, DYING TO SPEAK. AND WHEN OLLIE WANTS TO VOICE HIS OPINION--

--NOT EVEN DINAH'S BEAUTIFUL SONG CAN CONVINCE HIM OTHERWISE.

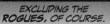

FLASH...

THE PREVIOUS FLASH DIED TO SAVE THE WORLD, PRETTY BIRD. AND EVEN THOUGH HE WAS MORE HAL'S BUD THAN MINE, HE WAS STILL A FRIEND.

AND NONE OF US CAN REMEMBER HIS REAL NAME--

--OR HIS GROWN-UP SIDEKICK'S.

WE ALL AGREED SUPERMAN WOULD TAKE POINT ON THIS.

OF COURSE THEY CAN'T. HAL ERASED THE KNOWLEDGE OF MY IDENTITY FROM EVERYONE. GIVING ME WHAT HE THOUGHT WOULD BE A NORMAL LIFE AGAIN. SO NOW THE JUSTICE LEAGUE AND A HANDFUL OF MY FELLOW SUPER-HERO FRIENDS HAVE BROUGHT ME UP TO THE WATCHTOWER.

SOMETHING WENT A LITTLE WRONG WITH HIS "SPELL." THE PART OF HIM THAT IS NOW THE SPECTRE...THREW A FEW WRENCHES INTO THE MIX. FOR AWHILE, I FORGOT EVERYTHING MYSELF.

FACT IS, AS OF NOW, NEXT TO THE FLASH FAMILY, ONLY ONE OTHER HERO KNOWS THE TRUTH.

WELCOME TO THE WATCHTOWER, FLASH.

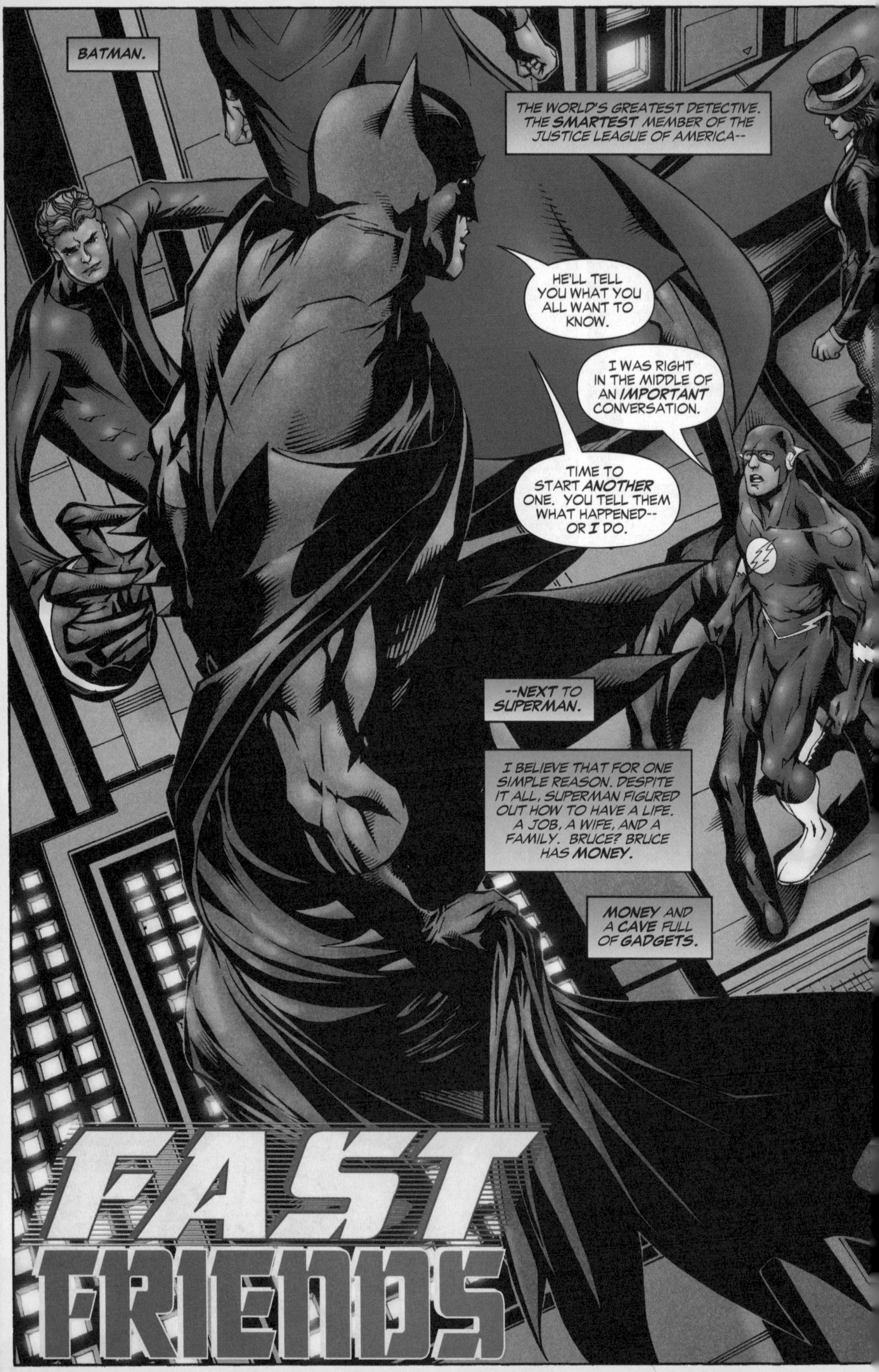
BATMAN.
THE WORLD'S GREATEST DETECTIVE. THE SMARTEST MEMBER OF THE JUSTICE LEAGUE OF AMERICA--
HE'LL TELL YOU WHAT YOU ALL WANT TO KNOW.
I WAS RIGHT IN THE MIDDLE OF AN IMPORTANT CONVERSATION.
TIME TO START ANOTHER ONE. YOU TELL THEM WHAT HAPPENED-- OR I DO.
--NEXT TO SUPERMAN.
I BELIEVE THAT FOR ONE SIMPLE REASON. DESPITE IT ALL, SUPERMAN FIGURED OUT HOW TO HAVE A LIFE. A JOB, A WIFE, AND A FAMILY. BRUCE? BRUCE HAS MONEY.
MONEY AND A CAVE FULL OF GADGETS.
FAST FRIENDS

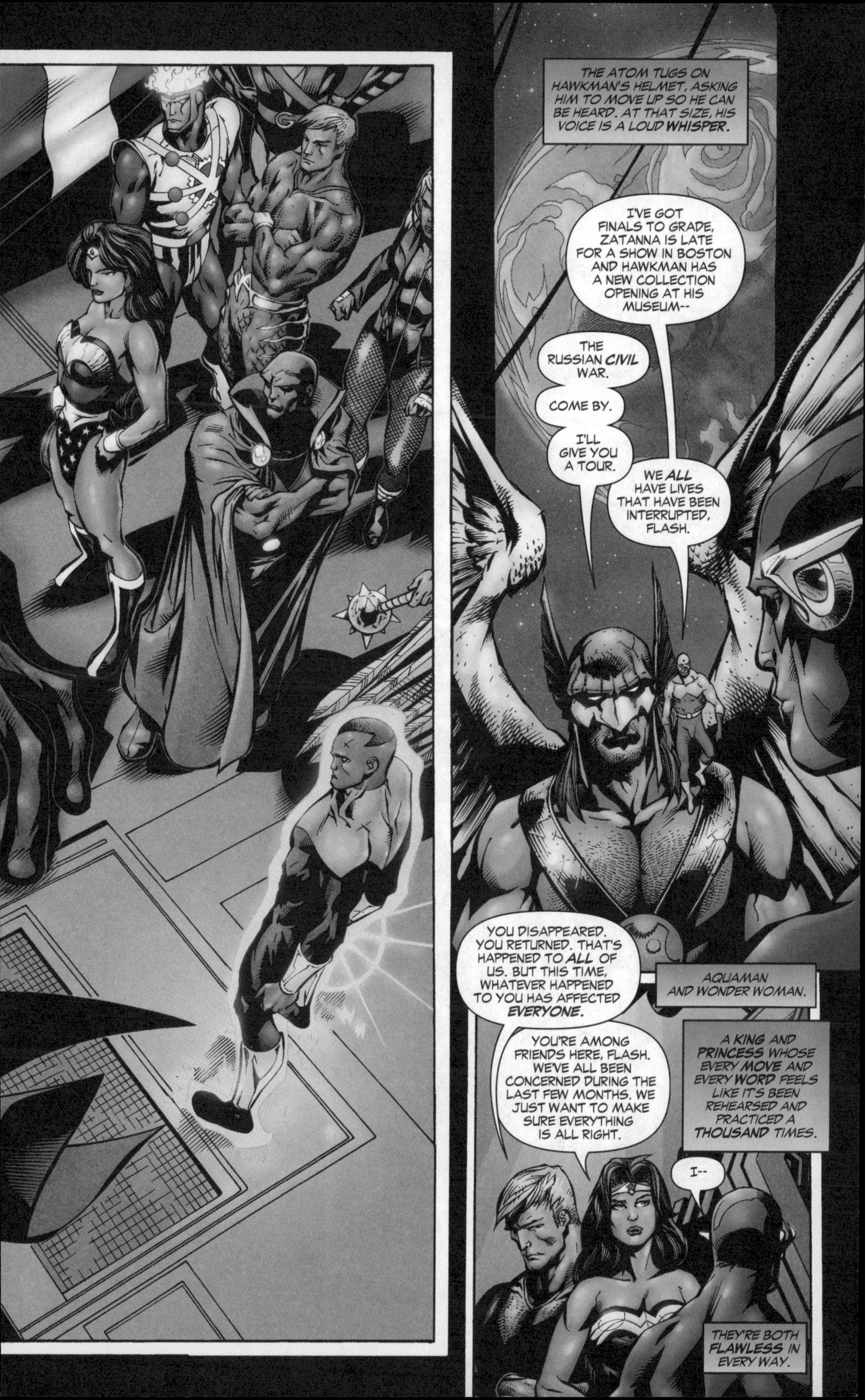
THE ATOM TUGS ON HAWKMAN'S HELMET, ASKING HIM TO MOVE UP SO HE CAN BE HEARD. AT THAT SIZE, HIS VOICE IS A LOUD WHISPER.
I'VE GOT FINALS TO GRADE, ZATANNA IS LATE FOR A SHOW IN BOSTON AND HAWKMAN HAS A NEW COLLECTION OPENING AT HIS MUSEUM--
THE RUSSIAN CIVIL WAR.
COME BY.
I'LL GIVE YOU A TOUR.
WE ALL HAVE LIVES THAT HAVE BEEN INTERRUPTED, FLASH.
YOU DISAPPEARED. YOU RETURNED. THAT'S HAPPENED TO ALL OF US. BUT THIS TIME, WHATEVER HAPPENED TO YOU HAS AFFECTED EVERYONE.
AQUAMAN AND WONDER WOMAN.
YOU'RE AMONG FRIENDS HERE, FLASH. WE'VE ALL BEEN CONCERNED DURING THE LAST FEW MONTHS. WE JUST WANT TO MAKE SURE EVERYTHING IS ALL RIGHT.
A KING AND PRINCESS WHOSE EVERY MOVE AND EVERY WORD FEELS LIKE IT'S BEEN REHEARSED AND PRACTICED A THOUSAND TIMES.
I--
THEY'RE BOTH FLAWLESS IN EVERY WAY.

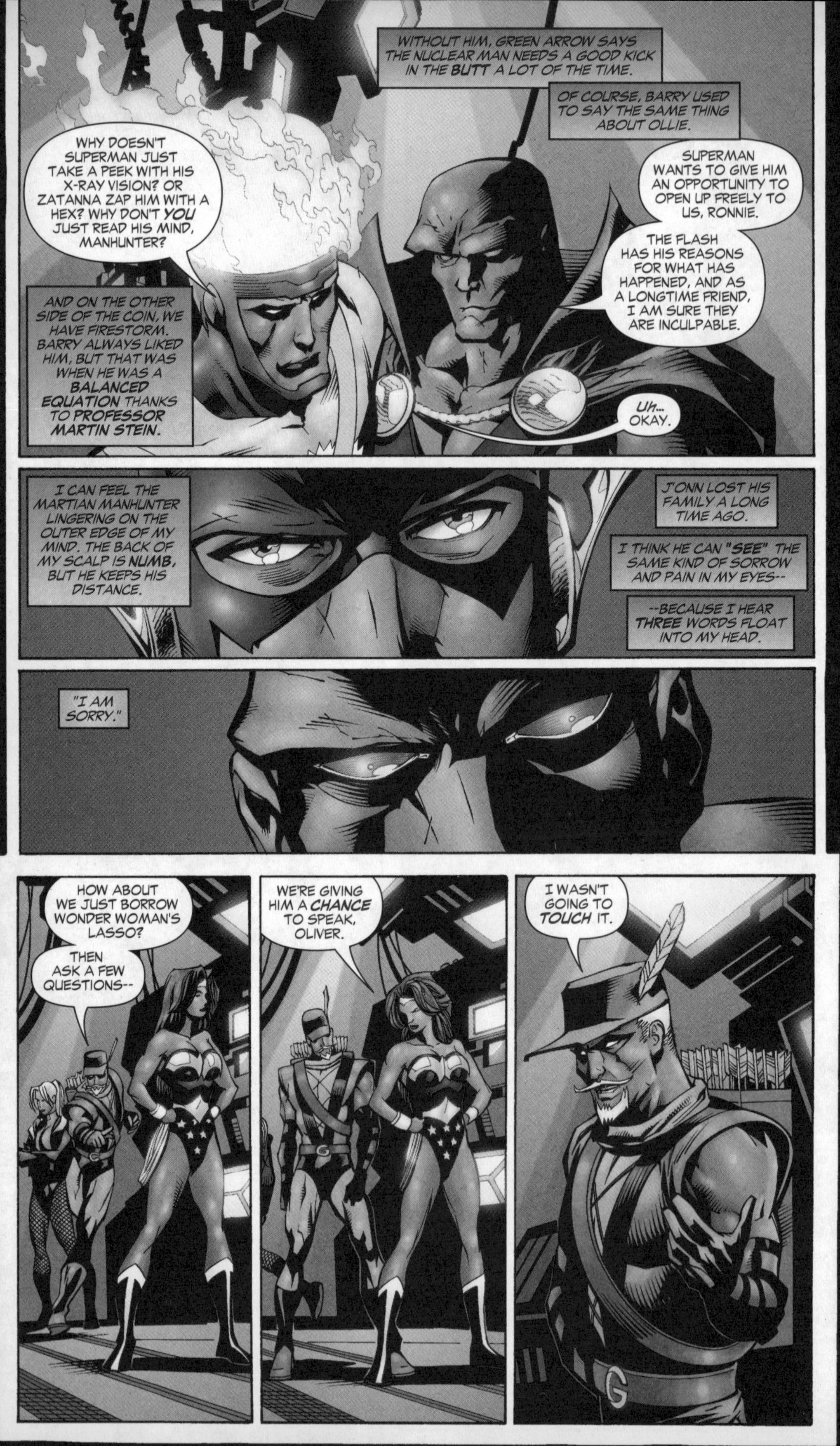
WITHOUT HIM, GREEN ARROW SAYS THE NUCLEAR MAN NEEDS A GOOD KICK IN THE BUTT A LOT OF THE TIME.
OF COURSE, BARRY USED TO SAY THE SAME THING ABOUT OLLIE.
WHY DOESN'T SUPERMAN JUST TAKE A PEEK WITH HIS X-RAY VISION? OR ZATANNA ZAP HIM WITH A HEX? WHY DON'T YOU JUST READ HIS MIND, MANHUNTER?
SUPERMAN WANTS TO GIVE HIM AN OPPORTUNITY TO OPEN UP FREELY TO US, RONNIE.
THE FLASH HAS HIS REASONS FOR WHAT HAS HAPPENED, AND AS A LONGTIME FRIEND, I AM SURE THEY ARE INCULPABLE.
AND ON THE OTHER SIDE OF THE COIN, WE HAVE FIRESTORM. BARRY ALWAYS LIKED HIM, BUT THAT WAS WHEN HE WAS A BALANCED EQUATION THANKS TO PROFESSOR MARTIN STEIN.
Uh... OKAY.
I CAN FEEL THE MARTIAN MANHUNTER LINGERING ON THE OUTER EDGE OF MY MIND. THE BACK OF MY SCALP IS NUMB, BUT HE KEEPS HIS DISTANCE.
J'ONN LOST HIS FAMILY A LONG TIME AGO.
I THINK HE CAN "SEE" THE SAME KIND OF SORROW AND PAIN IN MY EYES--
--BECAUSE I HEAR THREE WORDS FLOAT INTO MY HEAD.
"I AM SORRY."
HOW ABOUT WE JUST BORROW WONDER WOMAN'S LASSO?
THEN ASK A FEW QUESTIONS--
WE'RE GIVING HIM A CHANCE TO SPEAK, OLIVER.
I WASN'T GOING TO TOUCH IT.

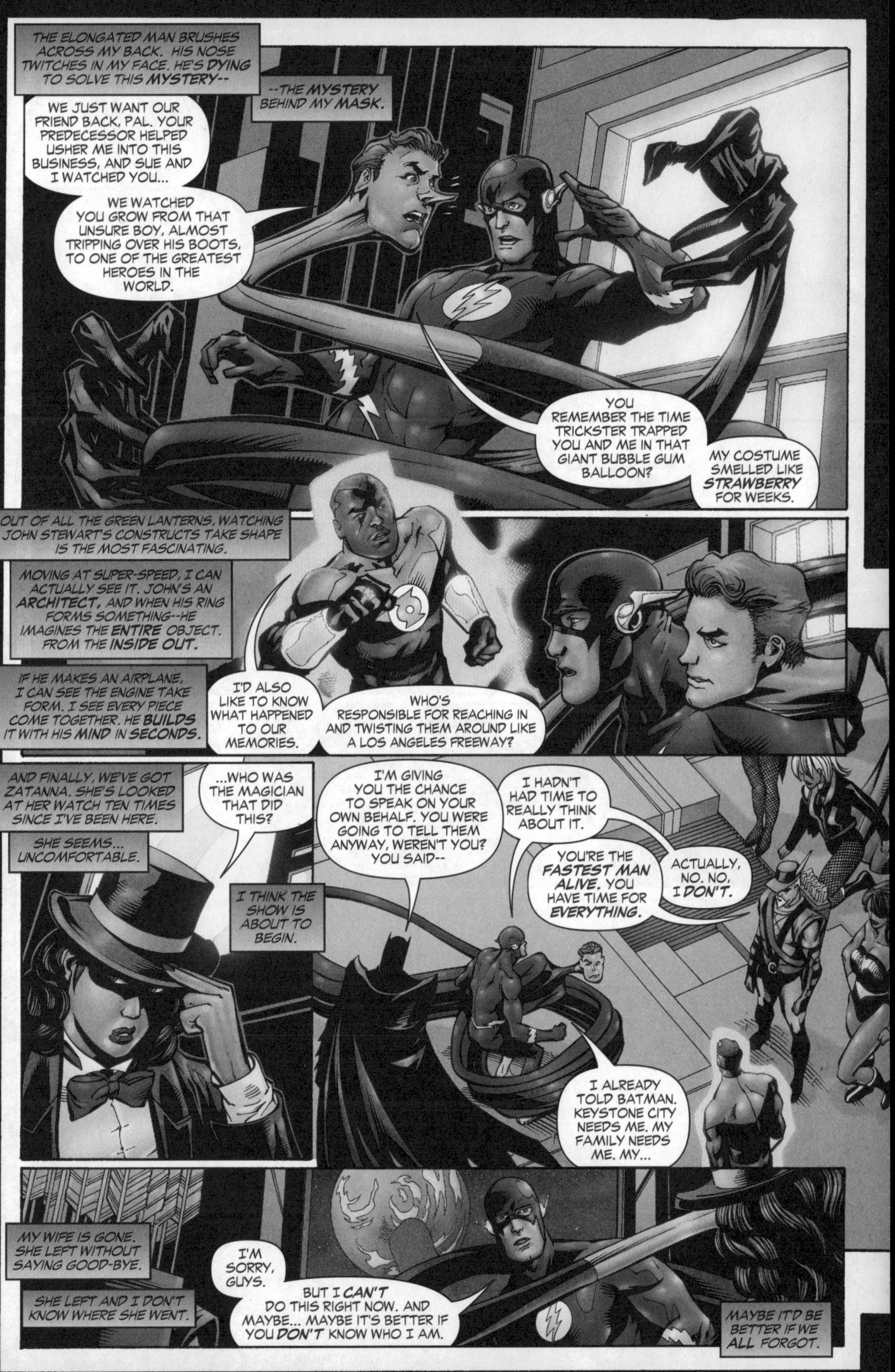

THE ELONGATED MAN BRUSHES ACROSS MY BACK. HIS NOSE TWITCHES IN MY FACE. HE'S DYING TO SOLVE THIS MYSTERY--
--THE MYSTERY BEHIND MY MASK.
WE JUST WANT OUR FRIEND BACK, PAL. YOUR PREDECESSOR HELPED USHER ME INTO THIS BUSINESS, AND SUE AND I WATCHED YOU...
WE WATCHED YOU GROW FROM THAT UNSURE BOY, ALMOST TRIPPING OVER HIS BOOTS, TO ONE OF THE GREATEST HEROES IN THE WORLD.
YOU REMEMBER THE TIME TRICKSTER TRAPPED YOU AND ME IN THAT GIANT BUBBLE GUM BALLOON?
MY COSTUME SMELLED LIKE STRAWBERRY FOR WEEKS.
OUT OF ALL THE GREEN LANTERNS, WATCHING JOHN STEWART'S CONSTRUCTS TAKE SHAPE IS THE MOST FASCINATING.
MOVING AT SUPER-SPEED, I CAN ACTUALLY SEE IT. JOHN'S AN ARCHITECT, AND WHEN HIS RING FORMS SOMETHING--HE IMAGINES THE ENTIRE OBJECT. FROM THE INSIDE OUT.
IF HE MAKES AN AIRPLANE, I CAN SEE THE ENGINE TAKE FORM. I SEE EVERY PIECE COME TOGETHER. HE BUILDS IT WITH HIS MIND IN SECONDS.
I'D ALSO LIKE TO KNOW WHAT HAPPENED TO OUR MEMORIES.
WHO'S RESPONSIBLE FOR REACHING IN AND TWISTING THEM AROUND LIKE A LOS ANGELES FREEWAY?
AND FINALLY, WE'VE GOT ZATANNA. SHE'S LOOKED AT HER WATCH TEN TIMES SINCE I'VE BEEN HERE.
SHE SEEMS... UNCOMFORTABLE.
...WHO WAS THE MAGICIAN THAT DID THIS?
I'M GIVING YOU THE CHANCE TO SPEAK ON YOUR OWN BEHALF. YOU WERE GOING TO TELL THEM ANYWAY, WEREN'T YOU? YOU SAID--
I HADN'T HAD TIME TO REALLY THINK ABOUT IT.
YOU'RE THE FASTEST MAN ALIVE. YOU HAVE TIME FOR EVERYTHING.
ACTUALLY, NO. NO, I DON'T.
I THINK THE SHOW IS ABOUT TO BEGIN.
I ALREADY TOLD BATMAN. KEYSTONE CITY NEEDS ME. MY FAMILY NEEDS ME. MY...
MY WIFE IS GONE. SHE LEFT WITHOUT SAYING GOOD-BYE.
SHE LEFT AND I DON'T KNOW WHERE SHE WENT.
I'M SORRY, GUYS.
BUT I CAN'T DO THIS RIGHT NOW. AND MAYBE... MAYBE IT'S BETTER IF YOU DON'T KNOW WHO I AM.
MAYBE IT'D BE BETTER IF WE ALL FORGOT.

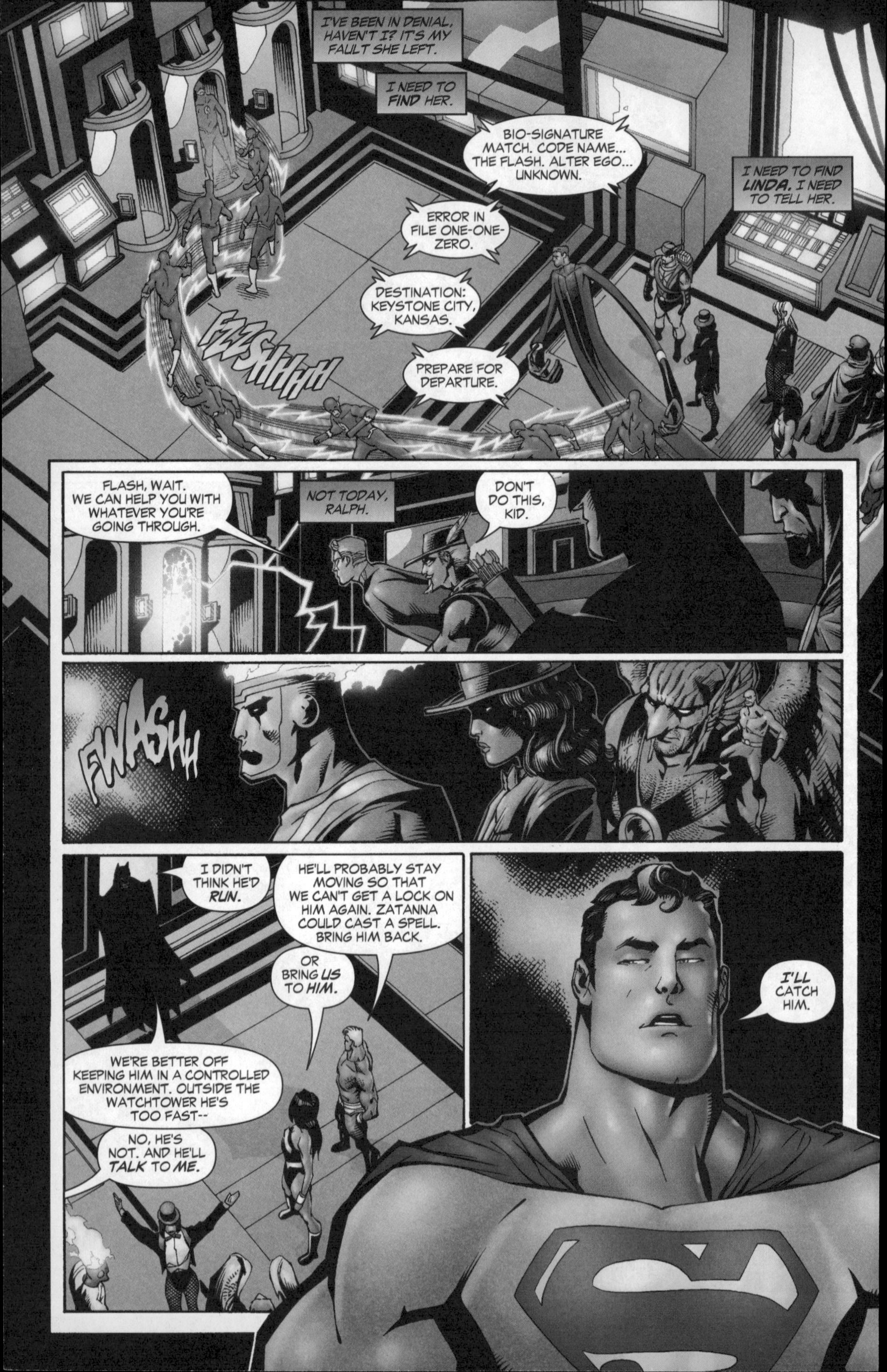
I'VE BEEN IN DENIAL, HAVEN'T I? IT'S MY FAULT SHE LEFT.
I NEED TO FIND HER.
BIO-SIGNATURE MATCH. CODE NAME... THE FLASH. ALTER EGO... UNKNOWN.
I NEED TO FIND LINDA. I NEED TO TELL HER.
ERROR IN FILE ONE-ONE-ZERO.
DESTINATION: KEYSTONE CITY, KANSAS.
FZZSHHHH
PREPARE FOR DEPARTURE.
FLASH, WAIT. WE CAN HELP YOU WITH WHATEVER YOU'RE GOING THROUGH.
NOT TODAY, RALPH.
DON'T DO THIS, KID.
FWASHH
I DIDN'T THINK HE'D RUN.
HE'LL PROBABLY STAY MOVING SO THAT WE CAN'T GET A LOCK ON HIM AGAIN. ZATANNA COULD CAST A SPELL. BRING HIM BACK.
OR BRING US TO HIM.
WE'RE BETTER OFF KEEPING HIM IN A CONTROLLED ENVIRONMENT. OUTSIDE THE WATCHTOWER HE'S TOO FAST--
NO, HE'S NOT. AND HE'LL TALK TO ME.
I'LL CATCH HIM.

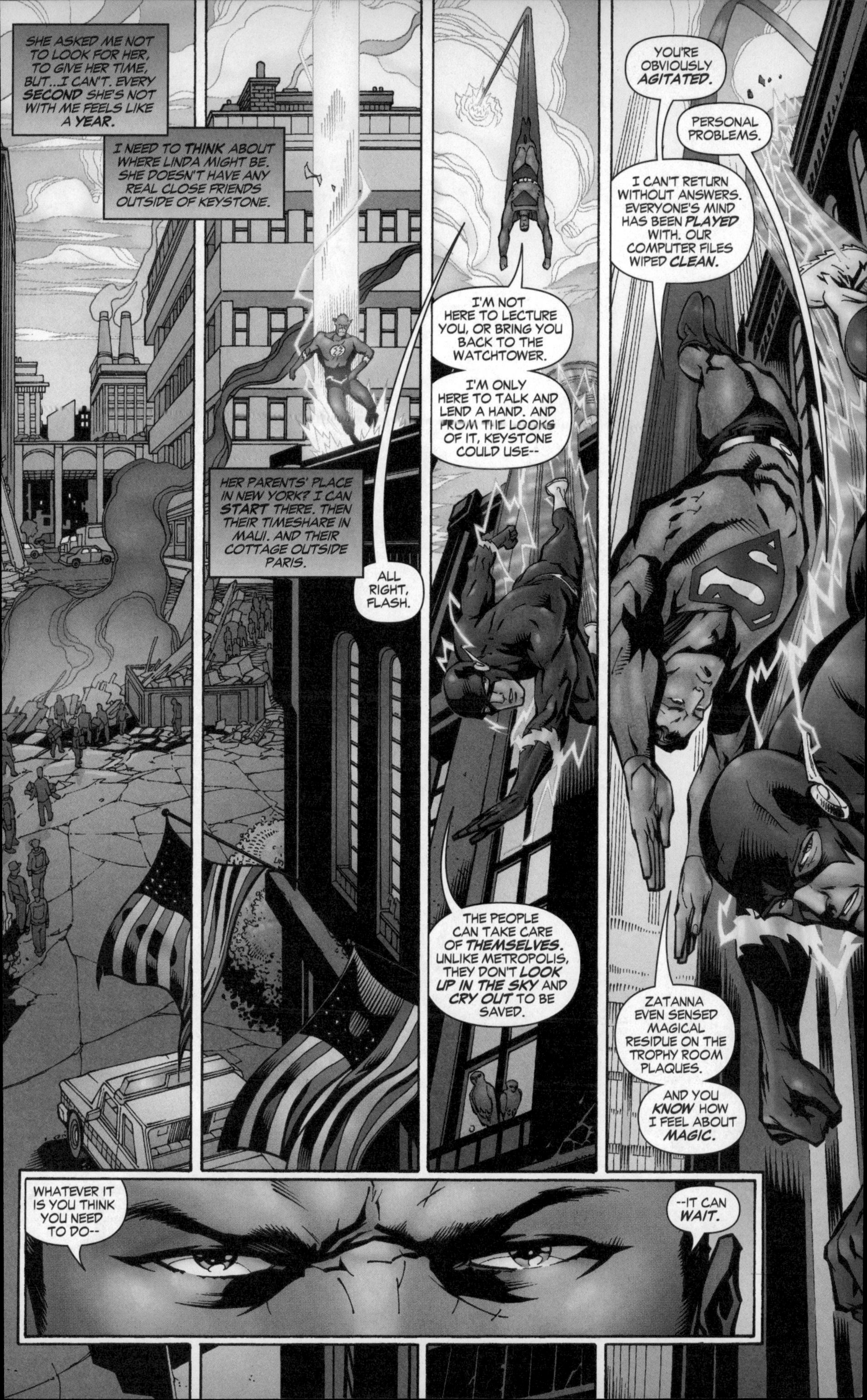

SHE ASKED ME NOT TO LOOK FOR HER, TO GIVE HER TIME, BUT...I CAN'T. EVERY SECOND SHE'S NOT WITH ME FEELS LIKE A YEAR.
I NEED TO THINK ABOUT WHERE LINDA MIGHT BE. SHE DOESN'T HAVE ANY REAL CLOSE FRIENDS OUTSIDE OF KEYSTONE.
HER PARENTS' PLACE IN NEW YORK? I CAN START THERE. THEN THEIR TIMESHARE IN MAUI. AND THEIR COTTAGE OUTSIDE PARIS.
I'M NOT HERE TO LECTURE YOU, OR BRING YOU BACK TO THE WATCHTOWER.
I'M ONLY HERE TO TALK AND LEND A HAND. AND FROM THE LOOKS OF IT, KEYSTONE COULD USE--
ALL RIGHT, FLASH.
THE PEOPLE CAN TAKE CARE OF THEMSELVES. UNLIKE METROPOLIS, THEY DON'T LOOK UP IN THE SKY AND CRY OUT TO BE SAVED.
YOU'RE OBVIOUSLY AGITATED.
PERSONAL PROBLEMS.
I CAN'T RETURN WITHOUT ANSWERS. EVERYONE'S MIND HAS BEEN PLAYED WITH. OUR COMPUTER FILES WIPED CLEAN.
ZATANNA EVEN SENSED MAGICAL RESIDUE ON THE TROPHY ROOM PLAQUES.
AND YOU KNOW HOW I FEEL ABOUT MAGIC.
WHATEVER IT IS YOU THINK YOU NEED TO DO--
--IT CAN WAIT.

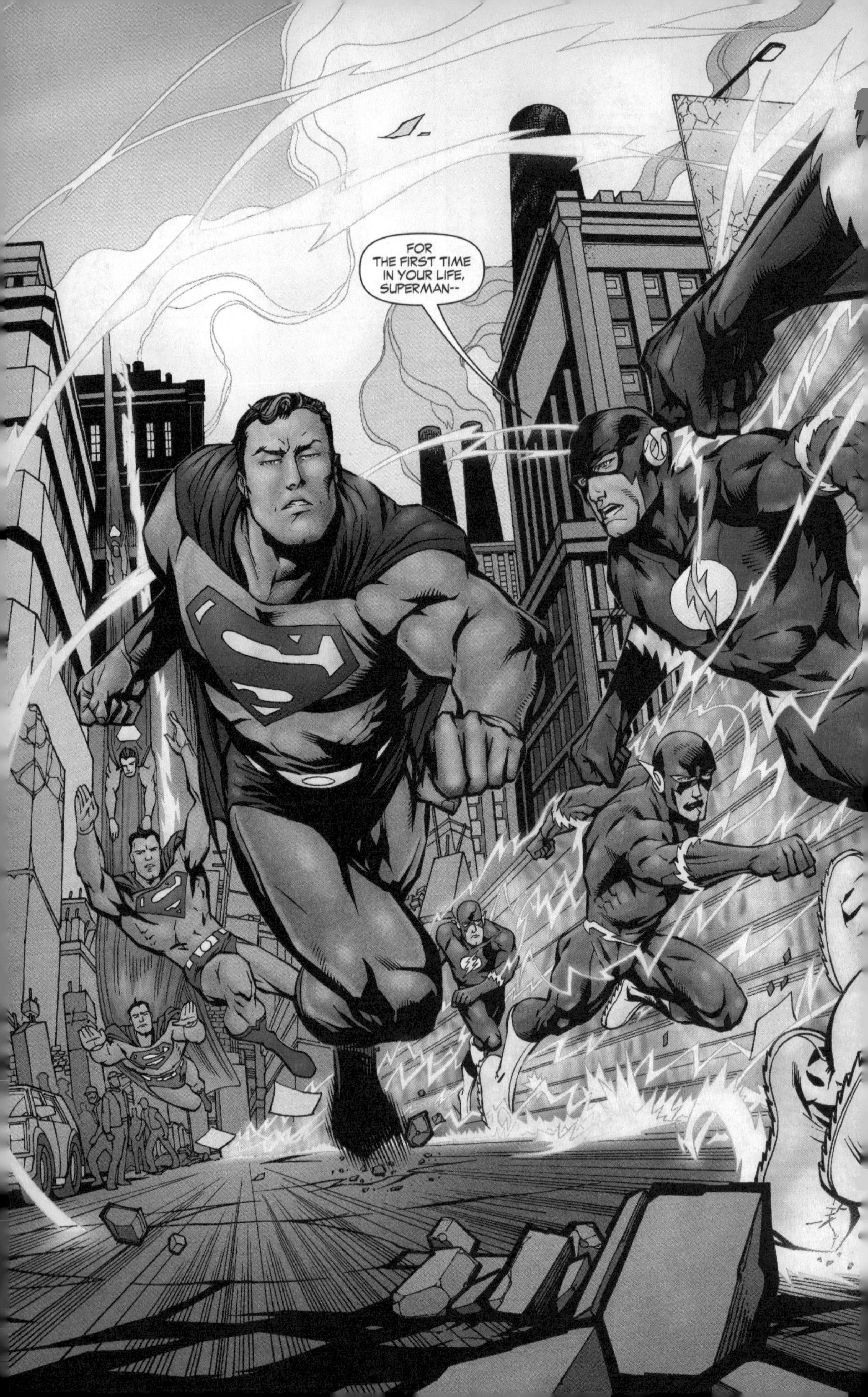
FOR THE FIRST TIME IN YOUR LIFE, SUPERMAN--

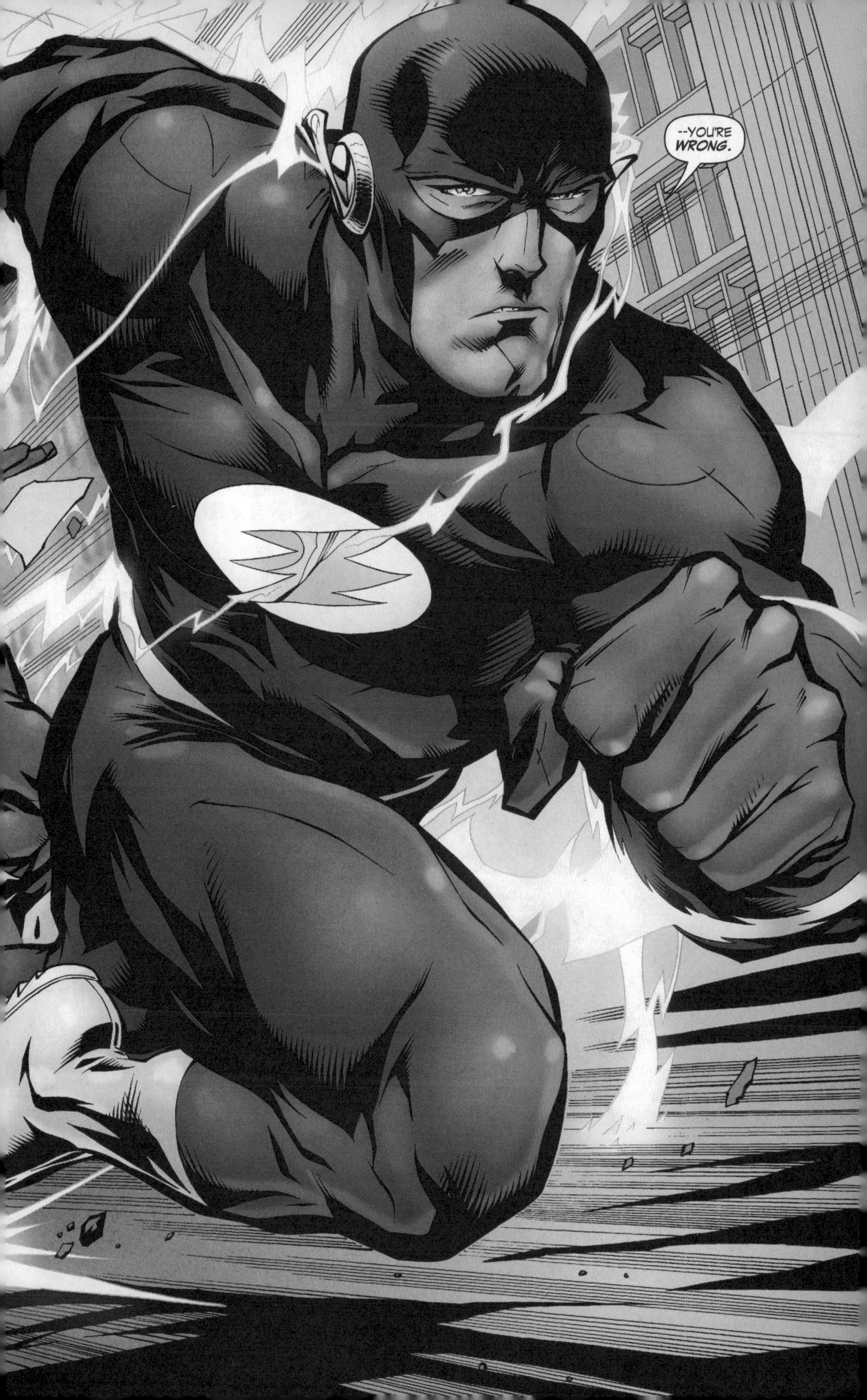
--YOU'RE WRONG.

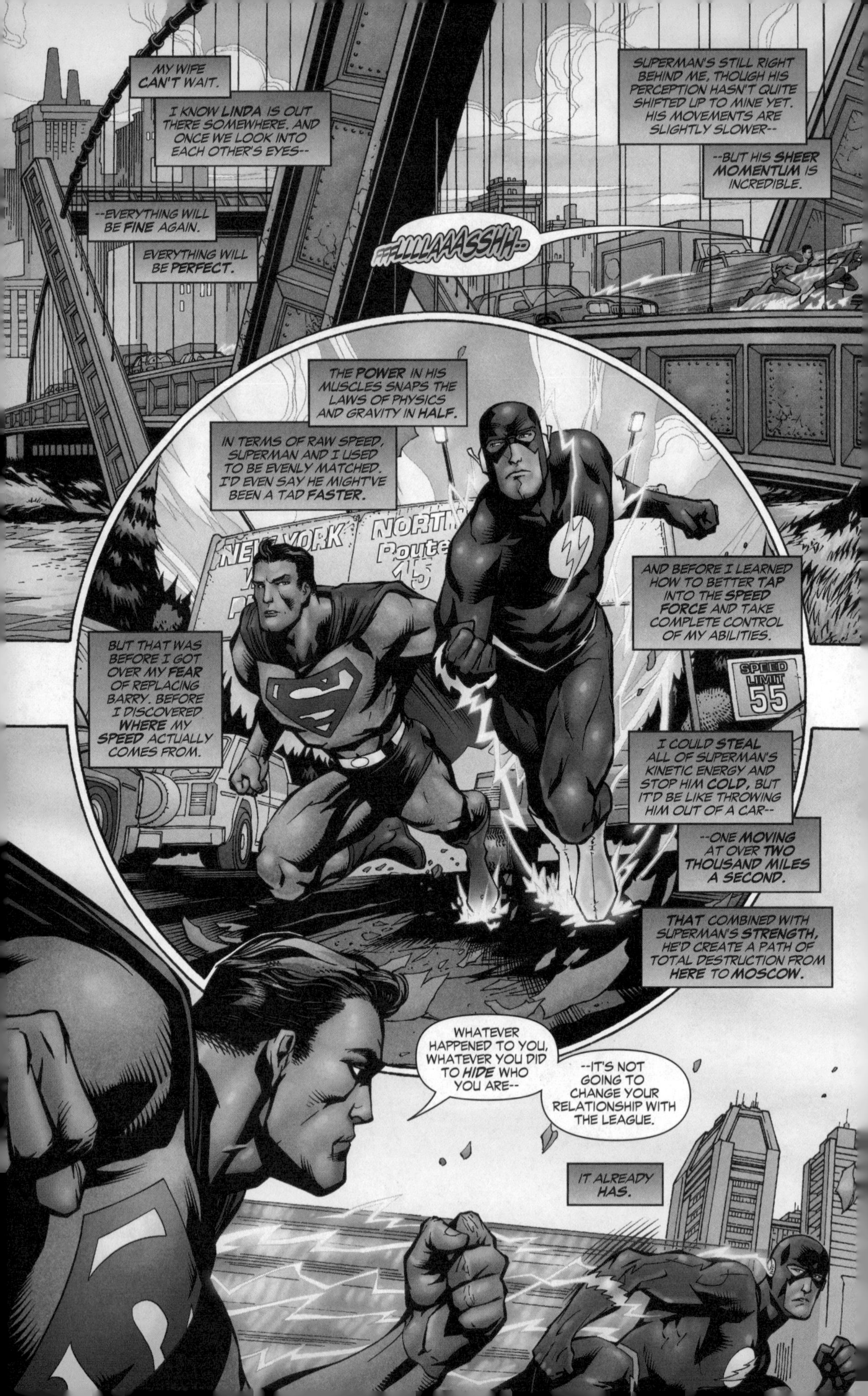
MY WIFE CAN'T WAIT.
I KNOW LINDA IS OUT THERE SOMEWHERE. AND ONCE WE LOOK INTO EACH OTHER'S EYES--
--EVERYTHING WILL BE FINE AGAIN.
EVERYTHING WILL BE PERFECT.
SUPERMAN'S STILL RIGHT BEHIND ME, THOUGH HIS PERCEPTION HASN'T QUITE SHIFTED UP TO MINE YET. HIS MOVEMENTS ARE SLIGHTLY SLOWER--
--BUT HIS SHEER MOMENTUM IS INCREDIBLE.
FFFLLLLAAASSHH-
THE POWER IN HIS MUSCLES SNAPS THE LAWS OF PHYSICS AND GRAVITY IN HALF.
IN TERMS OF RAW SPEED, SUPERMAN AND I USED TO BE EVENLY MATCHED. I'D EVEN SAY HE MIGHT'VE BEEN A TAD FASTER.
BUT THAT WAS BEFORE I GOT OVER MY FEAR OF REPLACING BARRY. BEFORE I DISCOVERED WHERE MY SPEED ACTUALLY COMES FROM.
AND BEFORE I LEARNED HOW TO BETTER TAP INTO THE SPEED FORCE AND TAKE COMPLETE CONTROL OF MY ABILITIES.
SPEED LIMIT 55
I COULD STEAL ALL OF SUPERMAN'S KINETIC ENERGY AND STOP HIM COLD, BUT IT'D BE LIKE THROWING HIM OUT OF A CAR--
--ONE MOVING AT OVER TWO THOUSAND MILES A SECOND.
THAT COMBINED WITH SUPERMAN'S STRENGTH, HE'D CREATE A PATH OF TOTAL DESTRUCTION FROM HERE TO MOSCOW.
WHATEVER HAPPENED TO YOU, WHATEVER YOU DID TO HIDE WHO YOU ARE--
--IT'S NOT GOING TO CHANGE YOUR RELATIONSHIP WITH THE LEAGUE.
IT ALREADY HAS.

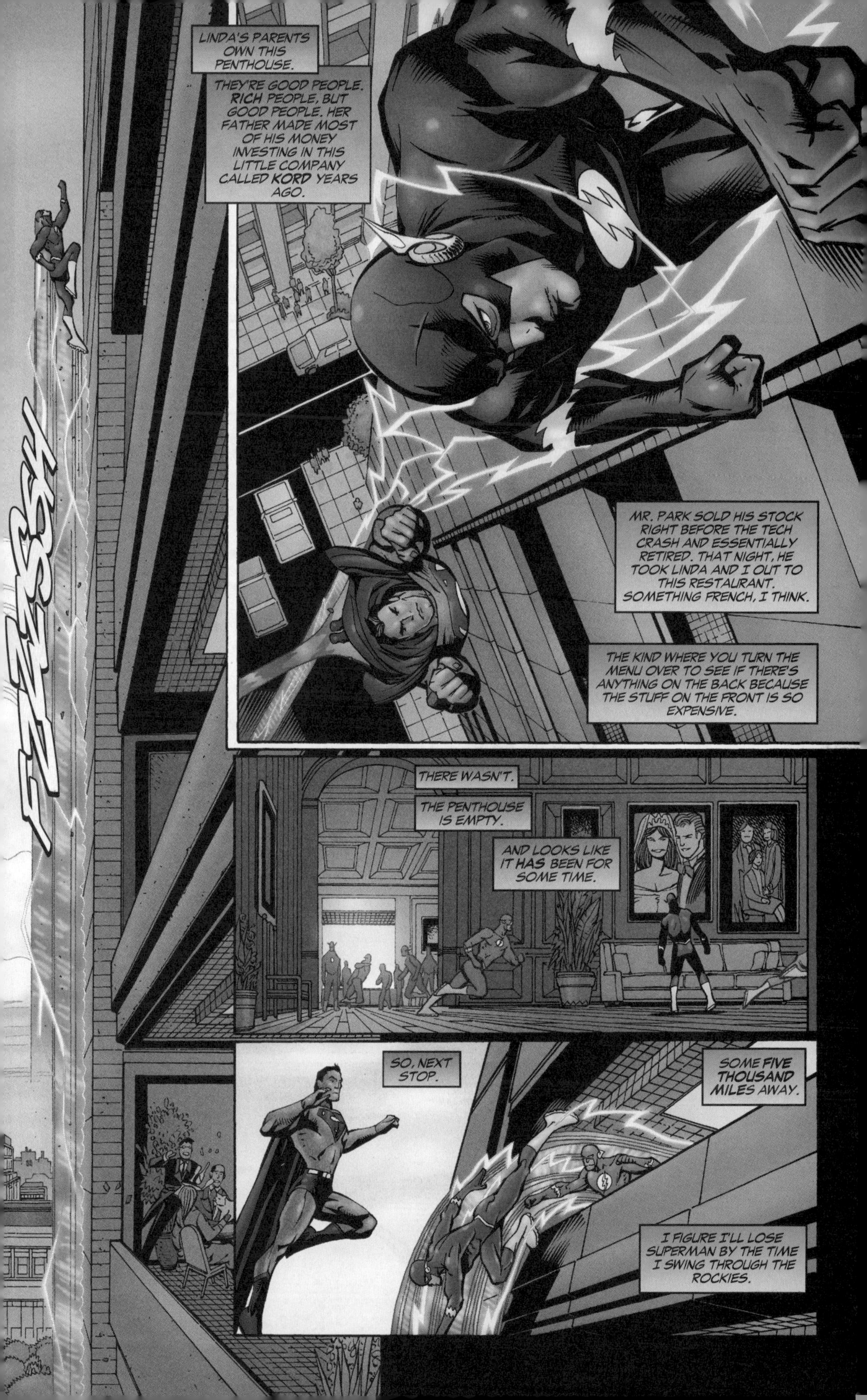
LINDA'S PARENTS OWN THIS PENTHOUSE.
THEY'RE GOOD PEOPLE. RICH PEOPLE, BUT GOOD PEOPLE. HER FATHER MADE MOST OF HIS MONEY INVESTING IN THIS LITTLE COMPANY CALLED KORD YEARS AGO.
MR. PARK SOLD HIS STOCK RIGHT BEFORE THE TECH CRASH AND ESSENTIALLY RETIRED. THAT NIGHT, HE TOOK LINDA AND I OUT TO THIS RESTAURANT. SOMETHING FRENCH, I THINK.
THE KIND WHERE YOU TURN THE MENU OVER TO SEE IF THERE'S ANYTHING ON THE BACK BECAUSE THE STUFF ON THE FRONT IS SO EXPENSIVE.
THERE WASN'T.
THE PENTHOUSE IS EMPTY.
AND LOOKS LIKE IT HAS BEEN FOR SOME TIME.
SO, NEXT STOP.
SOME FIVE THOUSAND MILES AWAY.
I FIGURE I'LL LOSE SUPERMAN BY THE TIME I SWING THROUGH THE ROCKIES.

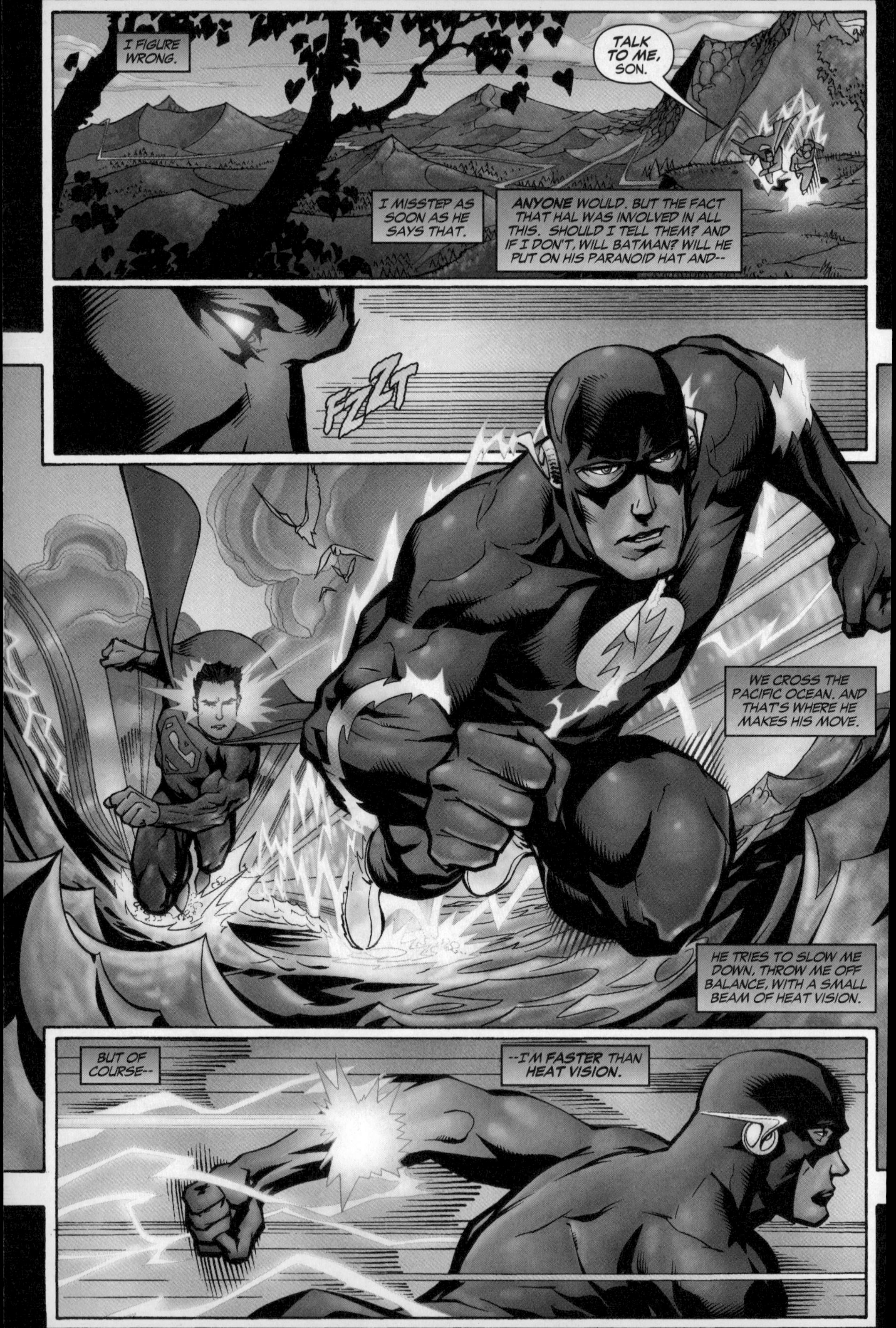

I FIGURE WRONG.
TALK TO ME, SON.
I MISSTEP AS SOON AS HE SAYS THAT.
ANYONE WOULD. BUT THE FACT THAT HAL WAS INVOLVED IN ALL THIS. SHOULD I TELL THEM? AND IF I DON'T, WILL BATMAN? WILL HE PUT ON HIS PARANOID HAT AND--
FZZZT
WE CROSS THE PACIFIC OCEAN. AND THAT'S WHERE HE MAKES HIS MOVE.
HE TRIES TO SLOW ME DOWN, THROW ME OFF BALANCE, WITH A SMALL BEAM OF HEAT VISION.
BUT OF COURSE--
--I'M FASTER THAN HEAT VISION.

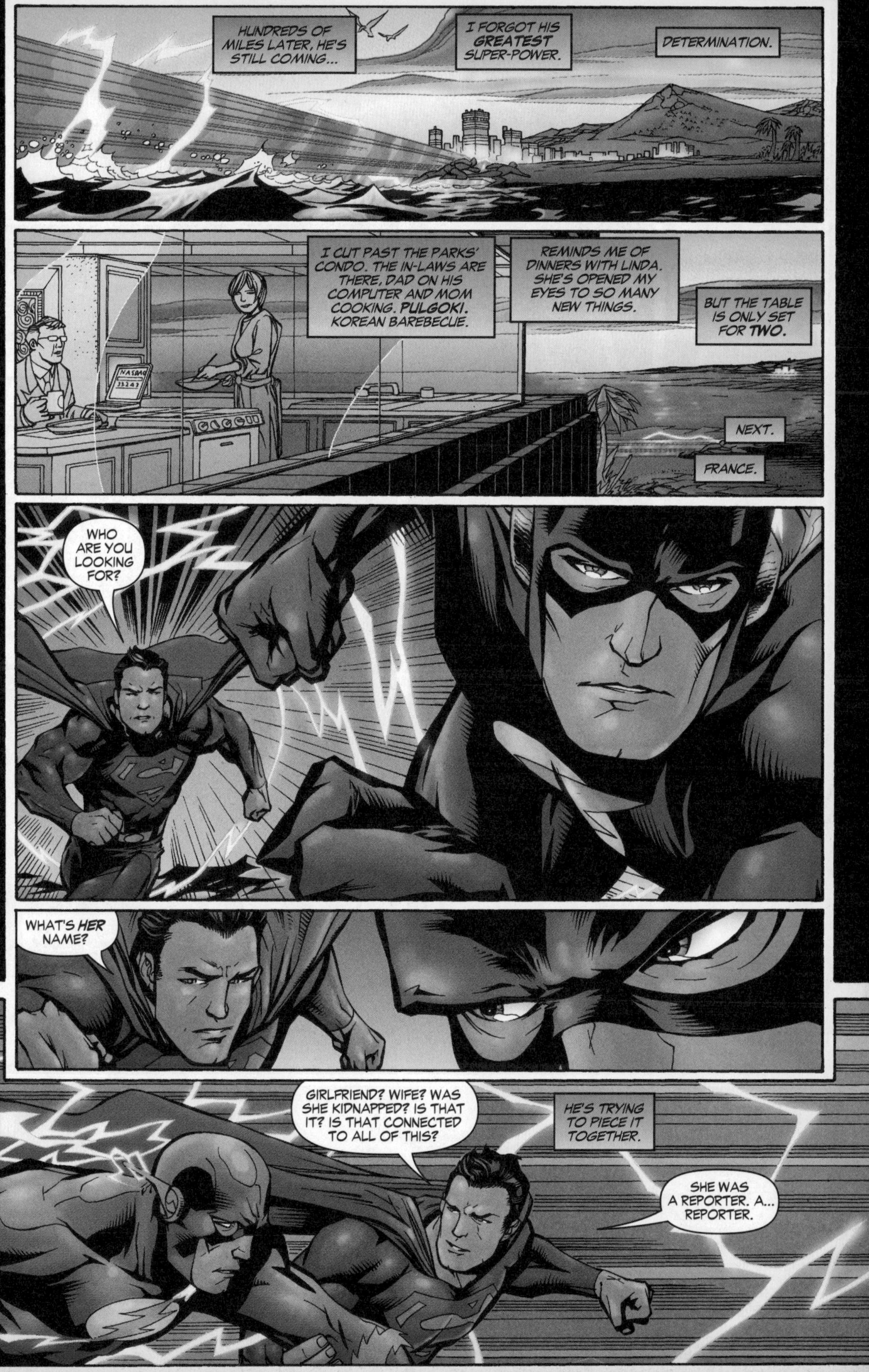

HUNDREDS OF MILES LATER, HE'S STILL COMING...
I FORGOT HIS GREATEST SUPER-POWER.
DETERMINATION.
I CUT PAST THE PARKS' CONDO. THE IN-LAWS ARE THERE, DAD ON HIS COMPUTER AND MOM COOKING. PULGOKI. KOREAN BAREBECUE.
REMINDS ME OF DINNERS WITH LINDA. SHE'S OPENED MY EYES TO SO MANY NEW THINGS.
BUT THE TABLE IS ONLY SET FOR TWO.
NEXT.
FRANCE.
WHO ARE YOU LOOKING FOR?
WHAT'S HER NAME?
GIRLFRIEND? WIFE? WAS SHE KIDNAPPED? IS THAT IT? IS THAT CONNECTED TO ALL OF THIS?
HE'S TRYING TO PIECE IT TOGETHER.
SHE WAS A REPORTER. A... REPORTER.

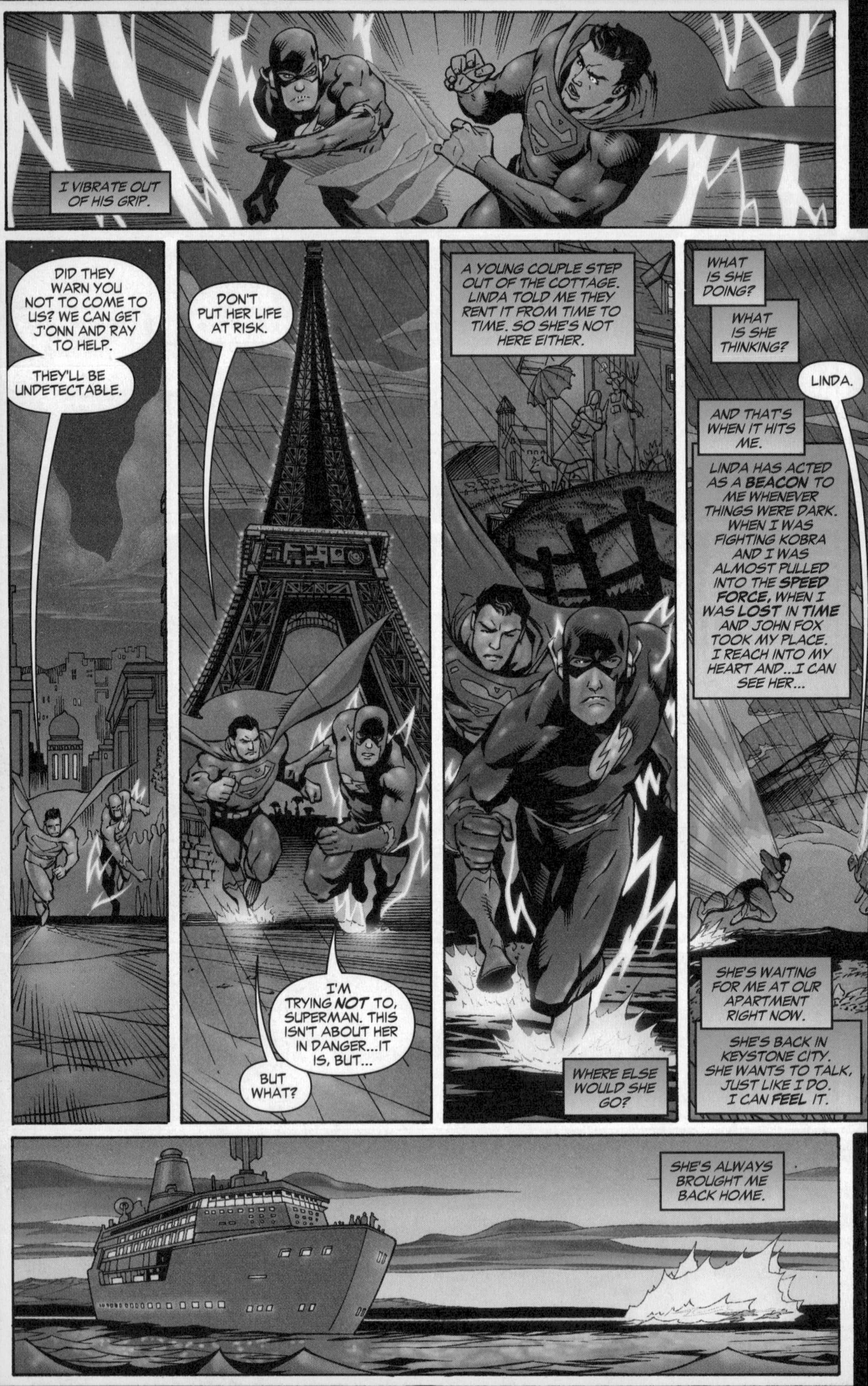
I VIBRATE OUT OF HIS GRIP.
DID THEY WARN YOU NOT TO COME TO US? WE CAN GET J'ONN AND RAY TO HELP.
THEY'LL BE UNDETECTABLE.
DON'T PUT HER LIFE AT RISK.
I'M TRYING NOT TO, SUPERMAN. THIS ISN'T ABOUT HER IN DANGER...IT IS, BUT...
BUT WHAT?
A YOUNG COUPLE STEP OUT OF THE COTTAGE. LINDA TOLD ME THEY RENT IT FROM TIME TO TIME. SO SHE'S NOT HERE EITHER.
WHERE ELSE WOULD SHE GO?
WHAT IS SHE DOING?
WHAT IS SHE THINKING?
LINDA.
AND THAT'S WHEN IT HITS ME.
LINDA HAS ACTED AS A BEACON TO ME WHENEVER THINGS WERE DARK. WHEN I WAS FIGHTING KOBRA AND I WAS ALMOST PULLED INTO THE SPEED FORCE, WHEN I WAS LOST IN TIME AND JOHN FOX TOOK MY PLACE. I REACH INTO MY HEART AND...I CAN SEE HER...
SHE'S WAITING FOR ME AT OUR APARTMENT RIGHT NOW.
SHE'S BACK IN KEYSTONE CITY. SHE WANTS TO TALK, JUST LIKE I DO. I CAN FEEL IT.
SHE'S ALWAYS BROUGHT ME BACK HOME.

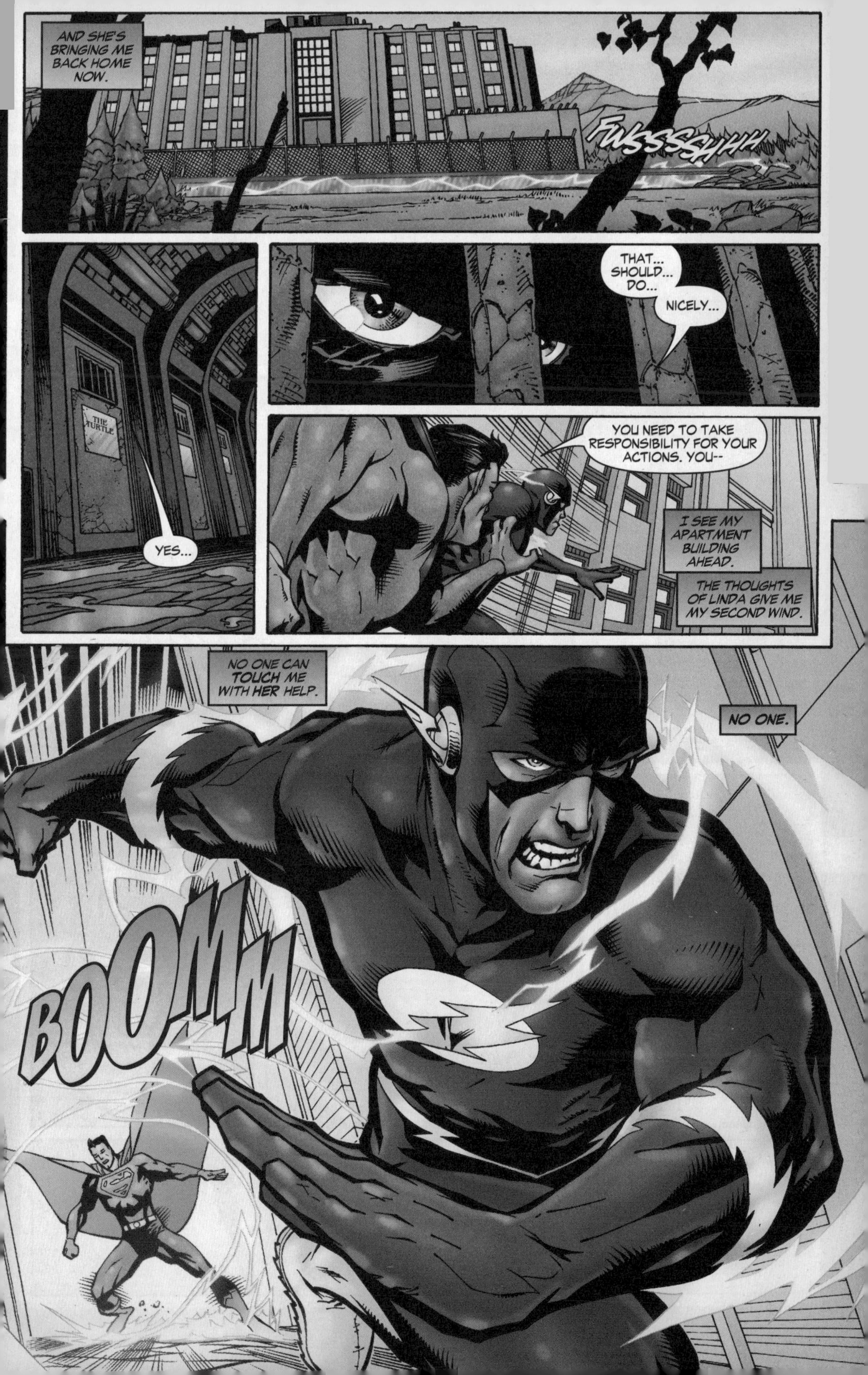
AND SHE'S BRINGING ME BACK HOME NOW.
FWSSSSHHH
YES...
THAT... SHOULD... DO...
NICELY...
YOU NEED TO TAKE RESPONSIBILITY FOR YOUR ACTIONS. YOU--
I SEE MY APARTMENT BUILDING AHEAD.
THE THOUGHTS OF LINDA GIVE ME MY SECOND WIND.
NO ONE CAN TOUCH ME WITH HER HELP.
NO ONE.
BOOMM

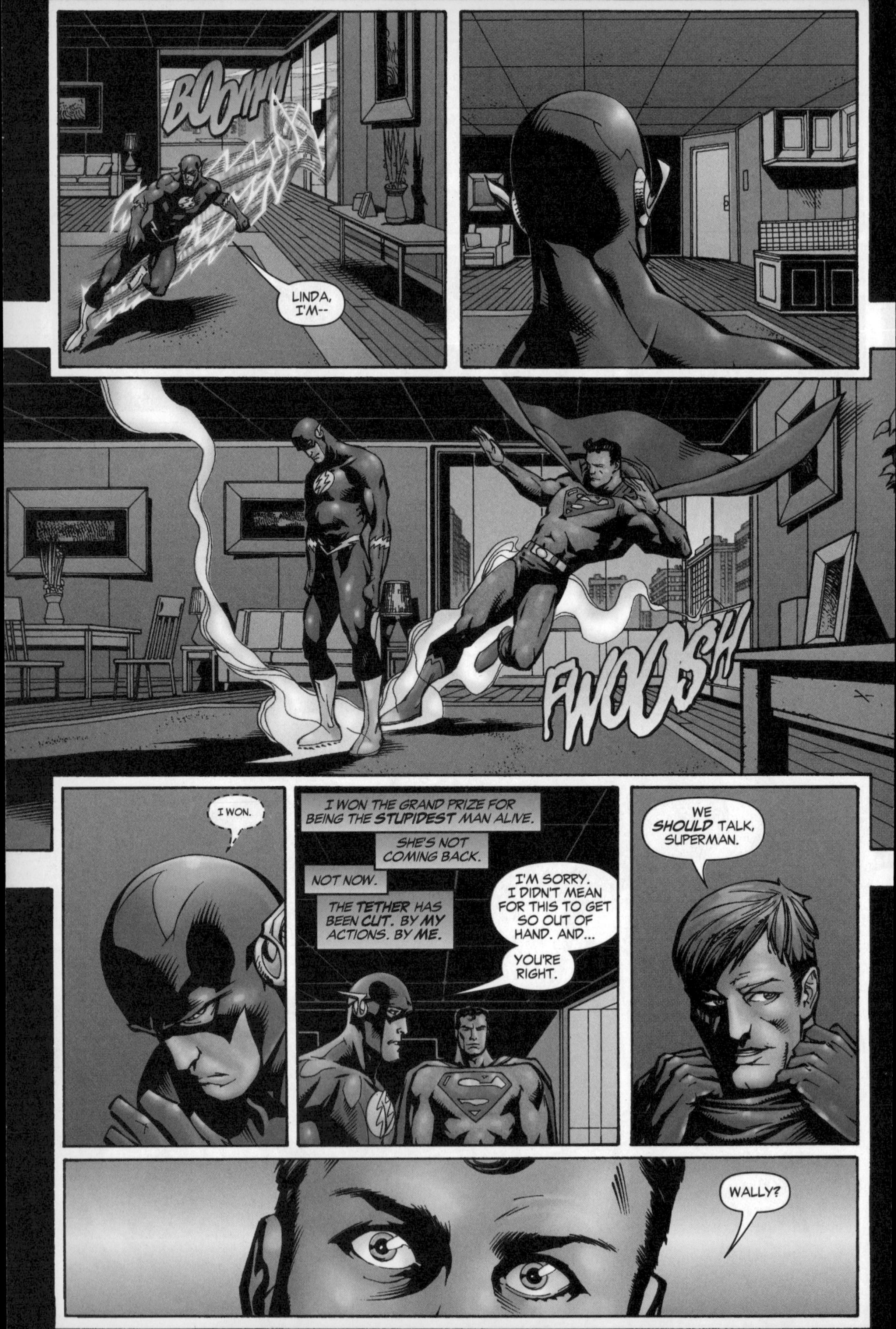
BOOMM
LINDA, I'M--
FWOOSH
I WON.
I WON THE GRAND PRIZE FOR BEING THE STUPIDEST MAN ALIVE.
SHE'S NOT COMING BACK.
NOT NOW.
THE TETHER HAS BEEN CUT. BY MY ACTIONS. BY ME.
I'M SORRY. I DIDN'T MEAN FOR THIS TO GET SO OUT OF HAND. AND...
YOU'RE RIGHT.
WE SHOULD TALK, SUPERMAN.
WALLY?

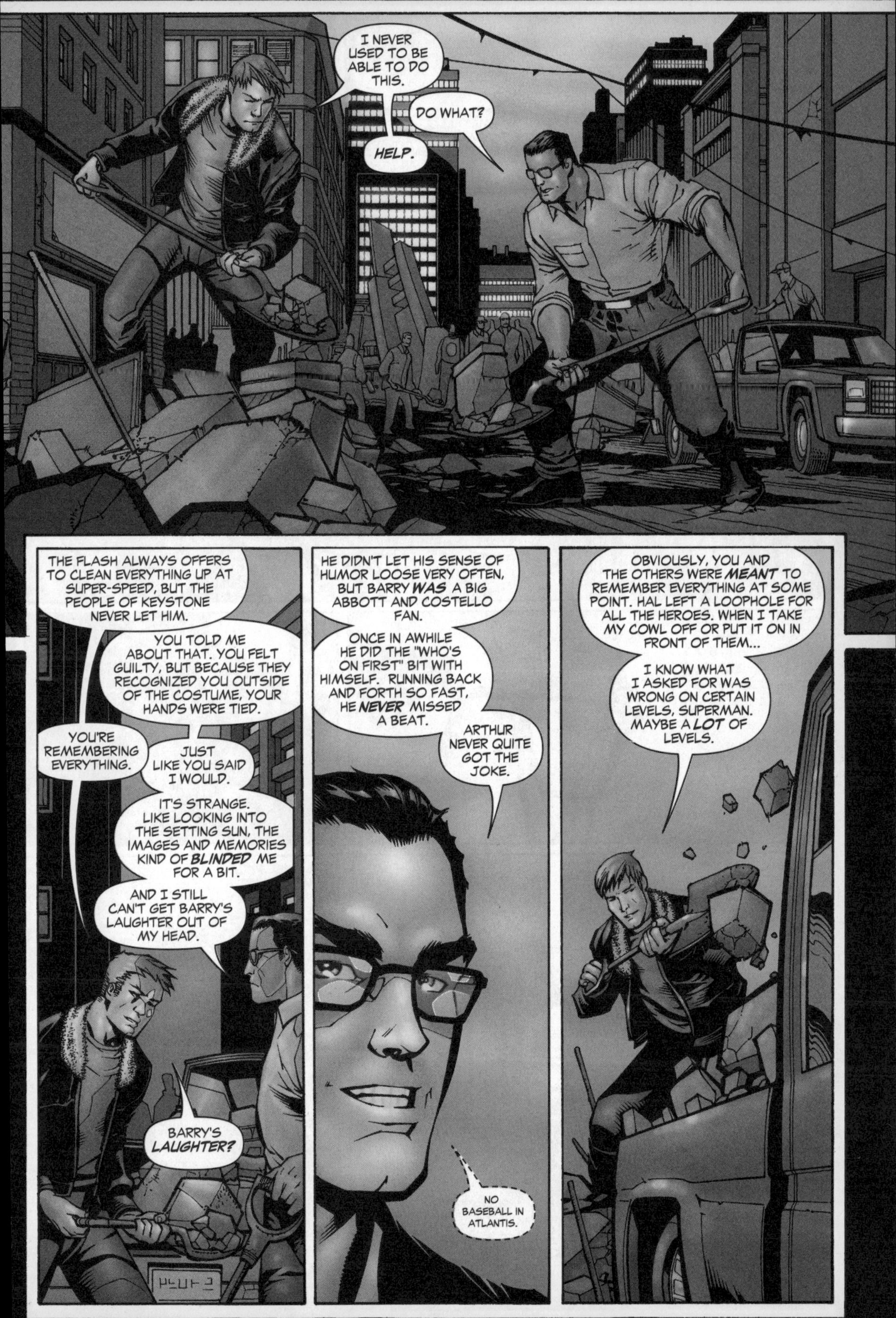
I NEVER USED TO BE ABLE TO DO THIS.
DO WHAT?
HELP.
THE FLASH ALWAYS OFFERS TO CLEAN EVERYTHING UP AT SUPER-SPEED, BUT THE PEOPLE OF KEYSTONE NEVER LET HIM.
YOU TOLD ME ABOUT THAT. YOU FELT GUILTY, BUT BECAUSE THEY RECOGNIZED YOU OUTSIDE OF THE COSTUME, YOUR HANDS WERE TIED.
YOU'RE REMEMBERING EVERYTHING.
JUST LIKE YOU SAID I WOULD.
IT'S STRANGE. LIKE LOOKING INTO THE SETTING SUN, THE IMAGES AND MEMORIES KIND OF BLINDED ME FOR A BIT.
AND I STILL CAN'T GET BARRY'S LAUGHTER OUT OF MY HEAD.
BARRY'S LAUGHTER?
HE DIDN'T LET HIS SENSE OF HUMOR LOOSE VERY OFTEN, BUT BARRY WAS A BIG ABBOTT AND COSTELLO FAN.
ONCE IN AWHILE HE DID THE "WHO'S ON FIRST" BIT WITH HIMSELF. RUNNING BACK AND FORTH SO FAST, HE NEVER MISSED A BEAT.
ARTHUR NEVER QUITE GOT THE JOKE.
NO BASEBALL IN ATLANTIS.
OBVIOUSLY, YOU AND THE OTHERS WERE MEANT TO REMEMBER EVERYTHING AT SOME POINT. HAL LEFT A LOOPHOLE FOR ALL THE HEROES. WHEN I TAKE MY COWL OFF OR PUT IT ON IN FRONT OF THEM...
I KNOW WHAT I ASKED FOR WAS WRONG ON CERTAIN LEVELS, SUPERMAN. MAYBE A LOT OF LEVELS.

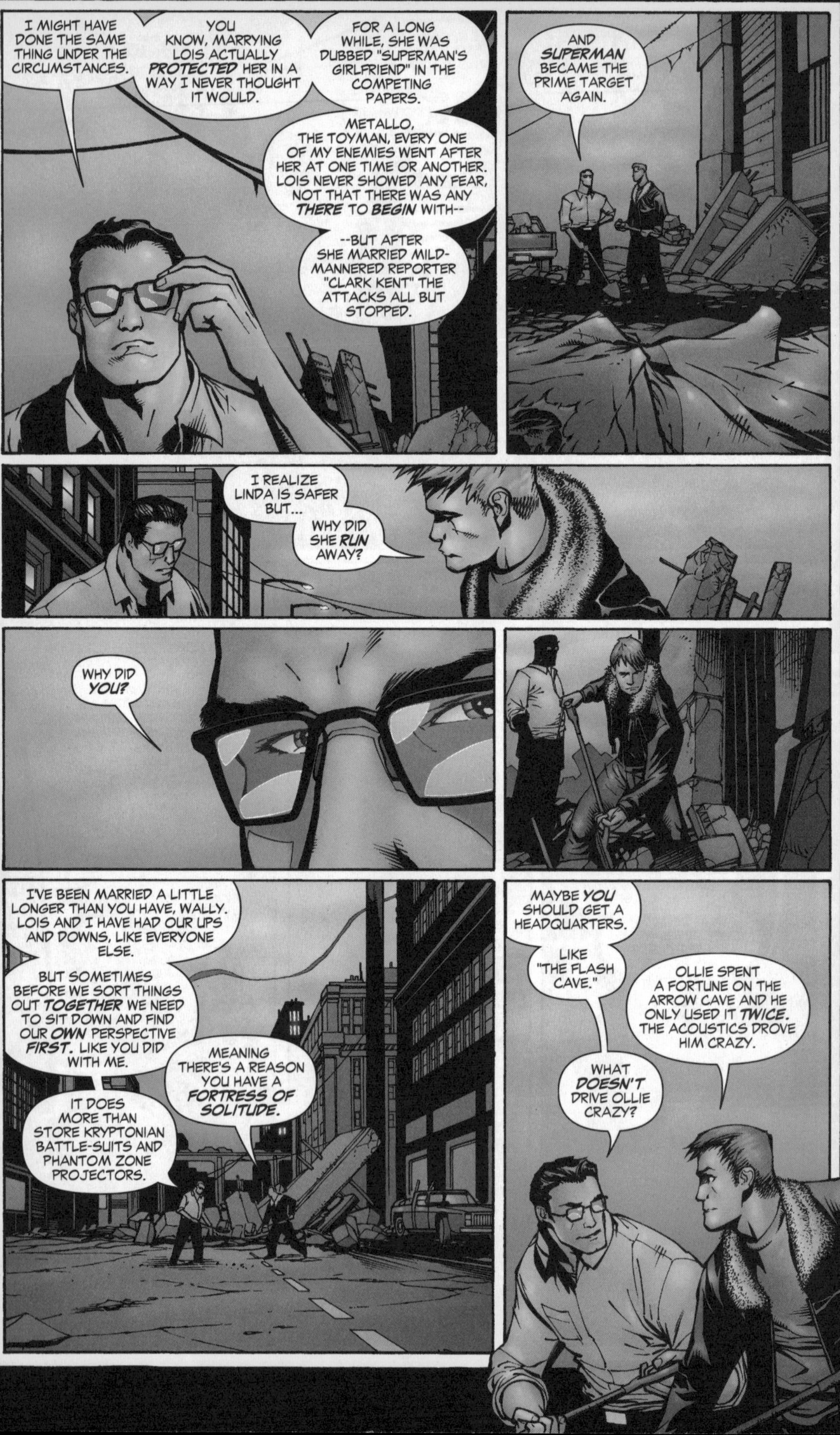
I MIGHT HAVE DONE THE SAME THING UNDER THE CIRCUMSTANCES.
YOU KNOW, MARRYING LOIS ACTUALLY PROTECTED HER IN A WAY I NEVER THOUGHT IT WOULD.
FOR A LONG WHILE, SHE WAS DUBBED "SUPERMAN'S GIRLFRIEND" IN THE COMPETING PAPERS.
METALLO, THE TOYMAN, EVERY ONE OF MY ENEMIES WENT AFTER HER AT ONE TIME OR ANOTHER. LOIS NEVER SHOWED ANY FEAR, NOT THAT THERE WAS ANY THERE TO BEGIN WITH--
--BUT AFTER SHE MARRIED MILD-MANNERED REPORTER "CLARK KENT" THE ATTACKS ALL BUT STOPPED.
AND SUPERMAN BECAME THE PRIME TARGET AGAIN.
I REALIZE LINDA IS SAFER BUT...
WHY DID SHE RUN AWAY?
WHY DID YOU?
I'VE BEEN MARRIED A LITTLE LONGER THAN YOU HAVE, WALLY. LOIS AND I HAVE HAD OUR UPS AND DOWNS, LIKE EVERYONE ELSE.
BUT SOMETIMES BEFORE WE SORT THINGS OUT TOGETHER WE NEED TO SIT DOWN AND FIND OUR OWN PERSPECTIVE FIRST. LIKE YOU DID WITH ME.
MEANING THERE'S A REASON YOU HAVE A FORTRESS OF SOLITUDE.
IT DOES MORE THAN STORE KRYPTONIAN BATTLE-SUITS AND PHANTOM ZONE PROJECTORS.
MAYBE YOU SHOULD GET A HEADQUARTERS.
LIKE "THE FLASH CAVE."
OLLIE SPENT A FORTUNE ON THE ARROW CAVE AND HE ONLY USED IT TWICE. THE ACOUSTICS DROVE HIM CRAZY.
WHAT DOESN'T DRIVE OLLIE CRAZY?

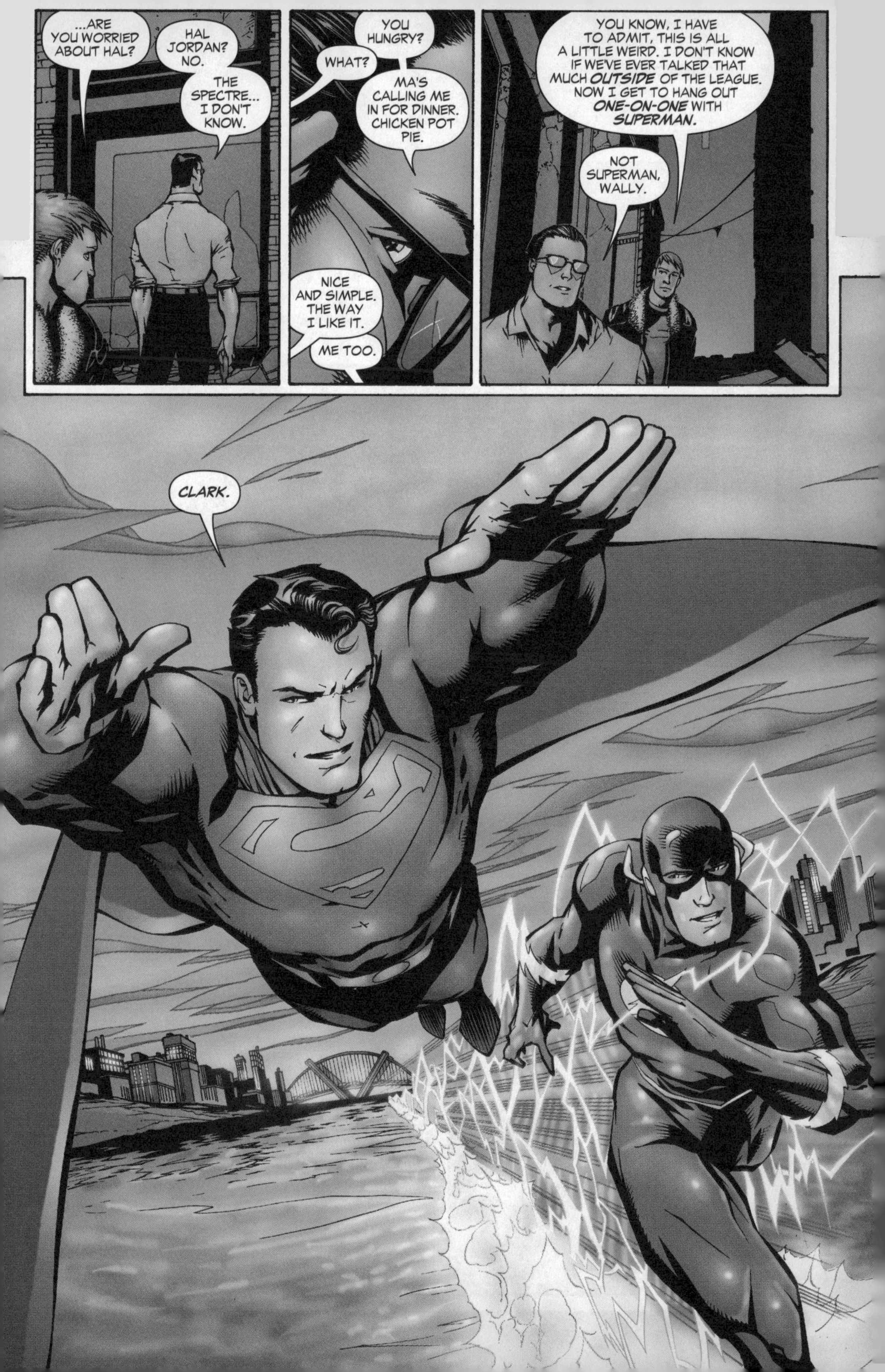
...ARE YOU WORRIED ABOUT HAL?
HAL JORDAN? NO.
THE SPECTRE... I DON'T KNOW.
YOU HUNGRY?
WHAT?
MA'S CALLING ME IN FOR DINNER. CHICKEN POT PIE.
NICE AND SIMPLE. THE WAY I LIKE IT.
ME TOO.
YOU KNOW, I HAVE TO ADMIT, THIS IS ALL A LITTLE WEIRD. I DON'T KNOW IF WE'VE EVER TALKED THAT MUCH OUTSIDE OF THE LEAGUE. NOW I GET TO HANG OUT ONE-ON-ONE WITH SUPERMAN.
NOT SUPERMAN, WALLY.
CLARK.

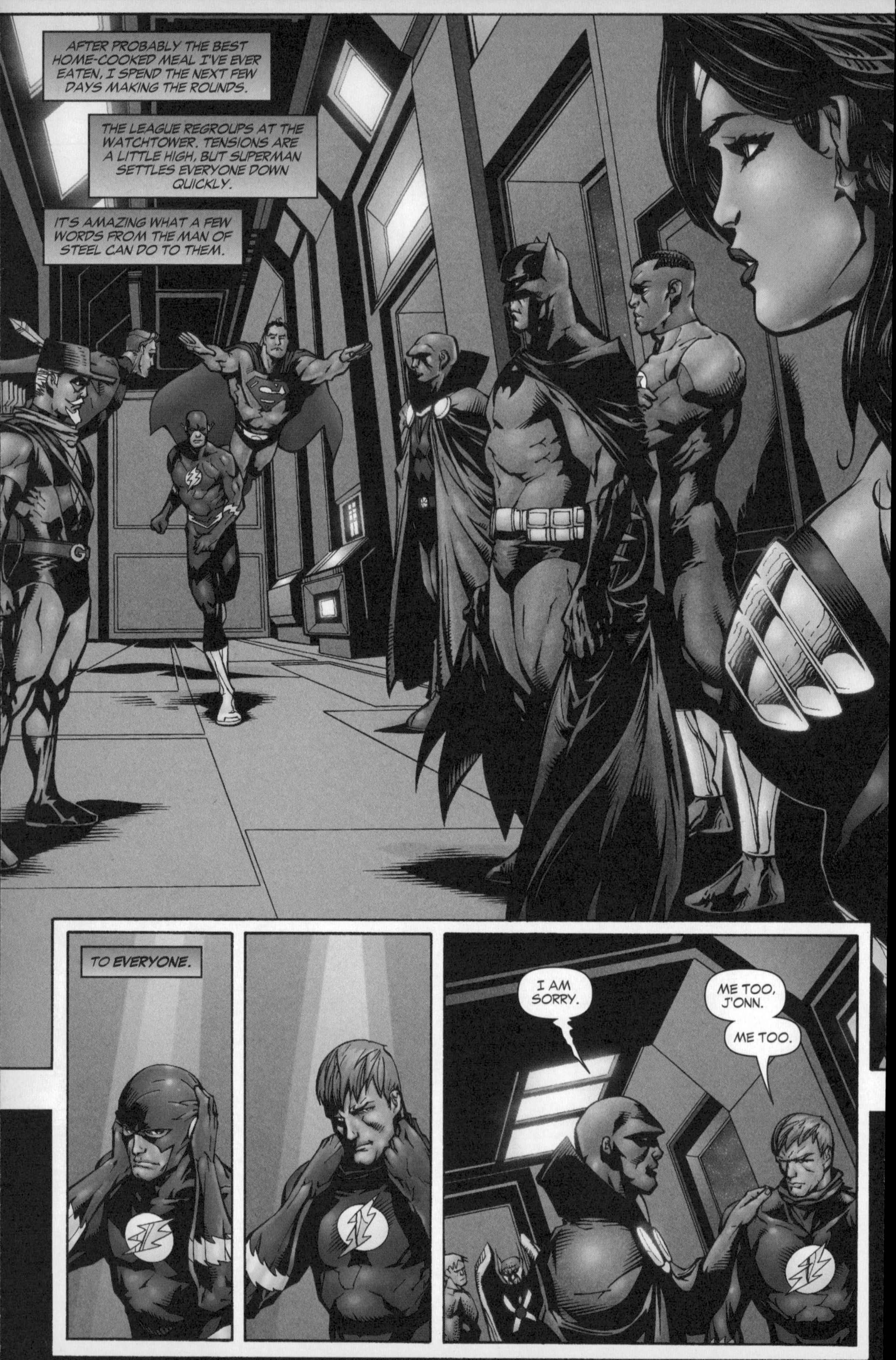
AFTER PROBABLY THE BEST HOME-COOKED MEAL I'VE EVER EATEN, I SPEND THE NEXT FEW DAYS MAKING THE ROUNDS.
THE LEAGUE REGROUPS AT THE WATCHTOWER. TENSIONS ARE A LITTLE HIGH, BUT SUPERMAN SETTLES EVERYONE DOWN QUICKLY.
IT'S AMAZING WHAT A FEW WORDS FROM THE MAN OF STEEL CAN DO TO THEM.
TO EVERYONE.
I AM SORRY.
ME TOO, J'ONN.
ME TOO.

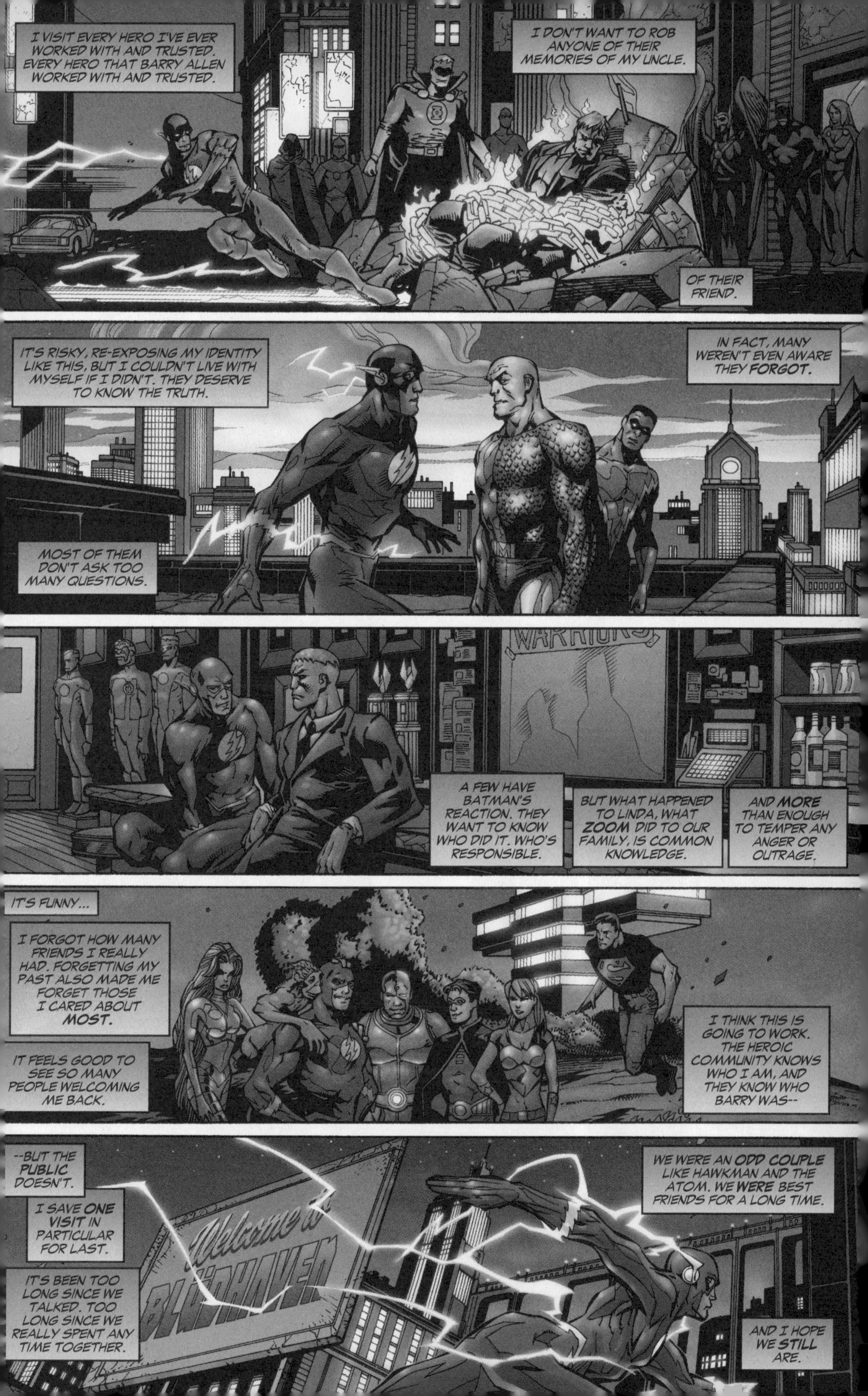
I VISIT EVERY HERO I'VE EVER WORKED WITH AND TRUSTED. EVERY HERO THAT BARRY ALLEN WORKED WITH AND TRUSTED.
I DON'T WANT TO ROB ANYONE OF THEIR MEMORIES OF MY UNCLE.
OF THEIR FRIEND.
IT'S RISKY, RE-EXPOSING MY IDENTITY LIKE THIS, BUT I COULDN'T LIVE WITH MYSELF IF I DIDN'T. THEY DESERVE TO KNOW THE TRUTH.
IN FACT, MANY WEREN'T EVEN AWARE THEY FORGOT.
MOST OF THEM DON'T ASK TOO MANY QUESTIONS.
WARRIORS
A FEW HAVE BATMAN'S REACTION. THEY WANT TO KNOW WHO DID IT. WHO'S RESPONSIBLE.
BUT WHAT HAPPENED TO LINDA, WHAT ZOOM DID TO OUR FAMILY, IS COMMON KNOWLEDGE.
AND MORE THAN ENOUGH TO TEMPER ANY ANGER OR OUTRAGE.
IT'S FUNNY...
I FORGOT HOW MANY FRIENDS I REALLY HAD. FORGETTING MY PAST ALSO MADE ME FORGET THOSE I CARED ABOUT MOST.
IT FEELS GOOD TO SEE SO MANY PEOPLE WELCOMING ME BACK.
I THINK THIS IS GOING TO WORK. THE HEROIC COMMUNITY KNOWS WHO I AM, AND THEY KNOW WHO BARRY WAS--
--BUT THE PUBLIC DOESN'T.
I SAVE ONE VISIT IN PARTICULAR FOR LAST.
IT'S BEEN TOO LONG SINCE WE TALKED. TOO LONG SINCE WE REALLY SPENT ANY TIME TOGETHER.
Welcome to BLÜDHAVEN
WE WERE AN ODD COUPLE LIKE HAWKMAN AND THE ATOM. WE WERE BEST FRIENDS FOR A LONG TIME.
AND I HOPE WE STILL ARE.

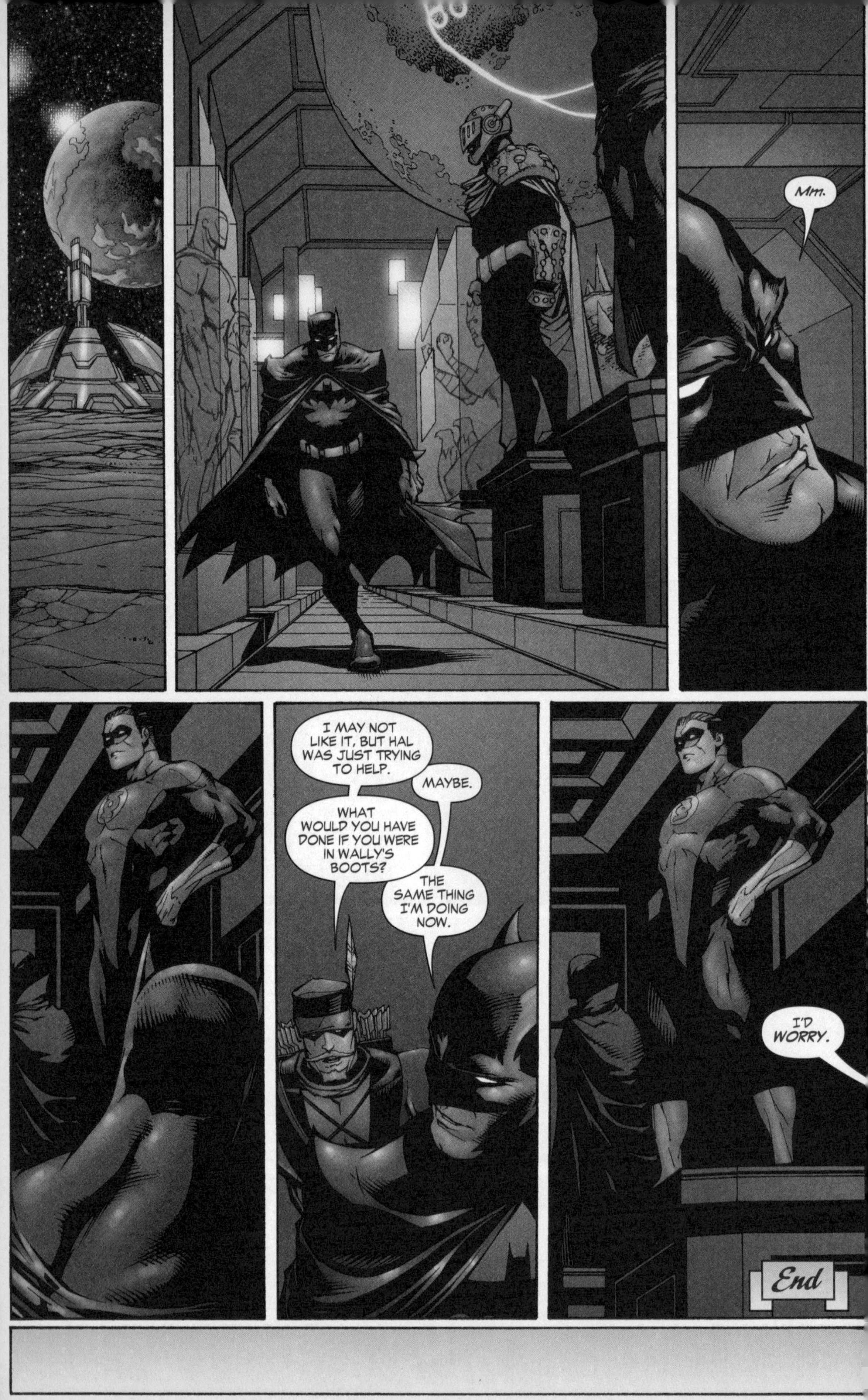
Mm.
I MAY NOT LIKE IT, BUT HAL WAS JUST TRYING TO HELP.
WHAT WOULD YOU HAVE DONE IF YOU WERE IN WALLY'S BOOTS?
MAYBE.
THE SAME THING I'M DOING NOW.
I'D WORRY.
End

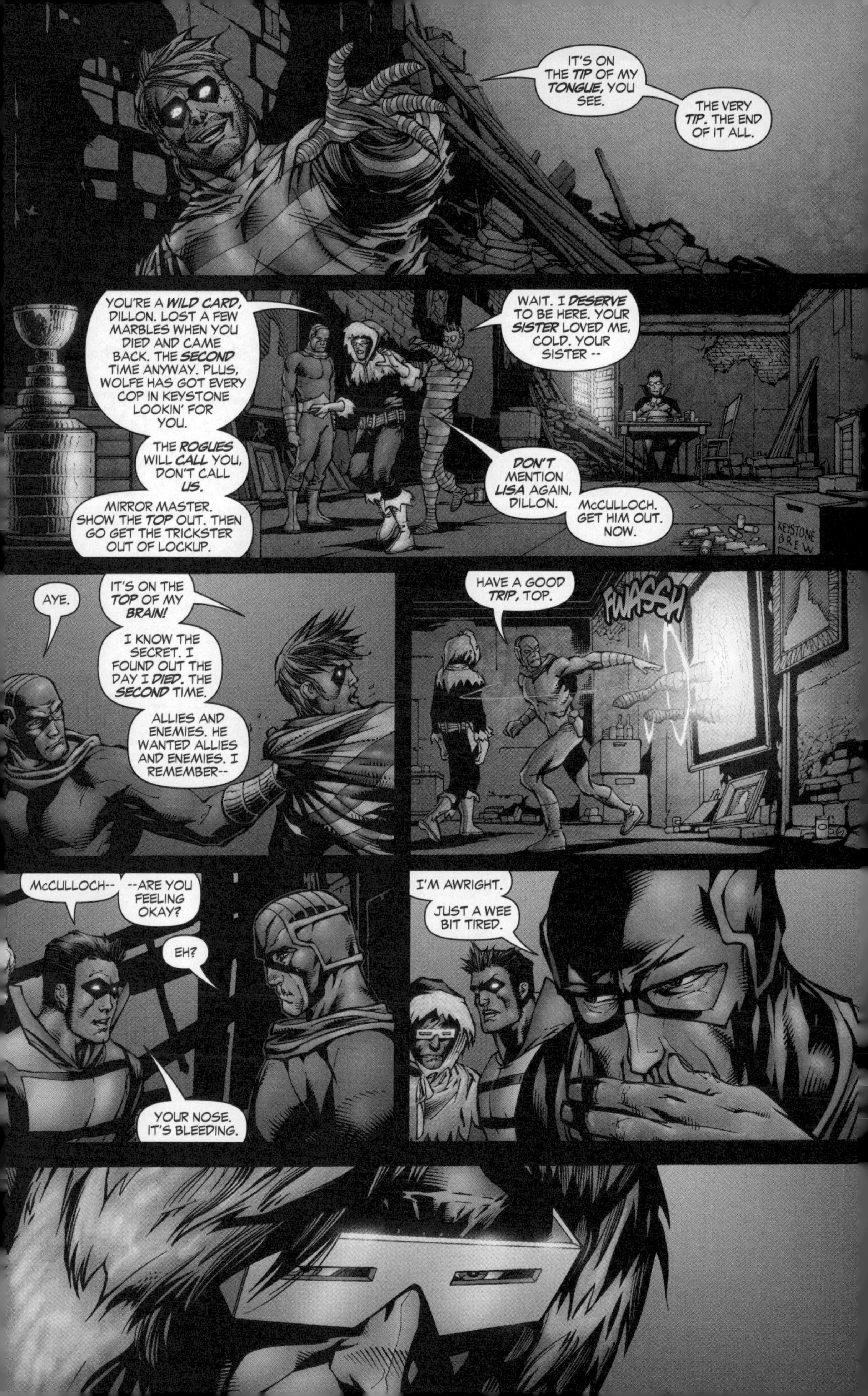
IT'S ON THE TIP OF MY TONGUE, YOU SEE.
THE VERY TIP. THE END OF IT ALL.
YOU'RE A WILD CARD, DILLON. LOST A FEW MARBLES WHEN YOU DIED AND CAME BACK. THE SECOND TIME ANYWAY. PLUS, WOLFE HAS GOT EVERY COP IN KEYSTONE LOOKIN' FOR YOU.
THE ROGUES WILL CALL YOU, DON'T CALL US.
MIRROR MASTER. SHOW THE TOP OUT. THEN GO GET THE TRICKSTER OUT OF LOCKUP.
WAIT. I DESERVE TO BE HERE. YOUR SISTER LOVED ME, COLD. YOUR SISTER --
DON'T MENTION LISA AGAIN, DILLON.
McCULLOCH. GET HIM OUT. NOW.
KEYSTONE BREW
AYE.
IT'S ON THE TOP OF MY BRAIN!
I KNOW THE SECRET. I FOUND OUT THE DAY I DIED. THE SECOND TIME.
ALLIES AND ENEMIES. HE WANTED ALLIES AND ENEMIES. I REMEMBER--
HAVE A GOOD TRIP, TOP.
FWASSH
McCULLOCH--
--ARE YOU FEELING OKAY?
EH?
YOUR NOSE. IT'S BLEEDING.
I'M AWRIGHT.
JUST A WEE BIT TIRED.

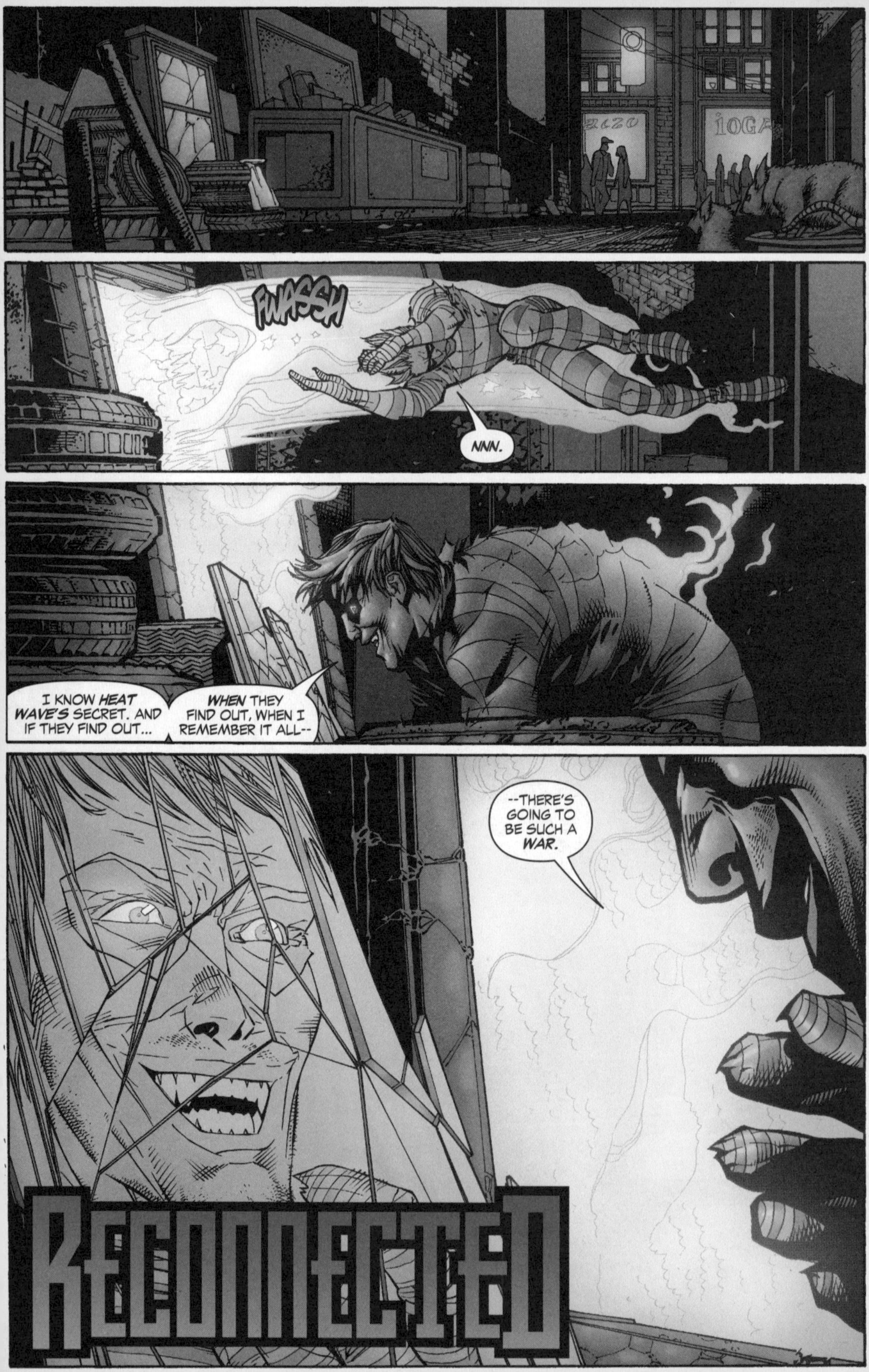

ZIZO
IOGA
FWASSH
NNN.
I KNOW HEAT WAVE'S SECRET. AND IF THEY FIND OUT...
WHEN THEY FIND OUT, WHEN I REMEMBER IT ALL--
--THERE'S GOING TO BE SUCH A WAR.
RECONNECTED

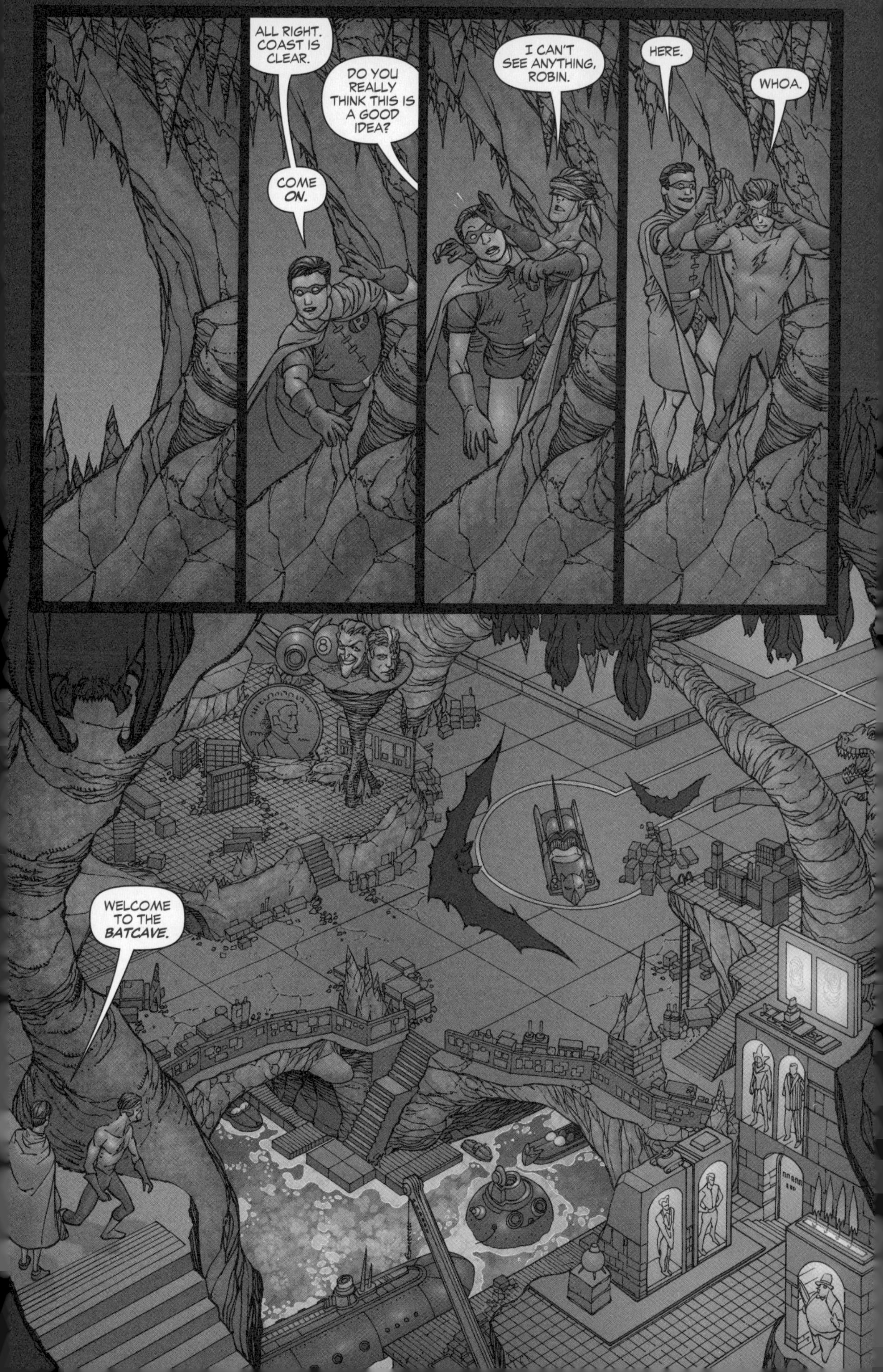
ALL RIGHT. COAST IS CLEAR.
DO YOU REALLY THINK THIS IS A GOOD IDEA?
COME ON.
I CAN'T SEE ANYTHING, ROBIN.
HERE.
WHOA.
WELCOME TO THE *BATCAVE.*

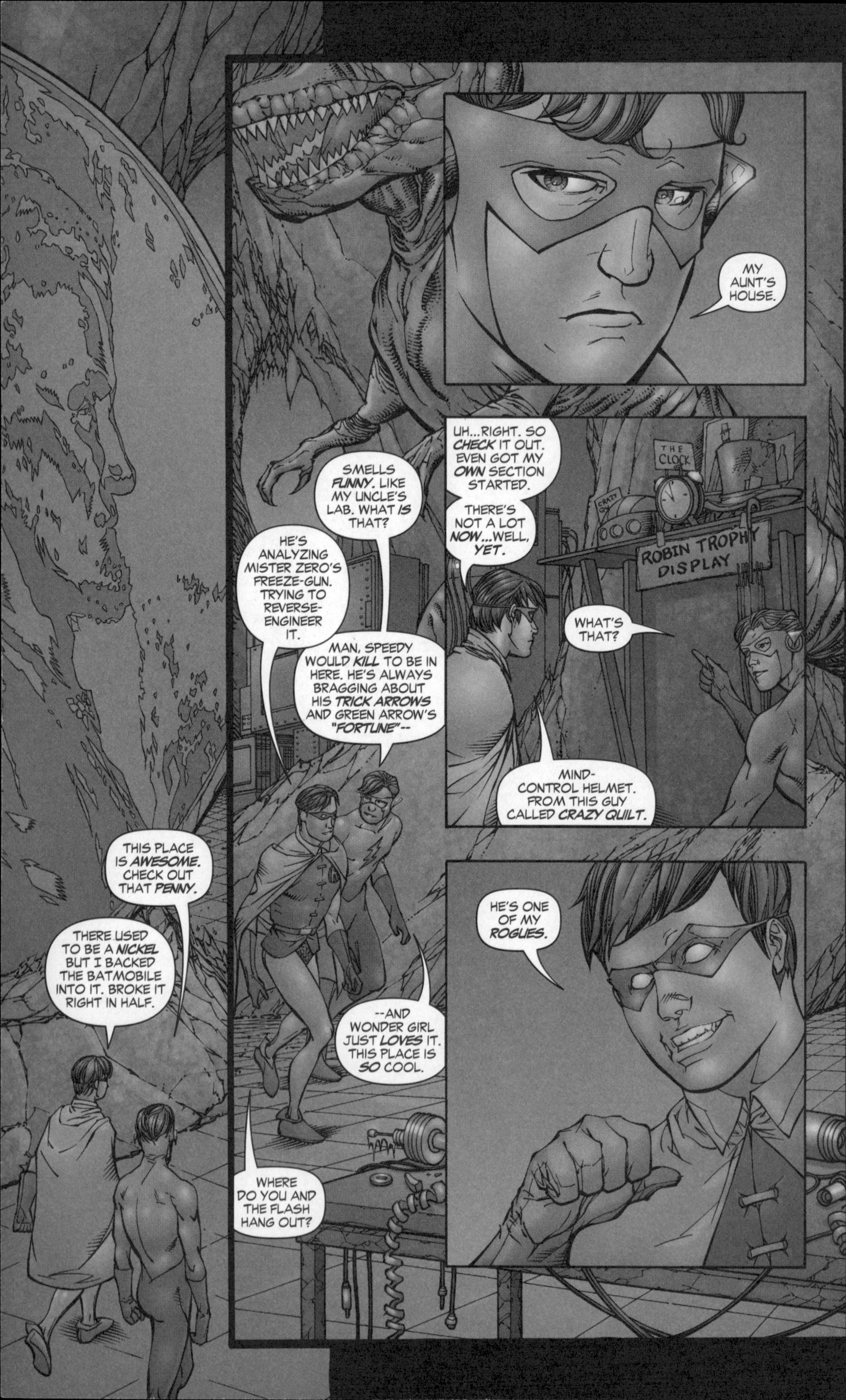
MY AUNT'S HOUSE.
UH...RIGHT. SO CHECK IT OUT. EVEN GOT MY OWN SECTION STARTED.
THERE'S NOT A LOT NOW...WELL, YET.
THE CLOCK
ROBIN TROPHY DISPLAY
WHAT'S THAT?
MIND-CONTROL HELMET. FROM THIS GUY CALLED CRAZY QUILT.
HE'S ONE OF MY ROGUES.
SMELLS FUNNY. LIKE MY UNCLE'S LAB. WHAT IS THAT?
HE'S ANALYZING MISTER ZERO'S FREEZE-GUN. TRYING TO REVERSE-ENGINEER IT.
MAN, SPEEDY WOULD KILL TO BE IN HERE. HE'S ALWAYS BRAGGING ABOUT HIS TRICK ARROWS AND GREEN ARROW'S "FORTUNE"--
--AND WONDER GIRL JUST LOVES IT. THIS PLACE IS SO COOL.
WHERE DO YOU AND THE FLASH HANG OUT?
THIS PLACE IS AWESOME. CHECK OUT THAT PENNY.
THERE USED TO BE A NICKEL BUT I BACKED THE BATMOBILE INTO IT. BROKE IT RIGHT IN HALF.

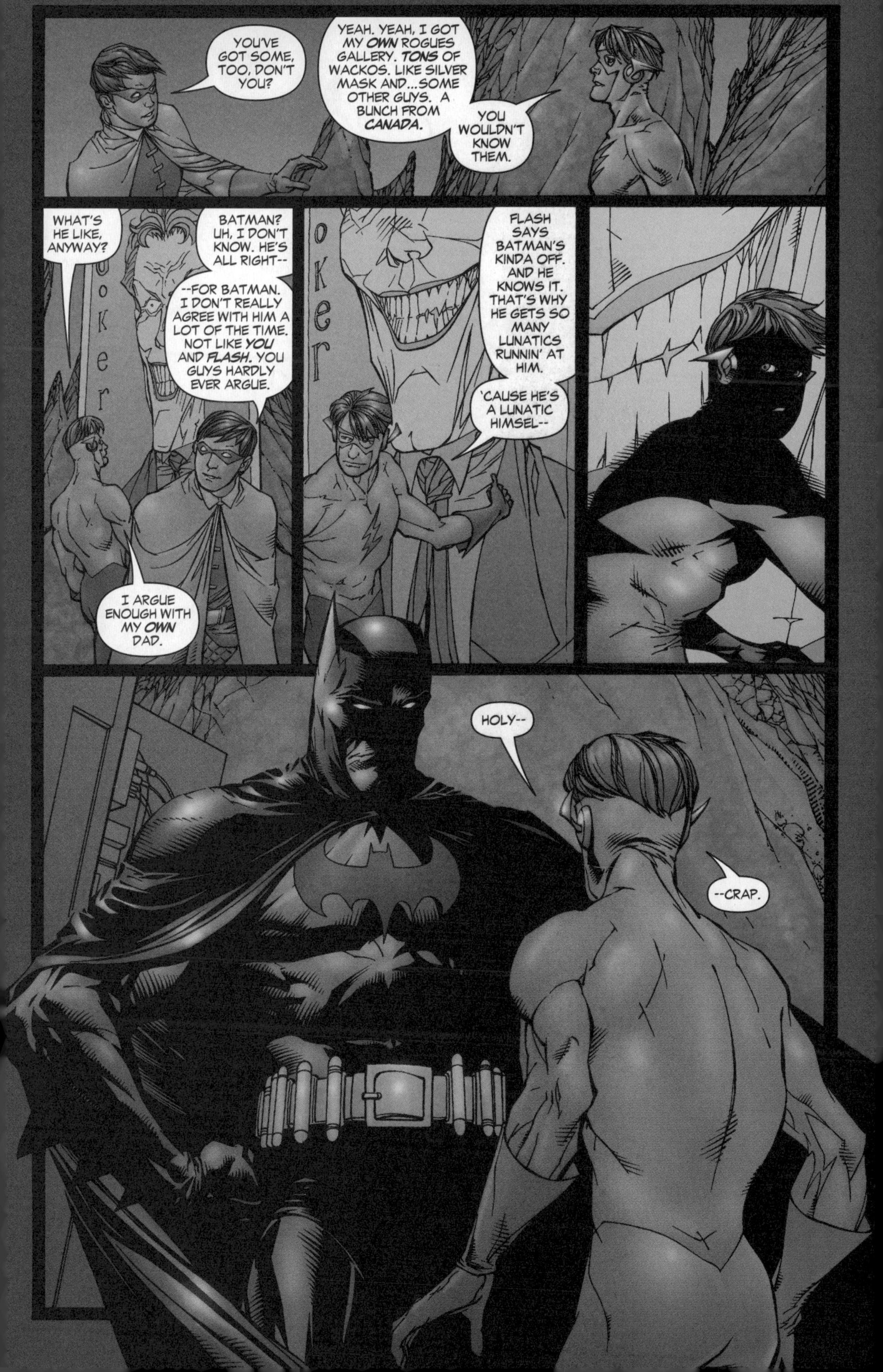
YOU'VE GOT SOME, TOO, DON'T YOU?
YEAH. YEAH, I GOT MY OWN ROGUES GALLERY. TONS OF WACKOS. LIKE SILVER MASK AND...SOME OTHER GUYS. A BUNCH FROM CANADA.
YOU WOULDN'T KNOW THEM.
WHAT'S HE LIKE, ANYWAY?
BATMAN? UH, I DON'T KNOW. HE'S ALL RIGHT--
--FOR BATMAN. I DON'T REALLY AGREE WITH HIM A LOT OF THE TIME. NOT LIKE YOU AND FLASH. YOU GUYS HARDLY EVER ARGUE.
I ARGUE ENOUGH WITH MY OWN DAD.
FLASH SAYS BATMAN'S KINDA OFF. AND HE KNOWS IT. THAT'S WHY HE GETS SO MANY LUNATICS RUNNIN' AT HIM.
'CAUSE HE'S A LUNATIC HIMSEL--
HOLY--
--CRAP.

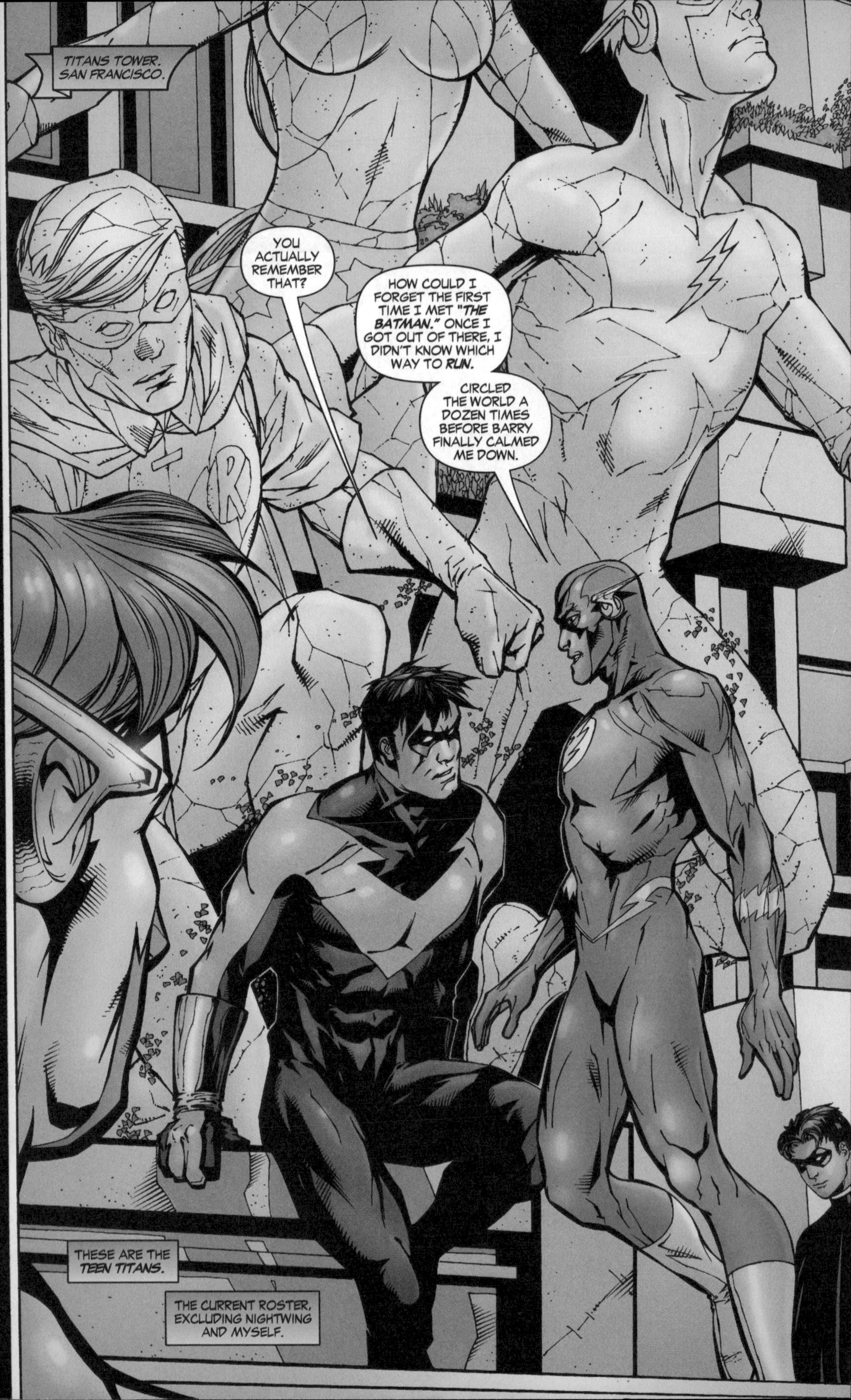
TITANS TOWER. SAN FRANCISCO.
YOU ACTUALLY REMEMBER THAT?
HOW COULD I FORGET THE FIRST TIME I MET "THE BATMAN." ONCE I GOT OUT OF THERE, I DIDN'T KNOW WHICH WAY TO RUN.
CIRCLED THE WORLD A DOZEN TIMES BEFORE BARRY FINALLY CALMED ME DOWN.
THESE ARE THE TEEN TITANS.
THE CURRENT ROSTER, EXCLUDING NIGHTWING AND MYSELF.

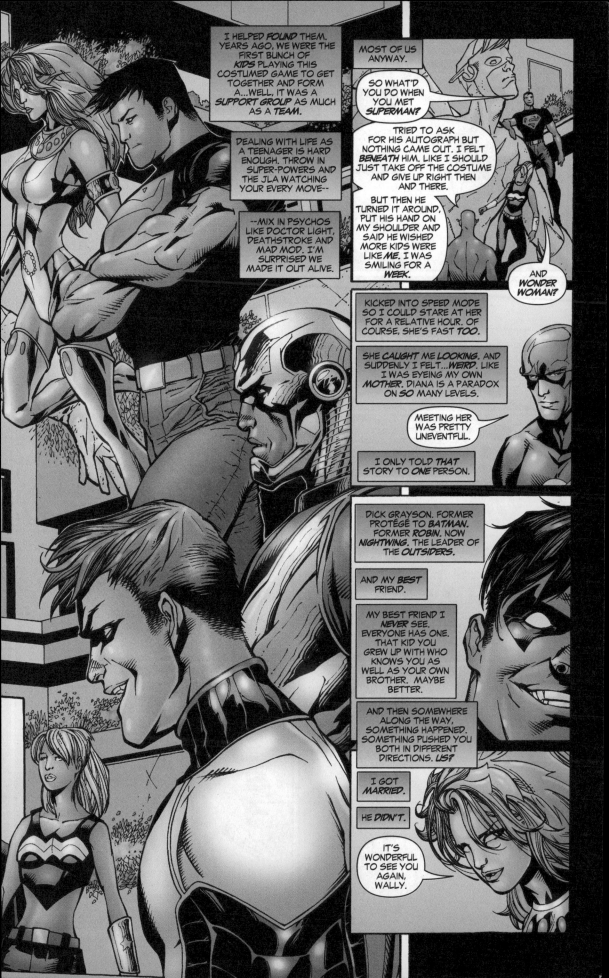

I HELPED *FOUND* THEM. YEARS AGO. WE WERE THE FIRST BUNCH OF *KIDS* PLAYING THIS COSTUMED GAME TO GET TOGETHER AND FORM A...WELL, IT WAS A *SUPPORT GROUP* AS MUCH AS A *TEAM.*

DEALING WITH LIFE AS A TEENAGER IS HARD ENOUGH. THROW IN SUPER-POWERS AND THE JLA WATCHING YOUR EVERY MOVE--

--MIX IN PSYCHOS LIKE DOCTOR LIGHT, DEATHSTROKE AND MAD MOD. I'M SURPRISED WE MADE IT OUT ALIVE.

MOST OF US ANYWAY.

SO WHAT'D YOU DO WHEN YOU MET *SUPERMAN?*

TRIED TO ASK FOR HIS AUTOGRAPH BUT NOTHING CAME OUT. I FELT *BENEATH* HIM. LIKE I SHOULD JUST TAKE OFF THE COSTUME AND GIVE UP RIGHT THEN AND THERE.

BUT THEN HE TURNED IT AROUND, PUT HIS HAND ON MY SHOULDER AND SAID HE WISHED MORE KIDS WERE LIKE *ME.* I WAS SMILING FOR A *WEEK.*

AND *WONDER WOMAN?*

KICKED INTO SPEED MODE SO I COULD STARE AT HER FOR A RELATIVE HOUR. OF COURSE, SHE'S FAST *TOO.*

SHE *CAUGHT ME LOOKING.* AND SUDDENLY I FELT...*WEIRD.* LIKE I WAS EYEING MY OWN *MOTHER.* DIANA IS A PARADOX ON *SO* MANY LEVELS.

MEETING HER WAS PRETTY UNEVENTFUL.

I ONLY TOLD *THAT* STORY TO *ONE* PERSON.

DICK GRAYSON. FORMER PROTÉGÉ TO *BATMAN.* FORMER *ROBIN.* NOW *NIGHTWING.* THE LEADER OF THE *OUTSIDERS.*

AND MY *BEST* FRIEND.

MY BEST FRIEND I *NEVER* SEE. EVERYONE HAS ONE. THAT KID YOU GREW UP WITH WHO KNOWS YOU AS WELL AS YOUR OWN BROTHER. MAYBE BETTER.

AND THEN SOMEWHERE ALONG THE WAY, SOMETHING HAPPENED. SOMETHING PUSHED YOU BOTH IN DIFFERENT DIRECTIONS. *US?*

I GOT *MARRIED.*

HE *DIDN'T.*

IT'S WONDERFUL TO SEE YOU AGAIN, WALLY.

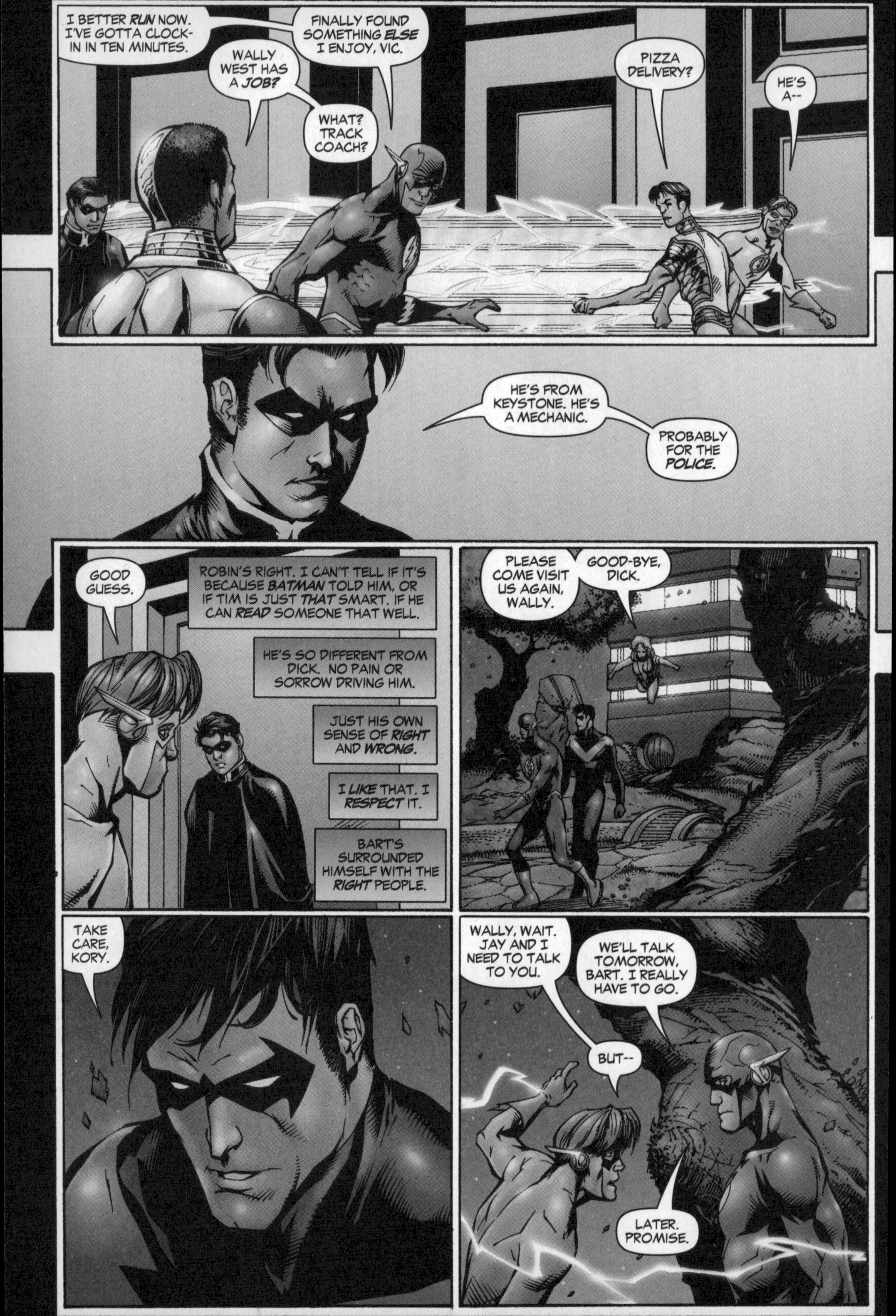
I BETTER RUN NOW. I'VE GOTTA CLOCK-IN IN TEN MINUTES.
WALLY WEST HAS A JOB?
FINALLY FOUND SOMETHING ELSE I ENJOY, VIC.
WHAT? TRACK COACH?
PIZZA DELIVERY?
HE'S A--
HE'S FROM KEYSTONE. HE'S A MECHANIC.
PROBABLY FOR THE POLICE.
GOOD GUESS.
ROBIN'S RIGHT. I CAN'T TELL IF IT'S BECAUSE BATMAN TOLD HIM, OR IF TIM IS JUST THAT SMART. IF HE CAN READ SOMEONE THAT WELL.
HE'S SO DIFFERENT FROM DICK. NO PAIN OR SORROW DRIVING HIM.
JUST HIS OWN SENSE OF RIGHT AND WRONG.
I LIKE THAT. I RESPECT IT.
BART'S SURROUNDED HIMSELF WITH THE RIGHT PEOPLE.
PLEASE COME VISIT US AGAIN, WALLY.
GOOD-BYE, DICK.
TAKE CARE, KORY.
WALLY, WAIT. JAY AND I NEED TO TALK TO YOU.
WE'LL TALK TOMORROW, BART. I REALLY HAVE TO GO.
BUT--
LATER. PROMISE.

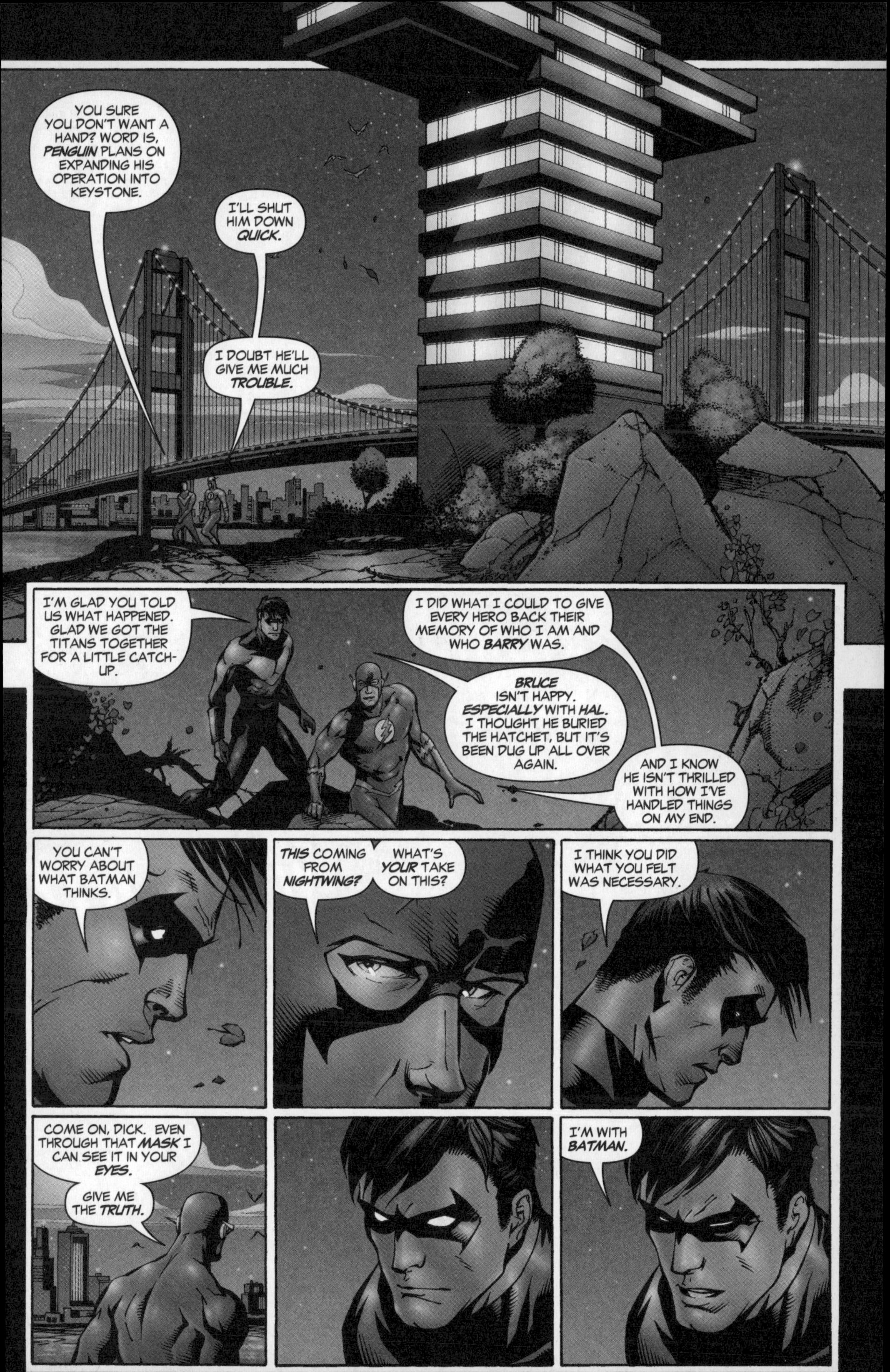

YOU SURE YOU DON'T WANT A HAND? WORD IS, PENGUIN PLANS ON EXPANDING HIS OPERATION INTO KEYSTONE.
I'LL SHUT HIM DOWN QUICK.
I DOUBT HE'LL GIVE ME MUCH TROUBLE.
I'M GLAD YOU TOLD US WHAT HAPPENED. GLAD WE GOT THE TITANS TOGETHER FOR A LITTLE CATCH-UP.
I DID WHAT I COULD TO GIVE EVERY HERO BACK THEIR MEMORY OF WHO I AM AND WHO BARRY WAS.
BRUCE ISN'T HAPPY. ESPECIALLY WITH HAL. I THOUGHT HE BURIED THE HATCHET, BUT IT'S BEEN DUG UP ALL OVER AGAIN.
AND I KNOW HE ISN'T THRILLED WITH HOW I'VE HANDLED THINGS ON MY END.
YOU CAN'T WORRY ABOUT WHAT BATMAN THINKS.
THIS COMING FROM NIGHTWING?
WHAT'S YOUR TAKE ON THIS?
I THINK YOU DID WHAT YOU FELT WAS NECESSARY.
COME ON, DICK. EVEN THROUGH THAT MASK I CAN SEE IT IN YOUR EYES.
GIVE ME THE TRUTH.
I'M WITH BATMAN.

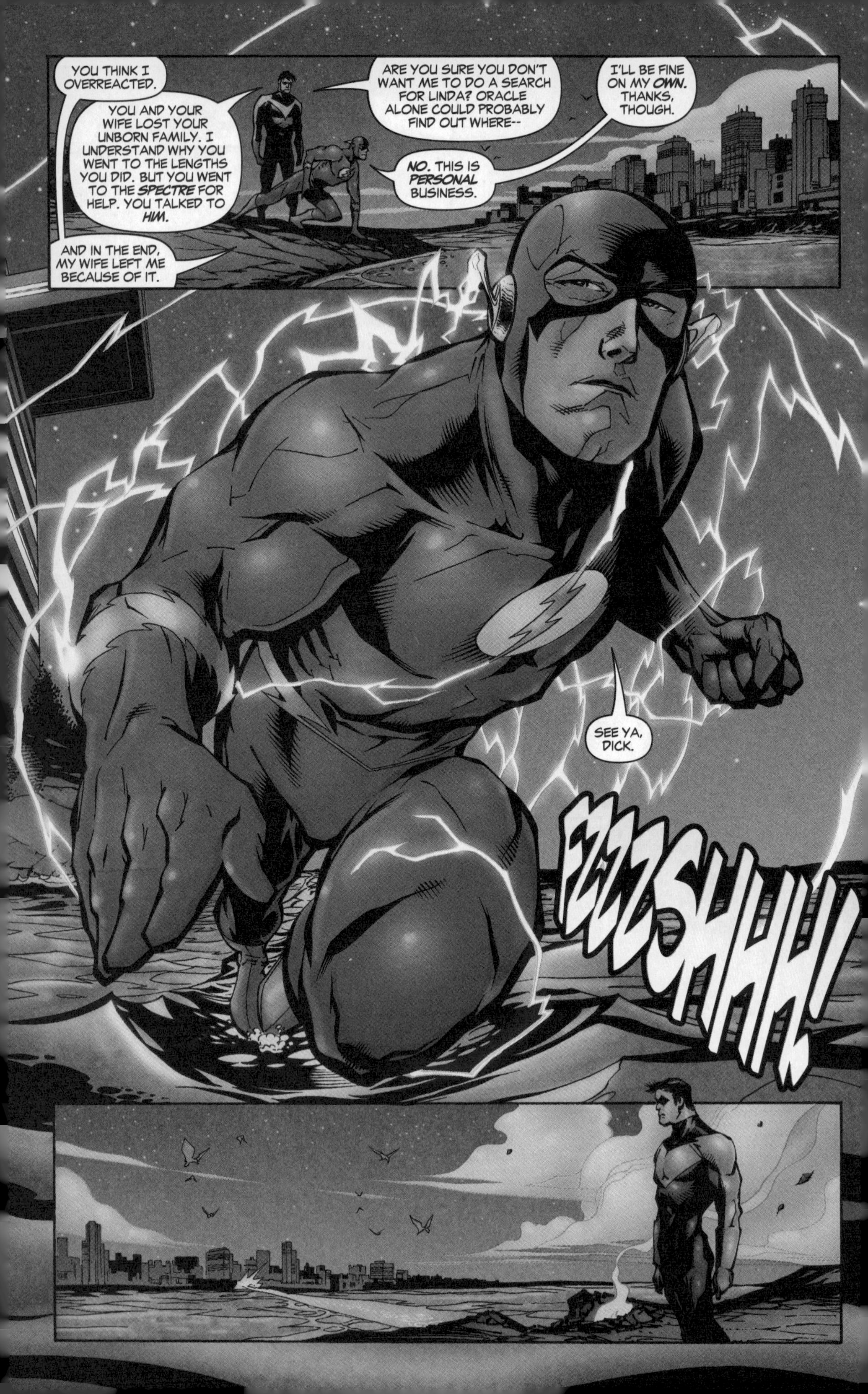
YOU THINK I OVERREACTED.
YOU AND YOUR WIFE LOST YOUR UNBORN FAMILY. I UNDERSTAND WHY YOU WENT TO THE LENGTHS YOU DID. BUT YOU WENT TO THE *SPECTRE* FOR HELP. YOU TALKED TO *HIM*.
AND IN THE END, MY WIFE LEFT ME BECAUSE OF IT.
ARE YOU SURE YOU DON'T WANT ME TO DO A SEARCH FOR LINDA? ORACLE ALONE COULD PROBABLY FIND OUT WHERE--
NO. THIS IS *PERSONAL* BUSINESS.
I'LL BE FINE ON MY *OWN*. THANKS, THOUGH.
SEE YA, DICK.
FZZZSHHH!

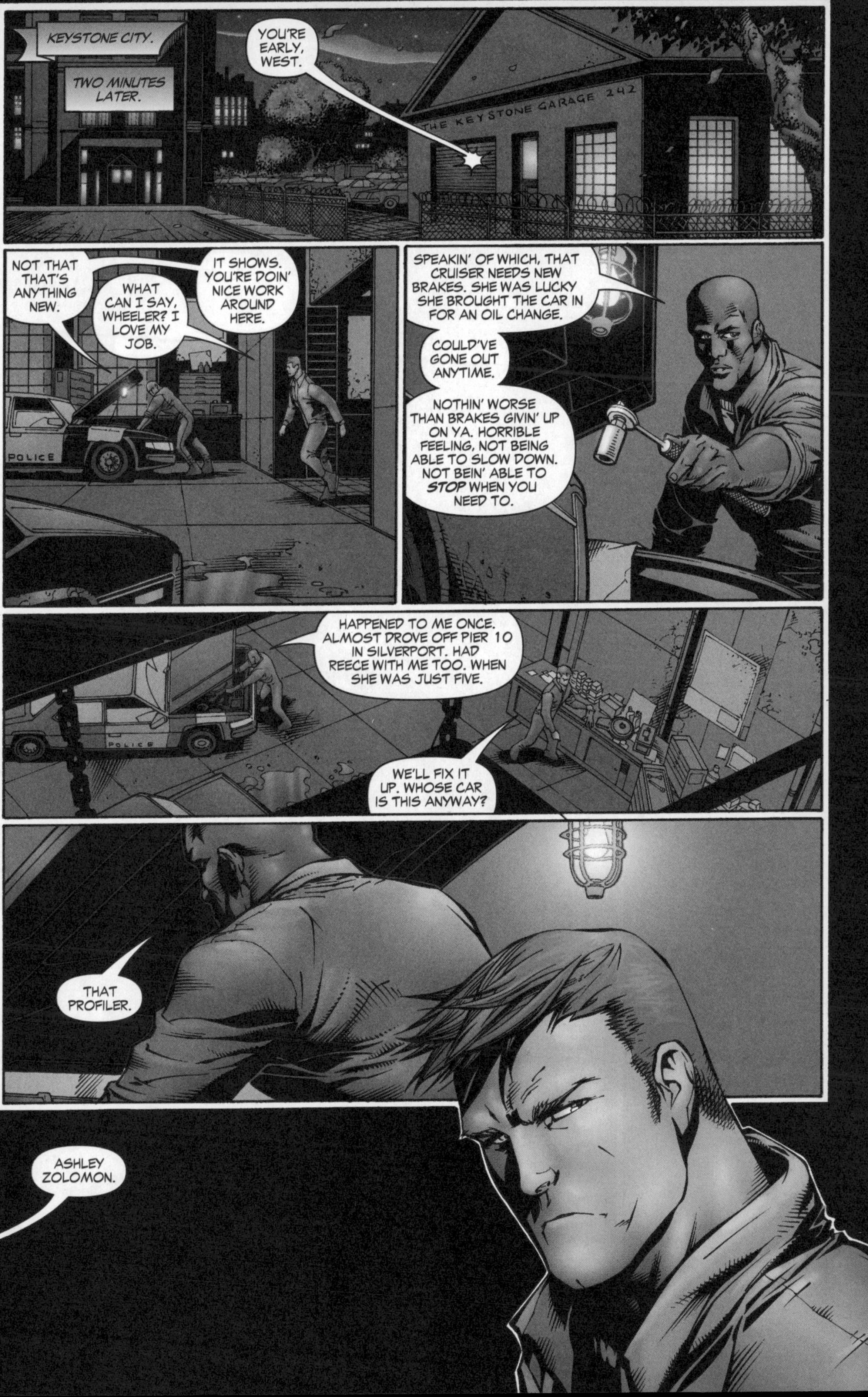
KEYSTONE CITY.
TWO MINUTES LATER.
THE KEYSTONE GARAGE 242
YOU'RE EARLY, WEST.
NOT THAT THAT'S ANYTHING NEW.
IT SHOWS. YOU'RE DOIN' NICE WORK AROUND HERE.
WHAT CAN I SAY, WHEELER? I LOVE MY JOB.
POLICE
SPEAKIN' OF WHICH, THAT CRUISER NEEDS NEW BRAKES. SHE WAS LUCKY SHE BROUGHT THE CAR IN FOR AN OIL CHANGE.
COULD'VE GONE OUT ANYTIME.
NOTHIN' WORSE THAN BRAKES GIVIN' UP ON YA. HORRIBLE FEELING, NOT BEING ABLE TO SLOW DOWN. NOT BEIN' ABLE TO STOP WHEN YOU NEED TO.
HAPPENED TO ME ONCE. ALMOST DROVE OFF PIER 10 IN SILVERPORT. HAD REECE WITH ME TOO. WHEN SHE WAS JUST FIVE.
POLICE
WE'LL FIX IT UP. WHOSE CAR IS THIS ANYWAY?
THAT PROFILER.
ASHLEY ZOLOMON.

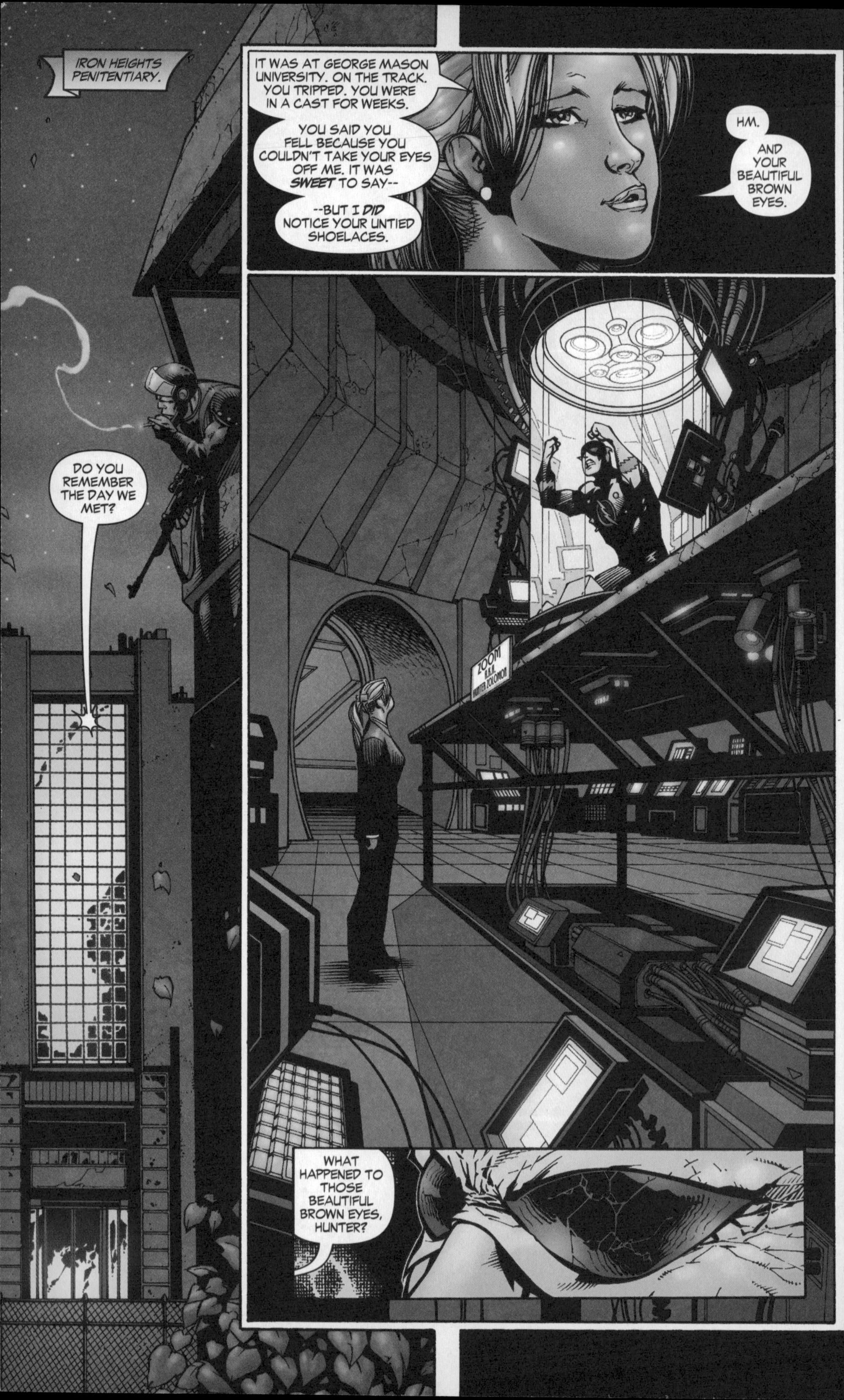
IRON HEIGHTS PENITENTIARY.
DO YOU REMEMBER THE DAY WE MET?
IT WAS AT GEORGE MASON UNIVERSITY. ON THE TRACK. YOU TRIPPED. YOU WERE IN A CAST FOR WEEKS.
YOU SAID YOU FELL BECAUSE YOU COULDN'T TAKE YOUR EYES OFF ME. IT WAS SWEET TO SAY--
--BUT I DID NOTICE YOUR UNTIED SHOELACES.
HM.
AND YOUR BEAUTIFUL BROWN EYES.
ZOOM A.K.A. HUNTER ZOLOMON
WHAT HAPPENED TO THOSE BEAUTIFUL BROWN EYES, HUNTER?

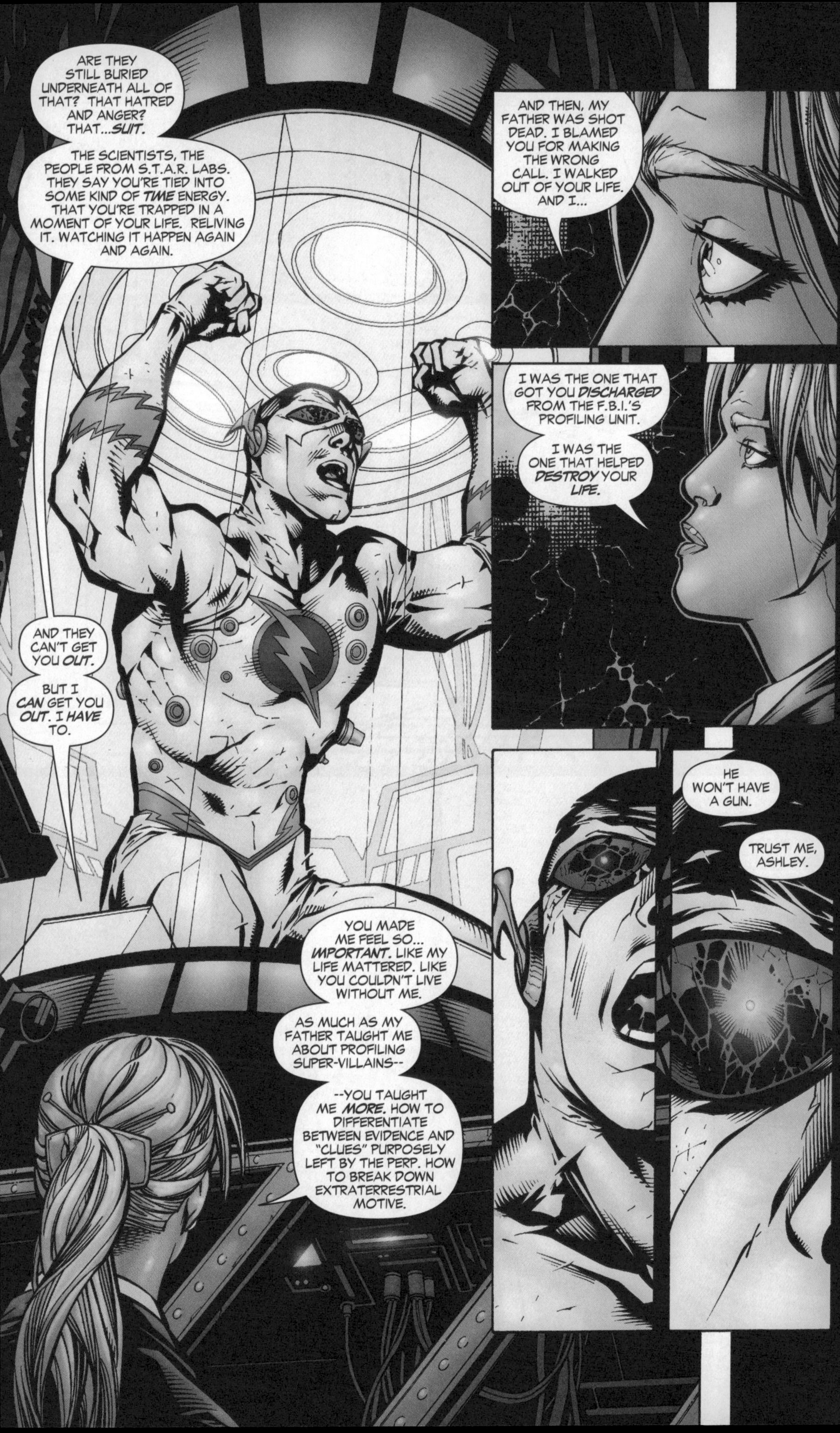
ARE THEY STILL BURIED UNDERNEATH ALL OF THAT? THAT HATRED AND ANGER? THAT...*SUIT*.
THE SCIENTISTS, THE PEOPLE FROM S.T.A.R. LABS. THEY SAY YOU'RE TIED INTO SOME KIND OF *TIME* ENERGY. THAT YOU'RE TRAPPED IN A MOMENT OF YOUR LIFE. RELIVING IT. WATCHING IT HAPPEN AGAIN AND AGAIN.
AND THEY CAN'T GET YOU *OUT*.
BUT I *CAN* GET YOU *OUT*. I *HAVE* TO.
AND THEN, MY FATHER WAS SHOT DEAD. I BLAMED YOU FOR MAKING THE WRONG CALL. I WALKED OUT OF YOUR LIFE. AND I...
I WAS THE ONE THAT GOT YOU *DISCHARGED* FROM THE F.B.I.'S PROFILING UNIT.
I WAS THE ONE THAT HELPED *DESTROY* YOUR *LIFE*.
YOU MADE ME FEEL SO... *IMPORTANT*. LIKE MY LIFE MATTERED. LIKE YOU COULDN'T LIVE WITHOUT ME.
AS MUCH AS MY FATHER TAUGHT ME ABOUT PROFILING SUPER-VILLAINS--
--YOU TAUGHT ME *MORE*. HOW TO DIFFERENTIATE BETWEEN EVIDENCE AND "CLUES" PURPOSELY LEFT BY THE PERP. HOW TO BREAK DOWN EXTRATERRESTRIAL MOTIVE.
HE WON'T HAVE A GUN.
TRUST ME, ASHLEY.

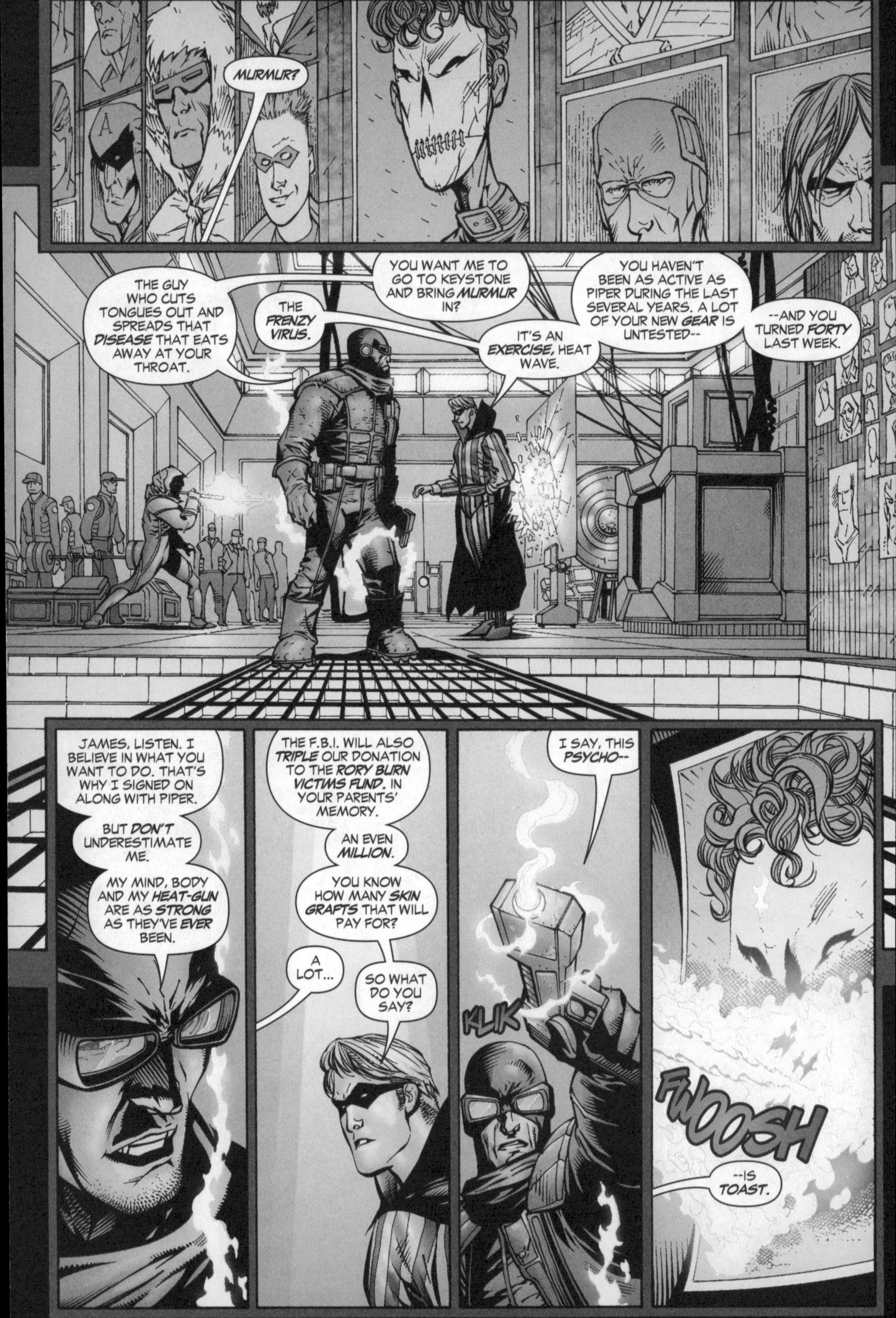
MURMUR?
THE GUY WHO CUTS TONGUES OUT AND SPREADS THAT DISEASE THAT EATS AWAY AT YOUR THROAT.
THE FRENZY VIRUS.
YOU WANT ME TO GO TO KEYSTONE AND BRING MURMUR IN?
IT'S AN EXERCISE, HEAT WAVE.
YOU HAVEN'T BEEN AS ACTIVE AS PIPER DURING THE LAST SEVERAL YEARS. A LOT OF YOUR NEW GEAR IS UNTESTED--
--AND YOU TURNED FORTY LAST WEEK.
JAMES, LISTEN. I BELIEVE IN WHAT YOU WANT TO DO. THAT'S WHY I SIGNED ON ALONG WITH PIPER.
BUT DON'T UNDERESTIMATE ME.
MY MIND, BODY AND MY HEAT-GUN ARE AS STRONG AS THEY'VE EVER BEEN.
THE F.B.I. WILL ALSO TRIPLE OUR DONATION TO THE RORY BURN VICTIMS FUND. IN YOUR PARENTS' MEMORY.
AN EVEN MILLION.
YOU KNOW HOW MANY SKIN GRAFTS THAT WILL PAY FOR?
A LOT...
SO WHAT DO YOU SAY?
I SAY, THIS PSYCHO--
KLIK
FWOOSH
--IS TOAST.

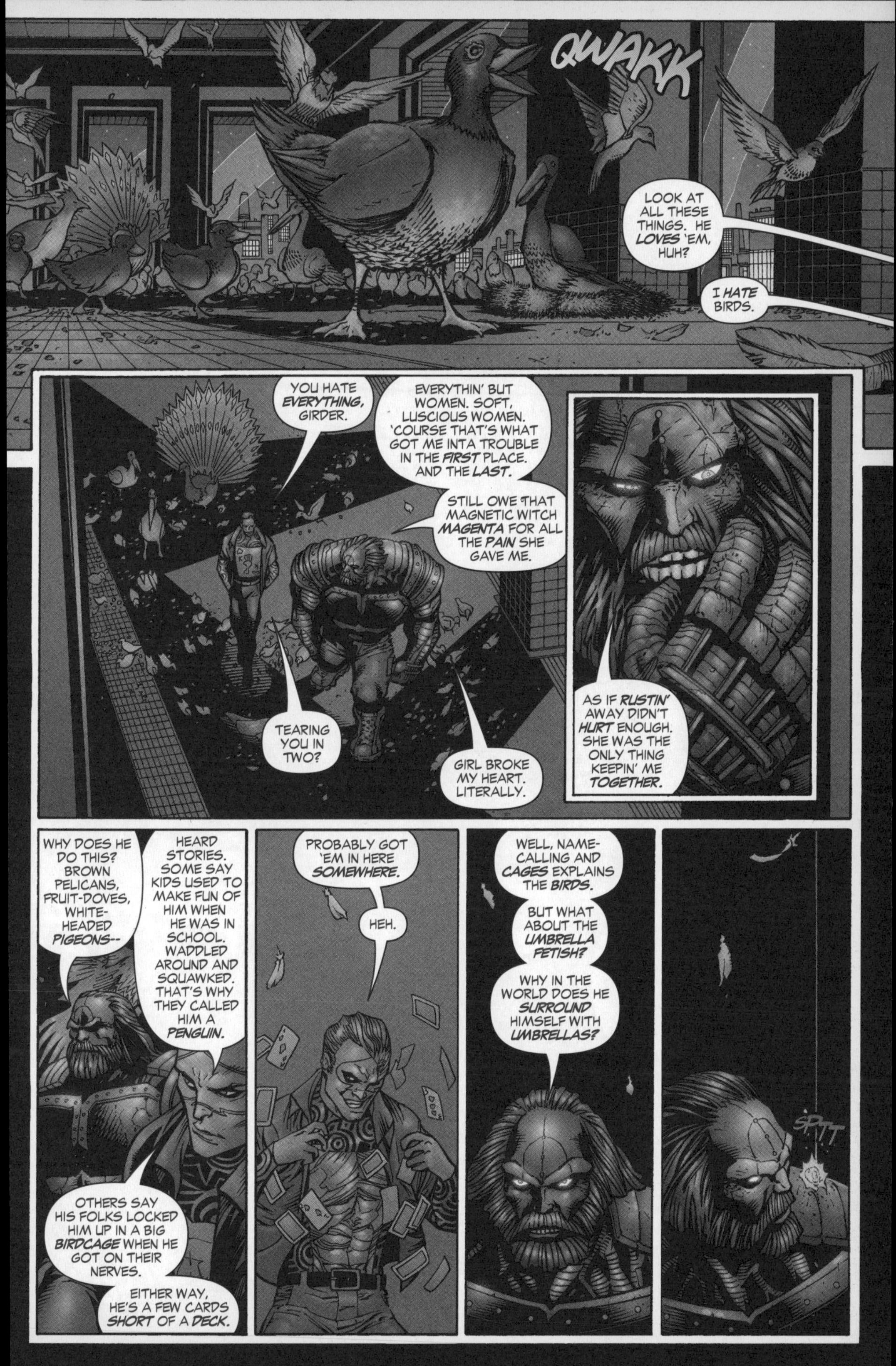
QWAKK
LOOK AT ALL THESE THINGS. HE LOVES 'EM, HUH?
I HATE BIRDS.
YOU HATE EVERYTHING, GIRDER.
EVERYTHIN' BUT WOMEN. SOFT, LUSCIOUS WOMEN. 'COURSE THAT'S WHAT GOT ME INTA TROUBLE IN THE FIRST PLACE. AND THE LAST.
STILL OWE THAT MAGNETIC WITCH MAGENTA FOR ALL THE PAIN SHE GAVE ME.
TEARING YOU IN TWO?
GIRL BROKE MY HEART. LITERALLY.
AS IF RUSTIN' AWAY DIDN'T HURT ENOUGH. SHE WAS THE ONLY THING KEEPIN' ME TOGETHER.
WHY DOES HE DO THIS? BROWN PELICANS, FRUIT-DOVES, WHITE-HEADED PIGEONS--
HEARD STORIES. SOME SAY KIDS USED TO MAKE FUN OF HIM WHEN HE WAS IN SCHOOL. WADDLED AROUND AND SQUAWKED. THAT'S WHY THEY CALLED HIM A PENGUIN.
OTHERS SAY HIS FOLKS LOCKED HIM UP IN A BIG BIRDCAGE WHEN HE GOT ON THEIR NERVES.
EITHER WAY, HE'S A FEW CARDS SHORT OF A DECK.
PROBABLY GOT 'EM IN HERE SOMEWHERE.
HEH.
WELL, NAME-CALLING AND CAGES EXPLAINS THE BIRDS.
BUT WHAT ABOUT THE UMBRELLA FETISH?
WHY IN THE WORLD DOES HE SURROUND HIMSELF WITH UMBRELLAS?
SPTT

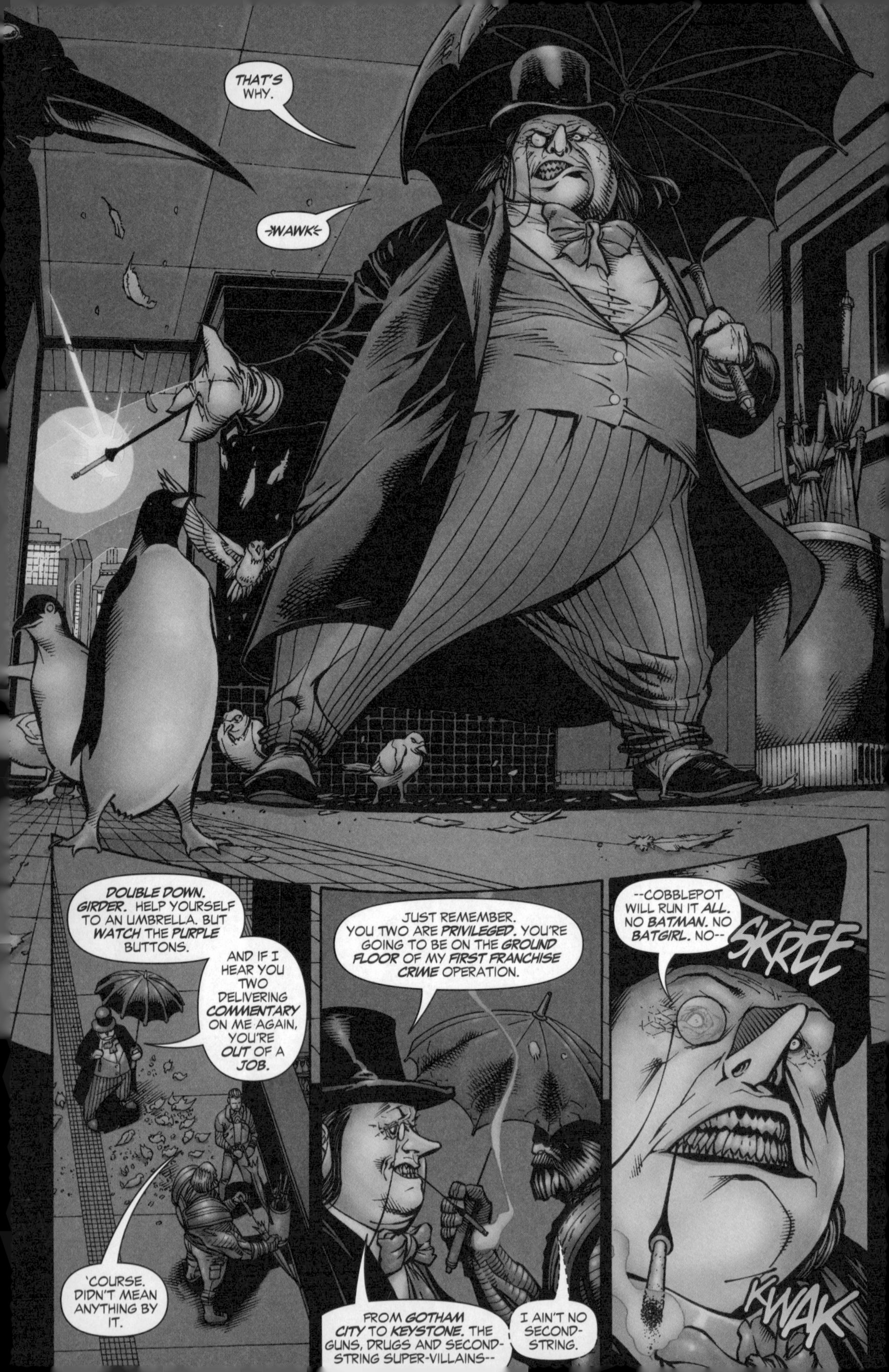
THAT'S WHY.
WAWK
DOUBLE DOWN. GIRDER. HELP YOURSELF TO AN UMBRELLA. BUT WATCH THE PURPLE BUTTONS.
AND IF I HEAR YOU TWO DELIVERING COMMENTARY ON ME AGAIN, YOU'RE OUT OF A JOB.
'COURSE. DIDN'T MEAN ANYTHING BY IT.
JUST REMEMBER. YOU TWO ARE PRIVILEGED. YOU'RE GOING TO BE ON THE GROUND FLOOR OF MY FIRST FRANCHISE CRIME OPERATION.
FROM GOTHAM CITY TO KEYSTONE. THE GUNS, DRUGS AND SECOND-STRING SUPER-VILLAINS--
I AIN'T NO SECOND-STRING.
--COBBLEPOT WILL RUN IT ALL. NO BATMAN. NO BATGIRL. NO--
SKREE
KWAK

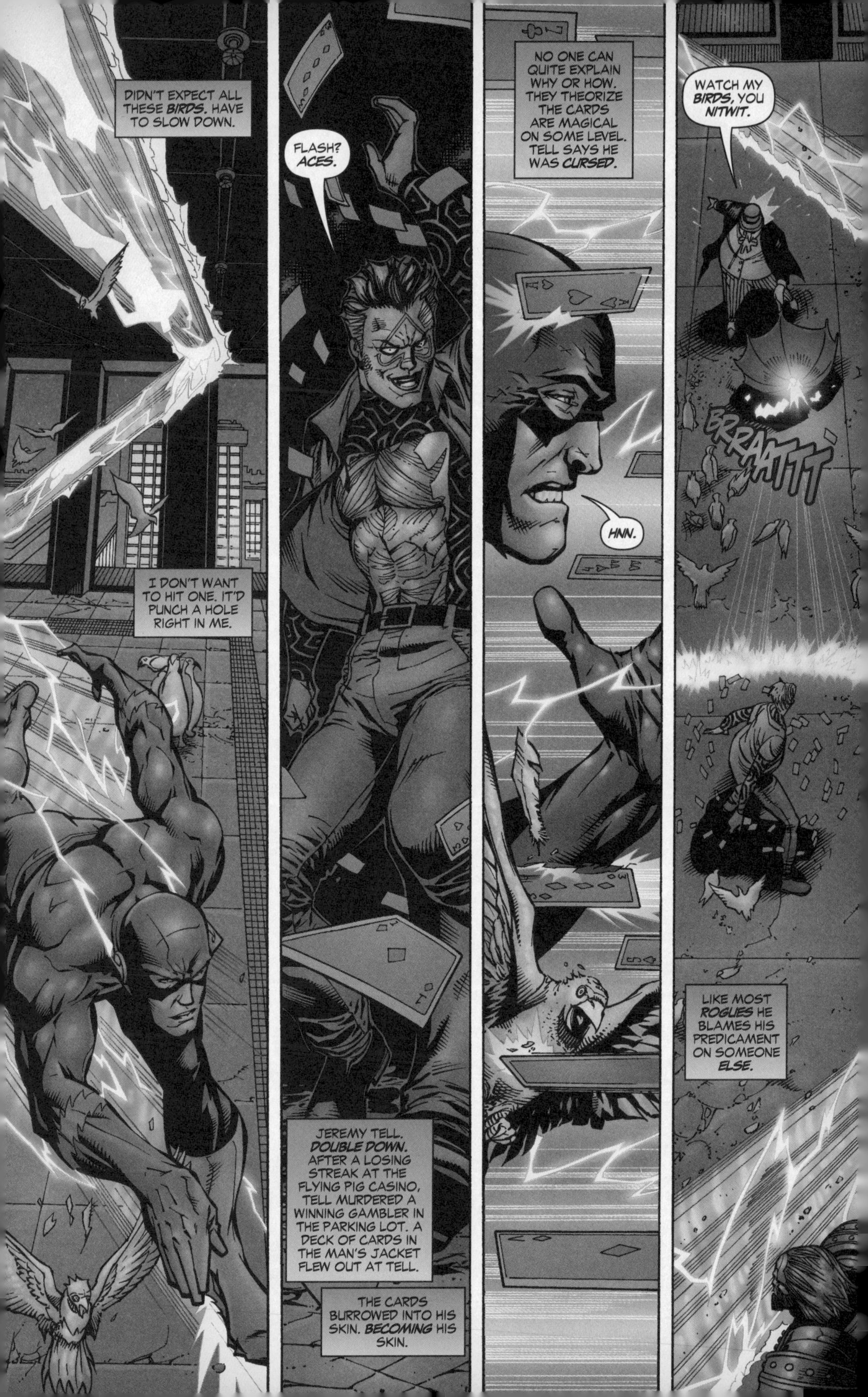
DIDN'T EXPECT ALL THESE *BIRDS*. HAVE TO SLOW DOWN.
I DON'T WANT TO HIT ONE. IT'D PUNCH A HOLE RIGHT IN ME.
FLASH? *ACES*.
JEREMY TELL. *DOUBLE DOWN.* AFTER A LOSING STREAK AT THE FLYING PIG CASINO, TELL MURDERED A WINNING GAMBLER IN THE PARKING LOT. A DECK OF CARDS IN THE MAN'S JACKET FLEW OUT AT TELL.
THE CARDS BURROWED INTO HIS SKIN. *BECOMING* HIS SKIN.
NO ONE CAN QUITE EXPLAIN WHY OR HOW. THEY THEORIZE THE CARDS ARE MAGICAL ON SOME LEVEL. TELL SAYS HE WAS *CURSED*.
HNN.
WATCH MY *BIRDS*, YOU *NITWIT*.
BRRAATTT
LIKE MOST *ROGUES* HE BLAMES HIS PREDICAMENT ON SOMEONE *ELSE*.

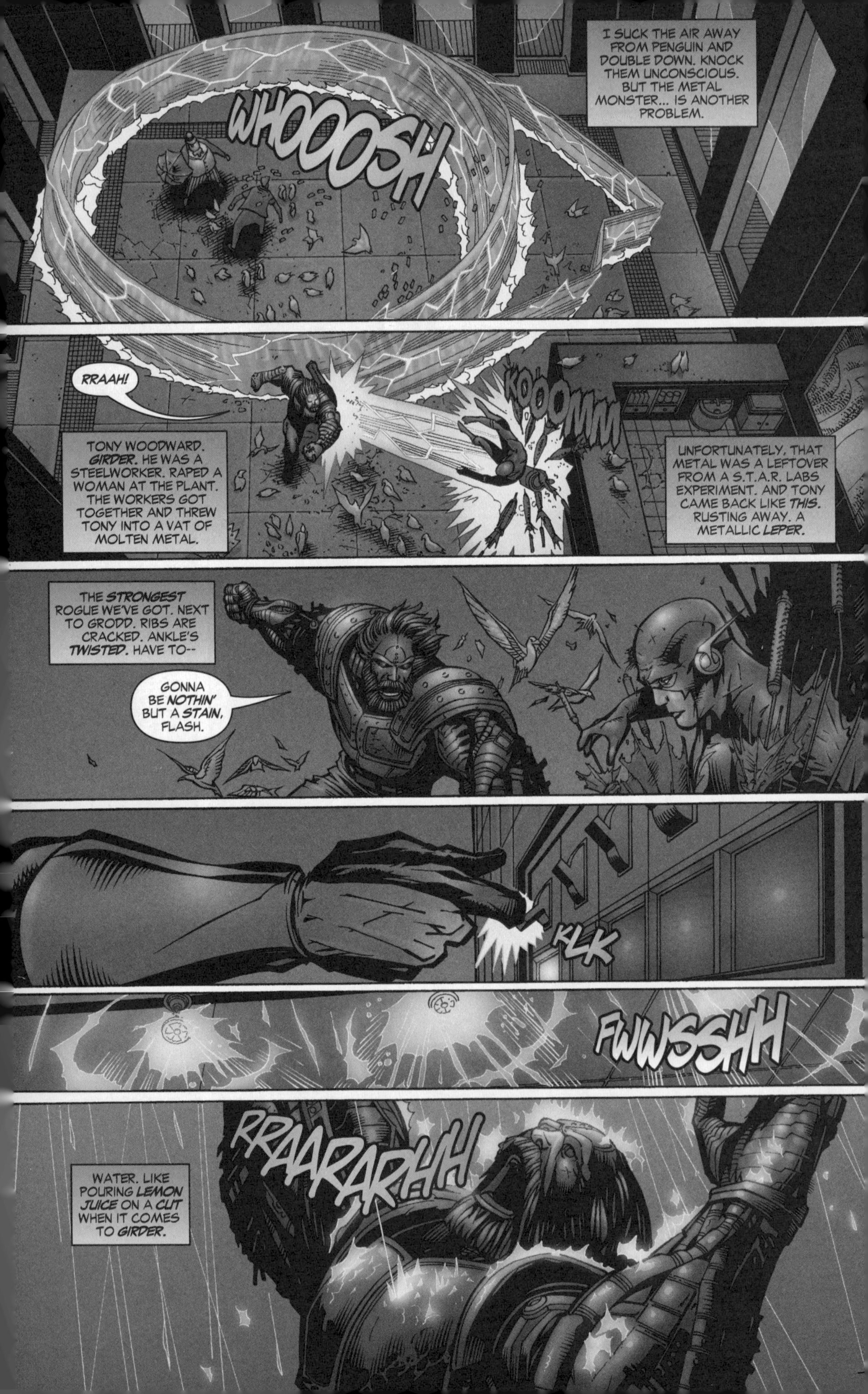
I SUCK THE AIR AWAY FROM PENGUIN AND DOUBLE DOWN. KNOCK THEM UNCONSCIOUS. BUT THE METAL MONSTER... IS ANOTHER PROBLEM.
WHOOOOSH
RRAAH!
TONY WOODWARD. GIRDER. HE WAS A STEELWORKER. RAPED A WOMAN AT THE PLANT. THE WORKERS GOT TOGETHER AND THREW TONY INTO A VAT OF MOLTEN METAL.
KOOOMM
UNFORTUNATELY, THAT METAL WAS A LEFTOVER FROM A S.T.A.R. LABS EXPERIMENT. AND TONY CAME BACK LIKE THIS. RUSTING AWAY. A METALLIC LEPER.
THE STRONGEST ROGUE WE'VE GOT. NEXT TO GRODD. RIBS ARE CRACKED. ANKLE'S TWISTED. HAVE TO--
GONNA BE NOTHIN' BUT A STAIN, FLASH.
KLK
FWWSSHH
RRAARARHH
WATER. LIKE POURING LEMON JUICE ON A CUT WHEN IT COMES TO GIRDER.

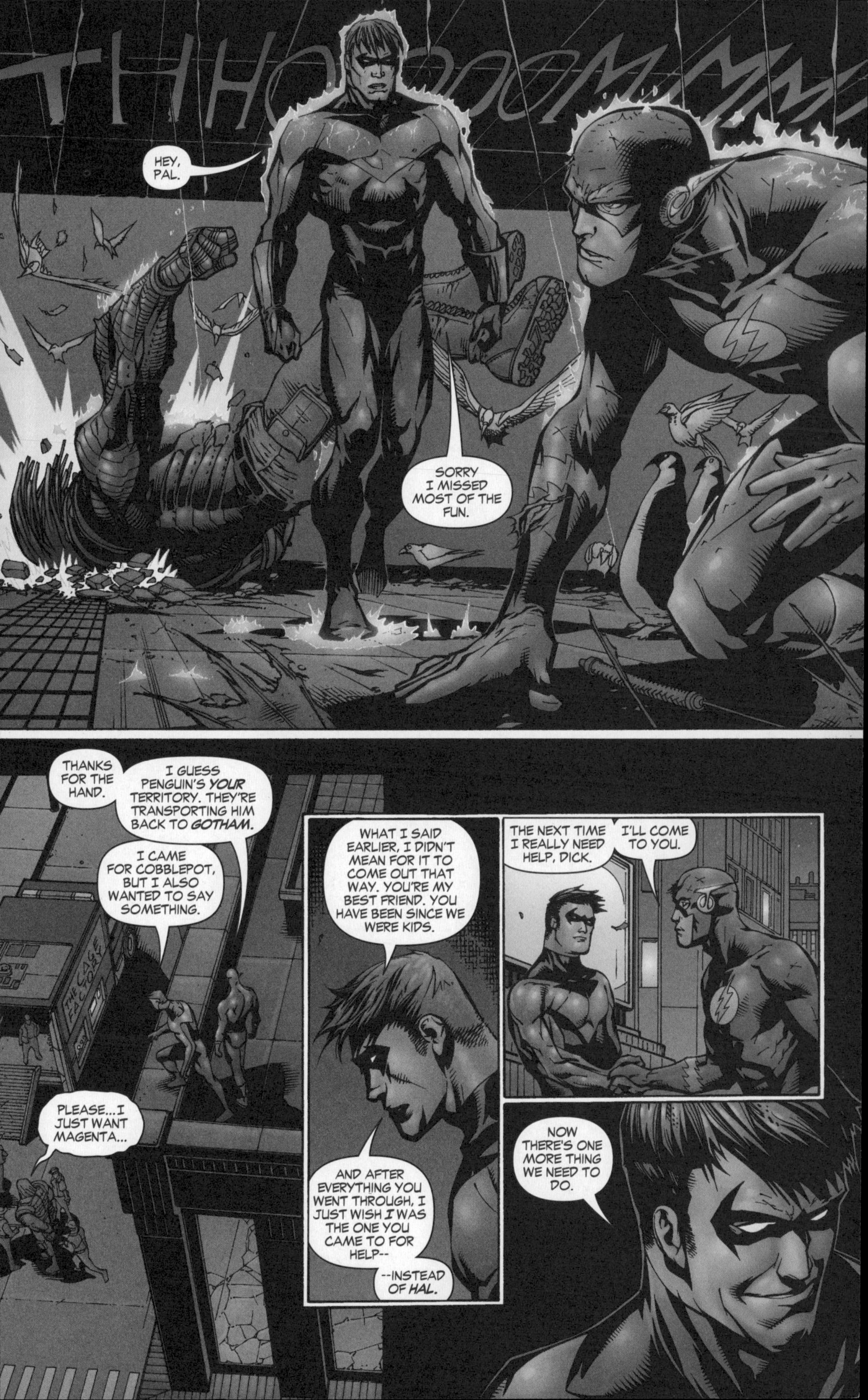
THHOOOOMMM
HEY, PAL.
SORRY I MISSED MOST OF THE FUN.
THANKS FOR THE HAND.
I GUESS PENGUIN'S *YOUR* TERRITORY. THEY'RE TRANSPORTING HIM BACK TO *GOTHAM*.
I CAME FOR COBBLEPOT, BUT I ALSO WANTED TO SAY SOMETHING.
THE CAGE FACTORY
PLEASE...I JUST WANT MAGENTA...
WHAT I SAID EARLIER, I DIDN'T MEAN FOR IT TO COME OUT THAT WAY. YOU'RE MY BEST FRIEND. YOU HAVE BEEN SINCE WE WERE KIDS.
AND AFTER EVERYTHING YOU WENT THROUGH, I JUST WISH *I* WAS THE ONE YOU CAME TO FOR HELP--
--INSTEAD OF *HAL*.
THE NEXT TIME I REALLY NEED HELP, DICK.
I'LL COME TO YOU.
NOW THERE'S ONE MORE THING WE NEED TO DO.

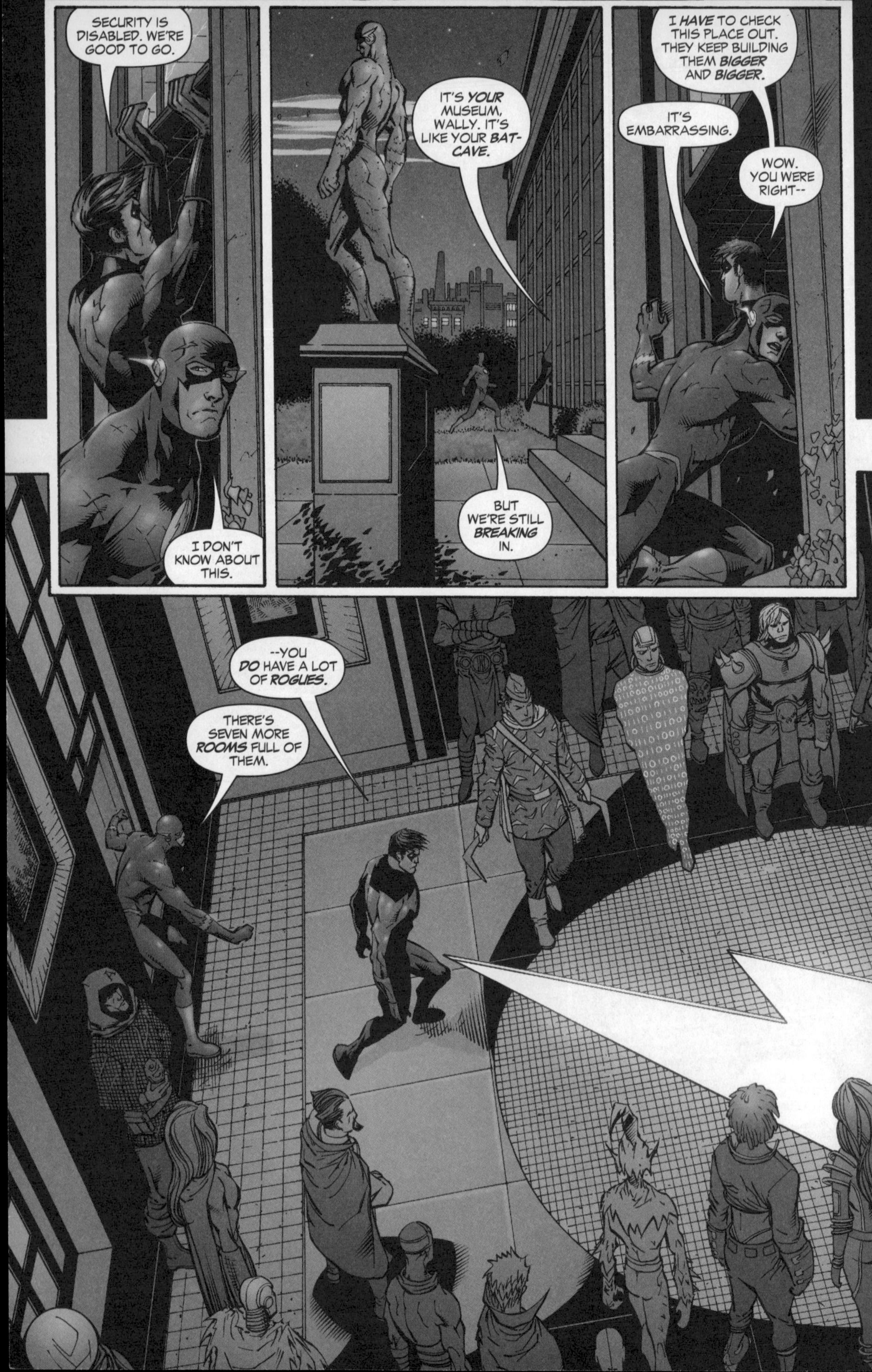
SECURITY IS DISABLED. WE'RE GOOD TO GO.
I DON'T KNOW ABOUT THIS.
IT'S YOUR MUSEUM, WALLY. IT'S LIKE YOUR BAT-CAVE.
BUT WE'RE STILL BREAKING IN.
I HAVE TO CHECK THIS PLACE OUT. THEY KEEP BUILDING THEM BIGGER AND BIGGER.
IT'S EMBARRASSING.
WOW. YOU WERE RIGHT--
--YOU DO HAVE A LOT OF ROGUES.
THERE'S SEVEN MORE ROOMS FULL OF THEM.

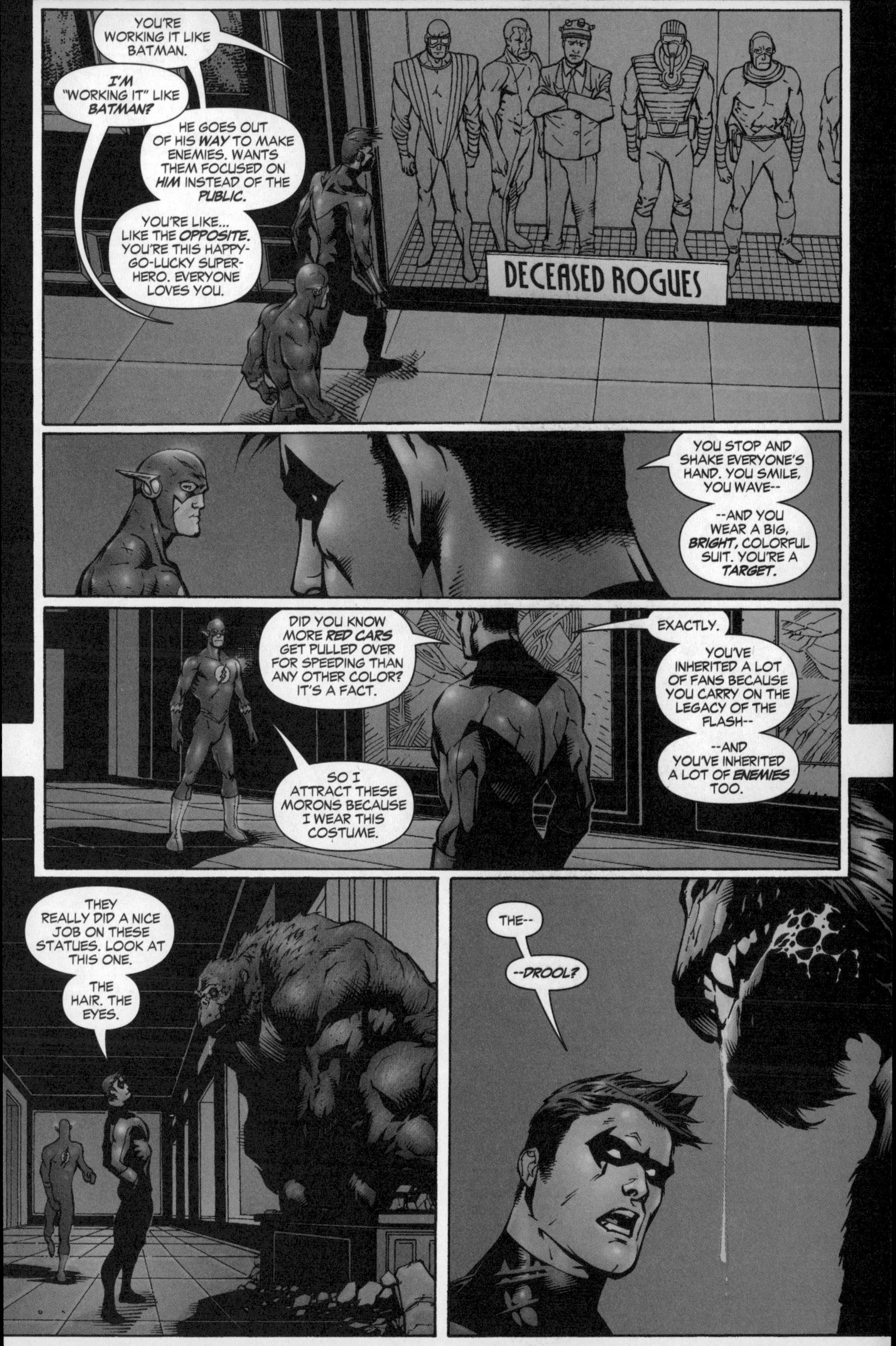
YOU'RE WORKING IT LIKE BATMAN.
I'M "WORKING IT" LIKE BATMAN?
HE GOES OUT OF HIS WAY TO MAKE ENEMIES. WANTS THEM FOCUSED ON HIM INSTEAD OF THE PUBLIC.
YOU'RE LIKE... LIKE THE OPPOSITE. YOU'RE THIS HAPPY-GO-LUCKY SUPER-HERO. EVERYONE LOVES YOU.
DECEASED ROGUES
YOU STOP AND SHAKE EVERYONE'S HAND. YOU SMILE, YOU WAVE--
--AND YOU WEAR A BIG, BRIGHT, COLORFUL SUIT. YOU'RE A TARGET.
DID YOU KNOW MORE RED CARS GET PULLED OVER FOR SPEEDING THAN ANY OTHER COLOR? IT'S A FACT.
SO I ATTRACT THESE MORONS BECAUSE I WEAR THIS COSTUME.
EXACTLY.
YOU'VE INHERITED A LOT OF FANS BECAUSE YOU CARRY ON THE LEGACY OF THE FLASH--
--AND YOU'VE INHERITED A LOT OF ENEMIES TOO.
THEY REALLY DID A NICE JOB ON THESE STATUES. LOOK AT THIS ONE.
THE HAIR. THE EYES.
THE--
--DROOL?

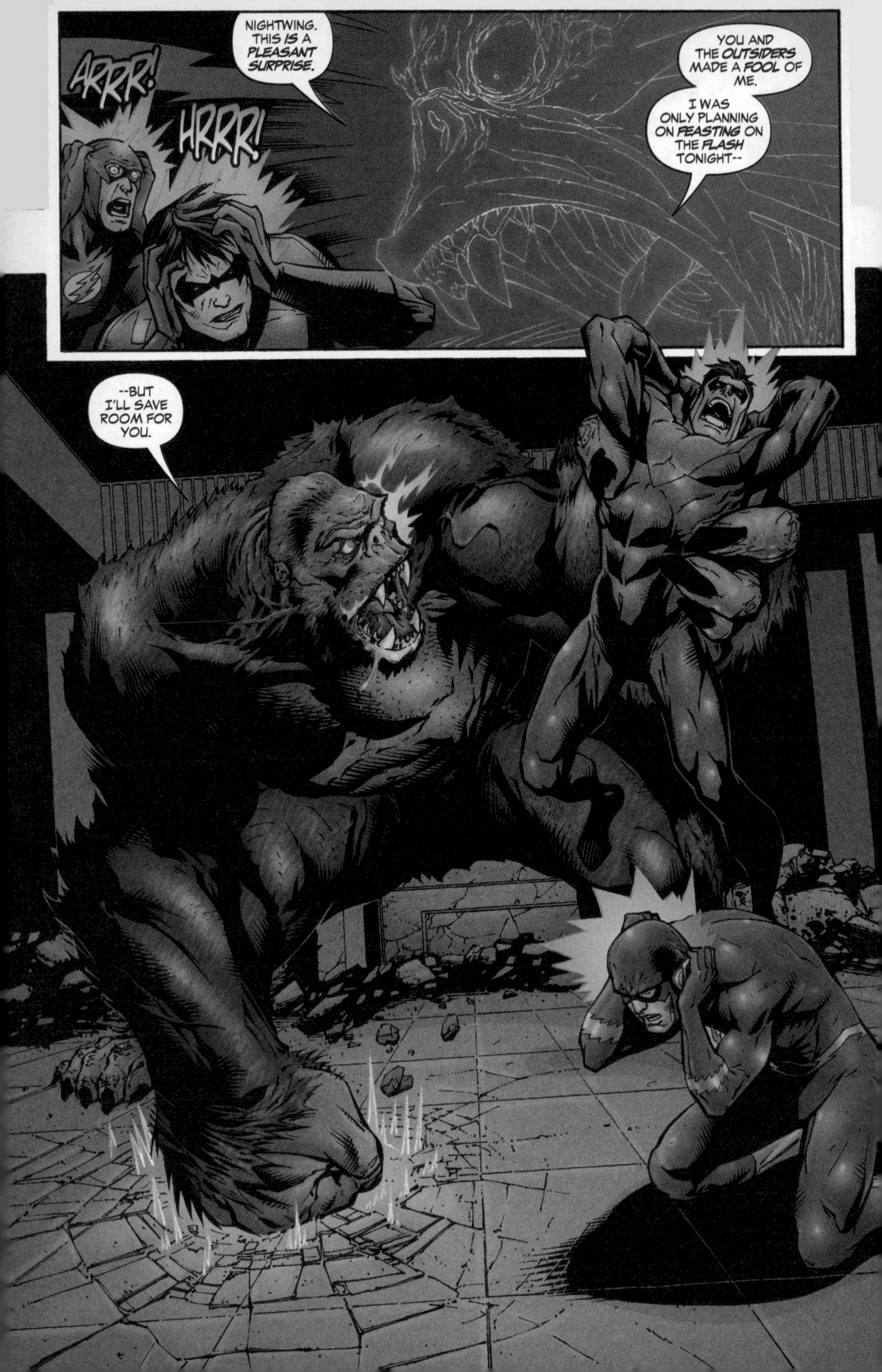

NIGHTWING. THIS IS A PLEASANT SURPRISE.
ARRR!
HRRR!
YOU AND THE OUTSIDERS MADE A FOOL OF ME.
I WAS ONLY PLANNING ON FEASTING ON THE FLASH TONIGHT--
--BUT I'LL SAVE ROOM FOR YOU.

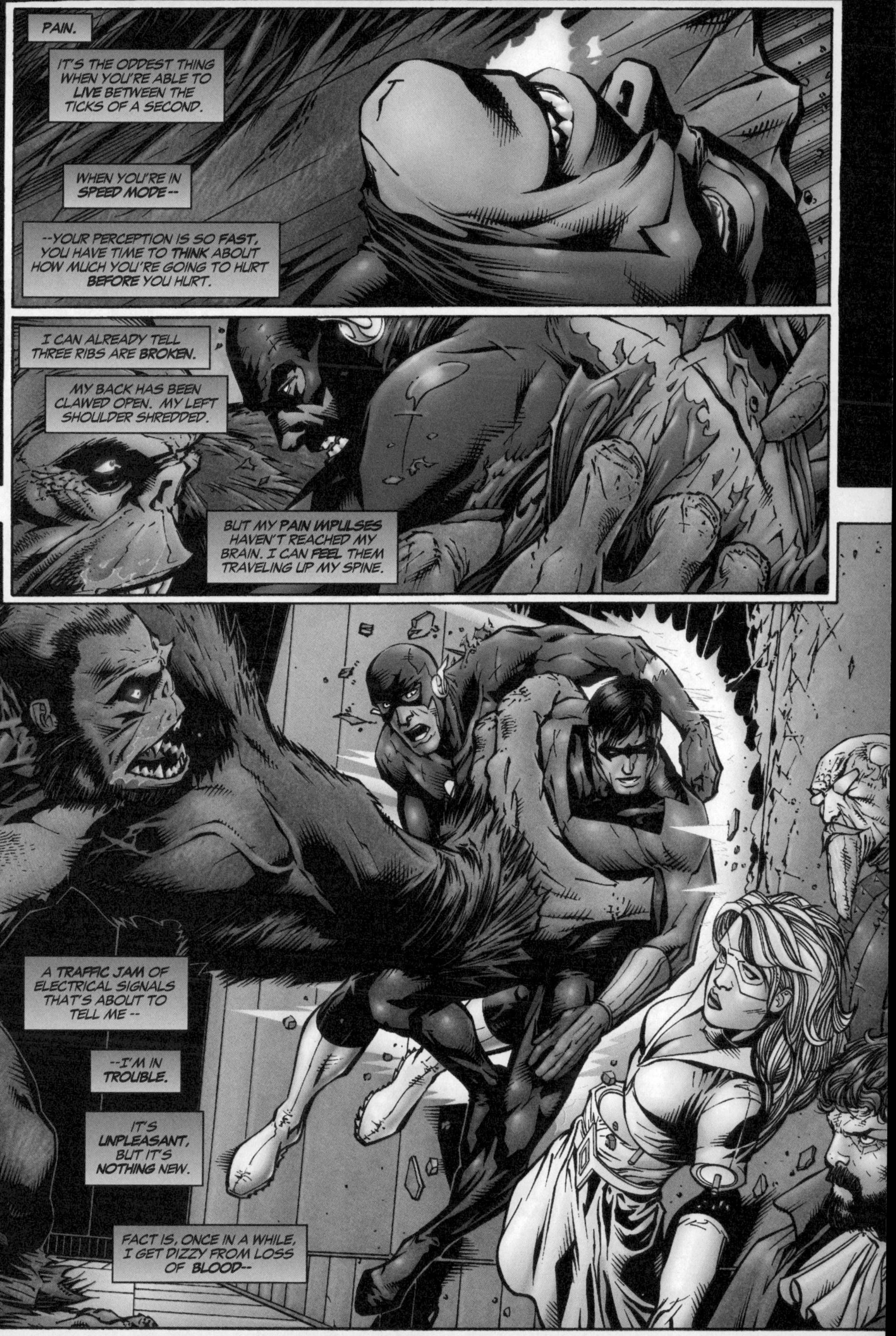
PAIN.
IT'S THE ODDEST THING WHEN YOU'RE ABLE TO LIVE BETWEEN THE TICKS OF A SECOND.
WHEN YOU'RE IN SPEED MODE--
--YOUR PERCEPTION IS SO FAST, YOU HAVE TIME TO THINK ABOUT HOW MUCH YOU'RE GOING TO HURT BEFORE YOU HURT.
I CAN ALREADY TELL THREE RIBS ARE BROKEN.
MY BACK HAS BEEN CLAWED OPEN. MY LEFT SHOULDER SHREDDED.
BUT MY PAIN IMPULSES HAVEN'T REACHED MY BRAIN. I CAN FEEL THEM TRAVELING UP MY SPINE.
A TRAFFIC JAM OF ELECTRICAL SIGNALS THAT'S ABOUT TO TELL ME --
--I'M IN TROUBLE.
IT'S UNPLEASANT, BUT IT'S NOTHING NEW.
FACT IS, ONCE IN A WHILE, I GET DIZZY FROM LOSS OF BLOOD--

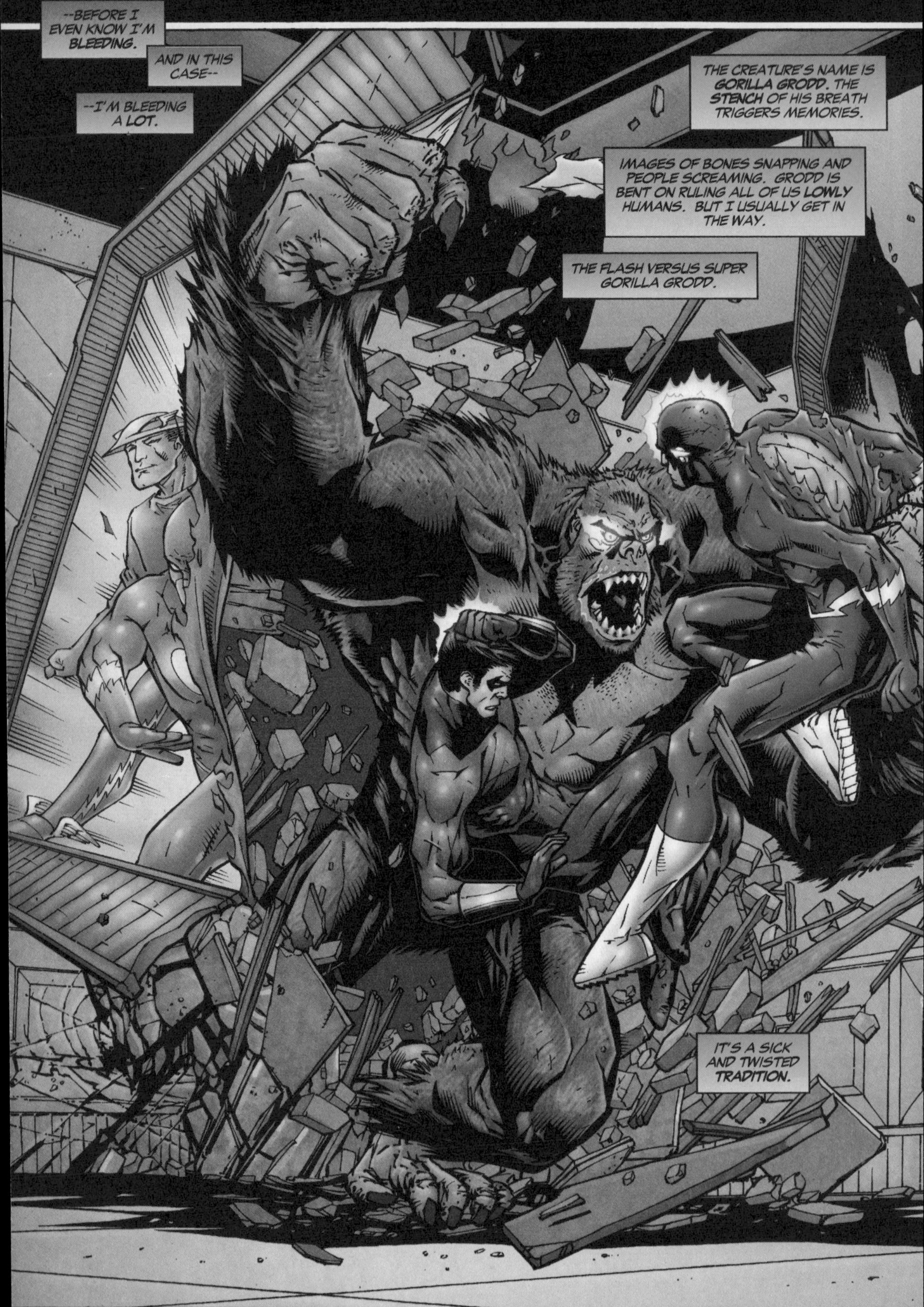
--BEFORE I EVEN KNOW I'M BLEEDING.
AND IN THIS CASE--
--I'M BLEEDING A LOT.
THE CREATURE'S NAME IS GORILLA GRODD. THE STENCH OF HIS BREATH TRIGGERS MEMORIES.
IMAGES OF BONES SNAPPING AND PEOPLE SCREAMING. GRODD IS BENT ON RULING ALL OF US LOWLY HUMANS. BUT I USUALLY GET IN THE WAY.
THE FLASH VERSUS SUPER GORILLA GRODD.
IT'S A SICK AND TWISTED TRADITION.

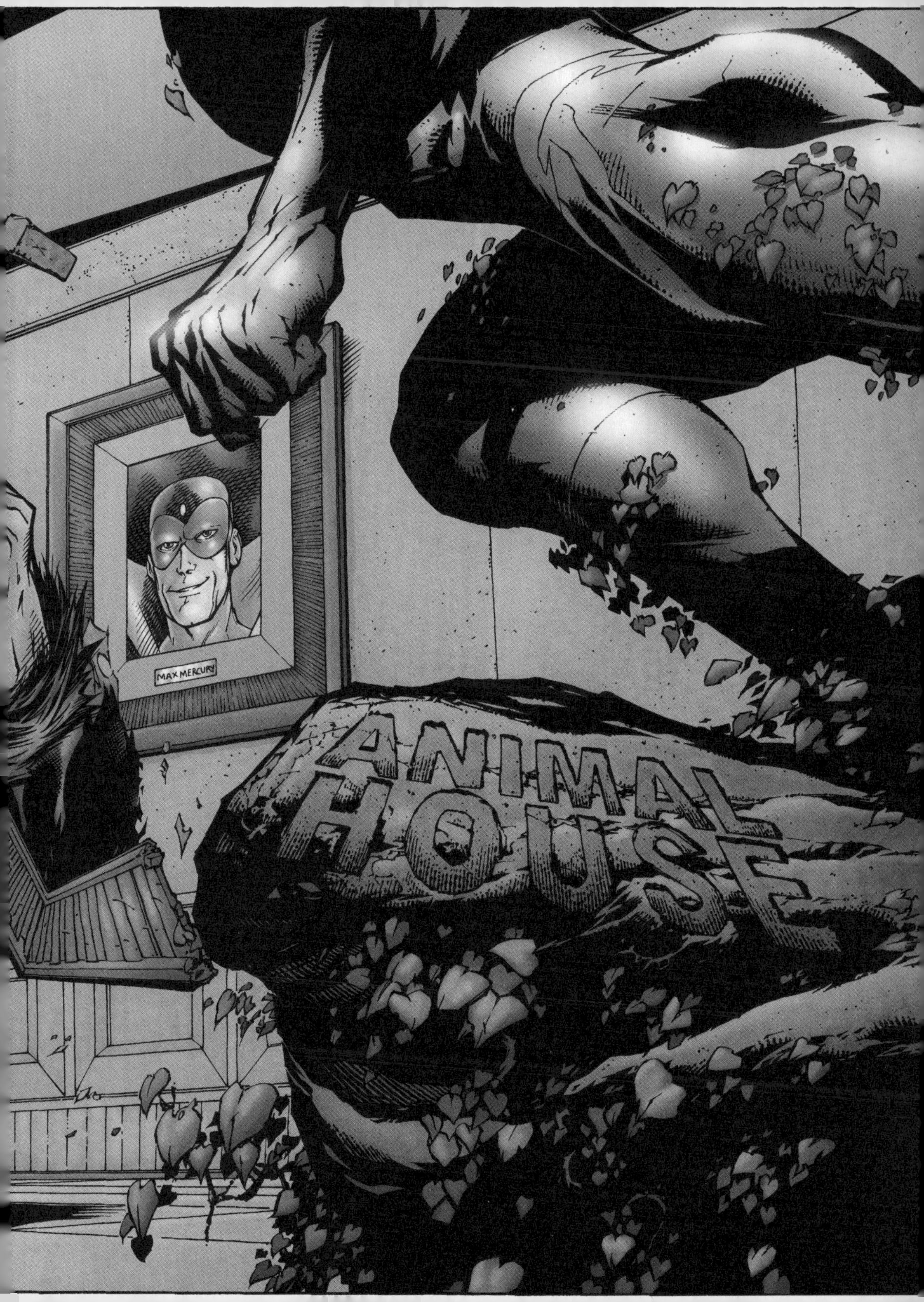
MAX MERCURY
ANIMAL HOUSE

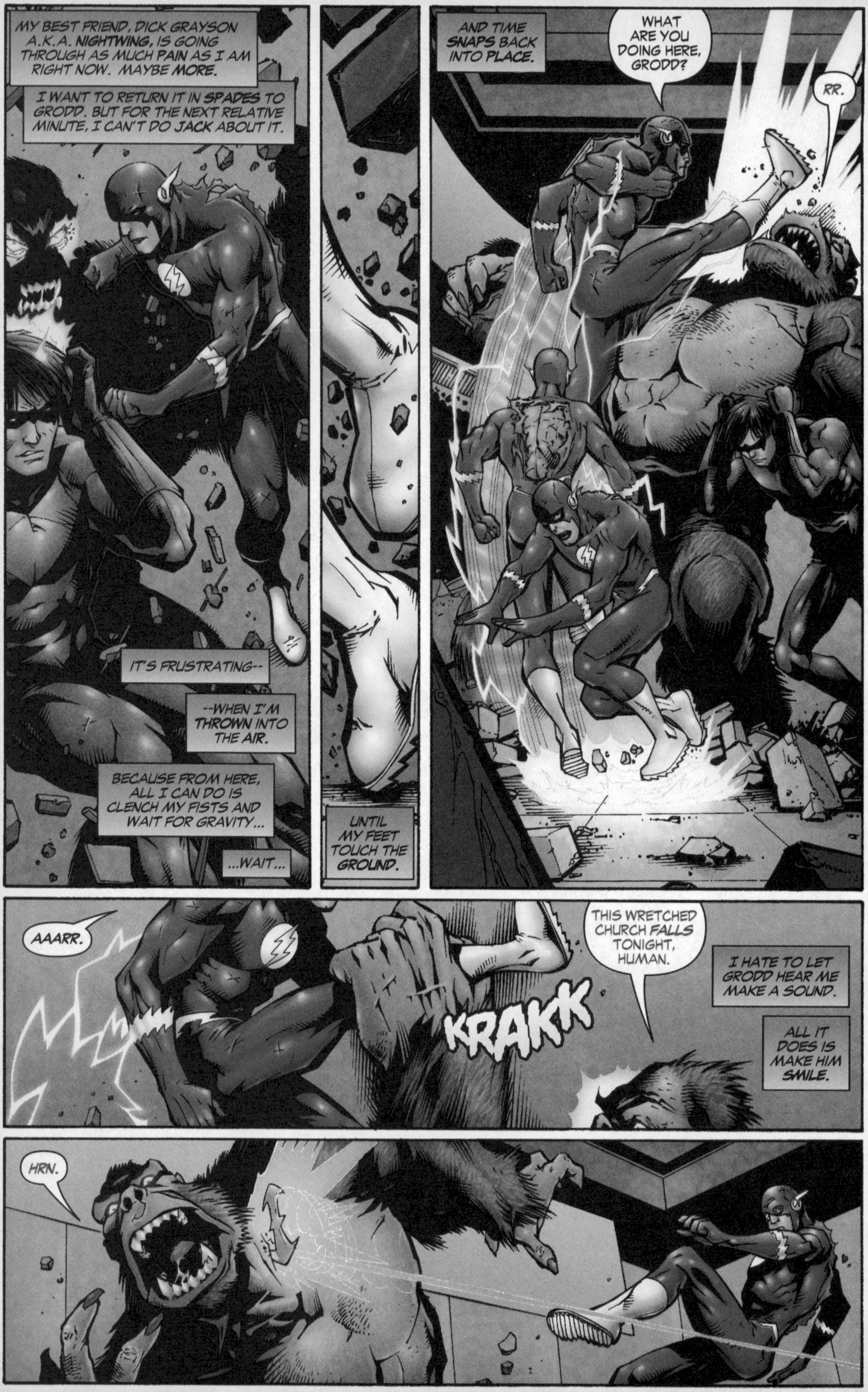

MY BEST FRIEND, DICK GRAYSON A.K.A. NIGHTWING, IS GOING THROUGH AS MUCH PAIN AS I AM RIGHT NOW. MAYBE MORE.
I WANT TO RETURN IT IN SPADES TO GRODD. BUT FOR THE NEXT RELATIVE MINUTE, I CAN'T DO JACK ABOUT IT.
IT'S FRUSTRATING--
--WHEN I'M THROWN INTO THE AIR.
BECAUSE FROM HERE, ALL I CAN DO IS CLENCH MY FISTS AND WAIT FOR GRAVITY...
...WAIT...
UNTIL MY FEET TOUCH THE GROUND.
AND TIME SNAPS BACK INTO PLACE.
WHAT ARE YOU DOING HERE, GRODD?
RR.
AAARR.
THIS WRETCHED CHURCH FALLS TONIGHT, HUMAN.
KRAKK
I HATE TO LET GRODD HEAR ME MAKE A SOUND.
ALL IT DOES IS MAKE HIM SMILE.
HRN.

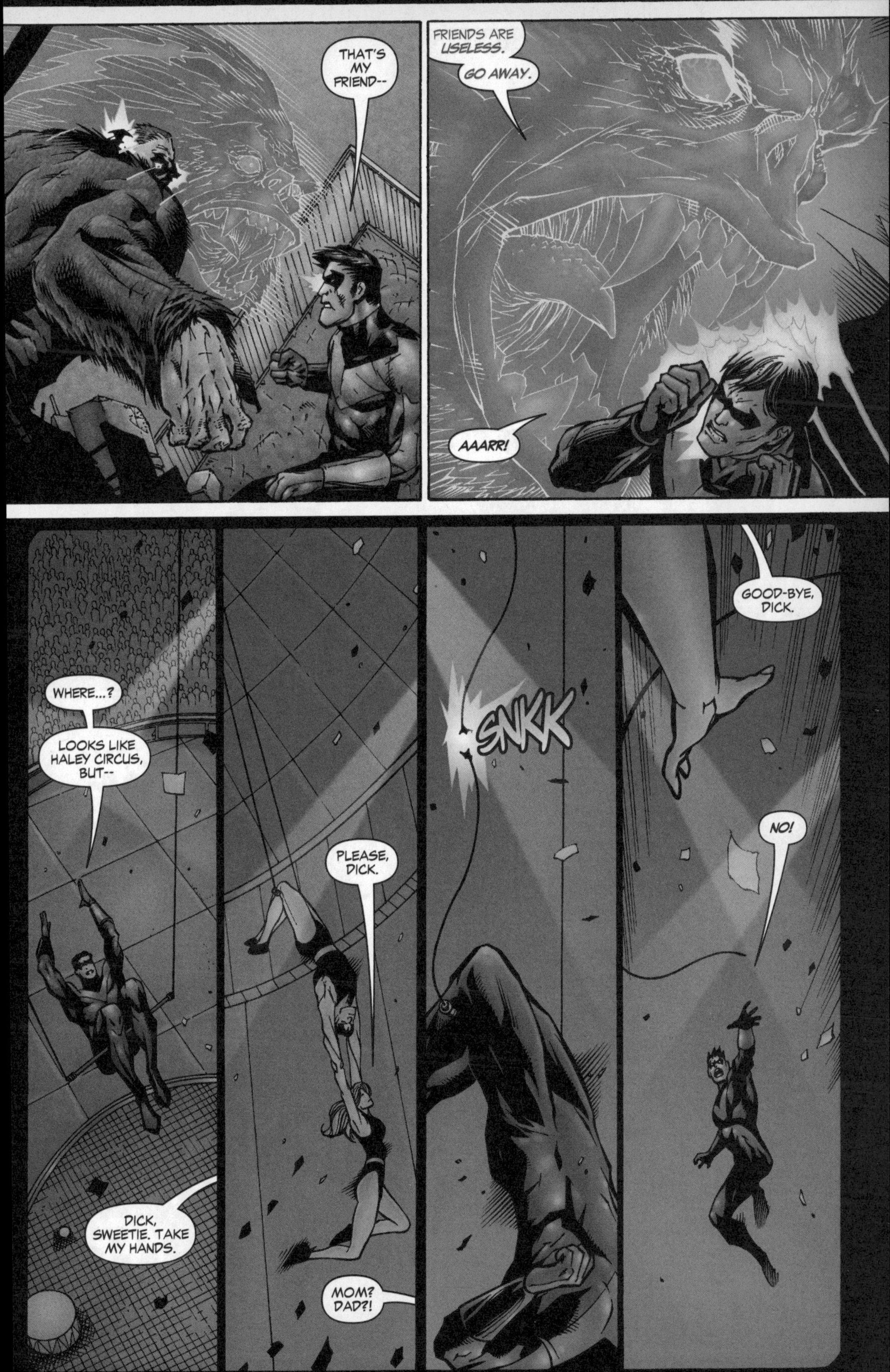
THAT'S MY FRIEND--
FRIENDS ARE USELESS.
GO AWAY.
AAARR!
WHERE...?
LOOKS LIKE HALEY CIRCUS, BUT--
DICK, SWEETIE. TAKE MY HANDS.
PLEASE, DICK.
MOM? DAD?!
SNKK
GOOD-BYE, DICK.
NO!

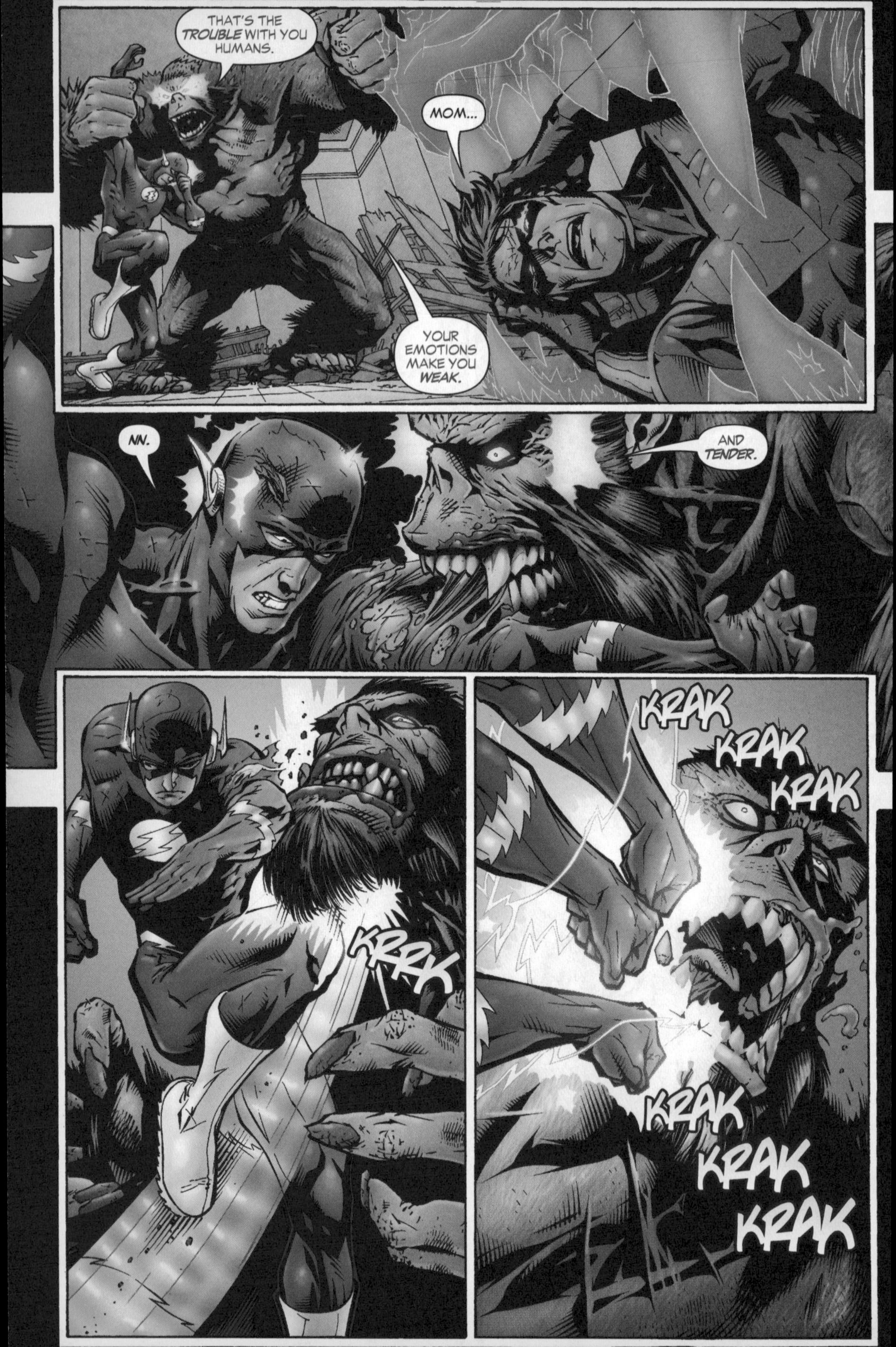
THAT'S THE TROUBLE WITH YOU HUMANS.
MOM...
YOUR EMOTIONS MAKE YOU WEAK.
NN.
AND TENDER.
KRRK
KRAK
KRAK
KRAK
KRAK
KRAK
KRAK

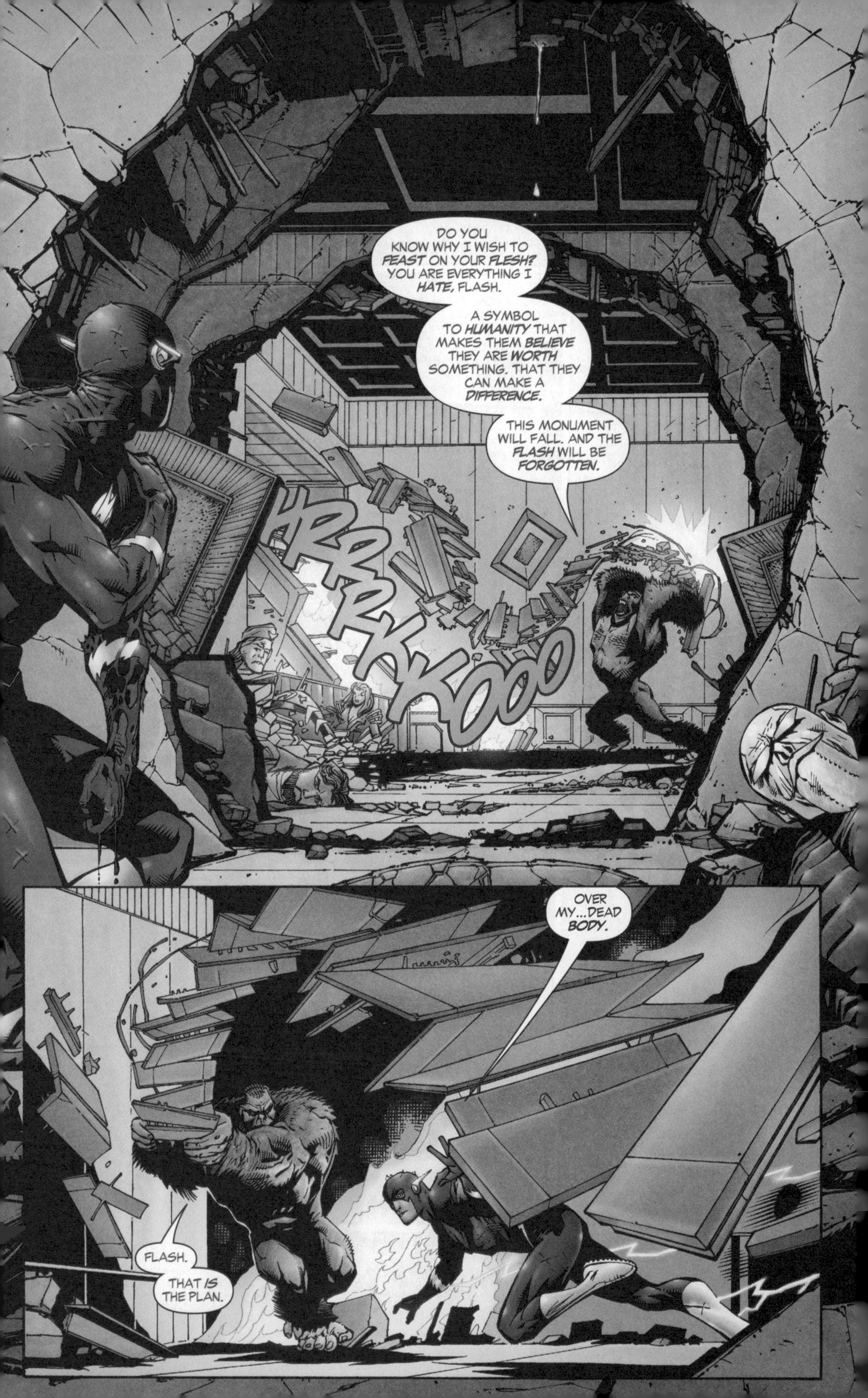

DO YOU KNOW WHY I WISH TO FEAST ON YOUR FLESH? YOU ARE EVERYTHING I HATE, FLASH.
A SYMBOL TO HUMANITY THAT MAKES THEM BELIEVE THEY ARE WORTH SOMETHING. THAT THEY CAN MAKE A DIFFERENCE.
THIS MONUMENT WILL FALL. AND THE FLASH WILL BE FORGOTTEN.
HRRRKKOOO
OVER MY...DEAD BODY.
FLASH.
THAT IS THE PLAN.

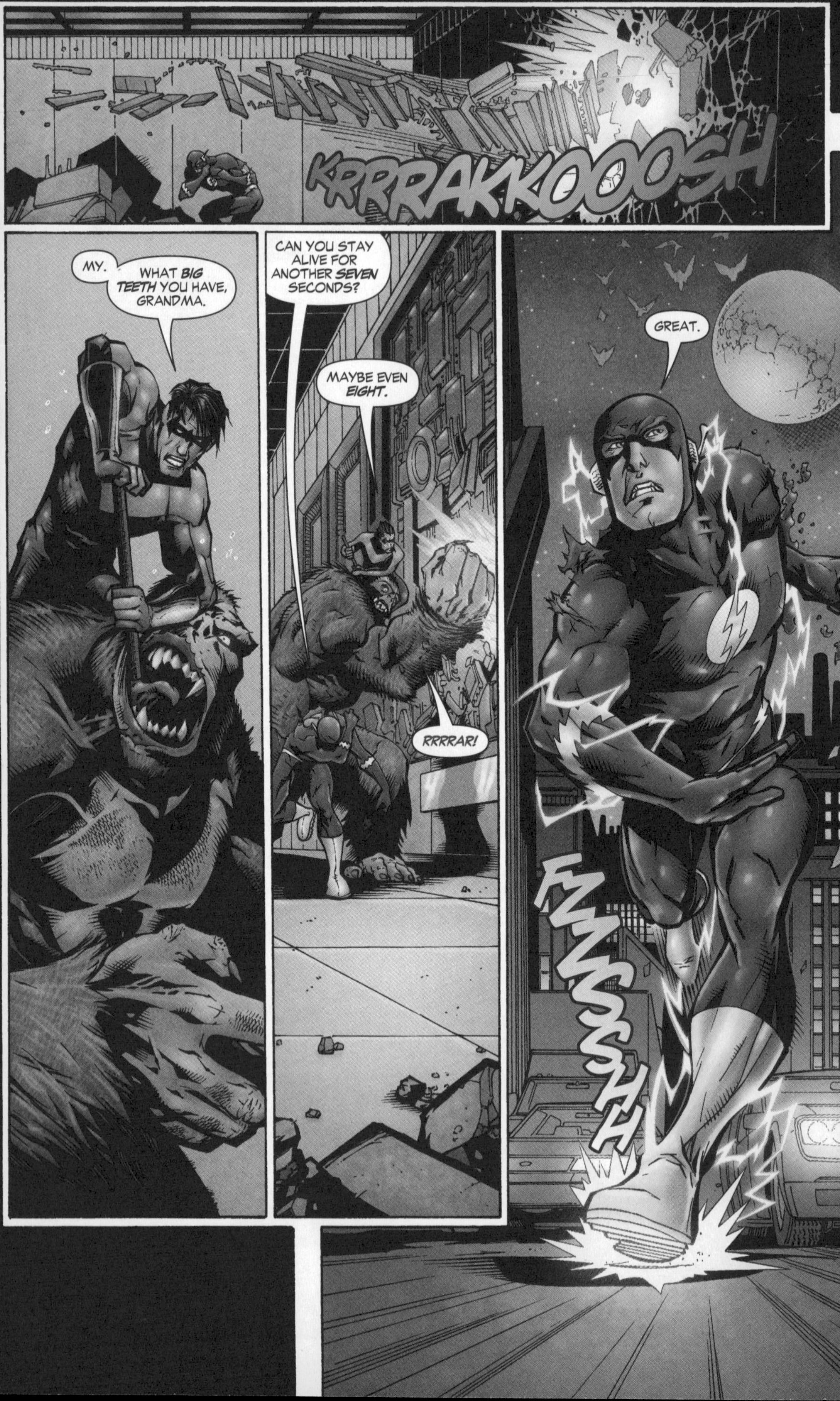
KRRRAKKOOOSH
MY.
WHAT BIG TEETH YOU HAVE, GRANDMA.
CAN YOU STAY ALIVE FOR ANOTHER SEVEN SECONDS?
MAYBE EVEN EIGHT.
RRRRAR!
GREAT.
FZZWSSHH

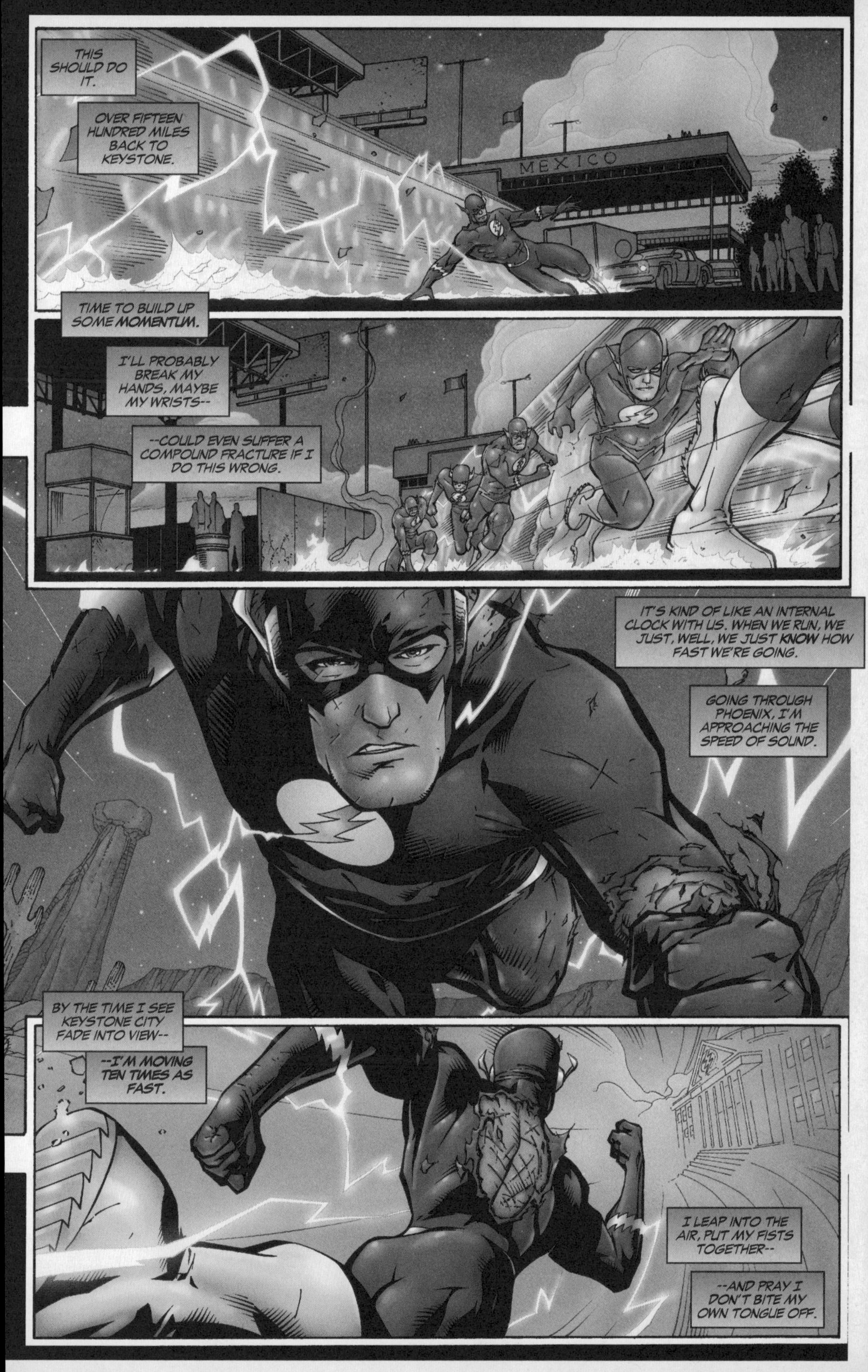
THIS SHOULD DO IT.
OVER FIFTEEN HUNDRED MILES BACK TO KEYSTONE.
MEXICO
TIME TO BUILD UP SOME MOMENTUM.
I'LL PROBABLY BREAK MY HANDS, MAYBE MY WRISTS--
--COULD EVEN SUFFER A COMPOUND FRACTURE IF I DO THIS WRONG.
IT'S KIND OF LIKE AN INTERNAL CLOCK WITH US. WHEN WE RUN, WE JUST, WELL, WE JUST KNOW HOW FAST WE'RE GOING.
GOING THROUGH PHOENIX, I'M APPROACHING THE SPEED OF SOUND.
BY THE TIME I SEE KEYSTONE CITY FADE INTO VIEW--
--I'M MOVING TEN TIMES AS FAST.
I LEAP INTO THE AIR, PUT MY FISTS TOGETHER--
--AND PRAY I DON'T BITE MY OWN TONGUE OFF.

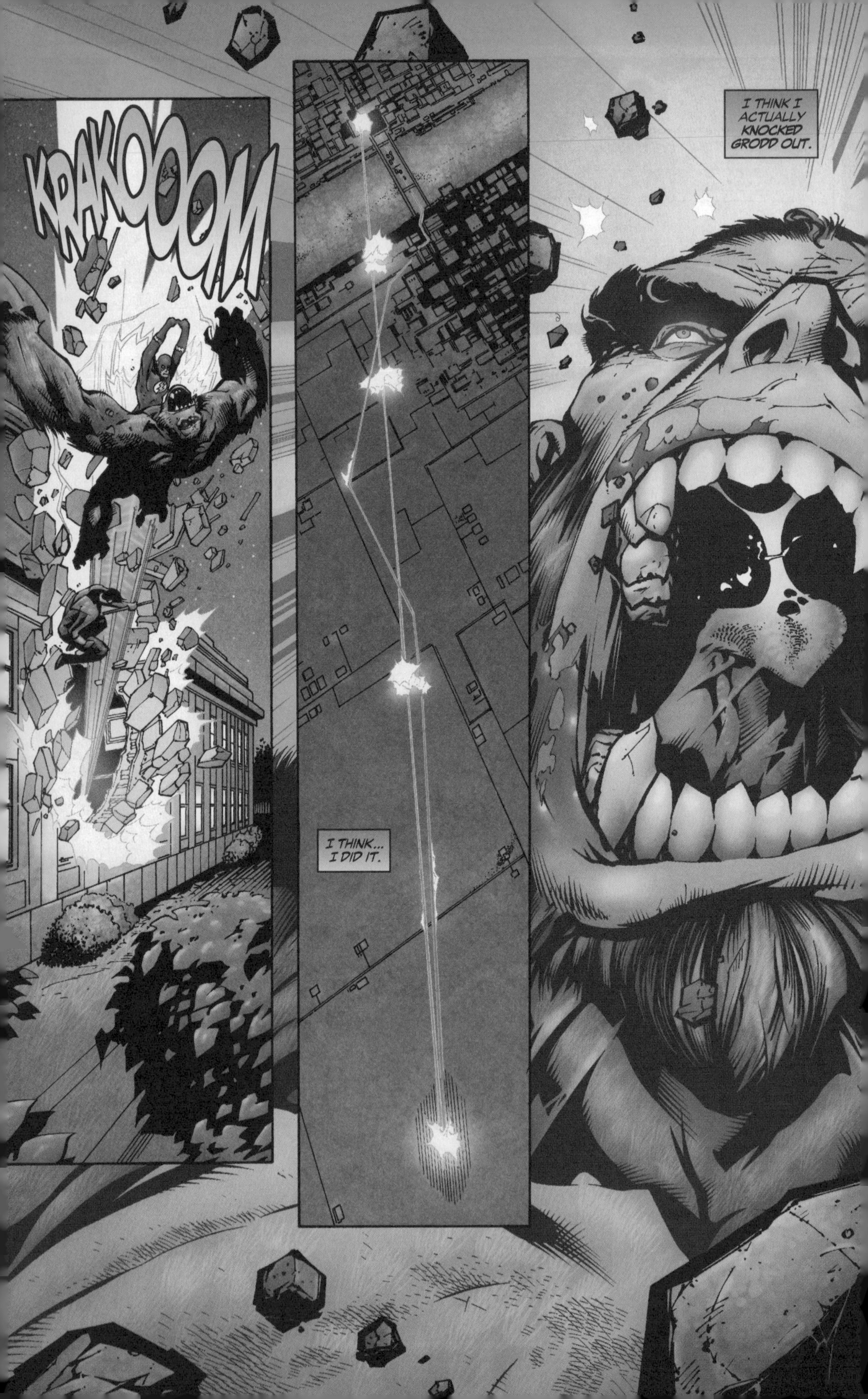
KRAKOOOM
I THINK... I DID IT.
I THINK I ACTUALLY KNOCKED GRODD OUT.

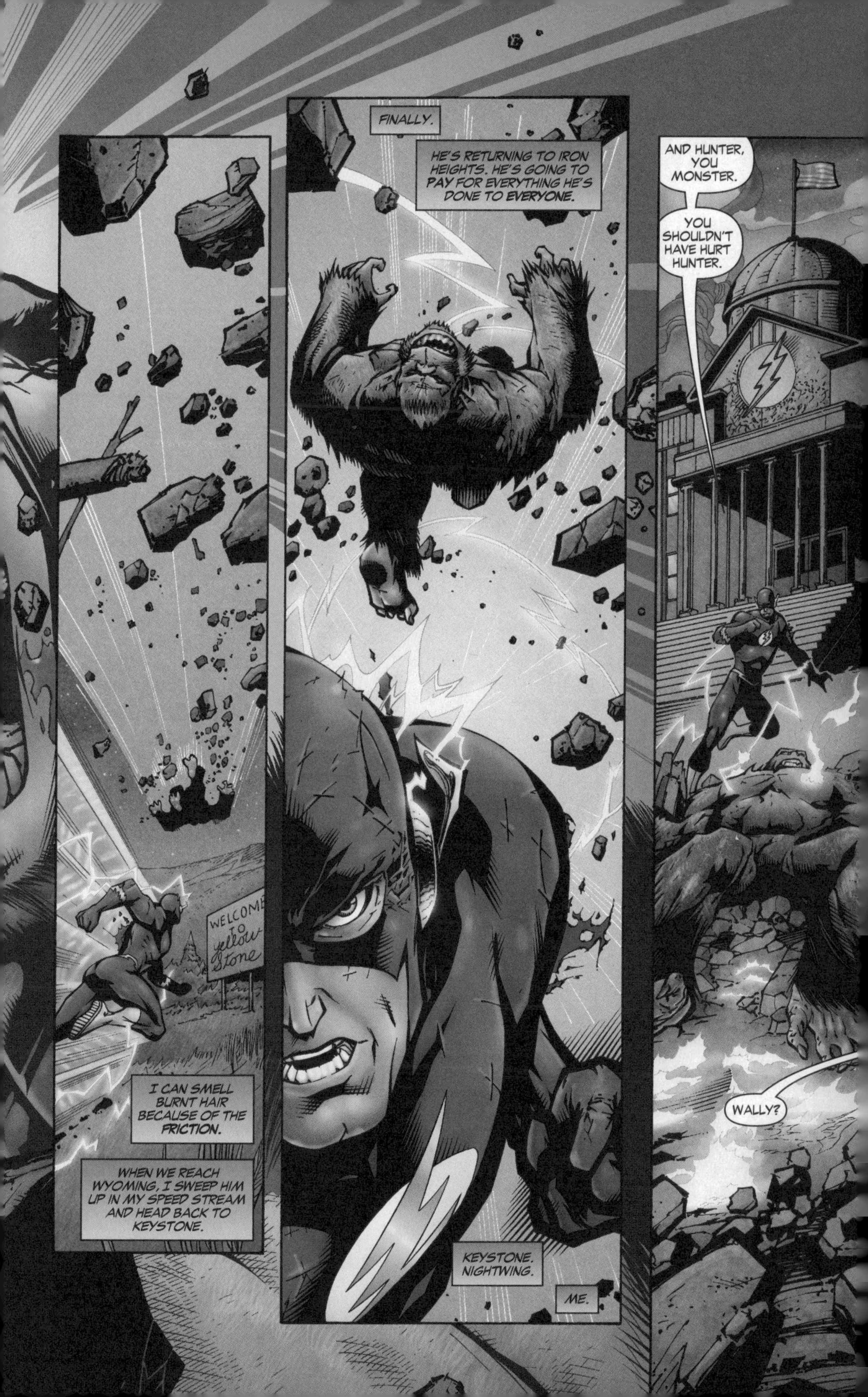
WELCOME TO yellow Stone
I CAN SMELL BURNT HAIR BECAUSE OF THE FRICTION.
WHEN WE REACH WYOMING, I SWEEP HIM UP IN MY SPEED STREAM AND HEAD BACK TO KEYSTONE.
FINALLY.
HE'S RETURNING TO IRON HEIGHTS. HE'S GOING TO PAY FOR EVERYTHING HE'S DONE TO EVERYONE.
KEYSTONE. NIGHTWING.
ME.
AND HUNTER, YOU MONSTER.
YOU SHOULDN'T HAVE HURT HUNTER.
WALLY?

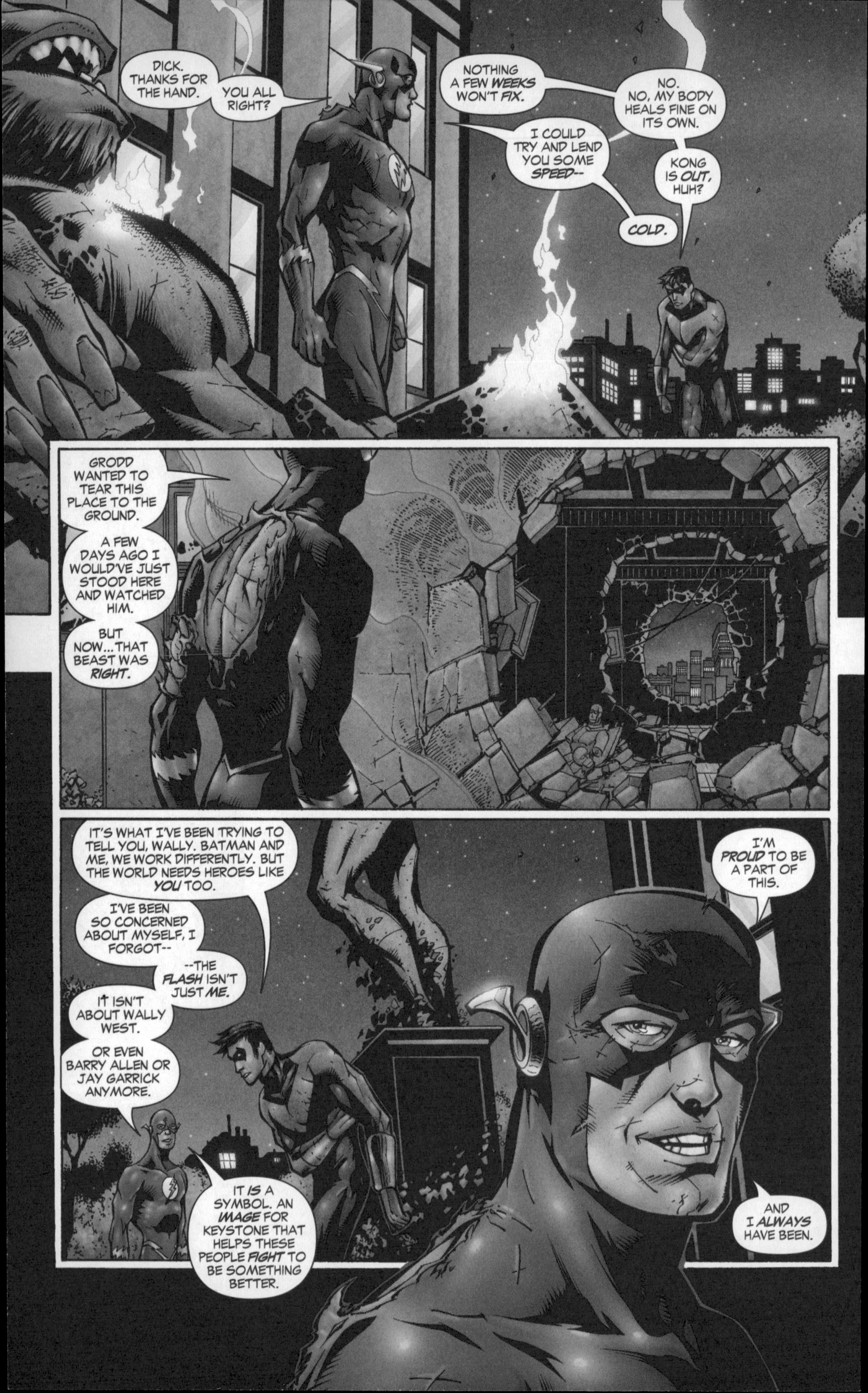
DICK. THANKS FOR THE HAND.
YOU ALL RIGHT?
NOTHING A FEW WEEKS WON'T FIX.
I COULD TRY AND LEND YOU SOME SPEED--
NO. NO, MY BODY HEALS FINE ON ITS OWN.
KONG IS OUT, HUH?
COLD.
GRODD WANTED TO TEAR THIS PLACE TO THE GROUND.
A FEW DAYS AGO I WOULD'VE JUST STOOD HERE AND WATCHED HIM.
BUT NOW...THAT BEAST WAS RIGHT.
IT'S WHAT I'VE BEEN TRYING TO TELL YOU, WALLY. BATMAN AND ME, WE WORK DIFFERENTLY. BUT THE WORLD NEEDS HEROES LIKE YOU TOO.
I'VE BEEN SO CONCERNED ABOUT MYSELF, I FORGOT--
--THE FLASH ISN'T JUST ME.
IT ISN'T ABOUT WALLY WEST.
OR EVEN BARRY ALLEN OR JAY GARRICK ANYMORE.
IT IS A SYMBOL. AN IMAGE FOR KEYSTONE THAT HELPS THESE PEOPLE FIGHT TO BE SOMETHING BETTER.
I'M PROUD TO BE A PART OF THIS.
AND I ALWAYS HAVE BEEN.

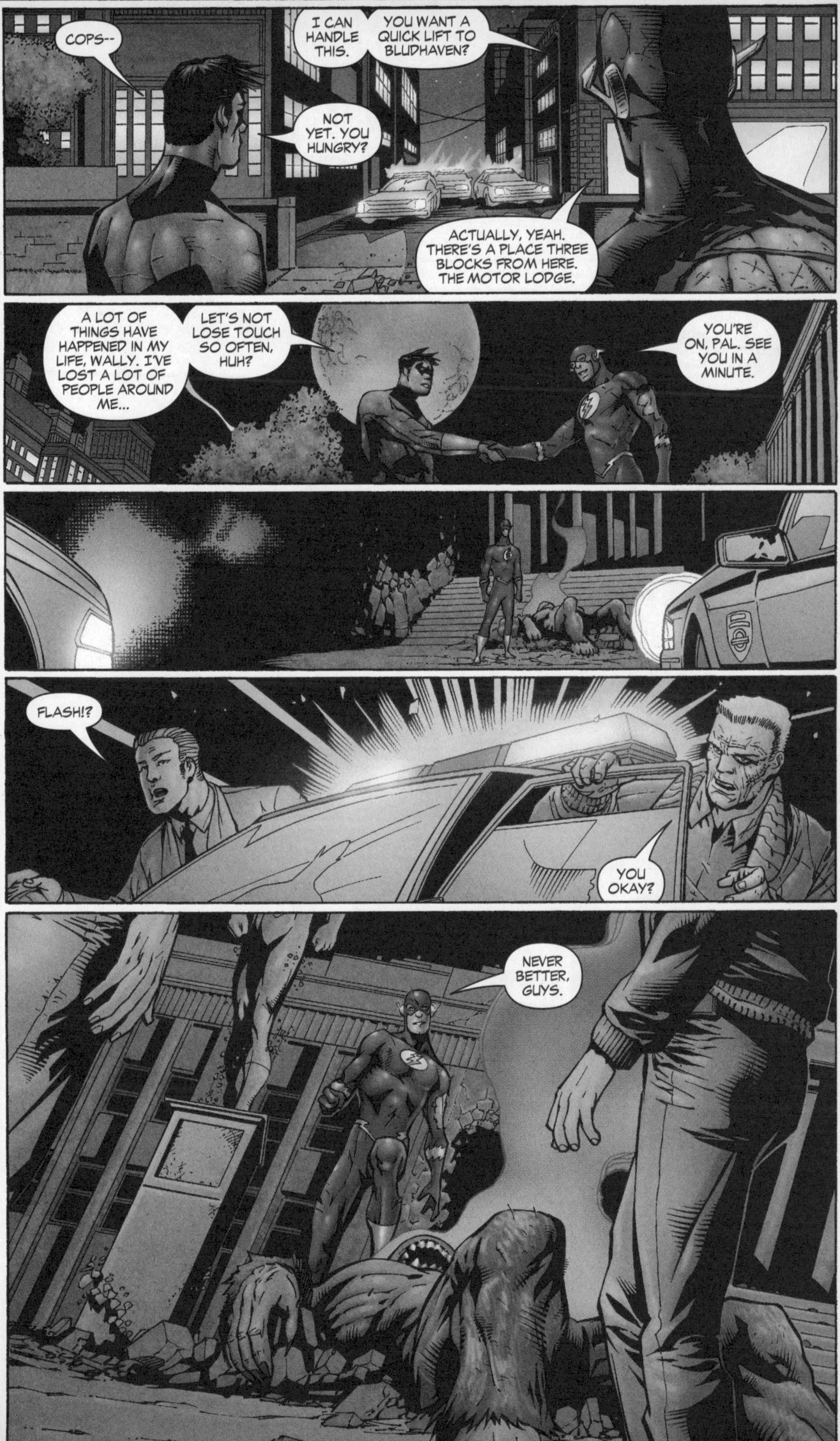
COPS--
I CAN HANDLE THIS.
YOU WANT A QUICK LIFT TO BLUDHAVEN?
NOT YET. YOU HUNGRY?
ACTUALLY, YEAH. THERE'S A PLACE THREE BLOCKS FROM HERE. THE MOTOR LODGE.
A LOT OF THINGS HAVE HAPPENED IN MY LIFE, WALLY. I'VE LOST A LOT OF PEOPLE AROUND ME...
LET'S NOT LOSE TOUCH SO OFTEN, HUH?
YOU'RE ON, PAL. SEE YOU IN A MINUTE.
FLASH!?
YOU OKAY?
NEVER BETTER, GUYS.

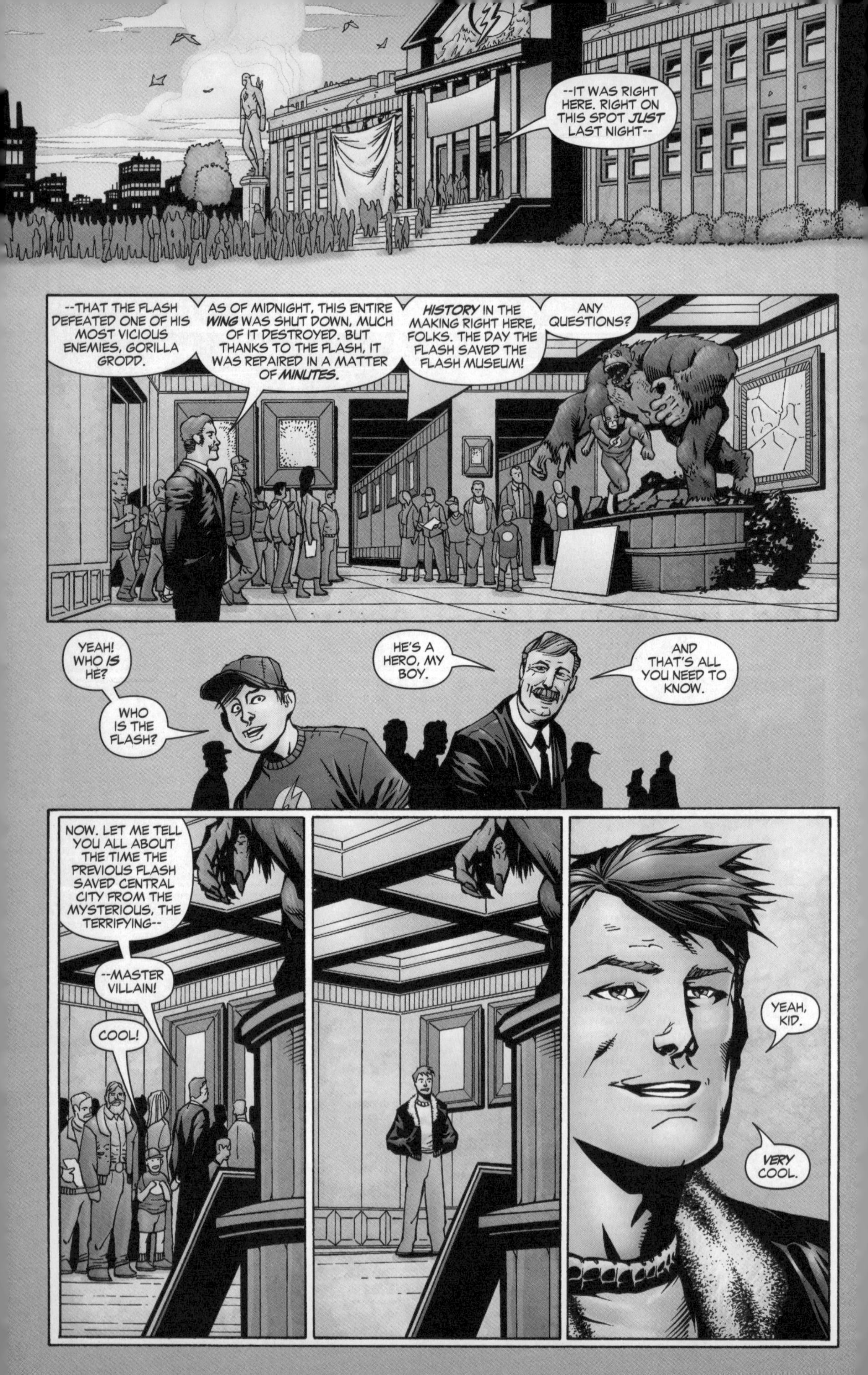
--IT WAS RIGHT HERE. RIGHT ON THIS SPOT JUST LAST NIGHT--
--THAT THE FLASH DEFEATED ONE OF HIS MOST VICIOUS ENEMIES, GORILLA GRODD.
AS OF MIDNIGHT, THIS ENTIRE WING WAS SHUT DOWN, MUCH OF IT DESTROYED. BUT THANKS TO THE FLASH, IT WAS REPAIRED IN A MATTER OF MINUTES.
HISTORY IN THE MAKING RIGHT HERE, FOLKS. THE DAY THE FLASH SAVED THE FLASH MUSEUM!
ANY QUESTIONS?
YEAH! WHO IS HE?
WHO IS THE FLASH?
HE'S A HERO, MY BOY.
AND THAT'S ALL YOU NEED TO KNOW.
NOW. LET ME TELL YOU ALL ABOUT THE TIME THE PREVIOUS FLASH SAVED CENTRAL CITY FROM THE MYSTERIOUS, THE TERRIFYING--
--MASTER VILLAIN!
COOL!
YEAH, KID.
VERY COOL.

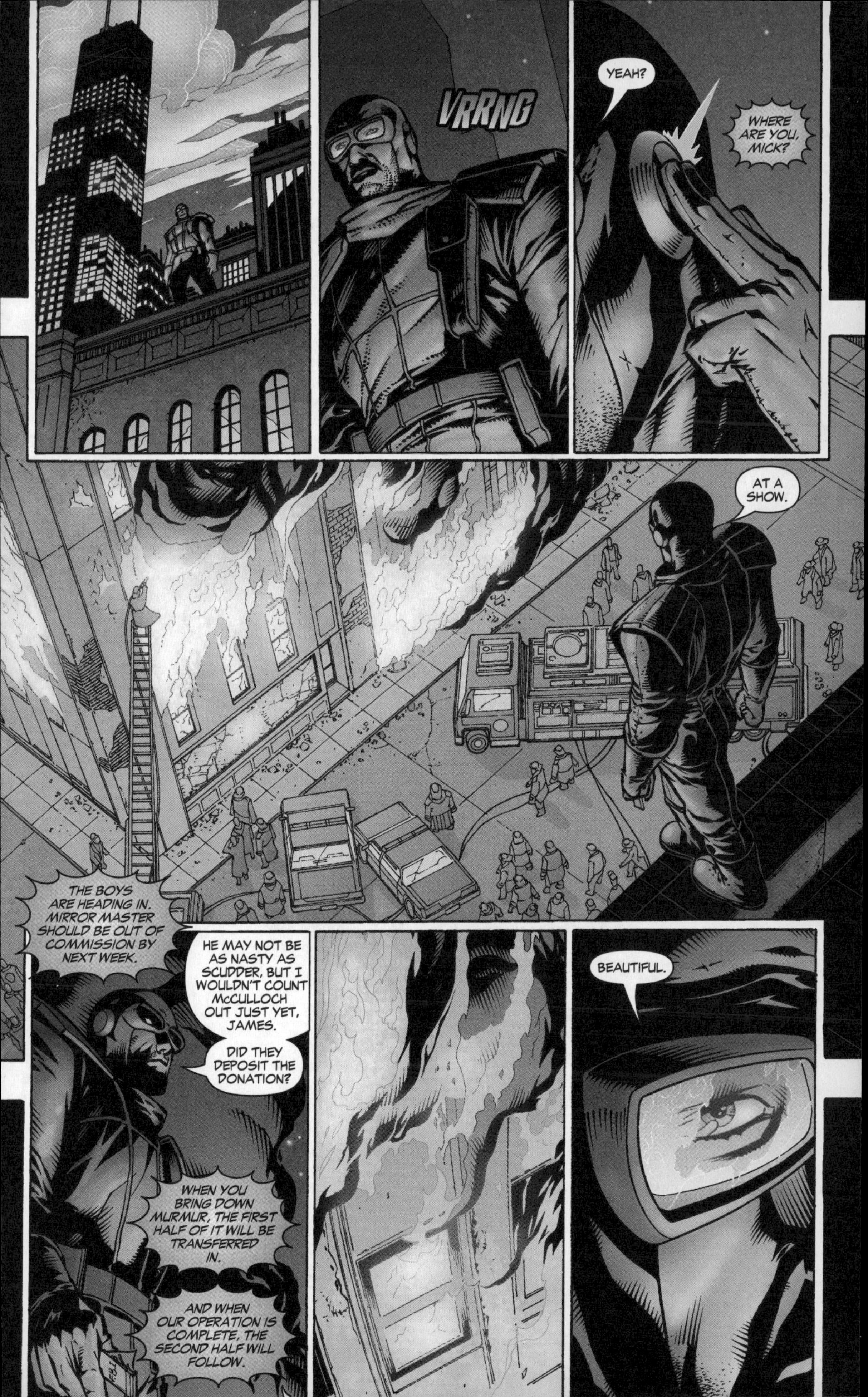
VRRNG
YEAH?
WHERE ARE YOU, MICK?
AT A SHOW.
THE BOYS ARE HEADING IN. MIRROR MASTER SHOULD BE OUT OF COMMISSION BY NEXT WEEK.
HE MAY NOT BE AS NASTY AS SCUDDER, BUT I WOULDN'T COUNT McCULLOCH OUT JUST YET, JAMES.
DID THEY DEPOSIT THE DONATION?
WHEN YOU BRING DOWN MURMUR, THE FIRST HALF OF IT WILL BE TRANSFERRED IN.
AND WHEN OUR OPERATION IS COMPLETE, THE SECOND HALF WILL FOLLOW.
BEAUTIFUL.

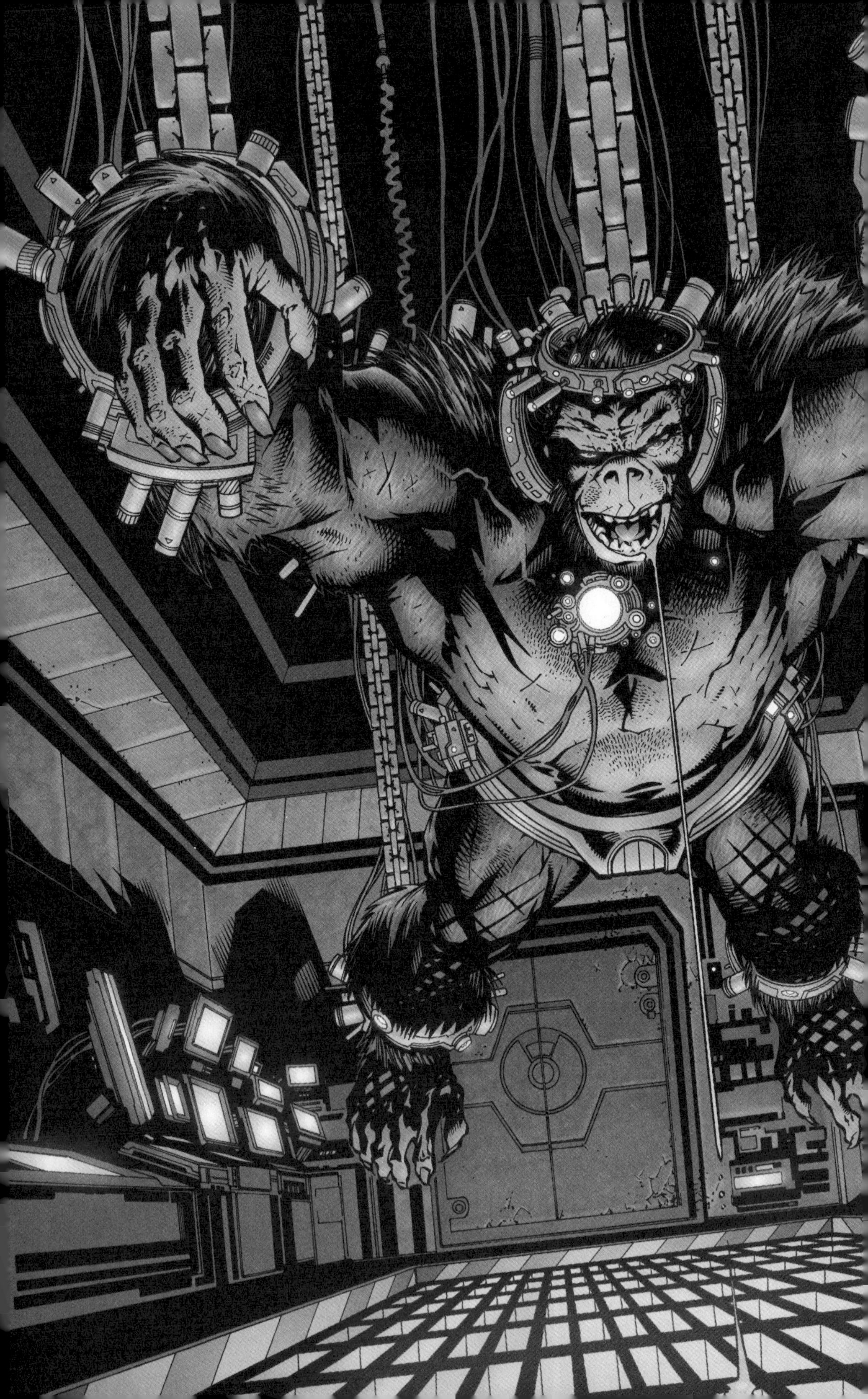

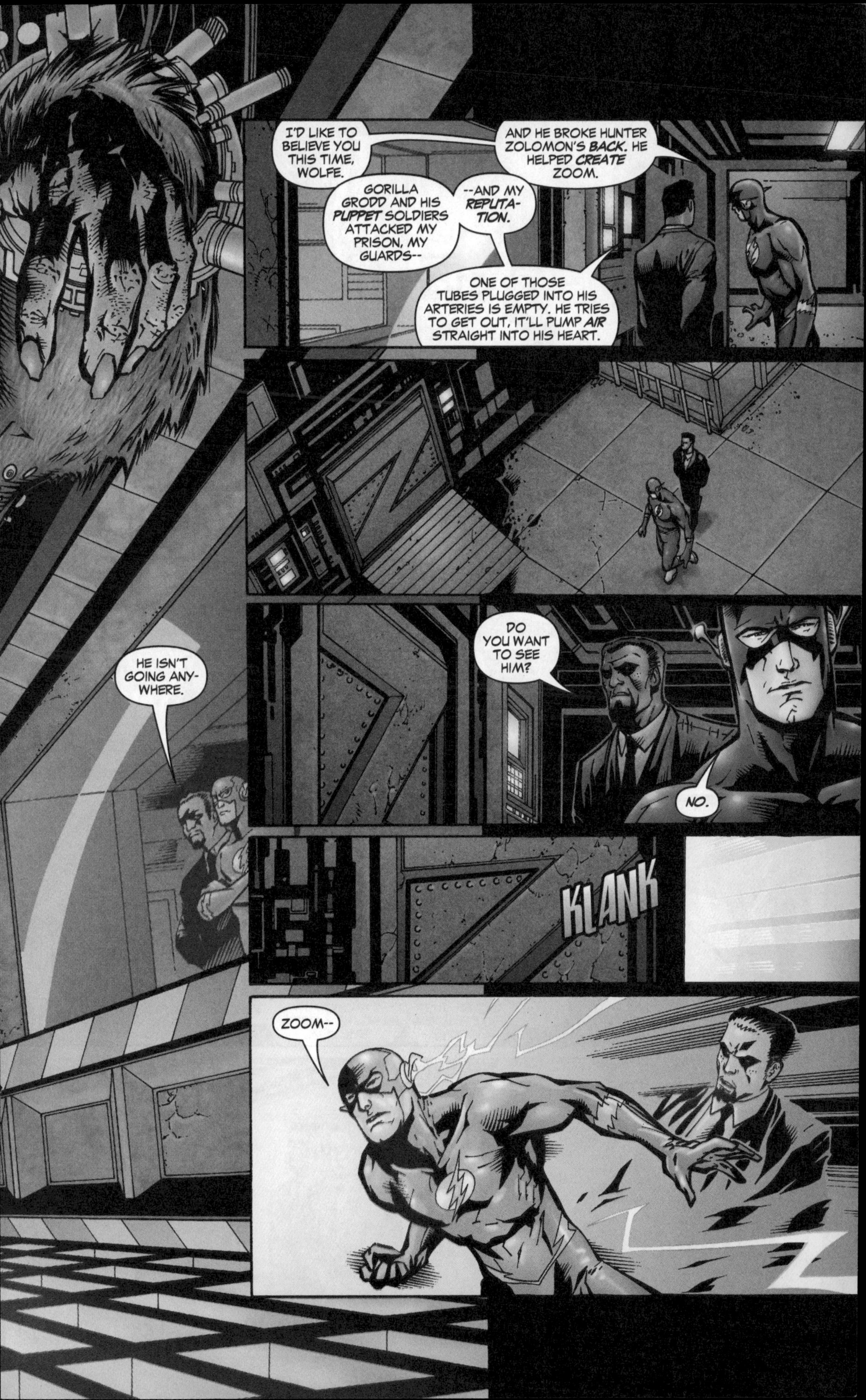
I'D LIKE TO BELIEVE YOU THIS TIME, WOLFE.
AND HE BROKE HUNTER ZOLOMON'S BACK. HE HELPED CREATE ZOOM.
GORILLA GRODD AND HIS PUPPET SOLDIERS ATTACKED MY PRISON, MY GUARDS--
--AND MY REPUTATION.
ONE OF THOSE TUBES PLUGGED INTO HIS ARTERIES IS EMPTY. HE TRIES TO GET OUT, IT'LL PUMP AIR STRAIGHT INTO HIS HEART.
DO YOU WANT TO SEE HIM?
NO.
HE ISN'T GOING ANYWHERE.
KLANK
ZOOM--

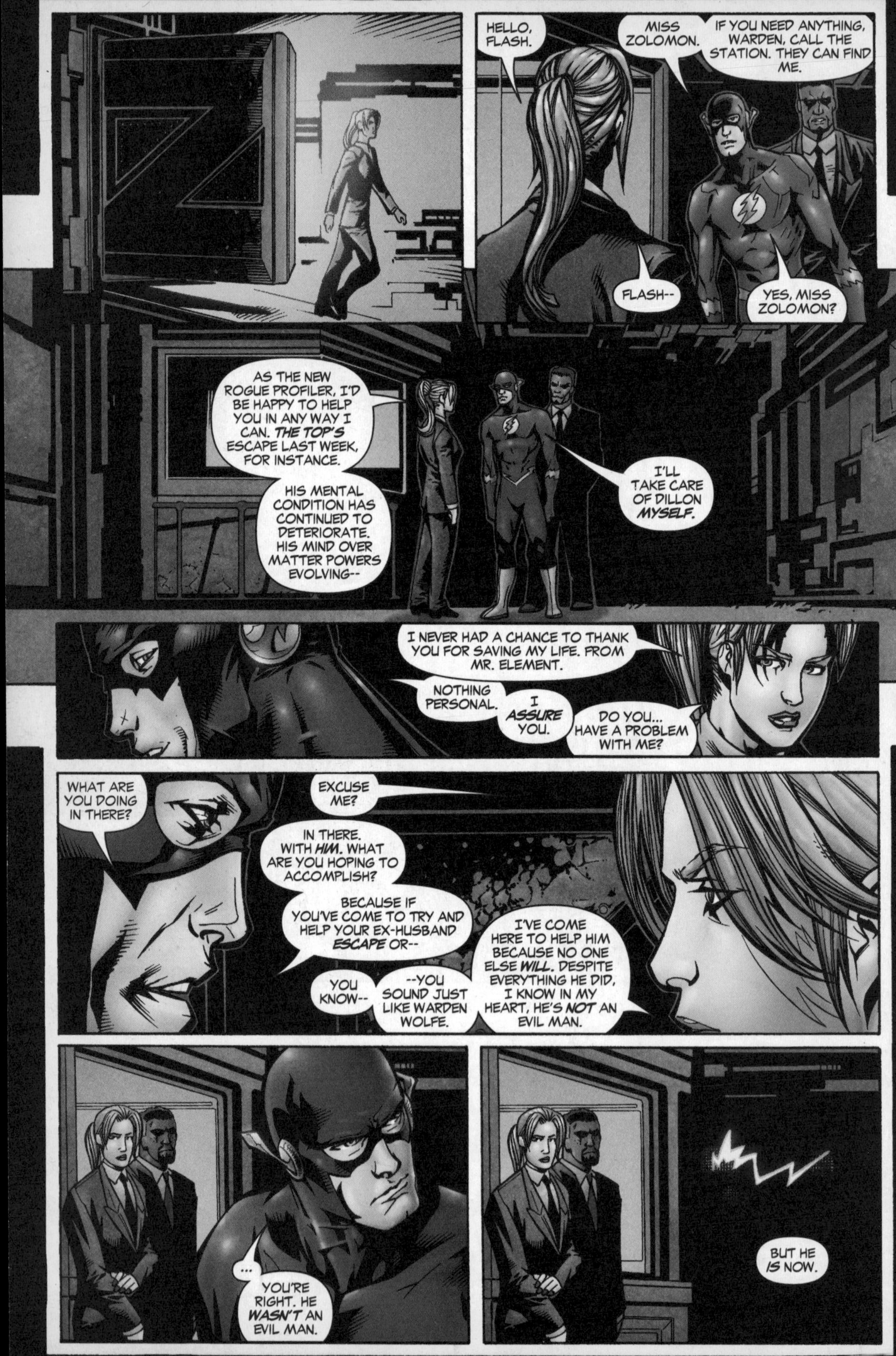
HELLO, FLASH.
MISS ZOLOMON.
IF YOU NEED ANYTHING, WARDEN, CALL THE STATION. THEY CAN FIND ME.
FLASH--
YES, MISS ZOLOMON?
AS THE NEW ROGUE PROFILER, I'D BE HAPPY TO HELP YOU IN ANY WAY I CAN. THE TOP'S ESCAPE LAST WEEK, FOR INSTANCE.
HIS MENTAL CONDITION HAS CONTINUED TO DETERIORATE. HIS MIND OVER MATTER POWERS EVOLVING--
I'LL TAKE CARE OF DILLON MYSELF.
I NEVER HAD A CHANCE TO THANK YOU FOR SAVING MY LIFE. FROM MR. ELEMENT.
NOTHING PERSONAL.
I ASSURE YOU.
DO YOU... HAVE A PROBLEM WITH ME?
WHAT ARE YOU DOING IN THERE?
EXCUSE ME?
IN THERE. WITH HIM. WHAT ARE YOU HOPING TO ACCOMPLISH?
BECAUSE IF YOU'VE COME TO TRY AND HELP YOUR EX-HUSBAND ESCAPE OR--
YOU KNOW--
--YOU SOUND JUST LIKE WARDEN WOLFE.
I'VE COME HERE TO HELP HIM BECAUSE NO ONE ELSE WILL. DESPITE EVERYTHING HE DID, I KNOW IN MY HEART, HE'S NOT AN EVIL MAN.
...
YOU'RE RIGHT. HE WASN'T AN EVIL MAN.
BUT HE IS NOW.

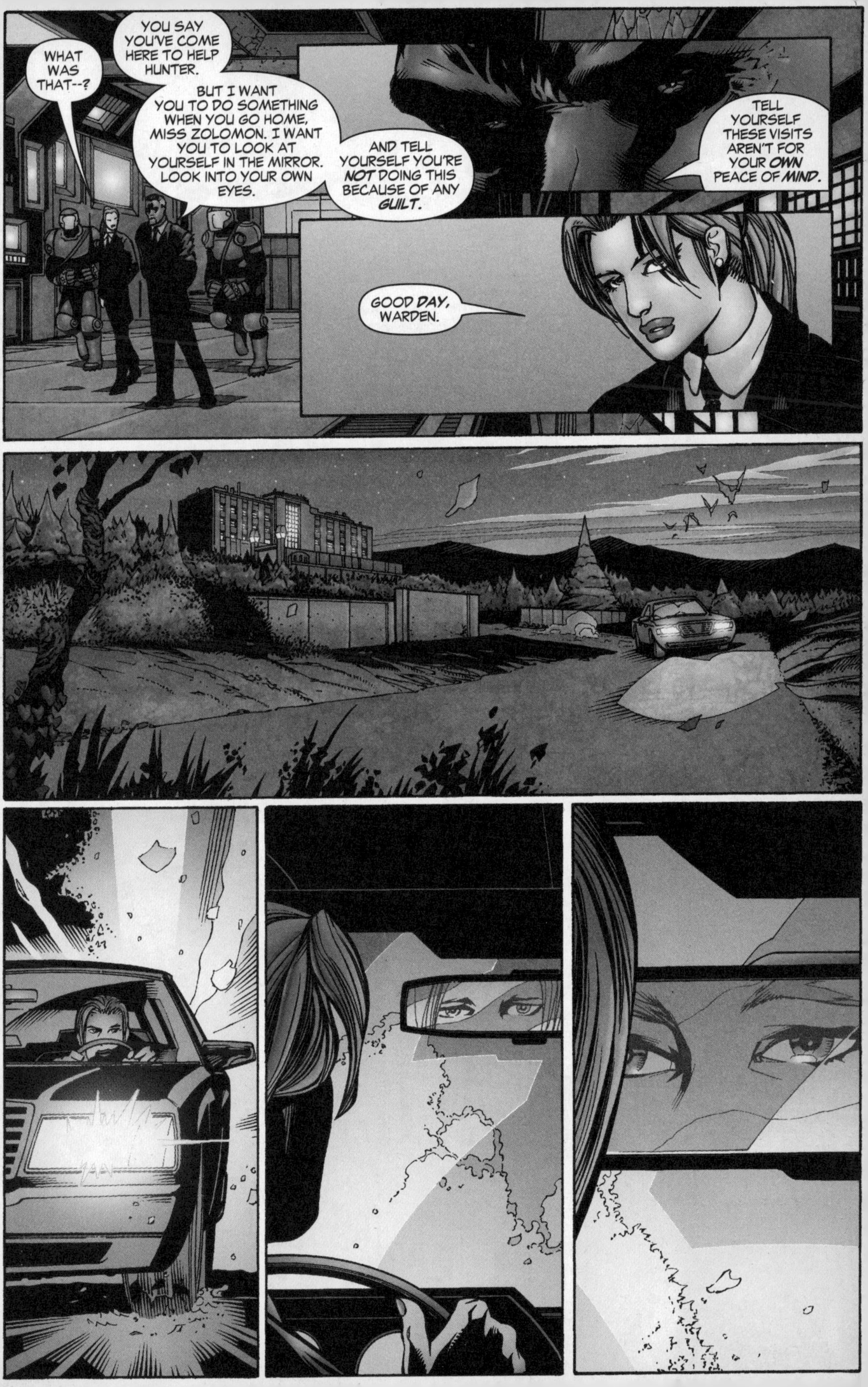
WHAT WAS THAT--?
YOU SAY YOU'VE COME HERE TO HELP HUNTER.
BUT I WANT YOU TO DO SOMETHING WHEN YOU GO HOME, MISS ZOLOMON. I WANT YOU TO LOOK AT YOURSELF IN THE MIRROR. LOOK INTO YOUR OWN EYES.
AND TELL YOURSELF YOU'RE NOT DOING THIS BECAUSE OF ANY GUILT.
TELL YOURSELF THESE VISITS AREN'T FOR YOUR OWN PEACE OF MIND.
GOOD DAY, WARDEN.

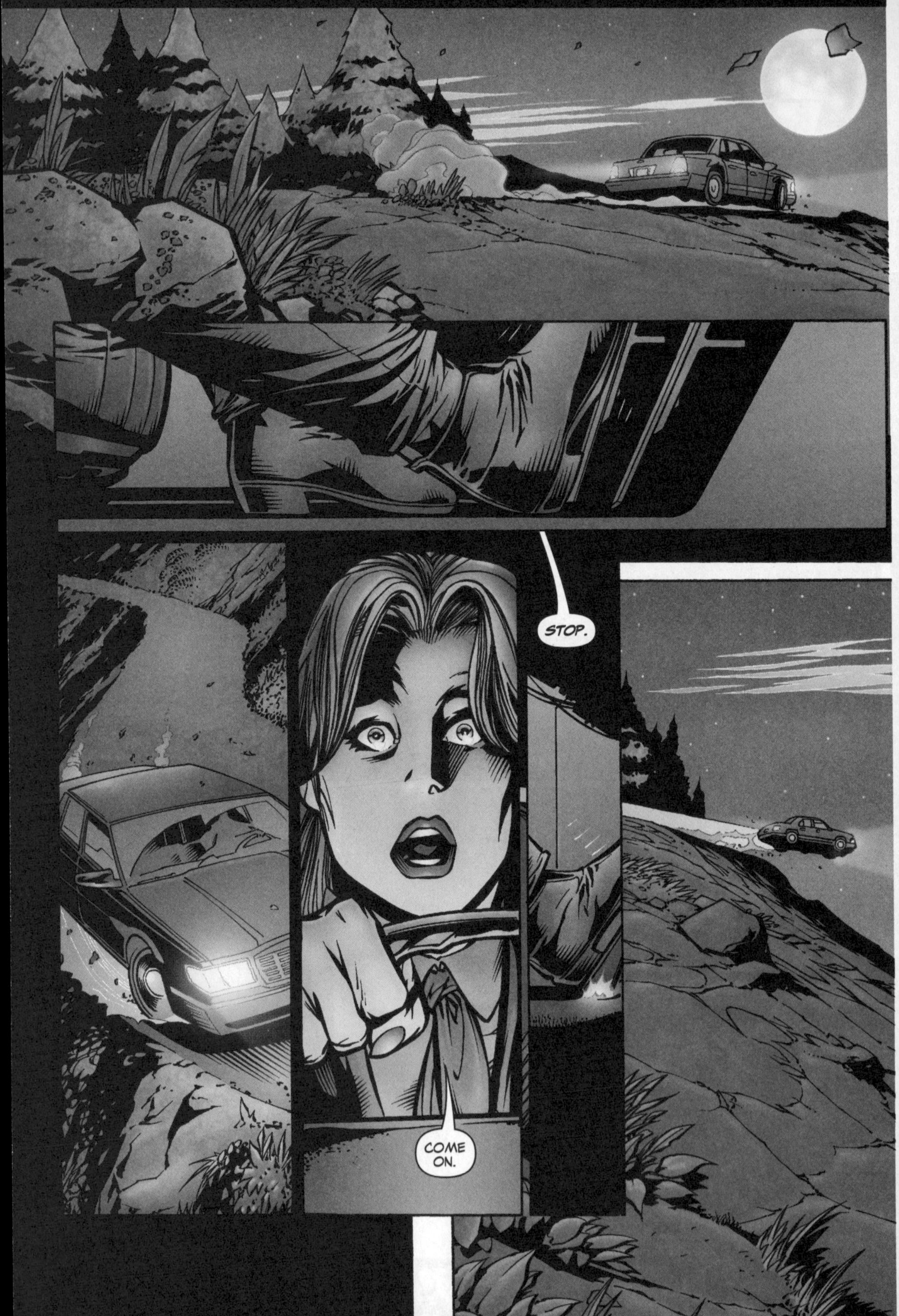
STOP.
COME ON.

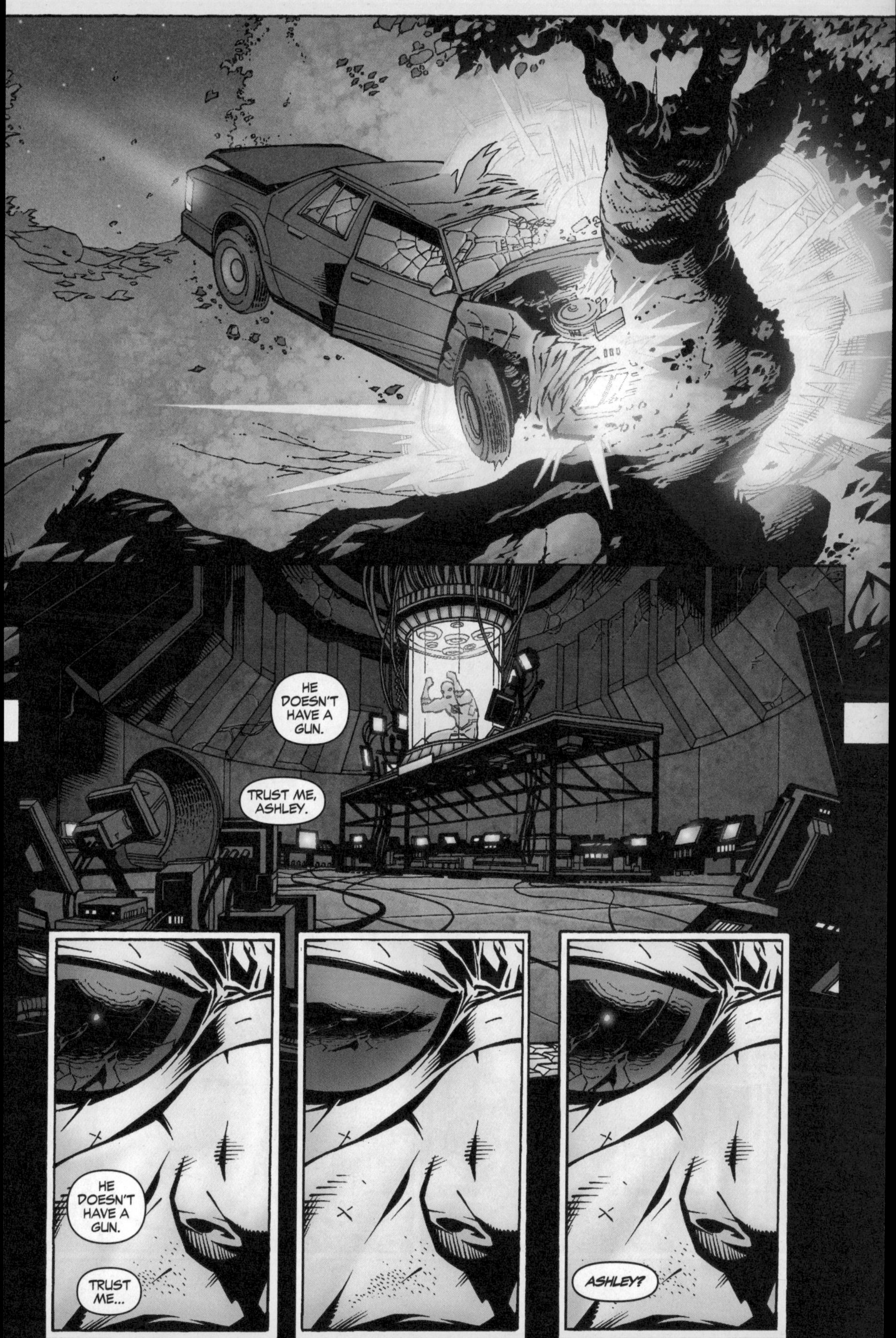
HE DOESN'T HAVE A GUN.
TRUST ME, ASHLEY.
HE DOESN'T HAVE A GUN.
TRUST ME...
ASHLEY?

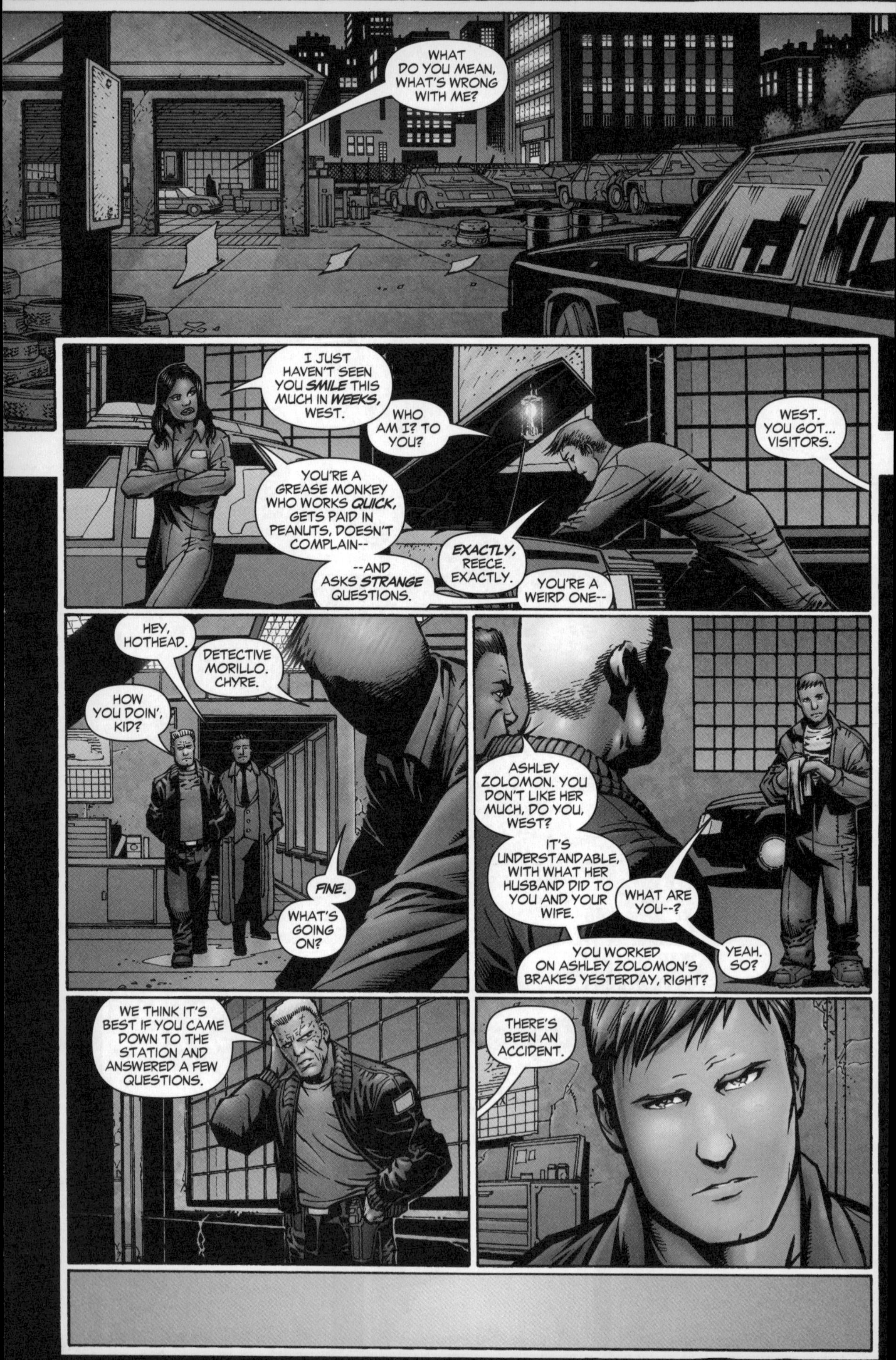
WHAT DO YOU MEAN, WHAT'S WRONG WITH ME?
I JUST HAVEN'T SEEN YOU SMILE THIS MUCH IN WEEKS, WEST.
WHO AM I? TO YOU?
YOU'RE A GREASE MONKEY WHO WORKS QUICK, GETS PAID IN PEANUTS, DOESN'T COMPLAIN--
--AND ASKS STRANGE QUESTIONS.
EXACTLY, REECE. EXACTLY.
YOU'RE A WEIRD ONE--
WEST. YOU GOT... VISITORS.
HEY, HOTHEAD.
DETECTIVE MORILLO. CHYRE.
HOW YOU DOIN', KID?
FINE.
WHAT'S GOING ON?
ASHLEY ZOLOMON. YOU DON'T LIKE HER MUCH, DO YOU, WEST?
IT'S UNDERSTANDABLE, WITH WHAT HER HUSBAND DID TO YOU AND YOUR WIFE.
WHAT ARE YOU--?
YOU WORKED ON ASHLEY ZOLOMON'S BRAKES YESTERDAY, RIGHT?
YEAH. SO?
WE THINK IT'S BEST IF YOU CAME DOWN TO THE STATION AND ANSWERED A FEW QUESTIONS.
THERE'S BEEN AN ACCIDENT.

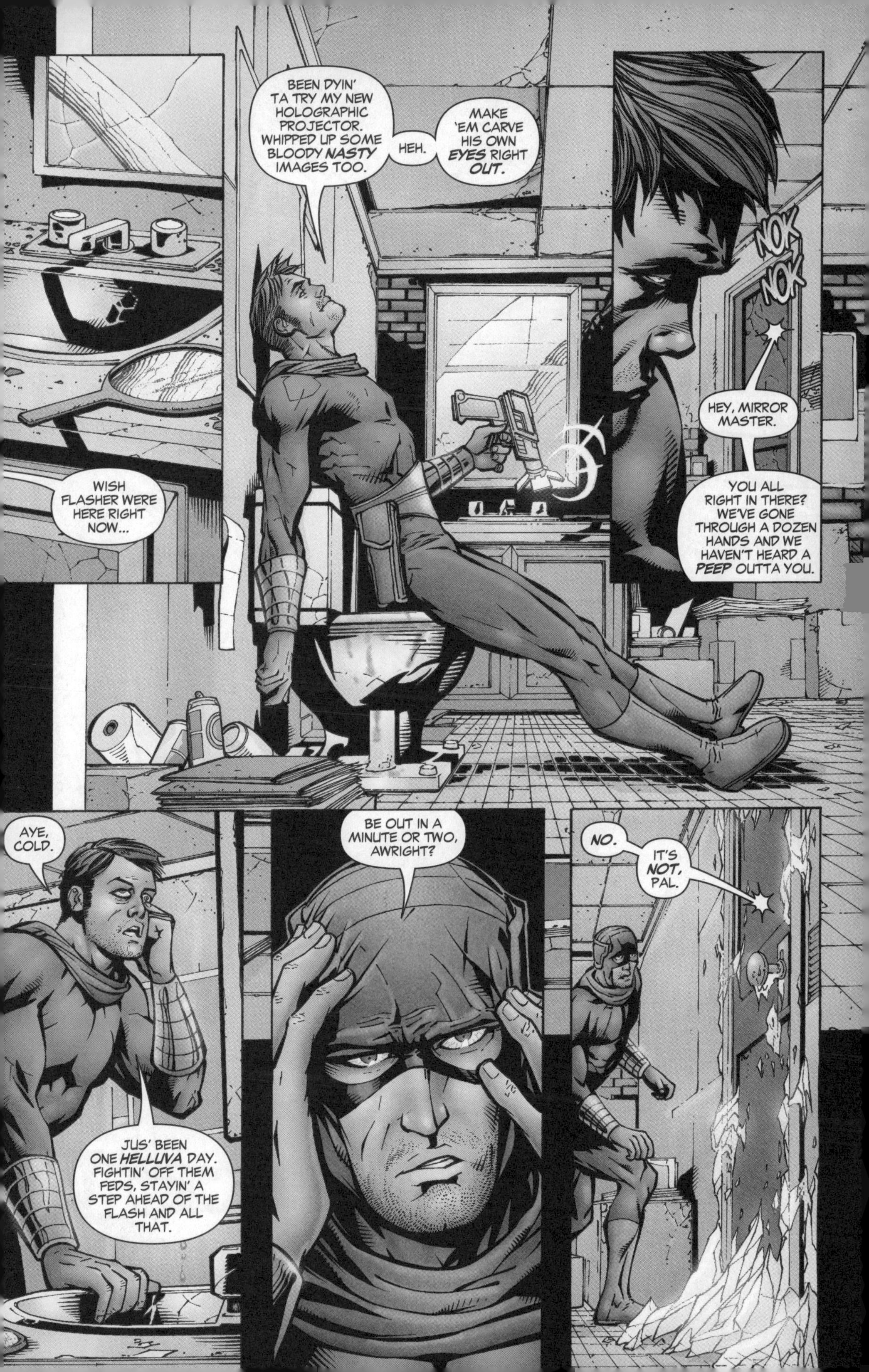

BEEN DYIN' TA TRY MY NEW HOLOGRAPHIC PROJECTOR. WHIPPED UP SOME BLOODY NASTY IMAGES TOO.
HEH.
MAKE 'EM CARVE HIS OWN EYES RIGHT OUT.
WISH FLASHER WERE HERE RIGHT NOW...
NOK NOK
HEY, MIRROR MASTER.
YOU ALL RIGHT IN THERE? WE'VE GONE THROUGH A DOZEN HANDS AND WE HAVEN'T HEARD A PEEP OUTTA YOU.
AYE, COLD.
JUS' BEEN ONE HELLUVA DAY. FIGHTIN' OFF THEM FEDS, STAYIN' A STEP AHEAD OF THE FLASH AND ALL THAT.
BE OUT IN A MINUTE OR TWO, AWRIGHT?
NO.
IT'S NOT, PAL.

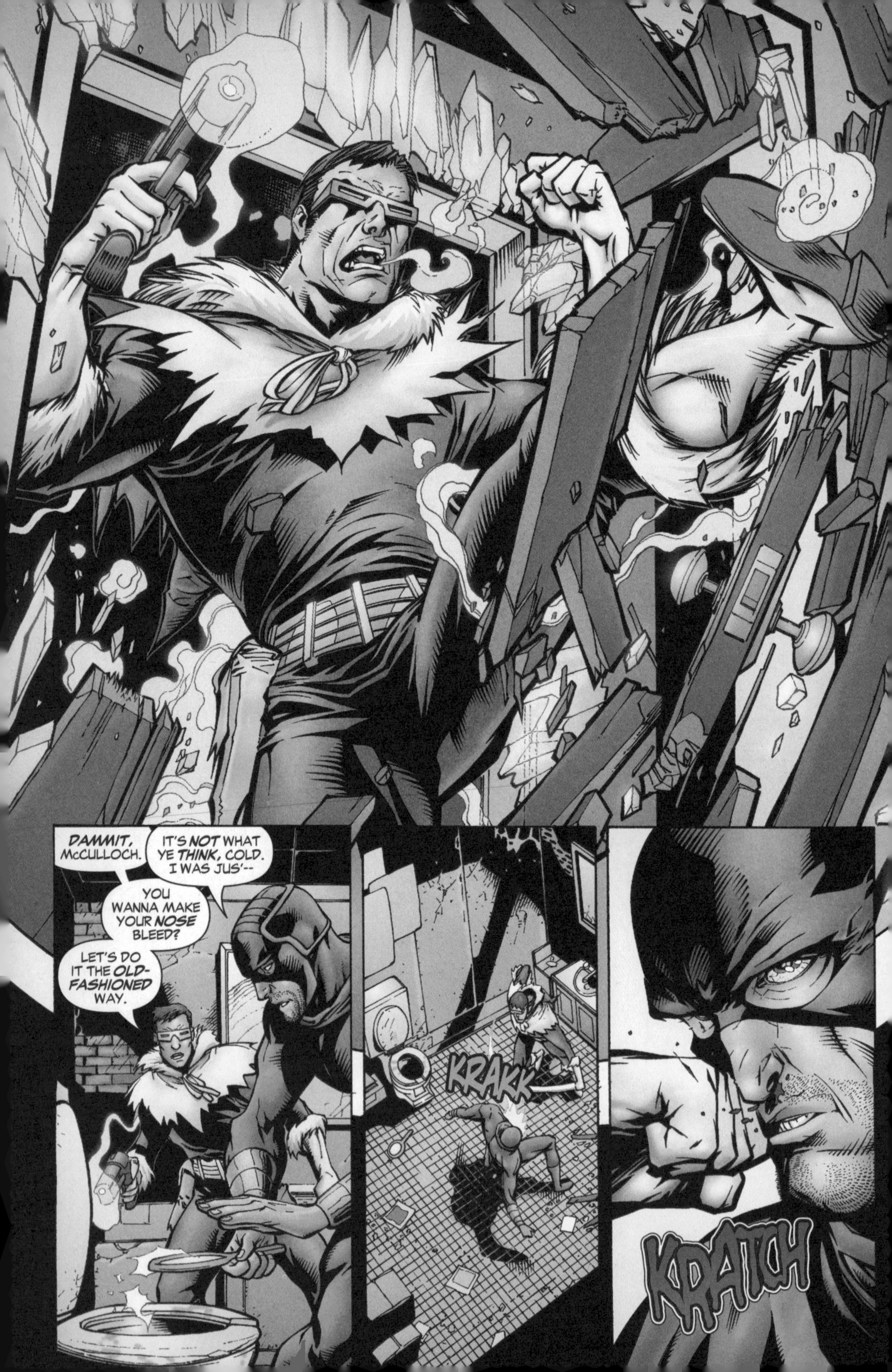
DAMMIT, McCULLOCH.
IT'S NOT WHAT YE THINK, COLD. I WAS JUS'--
YOU WANNA MAKE YOUR NOSE BLEED?
LET'S DO IT THE OLD-FASHIONED WAY.
KRAKK
KRATCH

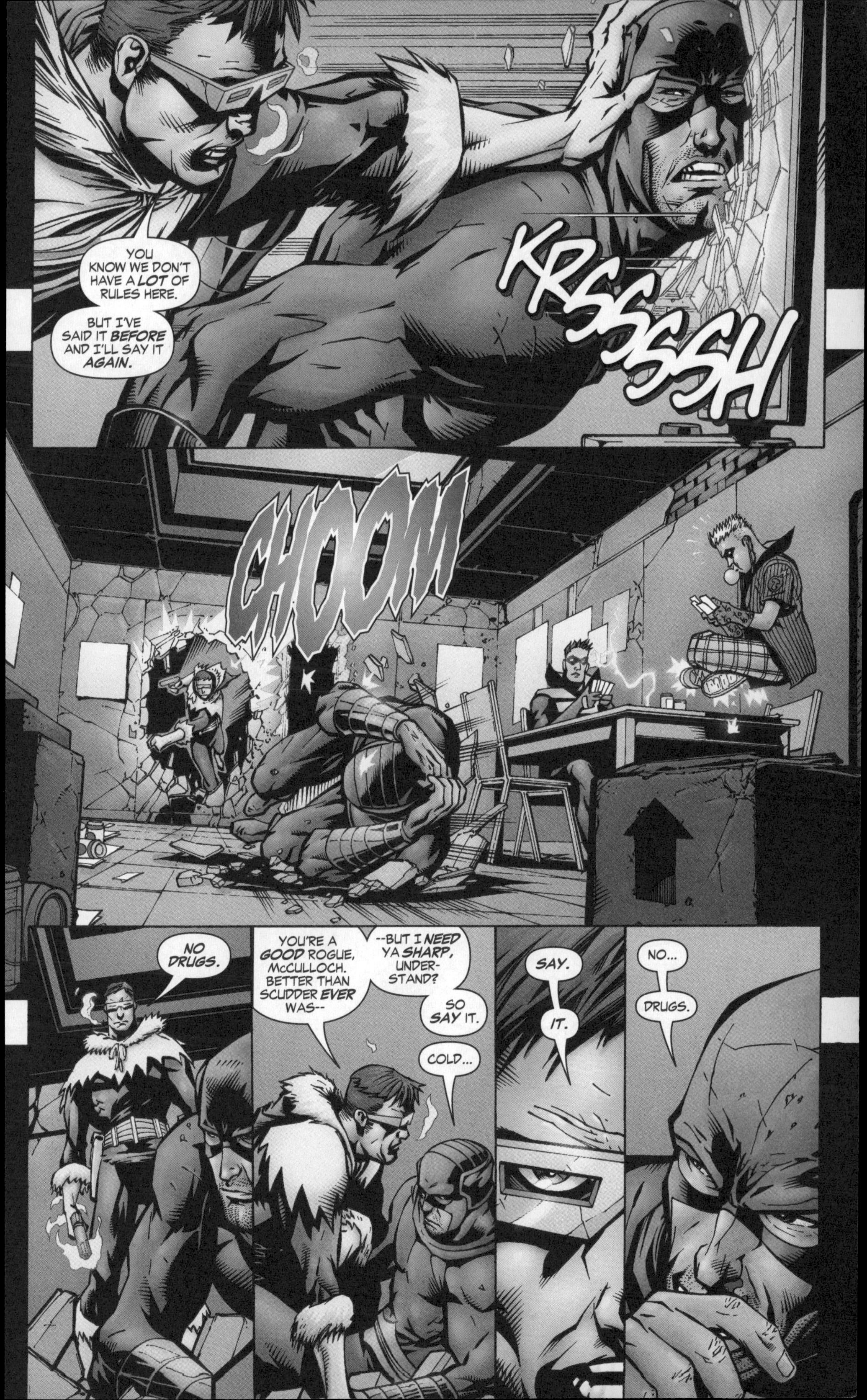
YOU KNOW WE DON'T HAVE A LOT OF RULES HERE.
BUT I'VE SAID IT BEFORE AND I'LL SAY IT AGAIN.
KRSSSSH
CHOOM
NO DRUGS.
YOU'RE A GOOD ROGUE, McCULLOCH. BETTER THAN SCUDDER EVER WAS--
--BUT I NEED YA SHARP, UNDER-STAND?
SO SAY IT.
COLD...
SAY.
IT.
NO...
DRUGS.

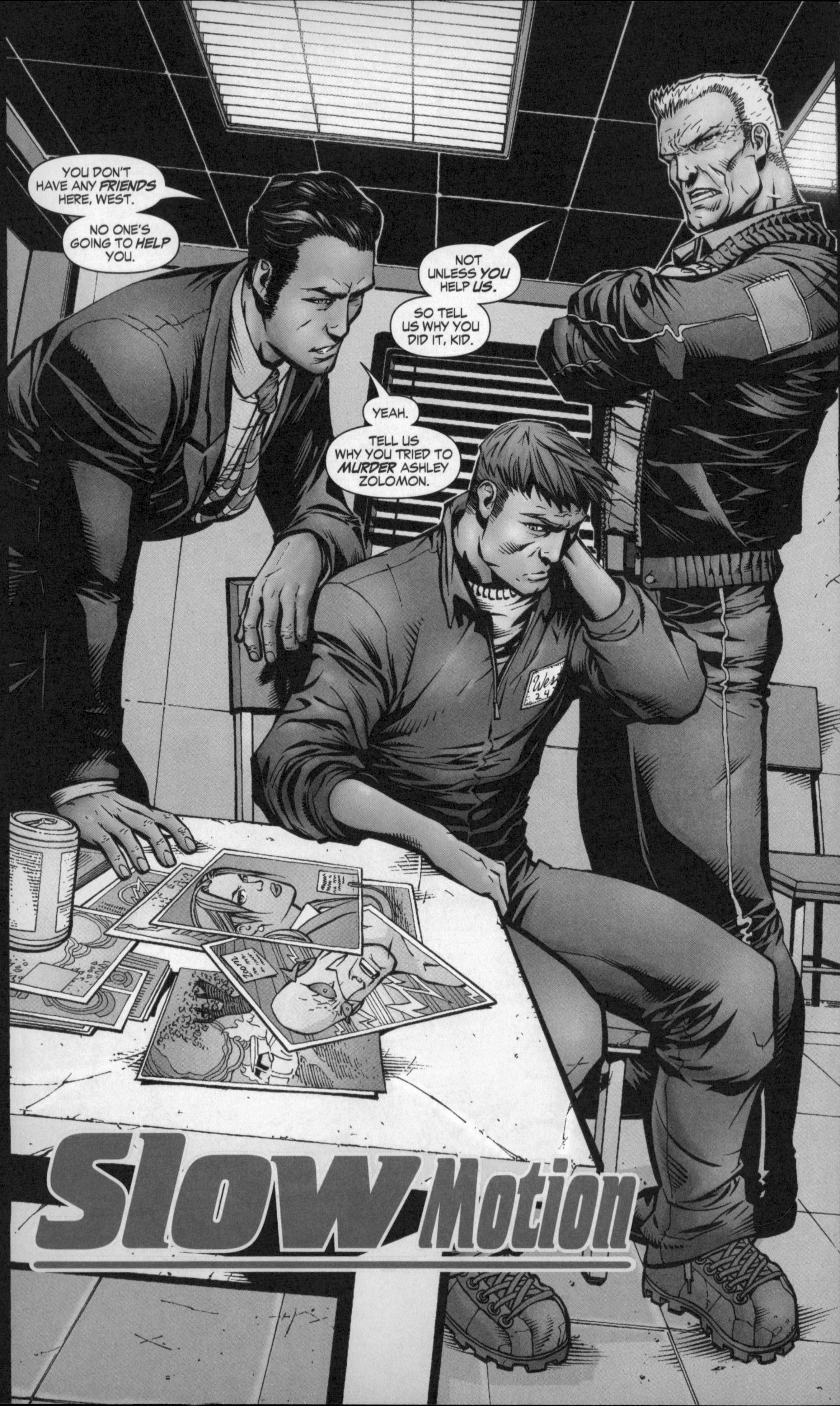
YOU DON'T HAVE ANY FRIENDS HERE, WEST.
NO ONE'S GOING TO HELP YOU.
NOT UNLESS YOU HELP US.
SO TELL US WHY YOU DID IT, KID.
YEAH.
TELL US WHY YOU TRIED TO MURDER ASHLEY ZOLOMON.
Slow Motion

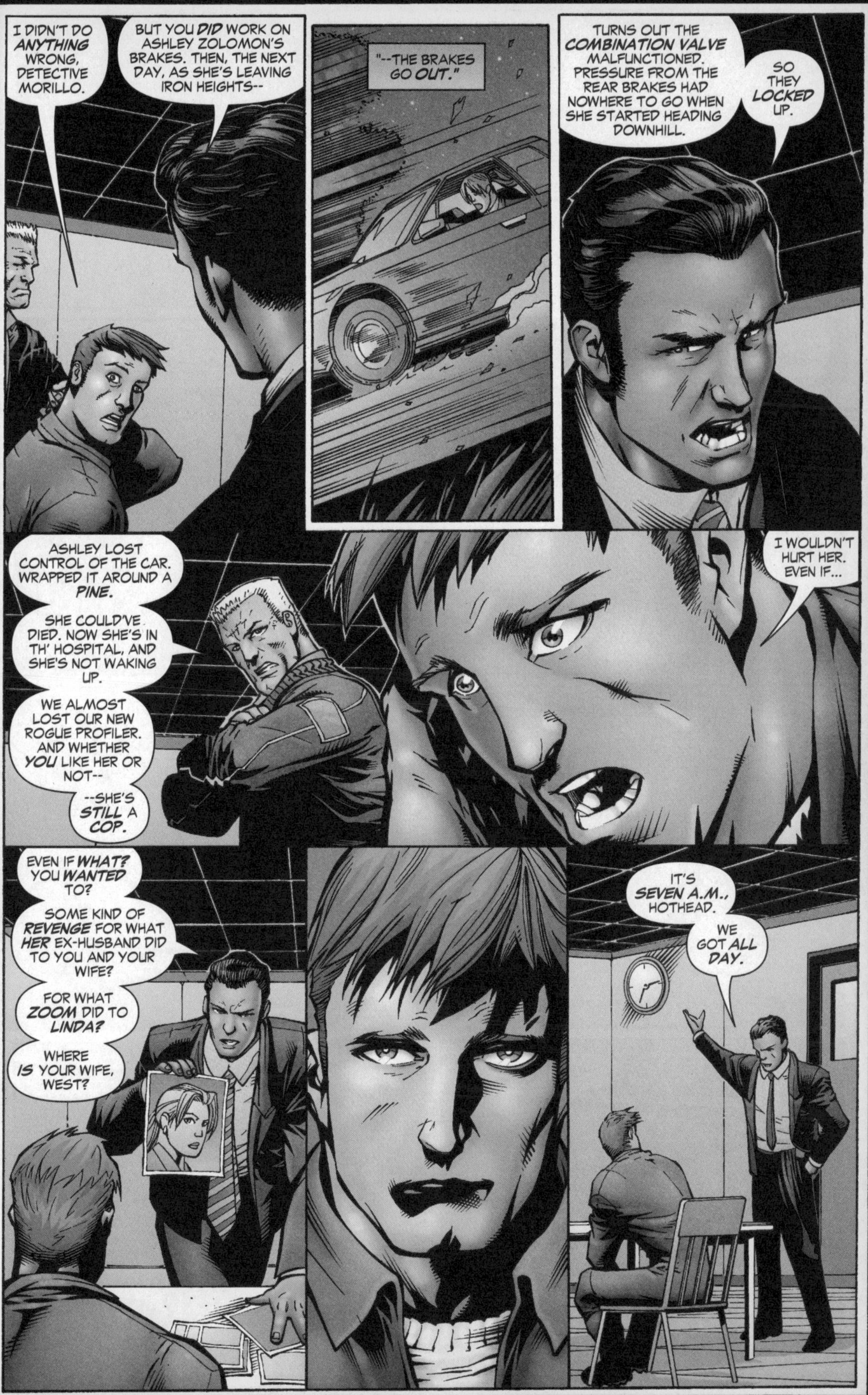

I DIDN'T DO ANYTHING WRONG, DETECTIVE MORILLO.
BUT YOU DID WORK ON ASHLEY ZOLOMON'S BRAKES. THEN, THE NEXT DAY, AS SHE'S LEAVING IRON HEIGHTS--
"--THE BRAKES GO OUT."
TURNS OUT THE COMBINATION VALVE MALFUNCTIONED. PRESSURE FROM THE REAR BRAKES HAD NOWHERE TO GO WHEN SHE STARTED HEADING DOWNHILL.
SO THEY LOCKED UP.
ASHLEY LOST CONTROL OF THE CAR. WRAPPED IT AROUND A PINE.
SHE COULD'VE DIED. NOW SHE'S IN TH' HOSPITAL, AND SHE'S NOT WAKING UP.
WE ALMOST LOST OUR NEW ROGUE PROFILER. AND WHETHER YOU LIKE HER OR NOT--
--SHE'S STILL A COP.
I WOULDN'T HURT HER. EVEN IF...
EVEN IF WHAT? YOU WANTED TO?
SOME KIND OF REVENGE FOR WHAT HER EX-HUSBAND DID TO YOU AND YOUR WIFE?
FOR WHAT ZOOM DID TO LINDA?
WHERE IS YOUR WIFE, WEST?
IT'S SEVEN A.M., HOTHEAD.
WE GOT ALL DAY.

CONGRATULATIONS, SAM!

YOU KNOW IF IT'S A *BOY* OR *GIRL* YET?

NO. WON'T KNOW FOR A FEW WEEKS.

WIFE WANTS TO WAIT THE FULL NINE MONTHS, BUT *ME?* I CAN'T STAND SUR-PRISES--

HEY!

THE PIPELINE USUALLY *STINKS*, ESPECIALLY WITH *GRODD* HERE, BUT THE TURTLE'S CELL IS PRETTY *RANK*.

I THINK THE OLD MAN *FINALLY* KICKED IT.

THE TURTLE

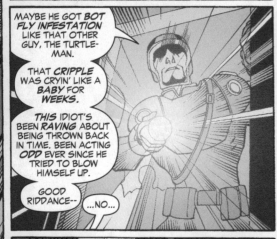

MAYBE HE GOT *BOT FLY* INFESTATION LIKE THAT OTHER GUY, THE TURTLE-MAN.

THAT *CRIPPLE* WAS CRYIN' LIKE A *BABY* FOR *WEEKS*.

THIS IDIOT'S BEEN *RAVING* ABOUT BEING THROWN BACK IN TIME. BEEN ACTING *ODD* EVER SINCE HE TRIED TO BLOW HIMSELF UP.

GOOD RIDDANCE--

...NO...

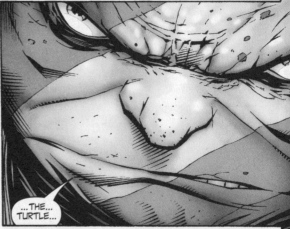

...THE... TURTLE...

LIVES.

RRNN.

ARRR.

MMM.

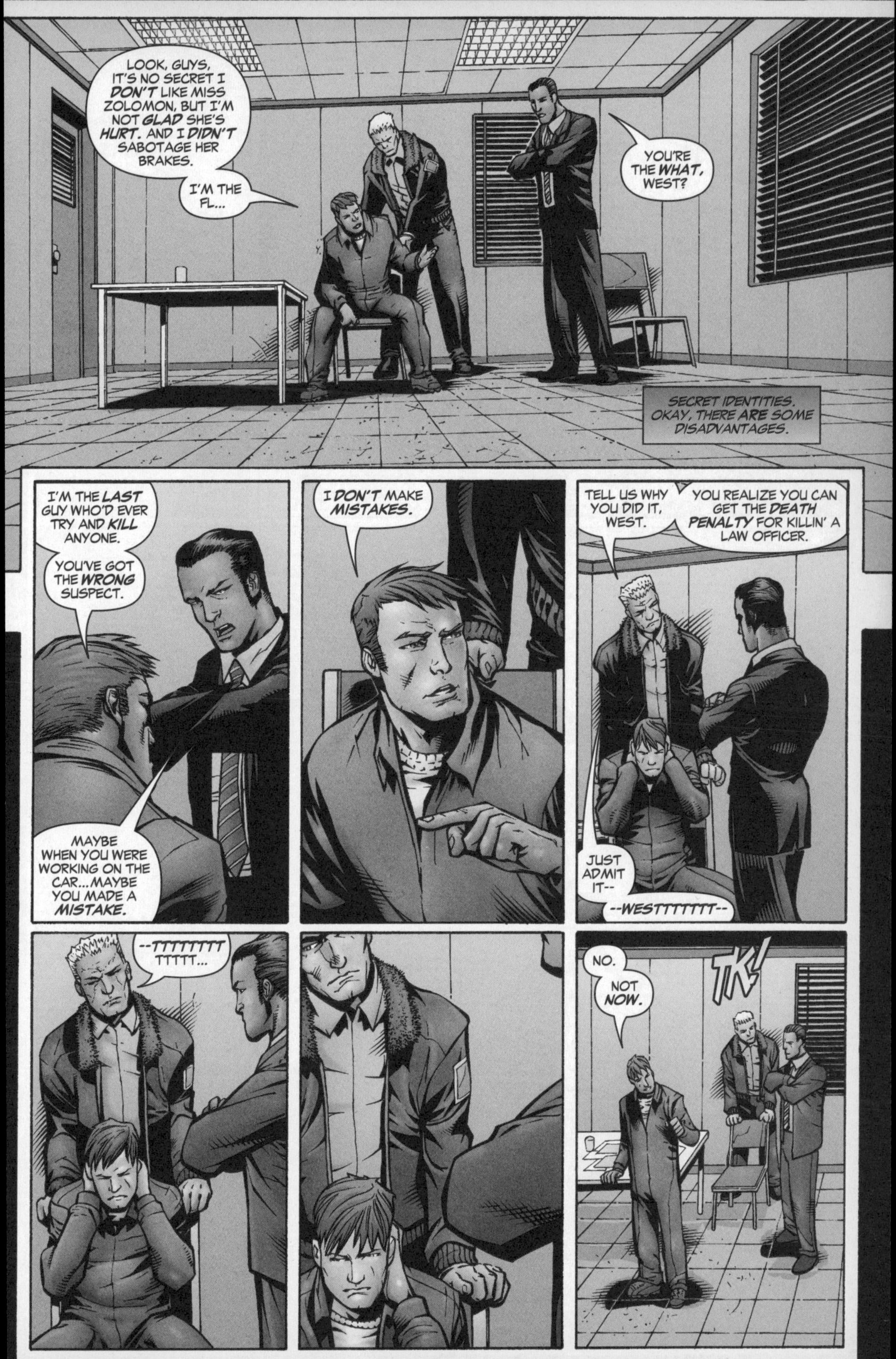
LOOK, GUYS, IT'S NO SECRET I DON'T LIKE MISS ZOLOMON, BUT I'M NOT GLAD SHE'S HURT. AND I DIDN'T SABOTAGE HER BRAKES.
I'M THE FL...
YOU'RE THE WHAT, WEST?
SECRET IDENTITIES. OKAY, THERE ARE SOME DISADVANTAGES.
I'M THE LAST GUY WHO'D EVER TRY AND KILL ANYONE.
YOU'VE GOT THE WRONG SUSPECT.
MAYBE WHEN YOU WERE WORKING ON THE CAR...MAYBE YOU MADE A MISTAKE.
I DON'T MAKE MISTAKES.
TELL US WHY YOU DID IT, WEST.
YOU REALIZE YOU CAN GET THE DEATH PENALTY FOR KILLIN' A LAW OFFICER.
JUST ADMIT IT--
--WESTTTTTTT--
--TTTTTTTT TTTTT...
NO.
NOT NOW.
TK!

TK!

WAIT A...

SOMETHING'S NOT RIGHT. CHYRE AND MORILLO HAVE STOPPED. THE CHATTER OUTSIDE HAS STOPPED. BUT THE CLOCK...

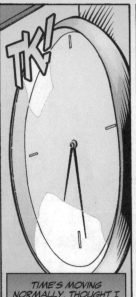

TK!

TIME'S MOVING NORMALLY. THOUGHT I KICKED INTO SPEED MODE BUT--

WHAT'S GOING ON?

KLIK

PUTTING ON THE SCARLET AND THE LIGHTNING IS USUALLY INSTINCTIVE. I CAN DO IT IN LESS THAN A MILLISECOND.

CHANGING BARELY REGISTERS. LIKE WHEN I'M RUNNING LONG DISTANCES. THE RELATIVE TIME WOULD BE DAYS, AND THAT WOULD DRIVE ME CRAZY.

BUT I CAN ZONE OUT AND MAKE IT SEEM INSTANT.

NOW...

ARMS AND LEGS WEIGH A THOUSAND POUNDS...

I FEEL LIKE--

--A REGULAR GUY.

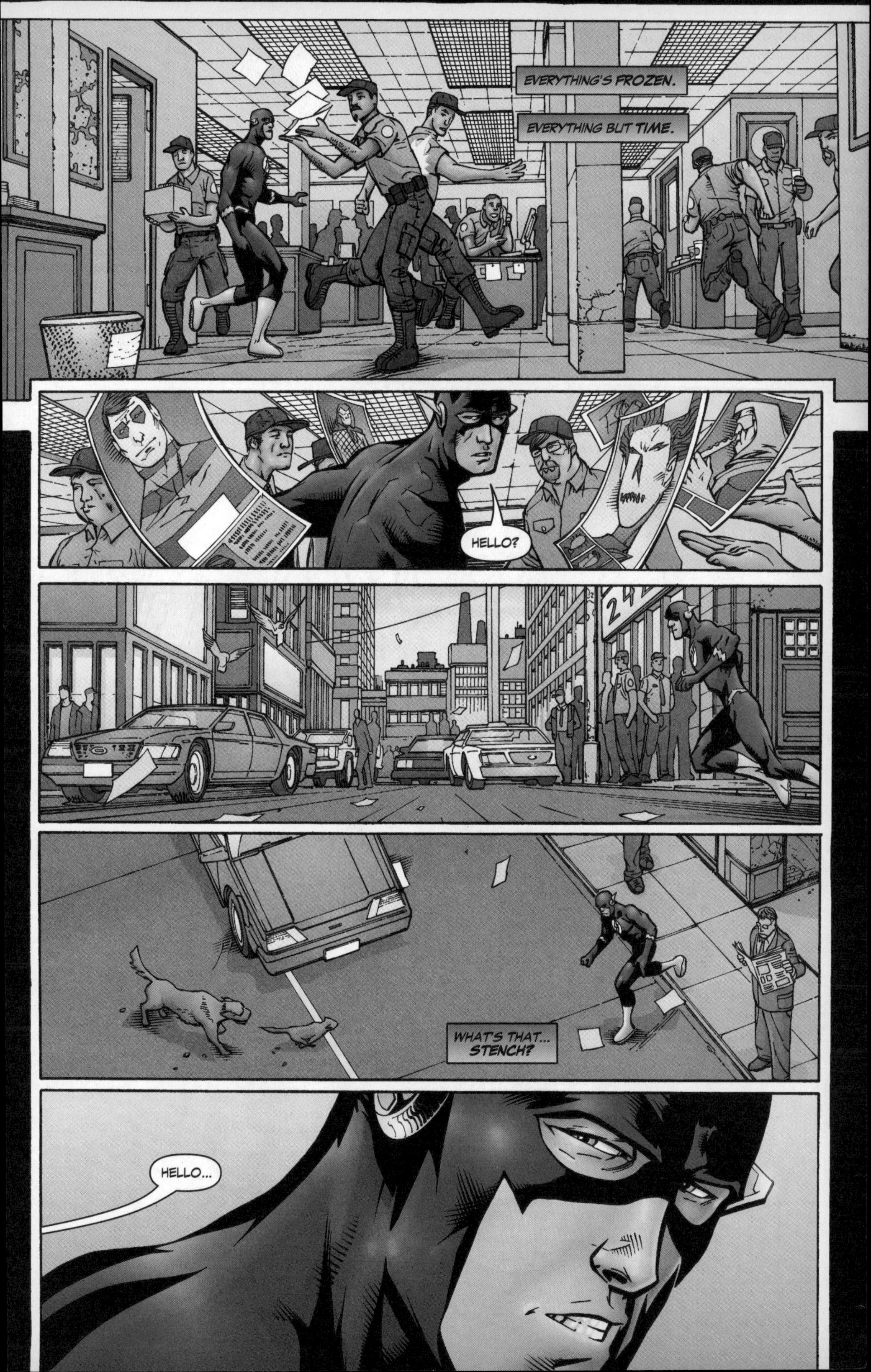
EVERYTHING'S FROZEN.
EVERYTHING BUT TIME.
HELLO?
WHAT'S THAT... STENCH?
HELLO...

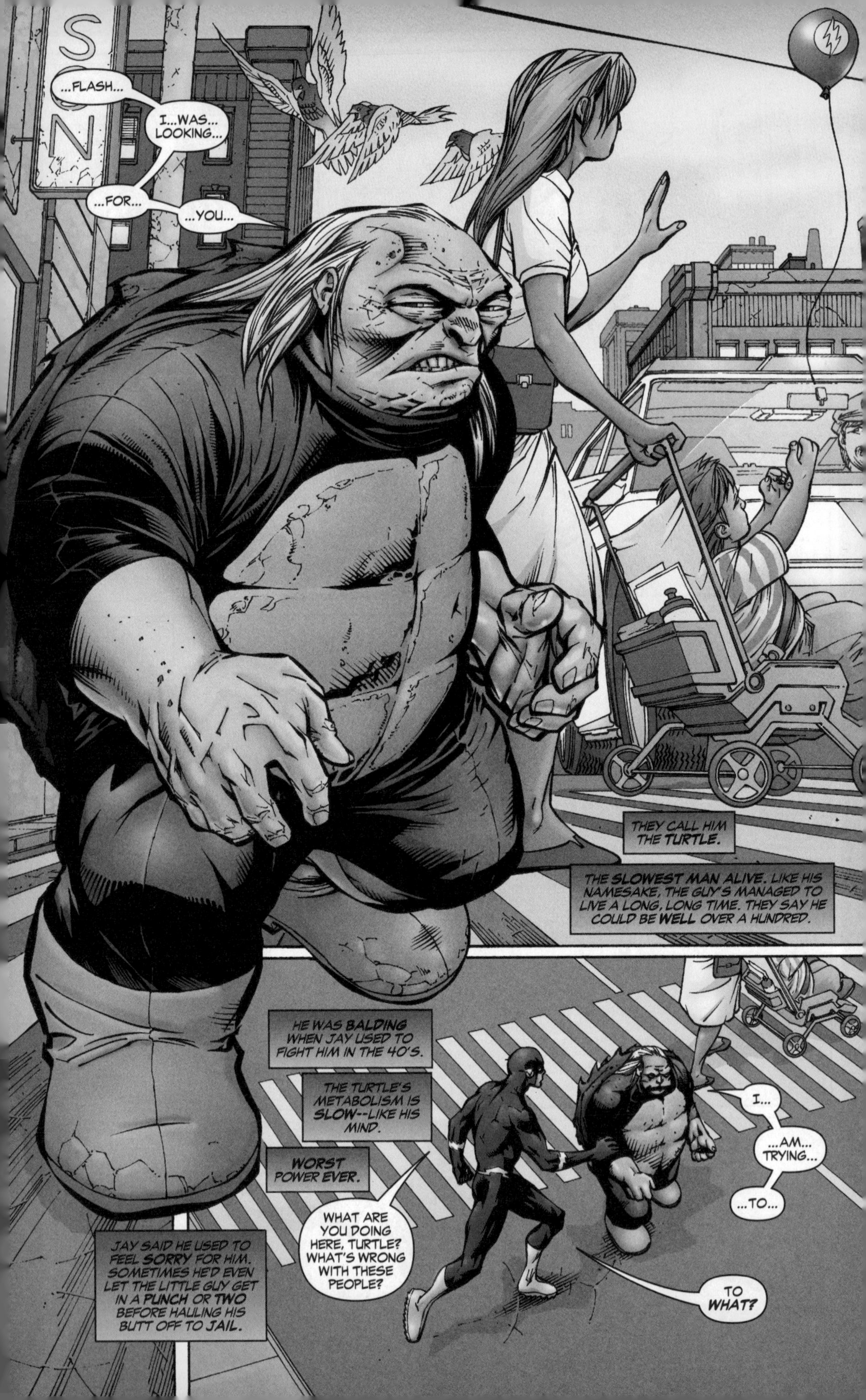
S
N
...FLASH...
I...WAS... LOOKING...
...FOR...
...YOU...
THEY CALL HIM THE TURTLE.
THE SLOWEST MAN ALIVE. LIKE HIS NAMESAKE, THE GUY'S MANAGED TO LIVE A LONG, LONG TIME. THEY SAY HE COULD BE WELL OVER A HUNDRED.
HE WAS BALDING WHEN JAY USED TO FIGHT HIM IN THE 40'S.
THE TURTLE'S METABOLISM IS SLOW--LIKE HIS MIND.
WORST POWER EVER.
JAY SAID HE USED TO FEEL SORRY FOR HIM. SOMETIMES HE'D EVEN LET THE LITTLE GUY GET IN A PUNCH OR TWO BEFORE HAULING HIS BUTT OFF TO JAIL.
WHAT ARE YOU DOING HERE, TURTLE? WHAT'S WRONG WITH THESE PEOPLE?
I...
...AM... TRYING...
...TO...
TO WHAT?

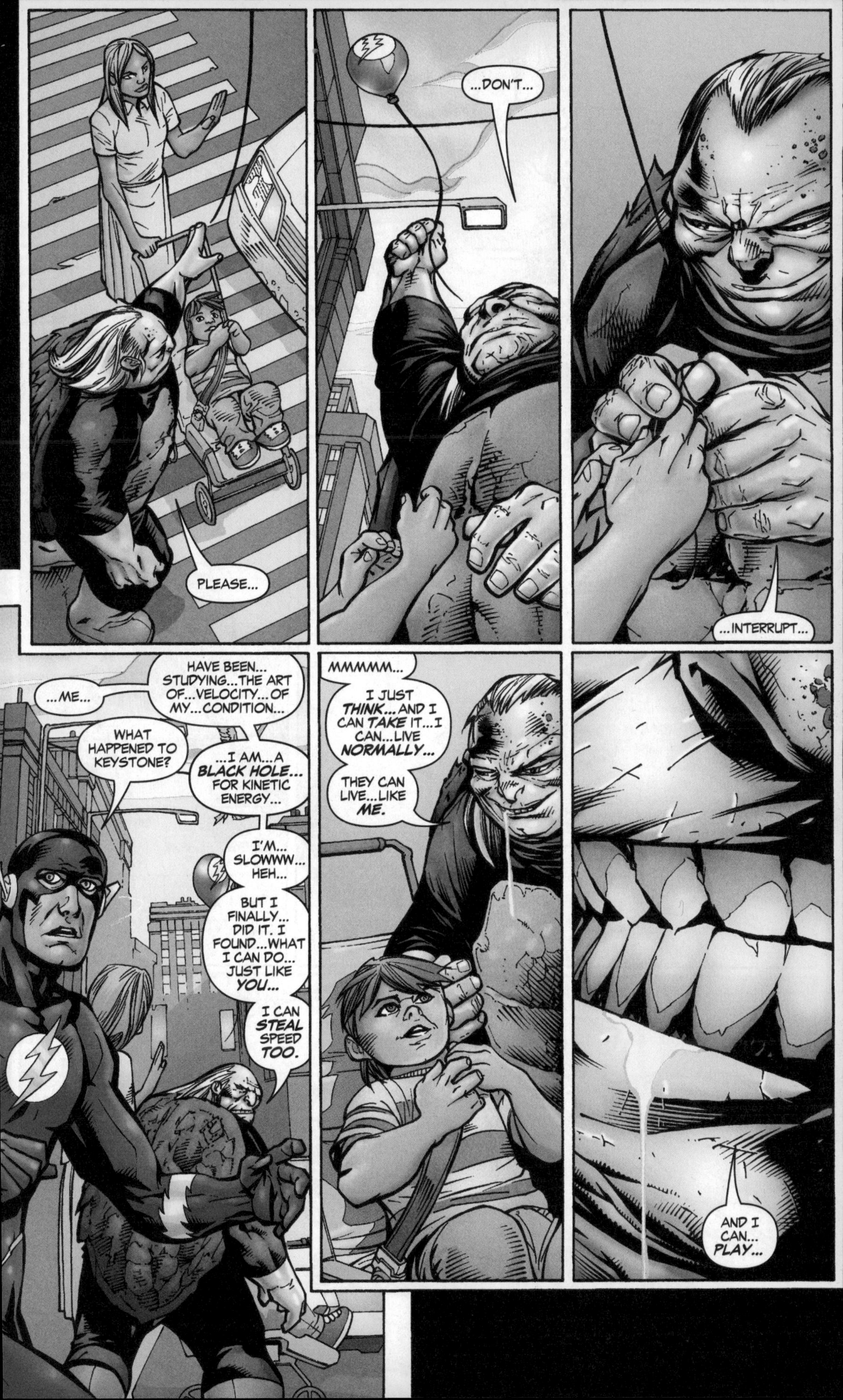
PLEASE...
...DON'T...
...INTERRUPT...
...ME...
HAVE BEEN... STUDYING...THE ART OF...VELOCITY...OF MY...CONDITION...
WHAT HAPPENED TO KEYSTONE?
...I AM...A BLACK HOLE... FOR KINETIC ENERGY...
I'M... SLOWWW... HEH...
BUT I FINALLY... DID IT. I FOUND...WHAT I CAN DO... JUST LIKE YOU...
I CAN STEAL SPEED TOO.
MMMMM...
I JUST THINK...AND I CAN TAKE IT...I CAN...LIVE NORMALLY...
THEY CAN LIVE...LIKE ME.
AND I CAN... PLAY...

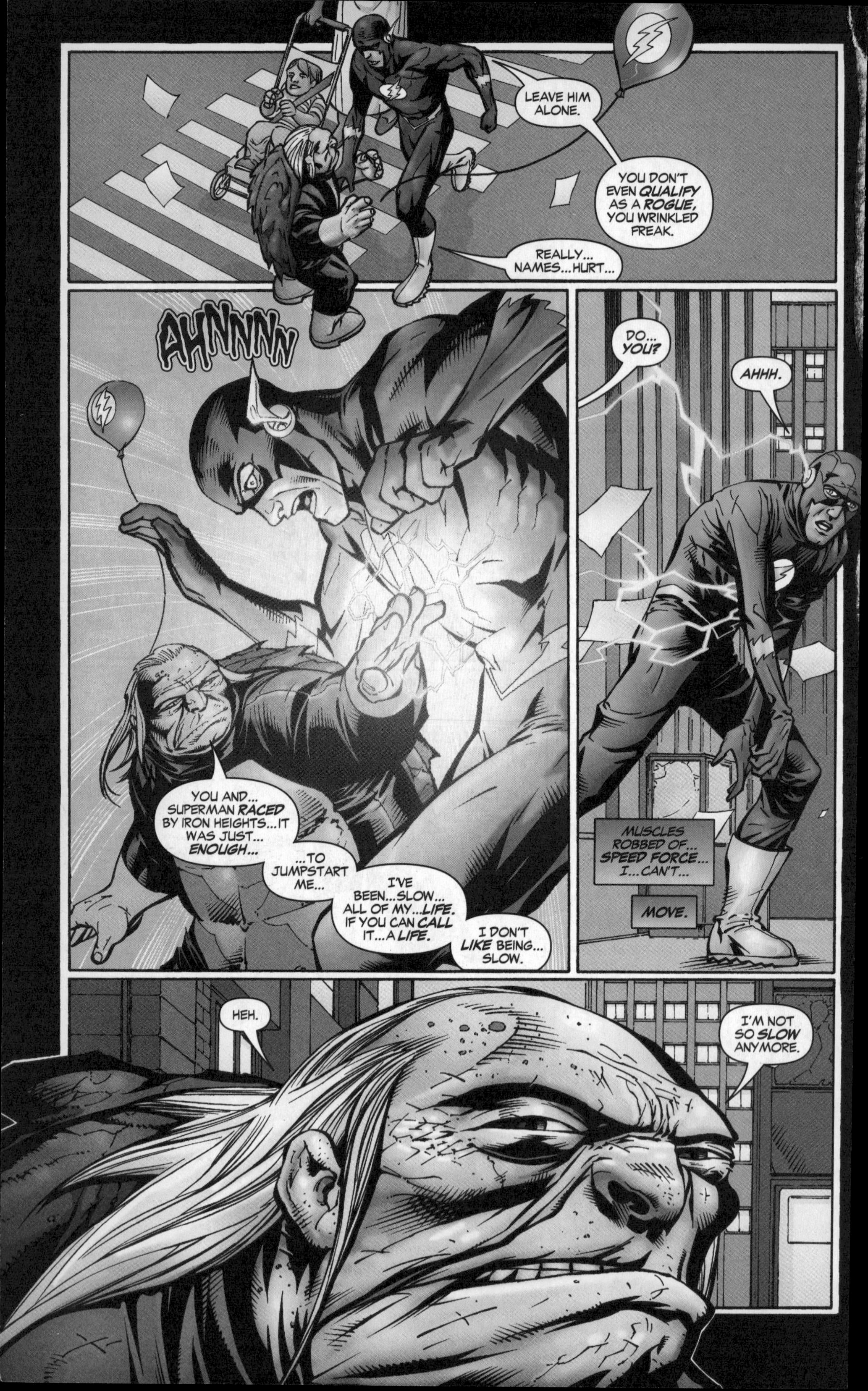
LEAVE HIM ALONE.
YOU DON'T EVEN QUALIFY AS A ROGUE, YOU WRINKLED FREAK.
REALLY... NAMES...HURT...
AHNNNN
YOU AND... SUPERMAN RACED BY IRON HEIGHTS...IT WAS JUST... ENOUGH...
...TO JUMPSTART ME...
I'VE BEEN...SLOW... ALL OF MY...LIFE. IF YOU CAN CALL IT...A LIFE.
I DON'T LIKE BEING... SLOW.
DO... YOU?
AHHH.
MUSCLES ROBBED OF... SPEED FORCE... I...CAN'T...
MOVE.
HEH.
I'M NOT SO SLOW ANYMORE.

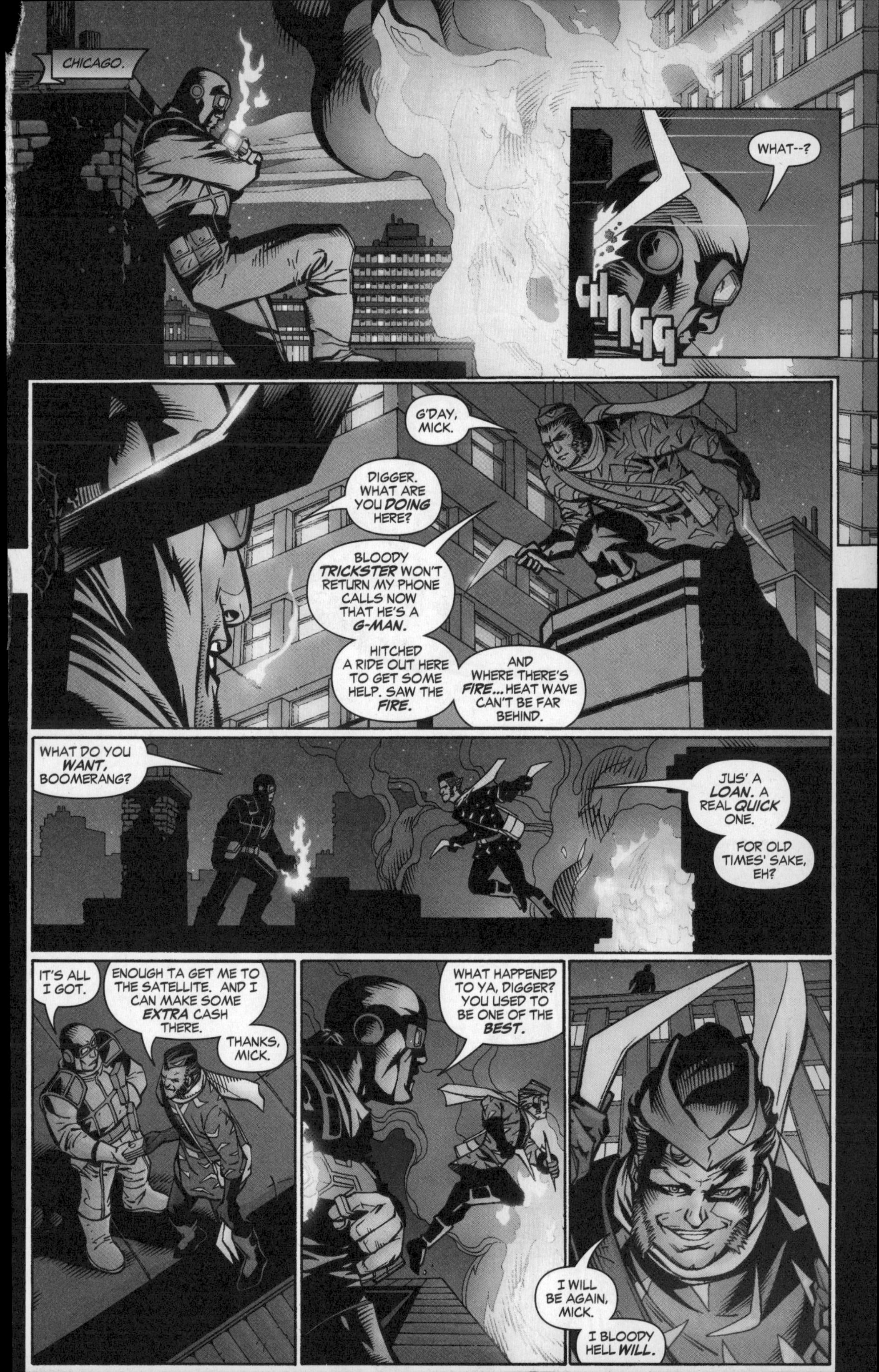
CHICAGO.
WHAT--?
CHNGG
G'DAY, MICK.
DIGGER. WHAT ARE YOU DOING HERE?
BLOODY TRICKSTER WON'T RETURN MY PHONE CALLS NOW THAT HE'S A G-MAN.
HITCHED A RIDE OUT HERE TO GET SOME HELP. SAW THE FIRE.
AND WHERE THERE'S FIRE... HEAT WAVE CAN'T BE FAR BEHIND.
WHAT DO YOU WANT, BOOMERANG?
JUS' A LOAN. A REAL QUICK ONE.
FOR OLD TIMES' SAKE, EH?
IT'S ALL I GOT.
ENOUGH TA GET ME TO THE SATELLITE. AND I CAN MAKE SOME EXTRA CASH THERE.
THANKS, MICK.
WHAT HAPPENED TO YA, DIGGER? YOU USED TO BE ONE OF THE BEST.
I WILL BE AGAIN, MICK.
I BLOODY HELL WILL.

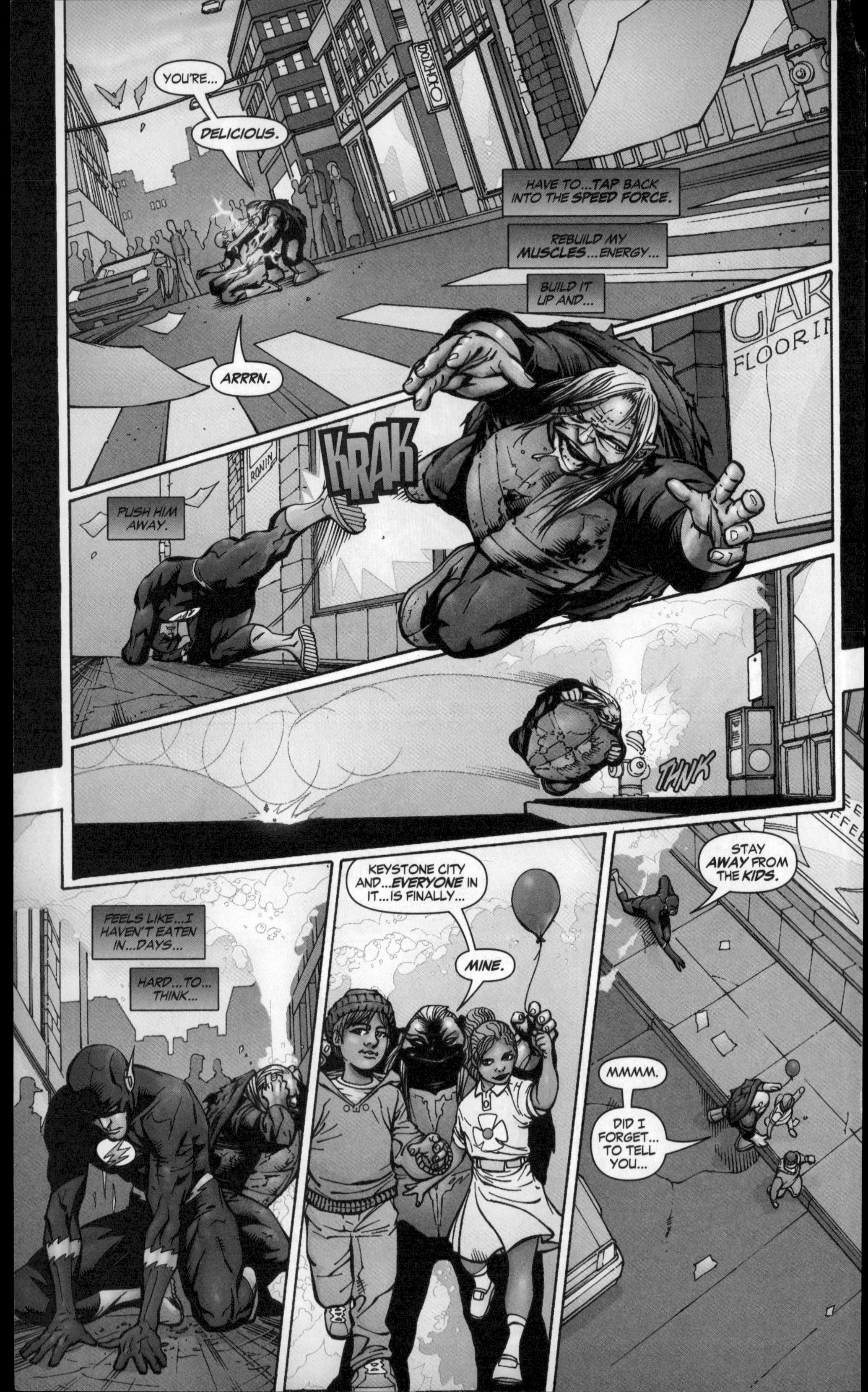

YOU'RE...
DELICIOUS.
KEYSTORE
HAVE TO...TAP BACK INTO THE SPEED FORCE.
REBUILD MY MUSCLES...ENERGY...
BUILD IT UP AND...
ARRRN.
FLOORIN
KRAK
RONIN
PUSH HIM AWAY.
THNK
FEELS LIKE...I HAVEN'T EATEN IN...DAYS...
HARD...TO... THINK...
KEYSTONE CITY AND...EVERYONE IN IT...IS FINALLY...
MINE.
STAY AWAY FROM THE KIDS.
MMMM.
DID I FORGET... TO TELL YOU...

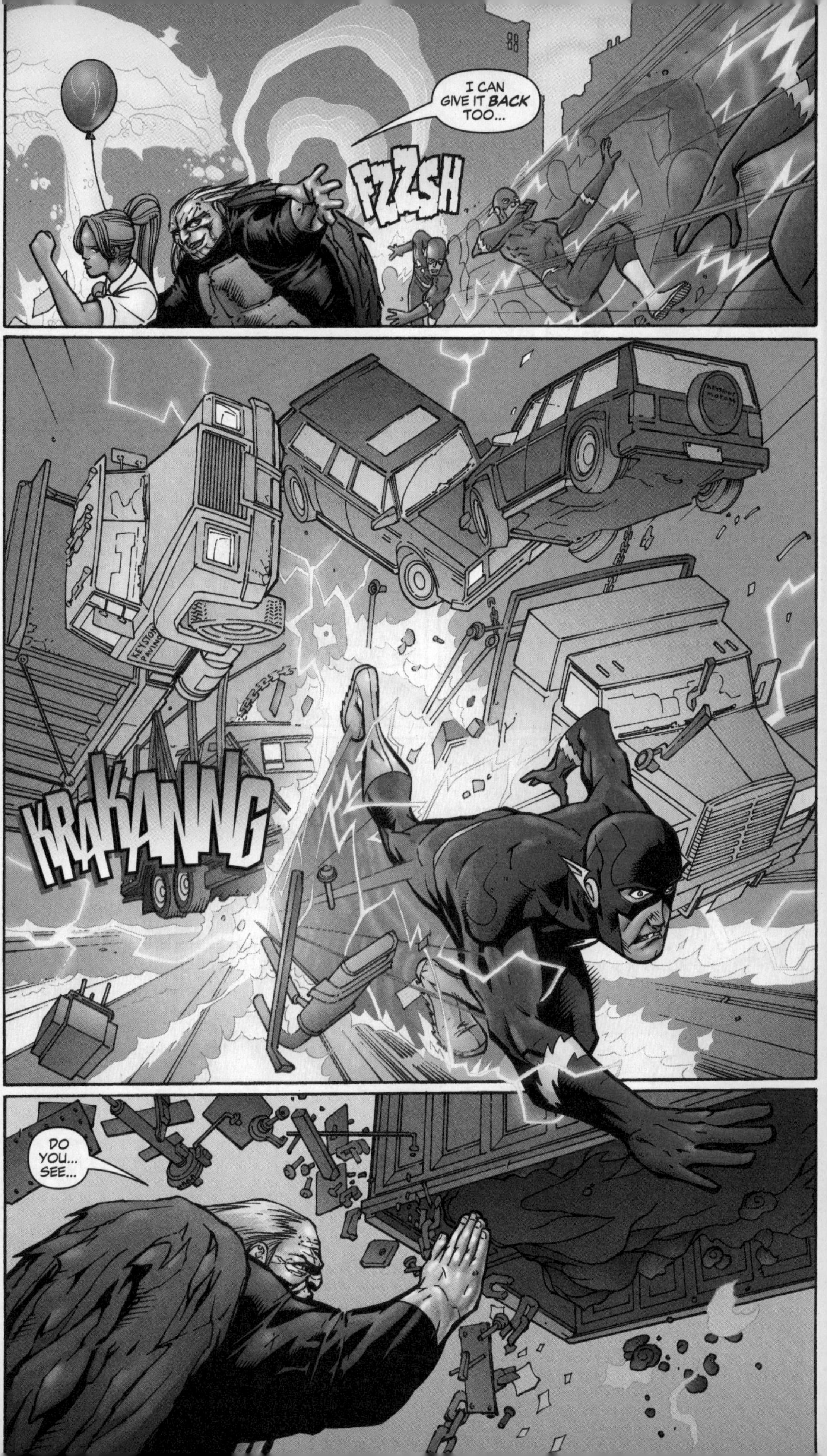

I CAN GIVE IT BACK TOO...
FZZSH
KRAKANNG
DO YOU... SEE...

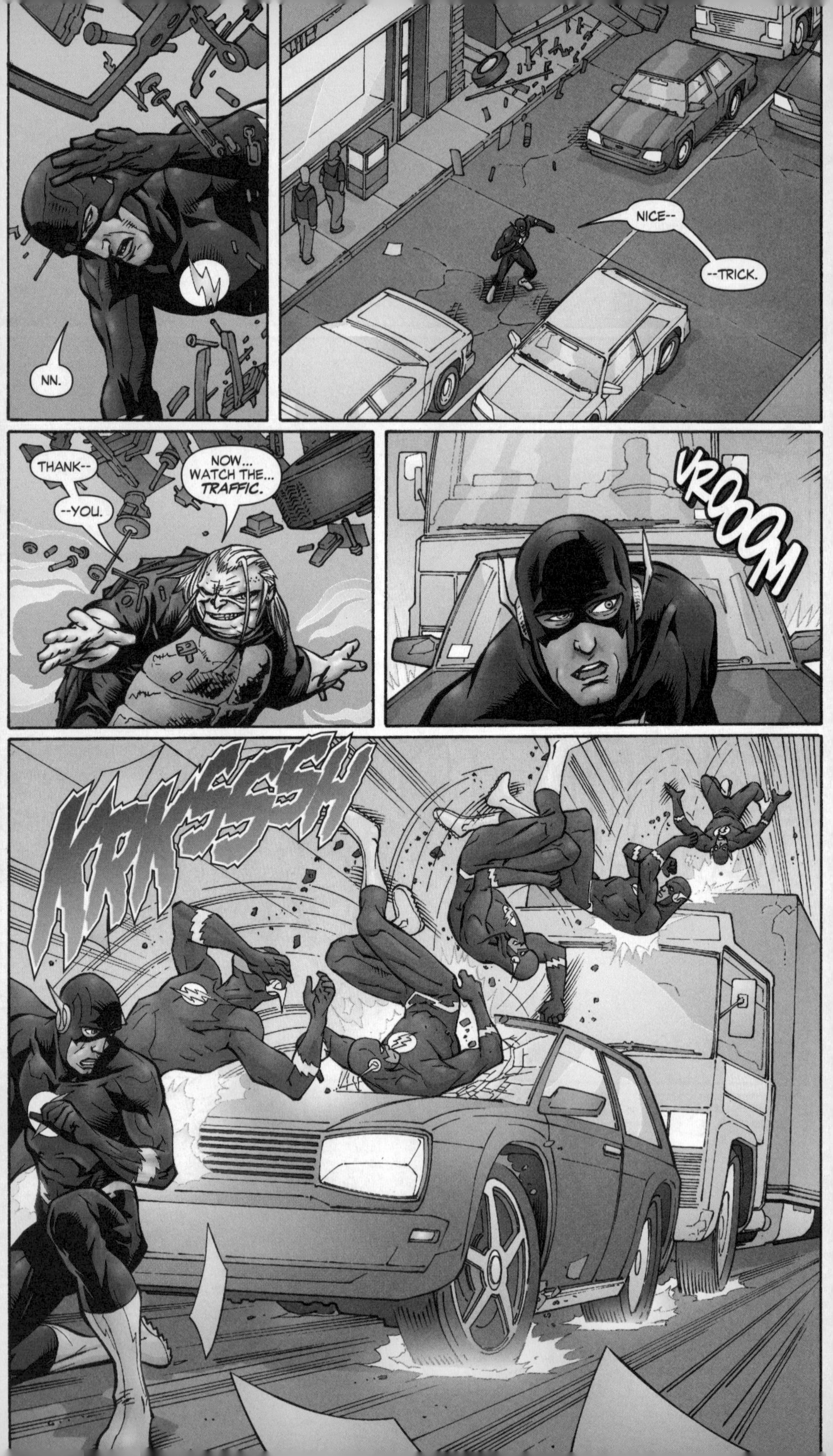
NN.
NICE--
--TRICK.
THANK--
--YOU.
NOW... WATCH THE... TRAFFIC.
VROOOOM
KRKSSSH

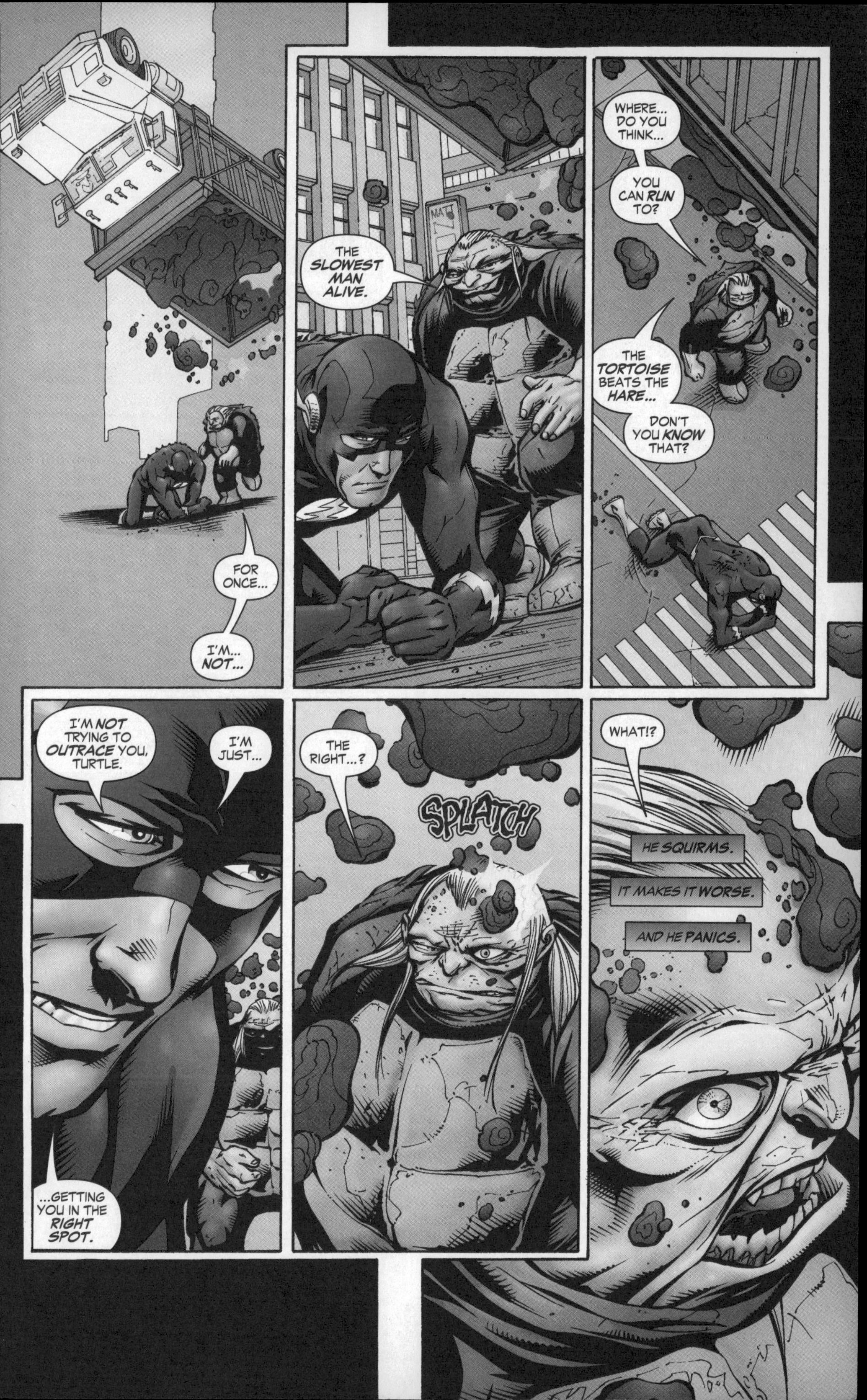

FOR ONCE...
I'M... NOT...
THE SLOWEST MAN ALIVE.
MATT
WHERE... DO YOU THINK...
YOU CAN RUN TO?
THE TORTOISE BEATS THE HARE...
DON'T YOU KNOW THAT?
I'M NOT TRYING TO OUTRACE YOU, TURTLE.
I'M JUST...
...GETTING YOU IN THE RIGHT SPOT.
THE RIGHT...?
SPLATCH
WHAT!?
HE SQUIRMS.
IT MAKES IT WORSE.
AND HE PANICS.

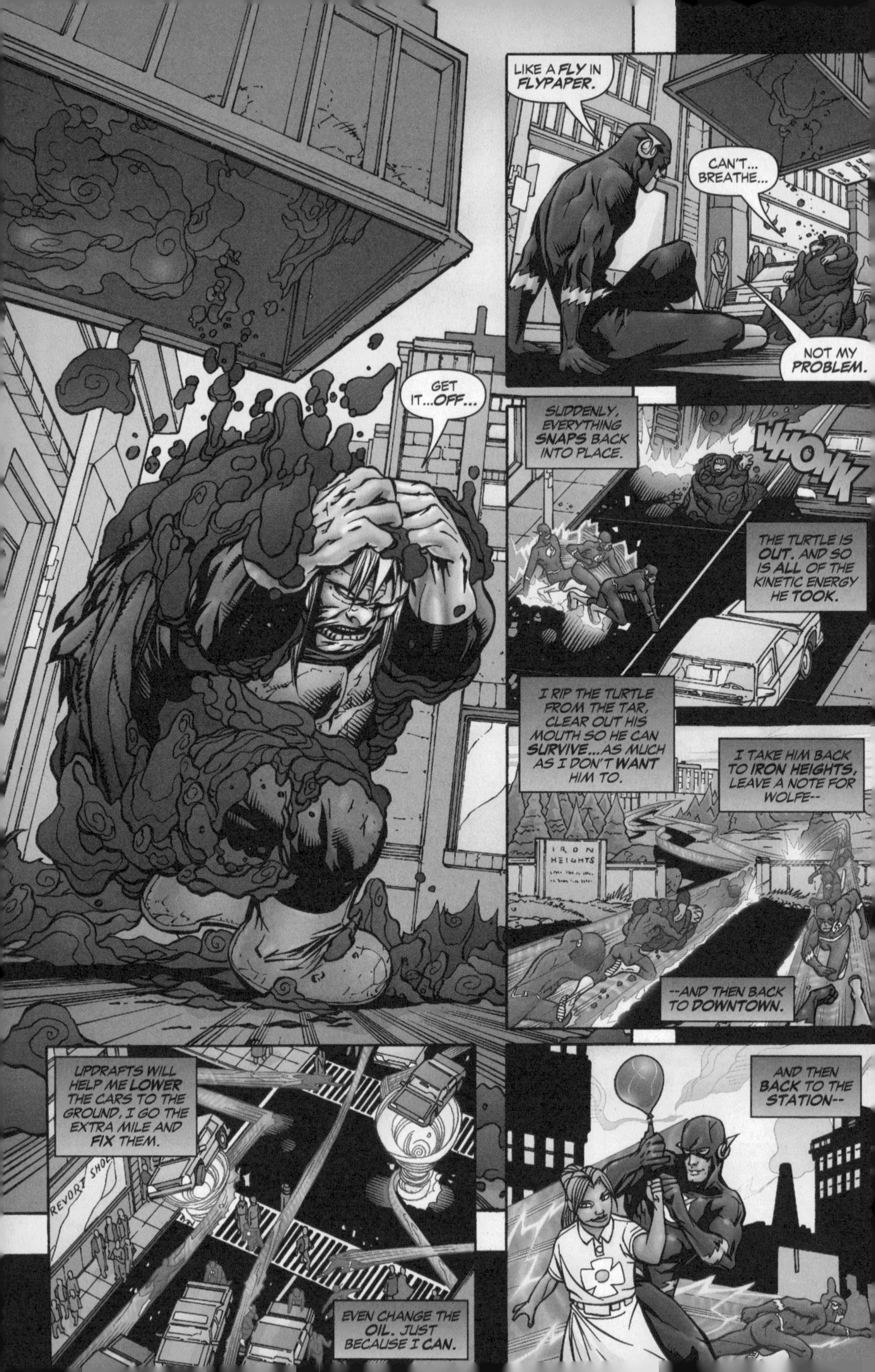
GET IT...OFF...
LIKE A FLY IN FLYPAPER.
CAN'T... BREATHE...
NOT MY PROBLEM.
SUDDENLY, EVERYTHING SNAPS BACK INTO PLACE.
WHONK
THE TURTLE IS OUT. AND SO IS ALL OF THE KINETIC ENERGY HE TOOK.
I RIP THE TURTLE FROM THE TAR, CLEAR OUT HIS MOUTH SO HE CAN SURVIVE...AS MUCH AS I DON'T WANT HIM TO.
I TAKE HIM BACK TO IRON HEIGHTS, LEAVE A NOTE FOR WOLFE--
IRON HEIGHTS
--AND THEN BACK TO DOWNTOWN.
UPDRAFTS WILL HELP ME LOWER THE CARS TO THE GROUND. I GO THE EXTRA MILE AND FIX THEM.
EVEN CHANGE THE OIL. JUST BECAUSE I CAN.
AND THEN BACK TO THE STATION--

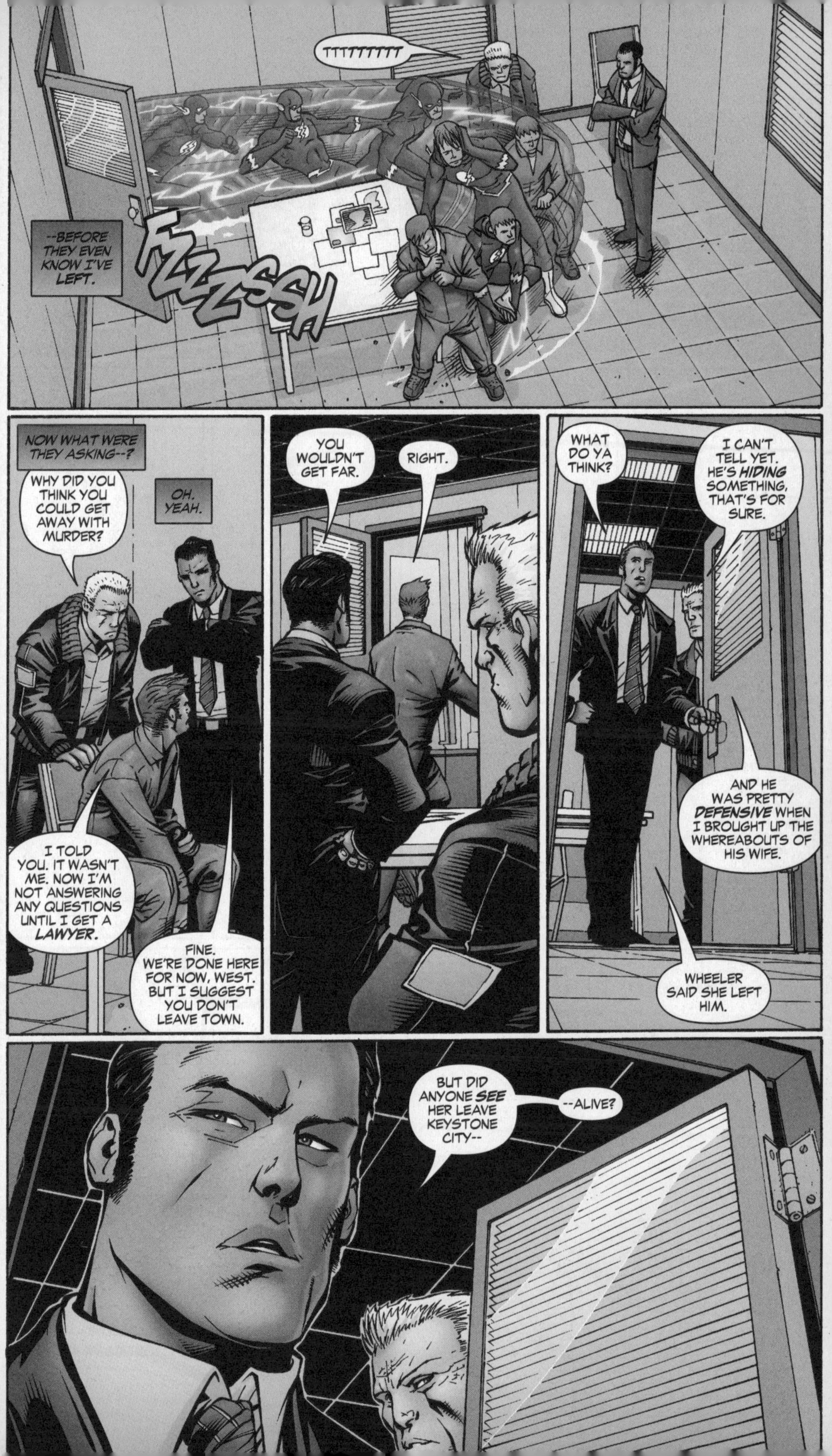
TTTTTTTTT
--BEFORE THEY EVEN KNOW I'VE LEFT.
FZZZSSH
NOW WHAT WERE THEY ASKING--?
WHY DID YOU THINK YOU COULD GET AWAY WITH MURDER?
OH. YEAH.
I TOLD YOU. IT WASN'T ME. NOW I'M NOT ANSWERING ANY QUESTIONS UNTIL I GET A LAWYER.
FINE. WE'RE DONE HERE FOR NOW, WEST. BUT I SUGGEST YOU DON'T LEAVE TOWN.
YOU WOULDN'T GET FAR.
RIGHT.
WHAT DO YA THINK?
I CAN'T TELL YET. HE'S HIDING SOMETHING, THAT'S FOR SURE.
AND HE WAS PRETTY DEFENSIVE WHEN I BROUGHT UP THE WHEREABOUTS OF HIS WIFE.
WHEELER SAID SHE LEFT HIM.
BUT DID ANYONE SEE HER LEAVE KEYSTONE CITY--
--ALIVE?

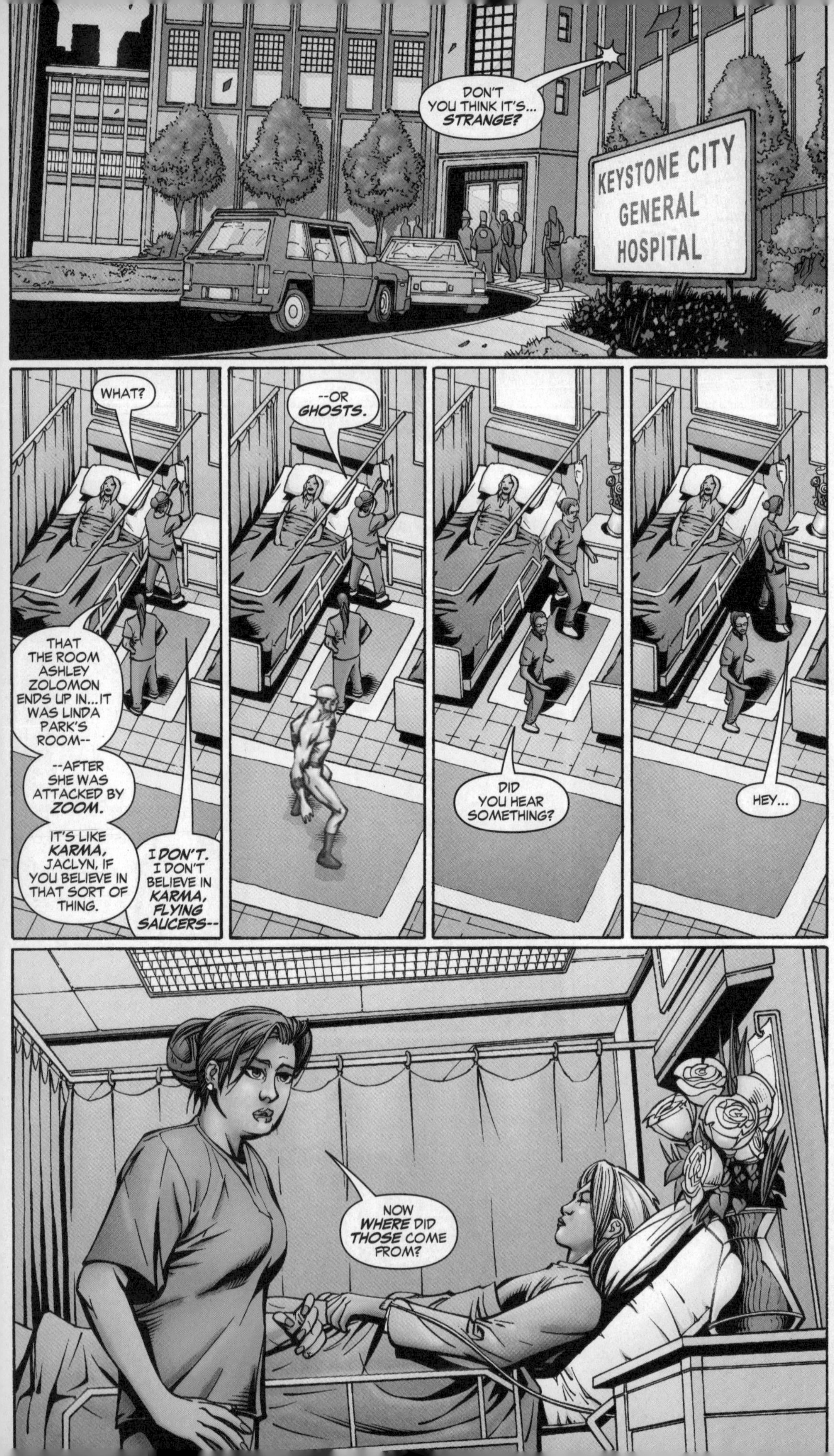
DON'T YOU THINK IT'S... STRANGE?
KEYSTONE CITY GENERAL HOSPITAL
WHAT?
THAT THE ROOM ASHLEY ZOLOMON ENDS UP IN...IT WAS LINDA PARK'S ROOM--
--AFTER SHE WAS ATTACKED BY ZOOM.
IT'S LIKE KARMA, JACLYN, IF YOU BELIEVE IN THAT SORT OF THING.
I DON'T. I DON'T BELIEVE IN KARMA, FLYING SAUCERS--
--OR GHOSTS.
DID YOU HEAR SOMETHING?
HEY...
NOW WHERE DID THOSE COME FROM?

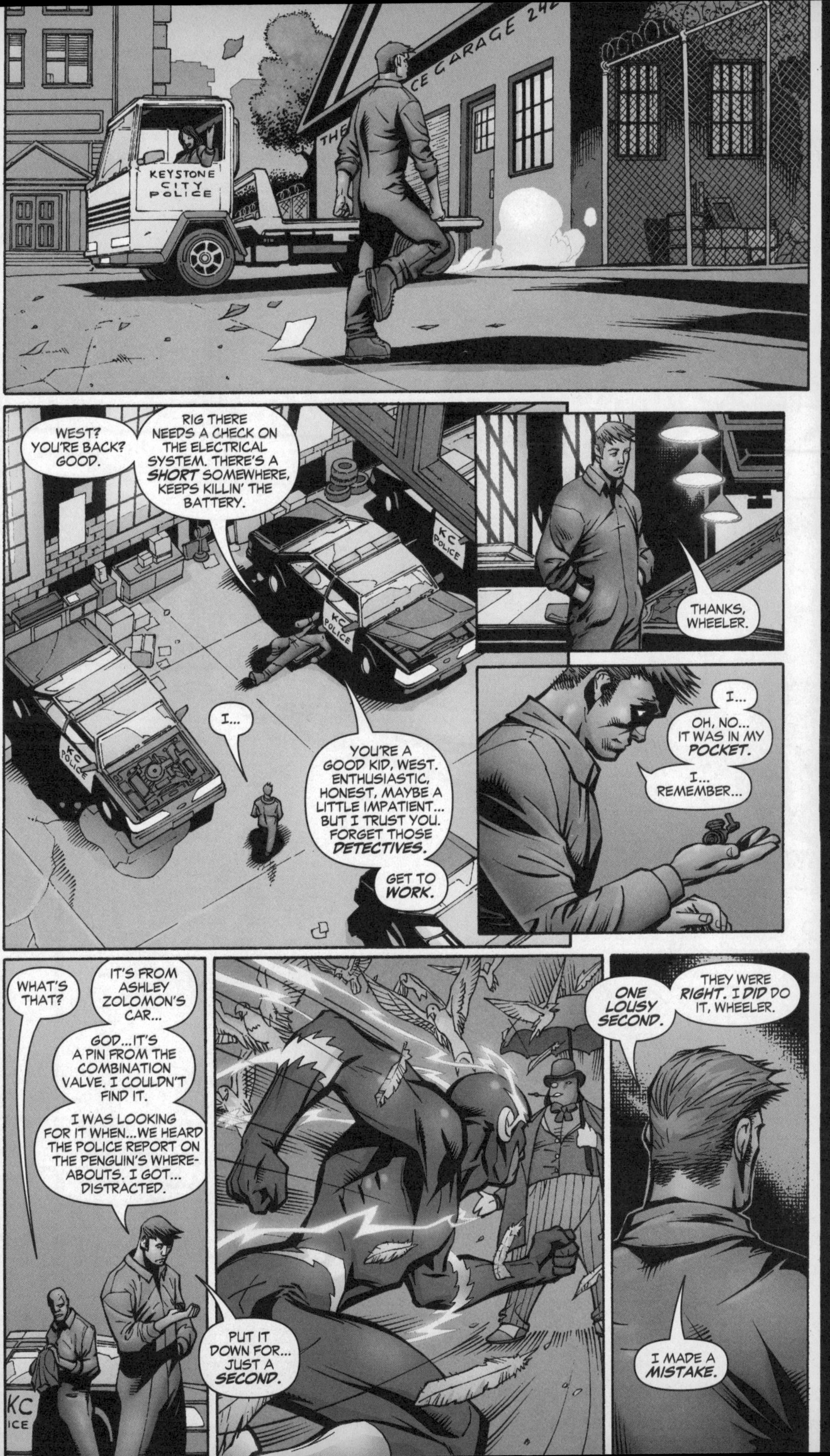
KEYSTONE CITY POLICE
WEST? YOU'RE BACK? GOOD.
RIG THERE NEEDS A CHECK ON THE ELECTRICAL SYSTEM. THERE'S A SHORT SOMEWHERE, KEEPS KILLIN' THE BATTERY.
THANKS, WHEELER.
I...
YOU'RE A GOOD KID, WEST. ENTHUSIASTIC, HONEST, MAYBE A LITTLE IMPATIENT... BUT I TRUST YOU. FORGET THOSE DETECTIVES.
GET TO WORK.
I...
OH, NO... IT WAS IN MY POCKET.
I... REMEMBER...
WHAT'S THAT?
IT'S FROM ASHLEY ZOLOMON'S CAR...
GOD...IT'S A PIN FROM THE COMBINATION VALVE. I COULDN'T FIND IT.
I WAS LOOKING FOR IT WHEN...WE HEARD THE POLICE REPORT ON THE PENGUIN'S WHERE-ABOUTS. I GOT... DISTRACTED.
PUT IT DOWN FOR... JUST A SECOND.
ONE LOUSY SECOND.
THEY WERE RIGHT. I DID DO IT, WHEELER.
I MADE A MISTAKE.

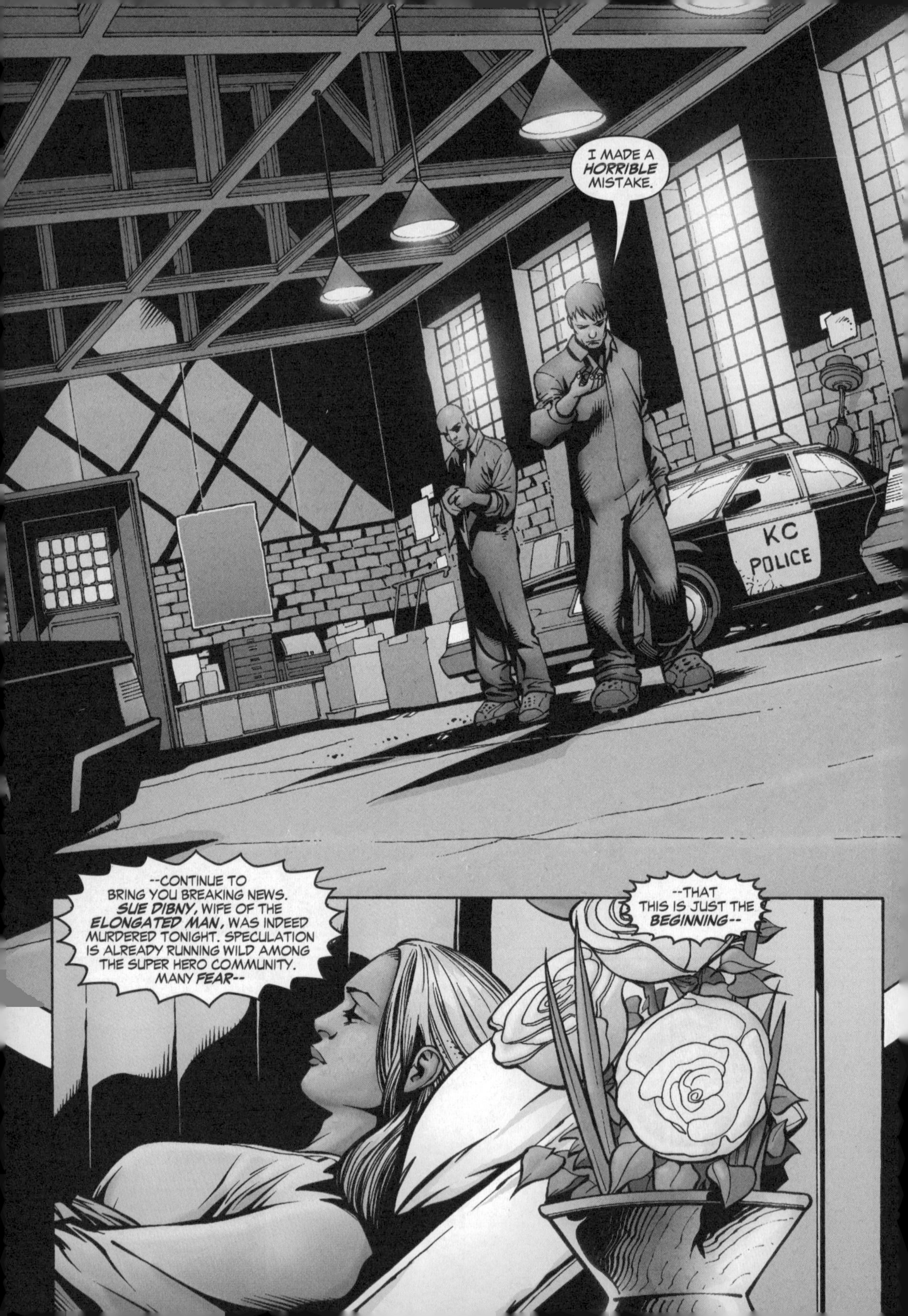
I MADE A HORRIBLE MISTAKE.
KC POLICE
--CONTINUE TO BRING YOU BREAKING NEWS. SUE DIBNY, WIFE OF THE ELONGATED MAN, WAS INDEED MURDERED TONIGHT. SPECULATION IS ALREADY RUNNING WILD AMONG THE SUPER HERO COMMUNITY. MANY FEAR--
--THAT THIS IS JUST THE BEGINNING--

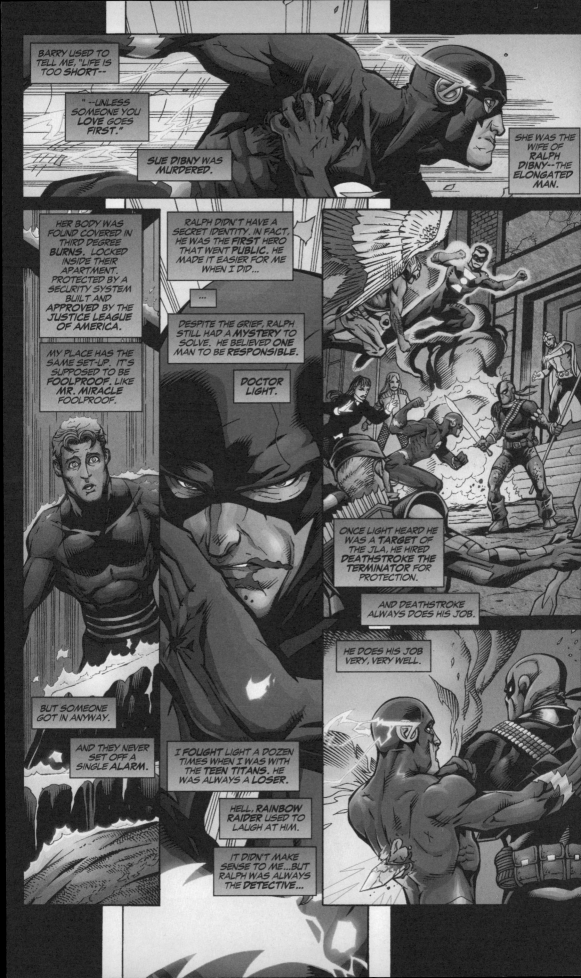

BARRY USED TO TELL ME, "LIFE IS TOO SHORT--

"--UNLESS SOMEONE YOU LOVE GOES FIRST."

SUE DIBNY WAS MURDERED.

SHE WAS THE WIFE OF RALPH DIBNY--THE ELONGATED MAN.

HER BODY WAS FOUND COVERED IN THIRD DEGREE BURNS. LOCKED INSIDE THEIR APARTMENT. PROTECTED BY A SECURITY SYSTEM BUILT AND APPROVED BY THE JUSTICE LEAGUE OF AMERICA.

RALPH DIDN'T HAVE A SECRET IDENTITY. IN FACT, HE WAS THE FIRST HERO THAT WENT PUBLIC. HE MADE IT EASIER FOR ME WHEN I DID...

...

DESPITE THE GRIEF, RALPH STILL HAD A MYSTERY TO SOLVE. HE BELIEVED ONE MAN TO BE RESPONSIBLE.

MY PLACE HAS THE SAME SET-UP. IT'S SUPPOSED TO BE FOOLPROOF. LIKE MR. MIRACLE FOOLPROOF.

DOCTOR LIGHT.

ONCE LIGHT HEARD HE WAS A TARGET OF THE JLA, HE HIRED DEATHSTROKE THE TERMINATOR FOR PROTECTION.

AND DEATHSTROKE ALWAYS DOES HIS JOB.

HE DOES HIS JOB VERY, VERY WELL.

BUT SOMEONE GOT IN ANYWAY.

AND THEY NEVER SET OFF A SINGLE ALARM.

I FOUGHT LIGHT A DOZEN TIMES WHEN I WAS WITH THE TEEN TITANS. HE WAS ALWAYS A LOSER.

HELL, RAINBOW RAIDER USED TO LAUGH AT HIM.

IT DIDN'T MAKE SENSE TO ME...BUT RALPH WAS ALWAYS THE DETECTIVE...

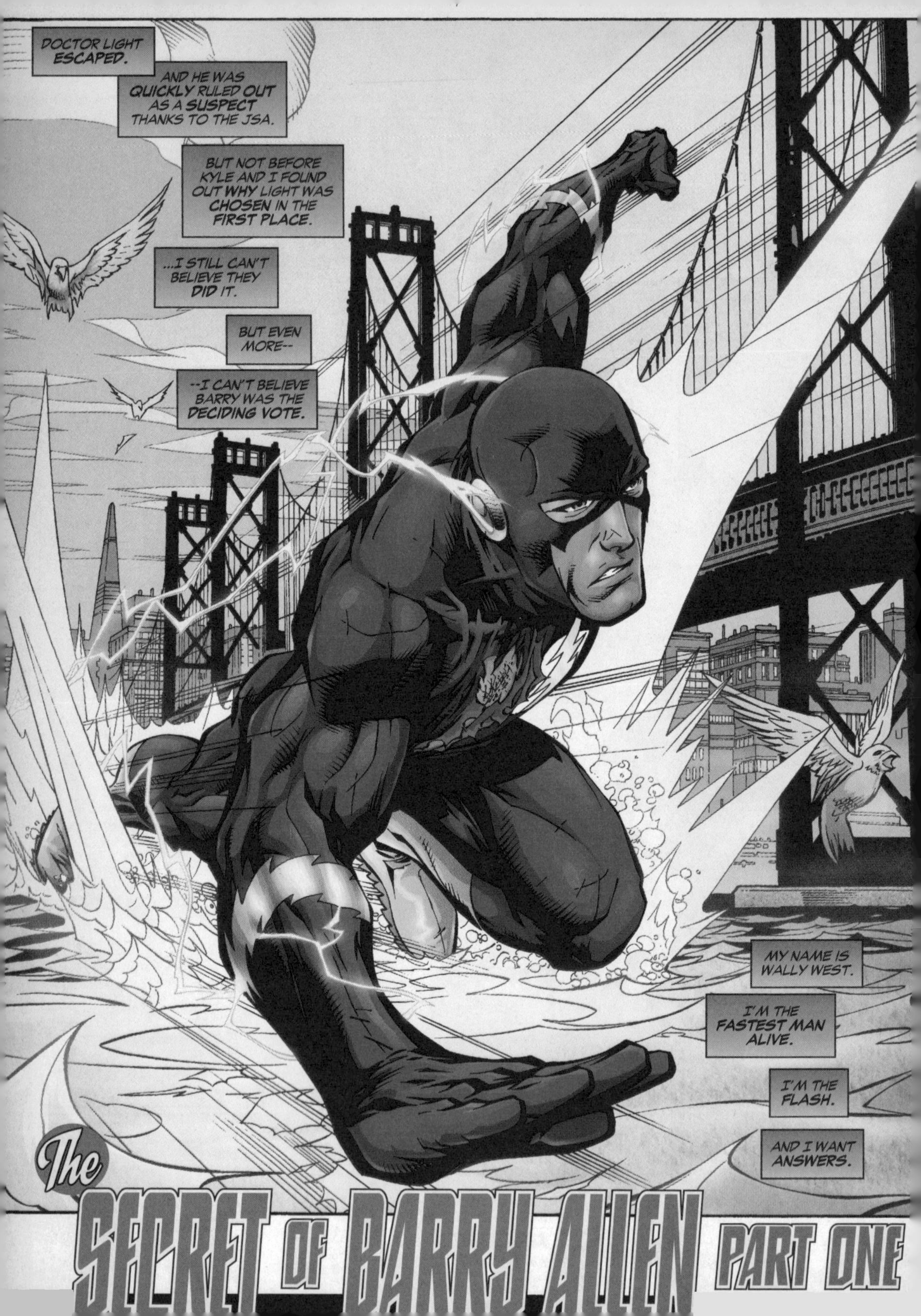
DOCTOR LIGHT ESCAPED.
AND HE WAS QUICKLY RULED OUT AS A SUSPECT THANKS TO THE JSA.
BUT NOT BEFORE KYLE AND I FOUND OUT WHY LIGHT WAS CHOSEN IN THE FIRST PLACE.
...I STILL CAN'T BELIEVE THEY DID IT.
BUT EVEN MORE--
--I CAN'T BELIEVE BARRY WAS THE DECIDING VOTE.
MY NAME IS WALLY WEST.
I'M THE FASTEST MAN ALIVE.
I'M THE FLASH.
AND I WANT ANSWERS.
The SECRET OF BARRY ALLEN PART ONE

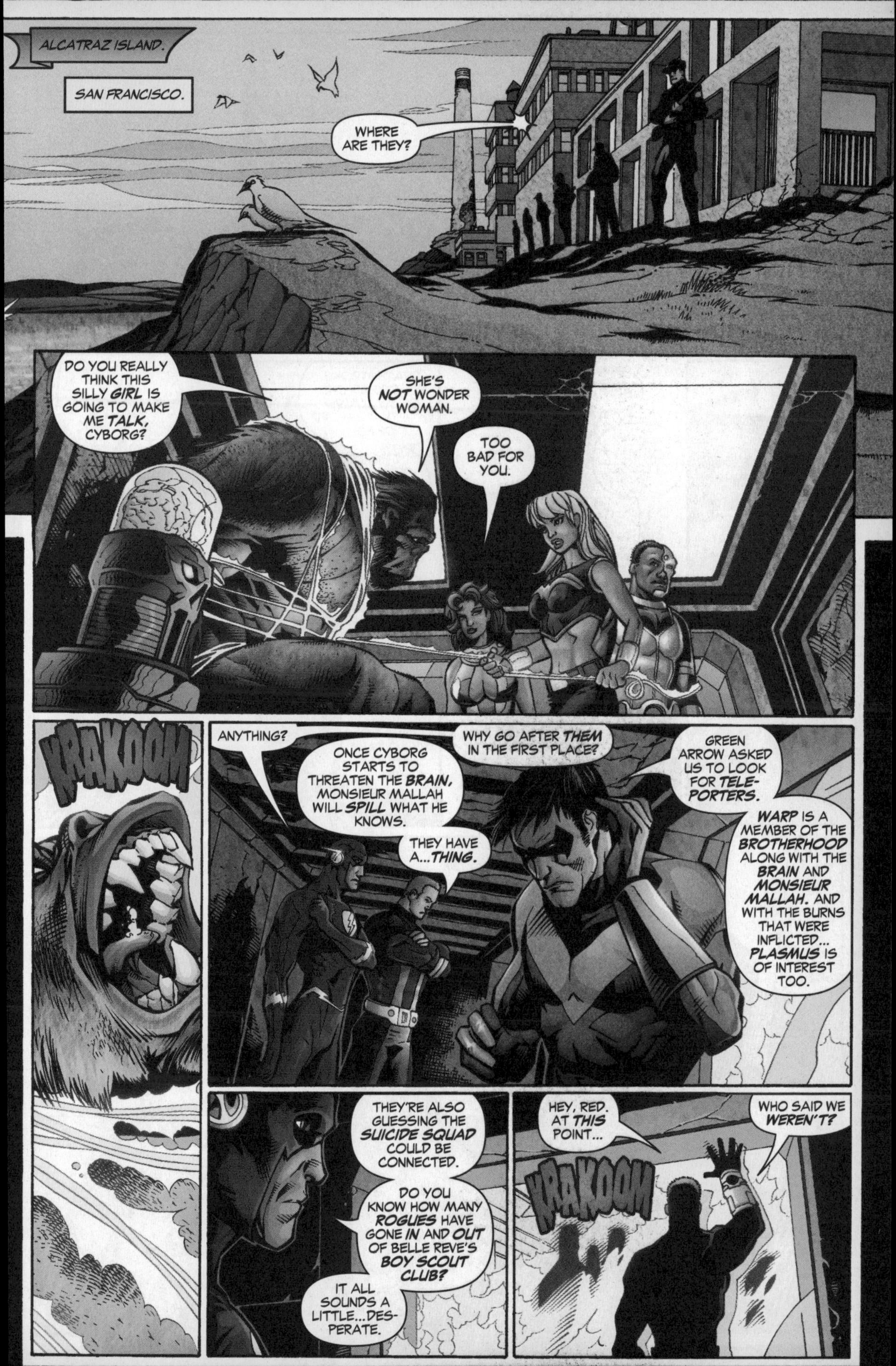
ALCATRAZ ISLAND.
SAN FRANCISCO.
WHERE ARE THEY?
DO YOU REALLY THINK THIS SILLY GIRL IS GOING TO MAKE ME TALK, CYBORG?
SHE'S NOT WONDER WOMAN.
TOO BAD FOR YOU.
KRAKOOM
ANYTHING?
ONCE CYBORG STARTS TO THREATEN THE BRAIN, MONSIEUR MALLAH WILL SPILL WHAT HE KNOWS.
THEY HAVE A...THING.
WHY GO AFTER THEM IN THE FIRST PLACE?
GREEN ARROW ASKED US TO LOOK FOR TELE-PORTERS.
WARP IS A MEMBER OF THE BROTHERHOOD ALONG WITH THE BRAIN AND MONSIEUR MALLAH. AND WITH THE BURNS THAT WERE INFLICTED... PLASMUS IS OF INTEREST TOO.
THEY'RE ALSO GUESSING THE SUICIDE SQUAD COULD BE CONNECTED.
DO YOU KNOW HOW MANY ROGUES HAVE GONE IN AND OUT OF BELLE REVE'S BOY SCOUT CLUB?
IT ALL SOUNDS A LITTLE...DES-PERATE.
HEY, RED. AT THIS POINT...
WHO SAID WE WEREN'T?
KRAKOOM

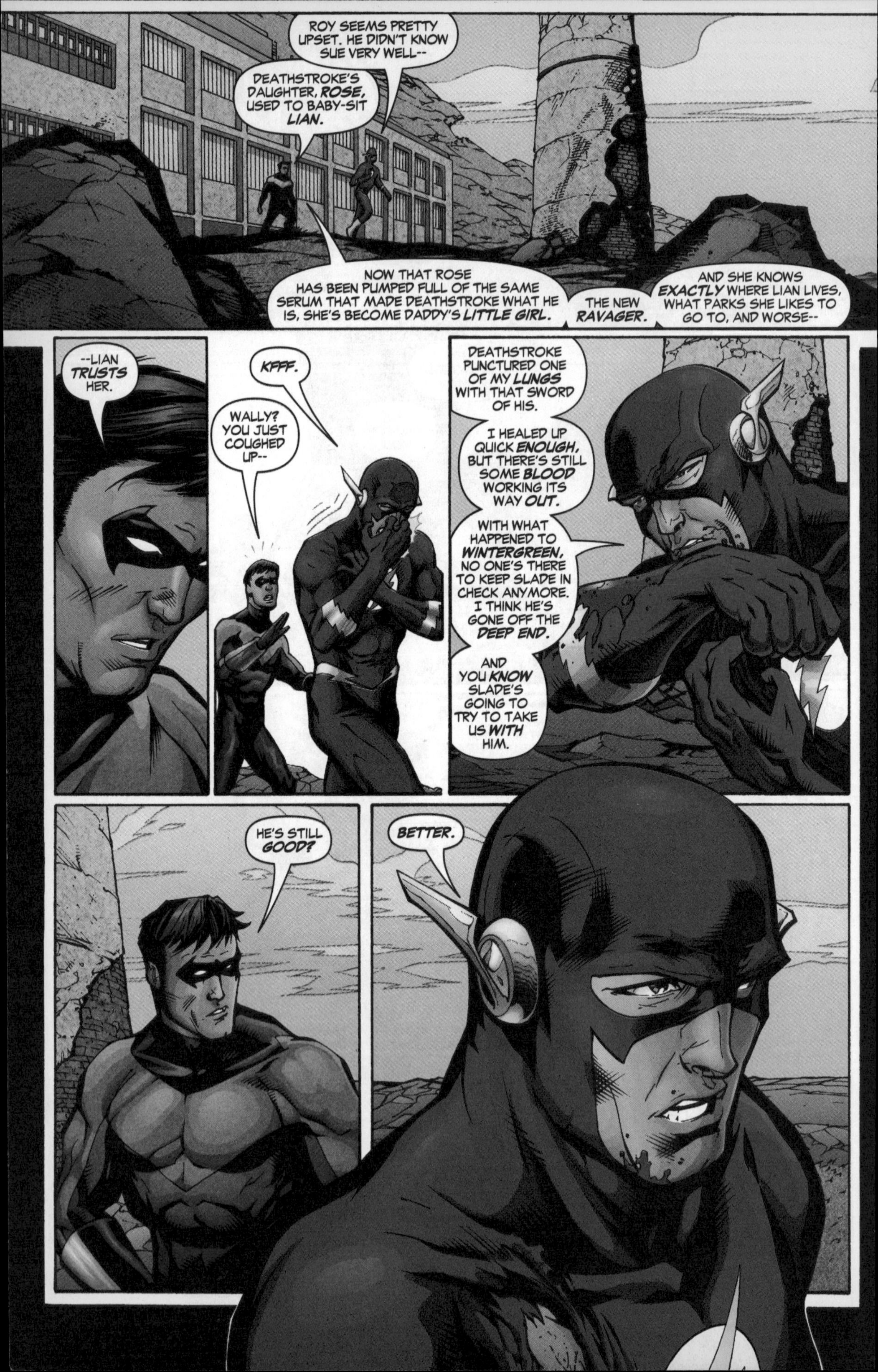
ROY SEEMS PRETTY UPSET. HE DIDN'T KNOW SUE VERY WELL--
DEATHSTROKE'S DAUGHTER, ROSE, USED TO BABY-SIT LIAN.
NOW THAT ROSE HAS BEEN PUMPED FULL OF THE SAME SERUM THAT MADE DEATHSTROKE WHAT HE IS, SHE'S BECOME DADDY'S LITTLE GIRL.
THE NEW RAVAGER.
AND SHE KNOWS EXACTLY WHERE LIAN LIVES, WHAT PARKS SHE LIKES TO GO TO, AND WORSE--
--LIAN TRUSTS HER.
KFFF.
WALLY? YOU JUST COUGHED UP--
DEATHSTROKE PUNCTURED ONE OF MY LUNGS WITH THAT SWORD OF HIS.
I HEALED UP QUICK ENOUGH, BUT THERE'S STILL SOME BLOOD WORKING ITS WAY OUT.
WITH WHAT HAPPENED TO WINTERGREEN, NO ONE'S THERE TO KEEP SLADE IN CHECK ANYMORE. I THINK HE'S GONE OFF THE DEEP END.
AND YOU KNOW SLADE'S GOING TO TRY TO TAKE US WITH HIM.
HE'S STILL GOOD?
BETTER.

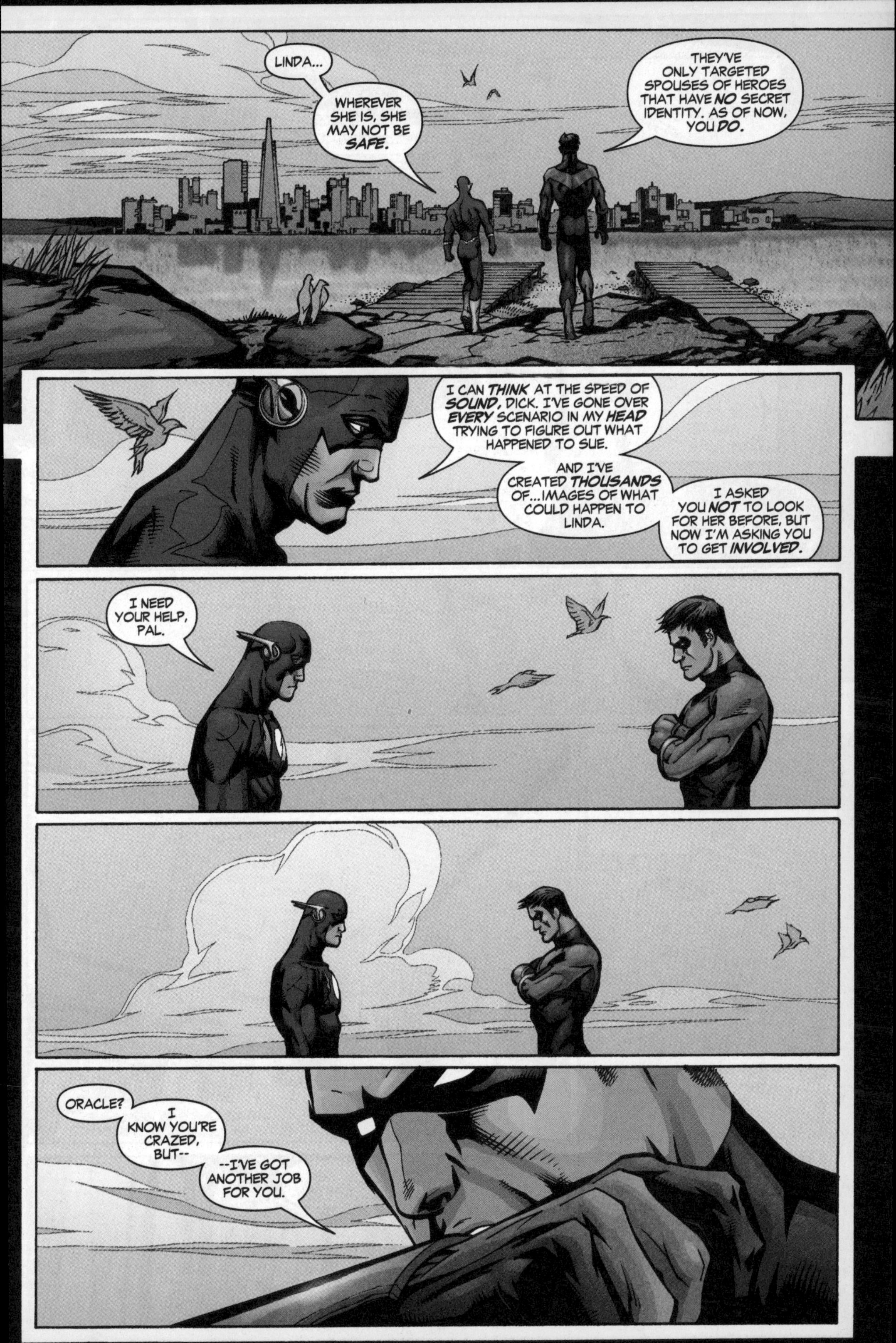
LINDA...
WHEREVER SHE IS, SHE MAY NOT BE SAFE.
THEY'VE ONLY TARGETED SPOUSES OF HEROES THAT HAVE NO SECRET IDENTITY. AS OF NOW, YOU DO.
I CAN THINK AT THE SPEED OF SOUND, DICK. I'VE GONE OVER EVERY SCENARIO IN MY HEAD TRYING TO FIGURE OUT WHAT HAPPENED TO SUE.
AND I'VE CREATED THOUSANDS OF...IMAGES OF WHAT COULD HAPPEN TO LINDA.
I ASKED YOU NOT TO LOOK FOR HER BEFORE, BUT NOW I'M ASKING YOU TO GET INVOLVED.
I NEED YOUR HELP, PAL.
ORACLE?
I KNOW YOU'RE CRAZED, BUT--
--I'VE GOT ANOTHER JOB FOR YOU.

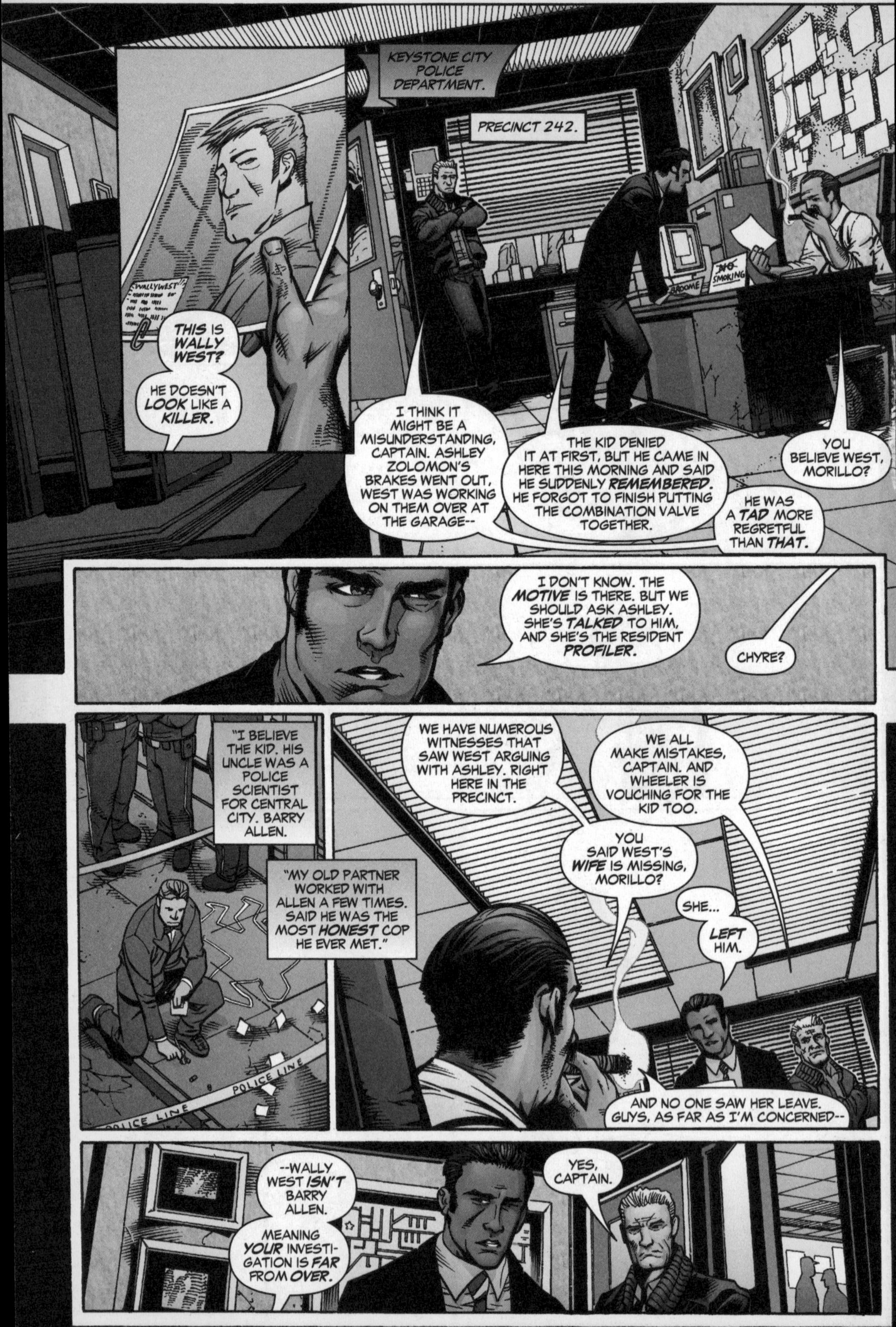
KEYSTONE CITY POLICE DEPARTMENT.
PRECINCT 242.
WALLY WEST
THIS IS WALLY WEST?
HE DOESN'T LOOK LIKE A KILLER.
BROOME
NO SMOKING
I THINK IT MIGHT BE A MISUNDERSTANDING, CAPTAIN. ASHLEY ZOLOMON'S BRAKES WENT OUT, WEST WAS WORKING ON THEM OVER AT THE GARAGE--
THE KID DENIED IT AT FIRST, BUT HE CAME IN HERE THIS MORNING AND SAID HE SUDDENLY REMEMBERED. HE FORGOT TO FINISH PUTTING THE COMBINATION VALVE TOGETHER.
YOU BELIEVE WEST, MORILLO?
HE WAS A TAD MORE REGRETFUL THAN THAT.
I DON'T KNOW. THE MOTIVE IS THERE. BUT WE SHOULD ASK ASHLEY. SHE'S TALKED TO HIM, AND SHE'S THE RESIDENT PROFILER.
CHYRE?
"I BELIEVE THE KID. HIS UNCLE WAS A POLICE SCIENTIST FOR CENTRAL CITY. BARRY ALLEN.
"MY OLD PARTNER WORKED WITH ALLEN A FEW TIMES. SAID HE WAS THE MOST HONEST COP HE EVER MET."
POLICE LINE
WE HAVE NUMEROUS WITNESSES THAT SAW WEST ARGUING WITH ASHLEY. RIGHT HERE IN THE PRECINCT.
WE ALL MAKE MISTAKES, CAPTAIN. AND WHEELER IS VOUCHING FOR THE KID TOO.
YOU SAID WEST'S WIFE IS MISSING, MORILLO?
SHE... LEFT HIM.
AND NO ONE SAW HER LEAVE. GUYS, AS FAR AS I'M CONCERNED--
--WALLY WEST ISN'T BARRY ALLEN.
MEANING YOUR INVESTIGATION IS FAR FROM OVER.
YES, CAPTAIN.

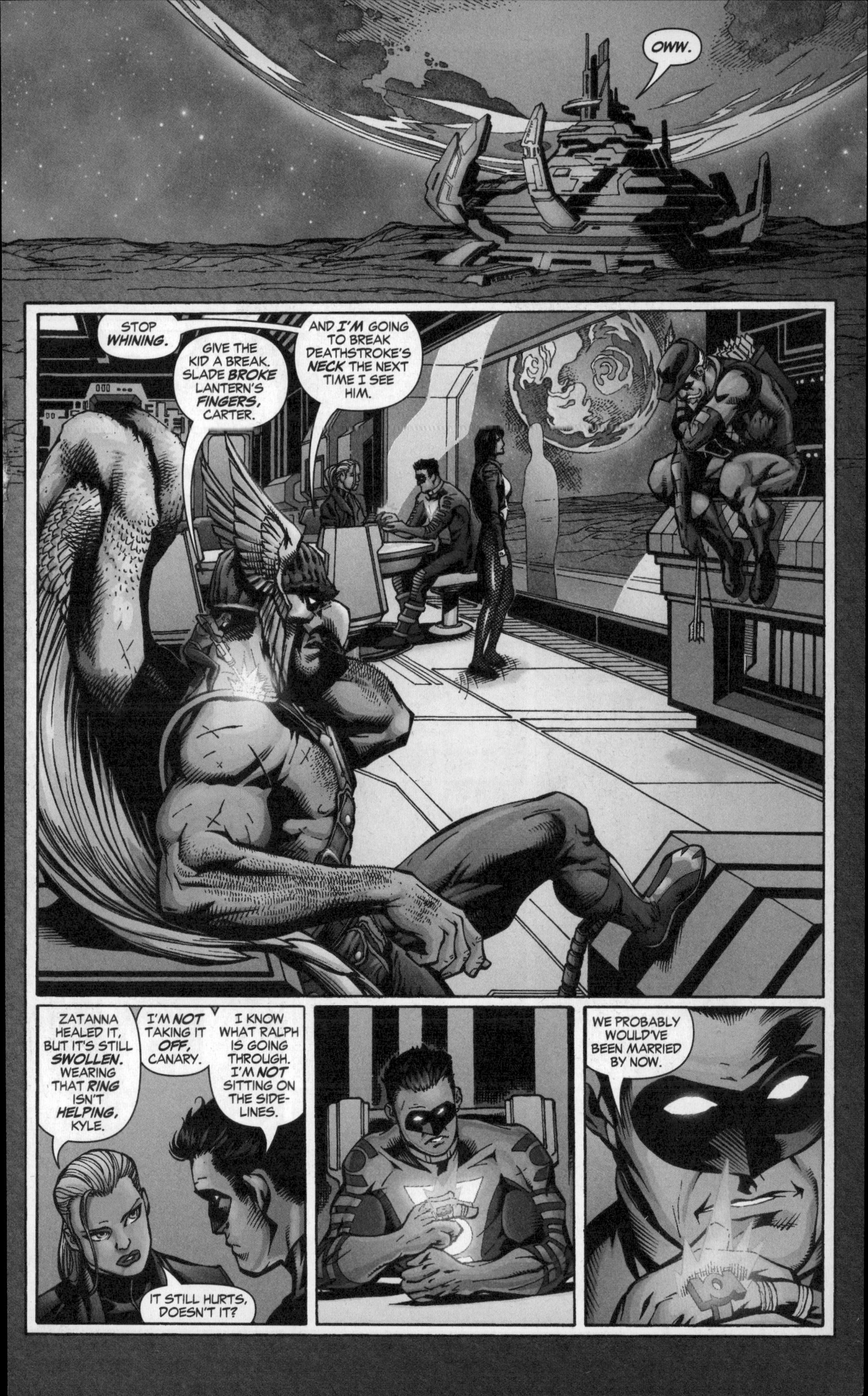
OWW.
STOP WHINING.
GIVE THE KID A BREAK. SLADE BROKE LANTERN'S FINGERS, CARTER.
AND I'M GOING TO BREAK DEATHSTROKE'S NECK THE NEXT TIME I SEE HIM.
ZATANNA HEALED IT, BUT IT'S STILL SWOLLEN. WEARING THAT RING ISN'T HELPING, KYLE.
I'M NOT TAKING IT OFF, CANARY.
I KNOW WHAT RALPH IS GOING THROUGH. I'M NOT SITTING ON THE SIDE-LINES.
IT STILL HURTS, DOESN'T IT?
WE PROBABLY WOULD'VE BEEN MARRIED BY NOW.

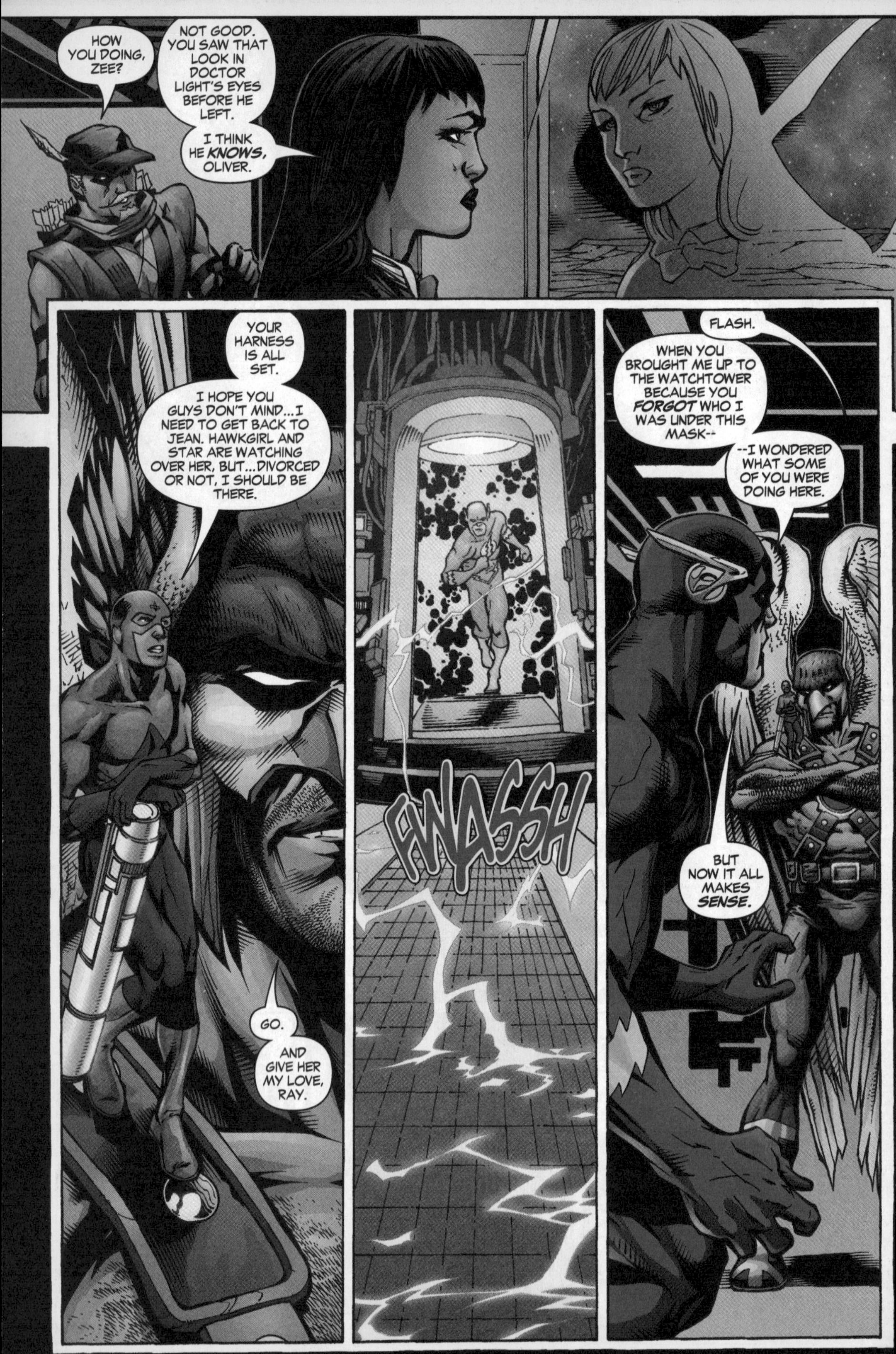
HOW YOU DOING, ZEE?
NOT GOOD. YOU SAW THAT LOOK IN DOCTOR LIGHT'S EYES BEFORE HE LEFT.
I THINK HE *KNOWS,* OLIVER.
YOUR HARNESS IS ALL SET.
I HOPE YOU GUYS DON'T MIND... I NEED TO GET BACK TO JEAN. HAWKGIRL AND STAR ARE WATCHING OVER HER, BUT... DIVORCED OR NOT, I SHOULD BE THERE.
GO.
AND GIVE HER MY LOVE, RAY.
FWASSH
FLASH.
WHEN YOU BROUGHT ME UP TO THE WATCHTOWER BECAUSE YOU *FORGOT* WHO I WAS UNDER THIS MASK--
--I WONDERED WHAT SOME OF YOU WERE DOING HERE.
BUT NOW IT ALL MAKES *SENSE.*

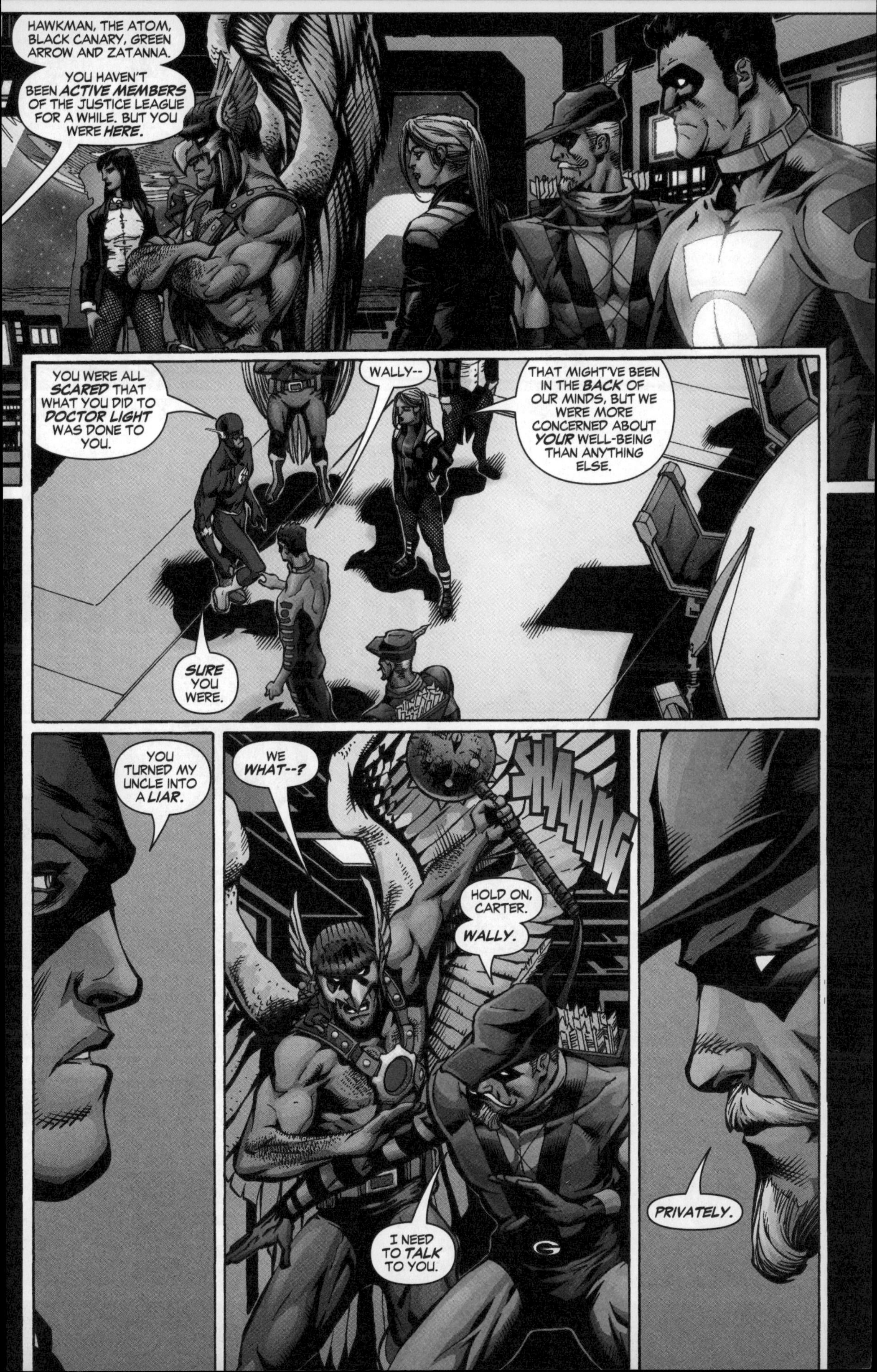
HAWKMAN, THE ATOM, BLACK CANARY, GREEN ARROW AND ZATANNA.
YOU HAVEN'T BEEN ACTIVE MEMBERS OF THE JUSTICE LEAGUE FOR A WHILE. BUT YOU WERE HERE.
YOU WERE ALL SCARED THAT WHAT YOU DID TO DOCTOR LIGHT WAS DONE TO YOU.
WALLY--
THAT MIGHT'VE BEEN IN THE BACK OF OUR MINDS, BUT WE WERE MORE CONCERNED ABOUT YOUR WELL-BEING THAN ANYTHING ELSE.
SURE YOU WERE.
YOU TURNED MY UNCLE INTO A LIAR.
WE WHAT--?
SHANNG
HOLD ON, CARTER.
WALLY.
I NEED TO TALK TO YOU.
PRIVATELY.

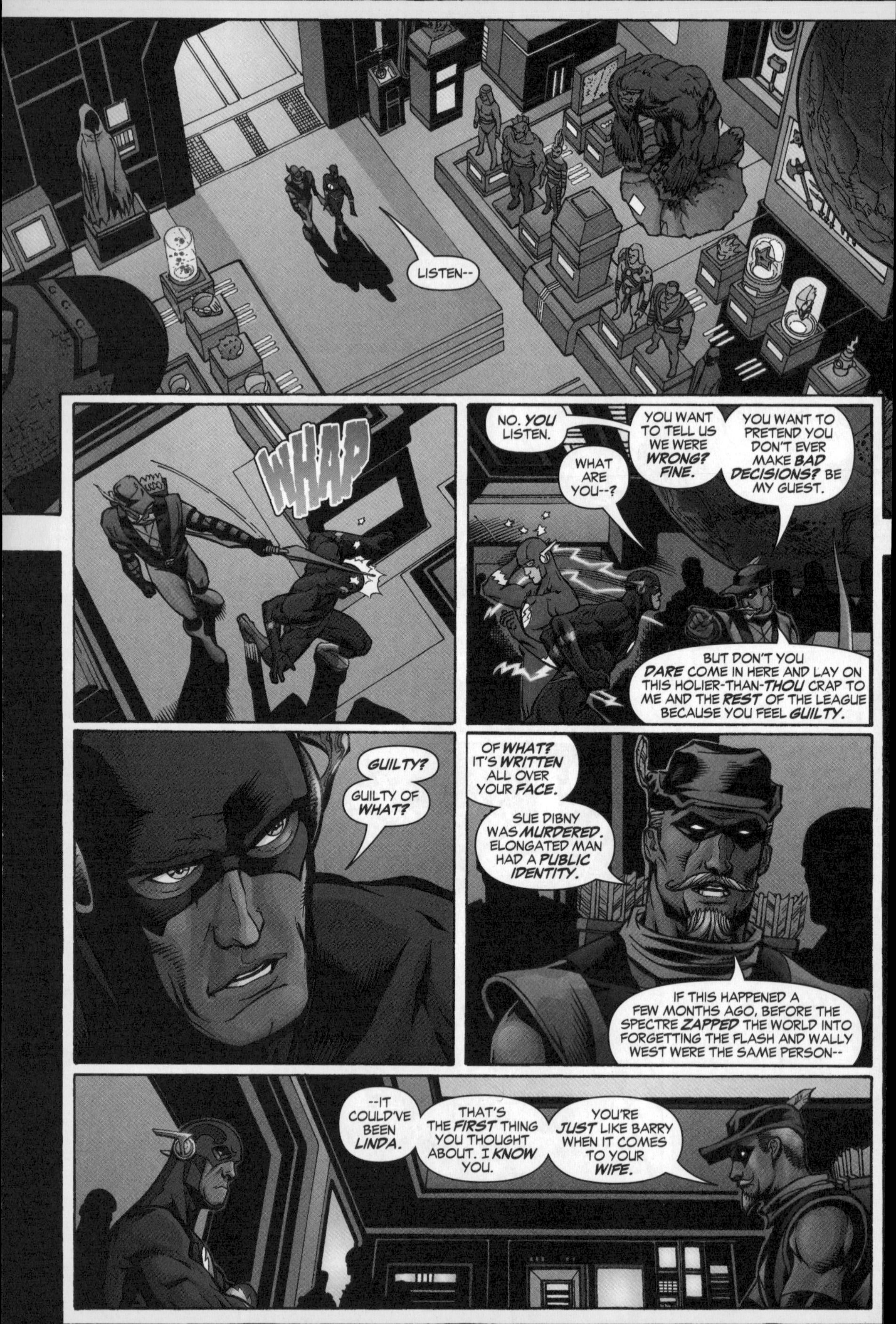
LISTEN--
WHAP
NO. YOU LISTEN.
WHAT ARE YOU--?
YOU WANT TO TELL US WE WERE WRONG? FINE.
YOU WANT TO PRETEND YOU DON'T EVER MAKE BAD DECISIONS? BE MY GUEST.
BUT DON'T YOU DARE COME IN HERE AND LAY ON THIS HOLIER-THAN-THOU CRAP TO ME AND THE REST OF THE LEAGUE BECAUSE YOU FEEL GUILTY.
GUILTY?
GUILTY OF WHAT?
OF WHAT? IT'S WRITTEN ALL OVER YOUR FACE.
SUE DIBNY WAS MURDERED. ELONGATED MAN HAD A PUBLIC IDENTITY.
IF THIS HAPPENED A FEW MONTHS AGO, BEFORE THE SPECTRE ZAPPED THE WORLD INTO FORGETTING THE FLASH AND WALLY WEST WERE THE SAME PERSON--
--IT COULD'VE BEEN LINDA.
THAT'S THE FIRST THING YOU THOUGHT ABOUT. I KNOW YOU.
YOU'RE JUST LIKE BARRY WHEN IT COMES TO YOUR WIFE.

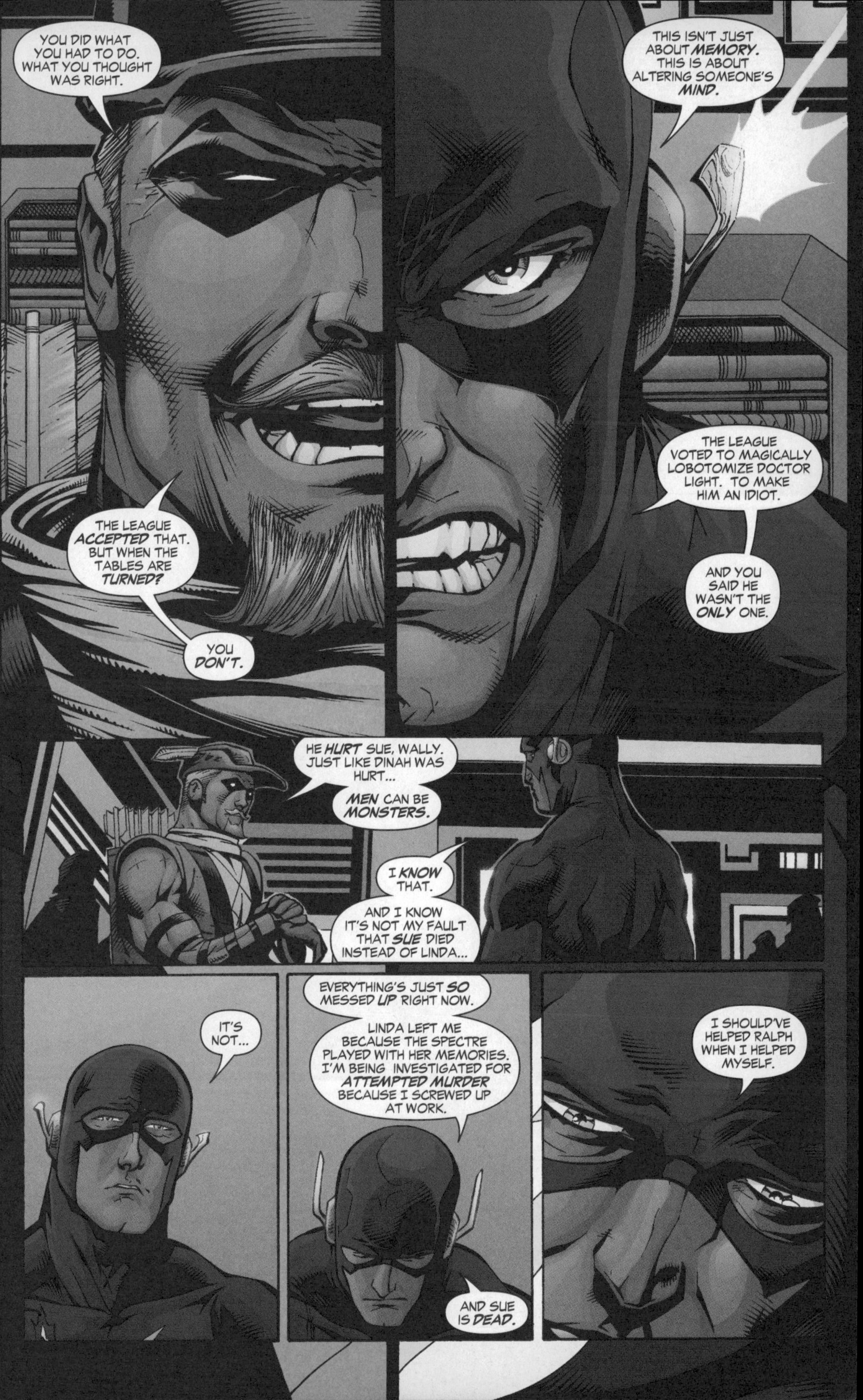

YOU DID WHAT YOU HAD TO DO. WHAT YOU THOUGHT WAS RIGHT.
THIS ISN'T JUST ABOUT MEMORY. THIS IS ABOUT ALTERING SOMEONE'S MIND.
THE LEAGUE VOTED TO MAGICALLY LOBOTOMIZE DOCTOR LIGHT. TO MAKE HIM AN IDIOT.
AND YOU SAID HE WASN'T THE ONLY ONE.
THE LEAGUE ACCEPTED THAT. BUT WHEN THE TABLES ARE TURNED?
YOU DON'T.
HE HURT SUE, WALLY. JUST LIKE DINAH WAS HURT...
MEN CAN BE MONSTERS.
I KNOW THAT.
AND I KNOW IT'S NOT MY FAULT THAT SUE DIED INSTEAD OF LINDA...
IT'S NOT...
EVERYTHING'S JUST SO MESSED UP RIGHT NOW.
LINDA LEFT ME BECAUSE THE SPECTRE PLAYED WITH HER MEMORIES. I'M BEING INVESTIGATED FOR ATTEMPTED MURDER BECAUSE I SCREWED UP AT WORK.
AND SUE IS DEAD.
I SHOULD'VE HELPED RALPH WHEN I HELPED MYSELF.

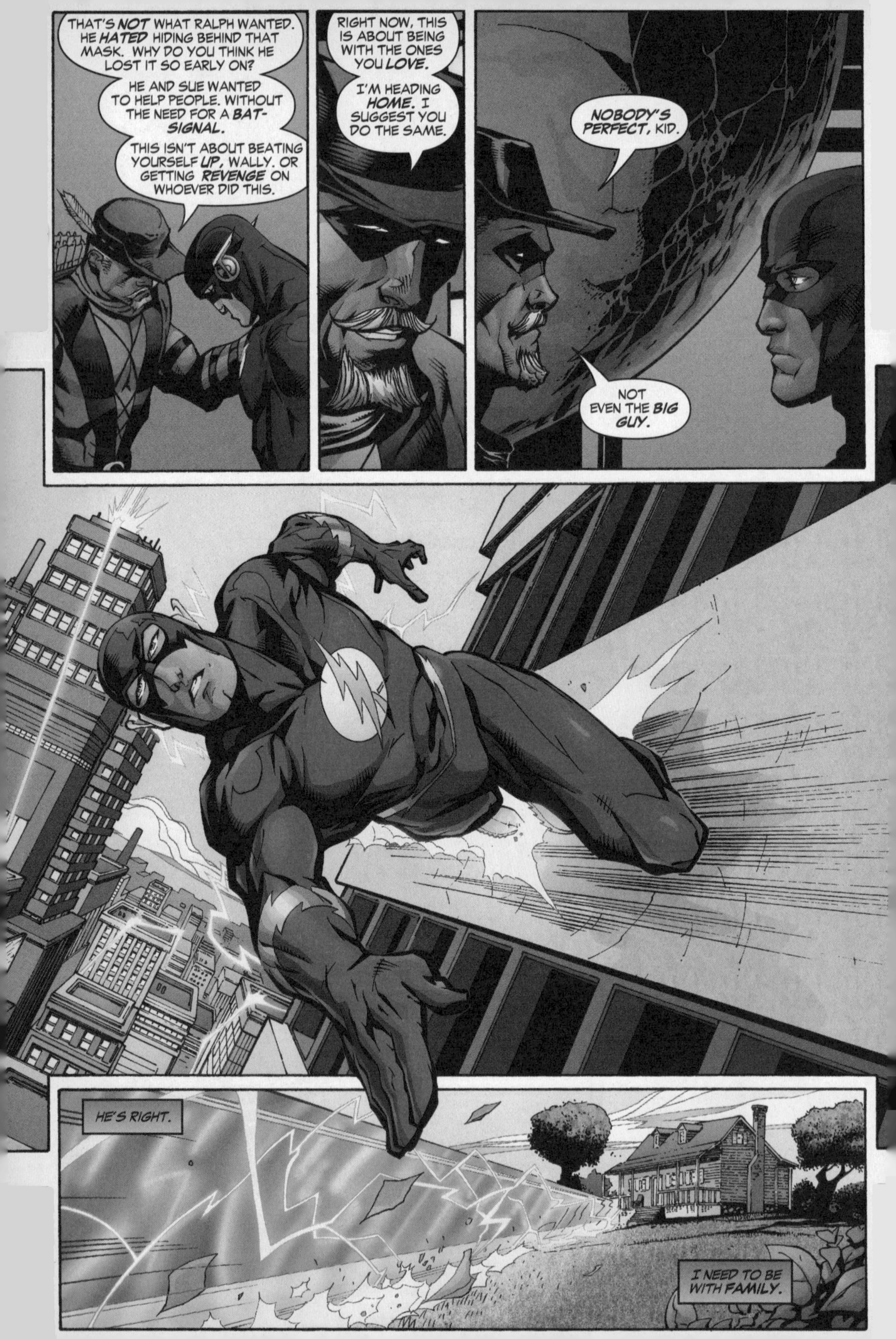
THAT'S NOT WHAT RALPH WANTED. HE HATED HIDING BEHIND THAT MASK. WHY DO YOU THINK HE LOST IT SO EARLY ON?
HE AND SUE WANTED TO HELP PEOPLE. WITHOUT THE NEED FOR A BAT-SIGNAL.
THIS ISN'T ABOUT BEATING YOURSELF UP, WALLY. OR GETTING REVENGE ON WHOEVER DID THIS.
RIGHT NOW, THIS IS ABOUT BEING WITH THE ONES YOU LOVE.
I'M HEADING HOME. I SUGGEST YOU DO THE SAME.
NOBODY'S PERFECT, KID.
NOT EVEN THE BIG GUY.
HE'S RIGHT.
I NEED TO BE WITH FAMILY.

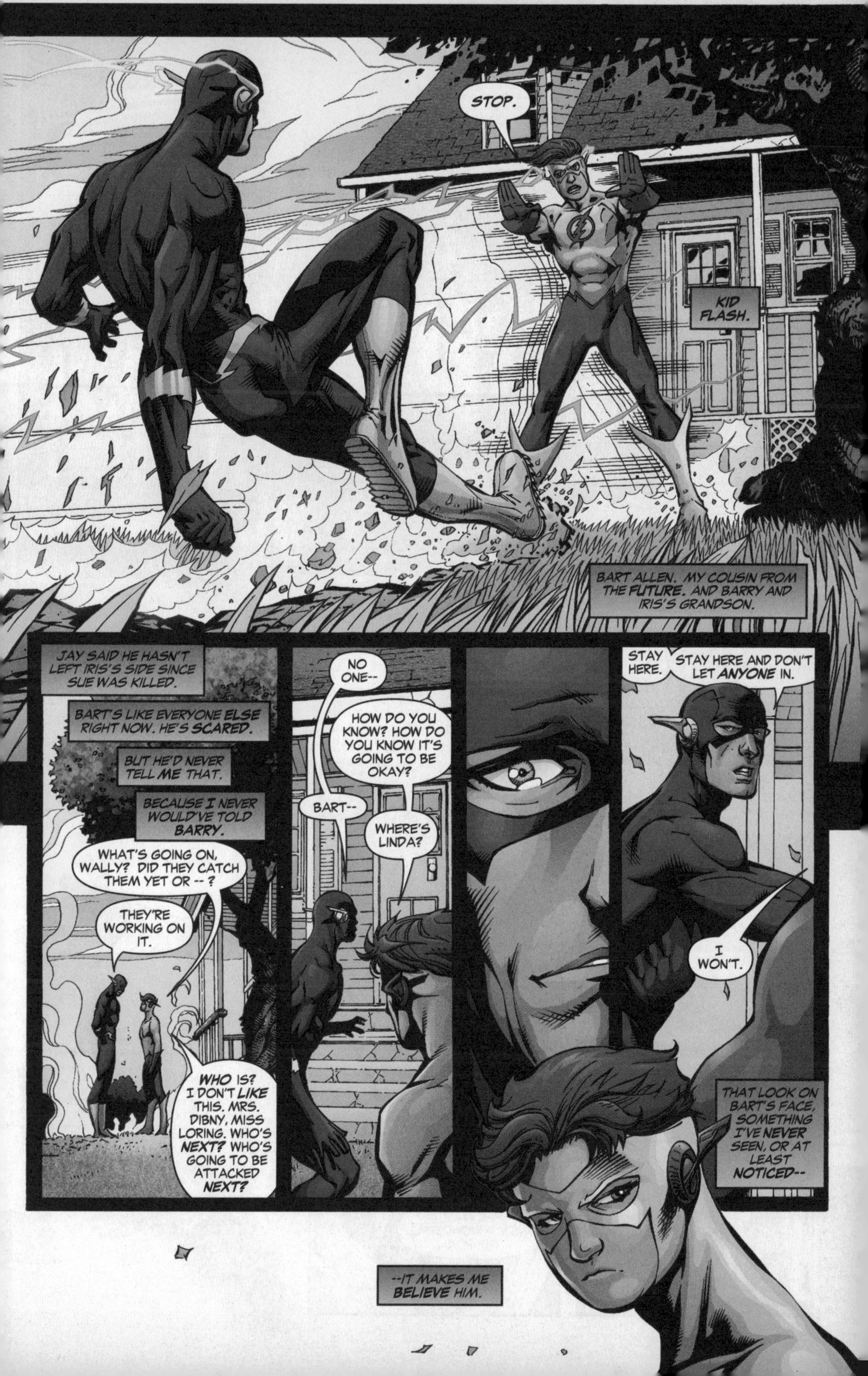
STOP.
KID FLASH.
BART ALLEN. MY COUSIN FROM THE FUTURE. AND BARRY AND IRIS'S GRANDSON.
JAY SAID HE HASN'T LEFT IRIS'S SIDE SINCE SUE WAS KILLED.
BART'S LIKE EVERYONE ELSE RIGHT NOW. HE'S SCARED.
BUT HE'D NEVER TELL ME THAT.
BECAUSE I NEVER WOULD'VE TOLD BARRY.
WHAT'S GOING ON, WALLY? DID THEY CATCH THEM YET OR -- ?
THEY'RE WORKING ON IT.
WHO IS? I DON'T LIKE THIS. MRS. DIBNY, MISS LORING. WHO'S NEXT? WHO'S GOING TO BE ATTACKED NEXT?
NO ONE--
HOW DO YOU KNOW? HOW DO YOU KNOW IT'S GOING TO BE OKAY?
BART--
WHERE'S LINDA?
STAY HERE.
STAY HERE AND DON'T LET ANYONE IN.
I WON'T.
THAT LOOK ON BART'S FACE, SOMETHING I'VE NEVER SEEN, OR AT LEAST NOTICED--
--IT MAKES ME BELIEVE HIM.

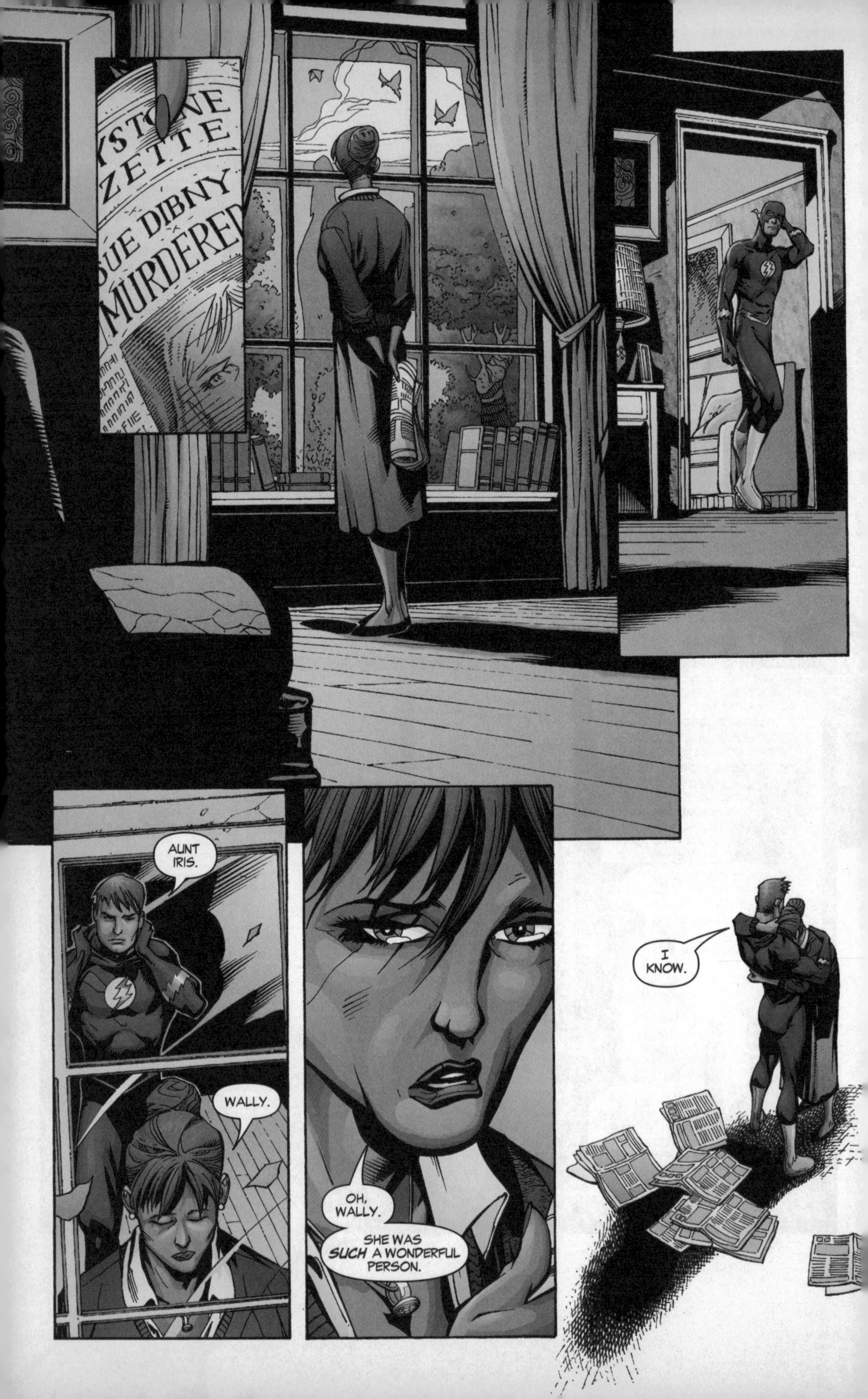

YSTONE
ZETTE
SUE DIBNY
MURDERED
AUNT IRIS.
WALLY.
OH, WALLY.
SHE WAS SUCH A WONDERFUL PERSON.
I KNOW.

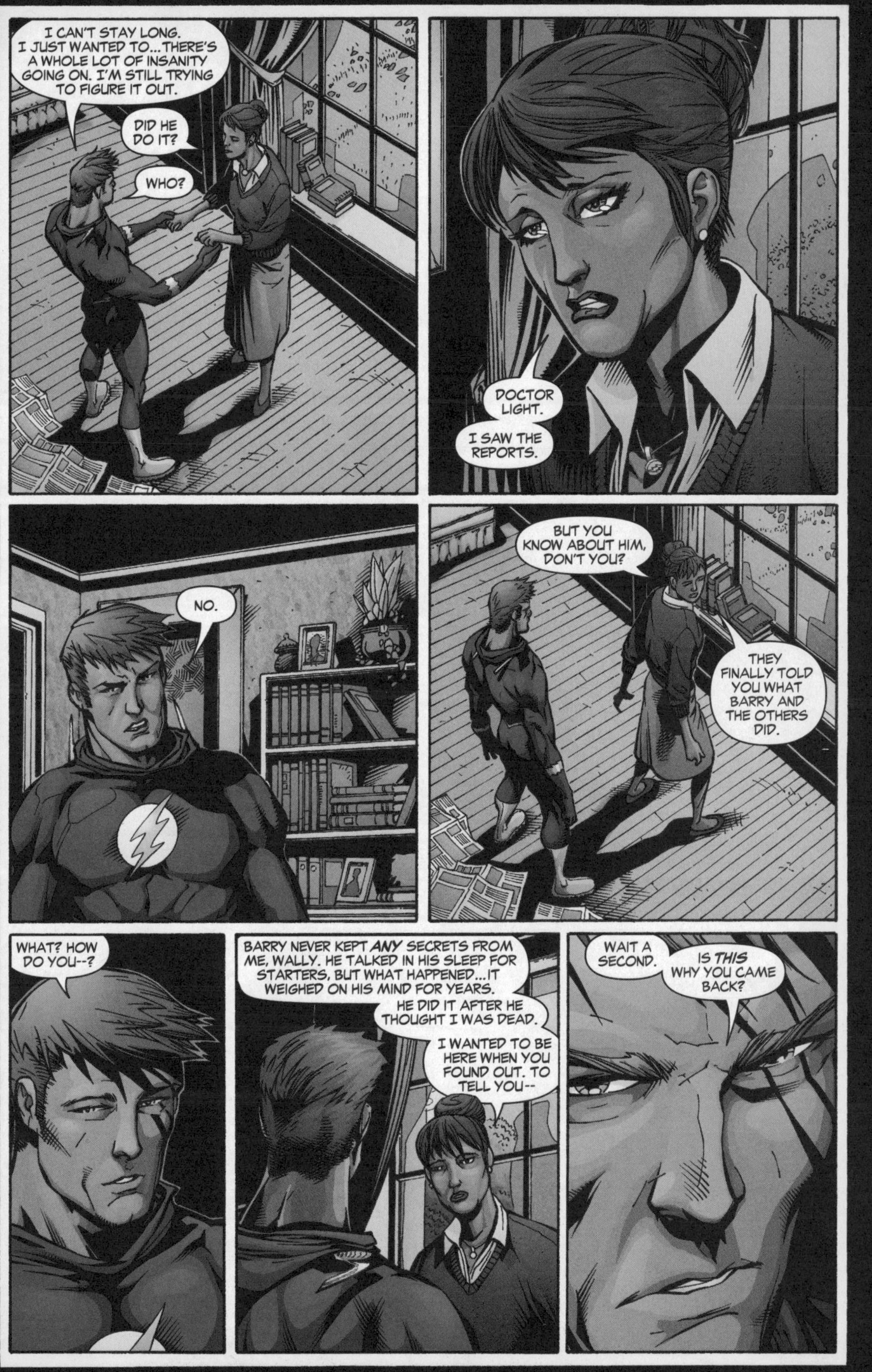
I CAN'T STAY LONG. I JUST WANTED TO... THERE'S A WHOLE LOT OF INSANITY GOING ON. I'M STILL TRYING TO FIGURE IT OUT.
DID HE DO IT?
WHO?
DOCTOR LIGHT.
I SAW THE REPORTS.
NO.
BUT YOU KNOW ABOUT HIM, DON'T YOU?
THEY FINALLY TOLD YOU WHAT BARRY AND THE OTHERS DID.
WHAT? HOW DO YOU--?
BARRY NEVER KEPT *ANY* SECRETS FROM ME, WALLY. HE TALKED IN HIS SLEEP FOR STARTERS, BUT WHAT HAPPENED...IT WEIGHED ON HIS MIND FOR YEARS.
HE DID IT AFTER HE THOUGHT I WAS DEAD.
I WANTED TO BE HERE WHEN YOU FOUND OUT. TO TELL YOU--
WAIT A SECOND.
IS *THIS* WHY YOU CAME BACK?

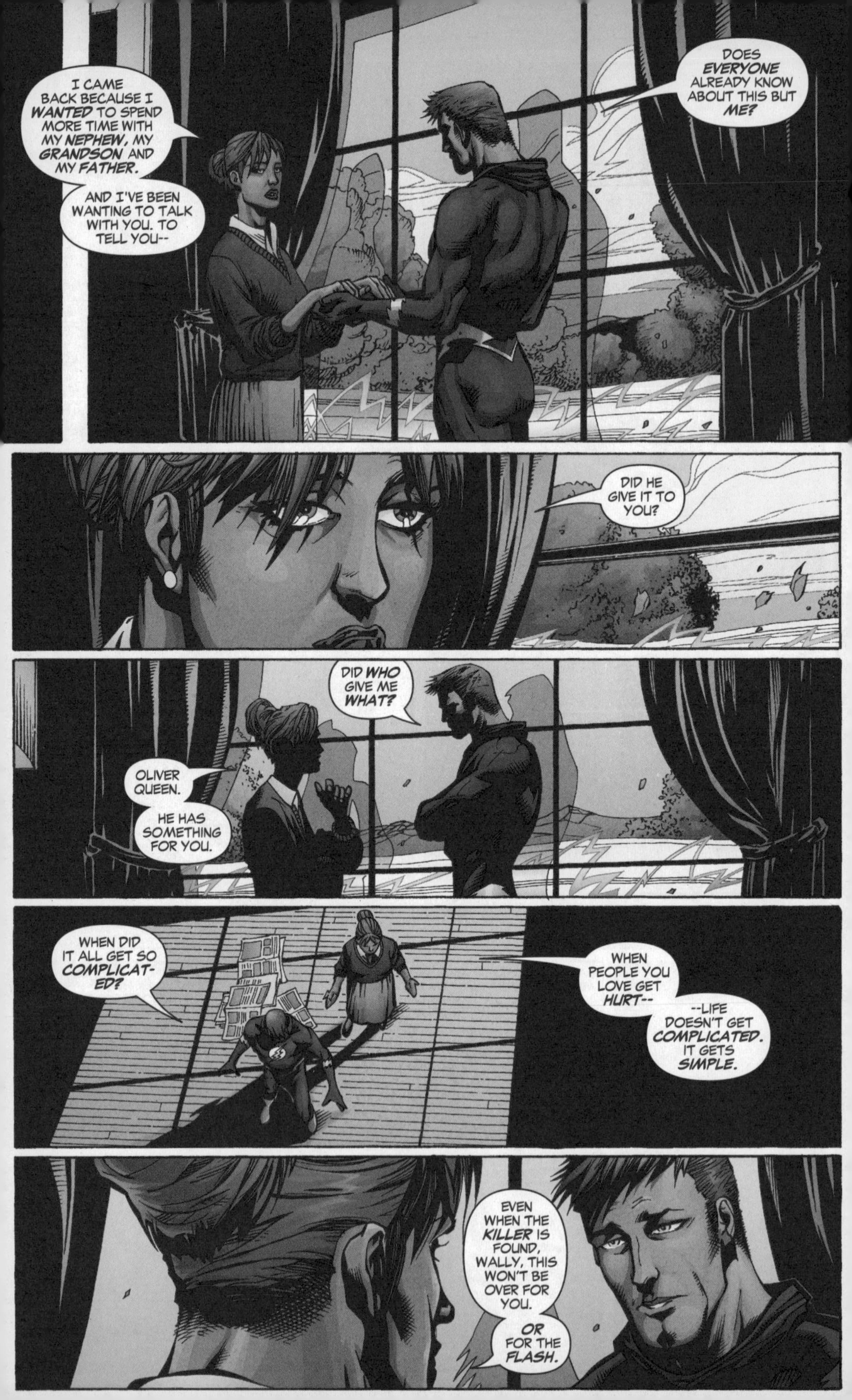

I CAME BACK BECAUSE I WANTED TO SPEND MORE TIME WITH MY NEPHEW, MY GRANDSON AND MY FATHER.
AND I'VE BEEN WANTING TO TALK WITH YOU. TO TELL YOU--
DOES EVERYONE ALREADY KNOW ABOUT THIS BUT ME?
DID HE GIVE IT TO YOU?
DID WHO GIVE ME WHAT?
OLIVER QUEEN.
HE HAS SOMETHING FOR YOU.
WHEN DID IT ALL GET SO COMPLICAT-ED?
WHEN PEOPLE YOU LOVE GET HURT--
--LIFE DOESN'T GET COMPLICATED. IT GETS SIMPLE.
EVEN WHEN THE KILLER IS FOUND, WALLY, THIS WON'T BE OVER FOR YOU.
OR FOR THE FLASH.

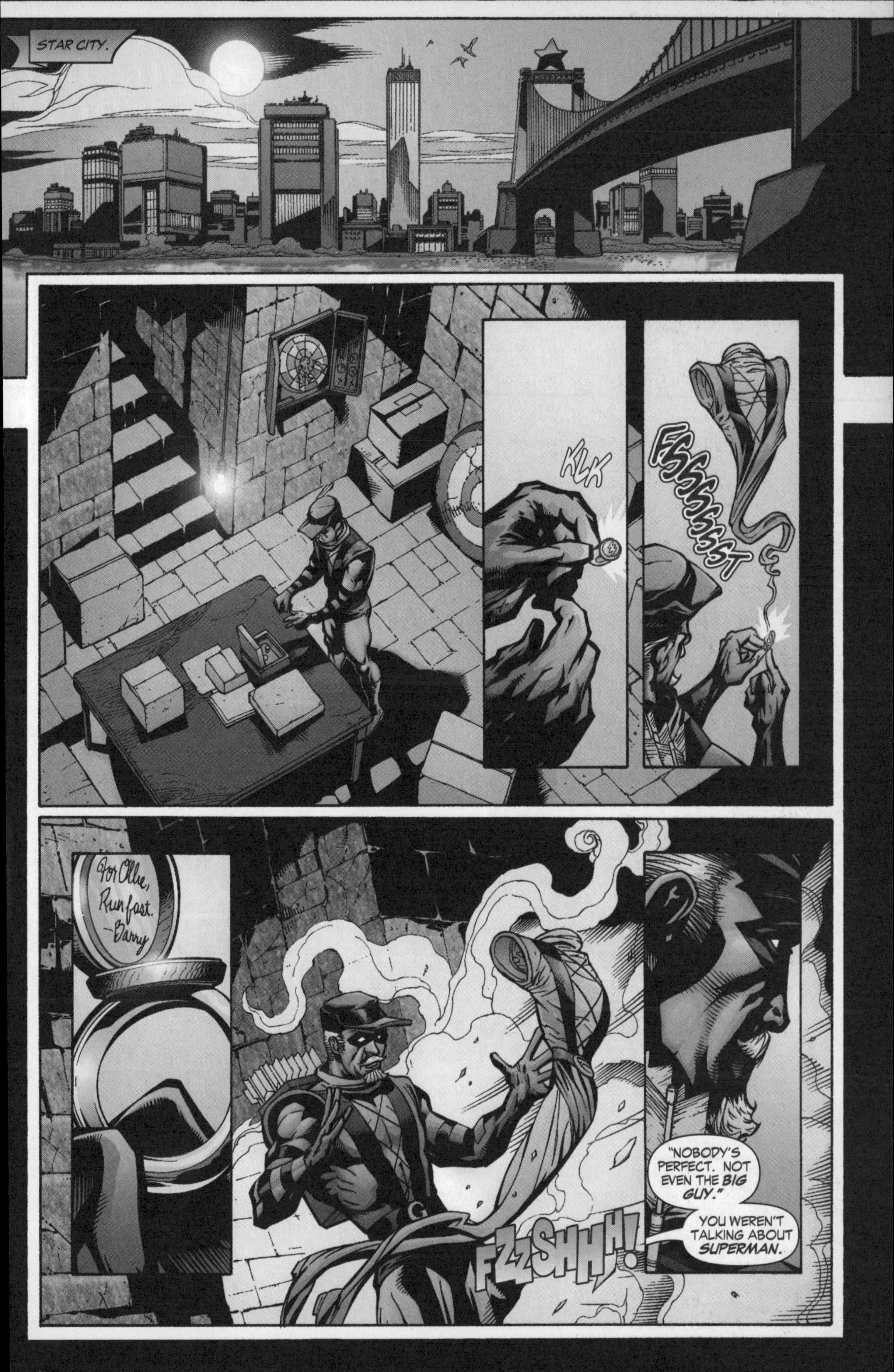
STAR CITY.
KLK
FSSSSSST
For Ollie, Run fast. —Barry
FZZSHHH!
"NOBODY'S PERFECT. NOT EVEN THE BIG GUY."
YOU WEREN'T TALKING ABOUT SUPERMAN.

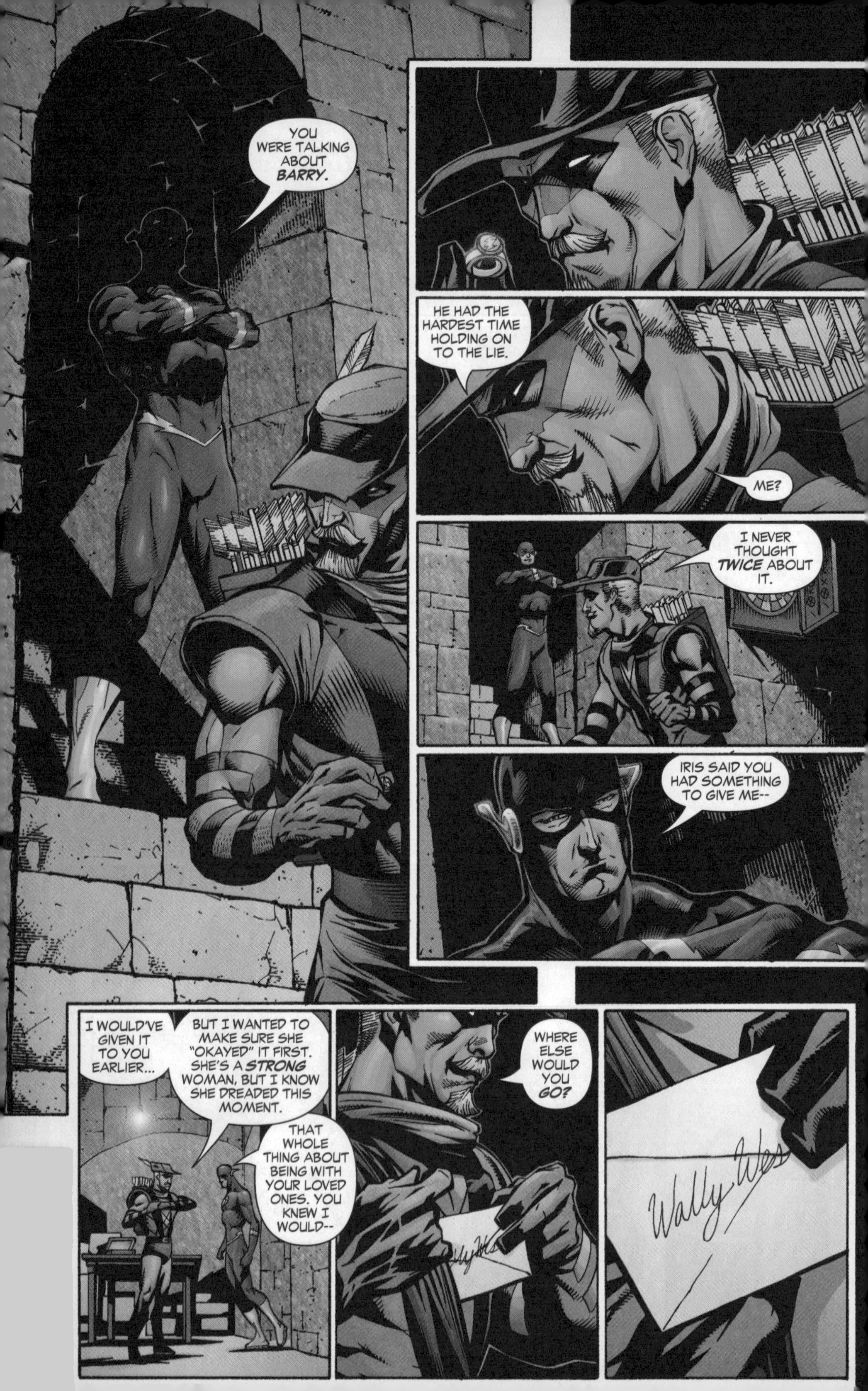
YOU WERE TALKING ABOUT BARRY.
HE HAD THE HARDEST TIME HOLDING ON TO THE LIE.
ME?
I NEVER THOUGHT TWICE ABOUT IT.
IRIS SAID YOU HAD SOMETHING TO GIVE ME--
I WOULD'VE GIVEN IT TO YOU EARLIER...
BUT I WANTED TO MAKE SURE SHE "OKAYED" IT FIRST. SHE'S A STRONG WOMAN, BUT I KNOW SHE DREADED THIS MOMENT.
THAT WHOLE THING ABOUT BEING WITH YOUR LOVED ONES. YOU KNEW I WOULD--
WHERE ELSE WOULD YOU GO?
Wally West

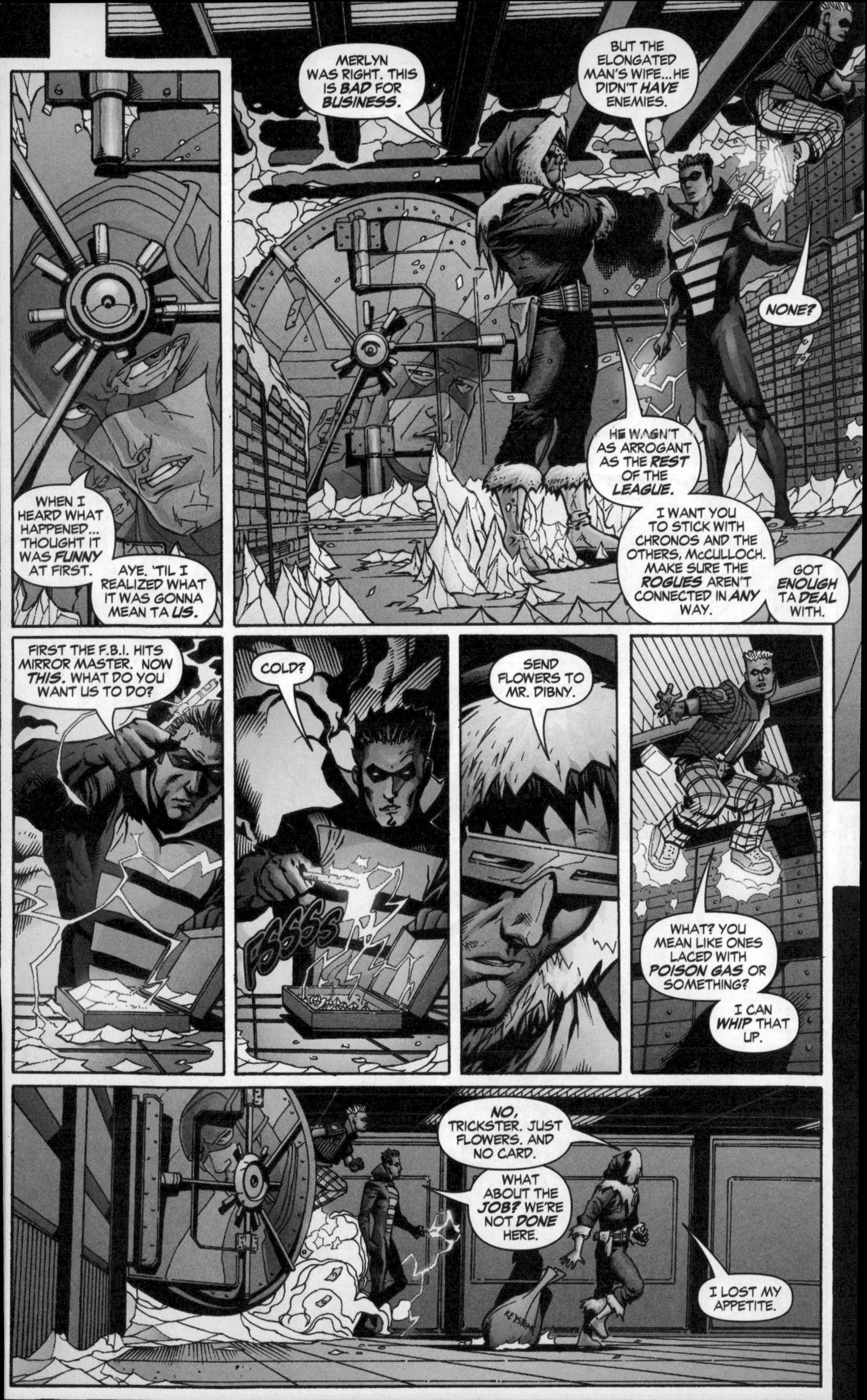

WHEN I HEARD WHAT HAPPENED... THOUGHT IT WAS FUNNY AT FIRST.
AYE. 'TIL I REALIZED WHAT IT WAS GONNA MEAN TA US.
MERLYN WAS RIGHT. THIS IS BAD FOR BUSINESS.
BUT THE ELONGATED MAN'S WIFE...HE DIDN'T HAVE ENEMIES.
NONE?
HE WASN'T AS ARROGANT AS THE REST OF THE LEAGUE.
I WANT YOU TO STICK WITH CHRONOS AND THE OTHERS, McCULLOCH. MAKE SURE THE ROGUES AREN'T CONNECTED IN ANY WAY.
GOT ENOUGH TA DEAL WITH.
FIRST THE F.B.I. HITS MIRROR MASTER. NOW THIS. WHAT DO YOU WANT US TO DO?
COLD?
FSSSS
SEND FLOWERS TO MR. DIBNY.
WHAT? YOU MEAN LIKE ONES LACED WITH POISON GAS OR SOMETHING?
I CAN WHIP THAT UP.
NO, TRICKSTER. JUST FLOWERS. AND NO CARD.
WHAT ABOUT THE JOB? WE'RE NOT DONE HERE.
I LOST MY APPETITE.
KEYSTONE

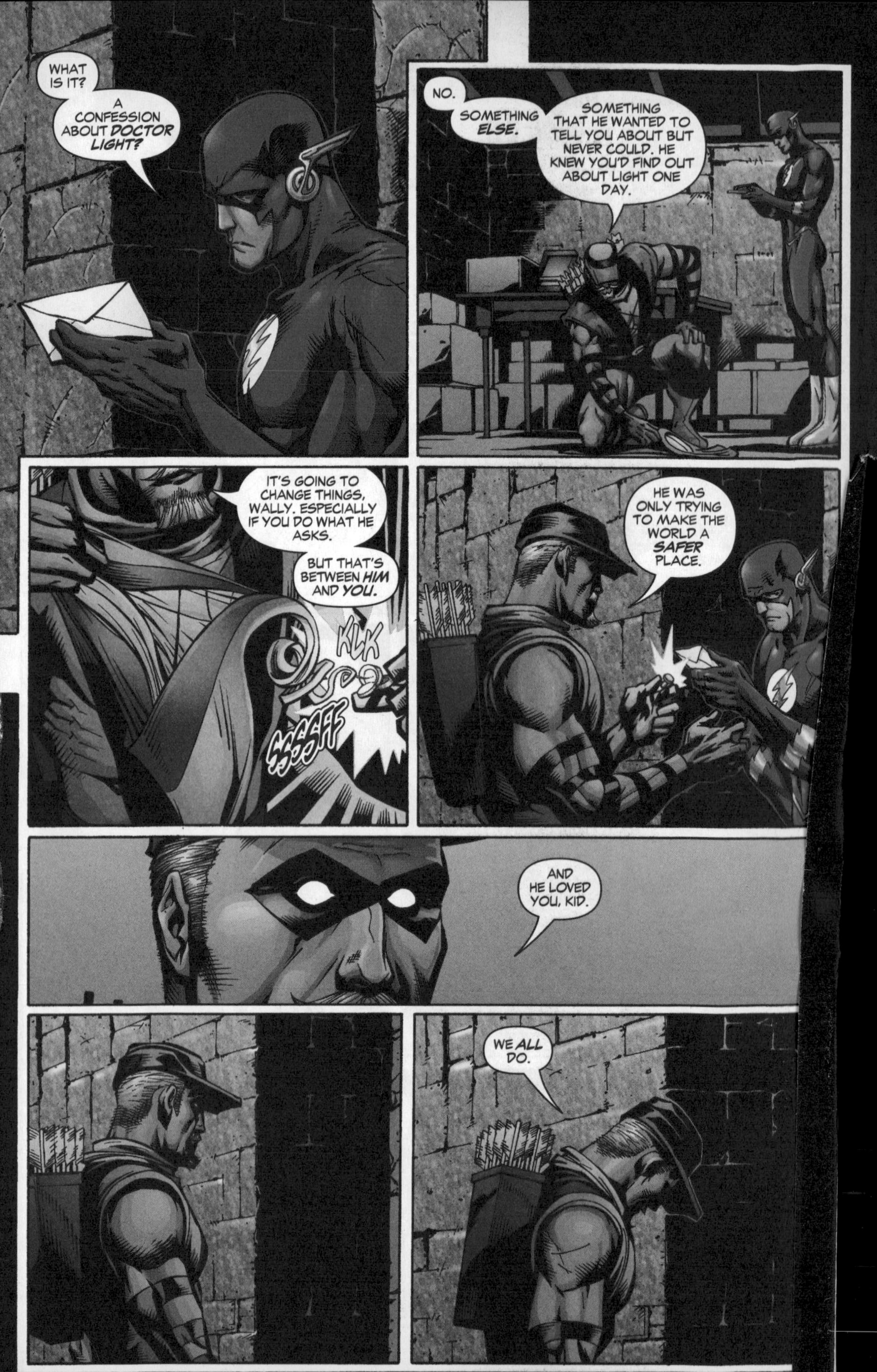
WHAT IS IT?
A CONFESSION ABOUT DOCTOR LIGHT?
NO.
SOMETHING ELSE.
SOMETHING THAT HE WANTED TO TELL YOU ABOUT BUT NEVER COULD. HE KNEW YOU'D FIND OUT ABOUT LIGHT ONE DAY.
IT'S GOING TO CHANGE THINGS, WALLY. ESPECIALLY IF YOU DO WHAT HE ASKS.
BUT THAT'S BETWEEN HIM AND YOU.
KLK
SSSSFF
HE WAS ONLY TRYING TO MAKE THE WORLD A SAFER PLACE.
AND HE LOVED YOU, KID.
WE ALL DO.

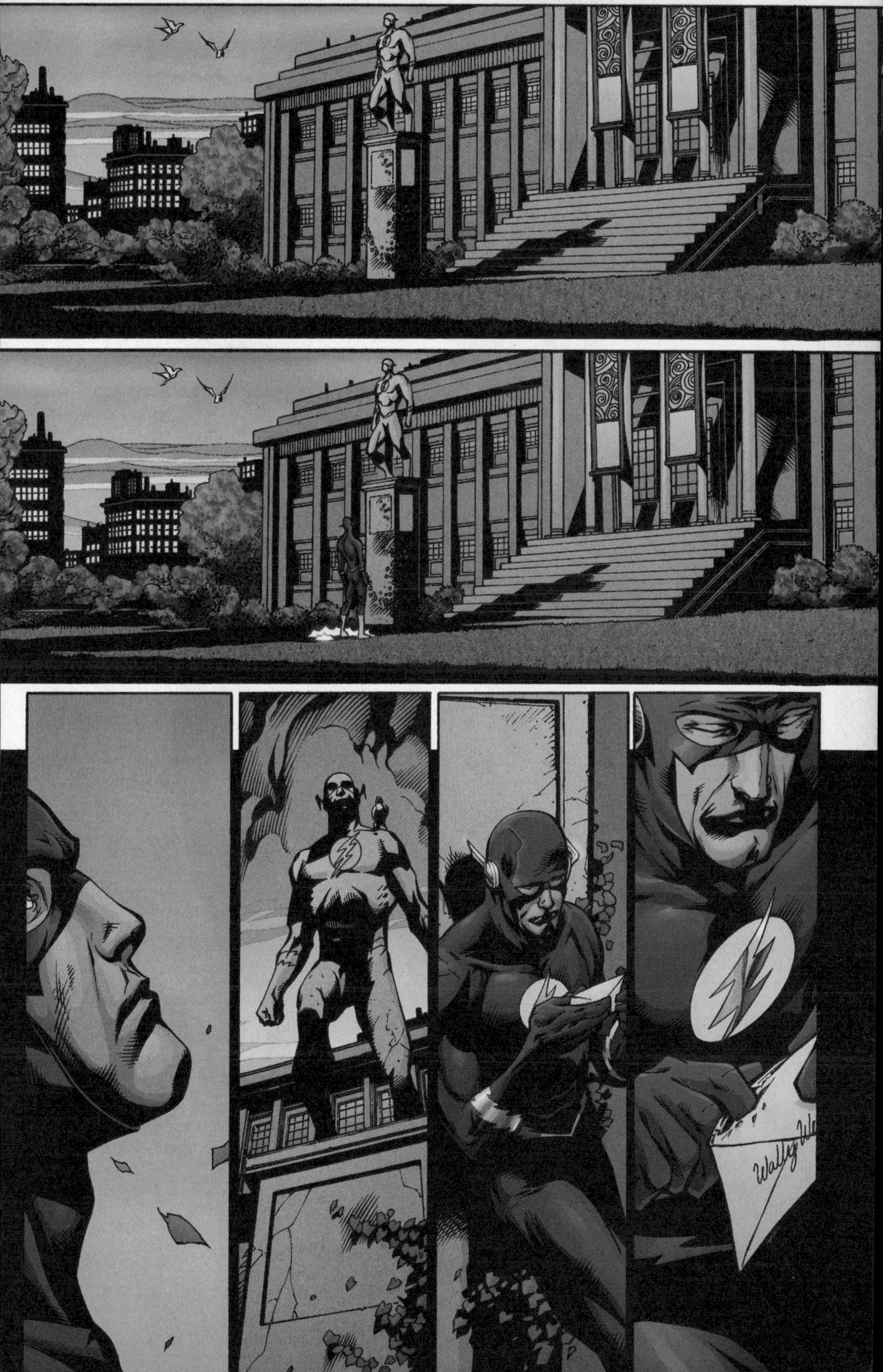
Wally

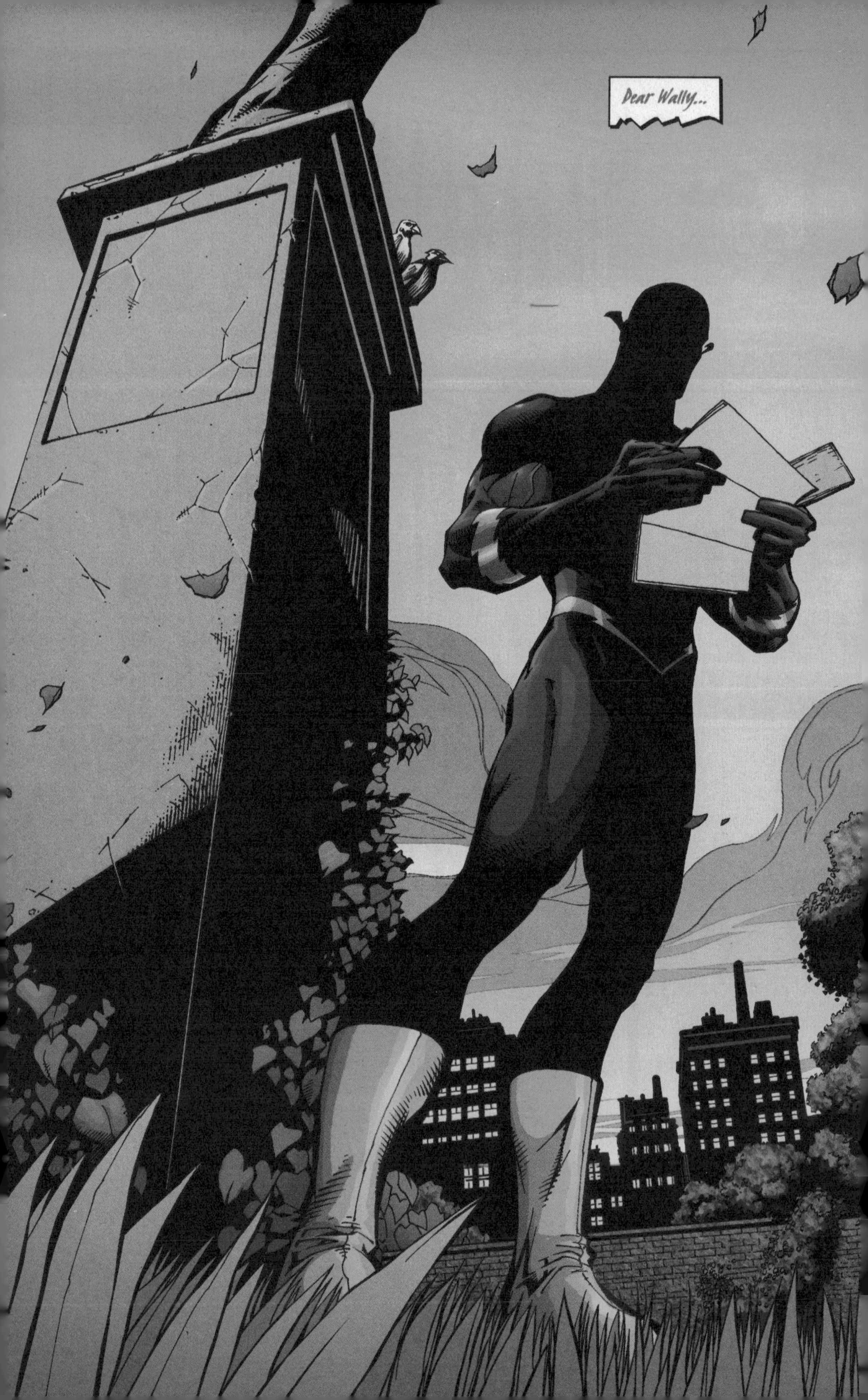
Dear Wally...

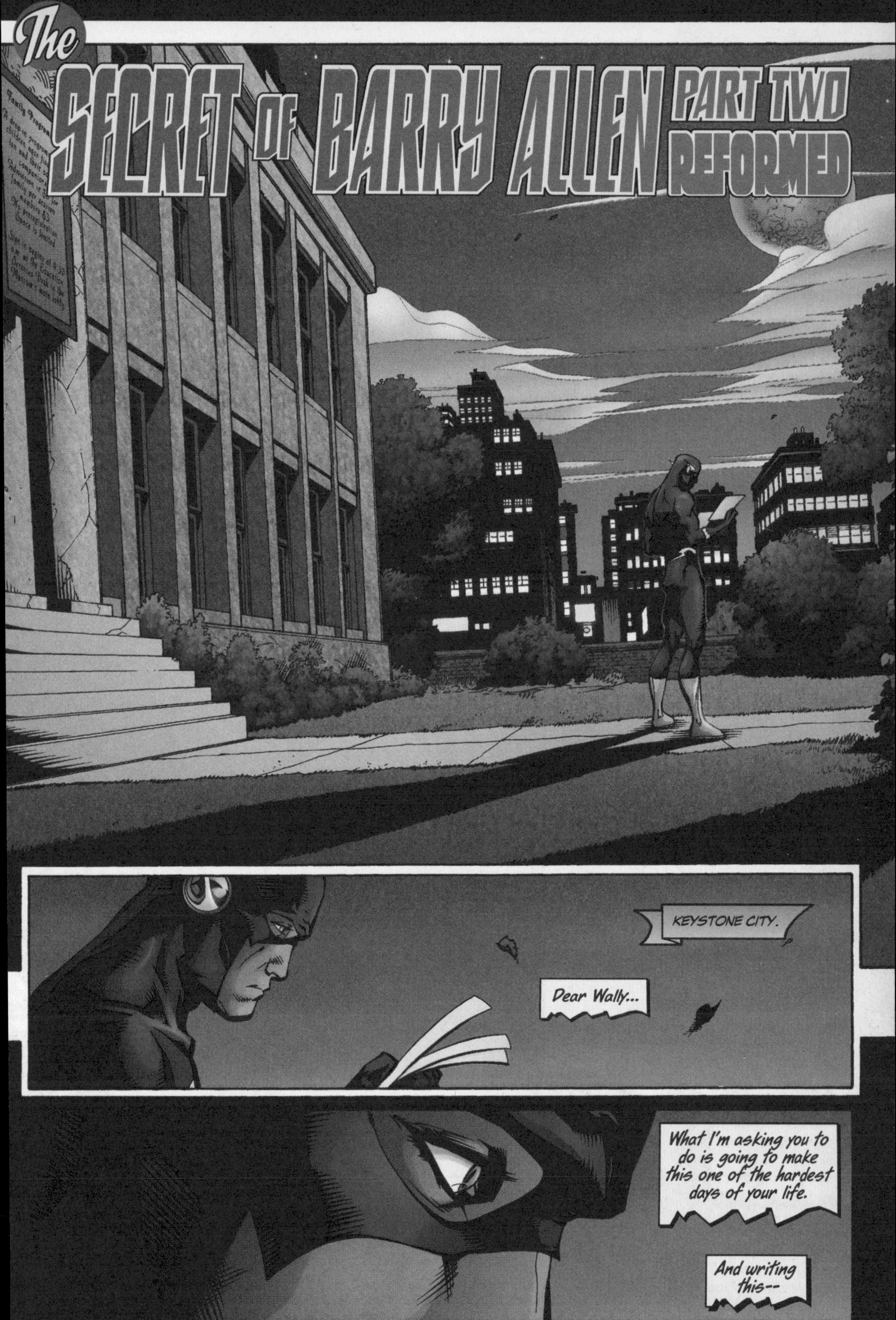
The
SECRET OF BARRY ALLEN
PART TWO
REFORMED
KEYSTONE CITY.
Dear Wally...
What I'm asking you to do is going to make this one of the hardest days of your life.
And writing this--

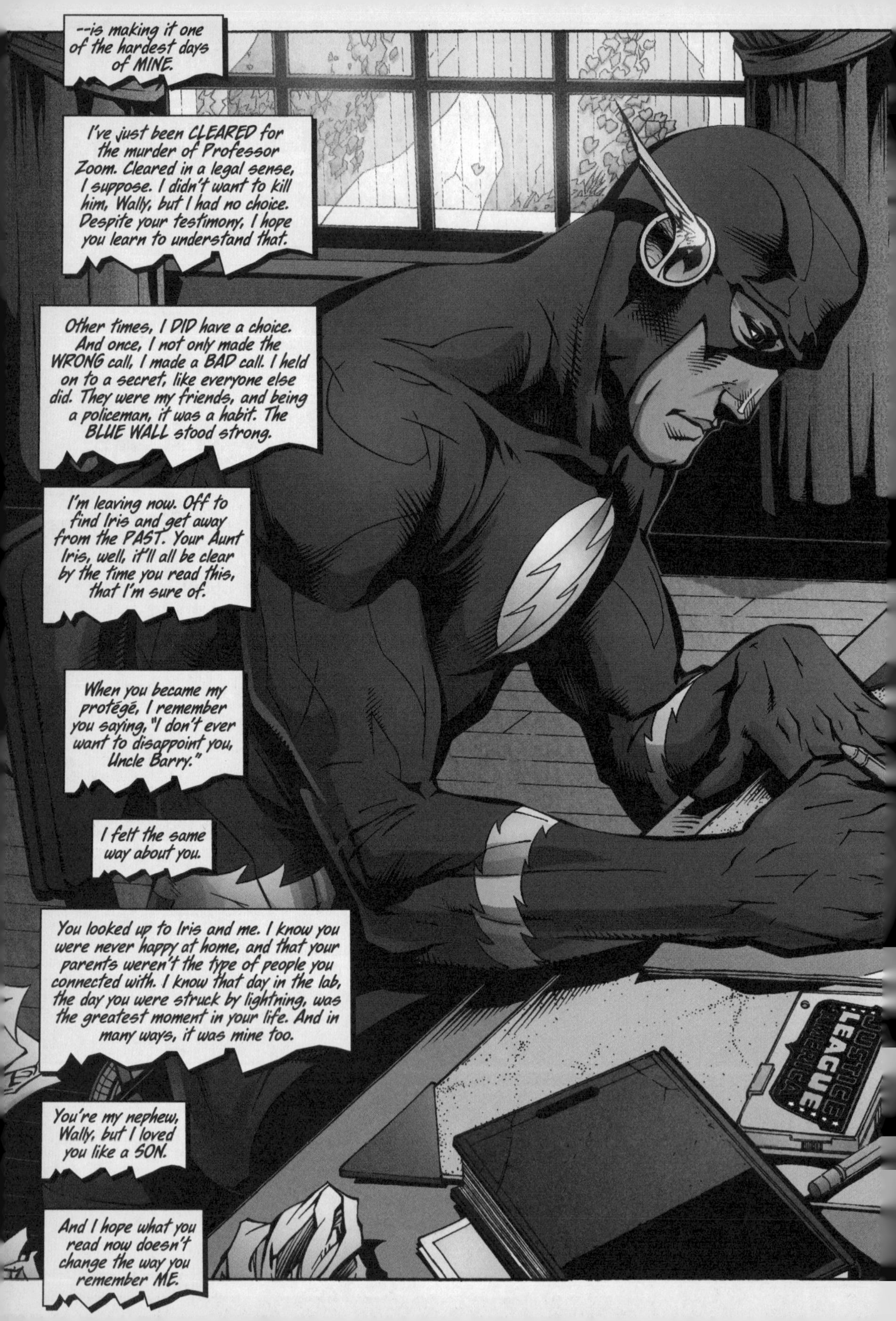
--is making it one of the hardest days of MINE.
I've just been CLEARED for the murder of Professor Zoom. Cleared in a legal sense, I suppose. I didn't want to kill him, Wally, but I had no choice. Despite your testimony, I hope you learn to understand that.
Other times, I DID have a choice. And once, I not only made the WRONG call, I made a BAD call. I held on to a secret, like everyone else did. They were my friends, and being a policeman, it was a habit. The BLUE WALL stood strong.
I'm leaving now. Off to find Iris and get away from the PAST. Your Aunt Iris, well, it'll all be clear by the time you read this, that I'm sure of.
When you became my protégé, I remember you saying, "I don't ever want to disappoint you, Uncle Barry."
I felt the same way about you.
You looked up to Iris and me. I know you were never happy at home, and that your parents weren't the type of people you connected with. I know that day in the lab, the day you were struck by lightning, was the greatest moment in your life. And in many ways, it was mine too.
You're my nephew, Wally, but I loved you like a SON.
And I hope what you read now doesn't change the way you remember ME.
JUSTICE LEAGUE AMERICA

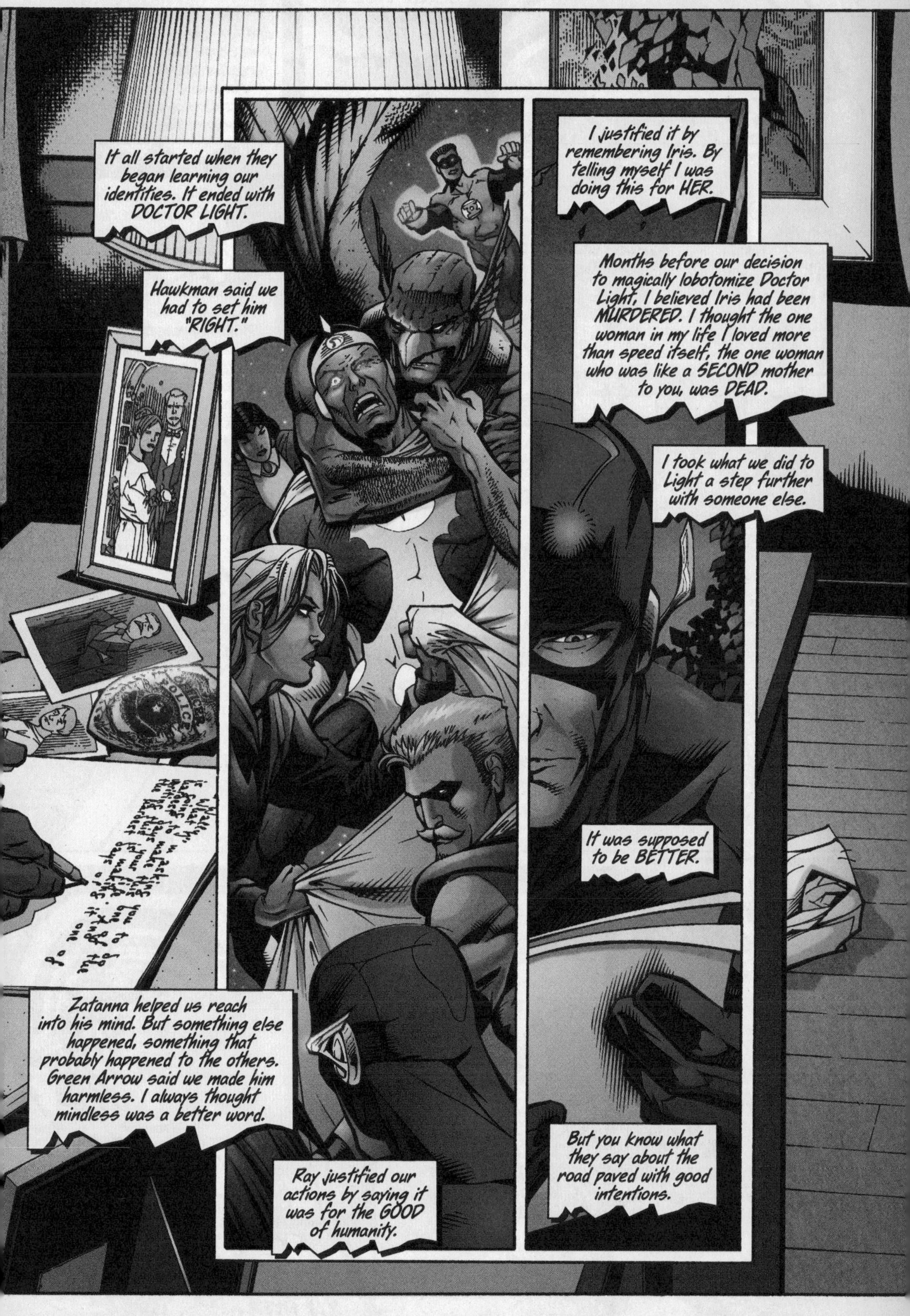
It all started when they began learning our identities. It ended with DOCTOR LIGHT.
Hawkman said we had to set him "RIGHT."
Zatanna helped us reach into his mind. But something else happened, something that probably happened to the others. Green Arrow said we made him harmless. I always thought mindless was a better word.
Ray justified our actions by saying it was for the GOOD of humanity.
I justified it by remembering Iris. By telling myself I was doing this for HER.
Months before our decision to magically lobotomize Doctor Light, I believed Iris had been MURDERED. I thought the one woman in my life I loved more than speed itself, the one woman who was like a SECOND mother to you, was DEAD.
I took what we did to Light a step further with someone else.
It was supposed to be BETTER.
But you know what they say about the road paved with good intentions.

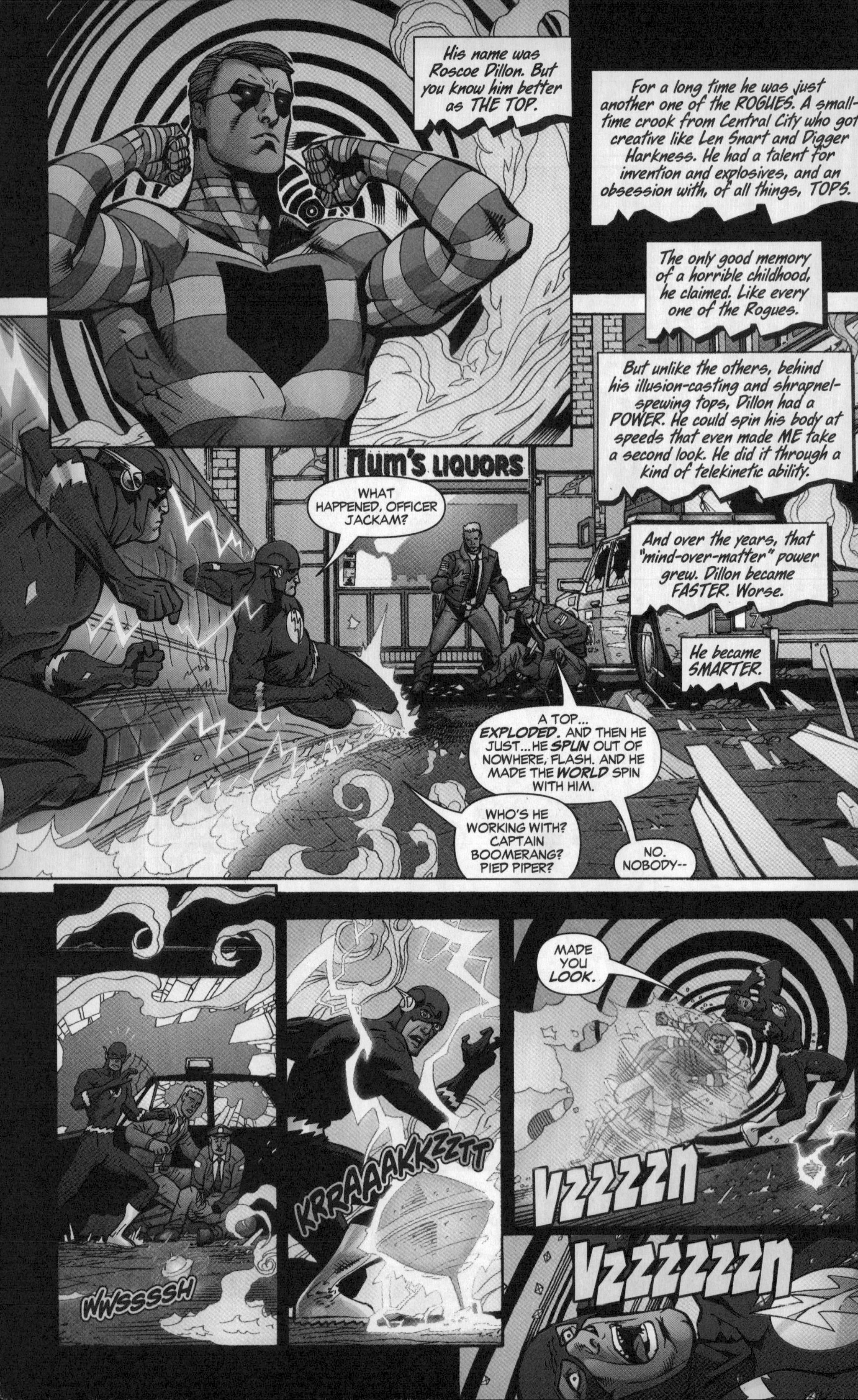

His name was Roscoe Dillon. But you know him better as THE TOP.
For a long time he was just another one of the ROGUES. A small-time crook from Central City who got creative like Len Snart and Digger Harkness. He had a talent for invention and explosives, and an obsession with, of all things, TOPS.
The only good memory of a horrible childhood, he claimed. Like every one of the Rogues.
But unlike the others, behind his illusion-casting and shrapnel-spewing tops, Dillon had a POWER. He could spin his body at speeds that even made ME take a second look. He did it through a kind of telekinetic ability.
Num's LIQUORS
WHAT HAPPENED, OFFICER JACKAM?
And over the years, that "mind-over-matter" power grew. Dillon became FASTER. Worse.
He became SMARTER.
A TOP... EXPLODED. AND THEN HE JUST...HE SPUN OUT OF NOWHERE, FLASH. AND HE MADE THE WORLD SPIN WITH HIM.
WHO'S HE WORKING WITH? CAPTAIN BOOMERANG? PIED PIPER?
NO. NOBODY--
WWSSSSH
KRRAAAKKZZTT
MADE YOU LOOK.
VZZZZN
VZZZZZZN

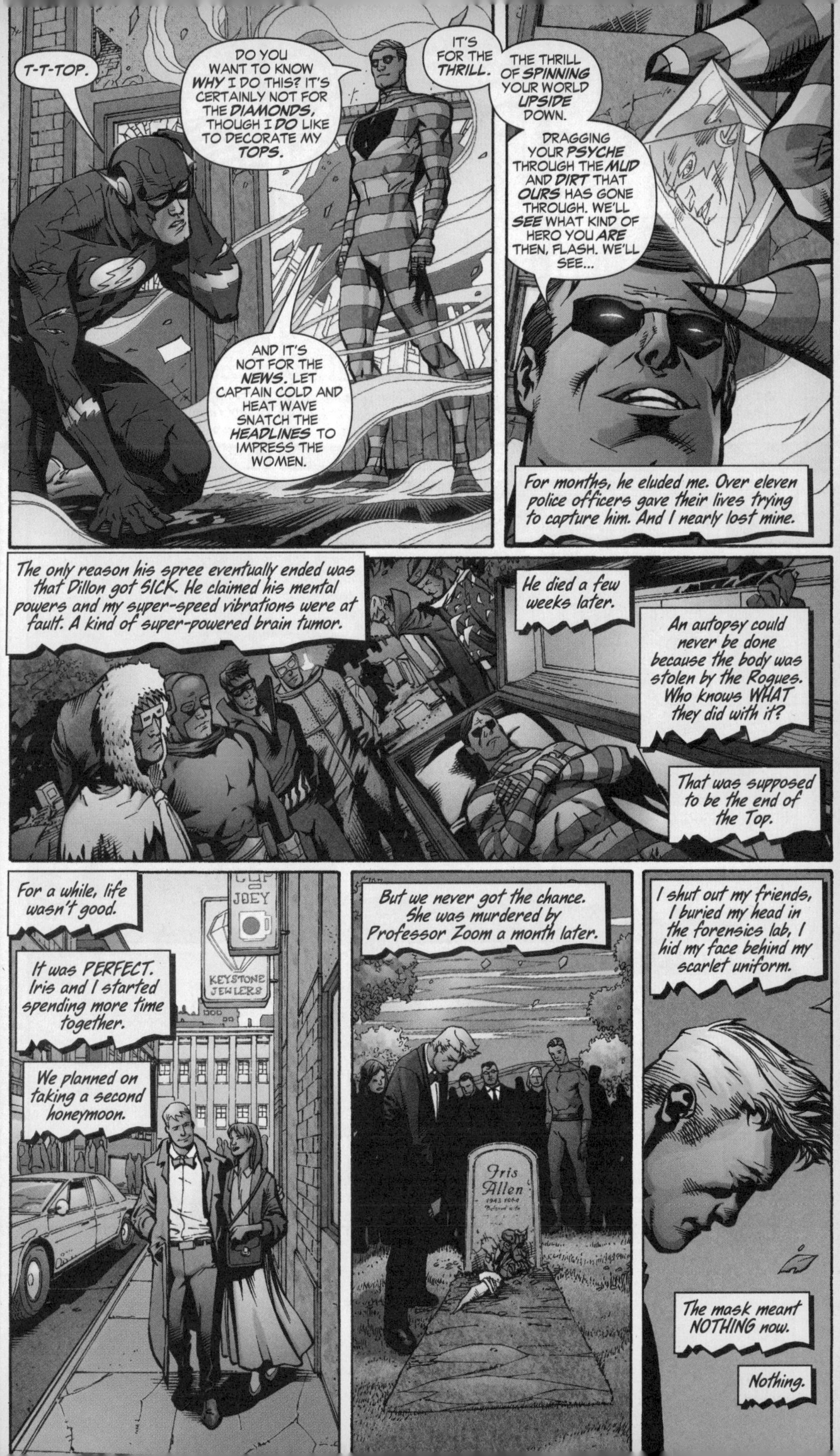
T-T-TOP.
DO YOU WANT TO KNOW WHY I DO THIS? IT'S CERTAINLY NOT FOR THE DIAMONDS, THOUGH I DO LIKE TO DECORATE MY TOPS.
AND IT'S NOT FOR THE NEWS. LET CAPTAIN COLD AND HEAT WAVE SNATCH THE HEADLINES TO IMPRESS THE WOMEN.
IT'S FOR THE THRILL.
THE THRILL OF SPINNING YOUR WORLD UPSIDE DOWN.
DRAGGING YOUR PSYCHE THROUGH THE MUD AND DIRT THAT OURS HAS GONE THROUGH. WE'LL SEE WHAT KIND OF HERO YOU ARE THEN, FLASH. WE'LL SEE...
For months, he eluded me. Over eleven police officers gave their lives trying to capture him. And I nearly lost mine.
The only reason his spree eventually ended was that Dillon got SICK. He claimed his mental powers and my super-speed vibrations were at fault. A kind of super-powered brain tumor.
He died a few weeks later.
An autopsy could never be done because the body was stolen by the Rogues. Who knows WHAT they did with it?
That was supposed to be the end of the Top.
For a while, life wasn't good.
JOEY
KEYSTONE JEWLERS
It was PERFECT. Iris and I started spending more time together.
We planned on taking a second honeymoon.
But we never got the chance. She was murdered by Professor Zoom a month later.
Iris Allen
I shut out my friends, I buried my head in the forensics lab, I hid my face behind my scarlet uniform.
The mask meant NOTHING now.
Nothing.

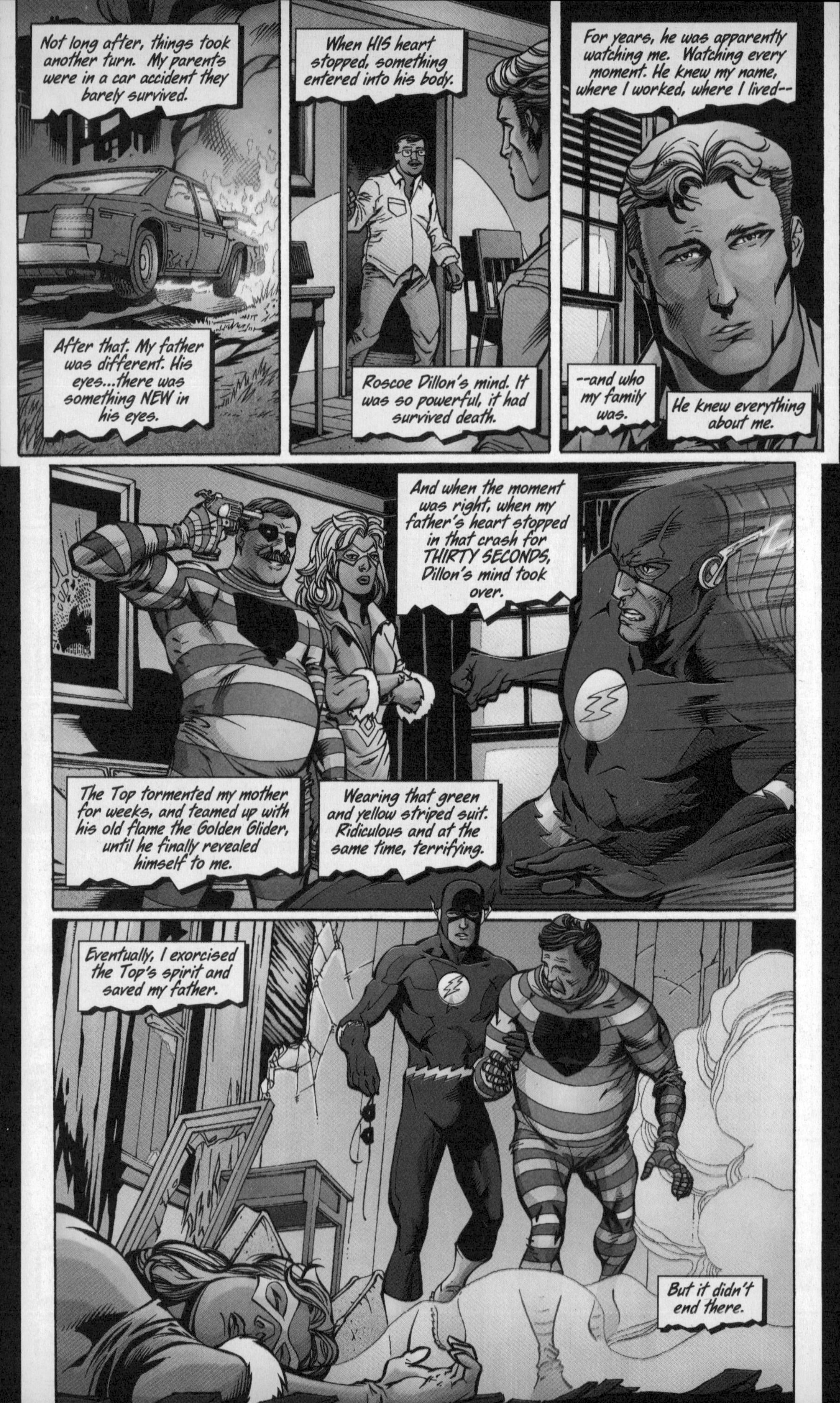
Not long after, things took another turn. My parents were in a car accident they barely survived.
After that. My father was different. His eyes...there was something NEW in his eyes.
When HIS heart stopped, something entered into his body.
Roscoe Dillon's mind. It was so powerful, it had survived death.
For years, he was apparently watching me. Watching every moment. He knew my name, where I worked, where I lived--
--and who my family was.
He knew everything about me.
And when the moment was right, when my father's heart stopped in that crash for THIRTY SECONDS, Dillon's mind took over.
The Top tormented my mother for weeks, and teamed up with his old flame the Golden Glider, until he finally revealed himself to me.
Wearing that green and yellow striped suit. Ridiculous and at the same time, terrifying.
Eventually, I exorcised the Top's spirit and saved my father.
But it didn't end there.

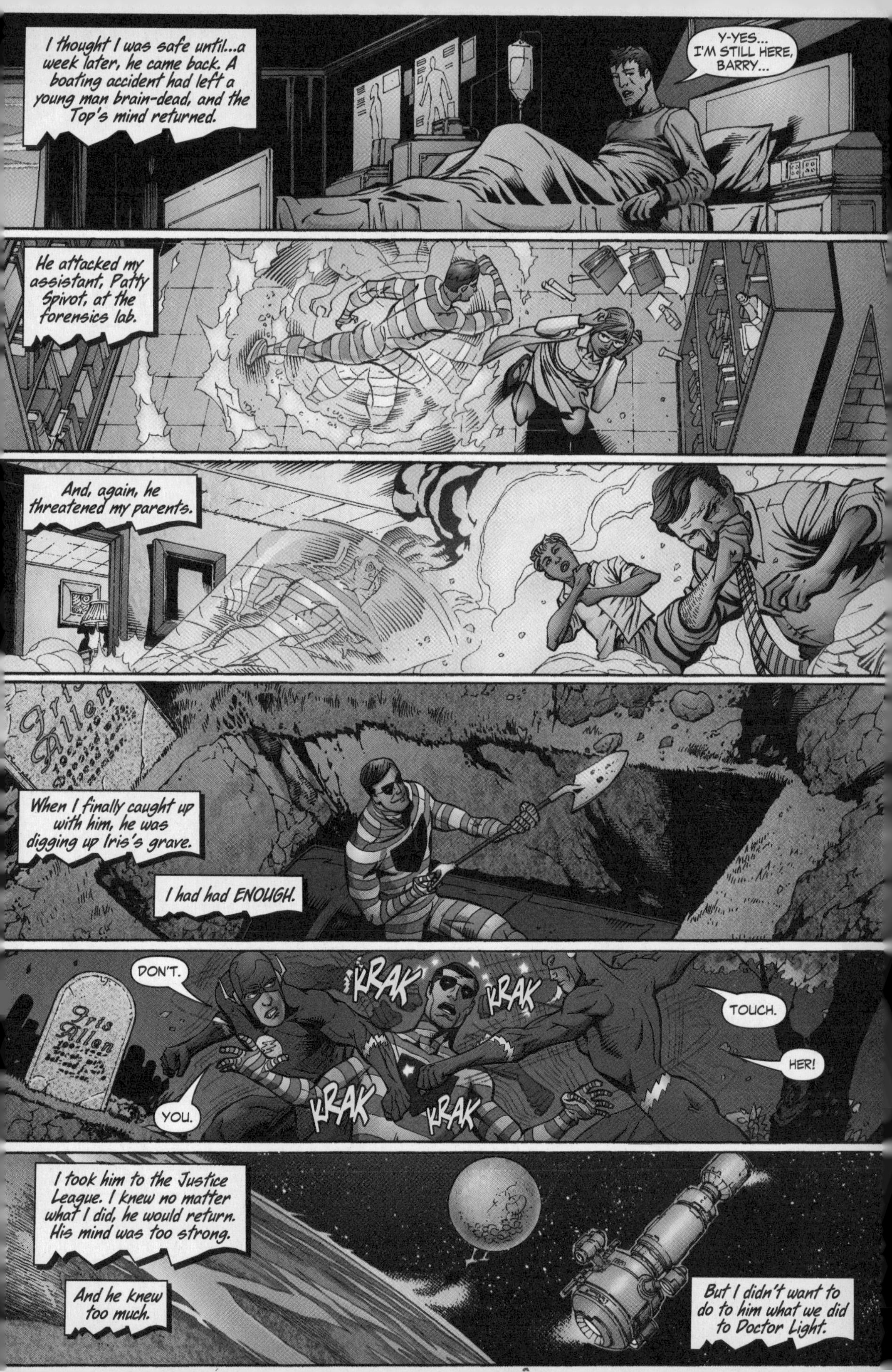
I thought I was safe until...a week later, he came back. A boating accident had left a young man brain-dead, and the Top's mind returned.
Y-YES... I'M STILL HERE, BARRY...
He attacked my assistant, Patty Spivot, at the forensics lab.
And, again, he threatened my parents.
When I finally caught up with him, he was digging up Iris's grave.
I had had ENOUGH.
DON'T.
KRAK
KRAK
TOUCH.
HER!
YOU.
KRAK
KRAK
I took him to the Justice League. I knew no matter what I did, he would return. His mind was too strong.
And he knew too much.
But I didn't want to do to him what we did to Doctor Light.

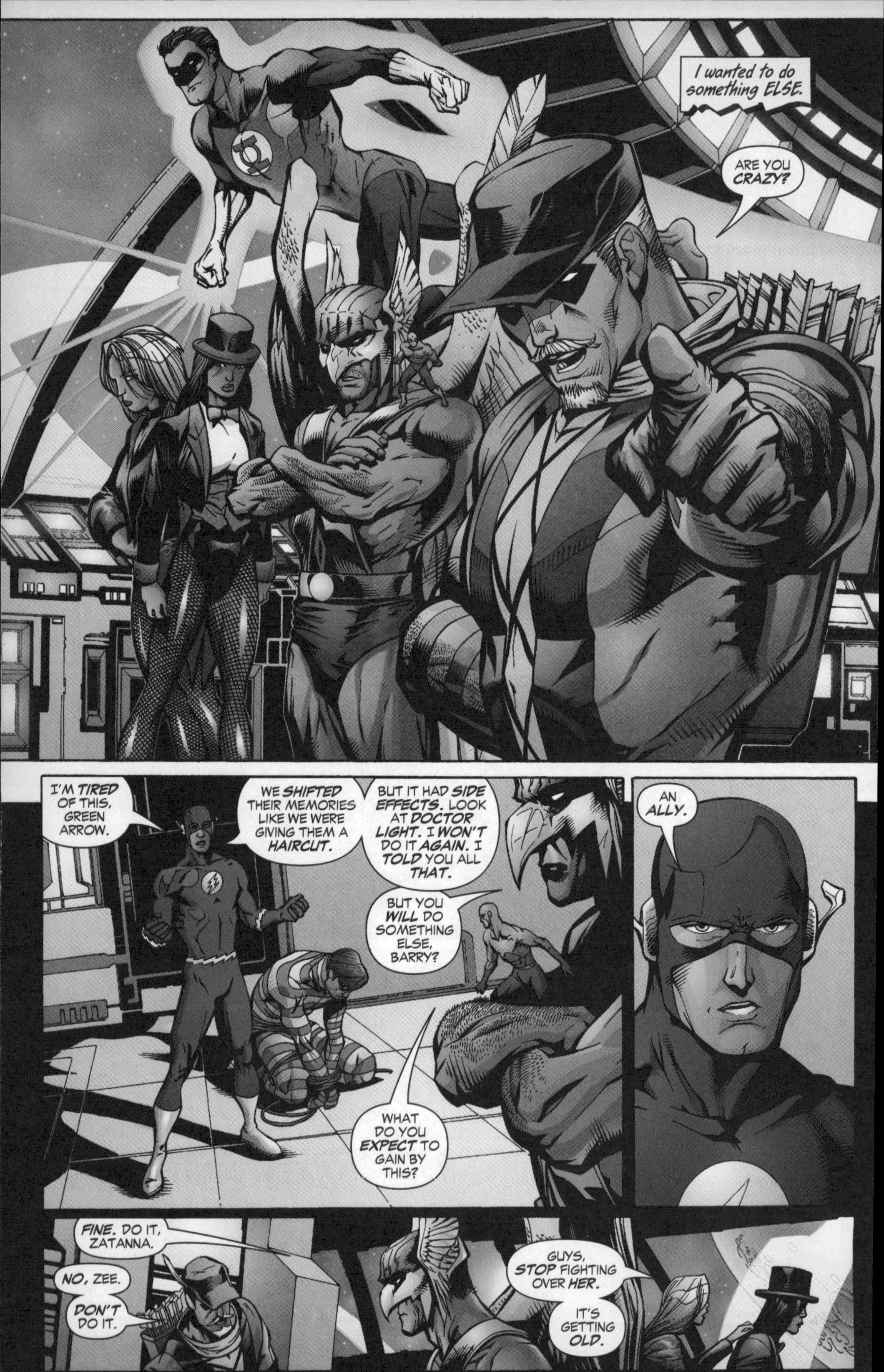
I wanted to do something ELSE.
ARE YOU CRAZY?
I'M TIRED OF THIS, GREEN ARROW.
WE SHIFTED THEIR MEMORIES LIKE WE WERE GIVING THEM A HAIRCUT.
BUT IT HAD SIDE EFFECTS. LOOK AT DOCTOR LIGHT. I WON'T DO IT AGAIN. I TOLD YOU ALL THAT.
BUT YOU WILL DO SOMETHING ELSE, BARRY?
WHAT DO YOU EXPECT TO GAIN BY THIS?
AN ALLY.
FINE. DO IT, ZATANNA.
NO, ZEE.
DON'T DO IT.
GUYS, STOP FIGHTING OVER HER.
IT'S GETTING OLD.

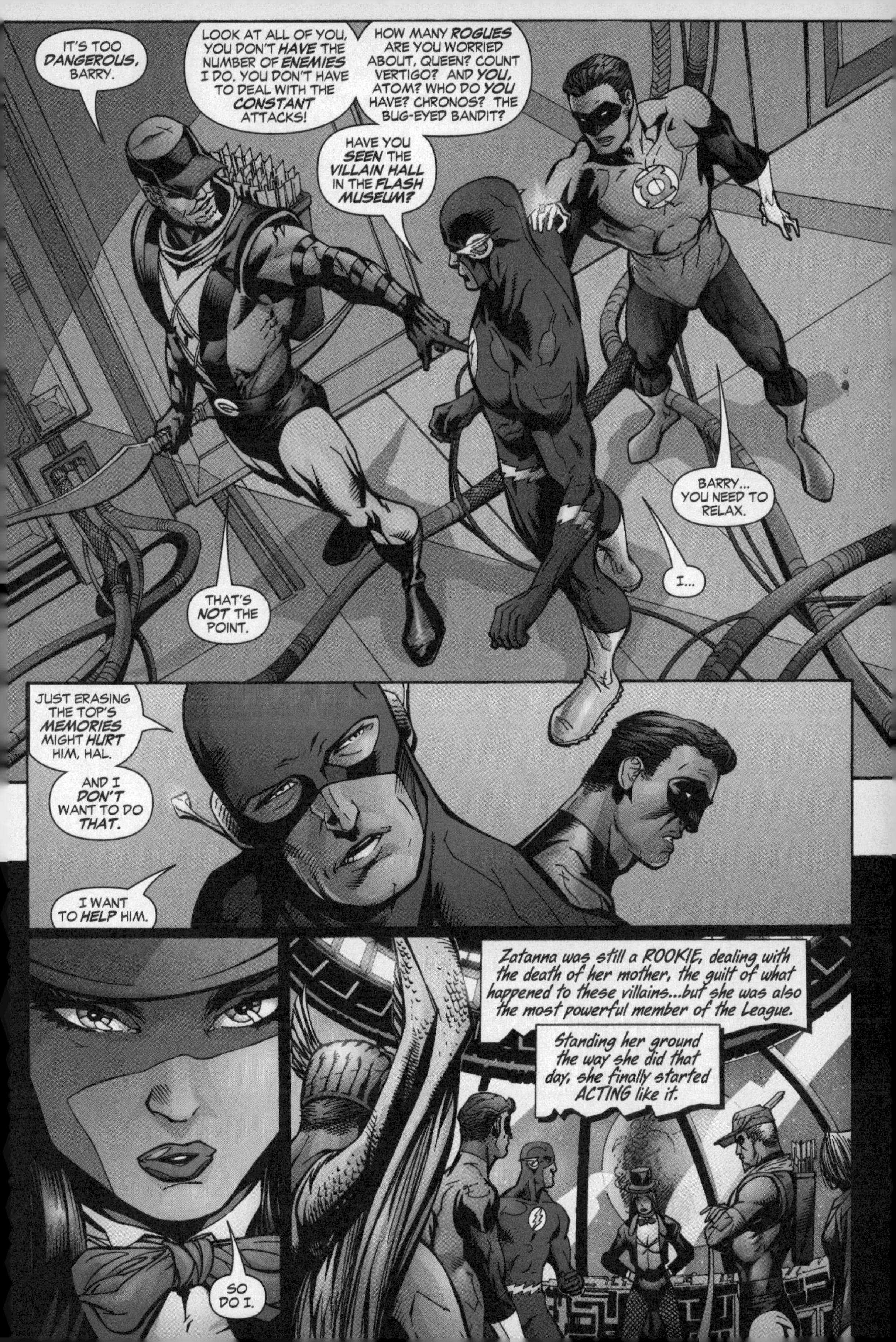
IT'S TOO DANGEROUS, BARRY.
LOOK AT ALL OF YOU, YOU DON'T HAVE THE NUMBER OF ENEMIES I DO. YOU DON'T HAVE TO DEAL WITH THE CONSTANT ATTACKS!
HOW MANY ROGUES ARE YOU WORRIED ABOUT, QUEEN? COUNT VERTIGO? AND YOU, ATOM? WHO DO YOU HAVE? CHRONOS? THE BUG-EYED BANDIT?
HAVE YOU SEEN THE VILLAIN HALL IN THE FLASH MUSEUM?
BARRY... YOU NEED TO RELAX.
THAT'S NOT THE POINT.
I...
JUST ERASING THE TOP'S MEMORIES MIGHT HURT HIM, HAL.
AND I DON'T WANT TO DO THAT.
I WANT TO HELP HIM.
SO DO I.
Zatanna was still a ROOKIE, dealing with the death of her mother, the guilt of what happened to these villains...but she was also the most powerful member of the League.
Standing her ground the way she did that day, she finally started ACTING like it.

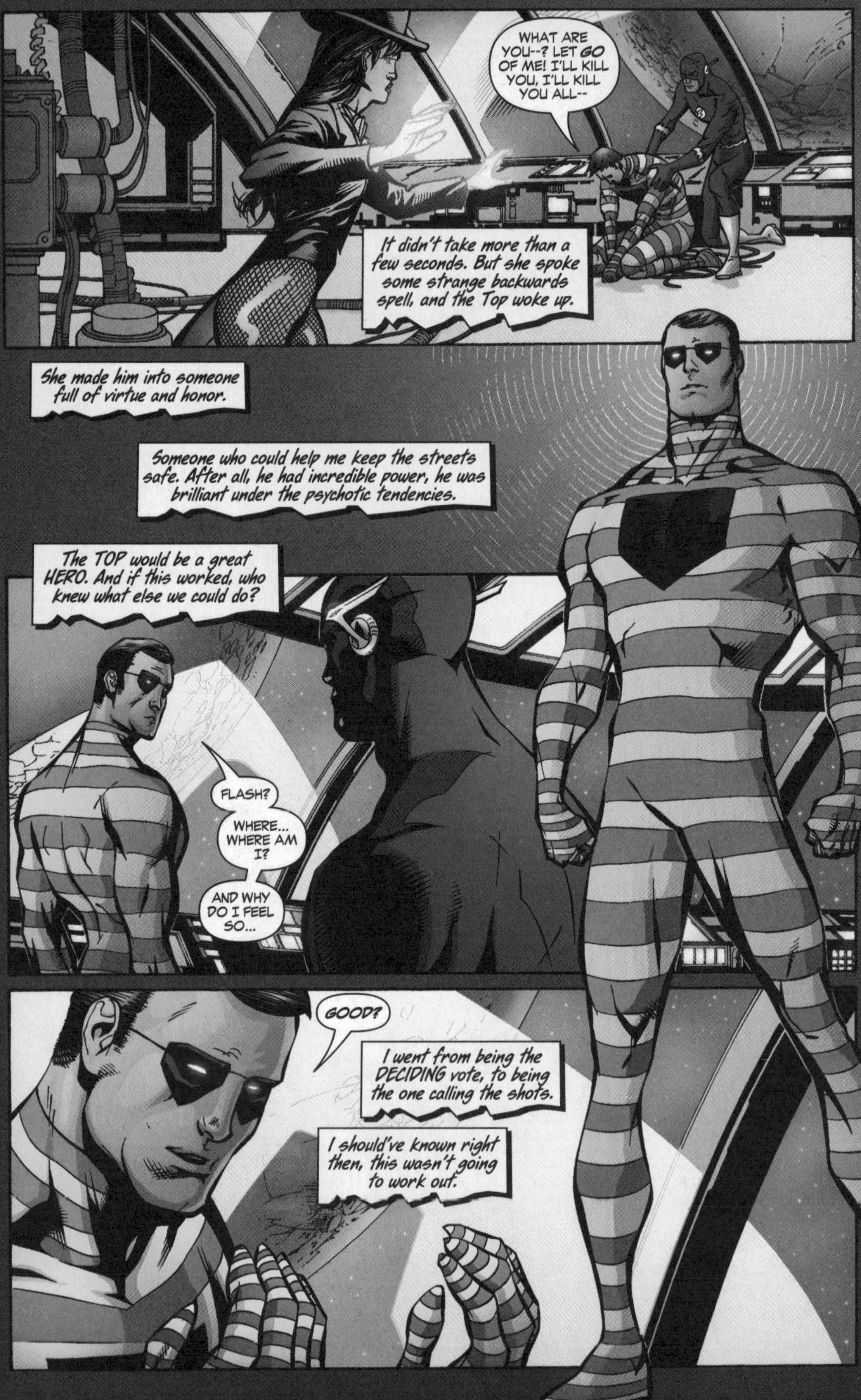
WHAT ARE YOU--? LET GO OF ME! I'LL KILL YOU, I'LL KILL YOU ALL--
It didn't take more than a few seconds. But she spoke some strange backwards spell, and the Top woke up.
She made him into someone full of virtue and honor.
Someone who could help me keep the streets safe. After all, he had incredible power, he was brilliant under the psychotic tendencies.
The TOP would be a great HERO. And if this worked, who knew what else we could do?
FLASH?
WHERE... WHERE AM I?
AND WHY DO I FEEL SO...
GOOD?
I went from being the DECIDING vote, to being the one calling the shots.
I should've known right then, this wasn't going to work out.

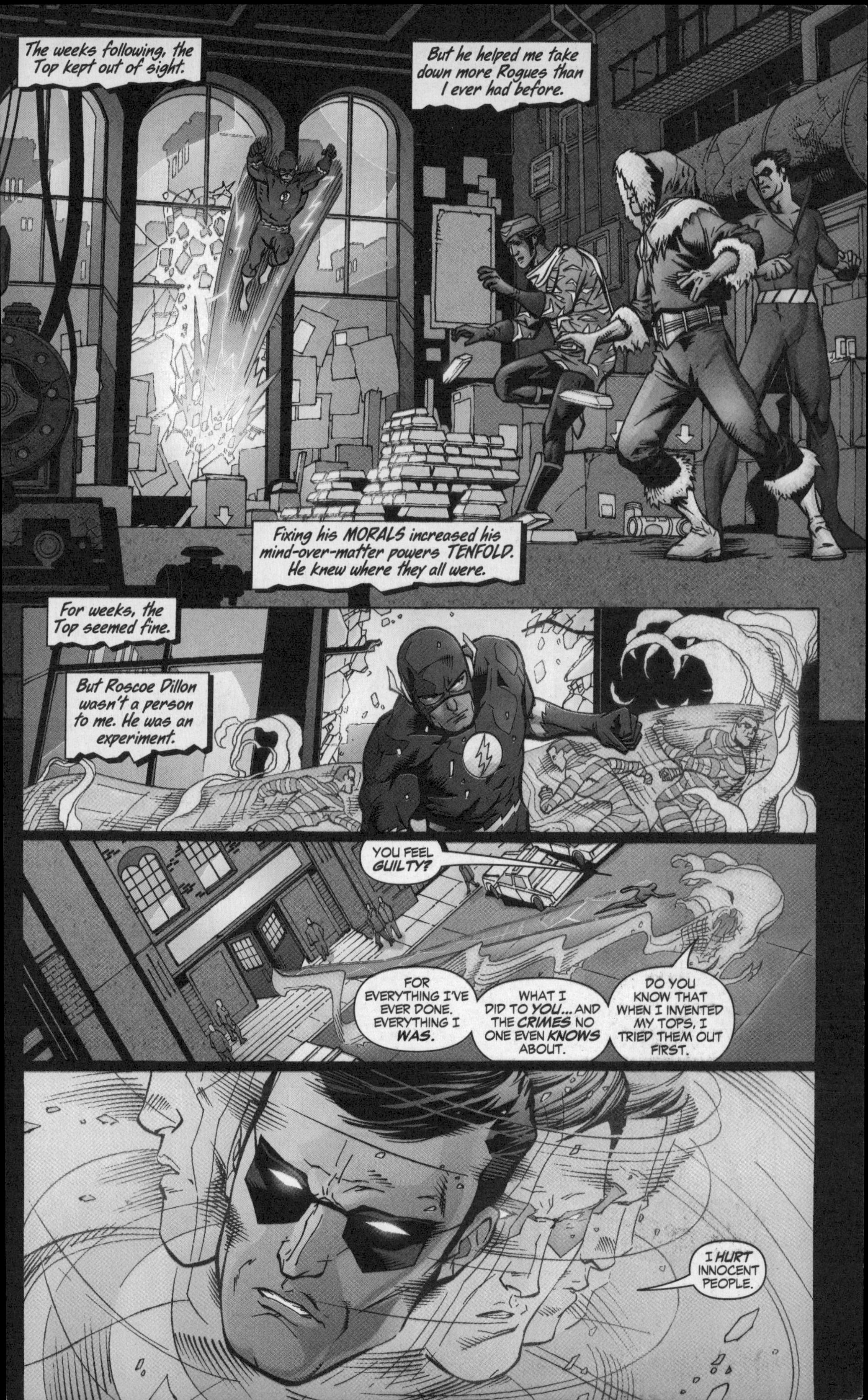

The weeks following, the Top kept out of sight.
But he helped me take down more Rogues than I ever had before.
Fixing his MORALS increased his mind-over-matter powers TENFOLD. He knew where they all were.
For weeks, the Top seemed fine.
But Roscoe Dillon wasn't a person to me. He was an experiment.
YOU FEEL GUILTY?
FOR EVERYTHING I'VE EVER DONE. EVERYTHING I WAS.
WHAT I DID TO YOU... AND THE CRIMES NO ONE EVEN KNOWS ABOUT.
DO YOU KNOW THAT WHEN I INVENTED MY TOPS, I TRIED THEM OUT FIRST.
I HURT INNOCENT PEOPLE.

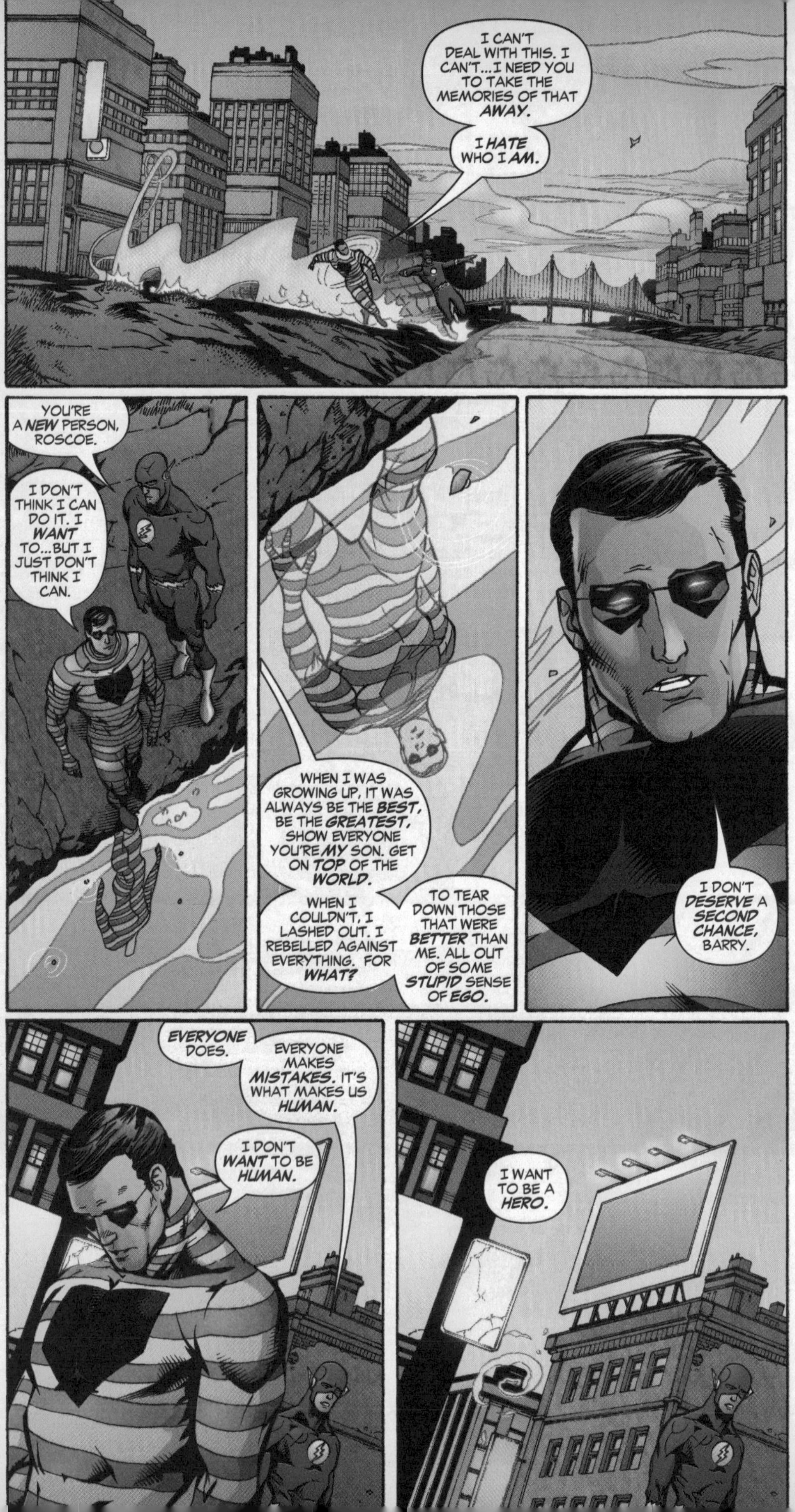
I CAN'T DEAL WITH THIS. I CAN'T...I NEED YOU TO TAKE THE MEMORIES OF THAT AWAY.
I HATE WHO I AM.
YOU'RE A NEW PERSON, ROSCOE.
I DON'T THINK I CAN DO IT. I WANT TO...BUT I JUST DON'T THINK I CAN.
WHEN I WAS GROWING UP, IT WAS ALWAYS BE THE BEST, BE THE GREATEST, SHOW EVERYONE YOU'RE MY SON. GET ON TOP OF THE WORLD.
WHEN I COULDN'T, I LASHED OUT. I REBELLED AGAINST EVERYTHING. FOR WHAT?
TO TEAR DOWN THOSE THAT WERE BETTER THAN ME. ALL OUT OF SOME STUPID SENSE OF EGO.
I DON'T DESERVE A SECOND CHANCE, BARRY.
EVERYONE DOES.
EVERYONE MAKES MISTAKES. IT'S WHAT MAKES US HUMAN.
I DON'T WANT TO BE HUMAN.
I WANT TO BE A HERO.

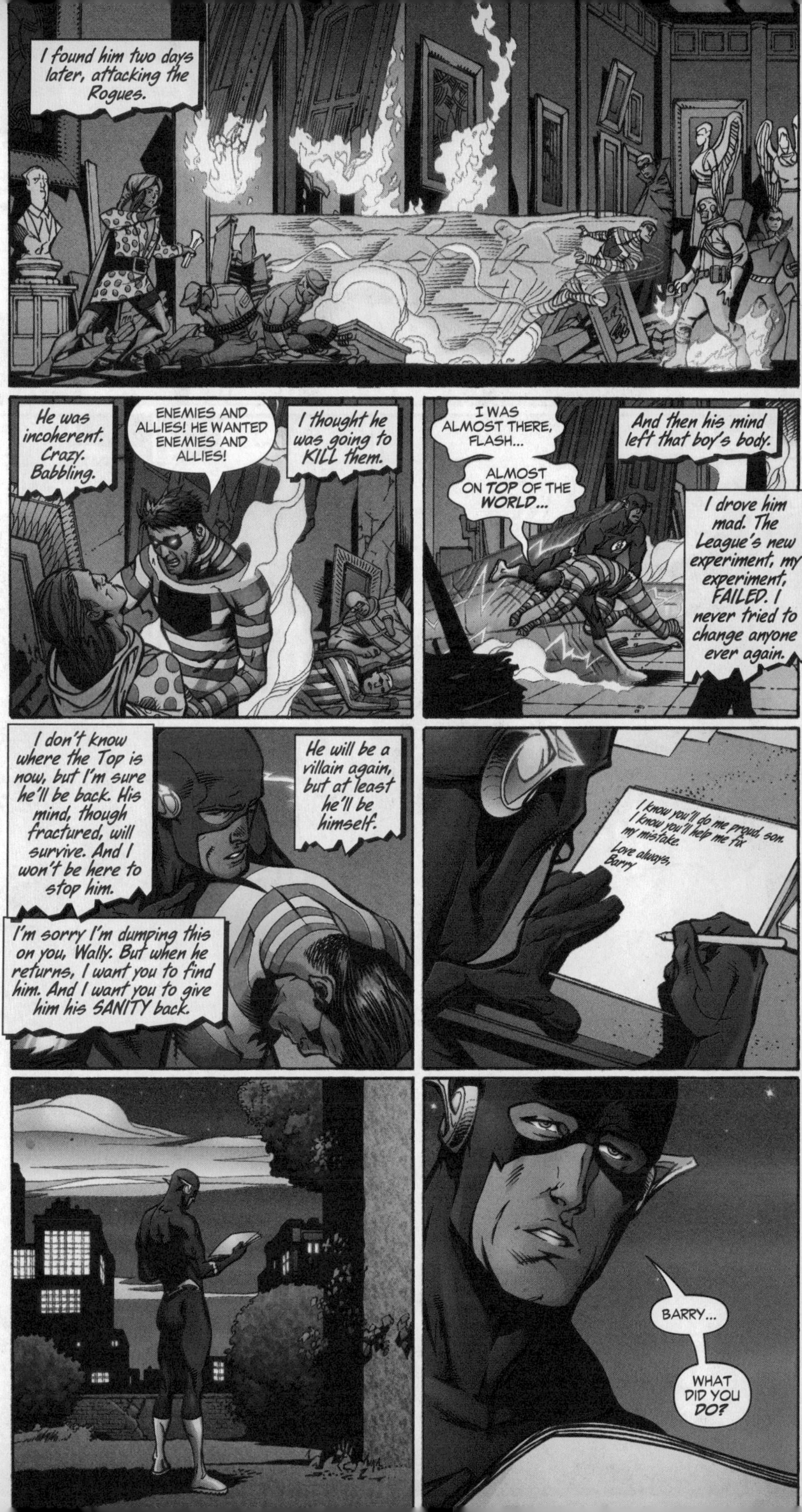

I found him two days later, attacking the Rogues.
He was incoherent. Crazy. Babbling.
ENEMIES AND ALLIES! HE WANTED ENEMIES AND ALLIES!
I thought he was going to KILL them.
I WAS ALMOST THERE, FLASH...
ALMOST ON TOP OF THE WORLD...
And then his mind left that boy's body.
I drove him mad. The League's new experiment, my experiment, FAILED. I never tried to change anyone ever again.
I don't know where the Top is now, but I'm sure he'll be back. His mind, though fractured, will survive. And I won't be here to stop him.
He will be a villain again, but at least he'll be himself.
I'm sorry I'm dumping this on you, Wally. But when he returns, I want you to find him. And I want you to give him his SANITY back.
I know you'll do me proud, son. I know you'll help me fix my mistake.
Love always, Barry
BARRY...
WHAT DID YOU DO?

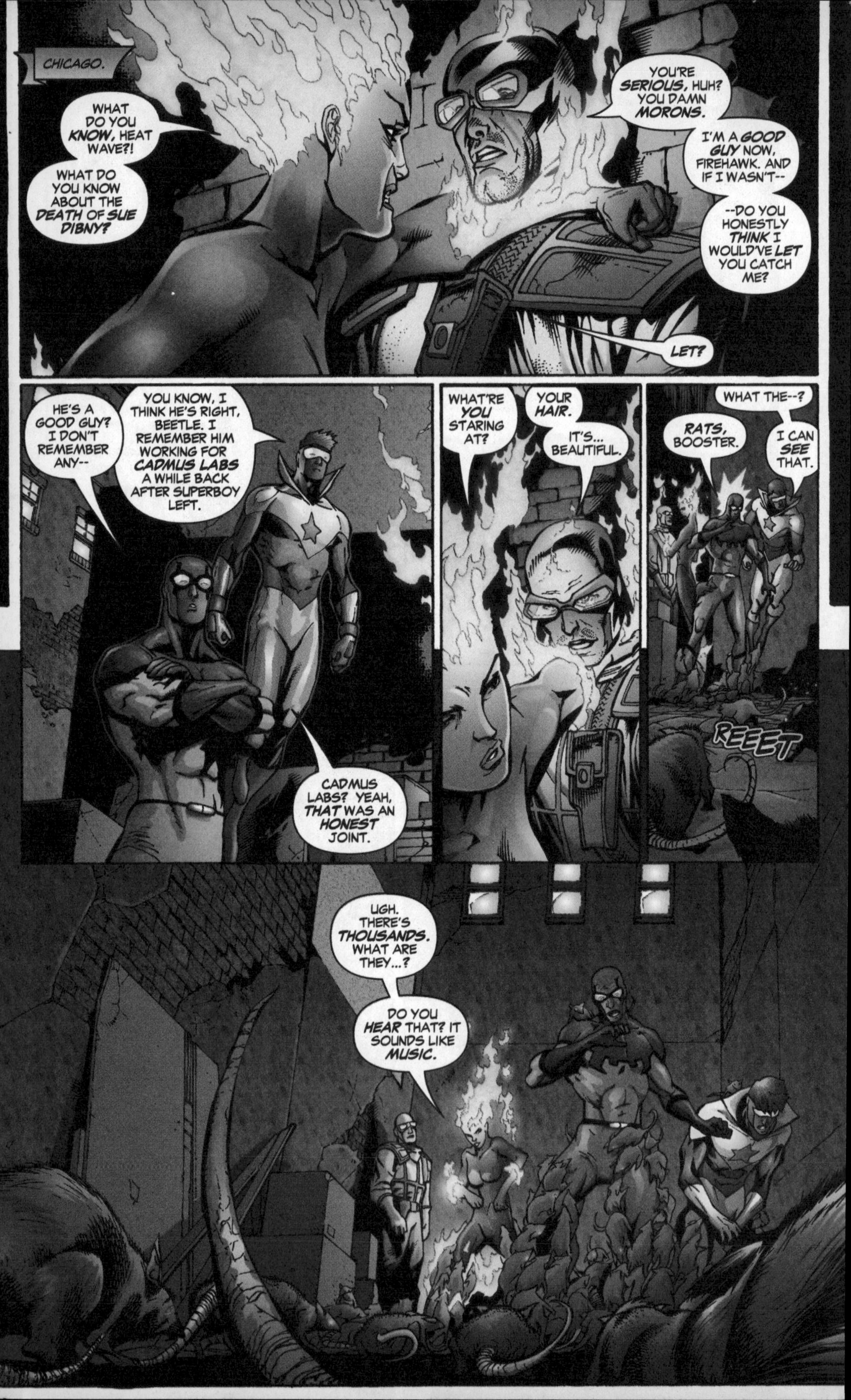
CHICAGO.
WHAT DO YOU KNOW, HEAT WAVE?!
WHAT DO YOU KNOW ABOUT THE DEATH OF SUE DIBNY?
YOU'RE SERIOUS, HUH? YOU DAMN MORONS.
I'M A GOOD GUY NOW, FIREHAWK. AND IF I WASN'T--
--DO YOU HONESTLY THINK I WOULD'VE LET YOU CATCH ME?
LET?
HE'S A GOOD GUY? I DON'T REMEMBER ANY--
YOU KNOW, I THINK HE'S RIGHT, BEETLE. I REMEMBER HIM WORKING FOR CADMUS LABS A WHILE BACK AFTER SUPERBOY LEFT.
CADMUS LABS? YEAH, THAT WAS AN HONEST JOINT.
WHAT'RE YOU STARING AT?
YOUR HAIR.
IT'S... BEAUTIFUL.
WHAT THE--?
RATS, BOOSTER.
I CAN SEE THAT.
REEET
UGH. THERE'S THOUSANDS. WHAT ARE THEY...?
DO YOU HEAR THAT? IT SOUNDS LIKE MUSIC.

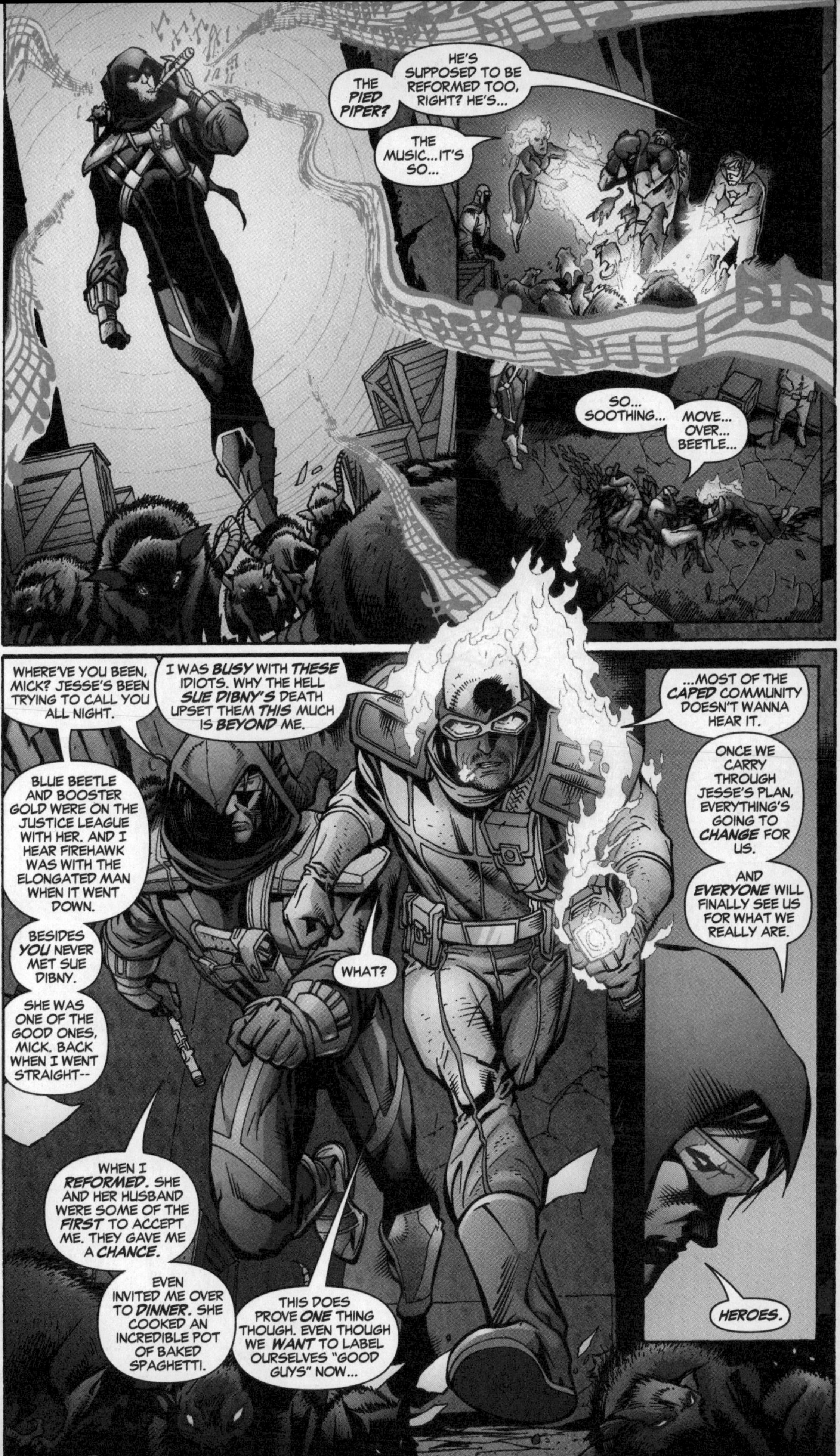
THE PIED PIPER?
HE'S SUPPOSED TO BE REFORMED TOO, RIGHT? HE'S...
THE MUSIC...IT'S SO...
SO... SOOTHING...
MOVE... OVER... BEETLE...
WHERE'VE YOU BEEN, MICK? JESSE'S BEEN TRYING TO CALL YOU ALL NIGHT.
I WAS BUSY WITH THESE IDIOTS. WHY THE HELL SUE DIBNY'S DEATH UPSET THEM THIS MUCH IS BEYOND ME.
BLUE BEETLE AND BOOSTER GOLD WERE ON THE JUSTICE LEAGUE WITH HER. AND I HEAR FIREHAWK WAS WITH THE ELONGATED MAN WHEN IT WENT DOWN.
BESIDES YOU NEVER MET SUE DIBNY.
SHE WAS ONE OF THE GOOD ONES, MICK. BACK WHEN I WENT STRAIGHT--
WHAT?
WHEN I REFORMED. SHE AND HER HUSBAND WERE SOME OF THE FIRST TO ACCEPT ME. THEY GAVE ME A CHANCE.
EVEN INVITED ME OVER TO DINNER. SHE COOKED AN INCREDIBLE POT OF BAKED SPAGHETTI.
THIS DOES PROVE ONE THING THOUGH. EVEN THOUGH WE WANT TO LABEL OURSELVES "GOOD GUYS" NOW...
...MOST OF THE CAPED COMMUNITY DOESN'T WANNA HEAR IT.
ONCE WE CARRY THROUGH JESSE'S PLAN, EVERYTHING'S GOING TO CHANGE FOR US.
AND EVERYONE WILL FINALLY SEE US FOR WHAT WE REALLY ARE.
HEROES.

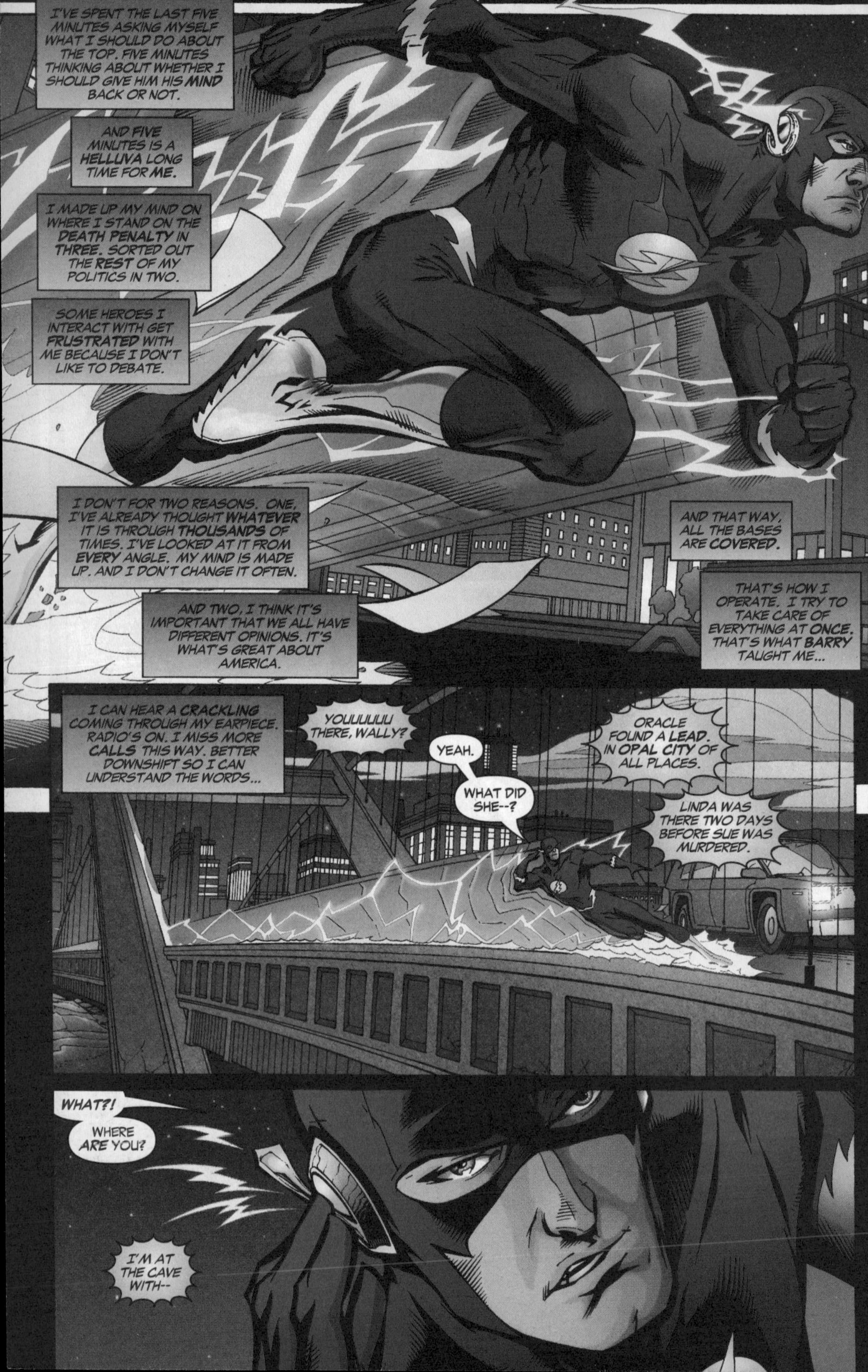
I'VE SPENT THE LAST FIVE MINUTES ASKING MYSELF WHAT I SHOULD DO ABOUT THE TOP. FIVE MINUTES THINKING ABOUT WHETHER I SHOULD GIVE HIM HIS MIND BACK OR NOT.
AND FIVE MINUTES IS A HELLUVA LONG TIME FOR ME.
I MADE UP MY MIND ON WHERE I STAND ON THE DEATH PENALTY IN THREE. SORTED OUT THE REST OF MY POLITICS IN TWO.
SOME HEROES I INTERACT WITH GET FRUSTRATED WITH ME BECAUSE I DON'T LIKE TO DEBATE.
I DON'T FOR TWO REASONS. ONE, I'VE ALREADY THOUGHT WHATEVER IT IS THROUGH THOUSANDS OF TIMES. I'VE LOOKED AT IT FROM EVERY ANGLE. MY MIND IS MADE UP. AND I DON'T CHANGE IT OFTEN.
AND TWO, I THINK IT'S IMPORTANT THAT WE ALL HAVE DIFFERENT OPINIONS. IT'S WHAT'S GREAT ABOUT AMERICA.
AND THAT WAY, ALL THE BASES ARE COVERED.
THAT'S HOW I OPERATE. I TRY TO TAKE CARE OF EVERYTHING AT ONCE. THAT'S WHAT BARRY TAUGHT ME...
I CAN HEAR A CRACKLING COMING THROUGH MY EARPIECE. RADIO'S ON. I MISS MORE CALLS THIS WAY. BETTER DOWNSHIFT SO I CAN UNDERSTAND THE WORDS...
YOUUUUUU THERE, WALLY?
YEAH.
WHAT DID SHE--?
ORACLE FOUND A LEAD. IN OPAL CITY OF ALL PLACES.
LINDA WAS THERE TWO DAYS BEFORE SUE WAS MURDERED.
WHAT?!
WHERE ARE YOU?
I'M AT THE CAVE WITH--

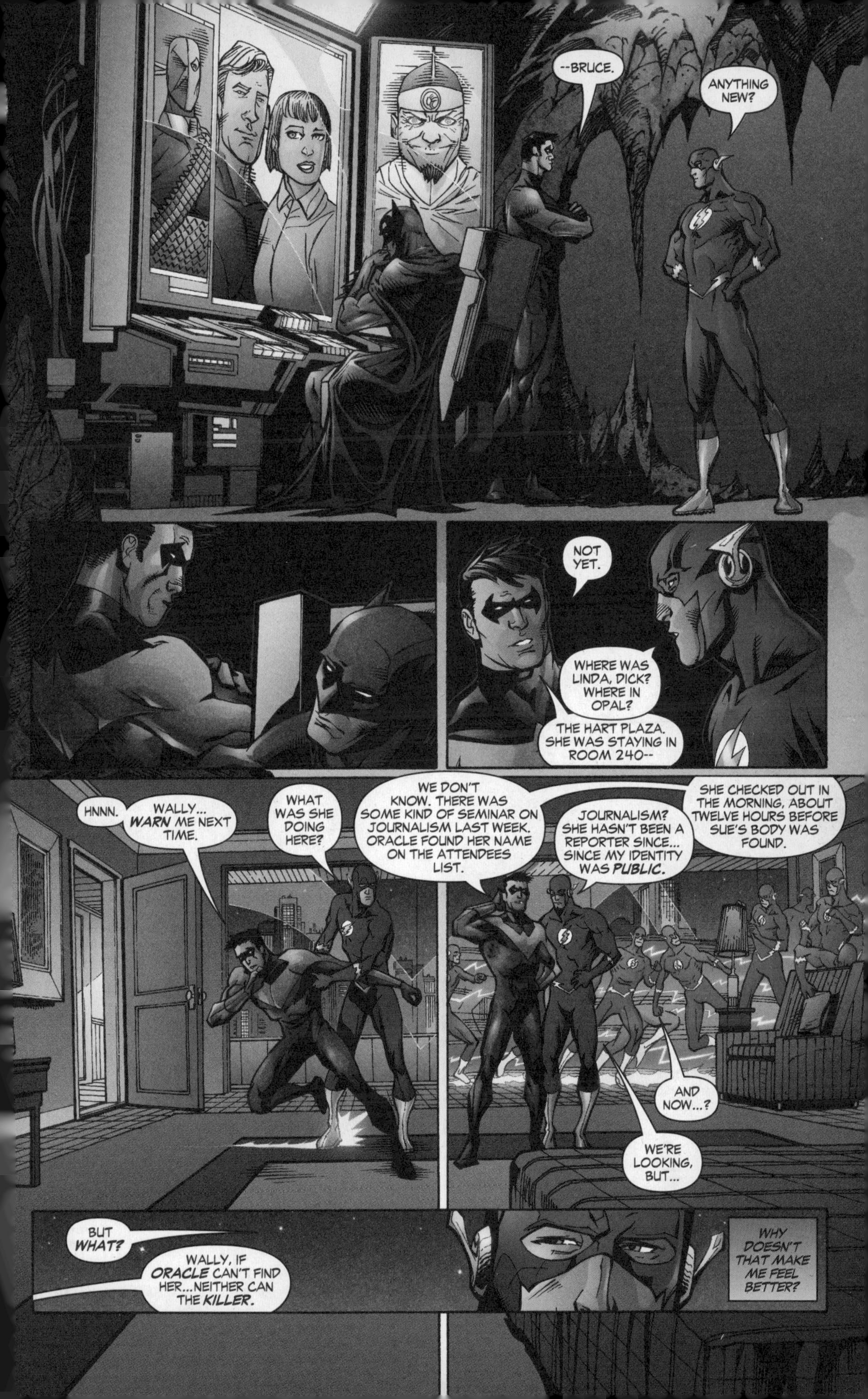

--BRUCE.
ANYTHING NEW?
NOT YET.
WHERE WAS LINDA, DICK? WHERE IN OPAL?
THE HART PLAZA. SHE WAS STAYING IN ROOM 240--
HNNN.
WALLY... WARN ME NEXT TIME.
WHAT WAS SHE DOING HERE?
WE DON'T KNOW. THERE WAS SOME KIND OF SEMINAR ON JOURNALISM LAST WEEK. ORACLE FOUND HER NAME ON THE ATTENDEES LIST.
SHE CHECKED OUT IN THE MORNING, ABOUT TWELVE HOURS BEFORE SUE'S BODY WAS FOUND.
JOURNALISM? SHE HASN'T BEEN A REPORTER SINCE... SINCE MY IDENTITY WAS PUBLIC.
AND NOW...?
WE'RE LOOKING, BUT...
BUT WHAT?
WALLY, IF ORACLE CAN'T FIND HER...NEITHER CAN THE KILLER.
WHY DOESN'T THAT MAKE ME FEEL BETTER?

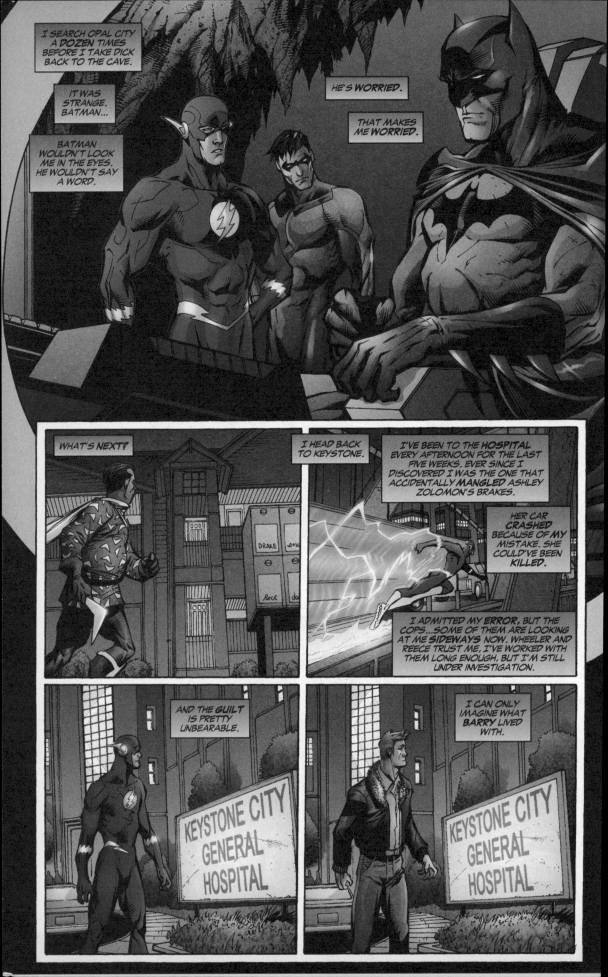

I SEARCH OPAL CITY A DOZEN TIMES BEFORE I TAKE DICK BACK TO THE CAVE.

IT WAS STRANGE. BATMAN...

BATMAN WOULDN'T LOOK ME IN THE EYES. HE WOULDN'T SAY A WORD.

HE'S WORRIED.

THAT MAKES ME WORRIED.

WHAT'S NEXT?

I HEAD BACK TO KEYSTONE.

I'VE BEEN TO THE HOSPITAL EVERY AFTERNOON FOR THE LAST FIVE WEEKS. EVER SINCE I DISCOVERED I WAS THE ONE THAT ACCIDENTALLY MANGLED ASHLEY ZOLOMON'S BRAKES.

HER CAR CRASHED BECAUSE OF MY MISTAKE. SHE COULD'VE BEEN KILLED.

I ADMITTED MY ERROR, BUT THE COPS...SOME OF THEM ARE LOOKING AT ME SIDEWAYS NOW. WHEELER AND REECE TRUST ME, I'VE WORKED WITH THEM LONG ENOUGH, BUT I'M STILL UNDER INVESTIGATION.

AND THE GUILT IS PRETTY UNBEARABLE.

I CAN ONLY IMAGINE WHAT BARRY LIVED WITH.

KEYSTONE CITY GENERAL HOSPITAL

KEYSTONE CITY GENERAL HOSPITAL

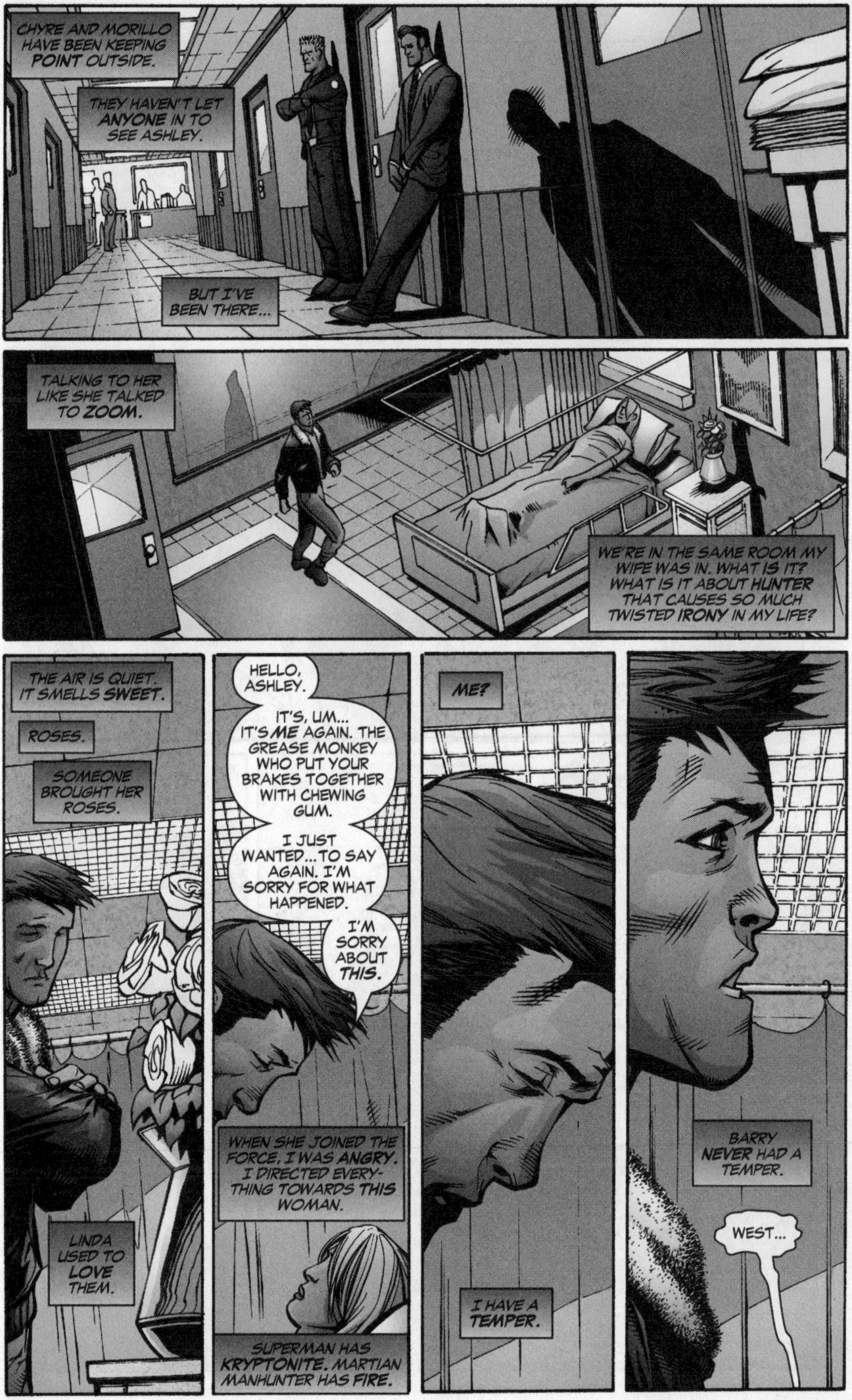
CHYRE AND MORILLO HAVE BEEN KEEPING POINT OUTSIDE.
THEY HAVEN'T LET ANYONE IN TO SEE ASHLEY.
BUT I'VE BEEN THERE...
TALKING TO HER LIKE SHE TALKED TO ZOOM.
WE'RE IN THE SAME ROOM MY WIFE WAS IN. WHAT IS IT? WHAT IS IT ABOUT HUNTER THAT CAUSES SO MUCH TWISTED IRONY IN MY LIFE?
THE AIR IS QUIET. IT SMELLS SWEET.
ROSES.
SOMEONE BROUGHT HER ROSES.
LINDA USED TO LOVE THEM.
HELLO, ASHLEY.
IT'S, UM... IT'S ME AGAIN. THE GREASE MONKEY WHO PUT YOUR BRAKES TOGETHER WITH CHEWING GUM.
I JUST WANTED...TO SAY AGAIN. I'M SORRY FOR WHAT HAPPENED.
I'M SORRY ABOUT THIS.
WHEN SHE JOINED THE FORCE, I WAS ANGRY. I DIRECTED EVERY-THING TOWARDS THIS WOMAN.
SUPERMAN HAS KRYPTONITE. MARTIAN MANHUNTER HAS FIRE.
ME?
I HAVE A TEMPER.
BARRY NEVER HAD A TEMPER.
WEST...

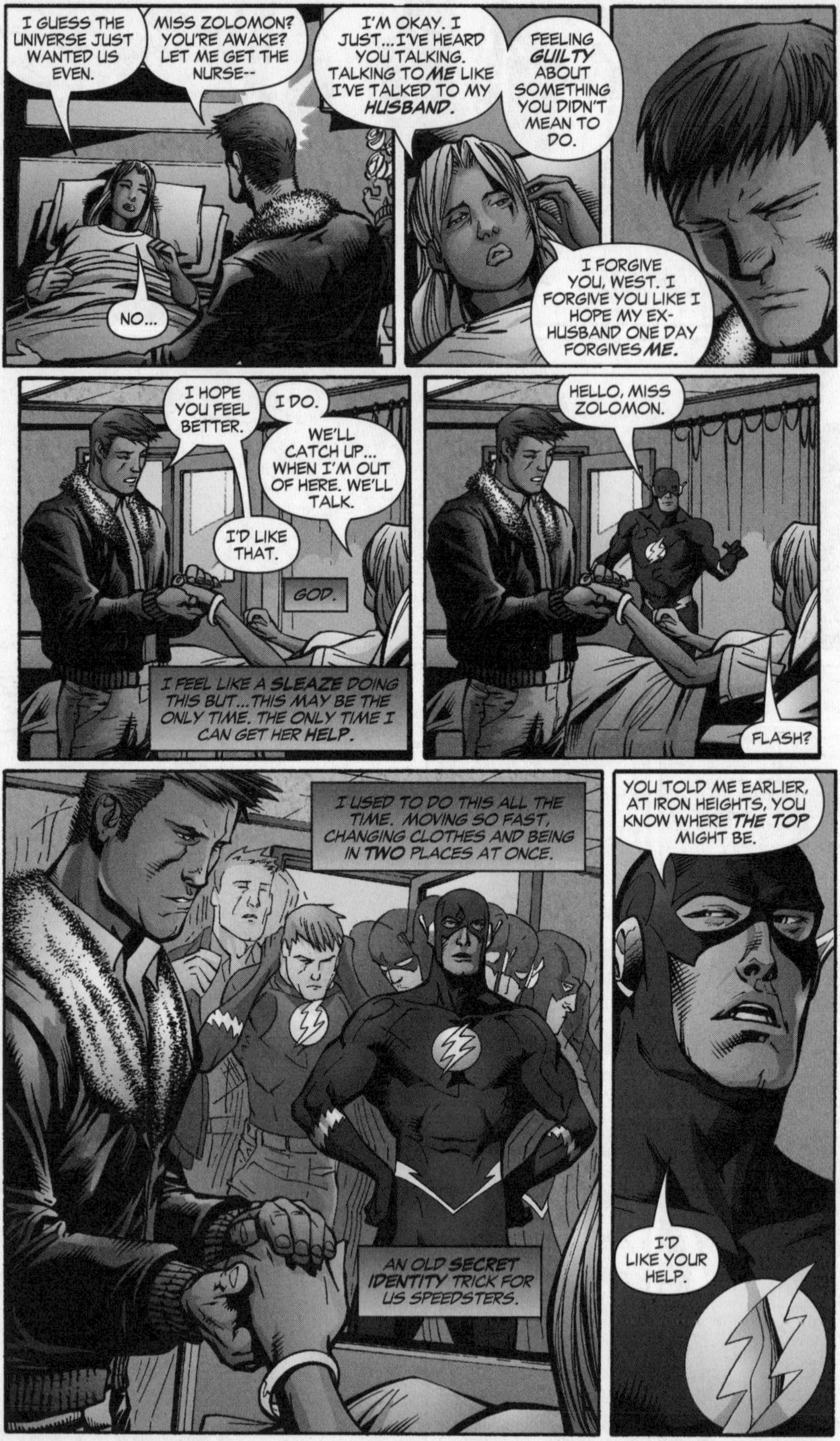
I GUESS THE UNIVERSE JUST WANTED US EVEN.
MISS ZOLOMON? YOU'RE AWAKE? LET ME GET THE NURSE--
NO...
I'M OKAY. I JUST...I'VE HEARD YOU TALKING. TALKING TO ME LIKE I'VE TALKED TO MY HUSBAND.
FEELING GUILTY ABOUT SOMETHING YOU DIDN'T MEAN TO DO.
I FORGIVE YOU, WEST. I FORGIVE YOU LIKE I HOPE MY EX-HUSBAND ONE DAY FORGIVES ME.
I HOPE YOU FEEL BETTER.
I DO.
WE'LL CATCH UP... WHEN I'M OUT OF HERE. WE'LL TALK.
I'D LIKE THAT.
GOD.
I FEEL LIKE A SLEAZE DOING THIS BUT...THIS MAY BE THE ONLY TIME. THE ONLY TIME I CAN GET HER HELP.
HELLO, MISS ZOLOMON.
FLASH?
I USED TO DO THIS ALL THE TIME. MOVING SO FAST, CHANGING CLOTHES AND BEING IN TWO PLACES AT ONCE.
AN OLD SECRET IDENTITY TRICK FOR US SPEEDSTERS.
YOU TOLD ME EARLIER, AT IRON HEIGHTS, YOU KNOW WHERE THE TOP MIGHT BE.
I'D LIKE YOUR HELP.

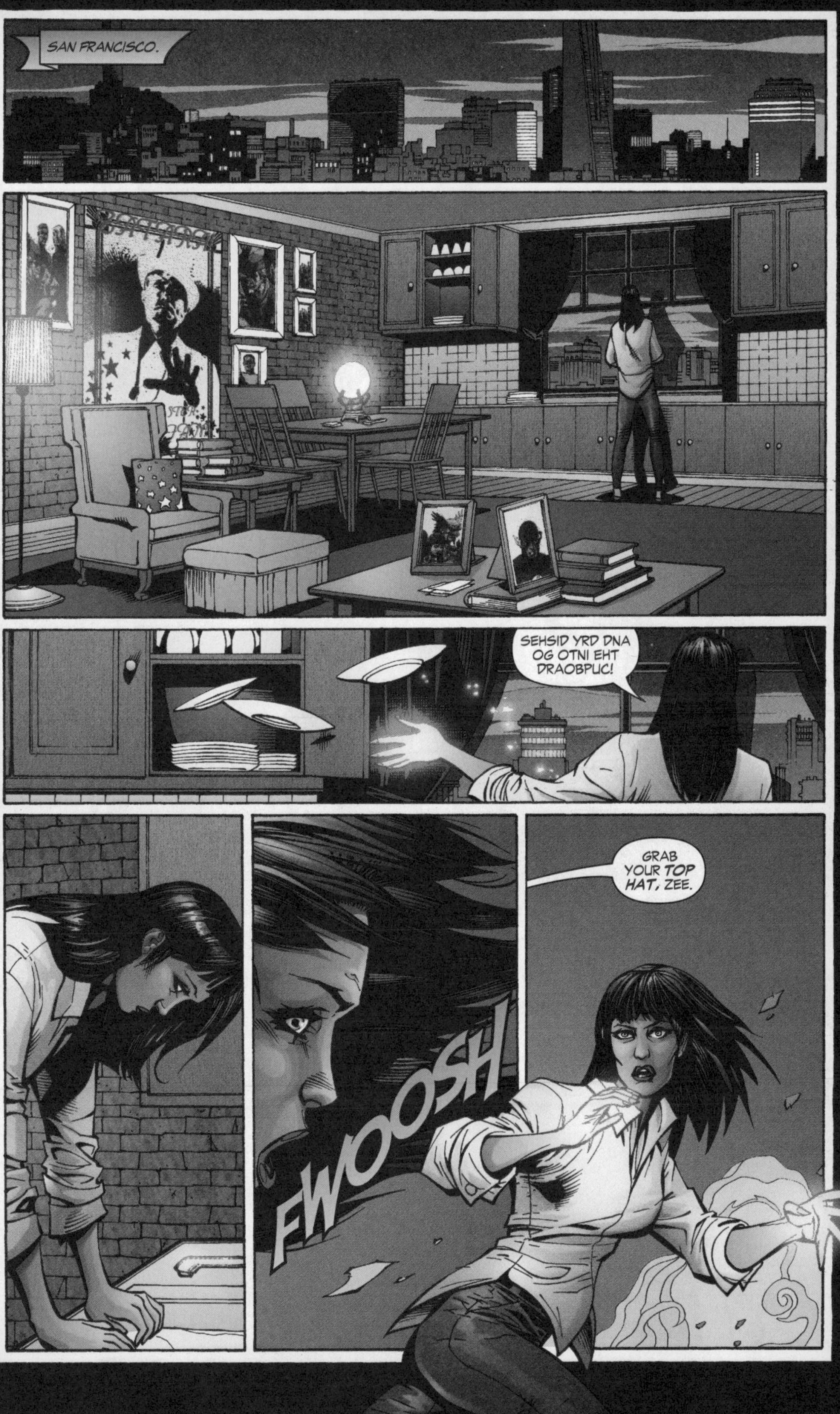
SAN FRANCISCO.
SEHSID YRD DNA OG OTNI EHT DRAOBPUC!
GRAB YOUR TOP HAT, ZEE.
FWOOSH

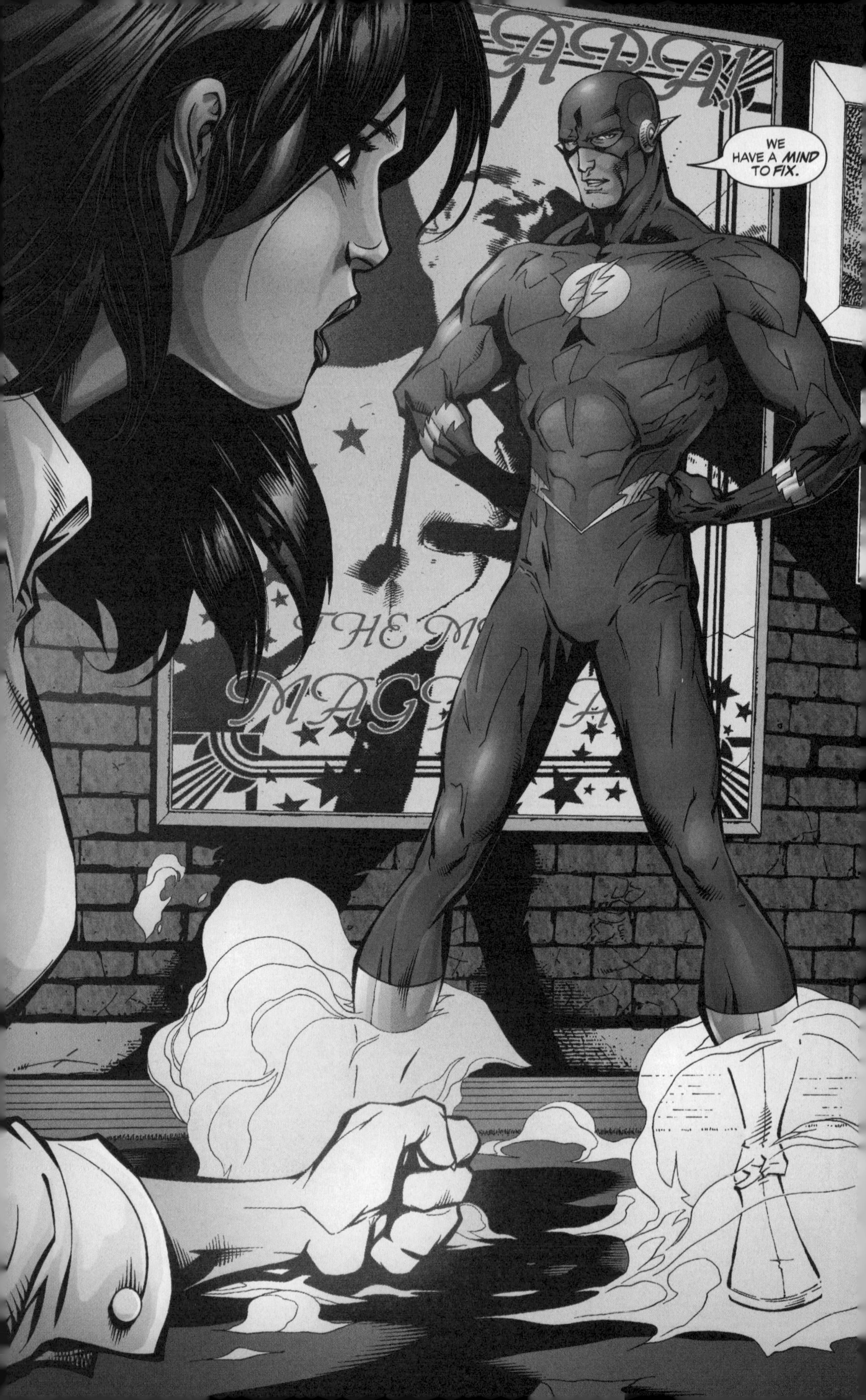
WE HAVE A MIND TO FIX.

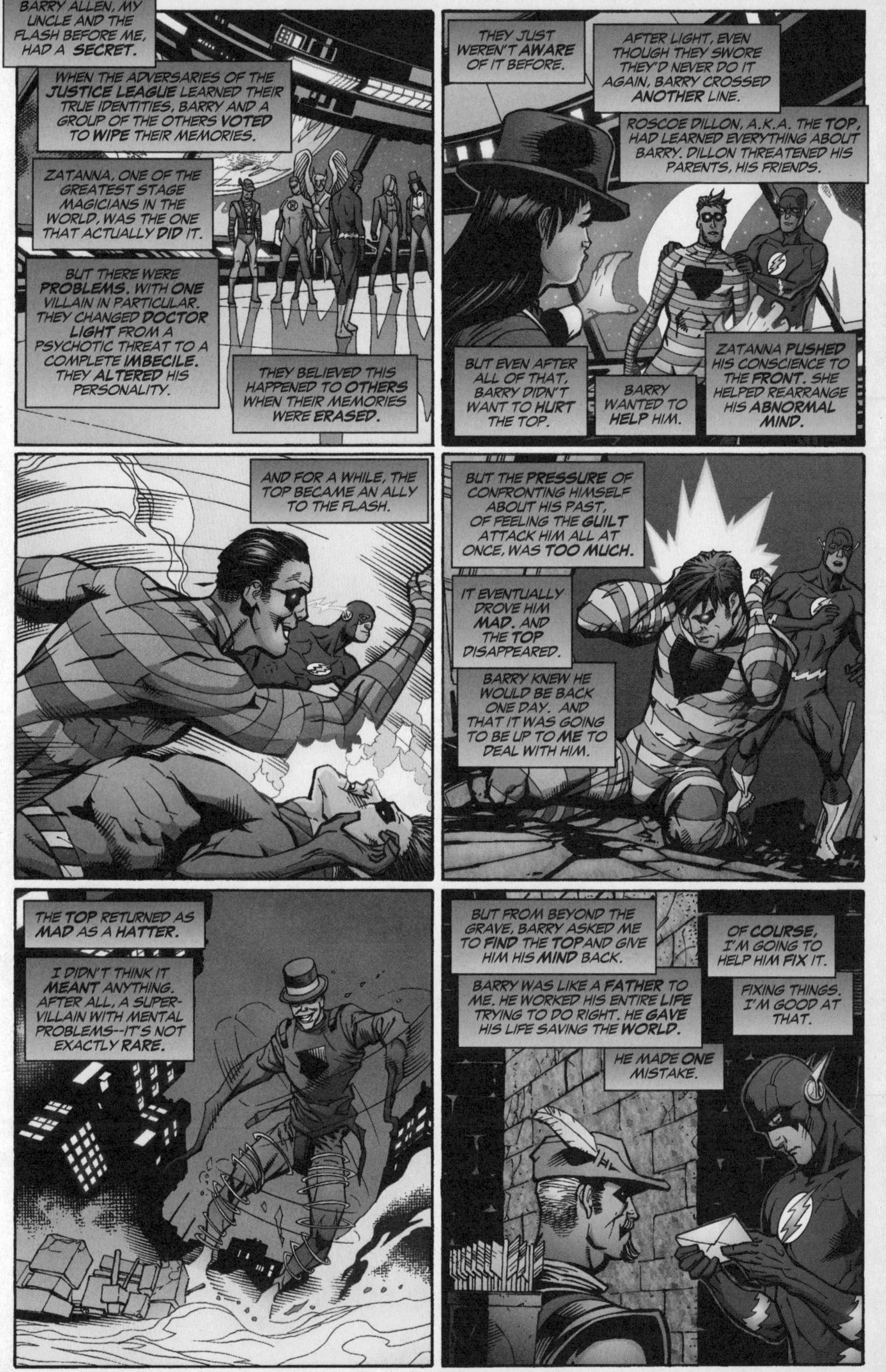

BARRY ALLEN, MY UNCLE AND THE FLASH BEFORE ME, HAD A SECRET.
WHEN THE ADVERSARIES OF THE JUSTICE LEAGUE LEARNED THEIR TRUE IDENTITIES, BARRY AND A GROUP OF THE OTHERS VOTED TO WIPE THEIR MEMORIES.
ZATANNA, ONE OF THE GREATEST STAGE MAGICIANS IN THE WORLD, WAS THE ONE THAT ACTUALLY DID IT.
BUT THERE WERE PROBLEMS. WITH ONE VILLAIN IN PARTICULAR. THEY CHANGED DOCTOR LIGHT FROM A PSYCHOTIC THREAT TO A COMPLETE IMBECILE. THEY ALTERED HIS PERSONALITY.
THEY BELIEVED THIS HAPPENED TO OTHERS WHEN THEIR MEMORIES WERE ERASED.
THEY JUST WEREN'T AWARE OF IT BEFORE.
AFTER LIGHT, EVEN THOUGH THEY SWORE THEY'D NEVER DO IT AGAIN, BARRY CROSSED ANOTHER LINE.
ROSCOE DILLON, A.K.A. THE TOP, HAD LEARNED EVERYTHING ABOUT BARRY. DILLON THREATENED HIS PARENTS, HIS FRIENDS.
BUT EVEN AFTER ALL OF THAT, BARRY DIDN'T WANT TO HURT THE TOP.
BARRY WANTED TO HELP HIM.
ZATANNA PUSHED HIS CONSCIENCE TO THE FRONT. SHE HELPED REARRANGE HIS ABNORMAL MIND.
AND FOR A WHILE, THE TOP BECAME AN ALLY TO THE FLASH.
BUT THE PRESSURE OF CONFRONTING HIMSELF ABOUT HIS PAST, OF FEELING THE GUILT ATTACK HIM ALL AT ONCE, WAS TOO MUCH.
IT EVENTUALLY DROVE HIM MAD. AND THE TOP DISAPPEARED.
BARRY KNEW HE WOULD BE BACK ONE DAY. AND THAT IT WAS GOING TO BE UP TO ME TO DEAL WITH HIM.
THE TOP RETURNED AS MAD AS A HATTER.
I DIDN'T THINK IT MEANT ANYTHING. AFTER ALL, A SUPER-VILLAIN WITH MENTAL PROBLEMS--IT'S NOT EXACTLY RARE.
BUT FROM BEYOND THE GRAVE, BARRY ASKED ME TO FIND THE TOP AND GIVE HIM HIS MIND BACK.
BARRY WAS LIKE A FATHER TO ME. HE WORKED HIS ENTIRE LIFE TRYING TO DO RIGHT. HE GAVE HIS LIFE SAVING THE WORLD.
HE MADE ONE MISTAKE.
OF COURSE, I'M GOING TO HELP HIM FIX IT.
FIXING THINGS. I'M GOOD AT THAT.

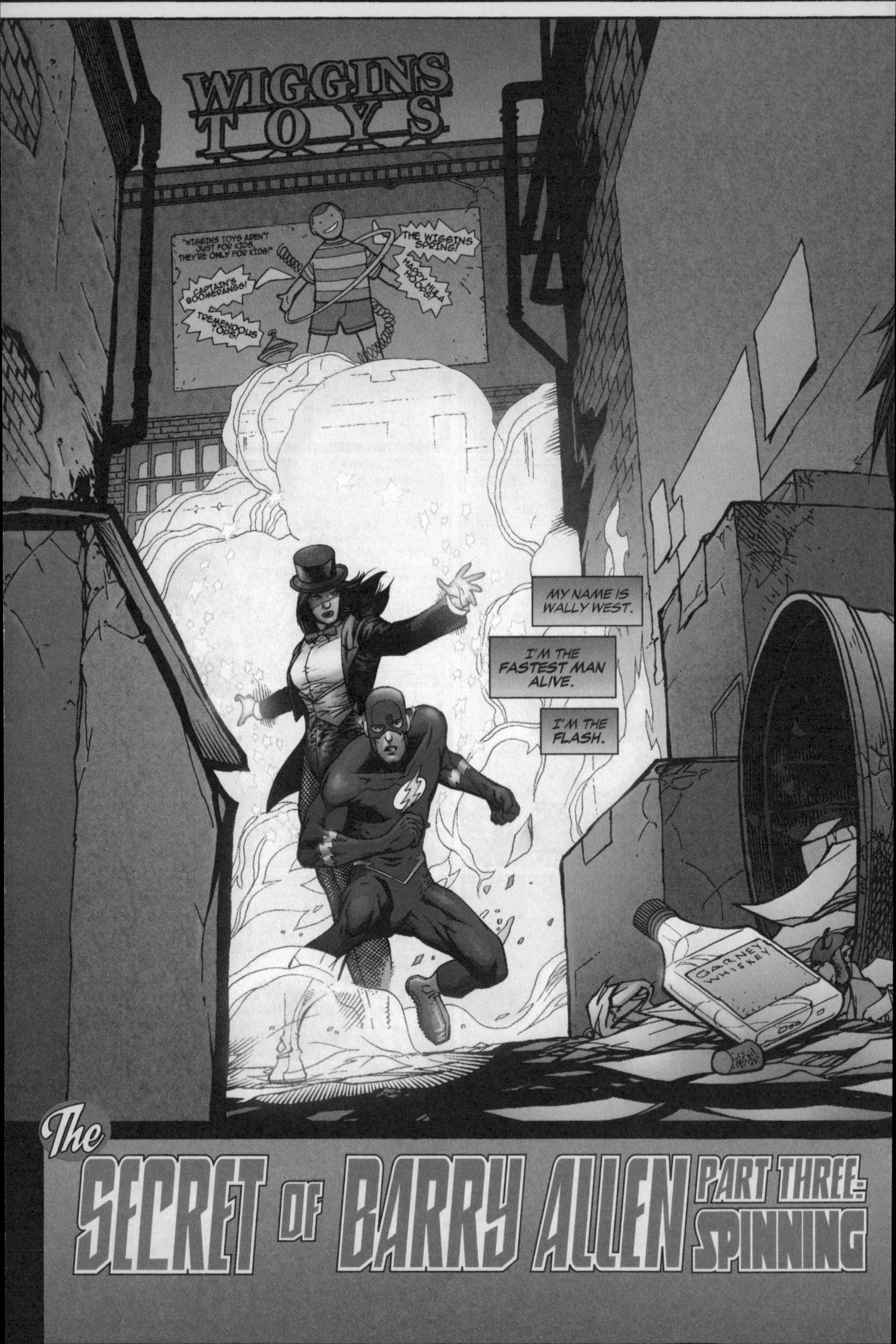
WIGGINS TOYS
"WIGGINS TOYS AREN'T JUST FOR KIDS, THEY'RE ONLY FOR KIDS!"
THE WIGGINS SPRING!
HAPPY HULA HOOPS!
CAPTAIN'S BOOMERANGS!
TREMENDOUS TOPS!
MY NAME IS WALLY WEST.
I'M THE FASTEST MAN ALIVE.
I'M THE FLASH.
GARNEY WHISKEY
The SECRET OF BARRY ALLEN PART THREE: SPINNING

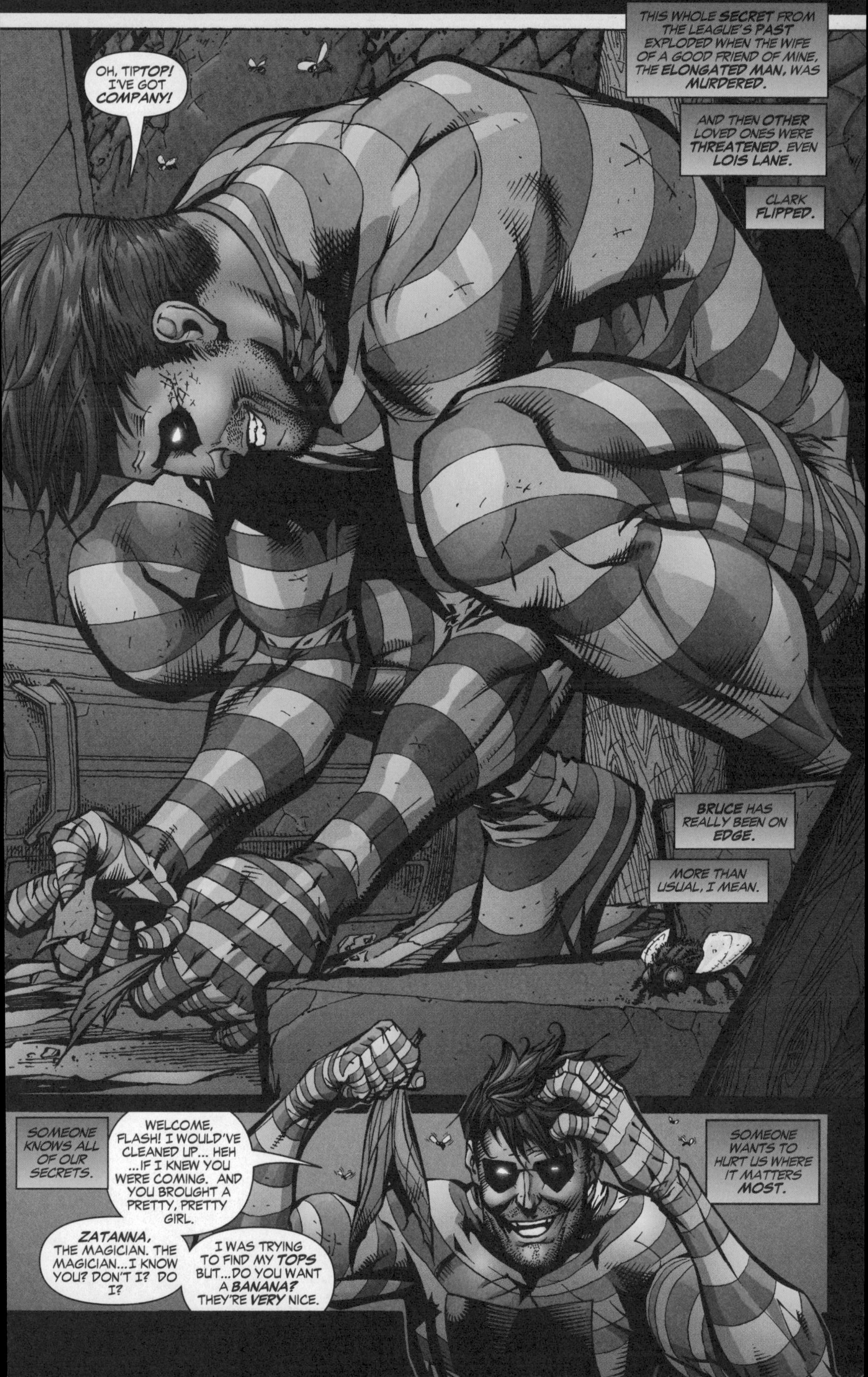

THIS WHOLE SECRET FROM THE LEAGUE'S PAST EXPLODED WHEN THE WIFE OF A GOOD FRIEND OF MINE, THE ELONGATED MAN, WAS MURDERED.
OH, TIPTOP! I'VE GOT COMPANY!
AND THEN OTHER LOVED ONES WERE THREATENED. EVEN LOIS LANE.
CLARK FLIPPED.
BRUCE HAS REALLY BEEN ON EDGE.
MORE THAN USUAL, I MEAN.
SOMEONE KNOWS ALL OF OUR SECRETS.
WELCOME, FLASH! I WOULD'VE CLEANED UP... HEH ...IF I KNEW YOU WERE COMING. AND YOU BROUGHT A PRETTY, PRETTY GIRL.
ZATANNA, THE MAGICIAN. THE MAGICIAN...I KNOW YOU? DON'T I? DO I?
I WAS TRYING TO FIND MY TOPS BUT...DO YOU WANT A BANANA? THEY'RE VERY NICE.
SOMEONE WANTS TO HURT US WHERE IT MATTERS MOST.

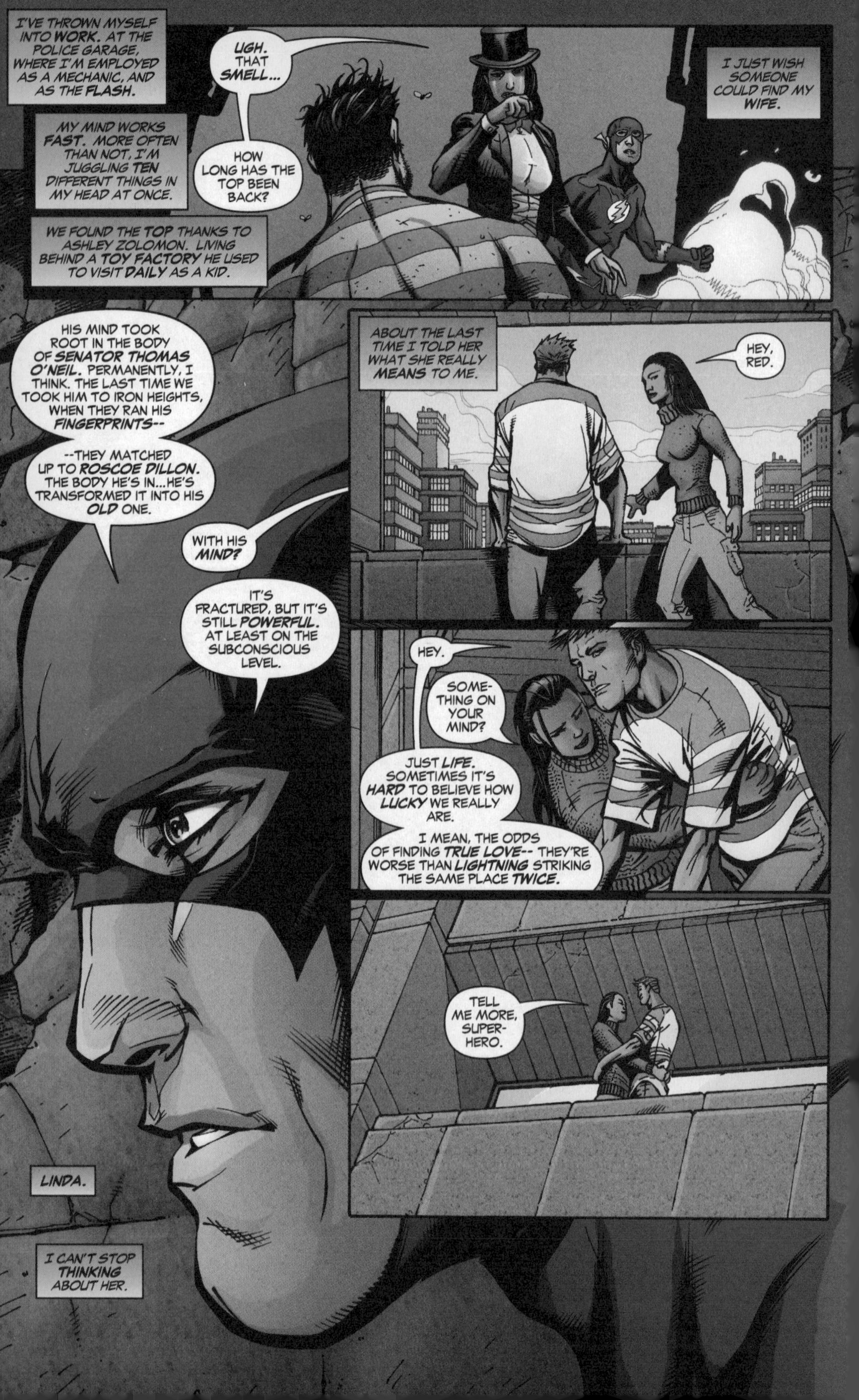
I'VE THROWN MYSELF INTO WORK. AT THE POLICE GARAGE, WHERE I'M EMPLOYED AS A MECHANIC, AND AS THE FLASH.
UGH. THAT SMELL...
MY MIND WORKS FAST. MORE OFTEN THAN NOT, I'M JUGGLING TEN DIFFERENT THINGS IN MY HEAD AT ONCE.
HOW LONG HAS THE TOP BEEN BACK?
WE FOUND THE TOP THANKS TO ASHLEY ZOLOMON. LIVING BEHIND A TOY FACTORY HE USED TO VISIT DAILY AS A KID.
I JUST WISH SOMEONE COULD FIND MY WIFE.
HIS MIND TOOK ROOT IN THE BODY OF SENATOR THOMAS O'NEIL. PERMANENTLY, I THINK. THE LAST TIME WE TOOK HIM TO IRON HEIGHTS, WHEN THEY RAN HIS FINGERPRINTS--
--THEY MATCHED UP TO ROSCOE DILLON. THE BODY HE'S IN...HE'S TRANSFORMED IT INTO HIS OLD ONE.
WITH HIS MIND?
IT'S FRACTURED, BUT IT'S STILL POWERFUL. AT LEAST ON THE SUBCONSCIOUS LEVEL.
ABOUT THE LAST TIME I TOLD HER WHAT SHE REALLY MEANS TO ME.
HEY, RED.
HEY.
SOME-THING ON YOUR MIND?
JUST LIFE. SOMETIMES IT'S HARD TO BELIEVE HOW LUCKY WE REALLY ARE.
I MEAN, THE ODDS OF FINDING TRUE LOVE-- THEY'RE WORSE THAN LIGHTNING STRIKING THE SAME PLACE TWICE.
TELL ME MORE, SUPER-HERO.
LINDA.
I CAN'T STOP THINKING ABOUT HER.

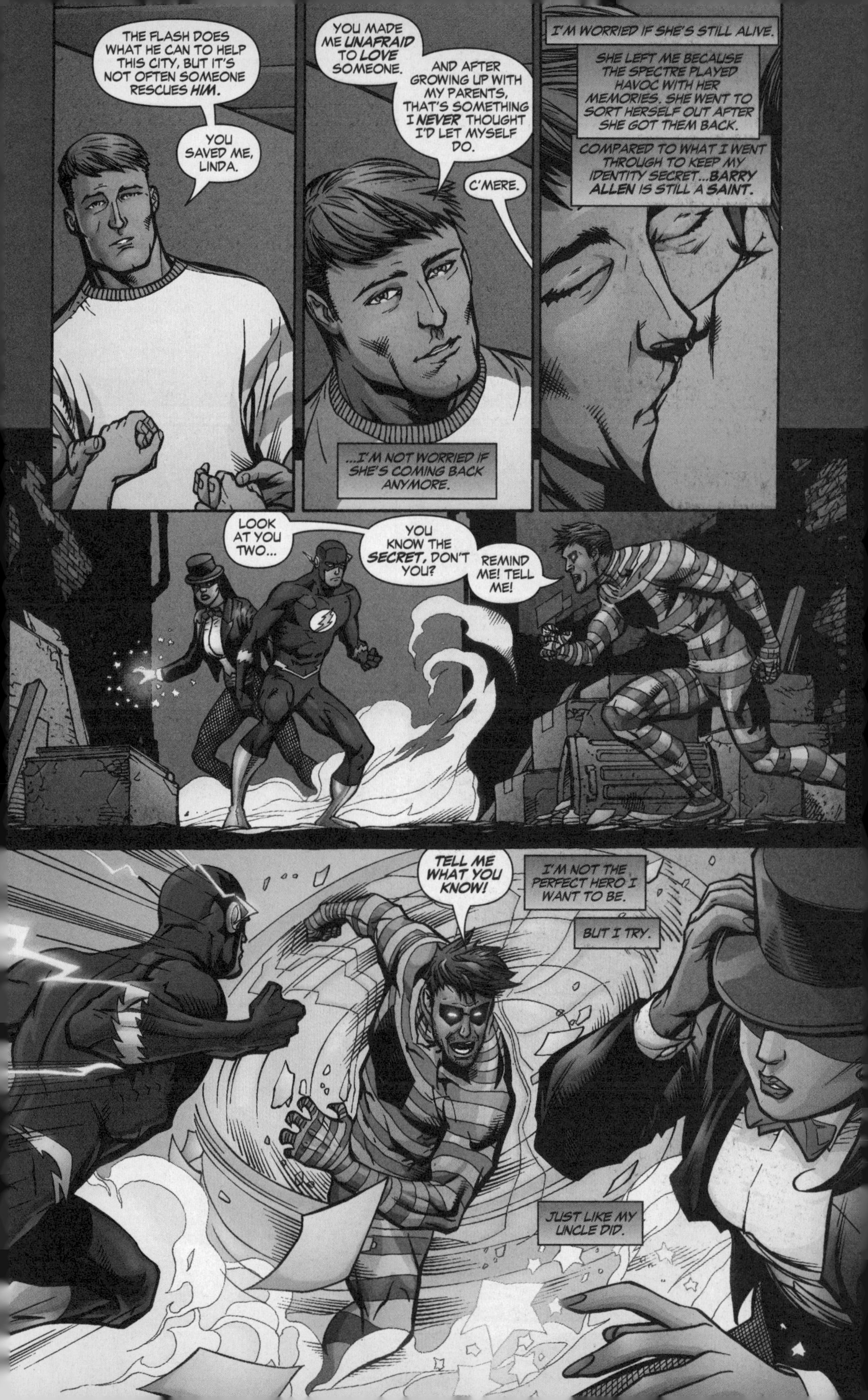
THE FLASH DOES WHAT HE CAN TO HELP THIS CITY, BUT IT'S NOT OFTEN SOMEONE RESCUES HIM.
YOU SAVED ME, LINDA.
YOU MADE ME UNAFRAID TO LOVE SOMEONE.
AND AFTER GROWING UP WITH MY PARENTS, THAT'S SOMETHING I NEVER THOUGHT I'D LET MYSELF DO.
C'MERE.
...I'M NOT WORRIED IF SHE'S COMING BACK ANYMORE.
I'M WORRIED IF SHE'S STILL ALIVE.
SHE LEFT ME BECAUSE THE SPECTRE PLAYED HAVOC WITH HER MEMORIES. SHE WENT TO SORT HERSELF OUT AFTER SHE GOT THEM BACK.
COMPARED TO WHAT I WENT THROUGH TO KEEP MY IDENTITY SECRET...BARRY ALLEN IS STILL A SAINT.
LOOK AT YOU TWO...
YOU KNOW THE SECRET, DON'T YOU?
REMIND ME! TELL ME!
TELL ME WHAT YOU KNOW!
I'M NOT THE PERFECT HERO I WANT TO BE.
BUT I TRY.
JUST LIKE MY UNCLE DID.

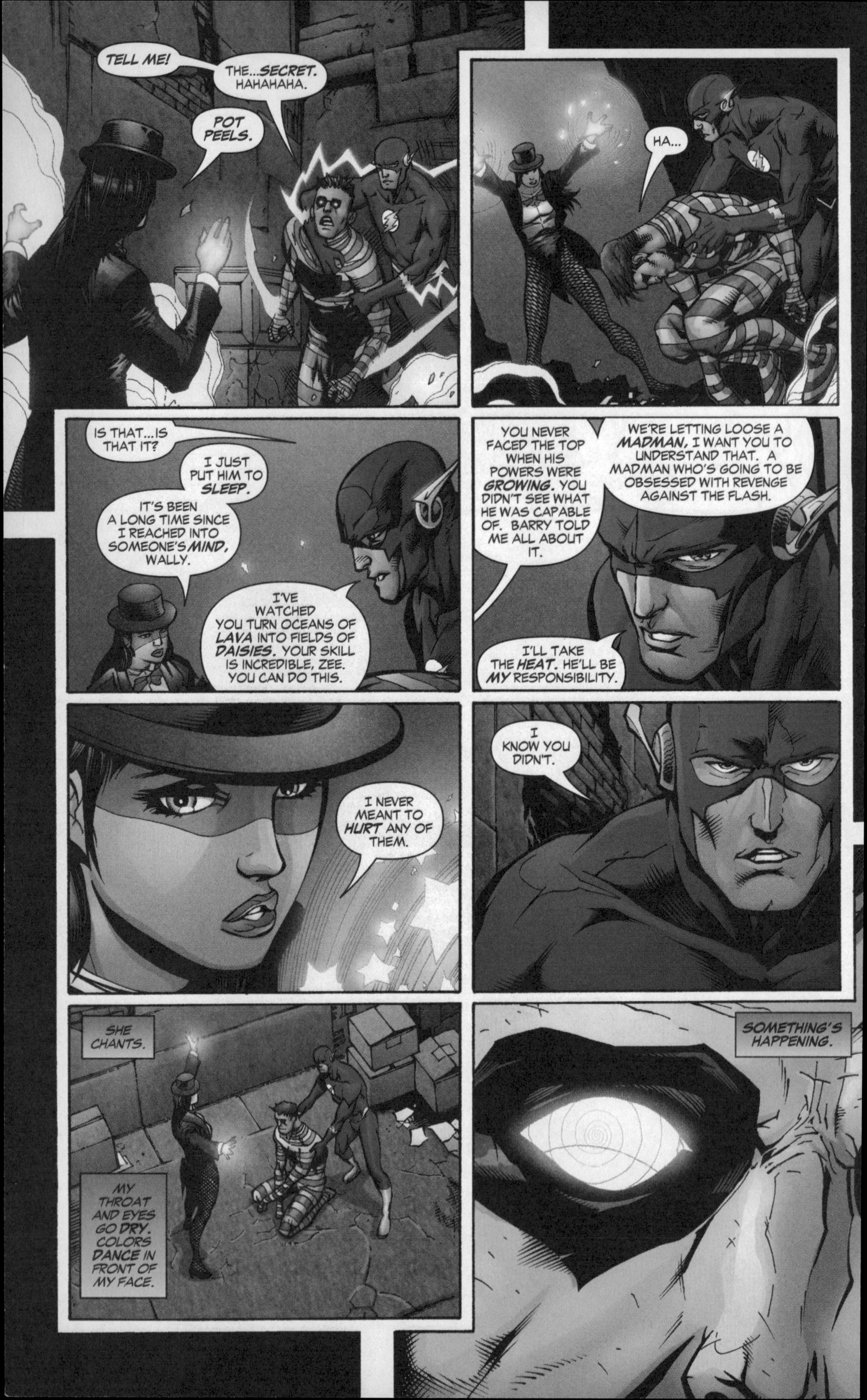
TELL ME!
THE...SECRET. HAHAHAHA.
POT PEELS.
HA...
IS THAT...IS THAT IT?
I JUST PUT HIM TO SLEEP.
IT'S BEEN A LONG TIME SINCE I REACHED INTO SOMEONE'S MIND, WALLY.
I'VE WATCHED YOU TURN OCEANS OF LAVA INTO FIELDS OF DAISIES. YOUR SKILL IS INCREDIBLE, ZEE. YOU CAN DO THIS.
YOU NEVER FACED THE TOP WHEN HIS POWERS WERE GROWING. YOU DIDN'T SEE WHAT HE WAS CAPABLE OF. BARRY TOLD ME ALL ABOUT IT.
WE'RE LETTING LOOSE A MADMAN, I WANT YOU TO UNDERSTAND THAT. A MADMAN WHO'S GOING TO BE OBSESSED WITH REVENGE AGAINST THE FLASH.
I'LL TAKE THE HEAT. HE'LL BE MY RESPONSIBILITY.
I NEVER MEANT TO HURT ANY OF THEM.
I KNOW YOU DIDN'T.
SHE CHANTS.
MY THROAT AND EYES GO DRY. COLORS DANCE IN FRONT OF MY FACE.
SOMETHING'S HAPPENING.

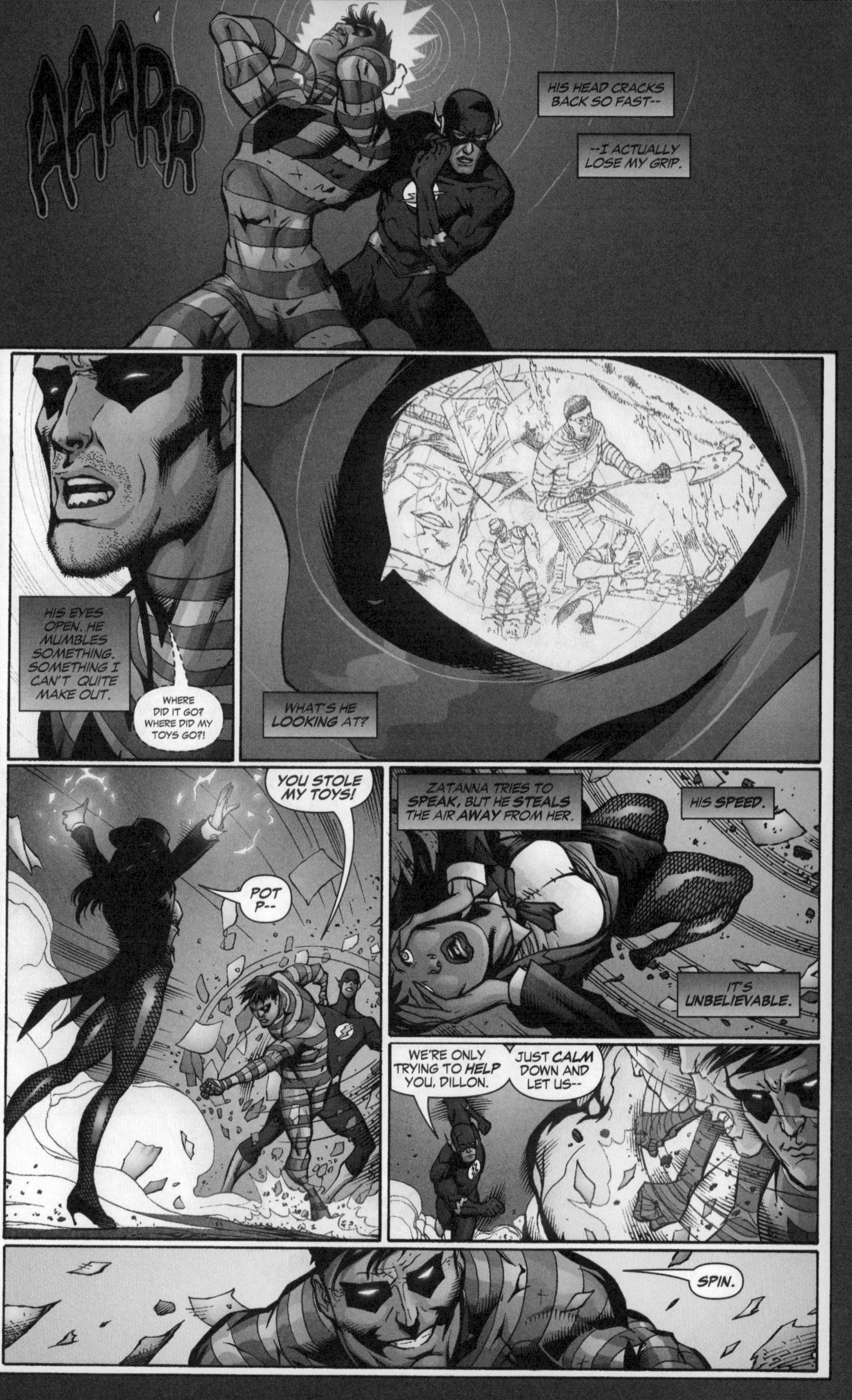
AAARR
HIS HEAD CRACKS BACK SO FAST--
--I ACTUALLY LOSE MY GRIP.
HIS EYES OPEN. HE MUMBLES SOMETHING. SOMETHING I CAN'T QUITE MAKE OUT.
WHERE DID IT GO? WHERE DID MY TOYS GO?!
WHAT'S HE LOOKING AT?
YOU STOLE MY TOYS!
POT P--
ZATANNA TRIES TO SPEAK, BUT HE STEALS THE AIR AWAY FROM HER.
HIS SPEED.
IT'S UNBELIEVABLE.
WE'RE ONLY TRYING TO HELP YOU, DILLON.
JUST CALM DOWN AND LET US--
SPIN.

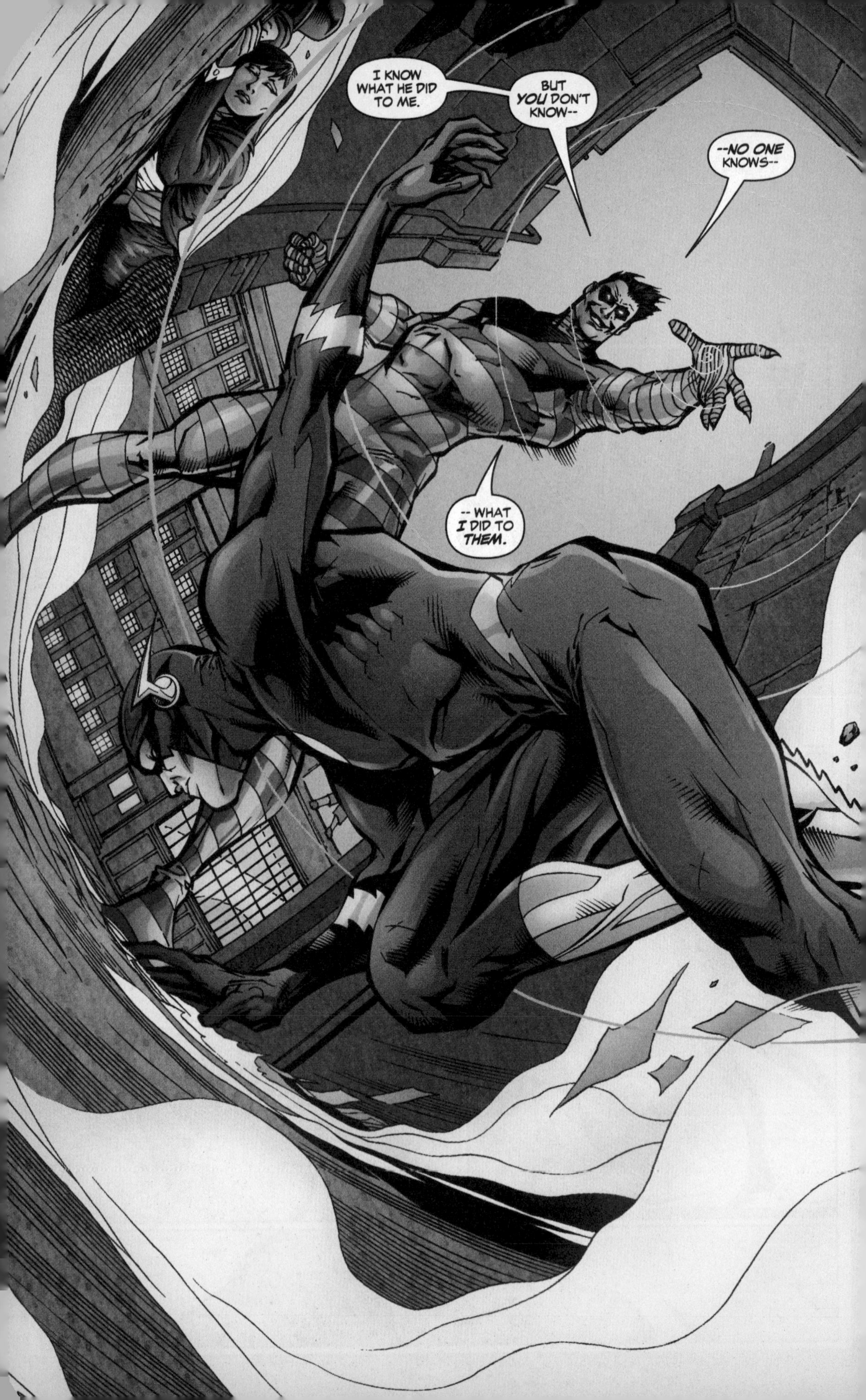
I KNOW WHAT HE DID TO ME.
BUT *YOU* DON'T KNOW--
--*NO ONE* KNOWS--
-- WHAT *I* DID TO *THEM*.

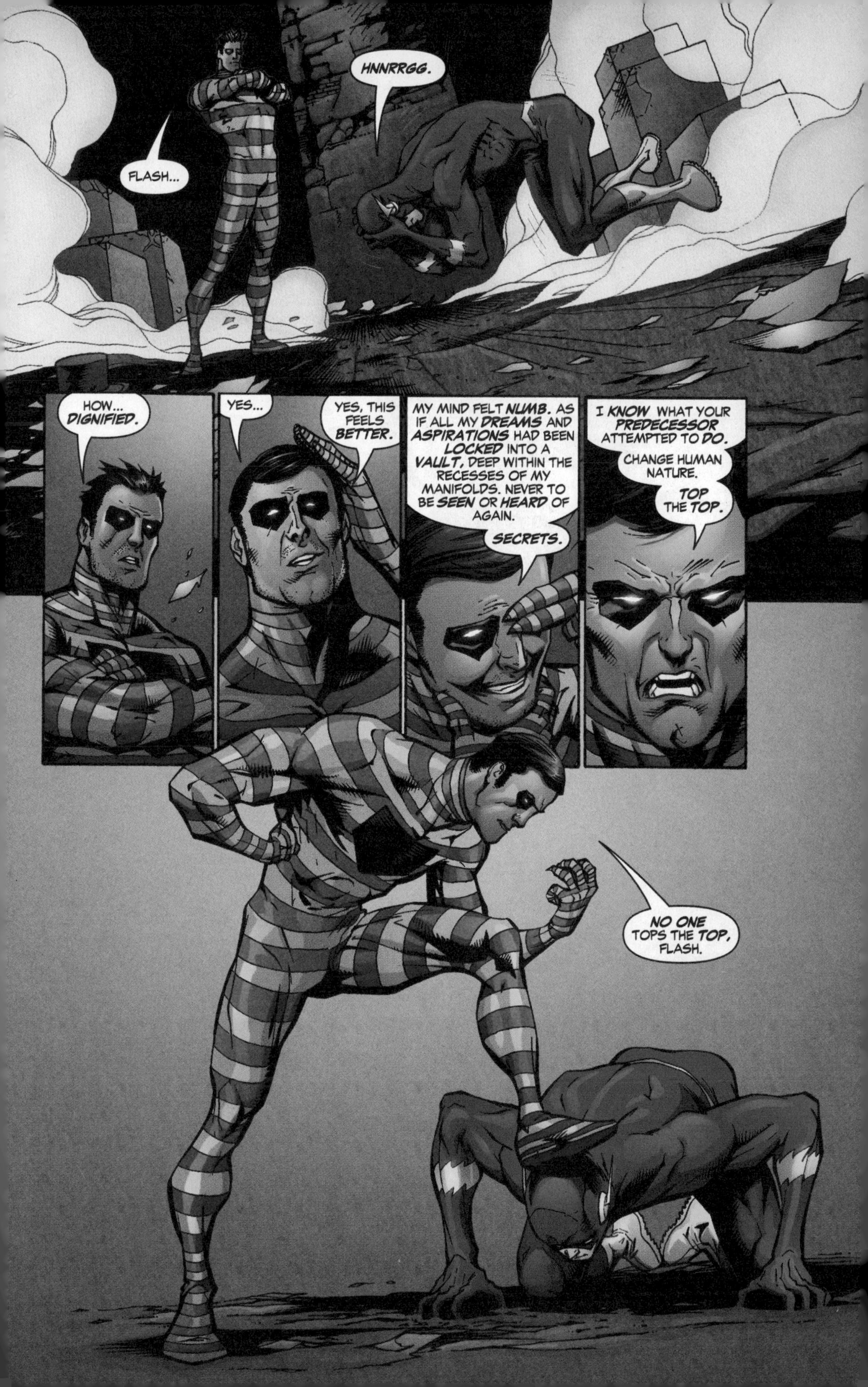
FLASH...
HNNRRGG.
HOW... DIGNIFIED.
YES...
YES, THIS FEELS BETTER.
MY MIND FELT NUMB. AS IF ALL MY DREAMS AND ASPIRATIONS HAD BEEN LOCKED INTO A VAULT, DEEP WITHIN THE RECESSES OF MY MANIFOLDS. NEVER TO BE SEEN OR HEARD OF AGAIN.
SECRETS.
I KNOW WHAT YOUR PREDECESSOR ATTEMPTED TO DO.
CHANGE HUMAN NATURE.
TOP THE TOP.
NO ONE TOPS THE TOP, FLASH.

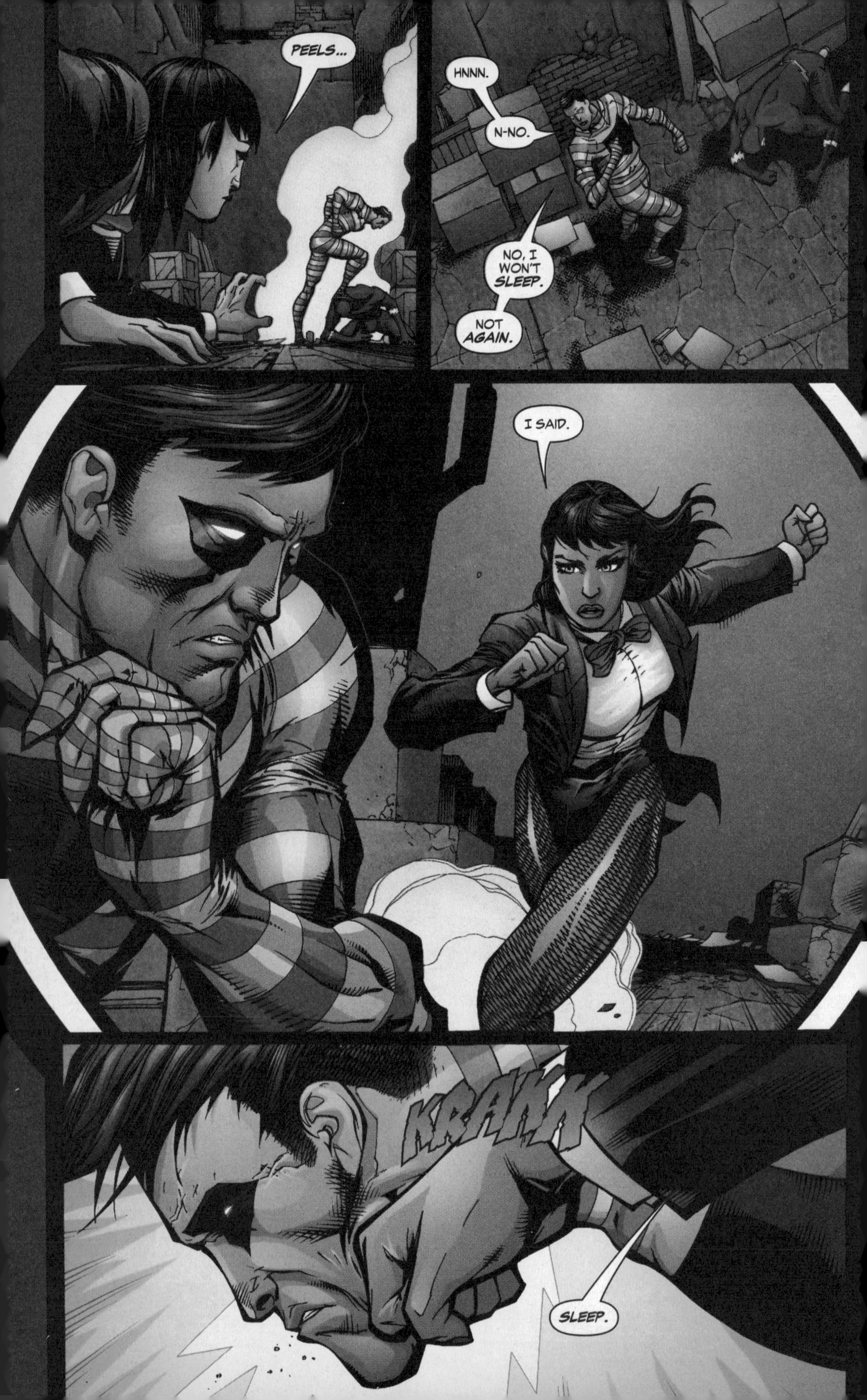
PEELS...
HNNN.
N-NO.
NO, I WON'T SLEEP.
NOT AGAIN.
I SAID.
KRAKK
SLEEP.

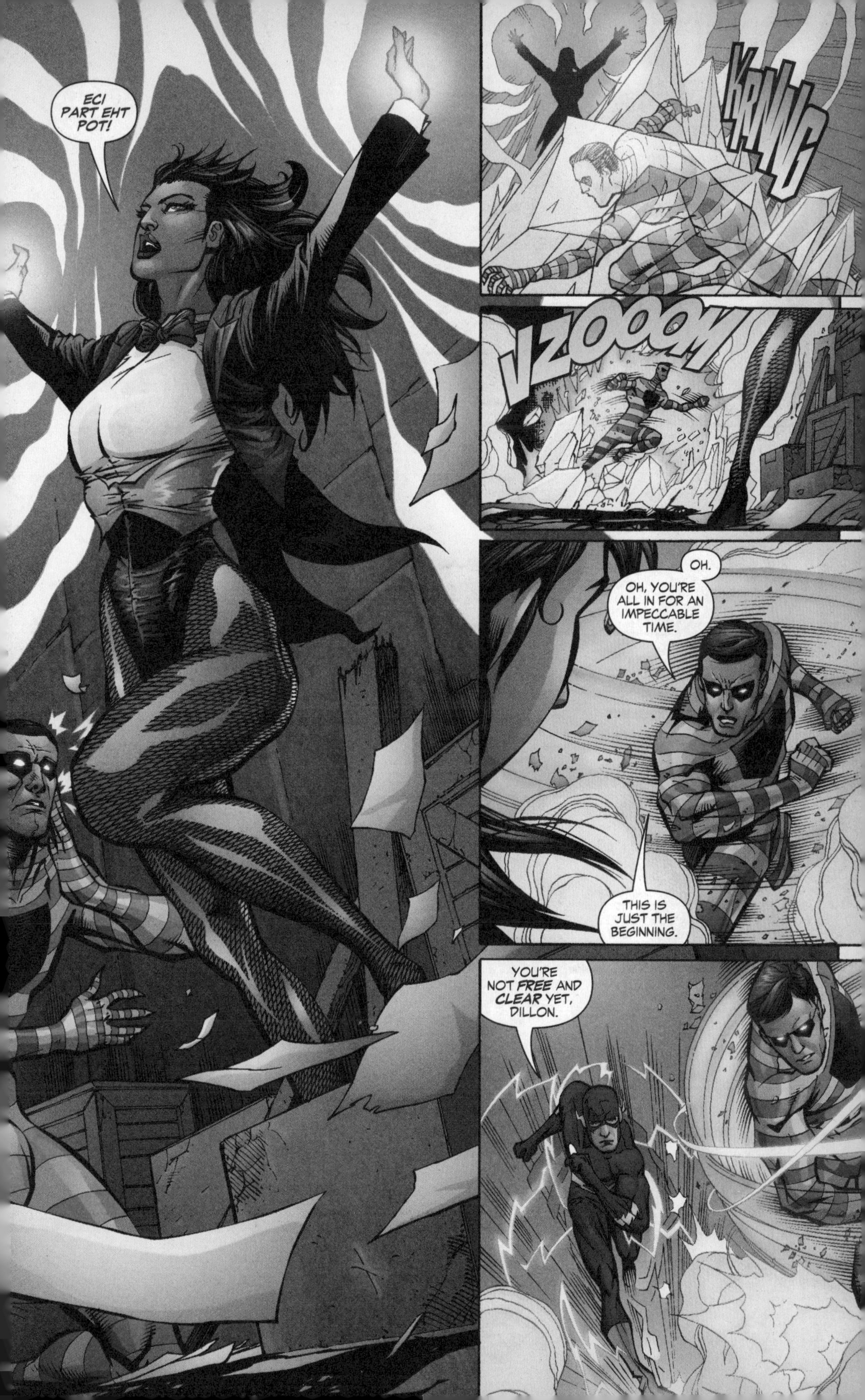
ECI PART EHT POT!
KRANG
VZOOOM
OH.
OH, YOU'RE ALL IN FOR AN IMPECCABLE TIME.
THIS IS JUST THE BEGINNING.
YOU'RE NOT FREE AND CLEAR YET, DILLON.

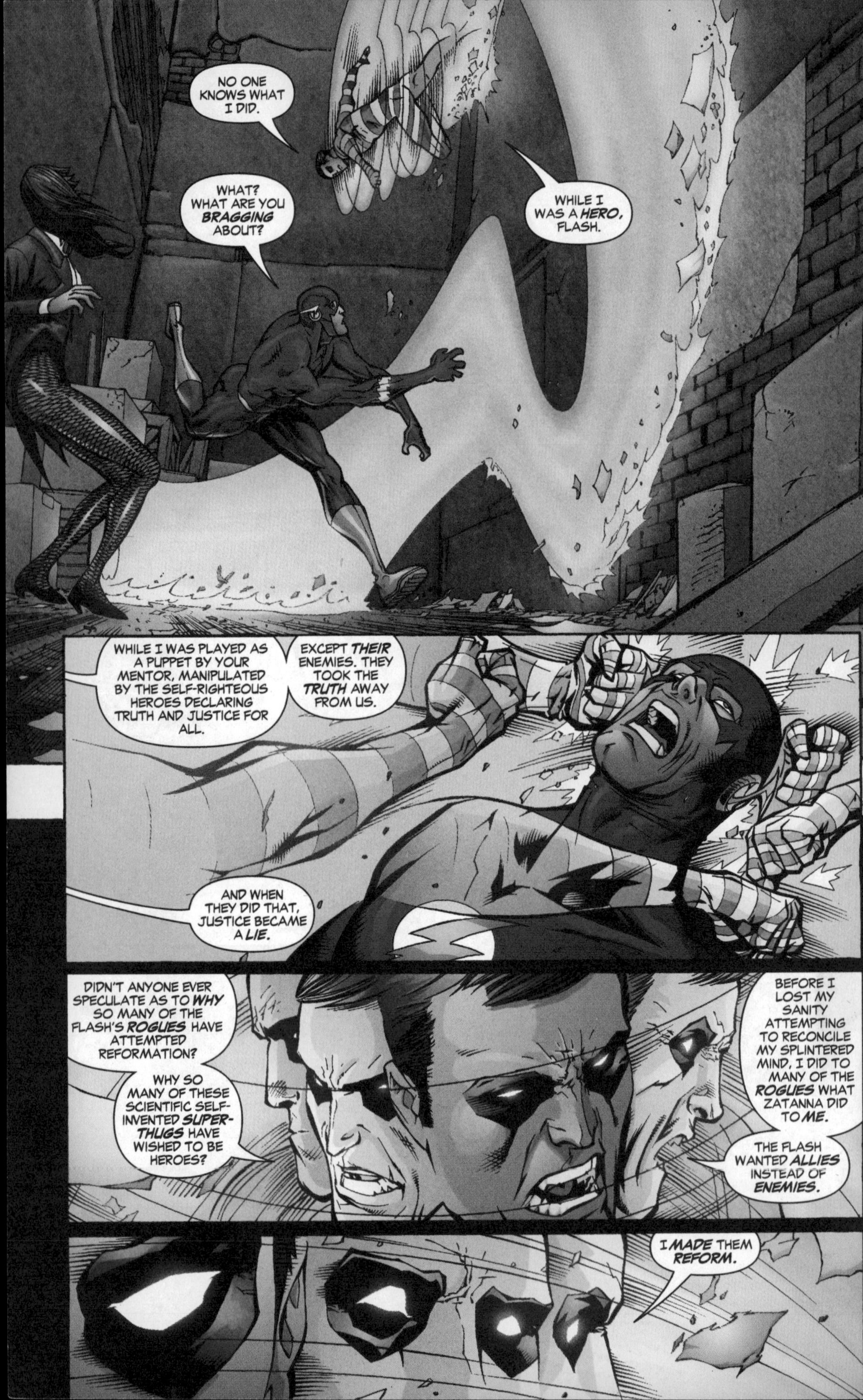
NO ONE KNOWS WHAT I DID.
WHAT? WHAT ARE YOU BRAGGING ABOUT?
WHILE I WAS A HERO, FLASH.
WHILE I WAS PLAYED AS A PUPPET BY YOUR MENTOR, MANIPULATED BY THE SELF-RIGHTEOUS HEROES DECLARING TRUTH AND JUSTICE FOR ALL.
EXCEPT THEIR ENEMIES. THEY TOOK THE TRUTH AWAY FROM US.
AND WHEN THEY DID THAT, JUSTICE BECAME A LIE.
DIDN'T ANYONE EVER SPECULATE AS TO WHY SO MANY OF THE FLASH'S ROGUES HAVE ATTEMPTED REFORMATION?
WHY SO MANY OF THESE SCIENTIFIC SELF-INVENTED SUPER-THUGS HAVE WISHED TO BE HEROES?
BEFORE I LOST MY SANITY ATTEMPTING TO RECONCILE MY SPLINTERED MIND, I DID TO MANY OF THE ROGUES WHAT ZATANNA DID TO ME.
THE FLASH WANTED ALLIES INSTEAD OF ENEMIES.
I MADE THEM REFORM.

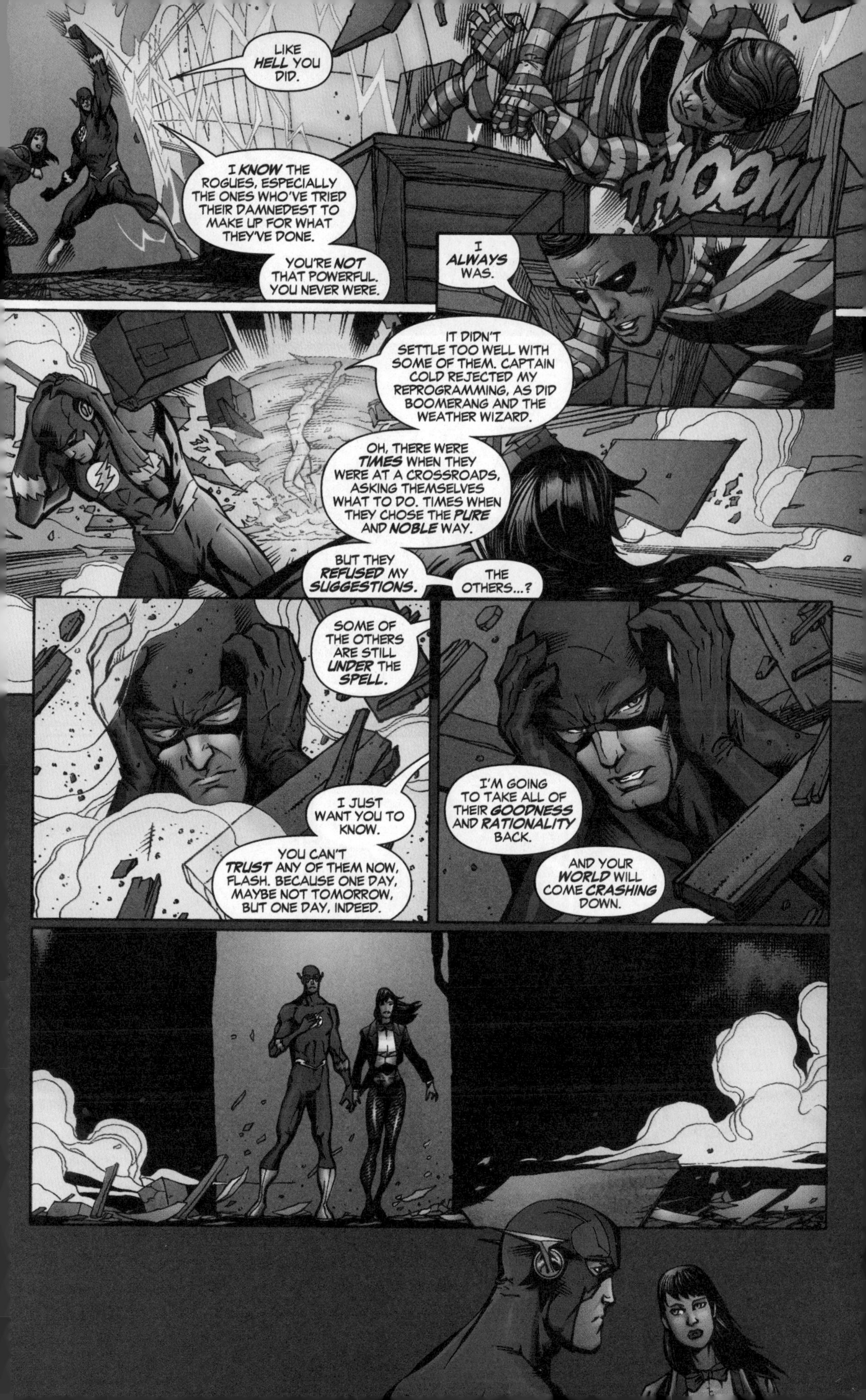
LIKE HELL YOU DID.
I KNOW THE ROGUES, ESPECIALLY THE ONES WHO'VE TRIED THEIR DAMNEDEST TO MAKE UP FOR WHAT THEY'VE DONE.
YOU'RE NOT THAT POWERFUL. YOU NEVER WERE.
THOOM
I ALWAYS WAS.
IT DIDN'T SETTLE TOO WELL WITH SOME OF THEM. CAPTAIN COLD REJECTED MY REPROGRAMMING, AS DID BOOMERANG AND THE WEATHER WIZARD.
OH, THERE WERE TIMES WHEN THEY WERE AT A CROSSROADS, ASKING THEMSELVES WHAT TO DO. TIMES WHEN THEY CHOSE THE PURE AND NOBLE WAY.
BUT THEY REFUSED MY SUGGESTIONS.
THE OTHERS...?
SOME OF THE OTHERS ARE STILL UNDER THE SPELL.
I JUST WANT YOU TO KNOW.
YOU CAN'T TRUST ANY OF THEM NOW, FLASH. BECAUSE ONE DAY, MAYBE NOT TOMORROW, BUT ONE DAY, INDEED.
I'M GOING TO TAKE ALL OF THEIR GOODNESS AND RATIONALITY BACK.
AND YOUR WORLD WILL COME CRASHING DOWN.

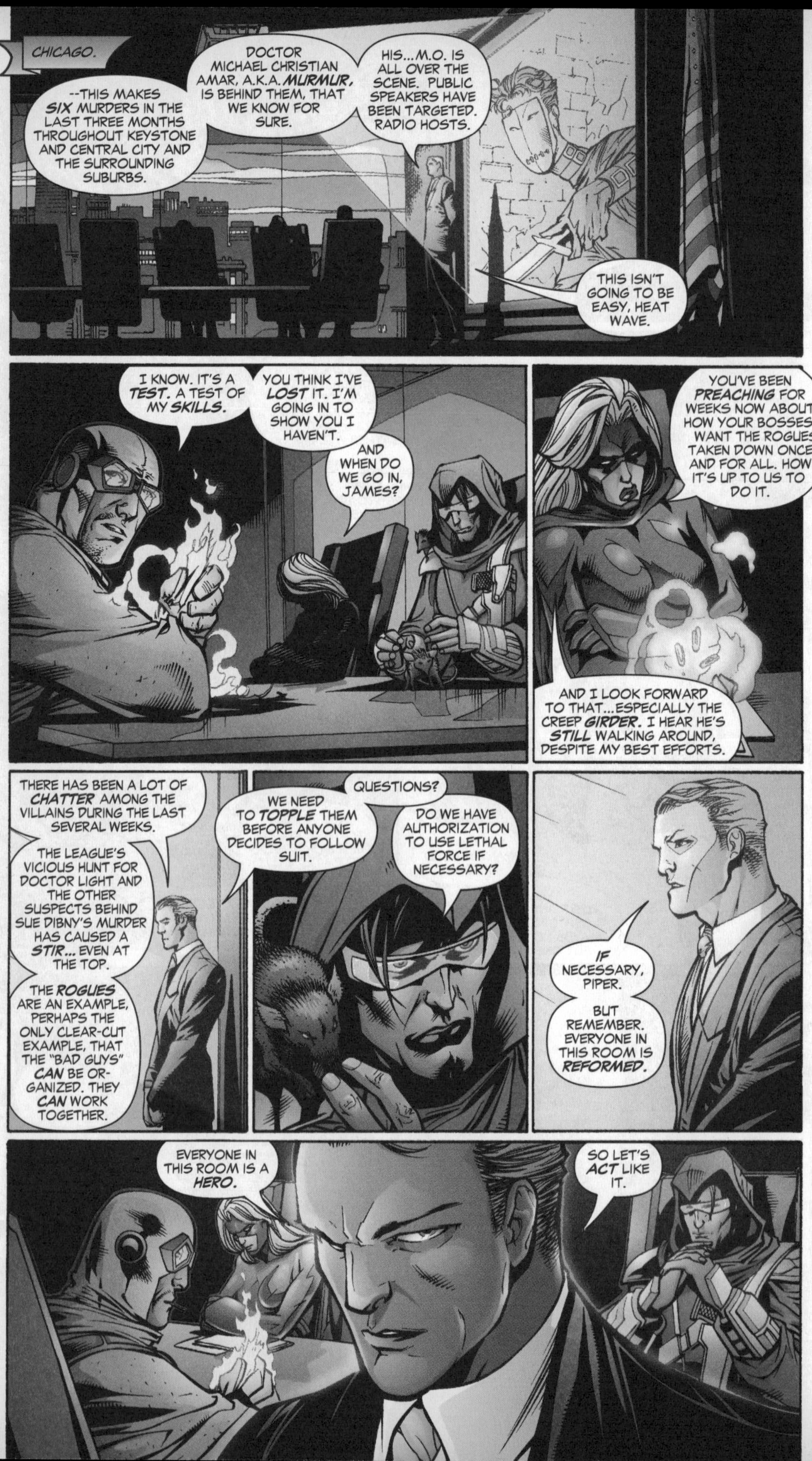
CHICAGO.
--THIS MAKES SIX MURDERS IN THE LAST THREE MONTHS THROUGHOUT KEYSTONE AND CENTRAL CITY AND THE SURROUNDING SUBURBS.
DOCTOR MICHAEL CHRISTIAN AMAR, A.K.A. MURMUR, IS BEHIND THEM, THAT WE KNOW FOR SURE.
HIS...M.O. IS ALL OVER THE SCENE. PUBLIC SPEAKERS HAVE BEEN TARGETED. RADIO HOSTS.
THIS ISN'T GOING TO BE EASY, HEAT WAVE.
I KNOW. IT'S A TEST. A TEST OF MY SKILLS.
YOU THINK I'VE LOST IT. I'M GOING IN TO SHOW YOU I HAVEN'T.
AND WHEN DO WE GO IN, JAMES?
YOU'VE BEEN PREACHING FOR WEEKS NOW ABOUT HOW YOUR BOSSES WANT THE ROGUES TAKEN DOWN ONCE AND FOR ALL. HOW IT'S UP TO US TO DO IT.
AND I LOOK FORWARD TO THAT...ESPECIALLY THE CREEP GIRDER. I HEAR HE'S STILL WALKING AROUND, DESPITE MY BEST EFFORTS.
THERE HAS BEEN A LOT OF CHATTER AMONG THE VILLAINS DURING THE LAST SEVERAL WEEKS.
THE LEAGUE'S VICIOUS HUNT FOR DOCTOR LIGHT AND THE OTHER SUSPECTS BEHIND SUE DIBNY'S MURDER HAS CAUSED A STIR... EVEN AT THE TOP.
THE ROGUES ARE AN EXAMPLE, PERHAPS THE ONLY CLEAR-CUT EXAMPLE, THAT THE "BAD GUYS" CAN BE ORGANIZED. THEY CAN WORK TOGETHER.
WE NEED TO TOPPLE THEM BEFORE ANYONE DECIDES TO FOLLOW SUIT.
QUESTIONS?
DO WE HAVE AUTHORIZATION TO USE LETHAL FORCE IF NECESSARY?
IF NECESSARY, PIPER.
BUT REMEMBER. EVERYONE IN THIS ROOM IS REFORMED.
EVERYONE IN THIS ROOM IS A HERO.
SO LET'S ACT LIKE IT.

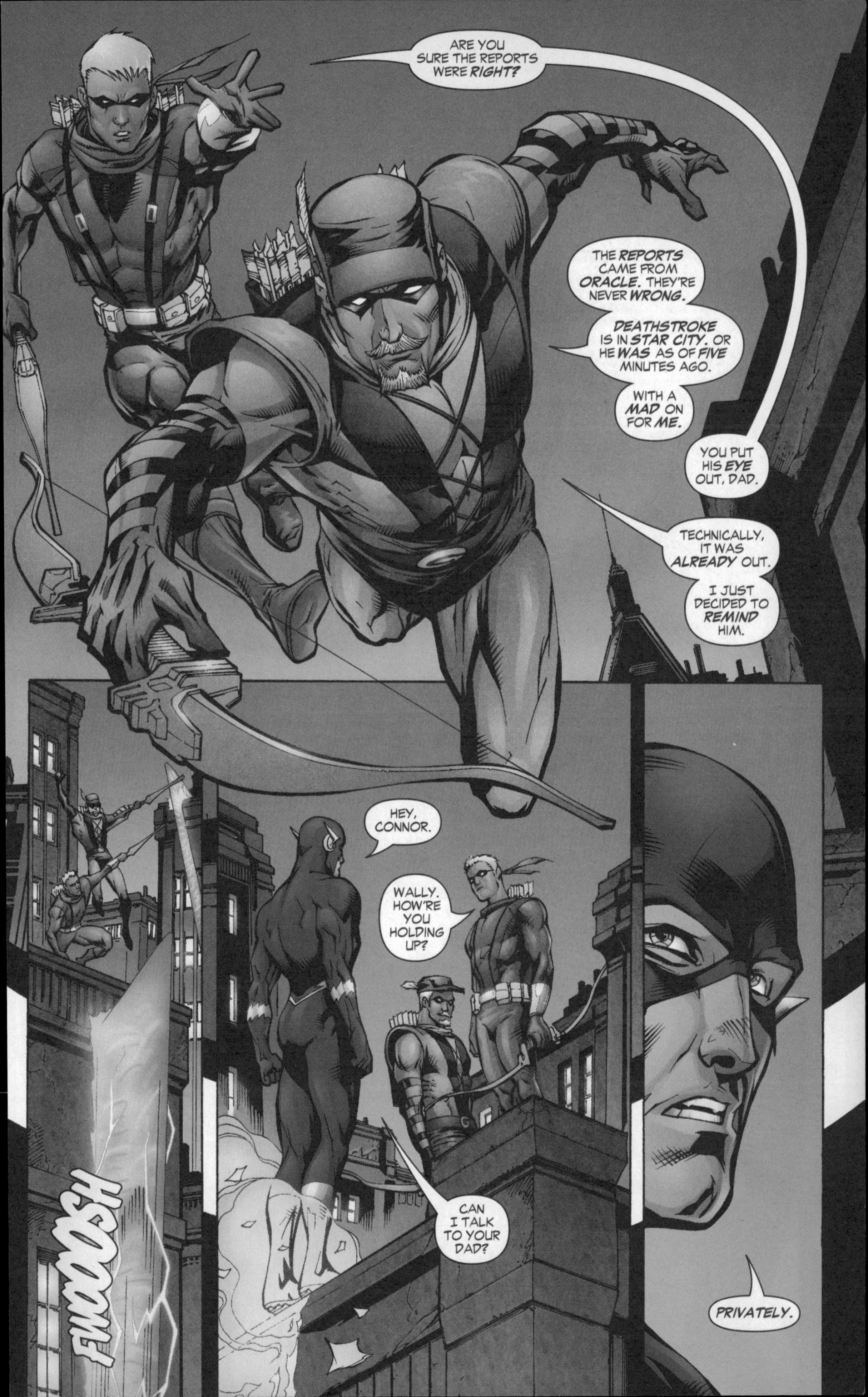

ARE YOU SURE THE REPORTS WERE RIGHT?
THE REPORTS CAME FROM ORACLE. THEY'RE NEVER WRONG.
DEATHSTROKE IS IN STAR CITY. OR HE WAS AS OF FIVE MINUTES AGO.
WITH A MAD ON FOR ME.
YOU PUT HIS EYE OUT, DAD.
TECHNICALLY, IT WAS ALREADY OUT.
I JUST DECIDED TO REMIND HIM.
FWOOOSH
HEY, CONNOR.
WALLY. HOW'RE YOU HOLDING UP?
CAN I TALK TO YOUR DAD?
PRIVATELY.

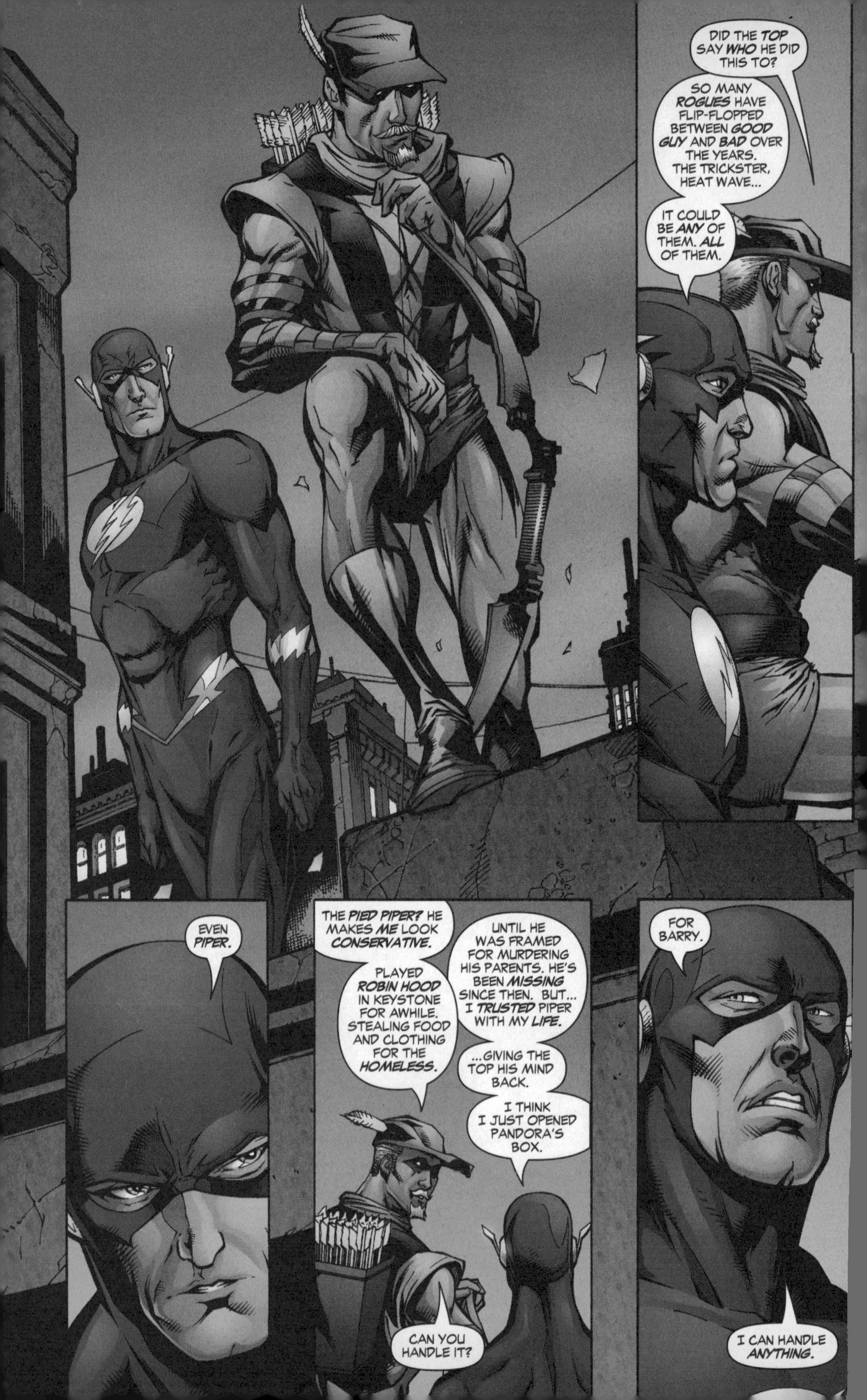
DID THE TOP SAY WHO HE DID THIS TO?
SO MANY ROGUES HAVE FLIP-FLOPPED BETWEEN GOOD GUY AND BAD OVER THE YEARS. THE TRICKSTER, HEAT WAVE...
IT COULD BE ANY OF THEM. ALL OF THEM.
EVEN PIPER.
THE PIED PIPER? HE MAKES ME LOOK CONSERVATIVE.
PLAYED ROBIN HOOD IN KEYSTONE FOR AWHILE. STEALING FOOD AND CLOTHING FOR THE HOMELESS.
UNTIL HE WAS FRAMED FOR MURDERING HIS PARENTS. HE'S BEEN MISSING SINCE THEN. BUT... I TRUSTED PIPER WITH MY LIFE.
...GIVING THE TOP HIS MIND BACK.
I THINK I JUST OPENED PANDORA'S BOX.
CAN YOU HANDLE IT?
FOR BARRY.
I CAN HANDLE ANYTHING.

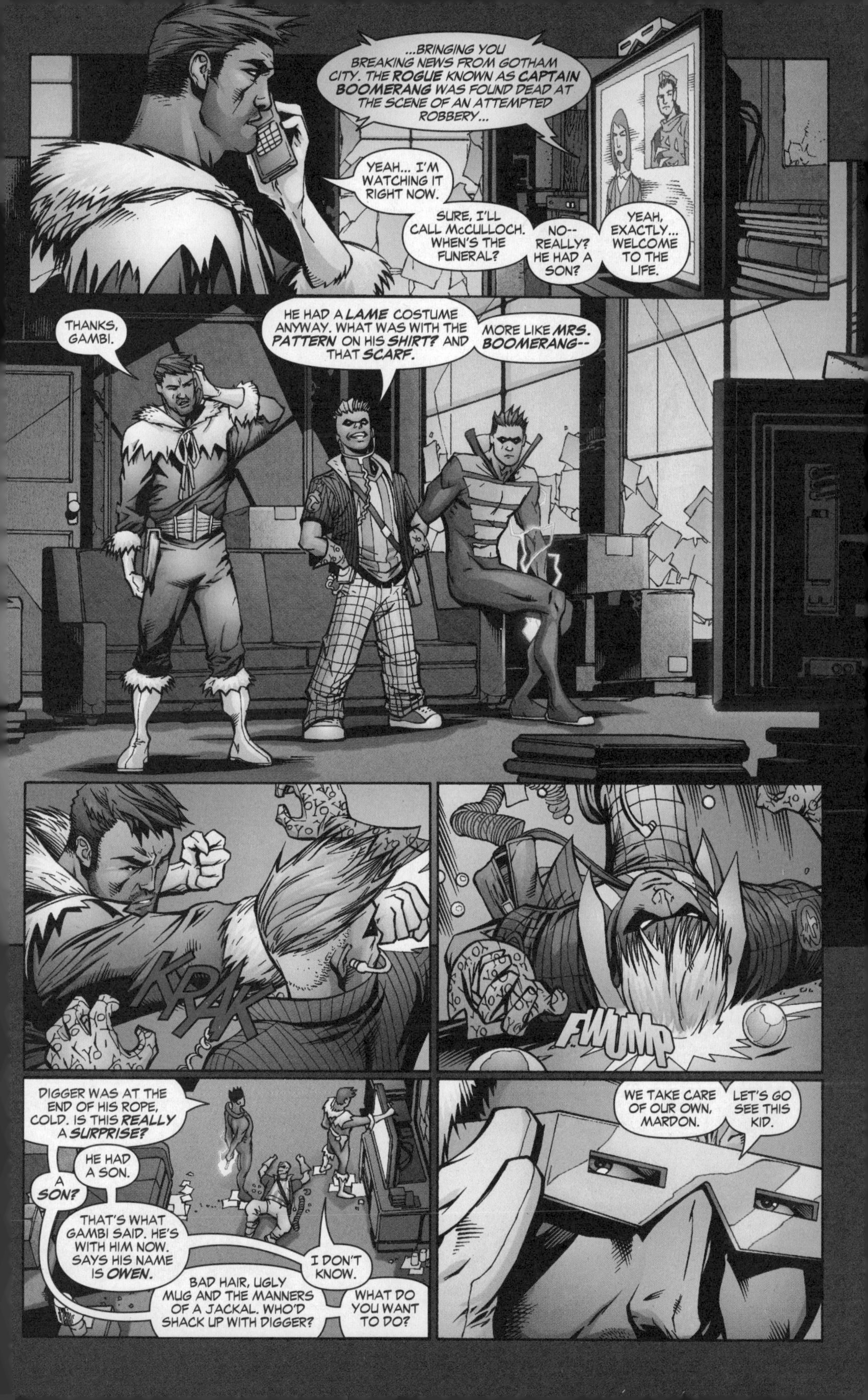
...BRINGING YOU BREAKING NEWS FROM GOTHAM CITY. THE ROGUE KNOWN AS CAPTAIN BOOMERANG WAS FOUND DEAD AT THE SCENE OF AN ATTEMPTED ROBBERY...
YEAH... I'M WATCHING IT RIGHT NOW.
SURE, I'LL CALL McCULLOCH. WHEN'S THE FUNERAL?
NO-- REALLY? HE HAD A SON?
YEAH, EXACTLY... WELCOME TO THE LIFE.
THANKS, GAMBI.
HE HAD A LAME COSTUME ANYWAY. WHAT WAS WITH THE PATTERN ON HIS SHIRT? AND THAT SCARF.
MORE LIKE MRS. BOOMERANG--
KRAK
FWUMP
DIGGER WAS AT THE END OF HIS ROPE, COLD. IS THIS REALLY A SURPRISE?
HE HAD A SON.
A SON?
THAT'S WHAT GAMBI SAID. HE'S WITH HIM NOW. SAYS HIS NAME IS OWEN.
BAD HAIR, UGLY MUG AND THE MANNERS OF A JACKAL. WHO'D SHACK UP WITH DIGGER?
I DON'T KNOW.
WHAT DO YOU WANT TO DO?
WE TAKE CARE OF OUR OWN, MARDON.
LET'S GO SEE THIS KID.

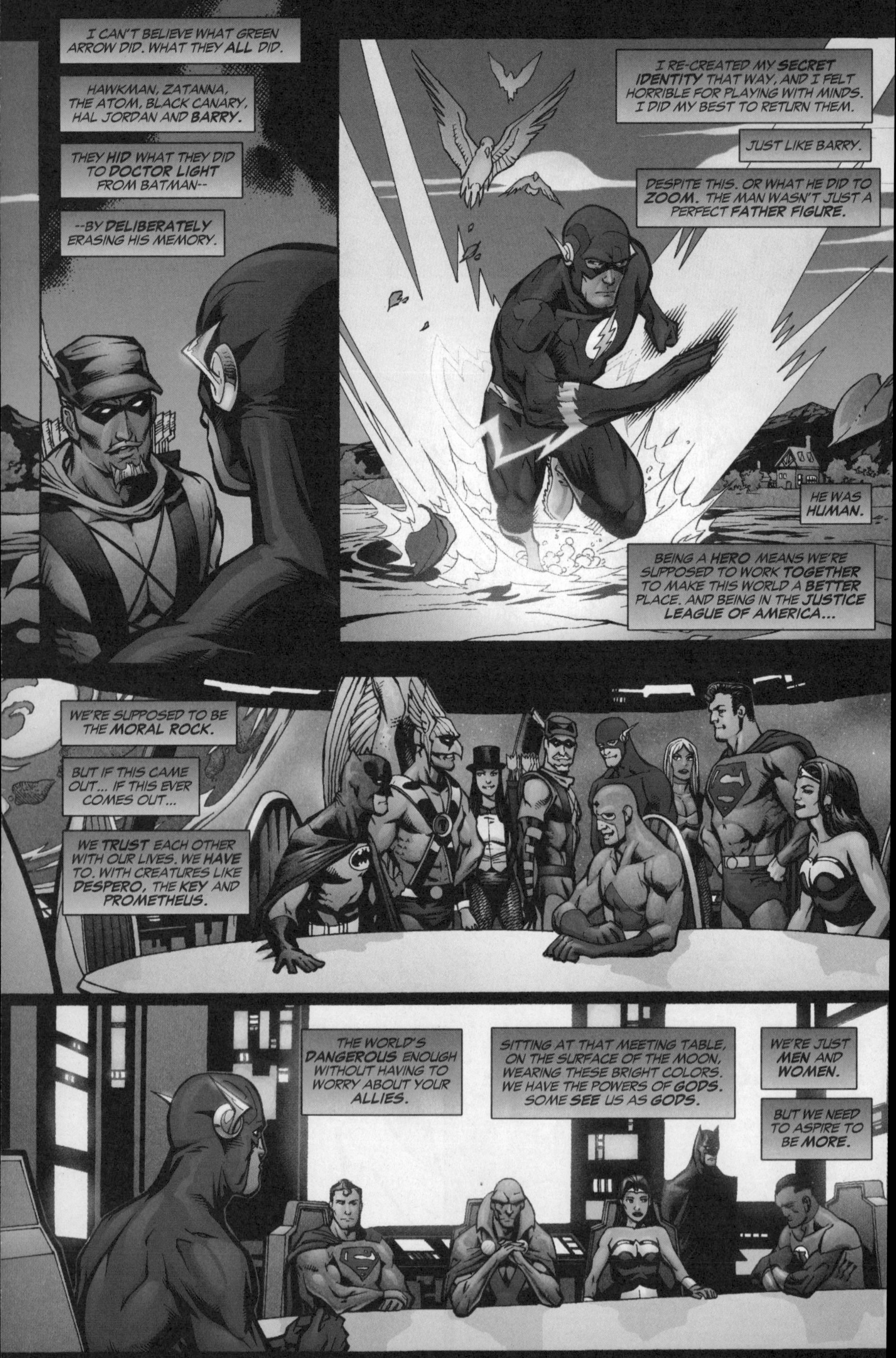
I CAN'T BELIEVE WHAT GREEN ARROW DID. WHAT THEY ALL DID.
HAWKMAN, ZATANNA, THE ATOM, BLACK CANARY, HAL JORDAN AND BARRY.
THEY HID WHAT THEY DID TO DOCTOR LIGHT FROM BATMAN--
--BY DELIBERATELY ERASING HIS MEMORY.
I RE-CREATED MY SECRET IDENTITY THAT WAY, AND I FELT HORRIBLE FOR PLAYING WITH MINDS. I DID MY BEST TO RETURN THEM.
JUST LIKE BARRY.
DESPITE THIS. OR WHAT HE DID TO ZOOM. THE MAN WASN'T JUST A PERFECT FATHER FIGURE.
HE WAS HUMAN.
BEING A HERO MEANS WE'RE SUPPOSED TO WORK TOGETHER TO MAKE THIS WORLD A BETTER PLACE. AND BEING IN THE JUSTICE LEAGUE OF AMERICA...
WE'RE SUPPOSED TO BE THE MORAL ROCK.
BUT IF THIS CAME OUT... IF THIS EVER COMES OUT...
WE TRUST EACH OTHER WITH OUR LIVES. WE HAVE TO. WITH CREATURES LIKE DESPERO, THE KEY AND PROMETHEUS.
THE WORLD'S DANGEROUS ENOUGH WITHOUT HAVING TO WORRY ABOUT YOUR ALLIES.
SITTING AT THAT MEETING TABLE, ON THE SURFACE OF THE MOON, WEARING THESE BRIGHT COLORS. WE HAVE THE POWERS OF GODS. SOME SEE US AS GODS.
WE'RE JUST MEN AND WOMEN.
BUT WE NEED TO ASPIRE TO BE MORE.

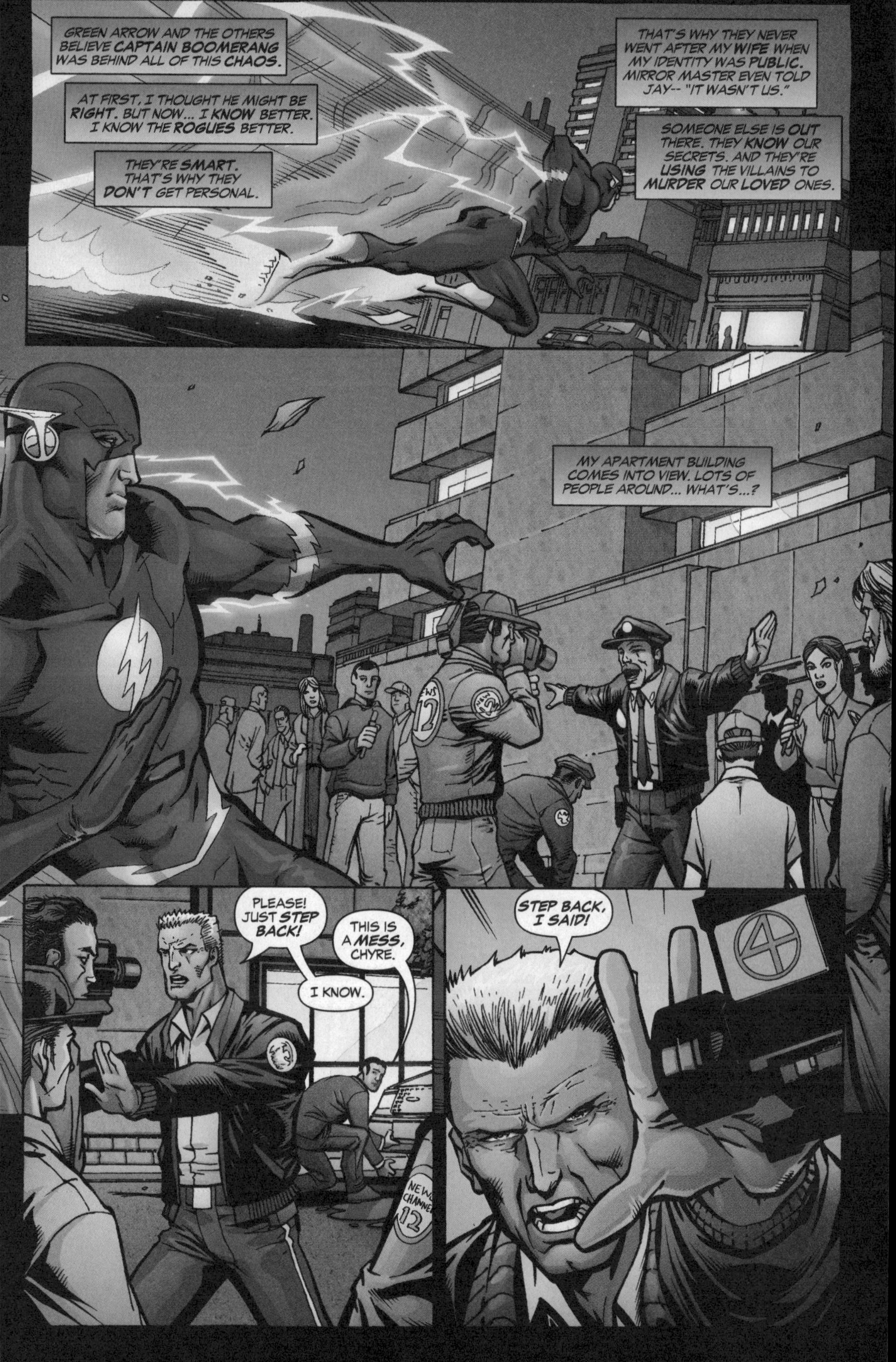

GREEN ARROW AND THE OTHERS BELIEVE CAPTAIN BOOMERANG WAS BEHIND ALL OF THIS CHAOS.
AT FIRST, I THOUGHT HE MIGHT BE RIGHT. BUT NOW... I KNOW BETTER. I KNOW THE ROGUES BETTER.
THEY'RE SMART. THAT'S WHY THEY DON'T GET PERSONAL.
THAT'S WHY THEY NEVER WENT AFTER MY WIFE WHEN MY IDENTITY WAS PUBLIC. MIRROR MASTER EVEN TOLD JAY-- "IT WASN'T US."
SOMEONE ELSE IS OUT THERE. THEY KNOW OUR SECRETS. AND THEY'RE USING THE VILLAINS TO MURDER OUR LOVED ONES.
MY APARTMENT BUILDING COMES INTO VIEW. LOTS OF PEOPLE AROUND... WHAT'S...?
PLEASE! JUST STEP BACK!
THIS IS A MESS, CHYRE.
I KNOW.
STEP BACK, I SAID!

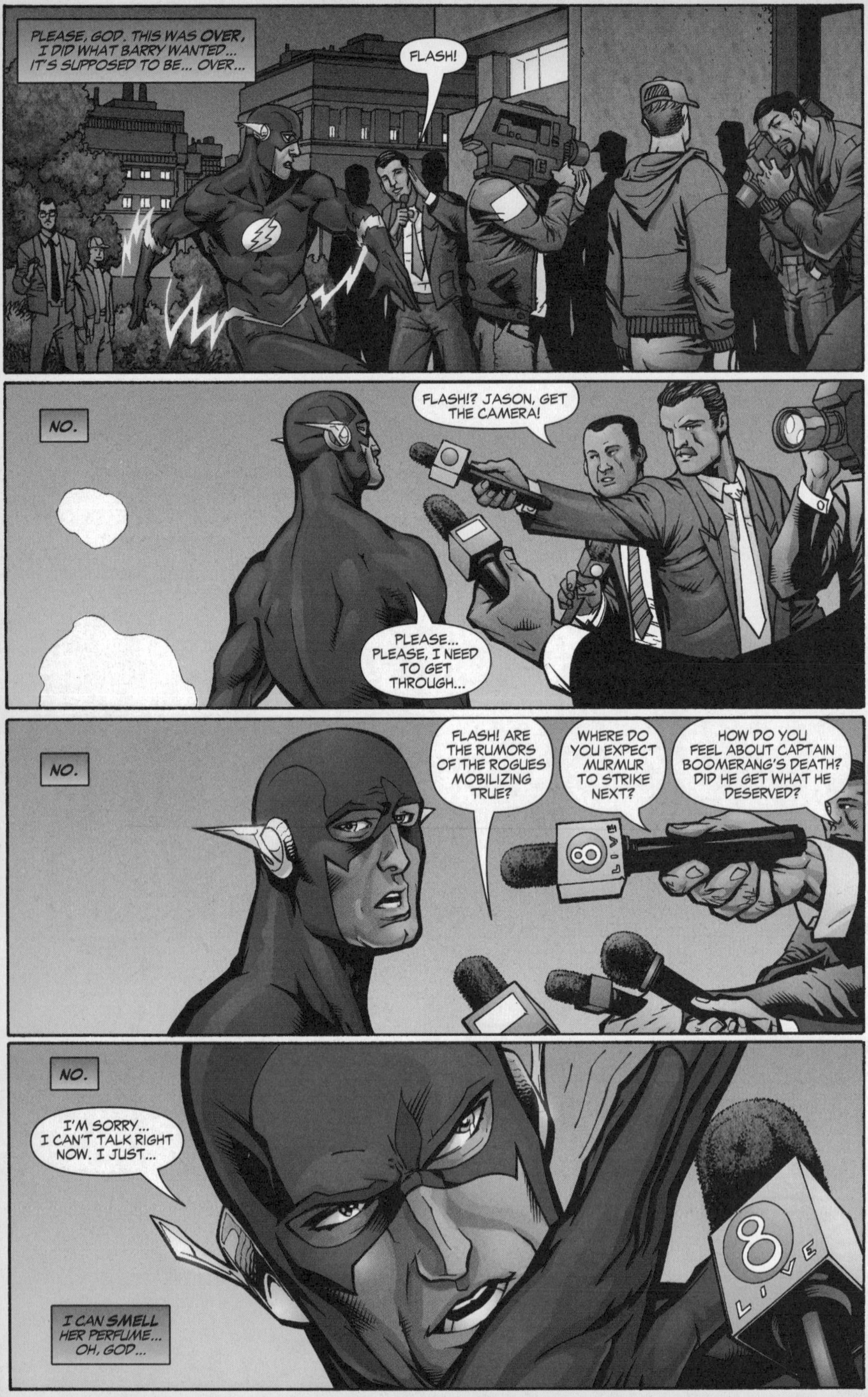
PLEASE, GOD. THIS WAS OVER, I DID WHAT BARRY WANTED... IT'S SUPPOSED TO BE... OVER...
FLASH!
NO.
FLASH!? JASON, GET THE CAMERA!
PLEASE... PLEASE, I NEED TO GET THROUGH...
NO.
FLASH! ARE THE RUMORS OF THE ROGUES MOBILIZING TRUE?
WHERE DO YOU EXPECT MURMUR TO STRIKE NEXT?
HOW DO YOU FEEL ABOUT CAPTAIN BOOMERANG'S DEATH? DID HE GET WHAT HE DESERVED?
8 LIVE
NO.
I'M SORRY... I CAN'T TALK RIGHT NOW. I JUST...
8 LIVE
I CAN SMELL HER PERFUME... OH, GOD...

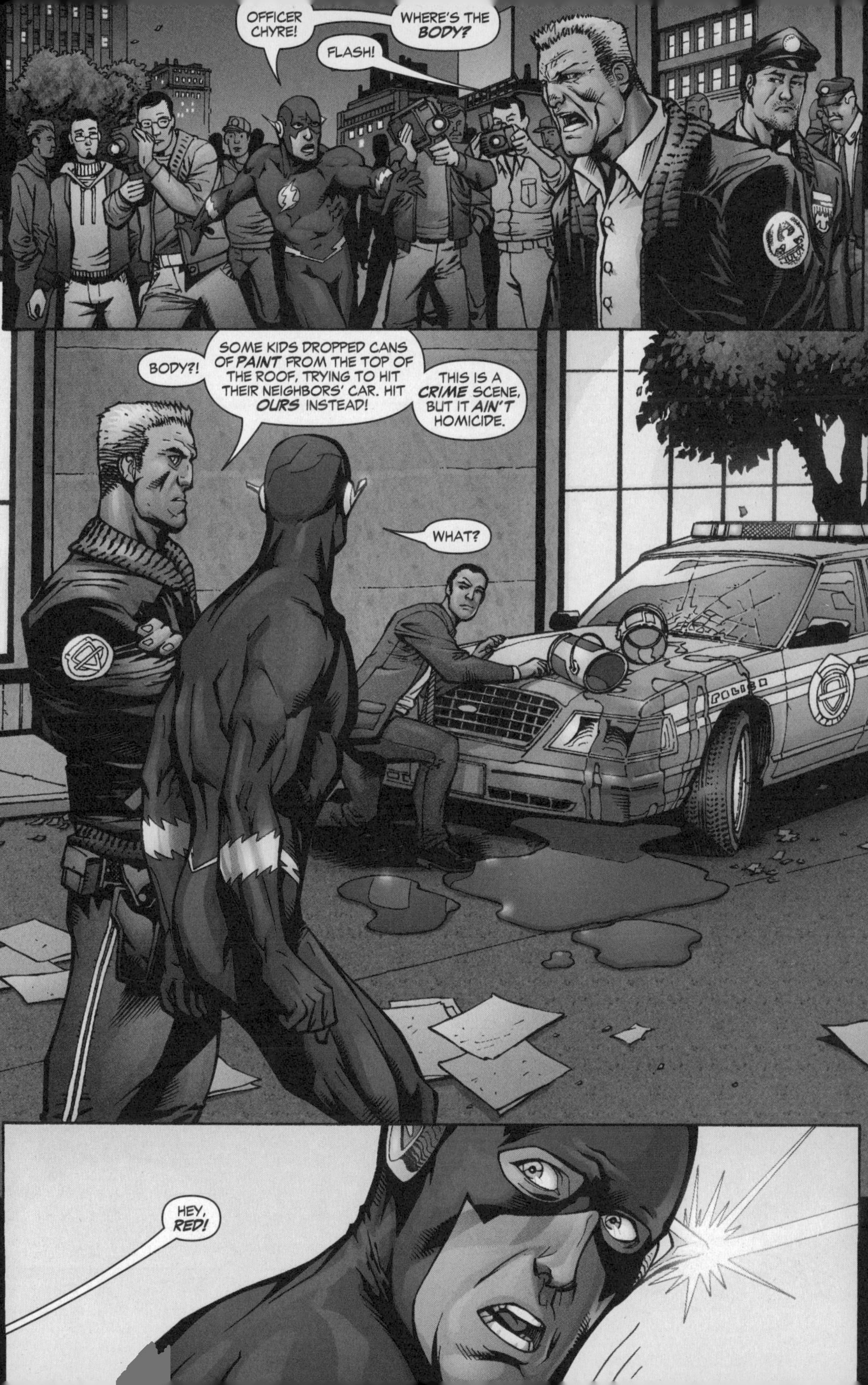
OFFICER CHYRE!
WHERE'S THE BODY?
FLASH!
BODY?!
SOME KIDS DROPPED CANS OF PAINT FROM THE TOP OF THE ROOF, TRYING TO HIT THEIR NEIGHBORS' CAR. HIT OURS INSTEAD!
THIS IS A CRIME SCENE, BUT IT AIN'T HOMICIDE.
WHAT?
HEY, RED!

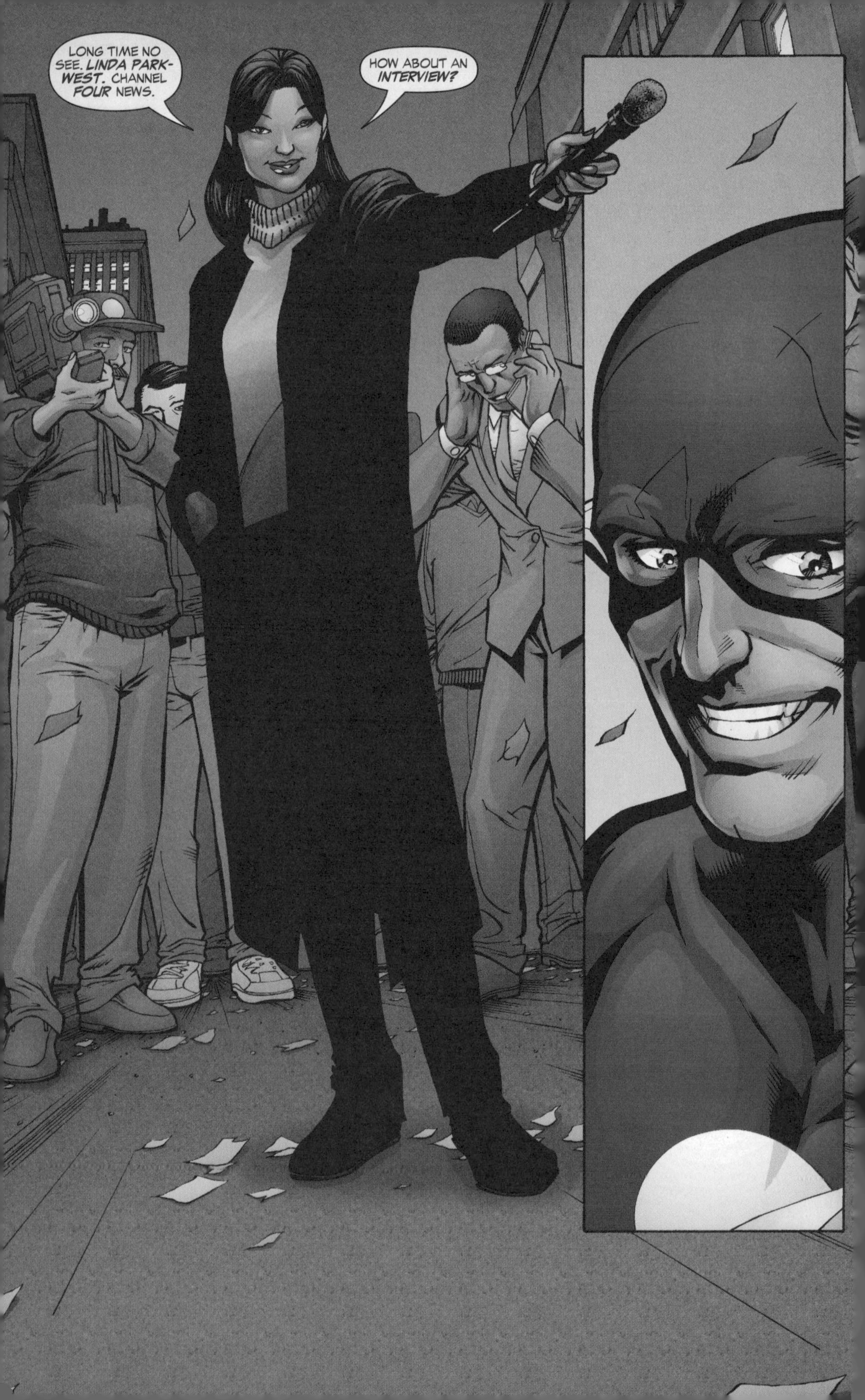
LONG TIME NO SEE. LINDA PARK-WEST. CHANNEL FOUR NEWS.
HOW ABOUT AN INTERVIEW?

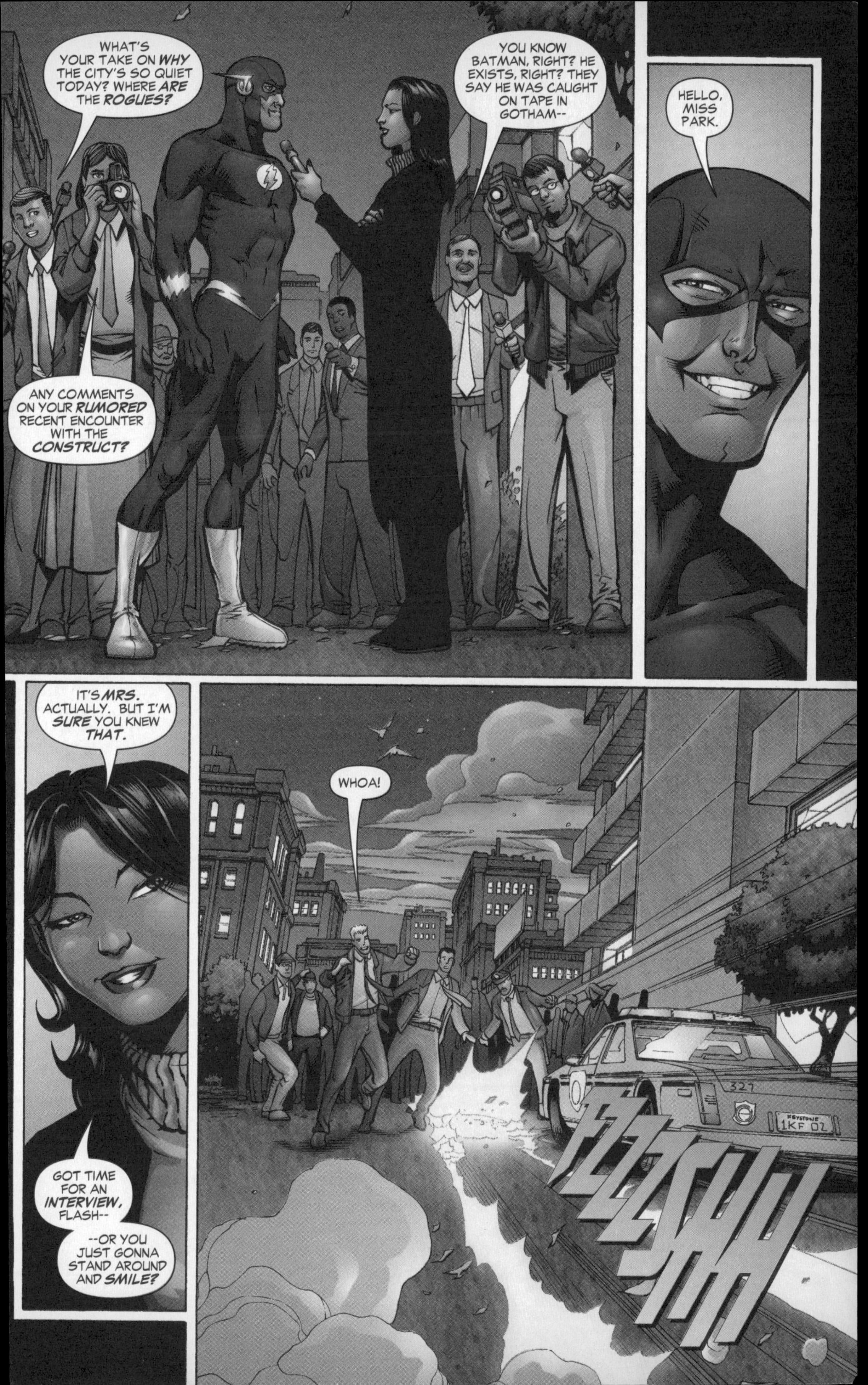

WHAT'S YOUR TAKE ON WHY THE CITY'S SO QUIET TODAY? WHERE ARE THE ROGUES?
ANY COMMENTS ON YOUR RUMORED RECENT ENCOUNTER WITH THE CONSTRUCT?
YOU KNOW BATMAN, RIGHT? HE EXISTS, RIGHT? THEY SAY HE WAS CAUGHT ON TAPE IN GOTHAM--
HELLO, MISS PARK.
IT'S MRS. ACTUALLY. BUT I'M SURE YOU KNEW THAT.
GOT TIME FOR AN INTERVIEW, FLASH--
--OR YOU JUST GONNA STAND AROUND AND SMILE?
WHOA!
KEYSTONE
1KF 02
ZZZSHH

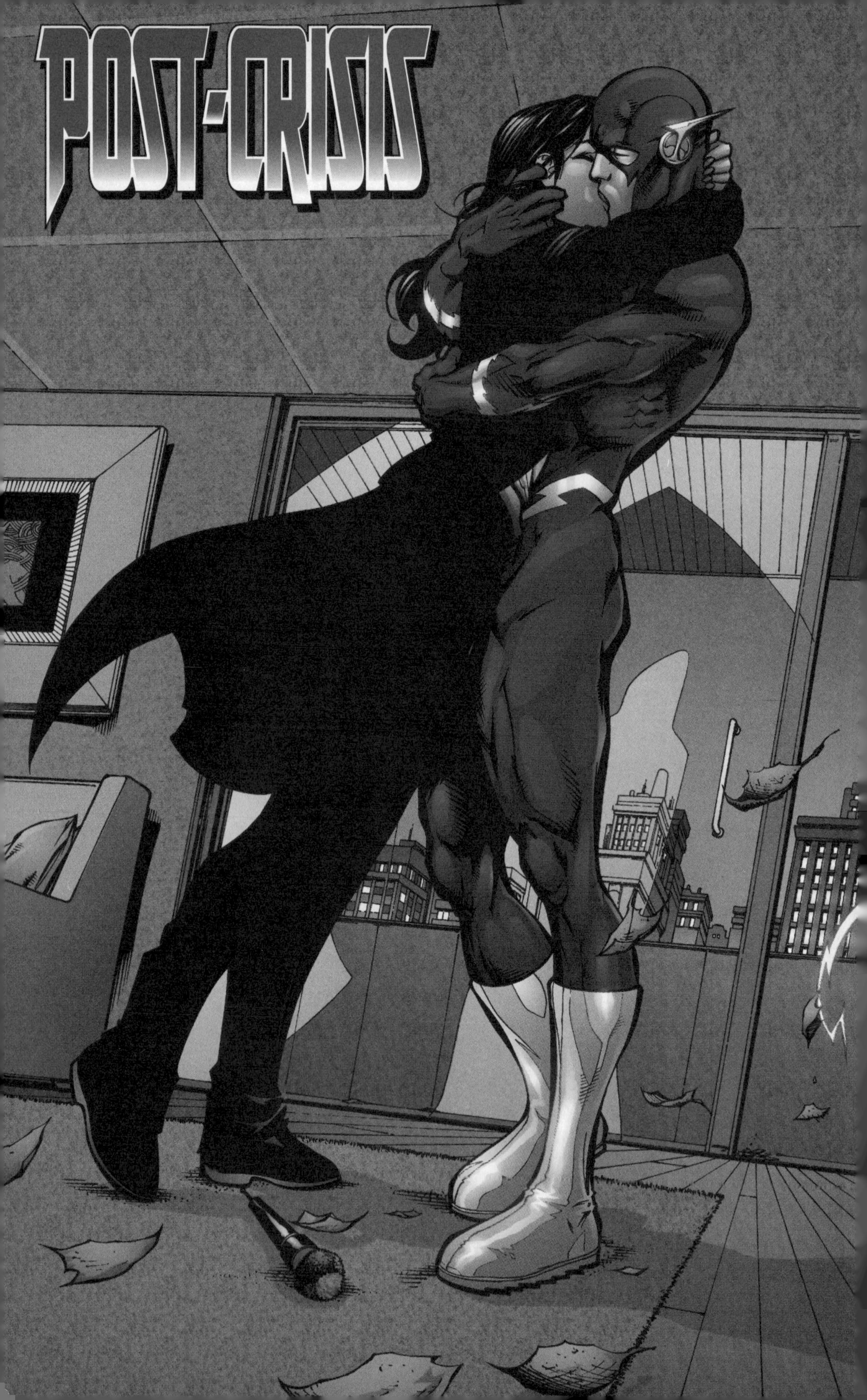
POST-CRISIS

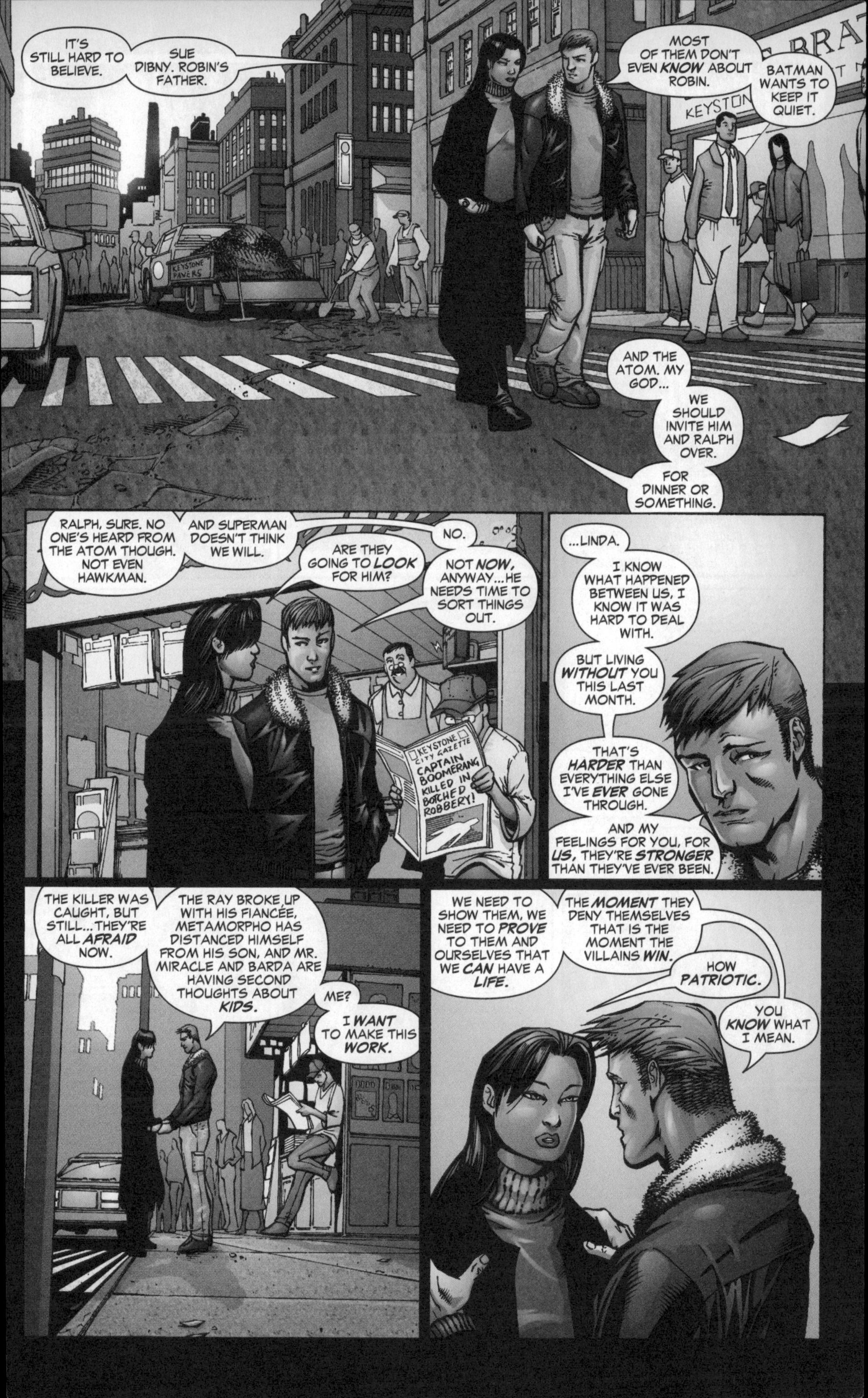

IT'S STILL HARD TO BELIEVE.
SUE DIBNY. ROBIN'S FATHER.
MOST OF THEM DON'T EVEN KNOW ABOUT ROBIN.
BATMAN WANTS TO KEEP IT QUIET.
KEYSTONE PAVERS
AND THE ATOM. MY GOD...
WE SHOULD INVITE HIM AND RALPH OVER.
FOR DINNER OR SOMETHING.
RALPH, SURE. NO ONE'S HEARD FROM THE ATOM THOUGH. NOT EVEN HAWKMAN.
AND SUPERMAN DOESN'T THINK WE WILL.
ARE THEY GOING TO LOOK FOR HIM?
NO.
NOT NOW, ANYWAY...HE NEEDS TIME TO SORT THINGS OUT.
KEYSTONE CITY GAZETTE
CAPTAIN BOOMERANG KILLED IN BOTCHED ROBBERY!
...LINDA.
I KNOW WHAT HAPPENED BETWEEN US, I KNOW IT WAS HARD TO DEAL WITH.
BUT LIVING WITHOUT YOU THIS LAST MONTH.
THAT'S HARDER THAN EVERYTHING ELSE I'VE EVER GONE THROUGH.
AND MY FEELINGS FOR YOU, FOR US, THEY'RE STRONGER THAN THEY'VE EVER BEEN.
THE KILLER WAS CAUGHT, BUT STILL... THEY'RE ALL AFRAID NOW.
THE RAY BROKE UP WITH HIS FIANCÉE, METAMORPHO HAS DISTANCED HIMSELF FROM HIS SON, AND MR. MIRACLE AND BARDA ARE HAVING SECOND THOUGHTS ABOUT KIDS.
ME?
I WANT TO MAKE THIS WORK.
WE NEED TO SHOW THEM, WE NEED TO PROVE TO THEM AND OURSELVES THAT WE CAN HAVE A LIFE.
THE MOMENT THEY DENY THEMSELVES THAT IS THE MOMENT THE VILLAINS WIN.
HOW PATRIOTIC.
YOU KNOW WHAT I MEAN.

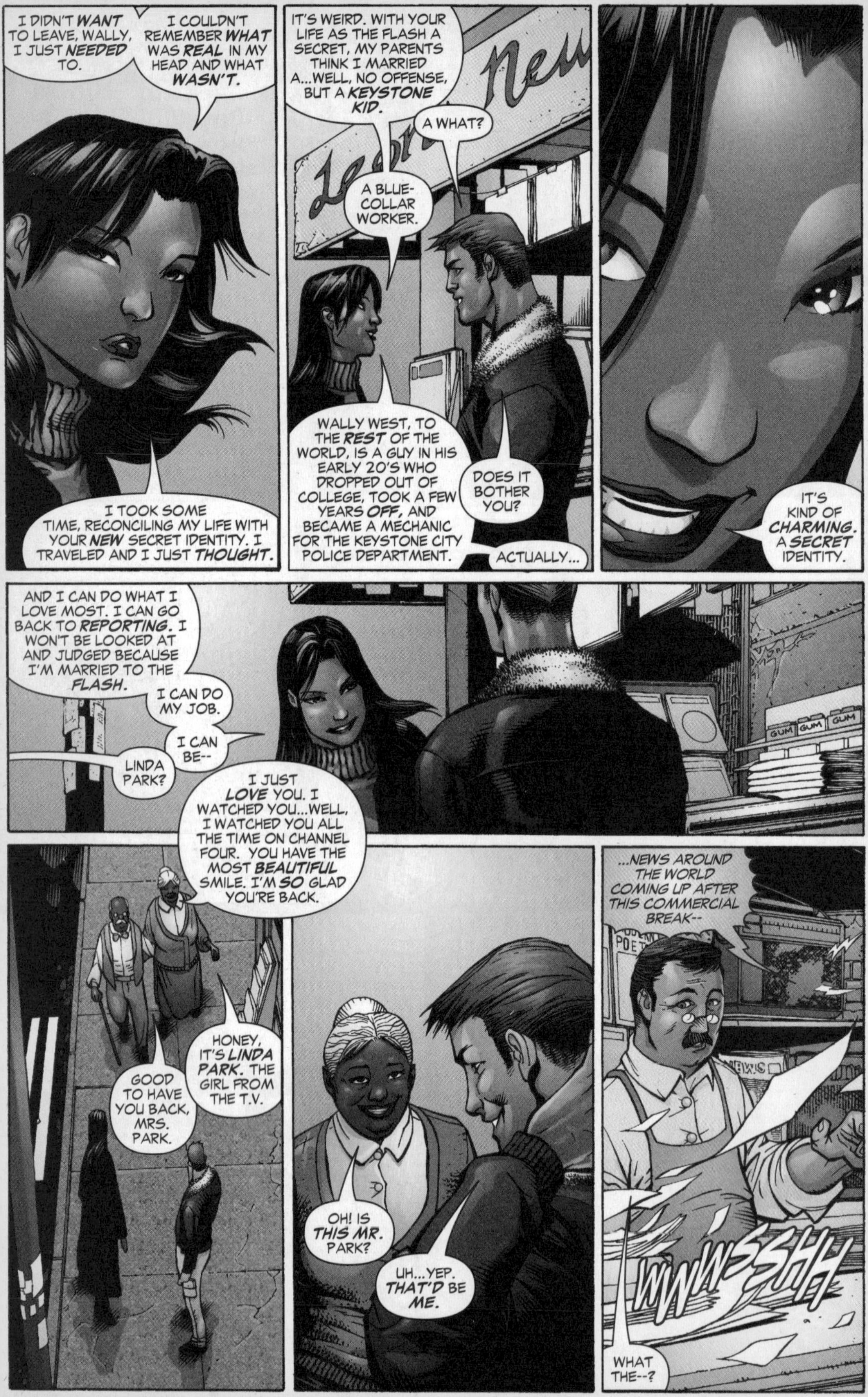

I DIDN'T WANT TO LEAVE, WALLY, I JUST NEEDED TO.
I COULDN'T REMEMBER WHAT WAS REAL IN MY HEAD AND WHAT WASN'T.
I TOOK SOME TIME, RECONCILING MY LIFE WITH YOUR NEW SECRET IDENTITY. I TRAVELED AND I JUST THOUGHT.
IT'S WEIRD. WITH YOUR LIFE AS THE FLASH A SECRET, MY PARENTS THINK I MARRIED A...WELL, NO OFFENSE, BUT A KEYSTONE KID.
A WHAT?
A BLUE-COLLAR WORKER.
WALLY WEST, TO THE REST OF THE WORLD, IS A GUY IN HIS EARLY 20'S WHO DROPPED OUT OF COLLEGE, TOOK A FEW YEARS OFF, AND BECAME A MECHANIC FOR THE KEYSTONE CITY POLICE DEPARTMENT.
DOES IT BOTHER YOU?
ACTUALLY...
IT'S KIND OF CHARMING. A SECRET IDENTITY.
AND I CAN DO WHAT I LOVE MOST. I CAN GO BACK TO REPORTING. I WON'T BE LOOKED AT AND JUDGED BECAUSE I'M MARRIED TO THE FLASH.
I CAN DO MY JOB.
I CAN BE--
LINDA PARK?
GUM
GUM
GUM
I JUST LOVE YOU. I WATCHED YOU...WELL, I WATCHED YOU ALL THE TIME ON CHANNEL FOUR. YOU HAVE THE MOST BEAUTIFUL SMILE. I'M SO GLAD YOU'RE BACK.
HONEY, IT'S LINDA PARK. THE GIRL FROM THE T.V.
GOOD TO HAVE YOU BACK, MRS. PARK.
OH! IS THIS MR. PARK?
UH...YEP. THAT'D BE ME.
...NEWS AROUND THE WORLD COMING UP AFTER THIS COMMERCIAL BREAK--
WWWSSHH
WHAT THE--?

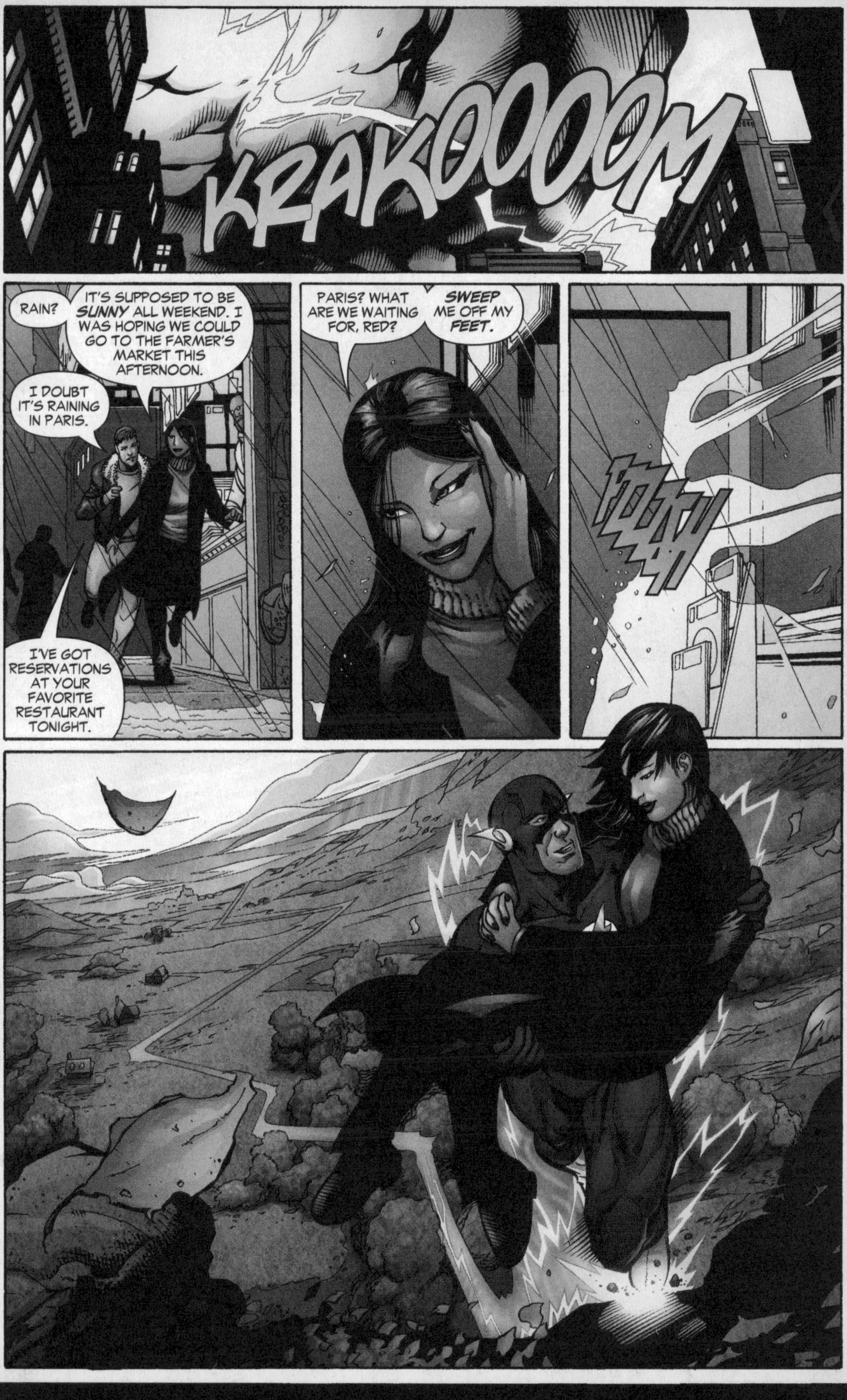
KRAKOOOOM
RAIN?
IT'S SUPPOSED TO BE SUNNY ALL WEEKEND. I WAS HOPING WE COULD GO TO THE FARMER'S MARKET THIS AFTERNOON.
I DOUBT IT'S RAINING IN PARIS.
I'VE GOT RESERVATIONS AT YOUR FAVORITE RESTAURANT TONIGHT.
PARIS? WHAT ARE WE WAITING FOR, RED?
SWEEP ME OFF MY FEET.

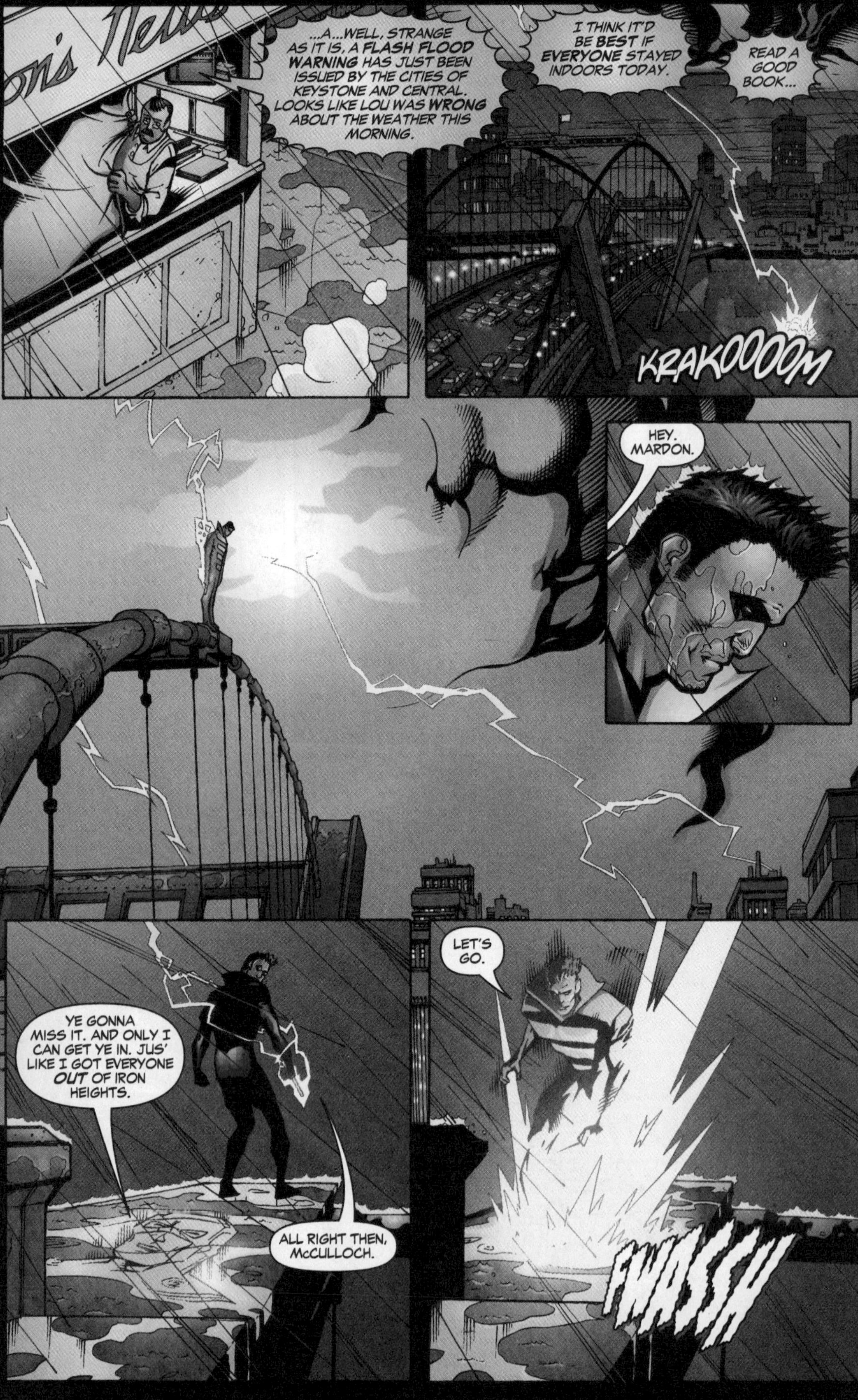

...A...WELL, STRANGE AS IT IS, A FLASH FLOOD WARNING HAS JUST BEEN ISSUED BY THE CITIES OF KEYSTONE AND CENTRAL. LOOKS LIKE LOU WAS WRONG ABOUT THE WEATHER THIS MORNING.
I THINK IT'D BE BEST IF EVERYONE STAYED INDOORS TODAY.
READ A GOOD BOOK...
KRAKOOOOM
HEY. MARDON.
YE GONNA MISS IT. AND ONLY I CAN GET YE IN. JUS' LIKE I GOT EVERYONE OUT OF IRON HEIGHTS.
ALL RIGHT THEN, McCULLOCH.
LET'S GO.
FWASSH

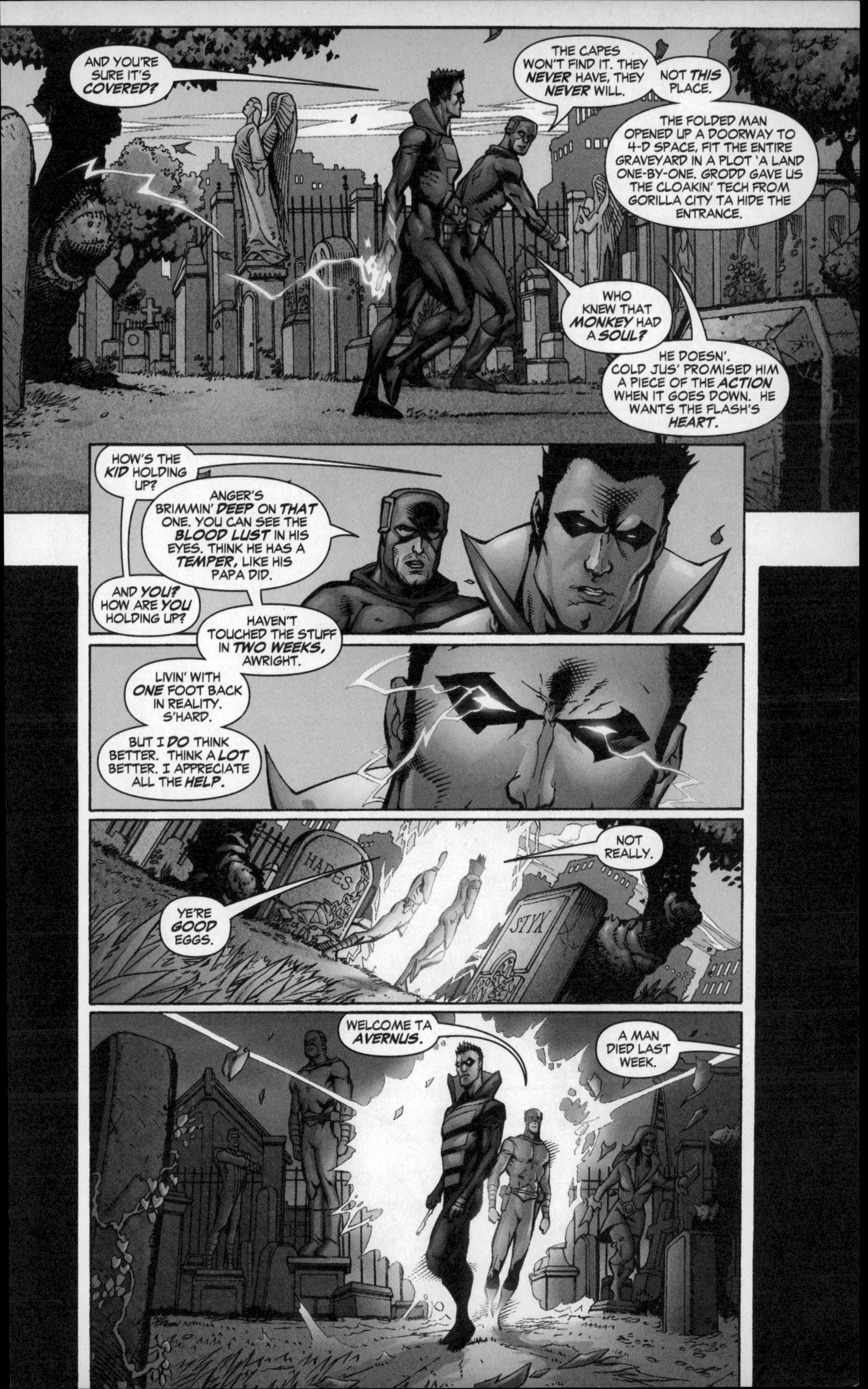
AND YOU'RE SURE IT'S COVERED?
THE CAPES WON'T FIND IT. THEY NEVER HAVE, THEY NEVER WILL.
NOT THIS PLACE.
THE FOLDED MAN OPENED UP A DOORWAY TO 4-D SPACE, FIT THE ENTIRE GRAVEYARD IN A PLOT 'A LAND ONE-BY-ONE. GRODD GAVE US THE CLOAKIN' TECH FROM GORILLA CITY TA HIDE THE ENTRANCE.
WHO KNEW THAT MONKEY HAD A SOUL?
HE DOESN'. COLD JUS' PROMISED HIM A PIECE OF THE ACTION WHEN IT GOES DOWN. HE WANTS THE FLASH'S HEART.
HOW'S THE KID HOLDING UP?
ANGER'S BRIMMIN' DEEP ON THAT ONE. YOU CAN SEE THE BLOOD LUST IN HIS EYES. THINK HE HAS A TEMPER, LIKE HIS PAPA DID.
AND YOU? HOW ARE YOU HOLDING UP?
HAVEN'T TOUCHED THE STUFF IN TWO WEEKS, AWRIGHT.
LIVIN' WITH ONE FOOT BACK IN REALITY. S'HARD.
BUT I DO THINK BETTER. THINK A LOT BETTER. I APPRECIATE ALL THE HELP.
HADES
STYX
YE'RE GOOD EGGS.
NOT REALLY.
WELCOME TA AVERNUS.
A MAN DIED LAST WEEK.

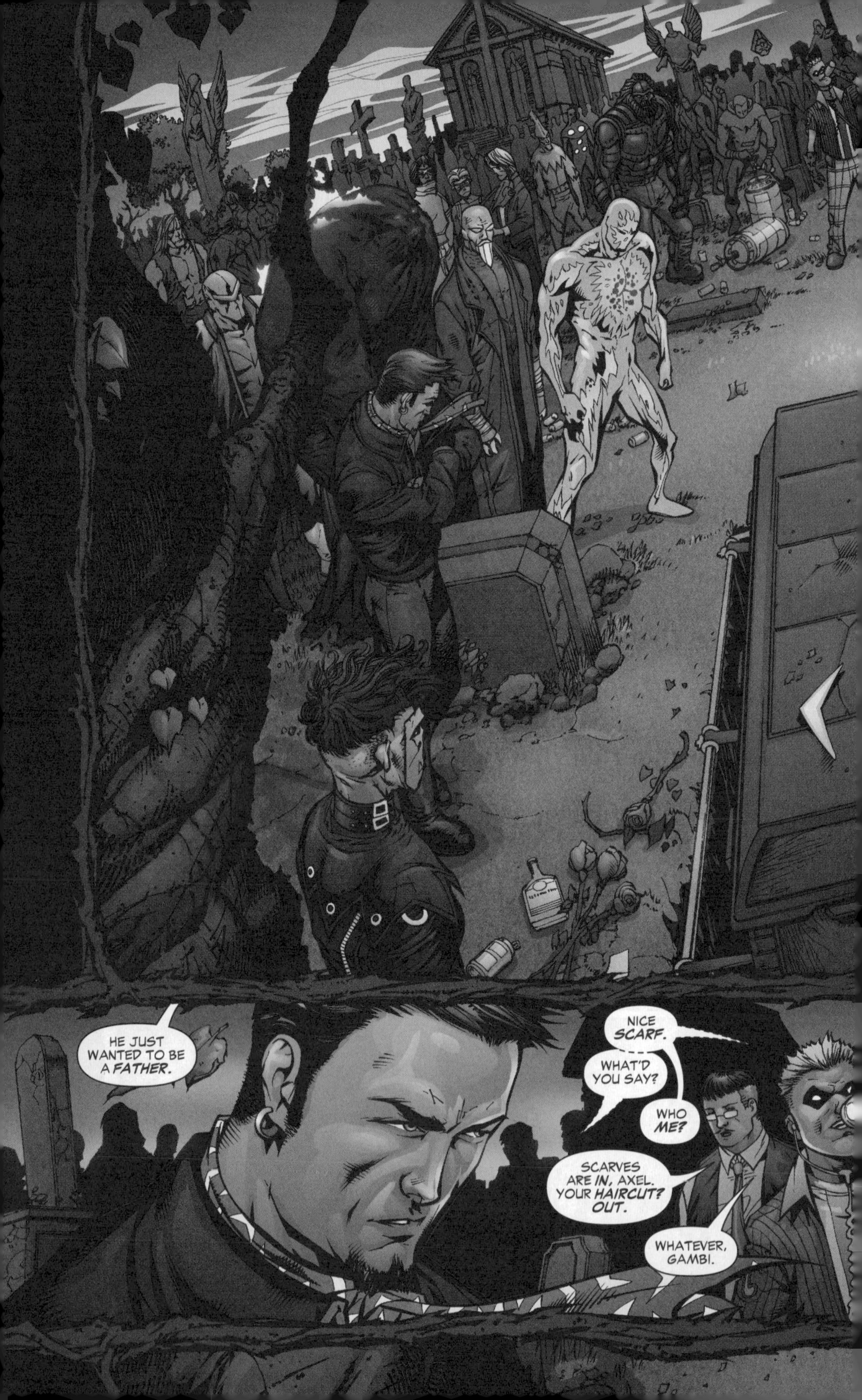
HE JUST WANTED TO BE A FATHER.
NICE SCARF.
WHAT'D YOU SAY?
WHO ME?
SCARVES ARE IN, AXEL. YOUR HAIRCUT? OUT.
WHATEVER, GAMBI.

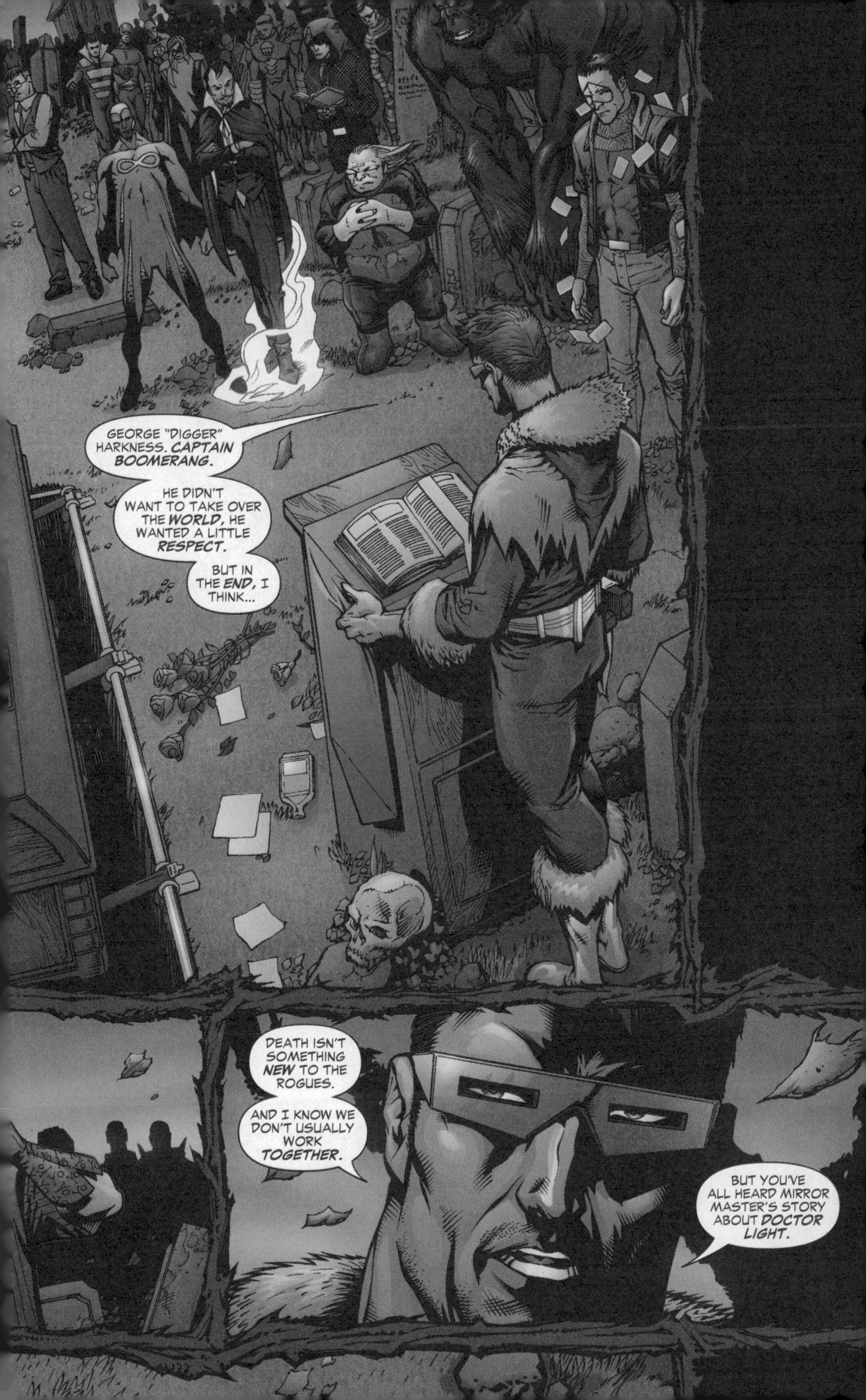
GEORGE "DIGGER" HARKNESS. CAPTAIN BOOMERANG.
HE DIDN'T WANT TO TAKE OVER THE WORLD, HE WANTED A LITTLE RESPECT.
BUT IN THE END, I THINK...
DEATH ISN'T SOMETHING NEW TO THE ROGUES.
AND I KNOW WE DON'T USUALLY WORK TOGETHER.
BUT YOU'VE ALL HEARD MIRROR MASTER'S STORY ABOUT DOCTOR LIGHT.

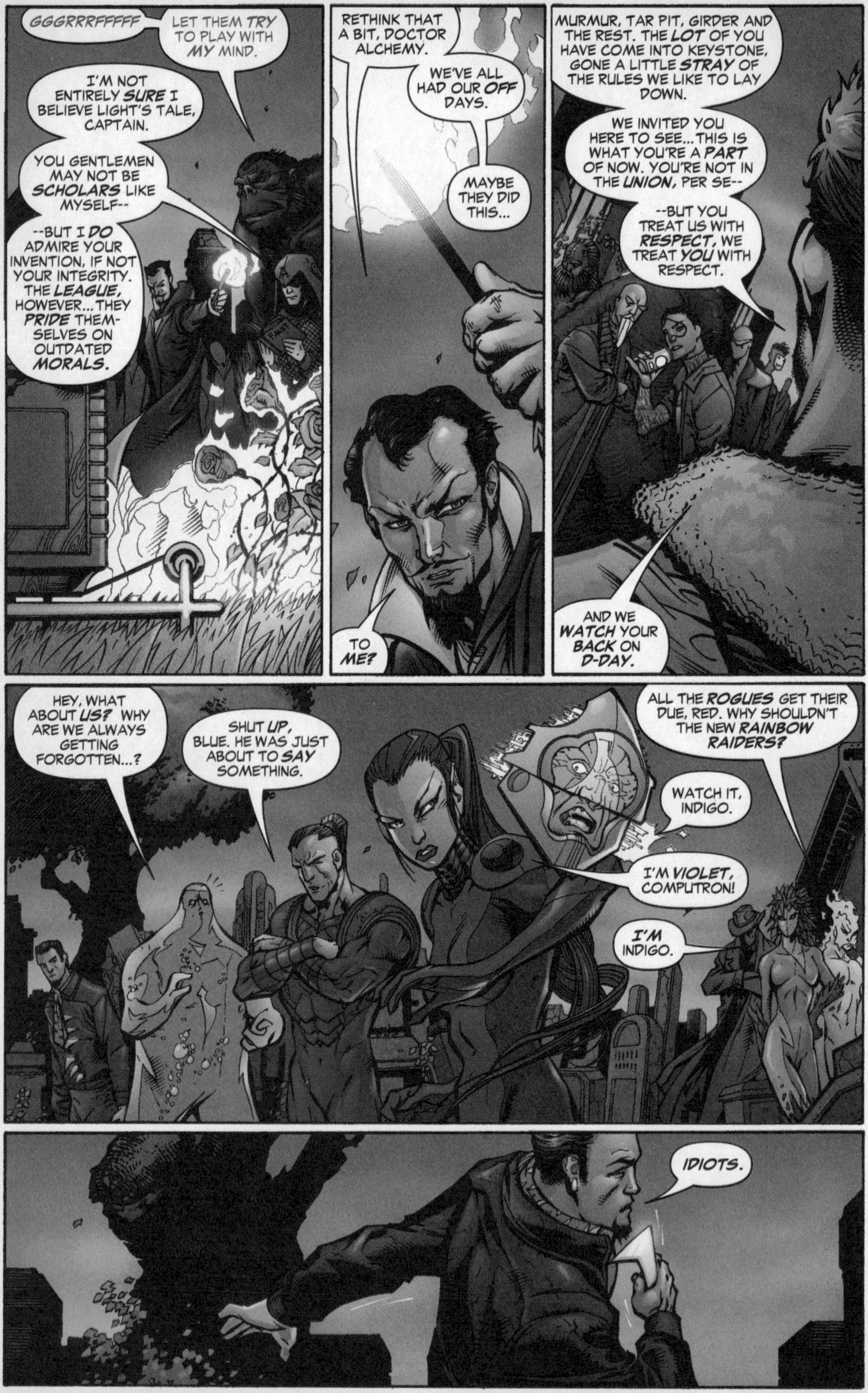
GGGRRRFFFFF
LET THEM TRY TO PLAY WITH MY MIND.
I'M NOT ENTIRELY SURE I BELIEVE LIGHT'S TALE, CAPTAIN.
YOU GENTLEMEN MAY NOT BE SCHOLARS LIKE MYSELF--
--BUT I DO ADMIRE YOUR INVENTION, IF NOT YOUR INTEGRITY. THE LEAGUE, HOWEVER... THEY PRIDE THEMSELVES ON OUTDATED MORALS.
RETHINK THAT A BIT, DOCTOR ALCHEMY.
WE'VE ALL HAD OUR OFF DAYS.
MAYBE THEY DID THIS...
TO ME?
MURMUR, TAR PIT, GIRDER AND THE REST. THE LOT OF YOU HAVE COME INTO KEYSTONE, GONE A LITTLE STRAY OF THE RULES WE LIKE TO LAY DOWN.
WE INVITED YOU HERE TO SEE... THIS IS WHAT YOU'RE A PART OF NOW. YOU'RE NOT IN THE UNION, PER SE--
--BUT YOU TREAT US WITH RESPECT, WE TREAT YOU WITH RESPECT.
AND WE WATCH YOUR BACK ON D-DAY.
HEY, WHAT ABOUT US? WHY ARE WE ALWAYS GETTING FORGOTTEN...?
SHUT UP, BLUE. HE WAS JUST ABOUT TO SAY SOMETHING.
ALL THE ROGUES GET THEIR DUE, RED. WHY SHOULDN'T THE NEW RAINBOW RAIDERS?
WATCH IT, INDIGO.
I'M VIOLET, COMPUTRON!
I'M INDIGO.
IDIOTS.

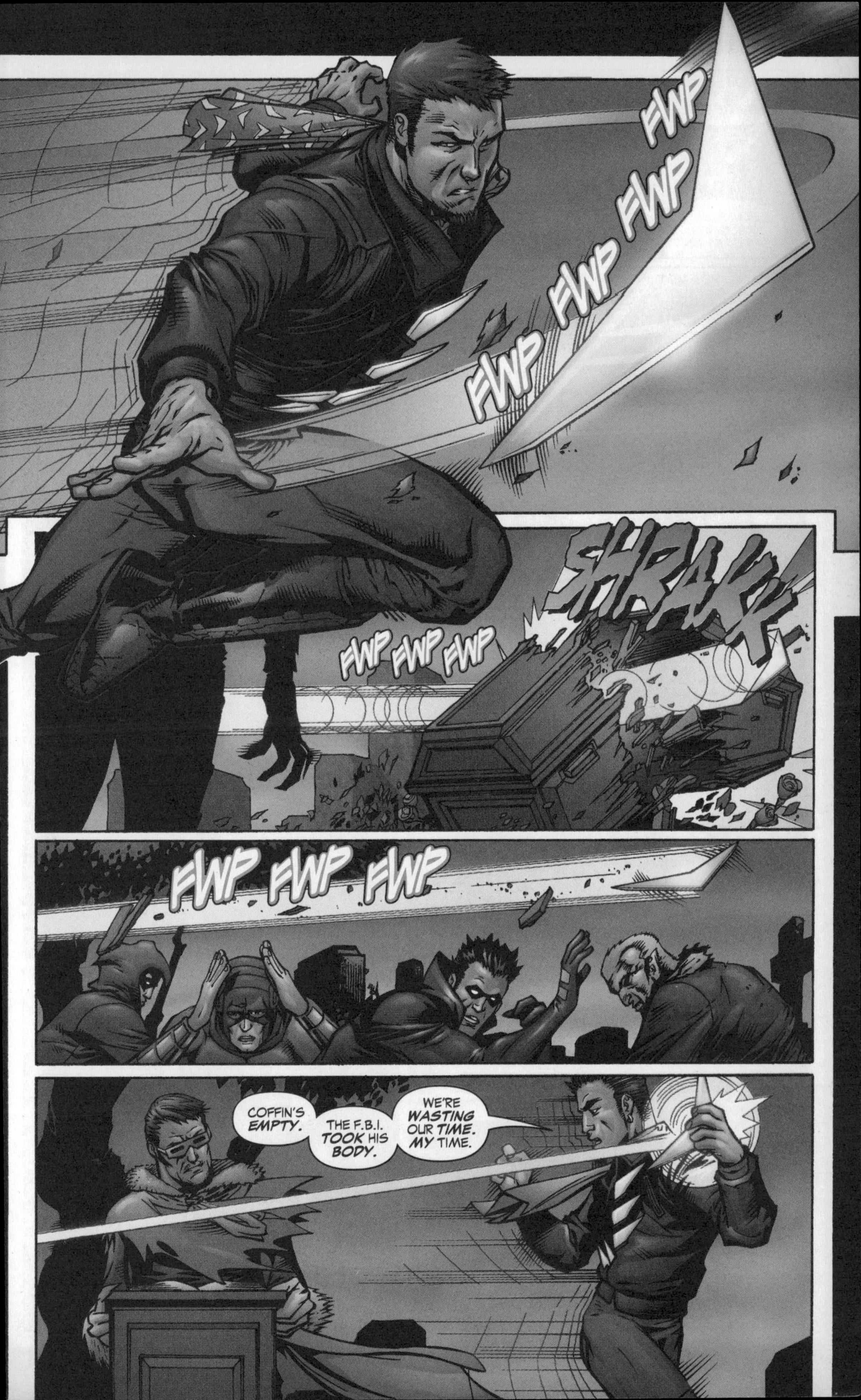
FWP
FWP FWP FWP FWP
SHRAKK
FWP FWP FWP
FWP FWP FWP
COFFIN'S EMPTY.
THE F.B.I. TOOK HIS BODY.
WE'RE WASTING OUR TIME. MY TIME.

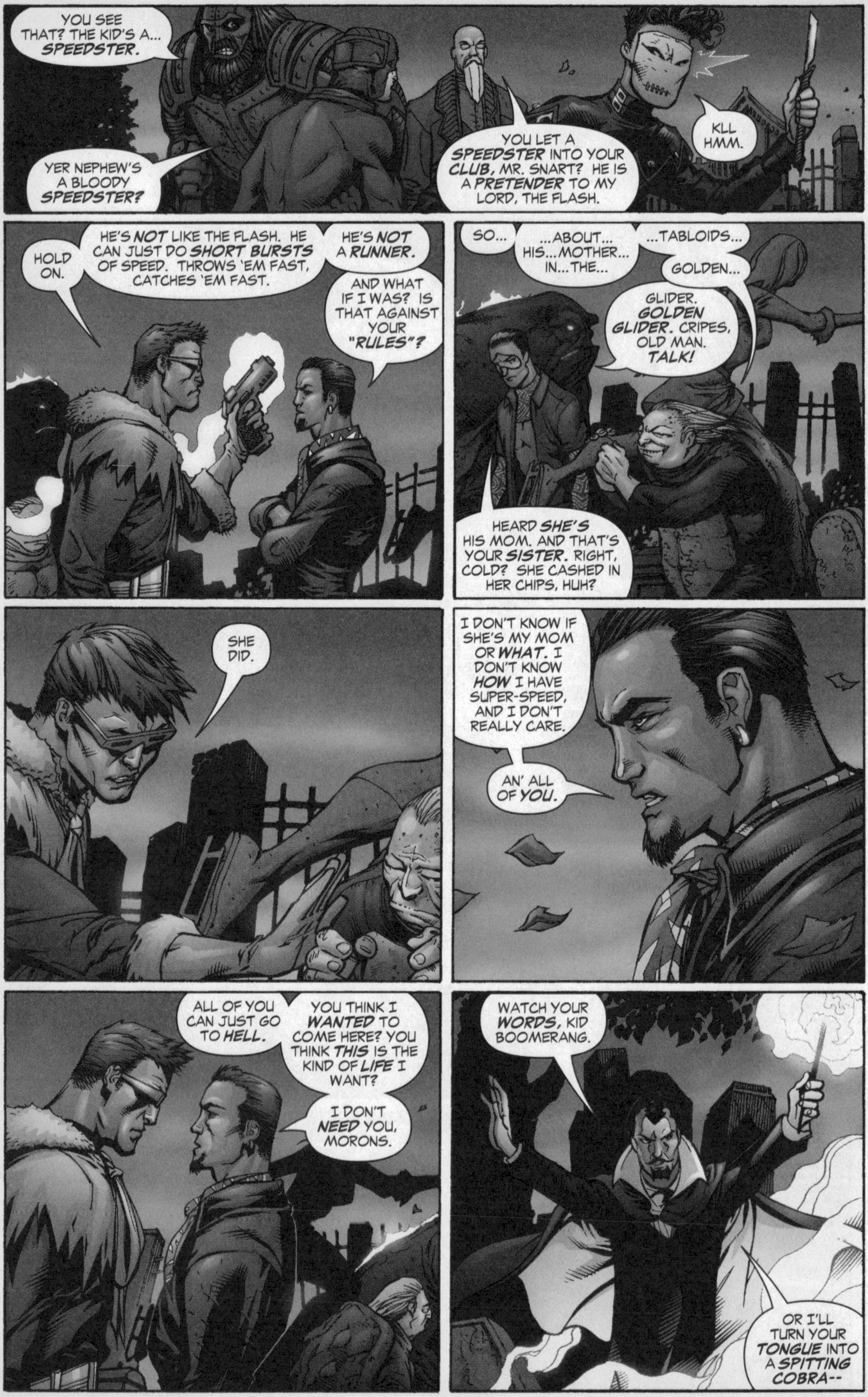
YOU SEE THAT? THE KID'S A... SPEEDSTER.
YER NEPHEW'S A BLOODY SPEEDSTER?
YOU LET A SPEEDSTER INTO YOUR CLUB, MR. SNART? HE IS A PRETENDER TO MY LORD, THE FLASH.
KLL HMM.
HOLD ON.
HE'S NOT LIKE THE FLASH. HE CAN JUST DO SHORT BURSTS OF SPEED. THROWS 'EM FAST, CATCHES 'EM FAST.
HE'S NOT A RUNNER.
AND WHAT IF I WAS? IS THAT AGAINST YOUR "RULES"?
SO...
...ABOUT... HIS...MOTHER... IN...THE...
...TABLOIDS...
GOLDEN...
GLIDER. GOLDEN GLIDER. CRIPES, OLD MAN. TALK!
HEARD SHE'S HIS MOM. AND THAT'S YOUR SISTER. RIGHT, COLD? SHE CASHED IN HER CHIPS, HUH?
SHE DID.
I DON'T KNOW IF SHE'S MY MOM OR WHAT. I DON'T KNOW HOW I HAVE SUPER-SPEED, AND I DON'T REALLY CARE.
AN' ALL OF YOU.
ALL OF YOU CAN JUST GO TO HELL.
YOU THINK I WANTED TO COME HERE? YOU THINK THIS IS THE KIND OF LIFE I WANT?
I DON'T NEED YOU, MORONS.
WATCH YOUR WORDS, KID BOOMERANG.
OR I'LL TURN YOUR TONGUE INTO A SPITTING COBRA--

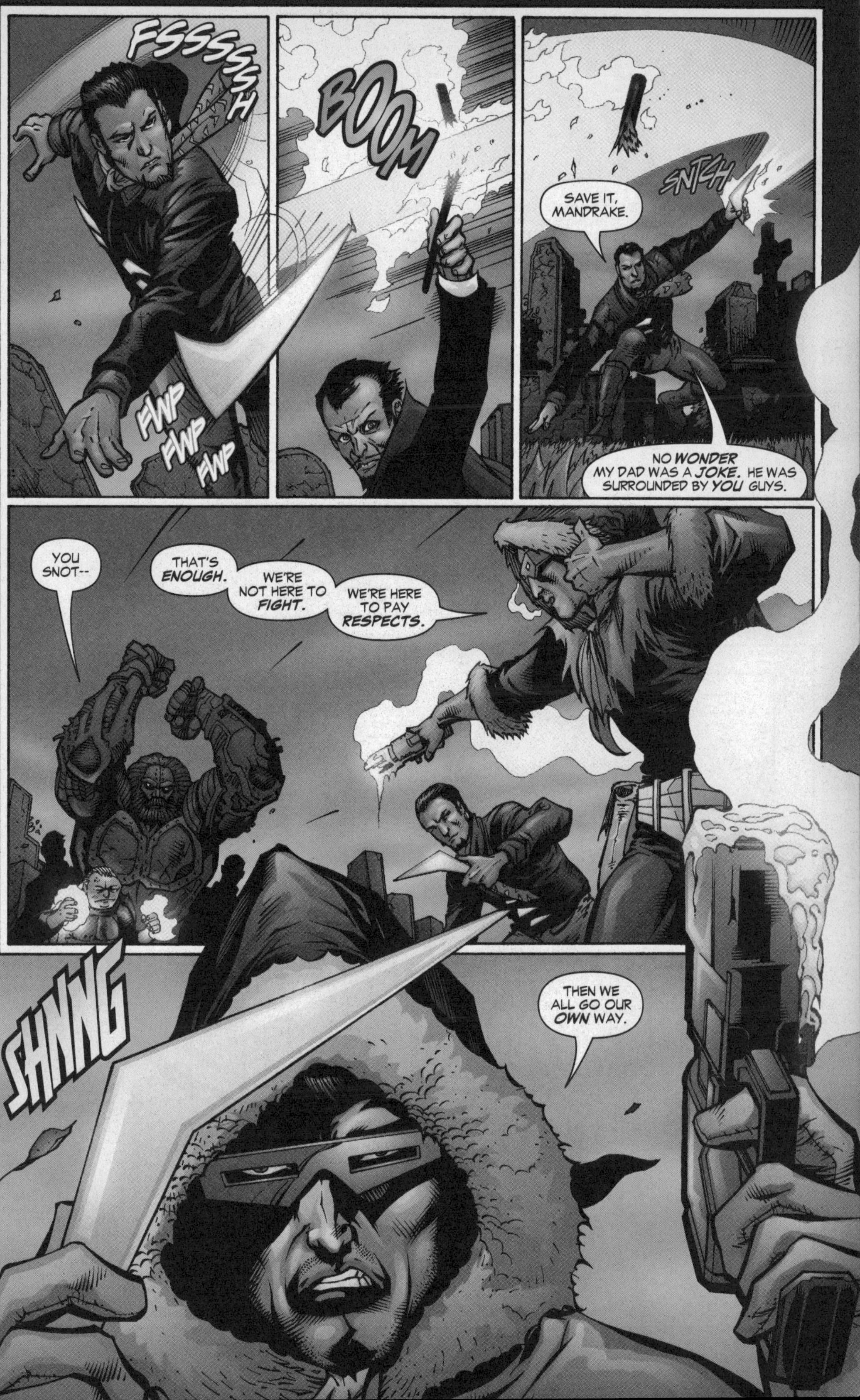
FSSSSSSH
FWP FWP FWP
BOOM
SNTCH
SAVE IT, MANDRAKE.
NO WONDER MY DAD WAS A JOKE. HE WAS SURROUNDED BY YOU GUYS.
YOU SNOT--
THAT'S ENOUGH.
WE'RE NOT HERE TO FIGHT.
WE'RE HERE TO PAY RESPECTS.
SHNNG
THEN WE ALL GO OUR OWN WAY.

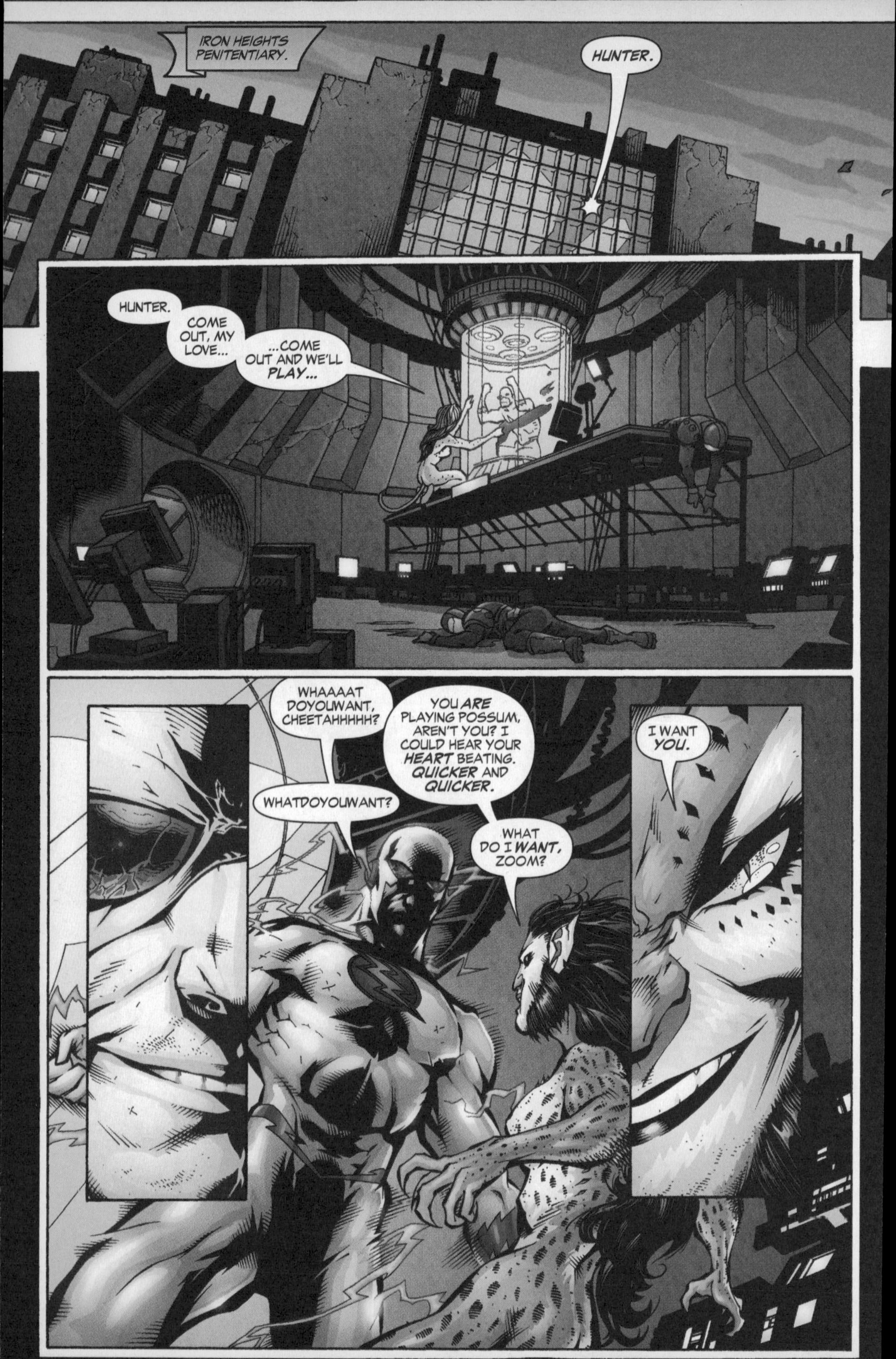
IRON HEIGHTS PENITENTIARY.
HUNTER.
HUNTER.
COME OUT, MY LOVE...
...COME OUT AND WE'LL PLAY...
WHAAAAT DOYOUWANT, CHEETAHHHHHH?
WHATDOYOUWANT?
YOU ARE PLAYING POSSUM, AREN'T YOU? I COULD HEAR YOUR HEART BEATING. QUICKER AND QUICKER.
WHAT DO I WANT, ZOOM?
I WANT YOU.

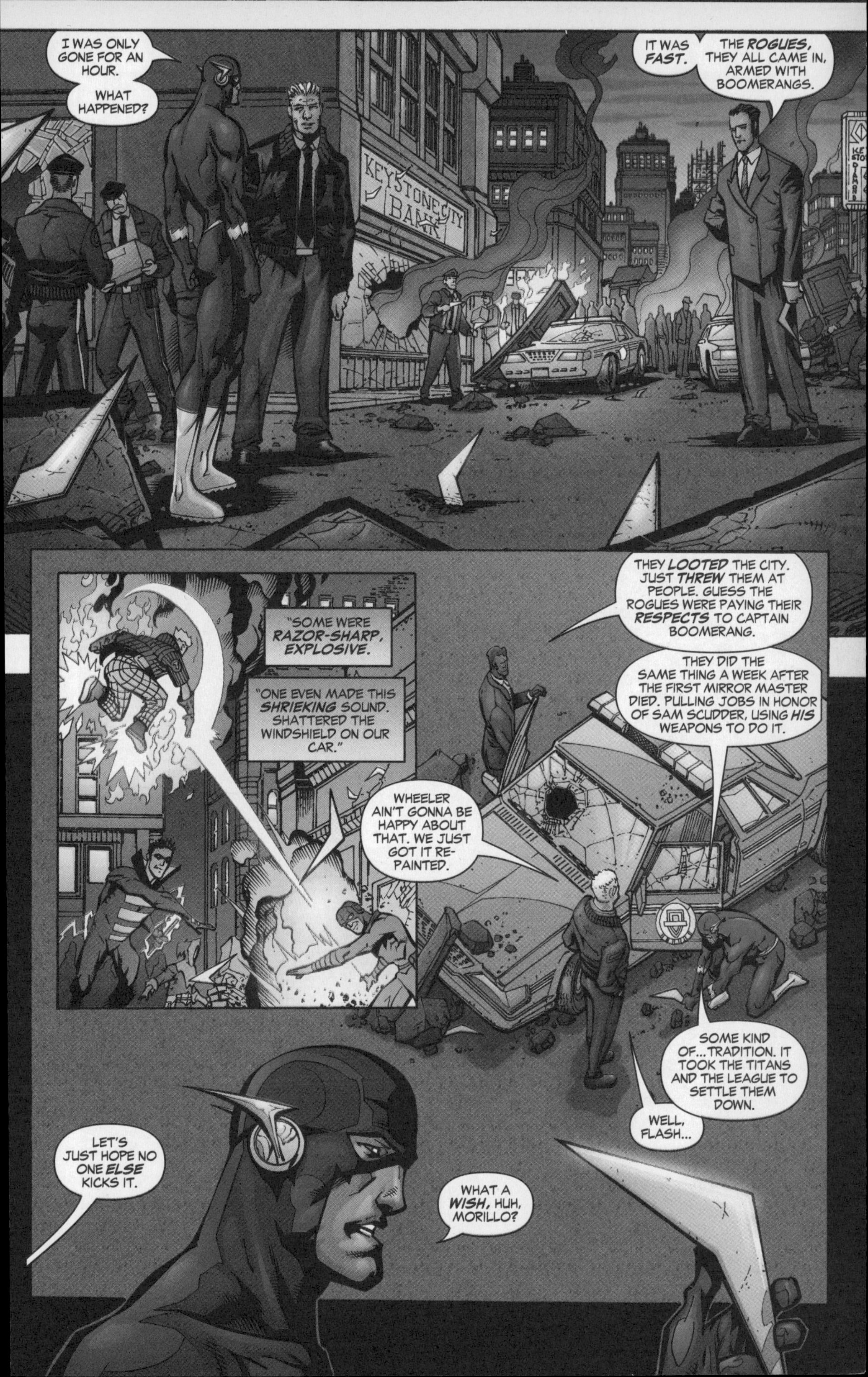

I WAS ONLY GONE FOR AN HOUR.
WHAT HAPPENED?
KEYSTONE CITY BANK
IT WAS FAST.
THE ROGUES, THEY ALL CAME IN, ARMED WITH BOOMERANGS.
THEY LOOTED THE CITY. JUST THREW THEM AT PEOPLE. GUESS THE ROGUES WERE PAYING THEIR RESPECTS TO CAPTAIN BOOMERANG.
"SOME WERE RAZOR-SHARP, EXPLOSIVE.
"ONE EVEN MADE THIS SHRIEKING SOUND. SHATTERED THE WINDSHIELD ON OUR CAR."
WHEELER AIN'T GONNA BE HAPPY ABOUT THAT. WE JUST GOT IT RE-PAINTED.
THEY DID THE SAME THING A WEEK AFTER THE FIRST MIRROR MASTER DIED. PULLING JOBS IN HONOR OF SAM SCUDDER, USING HIS WEAPONS TO DO IT.
SOME KIND OF... TRADITION. IT TOOK THE TITANS AND THE LEAGUE TO SETTLE THEM DOWN.
WELL, FLASH...
LET'S JUST HOPE NO ONE ELSE KICKS IT.
WHAT A WISH, HUH, MORILLO?

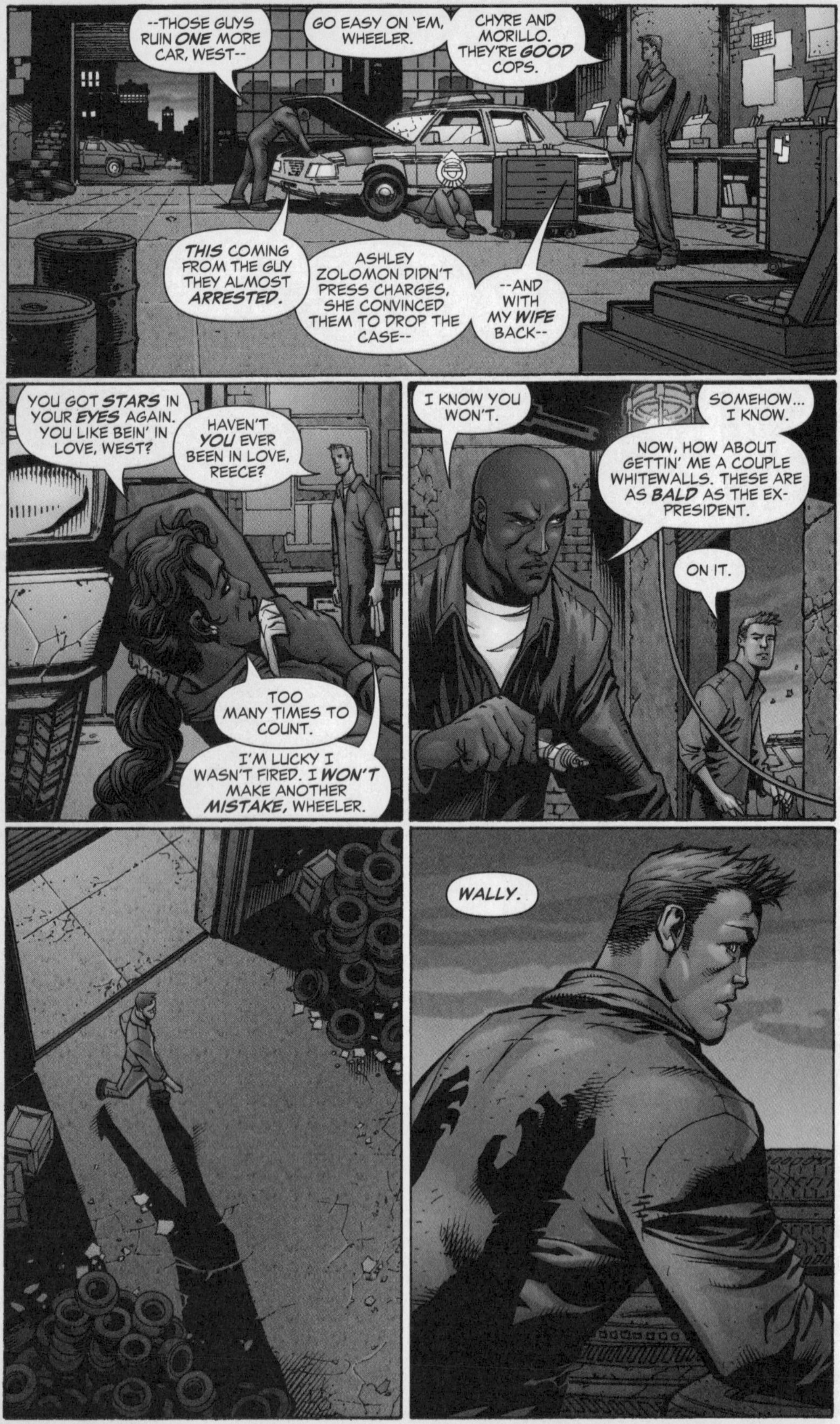
--THOSE GUYS RUIN ONE MORE CAR, WEST--
GO EASY ON 'EM, WHEELER.
CHYRE AND MORILLO. THEY'RE GOOD COPS.
THIS COMING FROM THE GUY THEY ALMOST ARRESTED.
ASHLEY ZOLOMON DIDN'T PRESS CHARGES, SHE CONVINCED THEM TO DROP THE CASE--
--AND WITH MY WIFE BACK--
YOU GOT STARS IN YOUR EYES AGAIN. YOU LIKE BEIN' IN LOVE, WEST?
HAVEN'T YOU EVER BEEN IN LOVE, REECE?
TOO MANY TIMES TO COUNT.
I'M LUCKY I WASN'T FIRED. I WON'T MAKE ANOTHER MISTAKE, WHEELER.
I KNOW YOU WON'T.
SOMEHOW... I KNOW.
NOW, HOW ABOUT GETTIN' ME A COUPLE WHITEWALLS. THESE ARE AS BALD AS THE EX-PRESIDENT.
ON IT.
WALLY.

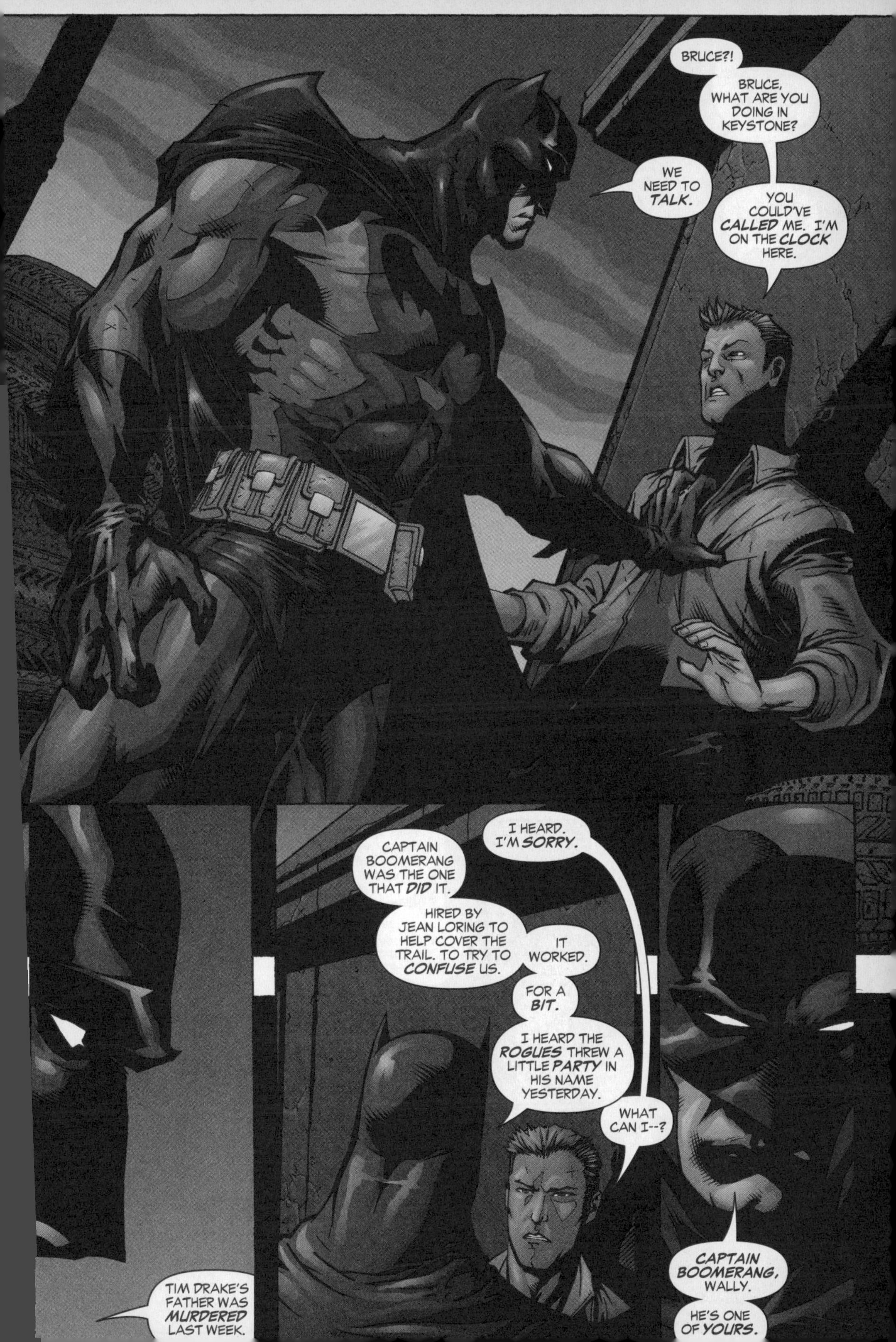
BRUCE?!
BRUCE, WHAT ARE YOU DOING IN KEYSTONE?
WE NEED TO TALK.
YOU COULD'VE CALLED ME. I'M ON THE CLOCK HERE.
TIM DRAKE'S FATHER WAS MURDERED LAST WEEK.
I HEARD. I'M SORRY.
CAPTAIN BOOMERANG WAS THE ONE THAT DID IT.
HIRED BY JEAN LORING TO HELP COVER THE TRAIL. TO TRY TO CONFUSE US.
IT WORKED.
FOR A BIT.
I HEARD THE ROGUES THREW A LITTLE PARTY IN HIS NAME YESTERDAY.
WHAT CAN I--?
CAPTAIN BOOMERANG, WALLY.
HE'S ONE OF YOURS.

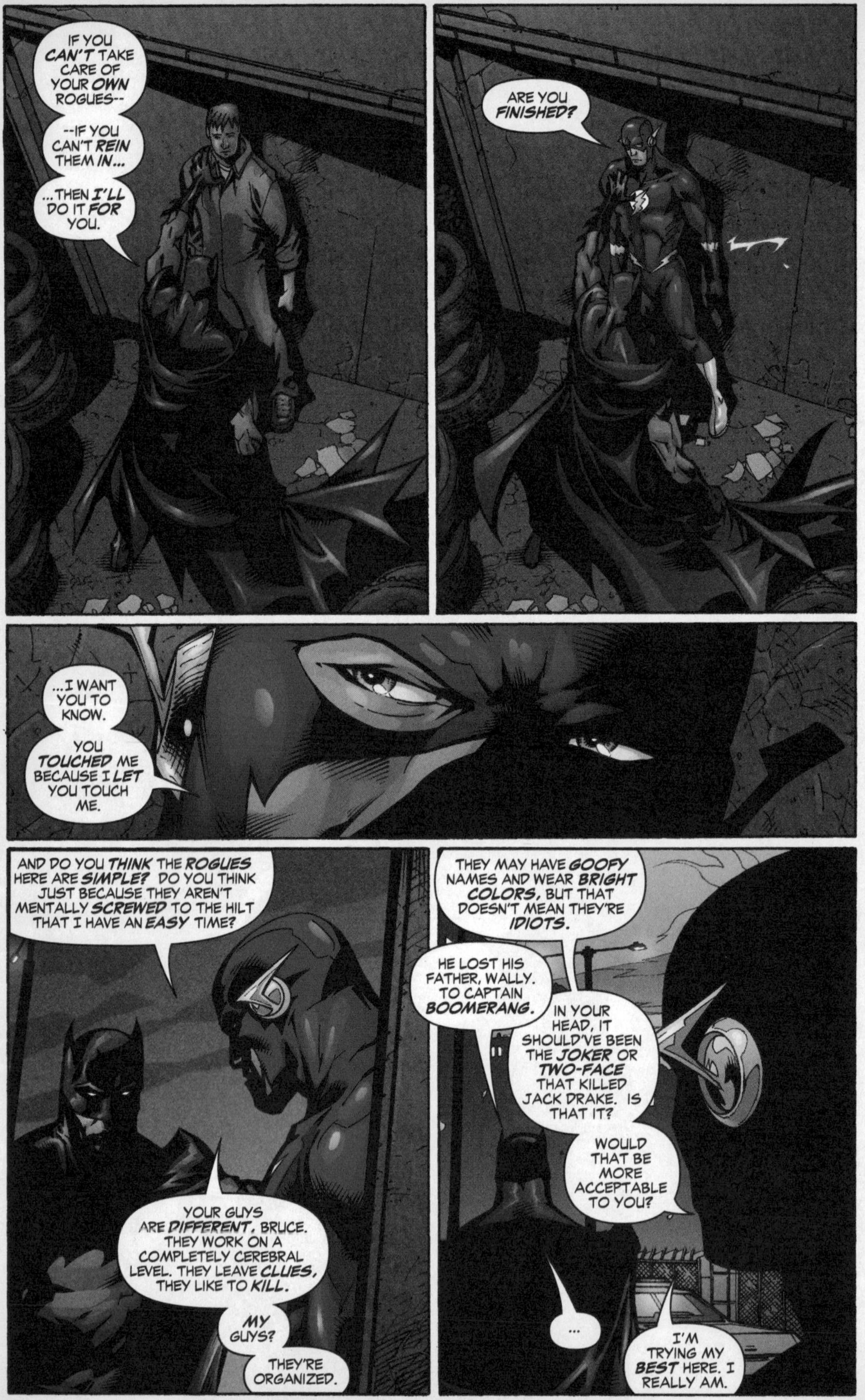
IF YOU CAN'T TAKE CARE OF YOUR OWN ROGUES--
--IF YOU CAN'T REIN THEM IN...
...THEN I'LL DO IT FOR YOU.
ARE YOU FINISHED?
...I WANT YOU TO KNOW.
YOU TOUCHED ME BECAUSE I LET YOU TOUCH ME.
AND DO YOU THINK THE ROGUES HERE ARE SIMPLE? DO YOU THINK JUST BECAUSE THEY AREN'T MENTALLY SCREWED TO THE HILT THAT I HAVE AN EASY TIME?
YOUR GUYS ARE DIFFERENT, BRUCE. THEY WORK ON A COMPLETELY CEREBRAL LEVEL. THEY LEAVE CLUES, THEY LIKE TO KILL.
MY GUYS?
THEY'RE ORGANIZED.
THEY MAY HAVE GOOFY NAMES AND WEAR BRIGHT COLORS, BUT THAT DOESN'T MEAN THEY'RE IDIOTS.
HE LOST HIS FATHER, WALLY. TO CAPTAIN BOOMERANG.
IN YOUR HEAD, IT SHOULD'VE BEEN THE JOKER OR TWO-FACE THAT KILLED JACK DRAKE. IS THAT IT?
WOULD THAT BE MORE ACCEPTABLE TO YOU?
...
I'M TRYING MY BEST HERE. I REALLY AM.

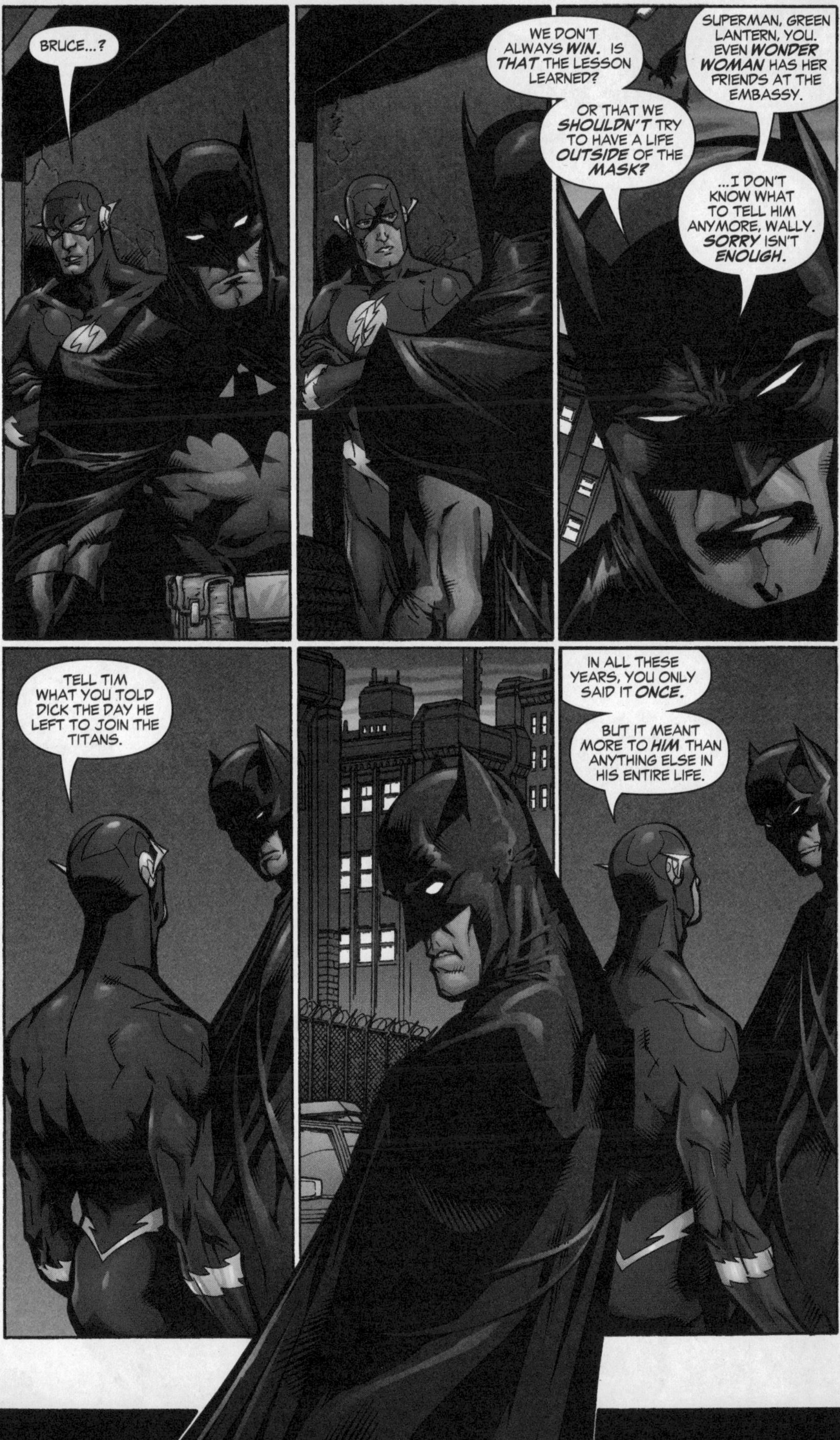
BRUCE...?
WE DON'T ALWAYS WIN. IS THAT THE LESSON LEARNED?
OR THAT WE SHOULDN'T TRY TO HAVE A LIFE OUTSIDE OF THE MASK?
SUPERMAN, GREEN LANTERN, YOU. EVEN WONDER WOMAN HAS HER FRIENDS AT THE EMBASSY.
...I DON'T KNOW WHAT TO TELL HIM ANYMORE, WALLY. SORRY ISN'T ENOUGH.
TELL TIM WHAT YOU TOLD DICK THE DAY HE LEFT TO JOIN THE TITANS.
IN ALL THESE YEARS, YOU ONLY SAID IT ONCE.
BUT IT MEANT MORE TO HIM THAN ANYTHING ELSE IN HIS ENTIRE LIFE.

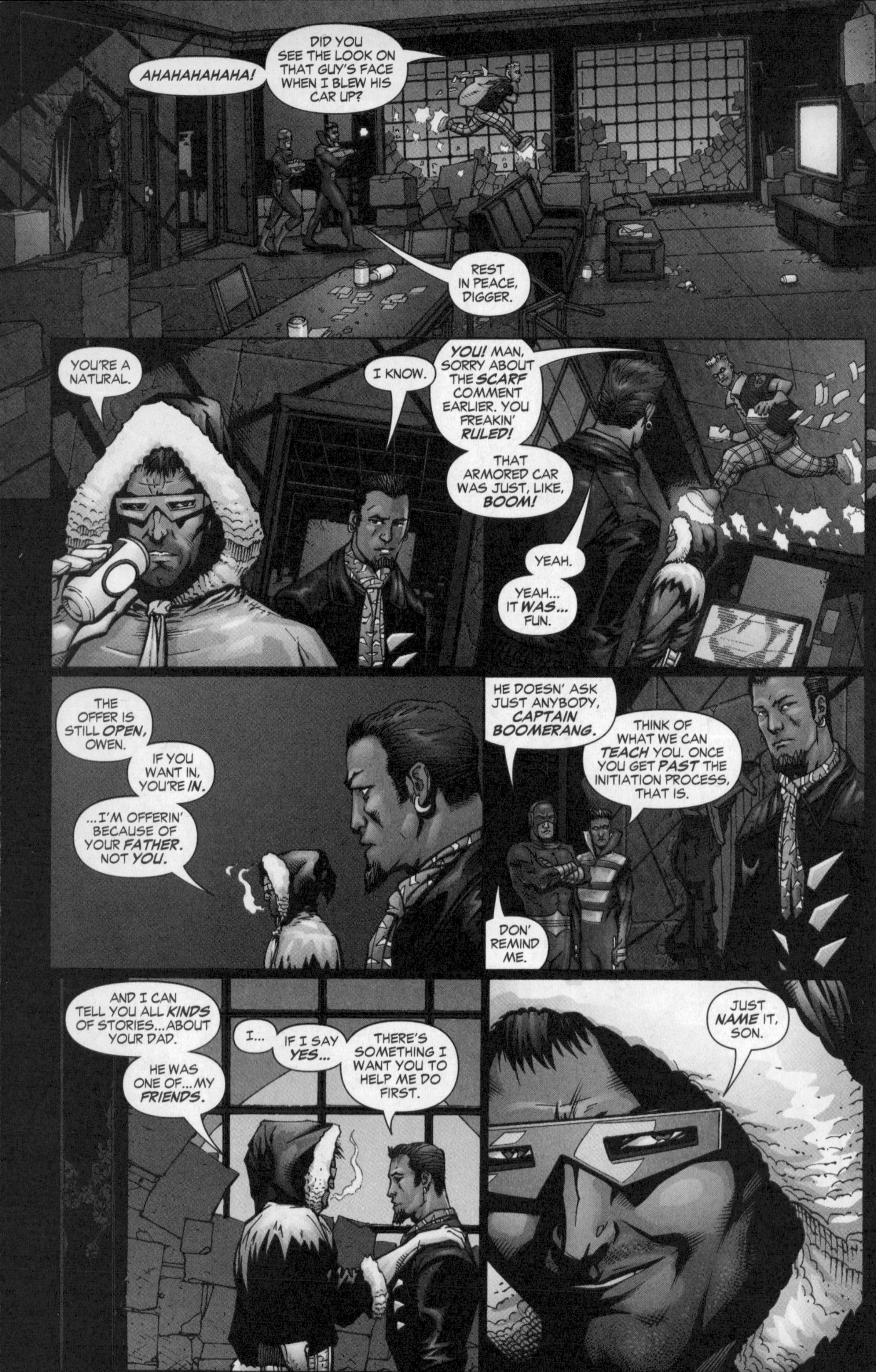
AHAHAHAHAHA!
DID YOU SEE THE LOOK ON THAT GUY'S FACE WHEN I BLEW HIS CAR UP?
REST IN PEACE, DIGGER.
YOU'RE A NATURAL.
I KNOW.
YOU! MAN, SORRY ABOUT THE SCARF COMMENT EARLIER. YOU FREAKIN' RULED!
THAT ARMORED CAR WAS JUST, LIKE, BOOM!
YEAH.
YEAH... IT WAS... FUN.
THE OFFER IS STILL OPEN, OWEN.
IF YOU WANT IN, YOU'RE IN.
...I'M OFFERIN' BECAUSE OF YOUR FATHER. NOT YOU.
HE DOESN' ASK JUST ANYBODY, CAPTAIN BOOMERANG.
THINK OF WHAT WE CAN TEACH YOU. ONCE YOU GET PAST THE INITIATION PROCESS, THAT IS.
DON' REMIND ME.
AND I CAN TELL YOU ALL KINDS OF STORIES...ABOUT YOUR DAD.
HE WAS ONE OF...MY FRIENDS.
I...
IF I SAY YES...
THERE'S SOMETHING I WANT YOU TO HELP ME DO FIRST.
JUST NAME IT, SON.

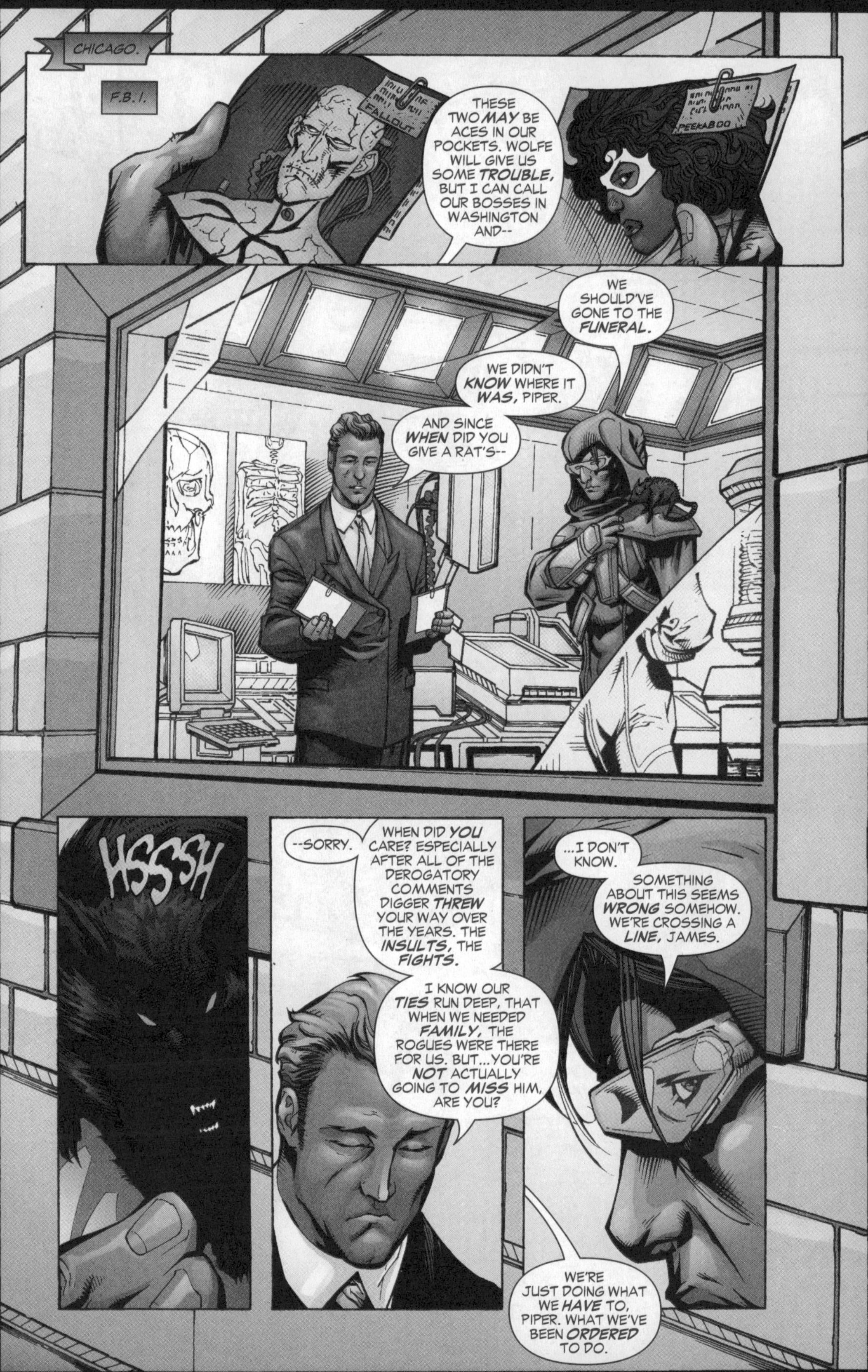

CHICAGO.
F.B.I.
FALLOUT
PEEKABOO
THESE TWO MAY BE ACES IN OUR POCKETS. WOLFE WILL GIVE US SOME TROUBLE, BUT I CAN CALL OUR BOSSES IN WASHINGTON AND--
WE SHOULD'VE GONE TO THE FUNERAL.
WE DIDN'T KNOW WHERE IT WAS, PIPER.
AND SINCE WHEN DID YOU GIVE A RAT'S--
HSSSH
--SORRY.
WHEN DID YOU CARE? ESPECIALLY AFTER ALL OF THE DEROGATORY COMMENTS DIGGER THREW YOUR WAY OVER THE YEARS. THE INSULTS, THE FIGHTS.
I KNOW OUR TIES RUN DEEP, THAT WHEN WE NEEDED FAMILY, THE ROGUES WERE THERE FOR US. BUT...YOU'RE NOT ACTUALLY GOING TO MISS HIM, ARE YOU?
...I DON'T KNOW.
SOMETHING ABOUT THIS SEEMS WRONG SOMEHOW. WE'RE CROSSING A LINE, JAMES.
WE'RE JUST DOING WHAT WE HAVE TO, PIPER. WHAT WE'VE BEEN ORDERED TO DO.

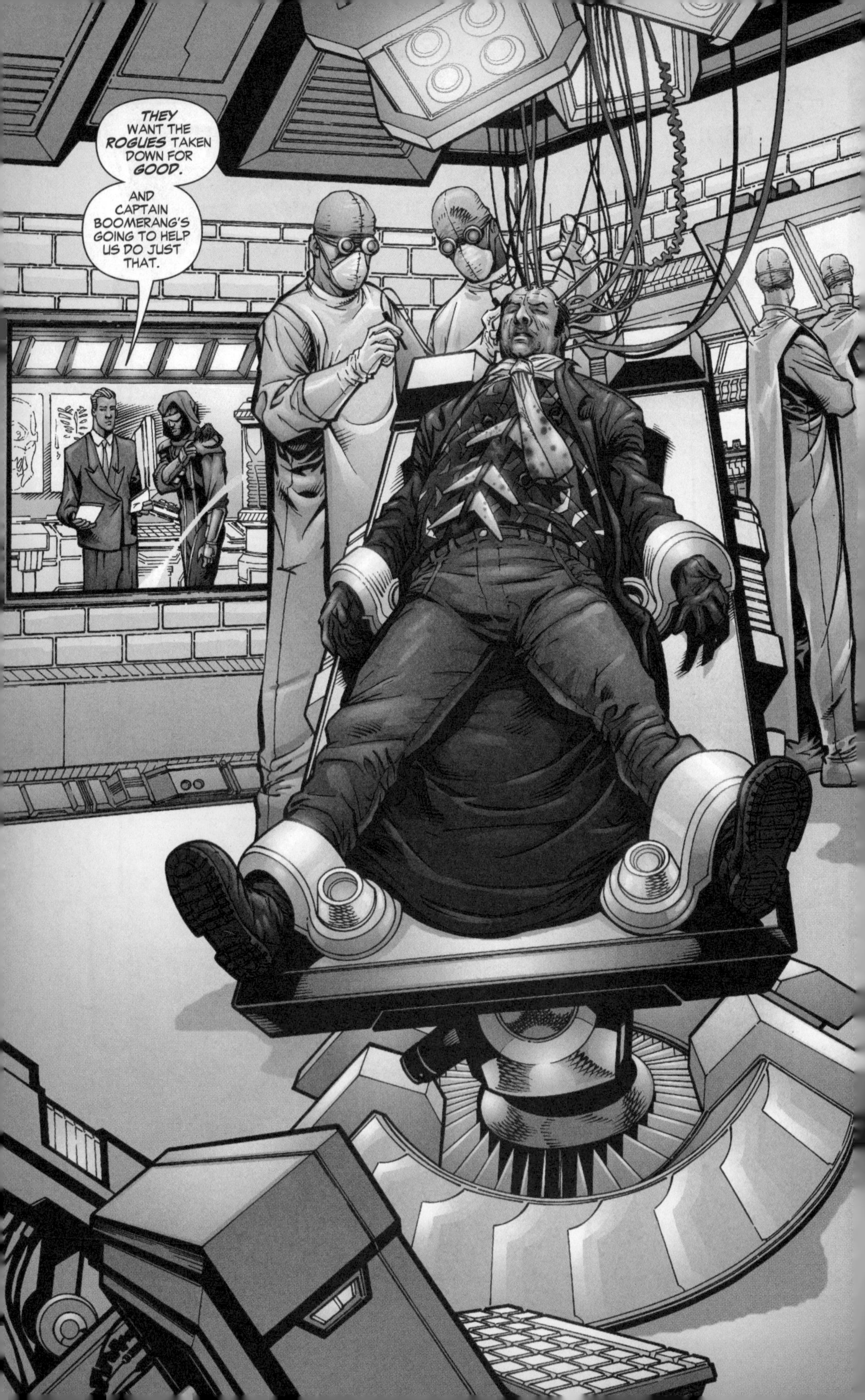

THEY WANT THE *ROGUES* TAKEN DOWN FOR *GOOD*.
AND CAPTAIN BOOMERANG'S GOING TO HELP US DO JUST THAT.

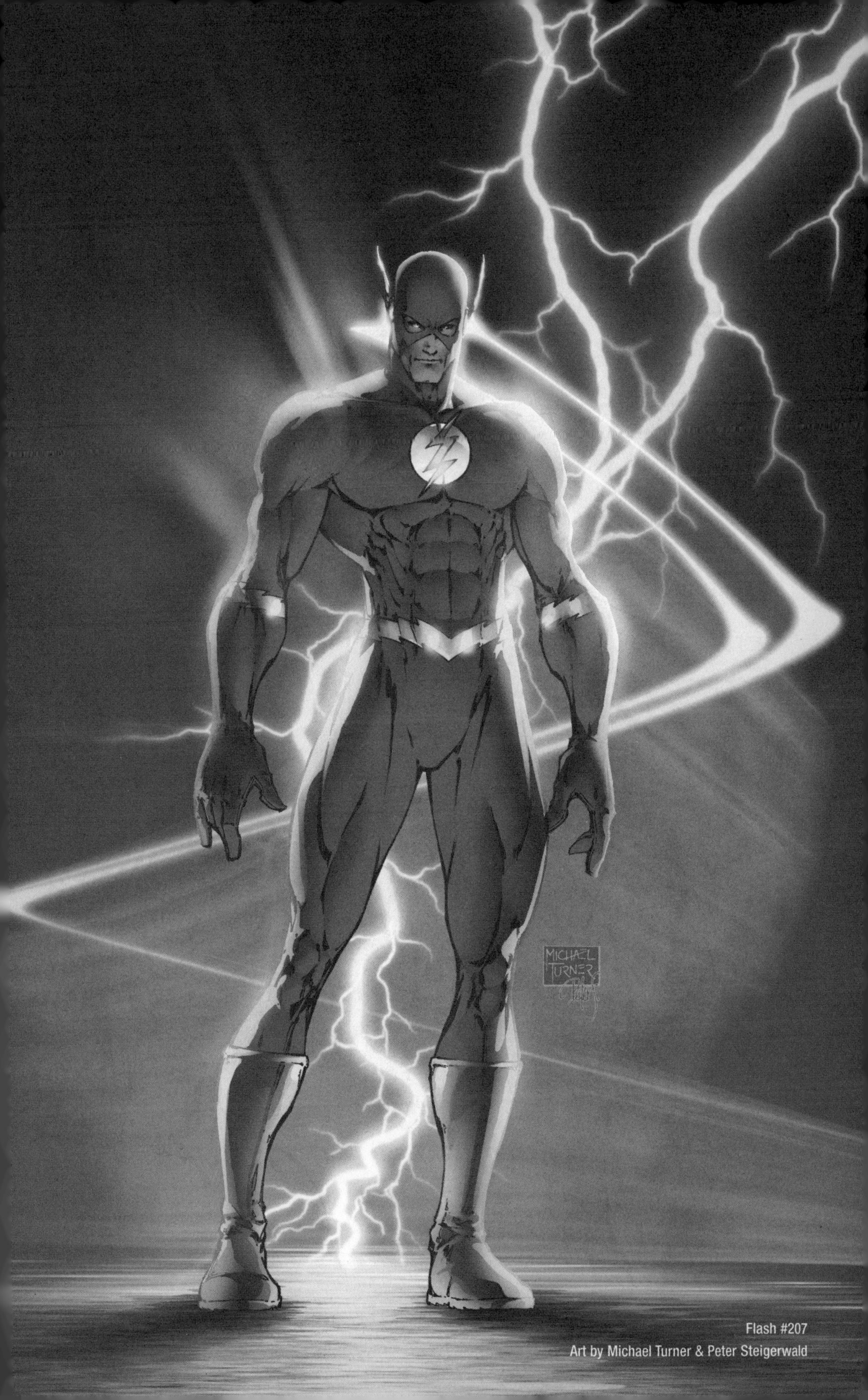
MICHAEL TURNER

Flash #207

Art by Michael Turner & Peter Steigerwald

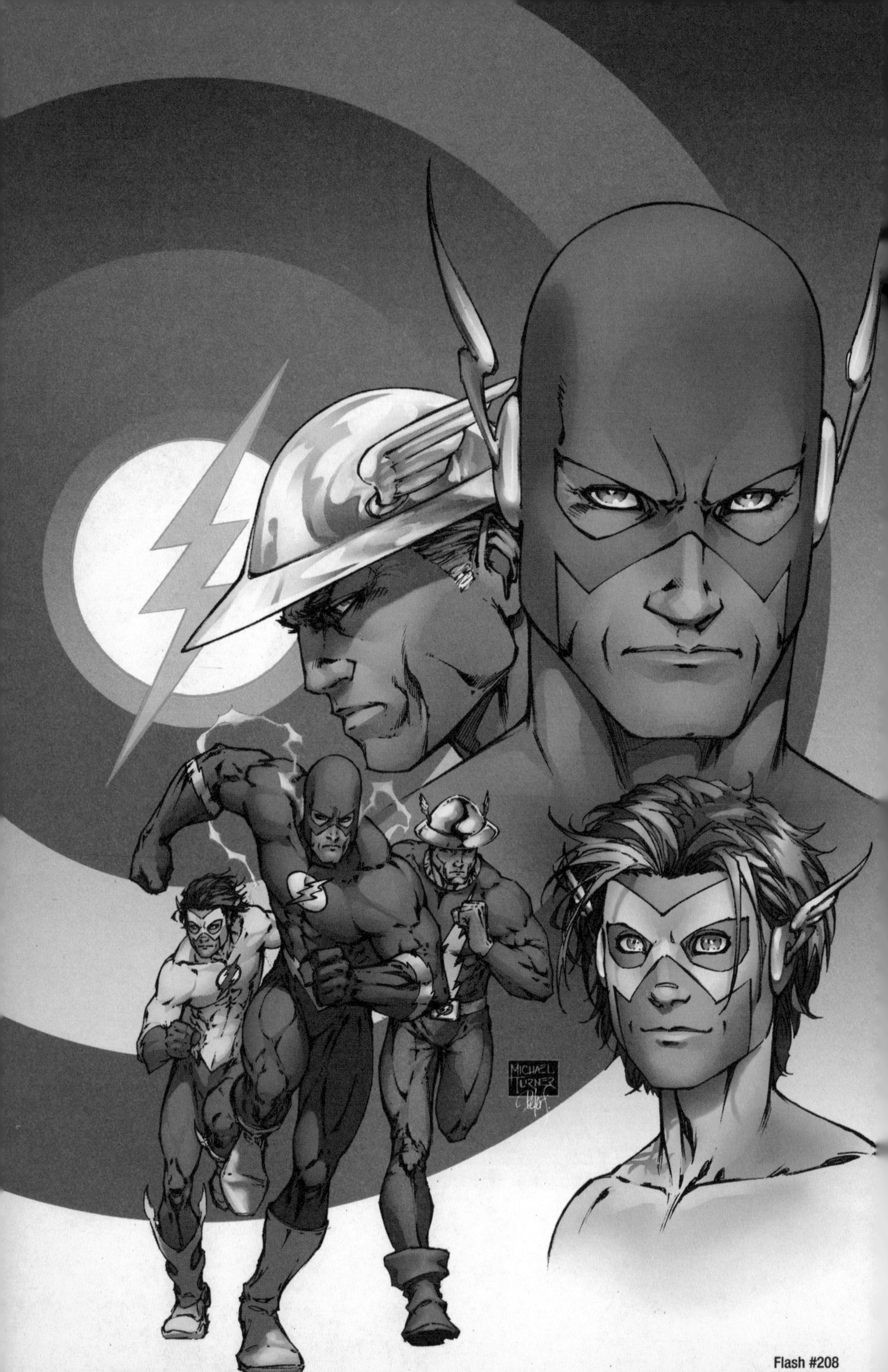
MICHAEL TURNER

Flash #208

Art by Michael Turner & Peter Steigerwald

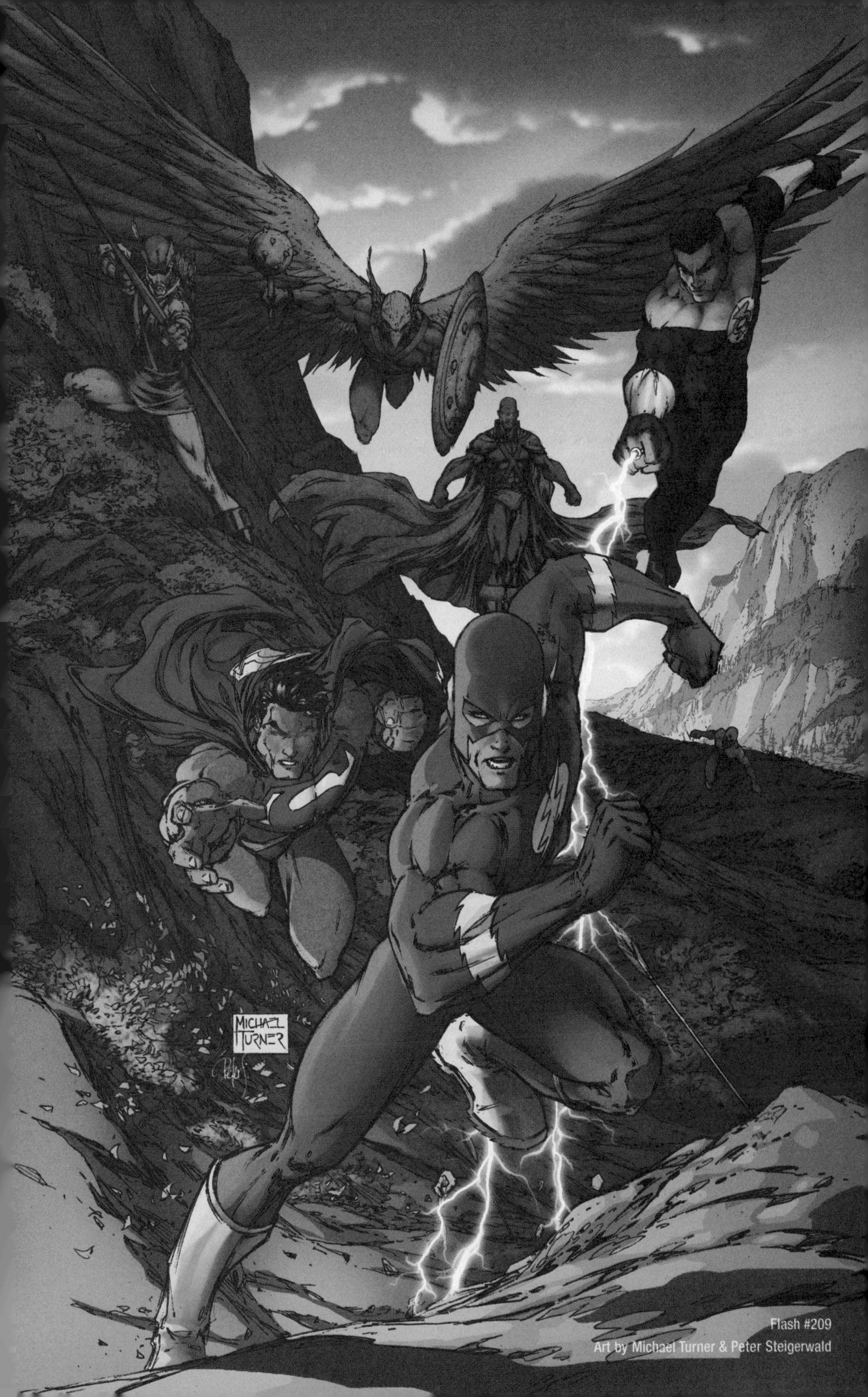
MICHAEL TURNER

Flash #209
Art by Michael Turner & Peter Steigerwald

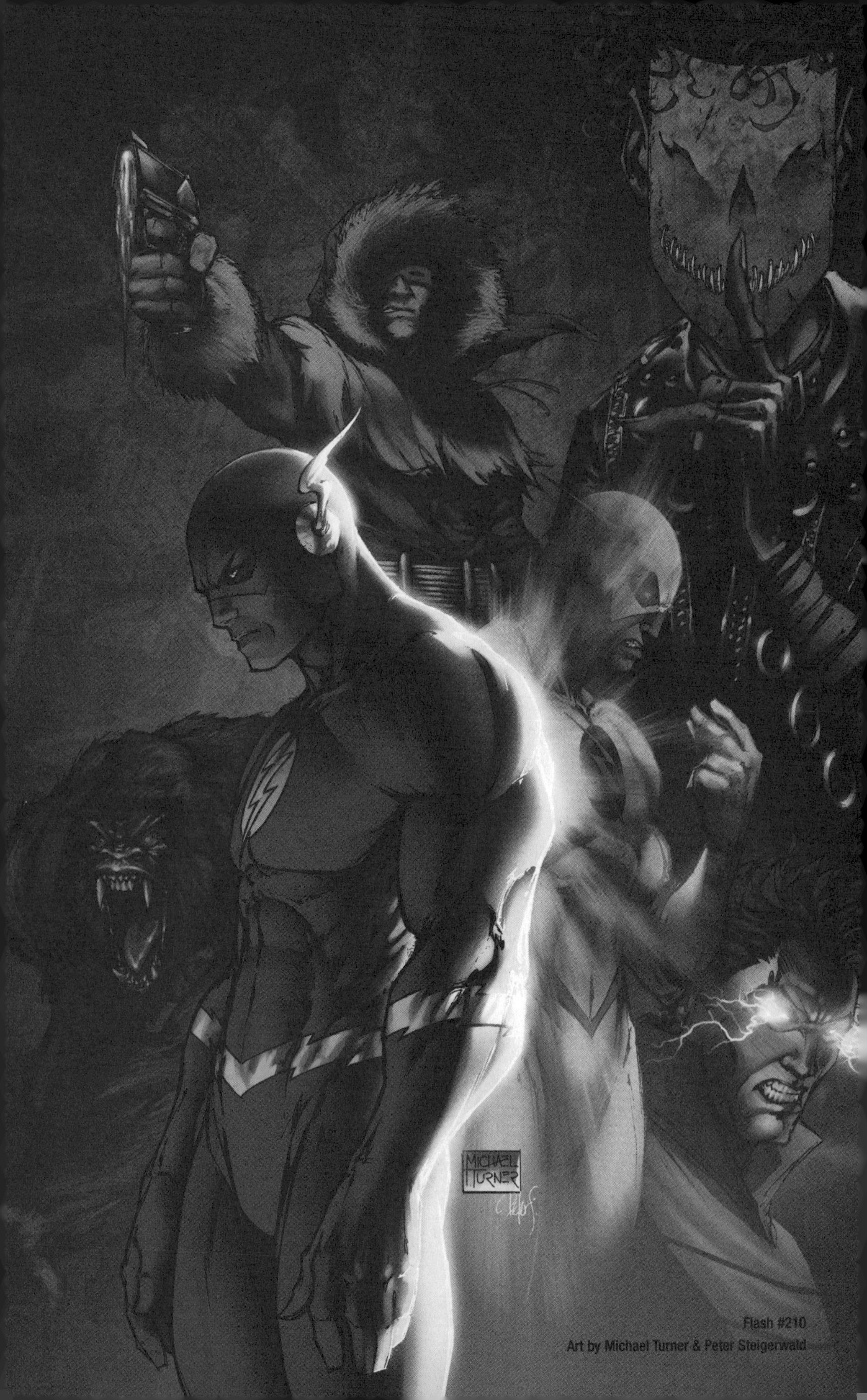
MICHAEL TURNER

Flash #210
Art by Michael Turner & Peter Steigerwald

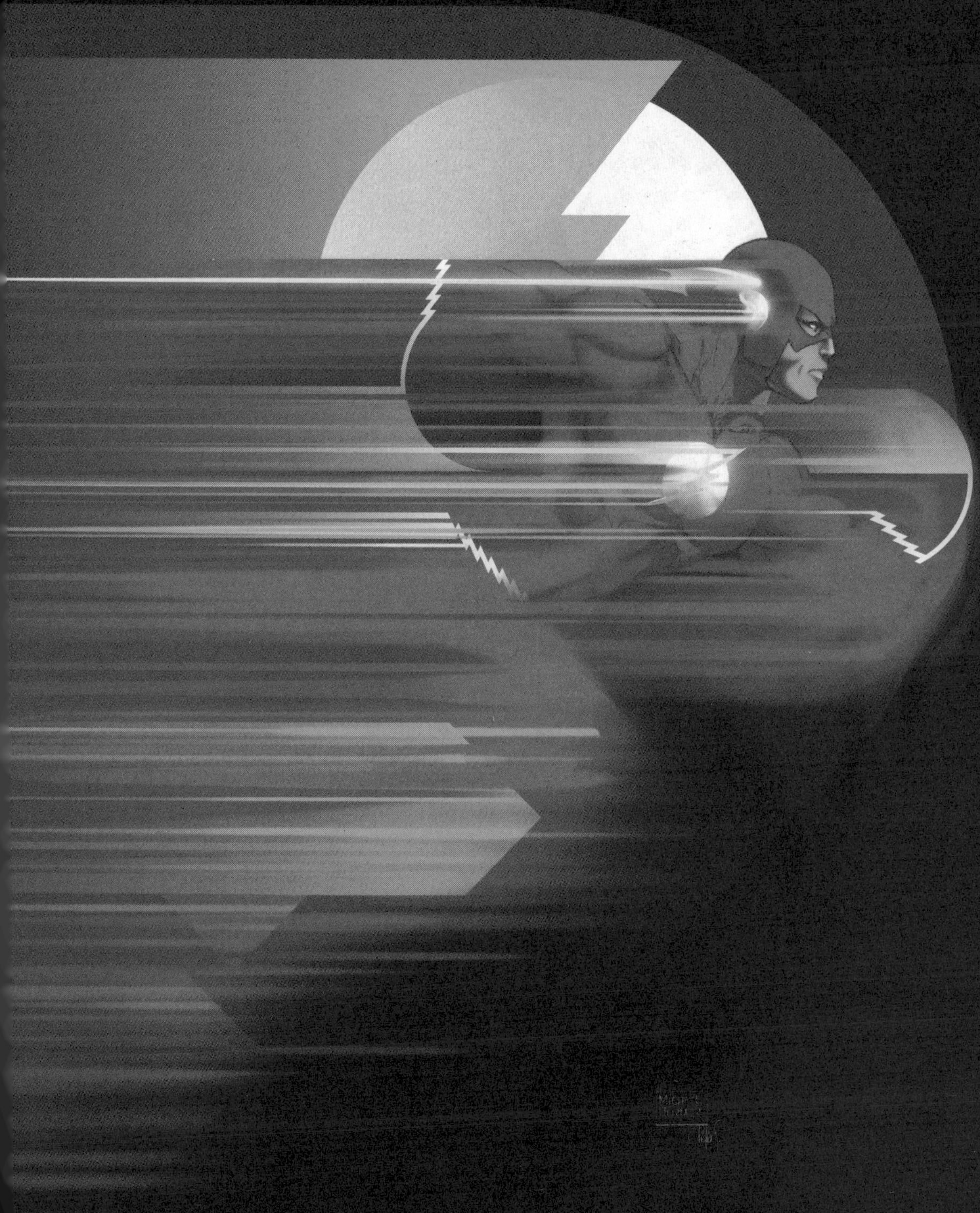

Flash #211

Art by Michael Turner & Peter Steigerwald

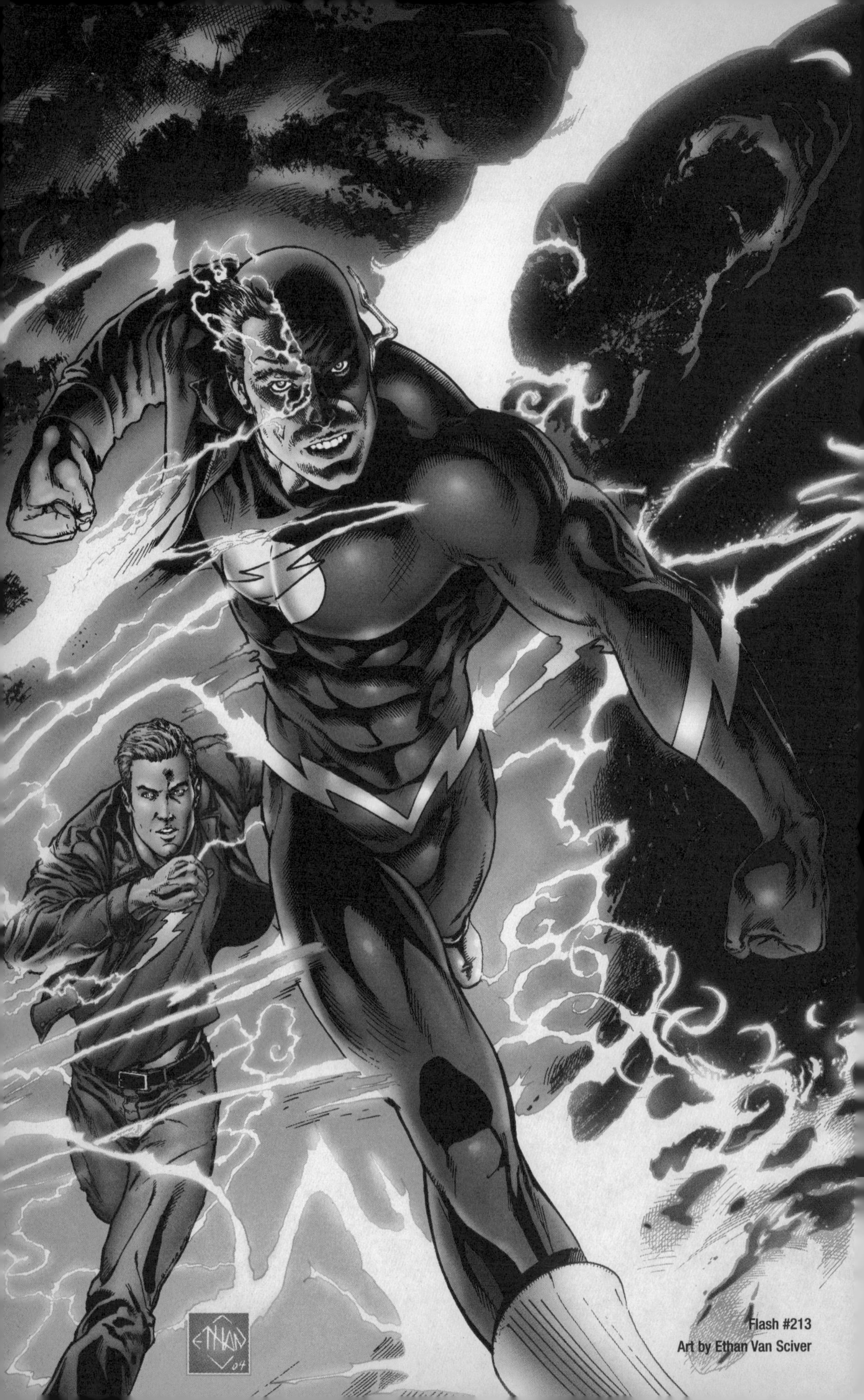

Flash #213
Art by Ethan Van Sciver

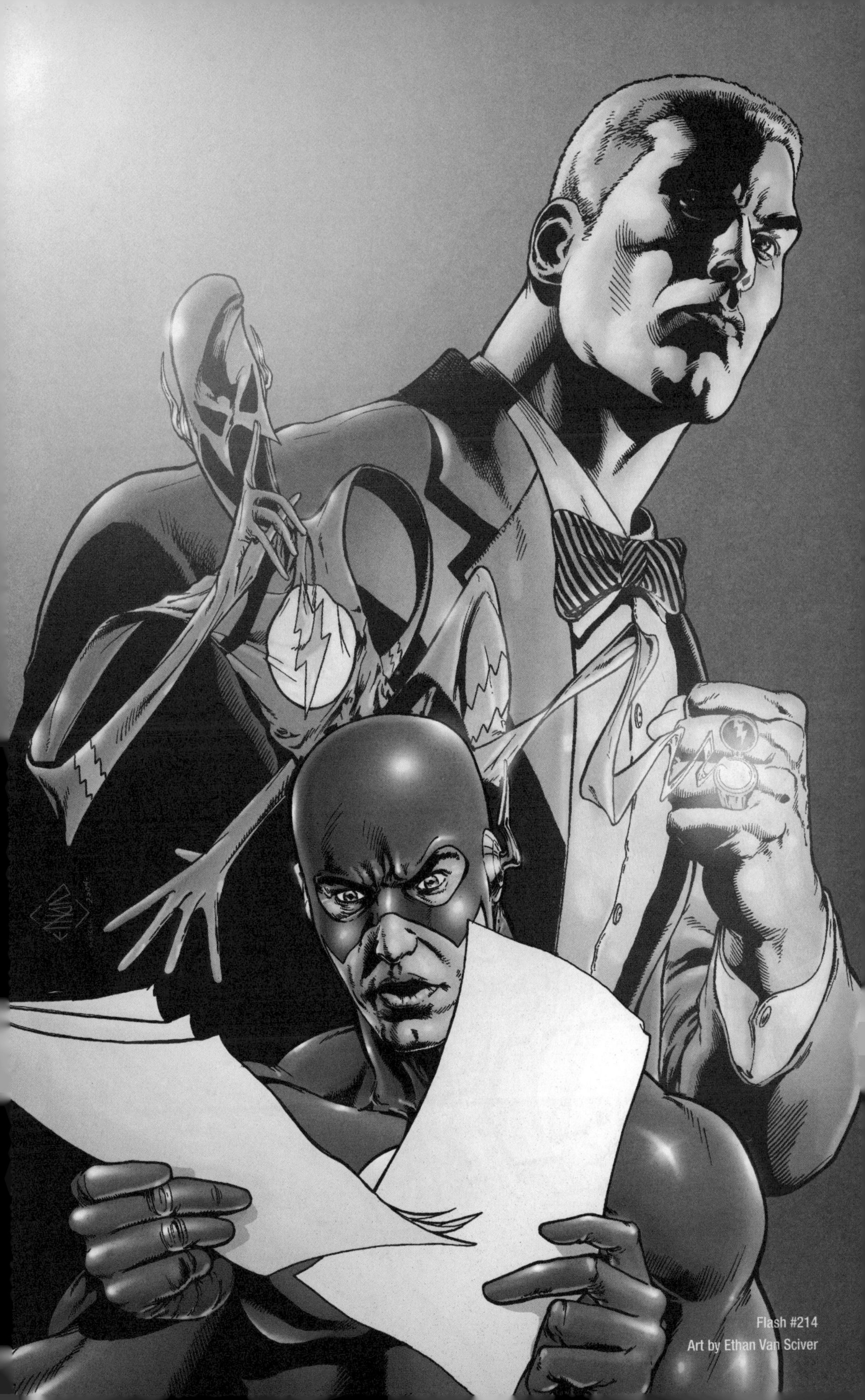

Flash #214
Art by Ethan Van Sciver

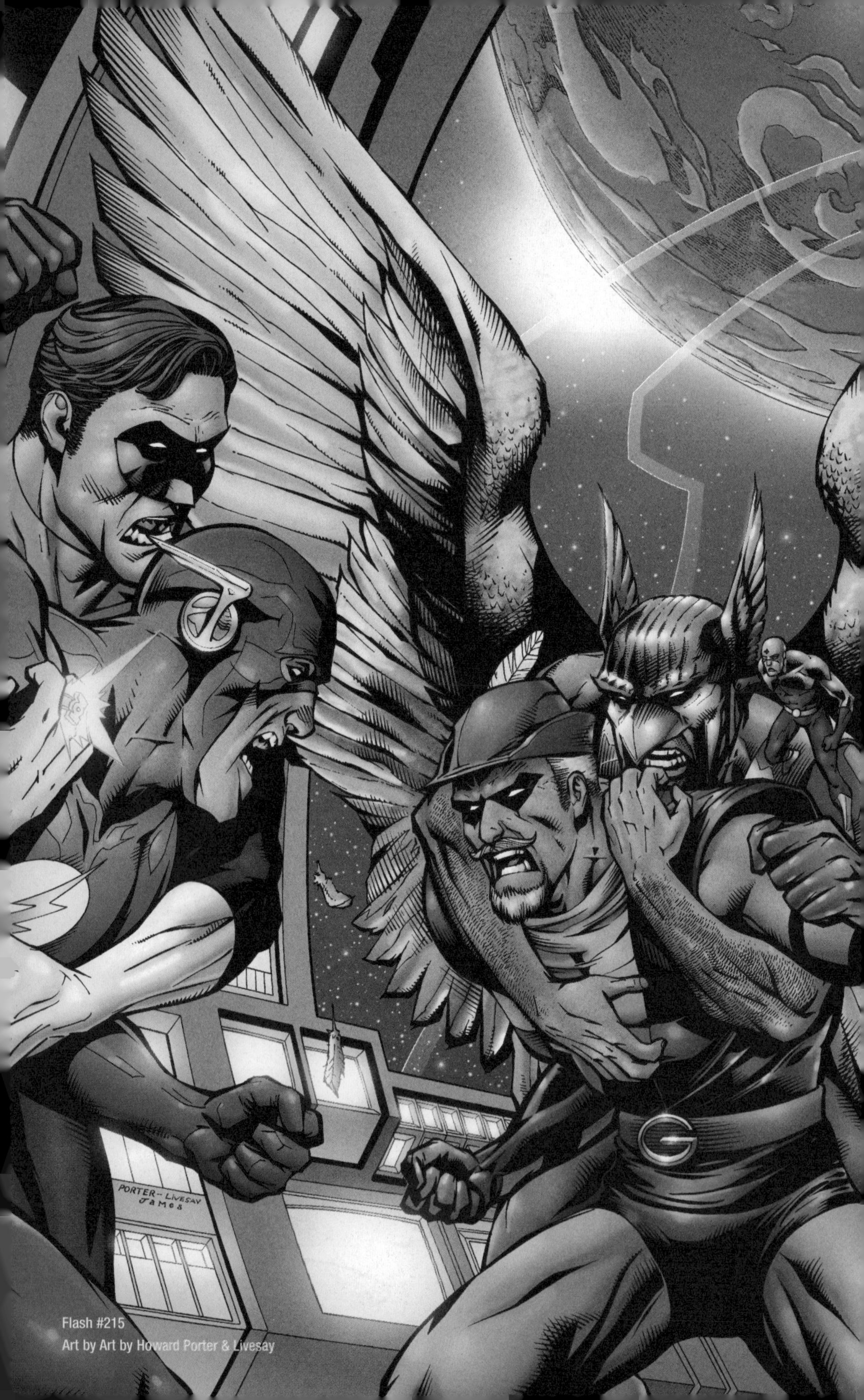
PORTER-LIVESAY
JAMES
Flash #215
Art by Art by Howard Porter & Livesay

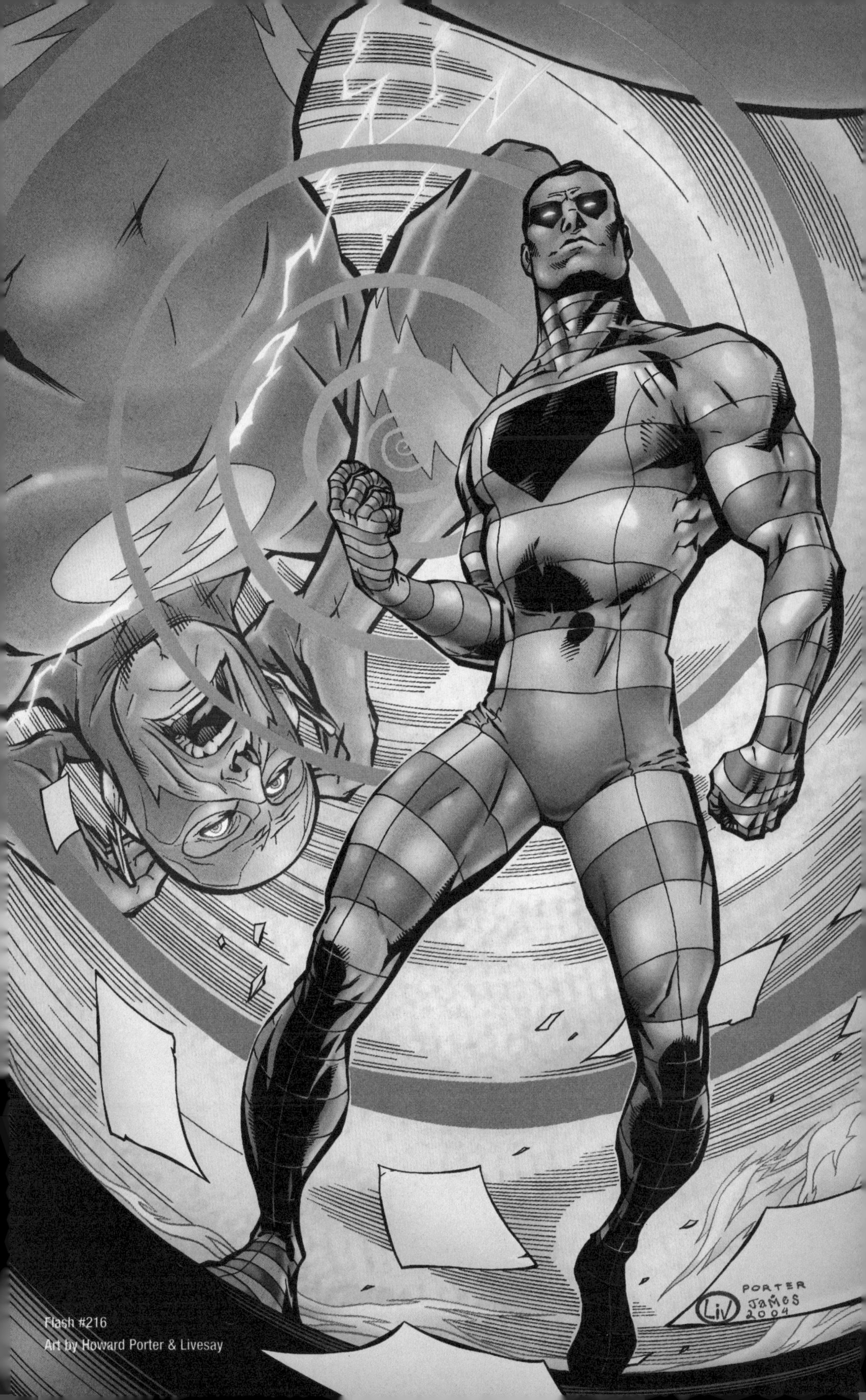
PORTER
JAMES
2004
LIV

Flash #216
Art by Howard Porter & Livesay

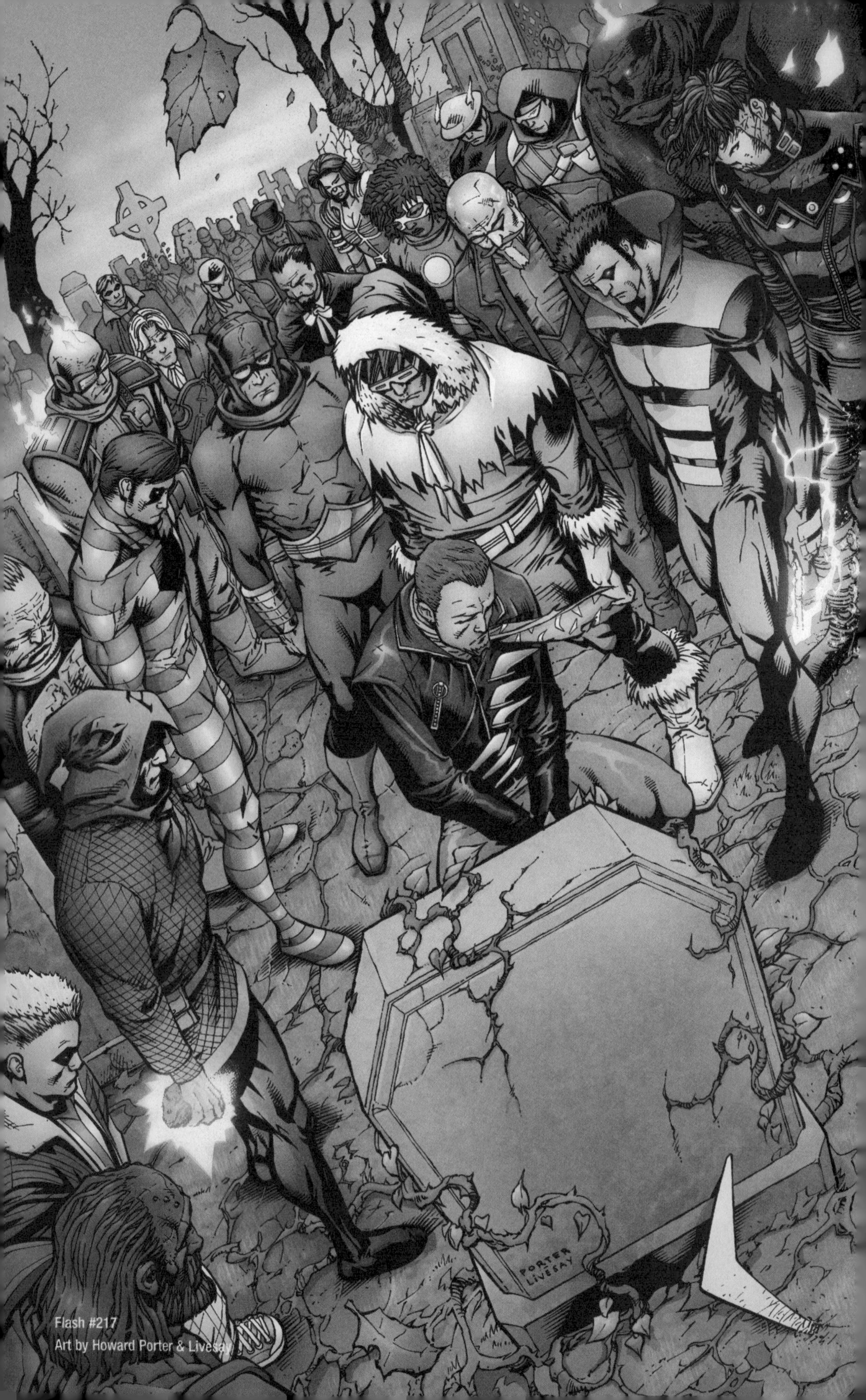
PORTER
LIVESAY

Flash #217
Art by Howard Porter & Livesay